STUDIES IN
THE PERIOD OF DAVID AND SOLOMON
AND OTHER ESSAYS

STUDIES IN
THE PERIOD OF DAVID AND SOLOMON
AND OTHER ESSAYS

Papers Read at the International Symposium for Biblical Studies,
Tokyo, 5-7 December, 1979

Edited by

TOMOO ISHIDA

EISENBRAUNS
WINONA LAKE, INDIANA
1982

Copyright © 1982
Yamakawa-Shuppansha, Ltd., Tokyo

Published by
Yamakawa-Shuppansha, Ltd.,
1-13-13 Uchikanda, Chiyoda-ku,
Tokyo, 101 Japan

Typeset by
Eisenbrauns,
Winona Lake, IN 46590
U. S. A.

Library of Congress Cataloging in Publication Data

International Symposium for Biblical Studies (1979: Tokyo, Japan)
    Studies in the period of David and Solomon and other essays

    Includes index.
    1. Bible. O.T.—Criticism, interpretation, etc.—Congresses.
2. Jews—History—1200-953 B.C.—Congresses. 3. David, King
of Israel—Congresses. 4. Solomon, King of Israel—
Congresses. 5. Jews—Kings and rulers—Biography—
Congresses. 6. Bible. O.T.—Biography—Congresses.
I. Ishida, Tomoo, 1931-   . II. Title.

BS1192.I58 1982 222′.409 82-11183
U.S. ISBN 0-931464-16-1

Distributed in North America by
Eisenbrauns, Winona Lake, IN 46590

Printed in U. S. A.

Contents

Preface ix

Opening Address xi

Abbreviations xiii

Part I: Studies in the Period of David and Solomon

Lyric Literature in the Davidic-Solomonic Period in the Light of
the History of Israelite Literature
by Masao Sekine 1

Wisdom Literature in the Reigns of David and Solomon
by R. N. Whybray 13

A Study of the Literary Structure of "The Succession Narrative"
by Kiyoshi K. Sacon 27

A Theologian of the Solomonic Era? A Plea for the Yahwist
by Werner H. Schmidt 55

Compact and Kingship: Stimuli for Hebrew Covenant Thinking
by Dennis J. McCarthy, S.J. 75

Zion in the Theology of the Davidic-Solomonic Empire
by J. J. M. Roberts 93

YHWH SABAOTH—The Heavenly King on the Cherubim
Throne
by Tryggve N. D. Mettinger 109

Female Cult Figurines in Late Canaan and Early Israel:
Archaeological Evidence
by Miriam Tadmor 139

Solomon's Succession to the Throne of David—A Political
Analysis
by Tomoo Ishida 175

A Political Look at the Kingdom of David and Solomon and Its
Relations with Egypt
by Abraham Malamat 189

The Interdependence of Internal Affairs and Foreign Policy
during the Davidic-Solomonic Period (with Special Regard
to the Phoenician Coast)
by Herbert Donner 205

Solomon's Trade in Horses and Chariots in Its International
Setting
by Yutaka Ikeda 215

Traditional Institutions and the Monarchy: Social and Political
Tensions in the Time of David and Solomon
by Hayim Tadmor 239

Compulsory Labor under David and Solomon
by J. Alberto Soggin 259

Monumental Architecture in Ancient Israel in the Period of
the United Monarchy
by William G. Dever 269

Part II: Biblical Studies and the Ancient Near East

Ebla and the Old Testament
by David Noel Freedman 309

Medicine in the Land and Times of the Old Testament
by J. V. Kinnier Wilson 337

Indexes

I. Texts

A. Biblical and Jewish Texts
  1. The Hebrew Bible (MT) 369
  2. The Greek Bible (LXX) 384
  3. The Vulgate 384
  4. The Apocrypha 384
  5. The New Testament 385
  6. The Mishnah 385
B. Non-Biblical Texts
  1. Akkadian Texts 385
  2. Hittite Texts 387
  3. West Semitic Texts 387

4. Egyptian Texts 388
5. Greek and Latin Texts 388

II. Words and Terms

A. Sumerian 388
B. Akkadian 389
C. Eblaite 389
D. Ugaritic and Other West Semitics 389
E. Hebrew 389
F. Egyptian 389
G. Words in Hebrew Letters 389

III. Authors 390

IV. Proper Names

A. Personal Names 398
B. Deities 400
C. Cities, Lands and Nations 401

V. Subjects 406

Preface

This volume is a collection of the papers offered at the International Symposium for Biblical Studies, which was held in Tokyo from December 5th to 7th, 1979. With regard to the purpose and organization of the Symposium, readers are suggested to refer to the Opening Address by Professor Masao Sekine, President of the Symposium, on the following pages.

I would like to thank all those who made this publication possible. I am particularly grateful to Prince Takahito Mikasa for a substantial grant which enabled us to publish the volume. I wish to thank Professor David Noel Freedman for his kind cooperation in copy-editing and typesetting of the volume at the American Schools of Oriental Research, Ann Arbor, and Eisenbrauns, Winona Lake. My special thanks are owed to Professor Masao Sekine, who entrusted me with the task of planning the Symposium and editing the volume in particular, and gave me precious advice and constant encouragement during the whole work. I also owe thanks to my students, Misses Fumi Karahashi and Keiko Sasaki and Messers. Masamichi Yamada and Shigeo Yamada, for having assisted me in compiling the indexes. Finally my thanks to staff members of ASOR, Eisenbrauns and Yamakawa-Shuppansha for the care taken in publishing this volume.

Tsukuba, May 1982
T. I.

Opening Address

MASAO SEKINE
President, International Symposium for Biblical Studies

Your Imperial Highness, Honorable colleagues, Ladies and Gentlemen, I have the honor to deliver you the opening address of the International Symposium for Biblical Studies. This is the first international meeting for Old Testament studies to be held in Japan. I am very happy that many distinguished colleagues from abroad readily accepted our invitation, came to Japan from far away and are present with us here.

It is clear that without cooperation of many friends and colleagues we could never hold this symposium. I should like to take this opportunity to express our special thanks to His Imperial Highness Prince Mikasa for the excellent initiative which he took for the realization of the symposium from the beginning of this enterprise. We also owe our heartfelt thanks to Dr. Sackler of Medical Tribune International and Mr. Yamagata of Medical Tribune Japan for their generous financial support which made us possible to hold the Symposium in Japan.

It was one of the inevitabilities of history that biblical studies scarcely made good progress in Japan until post-war years. For Japan does not belong to the cultural area which has a Judeo-Christian heritage. We have only about one million Christians even today, that is, less than one percent of the total population. Although the Japanese Christendom has had a notable influence upon our society in spite of its small number, it was not easy for us to develop biblical studies in the framework of this small community. However, after the general progress of scientific research in the field of humanities in Japan which had gone ahead, we have made some progress also in biblical studies in recent years, especially in cooperation with scholars of ancient Near Eastern studies. Some of the results have been presented to the international academic world in *The Annual of the Japanese Biblical Institute* (*AJBI*) over the last five years, in *Book List* published by the Society for Old Testament Study in Britain from some years ago and in *Old Testament Abstracts* published by the Catholic Biblical Association in the United States since last year. In the above publications, the members of the Japanese Biblical Institute have published the results of their researches in the field of biblical studies in European languages, while the members of the Society for Old Testament Studies in Japan have been invited to cooperate with British and American colleagues in order to make known to the international academic forum the essentials of the works on the Old Testament written in Japanese. I am very pleased, therefore, that we can open today this three-day symposium in Japan. This is really a timely project to stimulate us by cultivating the germ of biblical studies among us. At the same time, I shall be glad if we can serve the international academic world by offering a platform, on which important contributions to Old Testament studies would be made through the cooperation of all the participants, domestic as well as foreign.

Now I would like to explain briefly the outline of the symposium. The general theme of the symposium is "Archaeology and the Old Testament." The "archaeology" is meant in a broader sense. The symposium will be held in two parts, namely, special lectures and a forum. Special lectures will be given under the titles: "Ebla and the Old Testament" and "Medicine in the Land and Times of the Old Testament." Both topics were chosen as important examples of biblical researches made in close relation to ancient Near Eastern studies. The forum consists of fifteen papers dealing with the common theme: "The Period of David and Solomon." Our intention has been to clarify the characteristic features of the Davidic-Solomonic era, one of the most creative periods in the history of ancient Israel, by shedding light on it from every aspect. Broadly speaking, the literary problems will be discussed in the first four papers, then, the next four papers will be concerned with the problems of royal ideology and religion. After that, the political problems, inner-Israelite as well as international, will be dealt with by four papers. The last three papers will treat various aspects of the Israelite society in that period.

I am convinced that these lectures and papers and the intensive discussion which follows will enable us to deepen our understanding of biblical studies in general, and of the Davidic-Solomonic period in particular, to a great extent. I look forward to a profitable and also enjoyable symposium. Thank you!

(December 5th, 1979)

ABBREVIATIONS

AASOR	Annual of the American Schools of Oriental Research
AB	Anchor Bible
ABL	R. F. Harper, *Assyrian and Babylonian Letters* (Chicago, 1892-1914)
ADD	C. H. Johns, *Assyrian Deeds and Documents* (Cambridge, 1898-1923)
AfO	*Archiv für Orientforschung*
AHw	W. von Soden, *Akkadisches Handwörterbuch*
AION	*Annali dell'istituto orientali di Napoli*
AJA	*American Journal of Archaeology*
AJBA	*Australian Journal of Biblical Archaeology*
AJBI	*Annual of the Japanese Biblical Institute*
AJSL	*American Journal of Semitic Languages and Literature*
AKA	L. W. King, *The Annals of the Kings of Assyria* I (London, 1902)
AnBib	Analecta biblica
ANEP	J. B. Pritchard, ed., *Ancient Near East in Pictures*
ANET	J. B. Pritchard, ed., *Ancient Near Eastern Texts Relating to the Old Testament*, 3d ed. (Princeton, 1969)
AnOr	Analecta orientalia
AnSt	*Anatolian Studies*
AOAT	Alter Orient und Altes Testament
AOS	American Oriental Series
ARAB	D. D. Luckenbill, *Ancient Records of Assyria and Babylonia* 1-2 (Chicago, 1926-27)
ARI	A. K. Grayson, *Assyrian Royal Inscriptions* 1-2 (Wiesbaden, 1972-76)
ARM	*Archives royales de Mari*
ARW	*Archiv für Religionswissenschaft*
AS	Assyriological Studies (Chicago)
ASTI	*Annual of the Swedish Theological Institute*
ATANT	Abhandlungen zur Theologie des Alten und Neuen Testaments
ATD	Das Alte Testament Deutsch
BA	*The Biblical Archaeologist*
BAR	*The Biblical Archaeologist Reader*
BASOR	*Bulletin of the American Schools of Oriental Research*
BBB	Bonner biblische Beiträge
BBSt	L. W. King, *Babylonian Boundary Stones and Memorial Tablets in the British Museum* (London, 1912)
BeO	*Bibbia e oriente*

Bib	*Biblica*
BibOr	Biblica et orientalia
BJRL	*Bulletin of the John Rylands University Library of Manchester*
BKAT	Biblischer Kommentar: Altes Testament
BM	tablets in the collections of the British Museum
BO	*Bibliotheca orientalis*
BTAVO	Beihefte zum Tübinger Atlas des Vorderen Orients
BWANT	Beiträge zur Wissenschaft vom Alten und Neuen Testament
BZ	*Biblische Zeitschrift*
BZAW	Beihefte zur *ZAW*
CAD	*The Assyrian Dictionary of the Oriental Institute of the University of Chicago*
CAH	*Cambridge Ancient History*
CB OTS	Coniectanea biblica, Old Testament Series
CBQ	*Catholic Biblical Quarterly*
CRAIBL	*Comptes rendus de l'Académie des inscriptions et belles-lettres*
CT	*Cuneiform Texts from Babylonian Tablets . . . in the British Museum*
CTA	A. Herdner, *Corpus des tablettes en cunéiformes alphabétiques*
CUL	R. E. Whitaker, *A Concordance of the Ugaritic Literature* (Cambridge, MA, 1972)
DBSup	*Dictionnaire de la Bible, Supplément*
DCÉ	*Dictionnaire de la civilisation égyptienne*
EA	J. A. Knudtzon, *Die El-Amarna-Tafeln* (VAB 2, 1915)
EAEHL	*Encyclopedia of Archaeological Excavations in the Holy Land* 1-4 (Jerusalem, 1975-78)
EHAT	Exegetisches Handbuch zum Alten Testament
EncBib	*Encyclopaedia biblica* 1-7 (Jerusalem, 1950-76) (Hebrew)
EncJud	*Encyclopaedia judaica*
EvT	*Evangelische Theologie*
ExpTim	*Expository Times*
FRLANT	Forschungen zur Religion und Literatur des Alten und Neuen Testaments
GCCI	R. P. Dougherty, *Goucher College Cuneiform Inscriptions 1: Archives from Erech, Time of Nebuchadrezzar and Nabonidus* (New Haven, 1933)
HALAT	W. Baumgartner et al., *Hebräisches und aramäisches Lexicon zum Alten Testament*
HAT	Handbuch zum Alten Testament
HKAT	Handkommentar zum Alten Testament
HL	Hittite Laws

HSM	Harvard Semitic Monographs
HTR	*Harvard Theological Review*
HUCA	*Hebrew Union College Annual*
ICC	International Critical Commentary
IDB	G. A. Buttrick, ed., *Interpreter's Dictionary of the Bible* 1-4 (Nashville/New York, 1962)
IDBSup	*Supplementary Volume to IDB* (Nashville, 1976)
IEJ	*Israel Exploration Journal*
Int	*Interpretation*
JANES	*Journal of the Ancient Near Eastern Society of Columbia University*
JAOS	*Journal of the American Oriental Society*
JB	A. Jones, ed., *Jerusalem Bible*
JBL	*Journal of Biblical Literature*
JCS	*Journal of Cuneiform Studies*
JEA	*Journal of Egyptian Archaeology*
JEN	*Joint Expedition with the Iraq Museum at Nuzi*
JESHO	*Journal of Economic and Social History of the Orient*
JNES	*Journal of Near Eastern Studies*
JPOS	*Journal of the Palestine Oriental Society*
JQR	*Jewish Quarterly Review*
JRAS	*Journal of the Royal Asiatic Society*
JSOT	*Journal for the Study of the Old Testament*
JSOT SupS	*JSOT, Supplement Series*
JSS	*Journal of Semitic Studies*
JTC	*Journal for Theology and the Church*
K	tablets in the Kouyunjik collection of the British Museum
KAI	H. Donner and W. Röllig, *Kanaanäische und aramäische Inschriften* 1-3 (Wiesbaden, 1962-64)
KAT	E. Sellin, ed., Kommentar zum Alten Testament
KBo	*Keilschrifttexte aus Boghazköi*
KTU	M. Dietrich, O. Loretz, J. Sanmartín, eds., *Die keilalphabetischen Texte aus Ugarit* 1 (AOAT 24/1, 1976)
KUB	*Keilschrifturkunden aus Boghazköi*
LÄ	W. Helck et al., eds., *Lexikon der Ägyptologie* (Wiesbaden, 1972-)
MAOG	Mitteilungen der Altorientalischen Gesellschaft
MIO	*Mitteilungen des Instituts für Orientforschung*
MVAG	Mitteilungen der vorderasiatisch-ägyptischen Gesellschaft
ND	field numbers of tablets excavated at Nimrud
NEB	*New English Bible*
OIP	Oriental Institute Publications
OLZ	*Orientalistische Literaturzeitung*
Or	*Orientalia* (Rome)

OrAnt	*Oriens antiquus*
PBI Diss.	Pontifical Biblical Institute, Dissertation
PEQ	*Palestine Exploration Quarterly*
PJ	*Palästina-Jahrbuch*
PRU	*Le Palais royal d'Ugarit*
RA	*Revue d'assyriologie et d'archéologie orientale*
RB	*Revue biblique*
RechBib	*Recherches bibliques*
RHPR	*Revue d'histoire et de philosophie religieuses*
RLA	*Reallexikon der Assyriologie*
RLV	*Reallexikon der Vorgeschichte*
RSO	*Rivista degli studi orientali*
RSV	*Revised Standard Version*
SANT	Studien zum Alten und Neuen Testament
SBL DS	Society of Biblical Literature, Dissertation Series
SBM	Stuttgarter biblische Monographien
SBS	Stuttgarter Bibelstudien
SBT	Studies in Biblical Theology
SEÅ	*Svensk exegetisk årsbok*
SOTS MS	Society for Old Testament Study, Monograph Series
StOr	Studia orientalia
STU	*Schweizerische theologische Umschau*
TLZ	*Theologische Literaturzeitung*
TRu	*Theologische Rundschau*
TWAT	G. J. Botterweck and H. Ringgren, eds., *Theologisches Wörterbuch zum Alten Testament*
TZ	*Theologische Zeitschrift*
UF	*Ugarit-Forschungen*
UT	C. H. Gordon, *Ugaritic Textbook*
VAB	Vorderasiatische Bibliothek
VF	*Verkündigung und Forschung*
VT	*Vetus Testamentum*
VTSup	Supplements to *VT*
WMANT	Wissenschaftliche Monographien zum Alten und Neuen Testament
WO	*Die Welt des Orients*
ZA	*Zeitschrift für Assyriologie*
ZAW	*Zeitschrift für die alttestamentliche Wissenschaft*
ZDPV	*Zeitschrift des deutschen Palästina-Vereins*

Part I

Studies in the Period of David and Solomon

Lyric Literature in the Davidic-Solomonic Period in the Light of the History of Israelite Literature

MASAO SEKINE

The Japanese Biblical Institute, Tokyo

According to our original plan, epic literature in the period of David and Solomon was to be the first topic of the Forum, but as I have to be the first speaker for a compelling reason, I think I had better refer to epic and dramatic literature as well.

From Roman Jakobson we learn that epic literature is focused linguistically on the third person, while lyric literature is oriented towards the first person,[1] so that we come to the conclusion that epic and lyric literatures can be found in any literary work in the world insofar as the first and third persons are applied to the language in question. As for the third category, namely, dramatic literature, it exists in the latent form as soon as a dialogue is held between two persons. In actual fact, epic, lyric, and dramatic elements make their appearance intermingled, so that as a natural consequence we find such forms as epic elegy, lyrical ballad, and dramatic roman, as Emil Staiger pointed out in his famous work.[2] In spite of the complexity of the matters concerned, it is nontheless convenient to retain in ideal types the distinction of the above-mentioned three categories, as Albert Guerard maintains,[3] especially when the literatures of ancient peoples are to be studied.

In the history of ancient Japanese literature, epic literature was born in the process of consolidation of the nation as the result of the unity of tribes. We have the famous work of epic literature in the form of "Annals of Antiquities," that is, "*Kojiki*" in Japanese. After the national unity came into existence, the awakening of self-consciousness gave birth to the lyric literature in the collection of lyrical poems known as "*Manyōshū*." In other words, the nascence of the epic literature in Japan was motivated, as we see it, by the consciousness of the unity of tribes, while the maturity of the individual consciousness was the *sine qua non* of the florescence of our

---

[1] R. Jakobson, "Linguistics and Poetics," in *Style in Language* (ed. T. A. Sebeok; New York/London, 1960) 357.

[2] E. Staiger, *Grundbegriffe der Poetik* (5th ed.; Zürich, 1961) 237.

[3] A. Guerard, *Preface to World Literature* (New York, 1940) Part 2, Ch. 2.

lyrical poetry. It is of great interest to detect a similar phenomenal process in the history of Israelite literature.

I believe that the most exemplary work of epic literature in ancient Israel can be seen in the well-known "Song of Deborah" (Judg 5). It is noteworthy that this masterpiece of epic literature was produced during the process of unification of the tribal league called Israel.

The realized goal of this unification was the formation of the kingdom under Saul, a decisive event which exerted a far-reaching influence upon the subsequent periods of Israelite history. The finest pieces of lyric literature were born for the first time, in my opinion, in the laments of David on the occasion of the death of Jonathan, Saul's son, and of Abner, from whom he obviously expected much in the critical time of his political career. This corresponds precisely to the development from the epic to the lyric literature in the ancient literary history in Japan. It is clear, however, that the lyrical element can be found in cries and prayers to God in the premonarchic period, in which God was addressed in the second person. We hear for example the following prayer to God from the mouth of Joshua: "Alas, O Lord God, why didst thou bring this people across the Jordan only to hand us over to the Amorites to be destroyed?" (Josh 7:7). This reminds us again of the prayers called "*Norito*" of Japanese priests handed down from the oldest times, in which the lyrical element is conspicuous, as pointed out by the students of Japanese literary history. In spite of all this, the lyrical literature in its purest quality can be found in Japan in the above mentioned "*Manyōshū*", while the period of David and Solomon was the time when the lyricism in its genuine sense flourished in Israel for the first time.

David's lament over Saul and Jonathan (2 Sam 1:18ff.) begins, according to the reconstructed text by William Holladay,[4] who follows S. Gevirtz in outline,[5] as follows:

yĕlēl marr bĕkê yĕhûdâ
qĕšat nĕhî sĕpōd lĕ-yāšār.
A howling bitter weep, O Judah,
Harshness of wailing lament for the upright.

Holladay points out the assonance which exists between *yĕ-* at the beginning and end of the first line and makes an inclusio; he suggests a further inclusion in *yĕl-* and *lĕy-* of the first two lines. The musical harmony of sounds in poetry is the requisite element in lyrics, so that the assonance and wordplay pointed out by Holladay have much to do, in my opinion, with the lyrical character of this dirge, although Holladay takes no

---

[4] W. Holladay, "Form and Word-play in David's Lament over Saul and Jonathan," *VT* 20 (1970) 166.

[5] S. Gevirtz, *Patterns in the Early Poetry of Israel* (Chicago, 1963) 76.

account of this aspect of the poem at all. His emendation of the last word in the second line is worthy of note—Gevirtz reads "*yiśrāʾēl*"—because the "upright" (*yāšār*) can be construed to refer to Jonathan, from the beginning of this poem. That the "hills of Gilboa" and the "treacherous fields"—so I read in v. 21—are called out is important, insofar as the world of nature so often participates in lyrical poems, as we shall see later in the Song of Songs.

The central verse on which my main problem is based is v. 26. Holladay reads as follows:[6]

> ṣarr-lî ʿălêkā ʾāḥî
> yĕhônātān naʿamtā-llî mĕʾōd
> niplĕʾátâ ʾahăbātĕkā lî miʾʾahăbat nāšîm.

As Holladay regards *lî* in each line as enclitic, the number of units evens out as 3+3+4. It is very important to note chiastic assonances within each line, which were pointed out by him, especially from my standpoint, because the musicality of our lyrical lines can be recognized by his phonological analysis as the following chart indicates:

> -a-lî ʿā-lé-kā ʾa-ḥî
> -ĕ-ô- nā-tā- nā-tā- -ĕ-ô-
> n- ʾahăbāt- ʾahăbat n-

We can observe, especially in the second line, a good assonance and a wordplay: *e-o~e-o*, nata-nata, chiastically arranged. But Holladay's weakness may be seen in my opinion in the third line, as the elements of assonance, *n-*, are too far away from each other in this long line and can scarcely be perceived by the ear. This reflection leads us to a methodological scrutiny of Hebrew prosody. The recent works of some scholars (Loretz, Ridderbos, Hanson)[7] have respectively developed in their own ways an effective method of treating the Hebrew poetry. They agree in stressing the importance of dividing and counting the lines, the so-called stichos, or cola, starting from the observation of Ugaritic poetry. According to this method, which, strictly speaking, was inaugurated by the Albright school,[8] I read v. 26 as follows:

> ṣarr lî ʿălêkā ʾāḥî
> yĕhônātān nāʿamtā llî
> mĕʾōd niplĕʾátâ ʾahăbātĕkā llî
> miʾʾahăbat nāšîm.

---

[6] Holladay, *VT* 20 (1970) 183-84, 189.

[7] O. Loretz, *Das althebräische Liebespoesie* (Neukirchen-Vluyn, 1970); N. H. Ridderbos, *Die Psalmen: Stilistische Verfahren und Aufbau* (BZAW 117, 1972); P. D. Hanson, *The Dawn of Apocalyptic* (Philadelphia, 1975).

[8] Cf. W. F. Albright, *Yahweh and the Gods of Canaan* (London, 1968) Chap. 1.

I grieve for you, my brother,
Jonathan, you were delightful to me;
Your love for me was very wonderful,
surpassing the love of women.

The doubling of liquids and gutturals enhances the musicality of the verse. More important, however, is the end rhyme *hî-lî-lî* in the first three lines and the assonance *-m-* in the fourth line. We want to see further Jakobson's *"glissement,"*[9] that is, "sliding," in the *ʾahăbat* in the third and fourth lines. So we want to see here two-line poems, *"Zweizeiler,"* according to the terminology of Ridderbos. Worthy to note, perhaps, is the unbalanced meter according to our counting: 4+3/4+3, which reminds us of the qina-meter discovered first by Karl Budde,[10] 3+2, which stands in a sharp contrast to the balanced meter of the proverbs (2+2 or 3+3).The solecism in the position of *mĕʾōd* can be intentional, since the grammatical irregularities prove to be of advantage for the lyrical poetry (Staiger). The word *mĕʾōd* seldom appears at the head of a new stichos, but I have found the same usage at the second half of v. 9 in Ps 97.

In 2 Sam 3:33f. we read David's lament over the death of Abner:

hakĕmôt nābāl yāmût ʾabnēr
yādékā lō ʾăsûrôt
warraglékā lō linĕḫuštaim huggāšû
kinĕpôl (lipnê) bĕnê ʿawlā nāpāltā.
Must Abner die so base a death?
Your hands were not bound,
your feet not thrust into fetters;
you fell as one who falls as (before) wicked men.

I want to see here, with Hedwig Jahnow,[11] the meter 4+3/4+3, which is identical with that found in the lament over the death of Jonathan in 2 Sam 1:26. My assumption is that both laments derive from David himself. Even the most critical scholars are obliged to admit it.

The decisive factor for our main subject is the lyrical quality in both laments. David is unified with Jonathan and Abner in these poetic pieces, an epoch-making event in the history of Israelite literature. Jahnow speaks of *"ringender Individualismus"* in David's lament over Saul and Jonathan, as she maintains that the poem in 2 Sam 1:19-27 mourns over all the dead in battle at first, then gradually concentrates upon Saul and Jonathan and towards the end only upon Jonathan. Therefore the individualism in this poem is not quite free from collectivism, so that Jahnow calls this *"ringender Individualismus."* From the standpoint of the history of literature a lyrical poem can be very short, so that only v. 26 can be regarded as being

---

[9]Cf., e.g., Jakobson, *Questions de poétique* (Paris, 1973) 273ff.
[10]K. Budde, "Das hebräische Klagelied," *ZAW* 2 (1882) 1-52.
[11]H. Jahnow, *Das hebräische Leichenlied* (BZAW 36, 1923) 129.

purely lyrical, while epic and dramatic elements are permitted to be detected in other parts of this dirge. Even in v. 26 itself, epic and dramatic elements are to be seen. In terms of Wolfgang Kayser,[12] there are three stages of the lyrical; "*lyrisches Nennen*," "*lyrisches Ansprechen*," and "*liedhaftes Sprechen*" have to do with the three categories. In the lyrical, naming is included as an epical element and calling out as a dramatical element, while in the last stage, the singing narration, "I" welds with the object and all is internalized. This internalization is the core of lyrics, termed "*Erinnerung*" by Staiger, which means the remembering and making present of the past. In the laments of David, for example, he becomes one with Jonathan and Abner in singing narration of them, remembering and making present his beloved and valued. I should like to make an additional comment that the terminology of Staiger must be understood primarily according to its etymological meaning, namely "Erinnerung" in the sense of internalization.

But the main point I should like to make here is that mourning with the dirge and lament over the dead was in Israel a profane event, as the dead had nothing to do with the living God. It is very noteworthy that David made no use of the derivation of Jonathan's name in the course of this poem; there is no mention here of Yahweh or of what he has given, although the name Jonathan would have given the occasion to refer to the name of Yahweh and his donation. Obviously David has avoided intentionally to mention the divine name and his grace (Holladay).[13] On the other side, the dead were not deified in Israel, as Edmond Jacob remarked,[14] so that the other possibility for the dirge to be sung as a religious song was also excluded. But it is, in my opinion, just this secular quality of the poetry, through which the lyricism was introduced into Israel.

This thesis will be confirmed in the subsequent period, namely, in the time of Solomon. In the so-called Succession Narrative, whose literary character as entertainment was recently emphasized by David M. Gunn,[15] the lyrical element can be amply recognized. The portrayal of David at the time of Absalom's rebellion is most conspicuous. David left Jerusalem, fleeing away from Absalom. The moving scene is described as follows (2 Sam 15:30):

> David wept as he went up the slope of the Mount of Olives;
> he was bare-headed and went bare-foot. The people with him
> all had their heads uncovered and wept as they went.

Here we encounter a strong lyrical element in the stream of an epico-dramatical narration. More impressive are the words of David, when he was informed of the death of his favorite son (2 Sam 19:1):

---

[12]W. Kayser, *Das sprachliche Kunstwerk* (7th ed.; Bern/München, 1961) 339.

[13]Holladay, *VT* 20 (1970) 186.

[14]E. Jacob, "Mourning," *IDB* 3 (1962) 452-54.

[15]D. M. Gunn, *The Story of King David. Genre and Interpretation* (JSOT SupS 6, 1978) 29-30, 37-38.

O, my son! Absalom my son , my son Absalom! If only I had
died instead of you! O Absalom, my son, my son.

The repetition is, generally speaking, characteristic of lyrical poems, and
the wish to die is, in my opinion, a lyrical element peculiar to the Old
Testament. I want to remind you of the cases of Baalam (Num 23:10) and
of Elijah (I Kgs 19:4). Baalam's wish to die in his oracle as a seer is very
remarkable. Diether Vetter argues that his oracles take the style of dis-
putation and Baalam wants to make sure of the validity of his words at the
cost of his life.[16] We believe that we can see in his strong wish to die a
realistic character of lyricism in Israel. The same is likely true with Elijah's
wish to die. I think that I have shown the lyrical nature of the whole scene
of Elijah at Horeb.[17] In the case of David, his aspiration to die in his son's
place intensifies the lyrical element expressing forcibly the oneness of father
and son.

The most noteworthy for our main subject is undoubtedly the Song of
Songs. It is well known that this famous book has been interpreted from
many divergent viewpoints in the history of Bible studies. But in the last
two decades "allegorical" and "cultmythological" interpretations have gradually lost their supporters. The adequacy of "naturalistic" interpretation,
that is, the interpretation of the Song as love poetry is now almost
unanimously acknowleged. Regarding the foreign influence, the love language of ancient Israel shows a close affinity with the literature of Egypt of
the 18th Dynasty, which provides a corpus of parallel love songs. It is
interesting to note that the language of the Song has nothing to do with
fertility rites in Canaan, in contrast to the fact that we can assume
Canaanite influence upon the lyrico-mystical flavor of some psalms, as we
shall see later. Assyro-Babylonian literature also provides only a few songs
analogous to the Song.

John B. White[18] asserts in his erudite work published in 1978, following many other scholars, that the Song is a collection of poems or an
anthology of units. I am inclined, however, to assume a unity for the Song,
taking into consideration the results of J. Cheryl Exum's recent study[19]
which indicates that the first and the last poems (1:2-2:6; 8:4-14) form an
inclusio within which the other four poems occur in the structured correspondence. By the way, it seems very remarkable to be able to ascertain
nowadays that the method of inclusio plays a great role in many literary
works of the Old Testament. Further, I want to remind you that Exum,
from her viewpoint, disproves the claim of the dramatic construction and
that of a mere collection of the Song.

---

[16]D. Vetter, *Seherspruch und Segensschilderung* (Stuttgart, 1974) 15.

[17] Sekine, "Elias Verzweiflung—Erwägung zu 1. Kö XIX," *AJBI* 3 (1977) 52-68.

[18]J. B. White, *A Study of the Language of Love in the Song of Songs and Ancient Egyptian
Poetry* (SBL DS 38, 1978).

[19]J. C. Exum, "A Literary and Structural Analysis of the Song of Songs," *ZAW* 85 (1973)
47-79.

White speaks of Egyptian love lyrics throughout his research, but he does not put any emphasis on the lyrical character of the Song. Its lyrical high quality was profoundly elucidated by Gillis Gerleman[20] from a quite different angle from that of White. The hero and heroine appear in the Song of Songs sometimes as a king and a queen and in other times as gardeners and also as a shepherd and a shepherdess. According to Gerleman, the transformation of scenes is not one of dramatic changes, but should be understood as a literary travesty,[21] that is, the change of clothes of the hero and heroine represents the transmutation of the inner world of the poet. Alfred Hermann[22] had already found this travesty in the Egyptian poems of love, in which the outer scenes are only the expression of the lyrical feeling of the poets. According to Hermann, to whom Gerleman and White refer, lyric poetry is the linguistic resolution of human tension by means of literary forms. Many kinds of lyric poetry are enumerated and noted by Hermann, for example, magical saying, prayer, etc. But White, treading in the steps of Hermann, confirms that the strongest tension of love which exists in the human mind and demands *"Geistesbeschäftigung"* in the sense of André Jolles,[23] which means "basic mental concern," has created the lyrical poetry par exellence in Egypt. It is of course in conflict, whether the Song of Songs would be taken as popular or artistic poetry. The concensus in recent years has come to favour the second view, that the Song reflects a *"Kunstdichtung,"* which shows a high level of poetic development (Würthwein, Fohrer, Exum, Krinetzki),[24] while Wilhelm Rudolph and Moses H. Segal[25] champion the first view, that the Song exemplifies a collection of popular songs grown among common people. Prof. Kōchi Doi,[26] a Japanese literary scholar, once compared the Song of Songs with the Japanese *"nō"*-play which dramatizes popular songs handed down among common people. He maintained that Greek dramas gave influence upon the Song after the third century B.C. This presupposition is, however, difficult nowadays to accept. Further, White rejects the alternative of established categories, whether of popular or artistic poetry. He also assumes that the Song was preserved among the wisdom circles on account of the attribution of the Song to Solomon (1:1) and its affinity with some parts of the Proverbs (e.g. Prov 5:18-19: "And have joy in the wife of your youth, your lovely hind, your graceful doe. Her love will

---

[20]G. Gerleman, "Die Bildsprache des Hohenliedes und altägyptische Kunst," *ASTI* 1 (1962) 24-30; idem, *Das Hohelied* (BKAT 18/2-3, 1963-65).

[21]I want to add that White (*A Study of the Language of Love*, 146-48) treats the same phenomenon as "literary fictions."

[22]A. Hermann, *Altägyptische Liebesdichtung* (Wiesbaden, 1959).

[23]A. Jolles, *Einfache Formen* (5th ed.; Tübingen, 1974).

[24]E. Würthwein, *Die fünf Megilloth* (HAT 18, 1969) 26; G. Fohrer, *Einleitung in das AT* (Heidelberg, 1965) 330; L. Krinetzki, *Das Hohelied* (Düsseldorf, 1964) 46ff.

[25]W. Rudolph, *Das Hohelied* (KAT 17/1-3; 2nd ed., 1962) 100; M. H. Segal, "Song of Songs," *VT* 12 (1962) 470-90.

[26]K. Doi, *Solomon-no Uta* (Tokyo, 1926) (Japanese).

invigorate you always, through her love you will flourish continually").[27]
The latest article of M. Sadgrove[28] supports White's idea, presuming a
wisdom hand at work and interpreting the famous catchphrase "Love is
strong as death, ardour as vehement as Sheol" (8:6b) in the light of the
māšāl, or proverbial saying.

The proximity with wisdom can be discerned and the close relationship with wisdom, in some parts of the Song, can hardly be denied. It is
of no doubt, however, that the main parts of the Song of Songs were
written by other than wisdom circles and I believe that they are obviously
secular ones. The name of God is not explicitly mentioned in the whole
work. White confirms the following point: although the name of gods are
commonly mentioned in Egyptian love poetry, they are referred to in effect
as underscoring characteristic nonchalance on behalf of human love. As
regards the Song, he is of the opinion that the mere absence of God's name
may not approve it as "non-atheistic" literature, because he considers that
wisdom theology was expanded in the Song. This assertion seems to be
dubious.

The point I should like to make here is that the lyrical character of the
Song of Songs is in parallel with its secular nature as love poetry. It is
important, furthermore to mention that this secular character of the Song
can be sublimated and the high grade of lyricism in the Song of Songs
spiritualizes the love in this masterpiece of biblical literature. The world of
nature is not observed objectively by the poet, but penetrated with his
lyrical sentiment. I cite, for example, the unit 2:10-13:

My beloved answered, he said to me:
Rise up, my darling;
my fairest, come away.
For now the winter is past,
the rains are over and gone;
the flowers appear in the countryside;
the time is coming when the birds will sing,
and the turtle-doves cooing will be heard in our land;
when the green figs will ripen on the fig trees
and the vines give forth their fragrance.
Rise up, my darling;
my fairest, come away.

In this unit also we can see a neat inclusio.

The so-called umbra poetica, which elevates a lyrical nuance, also
plays an important role in some places, for example, 2:3; 4:6:

Like an apricot tree among the trees of the wood,
so is my beloved among boys.

---

[27]White, *A Study of the Language of Love*, 133.
[28]M. Sadgrove, *The Song of Songs as Wisdom* (JSOT SupS 11, 1979) 245ff.

To sit in its shadow was my delight,
and its fruit was sweet to my taste. (2:3)

While the day is cool and the shadows are dispersing,
I will go to the mountains of myrrh
and to the hills of frankincense. (4:6)

I want to add that a detailed analysis of 4:8 was made by Jakobson in one of his famous articles.[29]

The conclusive recognition that pure lyricism was also attained in the secular love songs deserves our attention in the history of Israelite literature, and my above-mentioned arguments derive from the assumption that the Song of Songs, or at least its important parts, dates from the time of Solomon. It is the most advantageous period, in which the court and the high intellectual class exerted decisive roles in cultural exchange and enlightened humanism in the history of ancient Israel.

Lyricism and mysticism have many features in common (Staiger). But I am of the opinion that love in the Song of Songs is spiritualized through its highest literary quality, while it has not yet obtained the mystic flavour in any degree. The spiritualized love is elevated in Israel to the mystical stage when it is turned to God.

The mystic character of Psalm 16 was observed in 1924 by Rudolf Kittel,[30] and in H. J. Franken's work on the mystical communion with God in the Book of Psalms in 1954,[31] when he first began to study this psalm. In his Psalm commentary Hans-Jojachim Kraus[32] found the sprout of mysticism in vv. 5-6 without referring to Kittel and Franken, while Mitchell Dahood[33] showed us linguistically the Canaanite background of this psalm. I am inclined to assume that clear Canaanite element and the undoubtedly lyrico-mystical sentiment of this remarkable piece of Psalms can be explained most naturally in terms of the characteristics of the Solomonic period. In this period Israel was imbued with the Canaanite influence on one side, and open to the eastern Mediterranean world on the other. The use of the past tense in vv. 2 and 6 is lyrical in its remembering of the past, and the repetition of the particle ʾp in vv. 6, 7, 9 heightens the lyrical tone of the whole poem. Dahood is of the opinion that this particle is attenuated and means only "and," but it seems to me that the problem of lyrical character of this psalm dropped out of his sight. I want to read, for example, v. 6 as follows:

---

[29]Jakobson, "Le parallélisme grammatical et ses aspects russes," *Questions de poétique* (Paris, 1973) 273ff.

[30]R. Kittel, *Die hellenistische Mysterienreligion und das Alte Testament* (Stuttgart, 1924) 86-87.

[31]H. J. Franken, *The Mystical Communion with JHWH in the Book of Psalms* (Leiden, 1954) 71ff.

[32]H. -J. Kraus, *Die Psalmen* (BKAT 15/1, 5th ed., 1978) 266.

[33]M. Dahood, *The Psalms* 1 (AB 16, 1966) 87ff.

The lines fell for me in pleasant places,
indeed I am well content with my inheritance.

The mystical feeling would be strongly felt also in v. 9:

Therefore my heart exults
and my spirit rejoices,
my body too rests unafraid.

Here I want to discuss a side issue to my main subject, but perhaps it is instructive for our common problem. From the standpoint of "climatology," I followed for long years a Japanese philosopher, the late Prof. Tetsurō Watsuji, who characterized the Middle East as a "desert," Europe as a "meadow," and the region from India to Japan as a "monsoon."[34] I cannot now enter into details, but it is necessary to add some remarks. Although I used the word *climatology*, it is not strict enough to designate the main issue of Watsuji, who is interested in the ontological problem of human existence standing under the influence of geographical-climatological conditions in the three important areas of the world. Quite recently, however, a Japanese agriculturist, Prof. Jirō Yiinuma scrutinized the theory of Watsuji and corrected it in many points.[35] I have learned from this scrutiny that Palestine belongs "climatologically" during the rainy season to the northern Mediterranean world, while in the dry season it has much in common with Mesopotamia and Egypt. This may be realized from the comparison of rainfall in Jerusalem and Nazareth with Cairo and Bagdad on one hand, and with Athens, Rome, and Marseille on the other. The rainfall of Elat and Jericho shows that the southern and eastern areas in Palestine also belong in the rainy season to the desert. The "climatological" viewpoint must of course be connected with the historical circumstances. The Mediterranean-Canaanite influence upon Israel was in the highest degree during the reign of Solomon.

Many scholars consider the possibility that Psalm 18 dates from the time of David. Franken again points out the mystical elements in this psalm. Compared with Psalm 16, the intimacy with God is less remarkable, although the opening of the Psalm "I love thee, O Lord my strength" is salient. The dating of Ps 63, which is undoubtedly most mystical in the whole Book of Psalms, is so uncertain that I am obliged to give up taking this psalm into consideration.

The lyrico-mystical character attains its summit in the eulogy of Wisdom in chap. 8 of the Book of Proverbs. In the light of the research of W. F. Albright[36] and Chrysta Kayatz,[37] it is not at all excluded that this

---

[34]T. Watsuji, *Hūdo* (Tokyo, 1935) (Japanese).

[35]J. Yiinuma, *Rekishi-nonakano Hūdo* (Tokyo, 1979) (Japanese).

[36]W. F. Albright, "Some Canaanite-Phoenician Sources of Hebrew Wisdom," *Wisdom in Israel and in the Ancient Near East* (VTSup 3, 1955) 7-9.

[37]C. Kayatz, *Studien zu Proverbien 1-9* (Neukirchen-Vluyn, 1970) especially 92ff.

chapter dates from the Solomonic period. As regards the understanding of Wisdom in this chapter, we owe revolutionary recognition to the study of Gerhard von Rad published in 1970.[38] According to him, Wisdom is grasped here as the *mysterium* of the created world, which appears in vv. 17 and 34 as the reciprocal eros between Wisdom and man. Wisdom as *mysterium* is further depicted in the image of God's darling (v. 30). When Wisdom is described as wooing love, we are faced with the most mystical scene in the history of Israel (von Rad). The lyrical sentiment is perceived when the poet speaks of the unspeakable as the alter ego of Wisdom. The poet and wisdom are unified here and the high degree of lyrico-mysticism makes it probable in the light of literary history of Israel to date this eulogy in the Solomonic period.

Franken writes about the lack of sexual patterns in the mysticism of the Old Testament.[39] Thus it is noteworthy that Israelite prophets, after Hosea, describe the relationship between God and Israel as husband and wife. I would like to question, as a problem in the history of Israelite literature, whether this imagery of prophets could be supported by the method of so-called *procédé anthologique*,[40] as having any connection with the lyrical images of love in the Davidic-Solomonic period.

POSTSCRIPT

Regarding the method of the history of Israelite literature, cf. my article, "Wie ist eine israelitische Literaturgeschichte möglich?" *Congress Volume Göttingen 1977* (VTSup 29, 1978) 285-97 and Chap. 3 of my book, *History of Old Testament Literature* 1-2 (Tokyo, 1978-80) (Japanese).

---

[38]Cf. G. von Rad, *Weisheit in Israel* (Neukirchen-Vluyn, 1970) especially 195ff., 203ff.

[39]Franken, *The Mystical Communion*, 70.

[40]Cf. A. Robert, "Littéraires (genres)," *DBSup* 5 (1957) 411ff.

Wisdom Literature in the Reigns of David and Solomon

R. N. WHYBRAY
University of Hull, England

It is understandable that in a symposium on the theme "The Reigns of David and Solomon" there should be a paper on the wisdom literature, just as there are papers on other aspects of literary activity in Israel during that period. But it ought to be understood from the outset that the title of this paper makes an assumption which requires examination: that our present knowledge of the history of wisdom literature in ancient Israel is sufficient to justify the identification of particular Old Testament wisdom texts as products of that comparatively short, though politically important, period in Israel's history. Is this assumption justified?

This question is only one aspect of a wider problem, one which is relevant to some of the other papers in this symposium: how far can *any* part of the literature of the Old Testament be confidently attributed to the reigns of David and Solomon? Several of the titles of these papers imply that there is in the Old Testament a whole range of Davidic-Solomonic literature—lyrical, narrative, and sapiential. What justification is there for this confidence? The books of the Old Testament are not as a rule provided with reliable colophons giving the dates of their composition. Moreover, many Old Testament books—especially the Psalms and other lyrical works, and the wisdom books—are almost entirely silent about datable historical events or specific historical situations. The problem of dating exists even in the case of the narrative works. The traditionally accepted hypothesis of a Solomonic date for the Succession Narrative, together with the hypposthesis of its literary integrity, has recently been seriously challenged; and W. H. Schmidt in another paper in this symposium has found it necessary to defend the traditional Davidic-Solomonic date of the "Yahwist," which also has recently been questioned.[1] The only evidence for dating these

---

[1] See W. H. Schmidt, "A Theologian of the Solomonic Era?" in this volume. On the Succession Narrative, see especially E. Würthwein, *Die Erzählung von der Thronfolge Davids. Theologische oder politische Geschichtsschreibung?* (Theologische Studien 115, 1974); T. Veijola, *Die ewige Dynastie: David und die Entstehung seiner Dynastie nach der deuteronomistischen Darstellung* (Helsinki, 1975); F. Langlamet, "Pour ou contre Salomon? La rédaction prosalomonienne de I Rois, I-II," *RB* 83 (1976) 321-79, 481-528; idem, "Absalom et les concubines de son père. Recherches sur II Sam. XVI, 21-22," *RB* 84 (1977) 161-209; D. M. Gunn, *The Story of King David. Genre and Interpretation* (JSOT SupS 6, 1978).

various works is of an indirect and to a large extent subjective kind—
internal indications of a particular point of view or *Sitz im Leben* and
stylistic and linguistic usage. All these clues have been and are subject to
debate, both as to their adequacy as clues and as to the conclusions to
which they point.

My concern in this paper is, however, solely with the wisdom literature.
Can one speak with confidence about "wisdom literature in the reigns of
David and Solomon"? The phrase implies that Israelite wisdom during
these two reigns had a distinctive character which can be distinguished
from that of the previous and the subsequent periods, and, in particular,
that these two reigns constitute a period of development or change of
direction as far as the wisdom tradition was concerned.

The most influential expression of the view that it is possible to speak
of, and to identify examples of, a Davidic-Solomonic body of literature is
to be found in the theory of a "Solomonic enlightenment" put forward by
Gerhard von Rad. In his article "The Beginnings of Historical Writing in
Ancient Israel"(1944),[2] writing of the Succession Narrative as marking a
new development in Israelite narrative composition, he referred to the
effect on Israel's cultural life of its achievement of statehood, and especially
of its sudden entry under Solomon into the international world of commerce and diplomacy. "This blossoming of economic life," he wrote, "was
naturally followed close behind by an intensive interchange of spiritual
ideas. . . . The court was a centre of international wisdom-lore, as the
Egyptian courts had been in an earlier age. . . . In short, the time of
Solomon was a period of 'enlightenment', of a sharp break with the ancient
patriarchal code of living."[3] Later, in his article "The Joseph Narrative and
Ancient Wisdom" (1953),[4] he again expressed these views on this subject,
this time with particular reference to Israelite wisdom literature; and he
reiterated them again in his final book *Wisdom in Israel* (1970),[5] though it
may be significant that in these two later works he preferred to speak
generally of "the early monarchy" rather than specifically of the reign of
Solomon as the period when Egyptian (and Near Eastern) culture generally
made its mark on Israelite culture.

---

[2]Originally published in German in *Archiv für Kulturgeschichte* 32 (Weimar, 1944) 1-42
under the title "Der Anfang der Geschichtsschreibung im alten Israel"; reprinted in G. von
Rad, *Gesammelte Studien zum Alten Testament* (München, 1958) 148-88. English translation
in G. von Rad, *The Problem of the Hexateuch and Other Essays* (Edinburgh/London, 1966)
166-204. Page references to this and other works cited in English translation are to the English
edition.

[3]"The Beginnings of Historical Writing," 203.

[4]Originally published in German under the title "Josephsgeschichte und ältere Chokma,"
Congress Volume, Copenhagen, 1953 (VTSup 1, 1953) 120-27: reprinted in *Gesammelte
Studien*, 272-80. English translation in *The Problem of the Hexateuch*, 292-300.

[5]*Wisdom in Israel* (London, 1972); originally published in German under the title *Weisheit
in Israel* (Neukirchen-Vluyn, 1970).

The theory of a "Solomonic enlightenment" was enthusiastically taken up and, as is often the case, taken for granted by many subsequent scholars, among whom I include myself, since my own early books *Wisdom in Proverbs* (1965)[6] and *The Succession Narrative* (1968)[7] largely presuppose it. Recently, however, the theory has been subjected to serious criticism, and one of the main purposes of this paper will be to attempt some reexamination of the evidence for and against it.

With regard to the wisdom literature the question is closely related to a larger one which has been vigorously debated in recent years: that of the origin of the wisdom tradition in Israel. It is also closely linked with an antecedent question: that of the definition of the terms *wisdom, wisdom tradition,* and *wisdom literature* as they are applied to the thought and literature of ancient Israel.[8] We shall bear these larger questions in mind as we proceed, but, in the compass of this paper, it will be prudent to begin from a narrower base and to consider simply the question of the character of "wisdom" in the reigns of David and Solomon as it is most frequently formulated, that is, the question whether those Old Testament texts most commonly supposed to be examples of *early* Israelite wisdom literature do in fact show signs of a close association with those two reigns any more than with other periods in the early history of Israel.

What are these texts? First and foremost we must consider Proverbs 10-29, chapters which according to most modern scholars—and it would be difficult to dispute this—contain the most ancient collections of proverbial literature in the Old Testament. This will be the text to which I shall mainly direct attention, although others must also be borne in mind. These include (1) parts of Proverbs 1-9, which according to some recent scholars[9] show the influence of ancient Egyptian wisdom "Instructions" and may be preexilic; and (2) a number of narrative texts which have been held by various scholars, especially by von Rad, to have been influenced by the same kind of "wisdom" teaching as we find in Proverbs 10-29—particularly the already mentioned "Joseph Narrative" (Genesis 37-50) and the Succession Narrative (2 Samuel 9-20 + 1 Kings 1-2 according to Rost).[10] But the most effective way of testing the theory that the reigns of David

---

[6] R. N. Whybray, *Wisdom in Proverbs: The Concept of Wisdom in Proverbs 1-9* (SBT 45, 1965, reprinted 1968).

[7] R. N. Whybray, *The Succession Narrative: A Study of II Samuel 9-20 and I Kings 1 and 2* (SBT 2/9, 1968).

[8] For my views on this subject see R. N. Whybray, *The Intellectual Tradition in the Old Testament* (BZAW 135, 1974).

[9] Especially R. N. Whybray, *Wisdom in Proverbs*; C. Kayatz, *Studien zu Proverbien 1-9: Eine form- und motivgeschichtliche Untersuchung unter Einbeziehung ägyptischen Vergleichsmaterials* (WMANT 22, 1966); B. Lang, *Die weisheitliche Lehrrede. Eine Untersuchung von Sprüche 1-7* (SBS 54, 1972).

[10] L. Rost, "Die Überlieferung von der Thronnachfolge Davids" (1926); reprinted in *Das kleine Credo und andere Studien zum Alten Testament* (Heidelberg, 1965) 119-253.

and Solomon saw significant developments in Israelite wisdom is to examine the material in Proverbs 10-29, which may without any possibility of contradiction be called "wisdom literature" *par excellence*. It constantly and consistently extols the advantages of acquiring something called "wisdom" (*hokmah*) and praises those who practice this wisdom (the *hăkamim*).

In the attempt made by von Rad and his disciples to demonstrate the close link between this type of "wisdom" and the period of David and Solomon, it has become customary to argue in the following way: (1) Large sections of the book of Proverbs show the influence of Egypt. (2) Solomon, and probably also his predecessor David, established close political and commercial ties with Egypt and also based much of their administrative system on Egyptian models. (3) Therefore, it is extremely probable that the similarity of the book of Proverbs to Egyptian literature is due to Egyptian cultural influence accompanying political, commercial, and administrative influence in its impact on Israel *during that period*.

On closer examination it becomes clear that there are some serious weaknesses in this argument.

(1) It makes the assumption that the Davidic-Solomonic period was the *only* period when relations between Egypt and Israel were sufficiently close to permit such cultural influences to operate. In other words, the admitted cultural and "wisdom" influence of Egypt on Israel need not have taken place during that period alone.[11]

(2) The theory does not sufficiently take into account other undoubted foreign influences on Israelite wisdom, such as that of Mesopotamia, which there is no special reason to date in this particular period.[12]

(3) The part played by the Canaanite cities of Palestine which David and Solomon incorporated into greater Israel also needs to be considered. These cities possessed a culture which was both older than and superior to that possessed by Israel at the beginning of the monarchy; and that culture was a mixed culture made up of several elements, including Egyptian,

---

[11]C. Loretz (*Qohelet und der alte Orient: Untersuchungen zu Stil und theologischer Thematik des Buches Qohelet* [Freiburg i. B., 1964] 93) points out that the Israelites must have been familiar with the scribal system of administration and so with the wisdom of the ancient Near East long before the time of David. For an up-to-date survey of Egyptian influence on Israel see R. J. Williams, " 'A People Come Out of Egypt', An Egyptologist Looks at the Old Testament," *Congress Volume, Edinburgh, 1974* (VTSup 28, 1975) 231-52.

[12]On Mesopotamian influence on Israelite wisdom literature see *inter alia* J. Hempel, *Die althebräische Literatur und ihr hellenistisch-jüdisches Nachleben* (Wildpark-Potsdam, 1930; reprinted Berlin, 1968) 51; W. Baumgartner, *Israelitische und altorientalische Weisheit* (Tübingen, 1933); idem, "Die israelitische Weisheitsliteratur," TRu 5 (1933) 259-88; G. Fohrer, "Tradition und Interpretation im Alten Testament" (1961); reprinted in *Studien zur alttestamentlichen Theologie und Geschichte (1949-1966)* (BZAW 115, 1969) 54-83; H. Cazelles, "Les débuts de la sagesse en Israël," *Les sagesses du proche-orient ancien. Colloque de Strasbourg, 17-19 mai 1962* (Paris, 1963) 27-40; G. Couturier, "Sagesse babylonienne et sagesse israélite," *Sciences Ecclésiastiques* (Montreal) 14 (1962) 293-310; Loretz, *Qohelet und der alte Orient*, 90-94; J. L. Crenshaw, "Prolegomena," *Studies in Ancient Israelite Wisdom* (ed. J. L. Crenshaw; New York, 1976) 7-8.

Mesopotamian, and indigenous elements. It is of course permissible to argue that this Canaanite influence was mainly brought to bear on Israel precisely during the period when these cities were incorporated into the state of Israel (i.e., that of David and Solomon); but, it is also possible *either* that these city-states began to influence Israel culturally *before* the time of David,[13] *or* that the full impact of Canaanite culture on Israel was not felt immediately after political unification: that a considerable period of interaction between the Israelite people and the citizens of the former Canaanite cities may have had to elapse before this could take place. If this was so, the main development of Israelite wisdom may well have taken place *after* the Davidic-Solomonic period.

(4) It is possible, as Albright has suggested,[14] that some parts of the book of Proverbs—he refers especially to chaps. 8 and 9—are directly dependent on Canaanite-Phoenician sources. If this is so, we may then be dealing to some extent also in Proverbs 10-29 with Canaanite literature from a period earlier than the reign of David, when Canaanite culture was at its peak; the only contribution which would have been made to this material in Israel in the period of David and Solomon would be its adaptation to Israelite needs: the "enlightenment" which produced it would have been in the first place a Canaanite one.

(5) The "Solomonic enlightenment" theory does not take sufficient account of the possibility of a native Israelite cultural development *earlier* than the period of the monarchy. The "enlightenment" theory in fact entails the view that a very rapid and unprecedented cultural development took place in Israel during the Davidic-Solomonic period which in the course of a comparatively short space of time turned Israel—or at least some of its leading citizens—from following what von Rad calls a "patriarchal code of living" ("Historical Writing," 203) to the practice of "an emancipated spirituality, modernised and freed from the cultus" (ibid., 204). It may be that history provides such examples of rapid cultural developments among other peoples, and we may perhaps compare the impact of western culture on Japan in the late nineteenth century; nevertheless the question must be asked whether there is really sufficient evidence to support the view that this is what happened to Israel under David and Solomon, or whether von Rad has to a large extent exaggerated the swiftness and completeness of the "cultural revolution". The possibility of the existence of a relatively highly developed premonarchical "folk wisdom" in Israel such as has been proposed by Gerstenberger, Wolff, and others therefore needs to be investigated further.

---

[13]Loretz, *Qohelet und der alte Orient*, 92-93; Cazelles, "Les débuts de la sagesse en Israël," 27-40 (he draws parallels especially between Israelite and Sumerian material, which he believes to have been mediated at an early date to Israel by the Canaanites); and W. F. Albright, "Some Canaanite-Phoenician Sources of Hebrew Wisdom," *Wisdom in Israel and the Ancient Near East* (VTSup 3, 1955) 1-15 are among those who support this view.

[14]"Some Canaantie-Phoenician Sources of Hebrew Wisdom," 1-15.

It must be admitted that these alternative views of Israel's early cultural development, like the view which they challenge, suffer from a paucity of precise and direct evidence, and it may be that we shall have to be content to remain uncertain about the course which it followed; but the theory of a sudden "cultural enlightenment" in the time of Solomon is, like the alternative views, no more than a rather bold hypothesis.

It is not possible in this short paper to follow up all the lines of investigation which have been suggested above. Some points may, however, be taken up in rather more detail.

(1) *Von Rad's theory of a "Solomonic enlightenment"*. An examination of the arguments put forward by von Rad to support the idea of a "Solomonic enlightenment" shows that the real basis for his case is to be found in his estimate of the character of certain *narrative works* (Succession Narrative, the so-called Story of David's Rise in 1 Samuel and the first part of 2 Samuel, the so-called Yahwistic History, the Joseph Story) rather than in the book of Proverbs. In his view of these narrative works he is very clearly dependent on the views of his teacher Albrecht Alt, who in his article "The Formation of the Israelite State in Palestine" (1930)[15] had argued, following Rost,[16] that the Succession Narrative marked the true beginning of continuous history writing in Israel, that it reflects a tremendous advance over the earlier "saga"-compositions, that it was written soon after the events which it describes, and that other narrative works—especially the Story of David's Rise and the account of Solomon's reign in 1 Kings 3-11—have similar characteristics and belong to the same period (1 Kings 3-11 being presumably slightly later). As has already been mentioned, the dates of all these works, and also of the Yahwistic History, have recently been seriously challenged, and it would be unwise to base arguments on these datings.

The theory of a Solomonic enlightenment, put forward in "The Beginnings of Historical Writing," was then applied by von Rad, first in "The Joseph Narrative and Ancient Wisdom" and then in his final work *Wisdom in Israel*, to the material in Proverbs 10-29, where he took up and accepted earlier work on Israelite wisdom literature which, following the discovery by Erman of the dependence of Prov 22:17-23:11 on the Egyptian *Instruction of Amenope*,[17] had reached the conclusion that Proverbs 10-29 *as a whole* emanated from the court and the wisdom schools of the early

---

[15] In A. Alt, *Essays on Old Testament History and Religion* (Oxford, 1966) 173-237, especially 205-37; originally published in German under the title *Die Staatenbildung der Israeliten in Palästina* (Leipzig, 1930); reprinted in A. Alt, *Kleine Schriften* 2 (München, 1959) 1-65.

[16] "Die Überlieferung von der Thronnachfolge Davids."

[17] A. Erman, "Eine ägyptische Quelle der 'Sprüche Salomos'," *Sitzungsberichte der Preussischen Akademie der Wissenschaften zu Berlin, Phil.-hist. Klasse* 15 (1924) 86-93.

monarchy which were based on Egyptian models. Von Rad did in fact admit[18] that some of the material in these chapters may be earlier than the period of the monarchy, but he specifically declined to pursue this possibility further on the grounds of the insufficiency of the evidence. For him, Proverbs 10-29 was "school wisdom." This statement, with its presupposition of the existence of a school system as early as the reign of Solomon, is itself open to question. But even supposing that it were correct, what is lacking in von Rad's argument is any direct evidence that Proverbs 10-29, whether in an earlier form or in its final form, comes precisely from the period of David and Solomon rather than from either an earlier or a later time.

In fact the case for a Solomonic dating of these chapters appears to rest entirely on two items of supposed evidence: the attribution of part or all of them to Solomon in the section headings in Prov 1:1; 10:1; 25:1, and the statements about Solomon's great wisdom in the account of Solomon's reign in 1 Kings (5:9-14; 10:1-10, 13, 23-24). R. B. Y. Scott, in an unjustly neglected article, "Solomon and the Beginnings of Wisdom in Israel",[19] discussed both of these. His view that the statements about Solomon's wisdom in 1 Kings have no historical value but come from a later time than Solomon is supported by Martin Noth in his commentary on 1 Kings 1-13,[20] the only difference between them being that Scott sees these statements as post-Deuteronomic interpolations, while Noth believed them to be pre-Deuteronomic. With regard to the attribution of proverbial collections to Solomon in Prov 1:1; 10:1; 25:1, Scott is surely right, in the light of the existence of a legendary tradition about Solomon's wisdom attested in 1 Kings 3-11 and of the Old Testament analogy of the attribution of law-codes to Moses and of the Psalms to David, in regarding these statements as part of that legendary tradition, and also right in regarding the reference to *Hezekiah* in this connection in Prov 25:1 as more significant and historically more reliable. The phrase "The proverbs of Solomon, which the men of Hezekiah edited (הֶעְתִּיקוּ)" is a much more precise reference to wisdom activity under Hezekiah than is the vague Solomonic attribution; and the allusion to wisdom literature as flourishing in the reign of Hezekiah accords well with the plausible theory that Hezekiah saw himself as a "new Solomon," which role may well have embraced the Solomon of legend as well as the Solomon of history. As for Egyptian influence on Judah in the reign of Hezekiah, this is well attested in the book of Isaiah, where the prophet refers on more than one occasion to a current over-

---

[18] *Wisdom in Israel*, 11-12 and n. 9.

[19] *Wisdom in Israel and the Ancient Near East* (VTSup 3, 1955) 262-79.

[20] *Könige* 1 (BKAT 9/1, 1968) 80-81, 208-209. See also his article "Die Bewährung von Salomos 'göttliche Weisheit'," *Wisdom in Israel and the Ancient Near East* (VTSup 3, 1955) 225-37.

reliance on Egypt,[21] and also refers, at least by implication, to an Israelite reliance upon Egypt's "wisdom".[22]

While then it would be imprudent to maintain that the legendary attribution of literary wisdom to Solomon is necessarily entirely without foundation, and even if we may go so far as to concede the possibility that his reign saw some kind of literary wisdom activity inspired by Egypt, the only reliable evidence for the date of the composition or editing of any part of the book of Proverbs concerns the reign of Hezekiah, and von Rad's theory of a Solomonic enlightenment must be judged, at least as far as the book of Proverbs is concerned, to be based on inadequate evidence.

(2) *The question of pre-Davidic wisdom in Israel.* The view that the reigns of David and Solomon were particularly crucial in the development of ancient Israelite wisdom makes two assumptions: (a) that proverbs such as those in Proverbs 10-29 are closely connected with the court and with wisdom schools of an Egyptianized kind, or at least written for cultured readers who had received a school education; and (b) that Israel before the time of David was too uncultured to have produced such fine literary work. These two points, though inter-related, may be considered separately.

(a) Recent study of preliterary cultures has shown that some preliterary, and even so-called primitive, peoples are capable of producing highly sophisticated "oral" literature, which may include what we should call wisdom literature. This discovery has already led to new insights into the date and composition of some of the extant literature of the ancient world, especially, through the researches of A. B. Lord (*The Singer of Tales*)[23] and others, with regard to the origin and character of some extant epic literature, in particular the Homeric poems. With regard to wisdom literature, the recent collection and recording of proverbial literature from preliterary Africa, Madagascar, and other areas has provided an opportunity to make comparisons between this and the proverbial literature of the ancient Near East, including that of Israel. The results of some of this work on African and other proverbs have been conveniently summarized, for the benefit of Old Testament scholars, by André Barucq in his article on the book of Proverbs in the *Supplément au Dictionnaire de la Bible.*[24] Claus Westermann has also written on this subject.[25] Barucq cites examples

---

[21]E.g., Isa 20:1-6; 30:1-7; 31:1.

[22]Isa 31:2. It is not certain whether the contemptuous reference to Egypt's wisdom and wise men in Isa 19:11-12 is the work of the prophet or not. See O. Kaiser, *Isaiah 13-39* (London, 1974) 97-104; original German edition, *Der Prophet Jesaja, Kapitel 13-39* (ATD 18, 1973); H. Wildberger, *Jesaja 13-27* (BKAT 10/2, 1978) 698-726.

[23]Cambridge, Mass., 1960.

[24]A. Barucq, "Proverbs (Livre des)," *DBSup* 8/47 (1972) 1415-19.

[25]C. Westermann, "Weisheit im Sprichwort," *Schalom: Studien zu Glaube und Geschichte Israels. Festschrift A. Jepsen* (ed. K. H. Bernhardt; Stuttgart, 1971) 73-85; reprinted in C. Westerman, *Forschung am Alten Testament. Gesammelte Studien* 2 (München, 1974) 149-61.

of African proverbs which are remarkably similar both in form and content with some of the proverbs in Proverbs 10-29. These African proverbs, composed, as he points out, without contact with any kind of school learning or with a privileged class or specific institution, have many of the stylistic features of proverbs in the biblical book of Proverbs, including rhythmical form, assonance, alliteration, play on words, and so on. Some of them are even couched in parallelistic form, a form of expression which, he asserts, should not be thought of as specifically the product of a narrow school-tradition especially characteristic of the learned literature of the ancient Near East, but corresponds to an universal human tendency. Thus one of the proverbs current among the Kabyles of North Africa, a branch of the Berber people, reads:

> To the intelligent man a wink is sufficient, but for the fool a blow with the fist is needed.

This saying, which not only has rhythmical form and parallelism but also draws the contrast between the wise man and the fool which is so characteristic of many proverbs in the Old Testament, may be compared with the following sayings from the book of Proverbs:

> On the lips of the intelligent man wisdom is found; but a rod is needed for the back of the witless man (10:13).

> A rebuke goes deeper into an intelligent man than a hundred blows into a fool (17:10).

From black Africa come such sayings as:

> A man may wash his body
> but he cannot wash away his fate.

> The enemy digs your grave
> but God digs you a way out of it.

> Rather than praising yourself,
> try to be praised by God.

Comparison with the biblical book of Proverbs will reveal strong similarities with these African sayings also; and many other examples could be given.

These similarities weaken the commonly held view that virtually all the proverbial literature of the Old Testament must come from the Davidic-Solomonic period, when Israel allegedly first felt the full impact of the influence of the literary wisdom tradition of ancient Near Eastern civilization, or from some *later* time. This view, first put forward by Gunkel,[26] was elaborated with great thoroughness by Hans-Jürgen Hermisson,[27] who went as far as to assert[28] that there are almost no clear examples of what he called "popular wisdom" (*Volkweisheit*) in the book of Proverbs. The meaning of this assertion of course depends on what is meant by "popular wisdom". Hermisson understood by it sayings unselfconsciously and spontaneously arising from the experiences of anonymous individuals (of any class) as distinct from sayings coined in a consciously literary form by the learned.[29]

The strong point of Hermisson's argument is that the examples of "popular wisdom" in the other, nonwisdom, books of the Old Testament do not correspond at all in form (though in fact they correspond to a large extent in theme[30] and also in the use of word play, assonance, etc.) to the material in the book of Proverbs. The latter is poetical and composed in parallel couplets, while the former is usually very short, prosaic (though often rhythmical) and lacking in parallelism. This is indeed a point of some importance, though it is somewhat weakened by Hermisson's own admission that the true "popular" sayings in the non-wisdom books of the Old Testament are very small in number, and therefore difficult to characterize adequately, and probably not truly representative of Israelite folk-wisdom.[31] It may, then, be by chance that sayings fully comparable with the material in the book of Proverbs do not occur there.

It is, however, possible that the reason for the difference in form between these "popular" sayings and the proverbs of Proverbs 10-29 is that the *Sitz im Leben* and function of the latter differed from that of the former, whose context in the narrative books is that of ordinary daily life. The material in the book of Proverbs may have had a rather more formal and serious function. But this is not to say that they are all "school wisdom" or "court wisdom" and so Davidic or post-Davidic in date. A number of scholars have recently argued for a premonarchical origin for this kind of material. In particular, Eberhard Gerstenberger attempted to show, on the basis of a comparison between the negative *Mahnwort* or "vetitive" in Proverbs (sayings beginning with "Do not . . .") and those so-called apodictic laws in the Pentateuch which begin with "Thou shalt not . . ." that the origins of both are to be found in a premonarchical "clan wisdom" (*Sippenweisheit*), which, he alleged, was a form of instruction given by the head of a clan or family to its younger members.[32] The

---

[26]H. Gunkel, *Die israelitische Literatur* (Die Kultur der Gegenwart 1/7, 1925, reprinted Darmstadt, 1963) 40.

[27]H.-J. Hermisson, *Studien zur israelitischen Spruchweisheit* (WMANT 28, 1968).

[28]Ibid., 92-94 and *passim*.

[29]Ibid., 27-36.

[30]Hermisson himself admits (ibid., 52-76) that many, though not all, of the themes covered in Proverbs 10-29 are relevant to *any* class in society.

[31]Ibid., 49-50.

[32]E. Gerstenberger, *Wesen und Herkunft des "apodiktischen Rechts"* (WMANT 20, 1965).

collections of sayings in Proverbs 10-29 as we now have them belong to a later stage, having been compiled by a later class of Israelite "wise men" corresponding to similar professional groups in the other cultural centres of the ancient Near East.[33] Gerstenberger's theory has not been widely accepted,[34] partly because the evidence for the existence of a family or clan institution such as that which he presupposes is dubious. Moreover, he did not deal at all with the other and much more frequent type of saying in the book of Proverbs, the "statement" or *Aussagewort*, which does not, at least ostensibly, claim to instruct but only states facts about life in general.

But a particular theory such as that of Gerstenberger is not essential to the view that some of the material in the book of Proverbs may come from the premonarchical period. There may have been circles in Israel well before the monarchy which created—and perhaps gathered into collections—proverbs in poetical and parallelistic form, which were quite distinct from ordinary sayings arising in daily life and had a more serious intention, but which did so—as occurred with other peoples—without the stimulus of the school-oriented and court-oriented milieux which are supposed to have existed in the time of David and Solomon. Such a phenomenon cannot of course be more than a possibility, and it is probably not possible to identify and define these circles; but it cannot be ruled out. The burden of proof surely lies with those who would date *all* or nearly all the sayings in Proverbs 10-29 in the period of the monarchy. I submit that it is difficult *a priori* to believe in a "Solomonic enlightenment" which suddenly produced literary wisdom of a highly polished kind *ab initio* and owed virtually nothing to any proverbial wisdom which may have existed in earlier generations.[35]

(b) This brings me to a discussion of the second assumption of the "Davidic-Solomonic" school of thought, that Israel before the time of David was incapable of producing the kind of material which we find in the book of Proverbs. This is, of course, manifestly not the case if my conclusions in the preceding section are accepted. But even if they are not, this assumption is still extremely precarious. The truth is that owing to the absence of contemporary historical sources we are not in a position to say very much with confidence about the life and history of premonarchical Israel, although every conceivable theory has been put forward about it on the basis of the extant literature of the Old Testament, and, to some extent, of the findings of archaeology. If we did possess any substantial knowledge about this period it would not have been possible, for example, for a

---

[33]Ibid., 144.

[34]See for example the criticisms in Whybray, *The Intellectual Tradition*, 113-116, and the review of Gerstenberger's book by H. B. Huffmon in *Int* 22 (1968) 201-204.

[35]The work of W. Richter, *Recht und Ethos: Versuch einer Ortung des weisheitlichen Mahnspruches* (SANT 15, 1966), which speaks of a "group ethic" rather than a "clan ethic," does not deal specifically with this point.

scholar like Mendenhall[36] to brush aside all the biblical sources which speak of an entry of the ancestors of the Israelites into Palestine from outside, and to maintain that most of them were there all the time, being simply dropouts from Canaanite urban life. Nor should we have the great and still continuing debate whether there was or was not some kind of Israelite tribal federation in existence before the monarchy such as that to which Noth applied the term "amphictyony".[37] But if we can say anything at all with confidence about the origins and early life and history of Israel, it is that the ancestors of the Israelites were not simple bedouin in process of sedentarization who had previously been unaffected by the surrounding cultures. Whether they were in origin (to quote a section heading from de Vaux's *History*)[38] Amorites or Aramaeans, there can be little doubt that they were, in the earliest centuries of which we have any record at all, in contact with, and to some extent part of, the cultural world of the civilized ancient Near East. Certainly their own traditions speak emphatically of early Mesopotamian connections, and also of an early contact with Egypt. And it is quite certain that for at least two centuries before the time of David they coexisted in Palestine with the Canaanites, and that, at least in such matters as religious practices and the arts of agriculture, they were profoundly influenced by them. Their own ethnic origins were almost certainly mixed. Whether or not they brought with them to Palestine some knowledge of Mesopotamian and/or Egyptian wisdom literature, a cultural as well as a religious influence of the Canaanites on them before the monarchical period is extremely probable. Although—perhaps by chance—very little *proverbial* wisdom has been discovered among extant Canaanite literary remains, there is now overwhelming evidence that in some Canaanite cities other forms of Mesopotamian wisdom literature were known and read;[39] and Egyptian influence was also marked.[40] On these grounds, therefore, we

---

[36]G. E. Mendenhall, "The Hebrew Conquest of Palestine," *BA* 25 (1962) 66-87; idem, *The Tenth Generation: The Origins of the Biblical Tradition* (Baltimore/London, 1973).

[37]M. Noth, *Das System der zwölf Stämme Israels* (Stuttgart, 1930, reprinted Darmstadt, 1966); idem, *The History of Israel* (2nd ed.; London, 1960) 85-109; originally published in German under the title *Geschichte Israels* (Göttingen, 1950; 2nd ed., 1954). Criticisms of this once dominant theory have been frequent in recent years; see *inter alia* R. de Vaux, *The Early History of Israel* (London, 1978) 695-715; originally published in French under the title *Histoire ancienne d'Israël* 2 (Paris, 1973); A. D. H. Mayes, *Israel in the Period of the Judges* (SBT 2/29, 1974); O. Bächli, *Amphiktyonie im Alten Testament: Forschungsgeschichtliche Studie zur Hypothese von Martin Noth* (*TZ* Sonderband 6, 1977). However, while Noth's theory at least in its original form now perhaps has few adherents, no alternative consensus has emerged.

[38]*The Early History of Israel*, 200-209.

[39]See for example Cazelles, "Les débuts de la sagesse en Israel"; J. Gray, "The Book of Job in the Context of Near Eastern Literature," *ZAW* 82 (1970) 251-69.

[40]See, for example, Albright, "Some Canaanite-Phoenician Sources of Hebrew Wisdom"; S. Morenz, "Ägyptologische Beiträge zur Erforschung der Weisheitsliteratur Israels," *Les sagesses du proche-orient ancien. Colloque de Strasbourg, 17-19 mai 1962* (Paris, 1963) 63-71.

may readily suppose that the premonarchical Israelites were capable of producing wisdom literature, even if a high culture is a prerequisite for this. It is accordingly quite possible that some of the material in the book of Proverbs may have been composed in premonarchical times on Canaanite, or on Egyptian or Mesopotamian models.

Conclusions. These observations are necessarily of a tentative character, since wisdom literature is notoriously difficult to date. But we may conclude from them at least this: that to speak of "the wisdom literature of the reigns of David and Solomon" is to assume a possibility of precision in dating which goes beyond the available evidence. On the one hand, the cultural contacts of the Israelites from the time of their settlement in Palestine with Canaanite culture, together with the probability of their adherence, even before their settlement, to the cultural world of the ancient Near East, makes it entirely possible that many of the proverbs in Proverbs 10-29 were composed *before* the institution of the monarchy. The relatively undeveloped state of their political organization before the advent of the monarchy in no way proves that their cultural level was low. Israelite wisdom literature of the premonarchical period may have been preserved only in oral forms, though it should not be assumed that they had no scribal culture. If, for example, the well-known reference in Judges 8:14 to the "young man" (נַעַר) of the city of Succoth who wrote down for Gideon the names of the seventy-seven officials and elders of the city may be regarded as reliable evidence, we may well have here a pre-Davidic reference to an Israelite professional scribe comparable to the Canaanite scribes of the period.[41] It is therefore quite possible that the beginnings of a *written* Israelite proverbial literature took place during this period.

It has been frequently asserted that the proverbial material in Proverbs 10-29 bears the marks of the monarchy. But this is by no means wholly true. Only the references to the king and his court—in a limited number of proverbs—point unequivocally to life under the kings. The great majority of the proverbs in these chapters simply reflect a sedentary society engaged in agriculture, with a fairly advanced technology and commerce. This picture certainly fits the period of the monarchy, but it is also compatible with the preceding period. Many of these proverbs *could* have been composed in the so-called period of the Judges. The contrast, culturally speaking, between premonarchical and monarchical Israel has been exaggerated. The advent of the monarchy seems to have produced no sudden change in traditional ways of life. For example, the story of the woman of Tekoa in 2 Samuel 14 points to a rather unsophisticated "wisdom tradition" poles apart from the "wisdom" of the royal counsellors, Ahithophel and Hushai depicted in 2 Samuel 17. Both stories refer to the reign of David, and both occur in the Succession Narrative.

---

[41]See Hermisson, *Studien zur israelitischen Spruchweisheit*, 99-103 and the bibliographical references there.

On the other hand, the division which has been made between the Davidic-Solomonic period and the *later* monarchy is an even more artificial one from the cultural point of view. Apart from the attribution of some collections in the book of Proverbs to Solomon, the very dubious historical value of which has already been noted, there is no evidence whatever that any of these proverbs was actually composed during either of these two reigns. The only solid evidence which we have for dating any of them is the reference to the men of *Hezekiah* in Proverbs 25:1. As far as the proverbial wisdom of Proverbs 10-29 is concerned, then, the reigns of David and Solomon may well have been a period in which a powerful stimulus was given, through the establishment of a royal court with its foreign connections, to the development of Israelite wisdom literature, but we cannot speak with any certitude of any extant Israelite wisdom literature which was actually composed or compiled during the reign of either David or Solomon.

A Study of the Literary Structure of "The Succession Narrative"

KIYOSHI K. SACON

Tokyo Union Theological Seminary

I. PROLOGUE

The intent of this study is to explore the structure of what is generally called the "Succession Narrative" (SN) from the synchronic and literary (and not structuralistic[1]) viewpoint.

Needless to say, there are many complex problems and issues with regard to the SN after they are delimited to those of literary level. To set aside issues of genre, literary character, and related problems around the recurrent discussion of historiography, one main issue remains, the boundaries of the SN. There is a trend to enlarge the boundaries particularly in the beginning. Whybray may well be identified as one of the few recent supporters to take the extent of the SN as 2 Samuel 9-20 and 1 Kings 1-2.[2]

Though an attempt to look for the beginning of the SN somewhere in 2 Samuel 6 was formerly made by Wellhausen,[3] it is in L. Rost's work in 1926 that 2 Sam 6:16, 20-23, 7:11b, 16 were extracted and regarded as the beginning of the story of the royal succession of David.[4] Strongly supported by von Rad's work,[5] which interpreted the SN with an additional interpretative perspective in the cultural-historical and intellectual-historical context, Rost's view has occupied the "quasi-canonical status in biblical studies for the best part of forty years."[6]

As for the inclusion of 2 Samuel 7 within the SN, Ridout may be a recent representative in the sense that he argues it totally from his rhetorical-critical methodology, though this does not seem to be widely accepted.[7]

---

[1]Cf., e.g., E. R. Leach, "The Legitimacy of Solomon: Some Structural Aspects of Old Testament History," *European Journal of Sociology* 7 (1966) 58-101.

[2]R. N. Whybray, *The Succession Narrative: A Study of II Sam. 9-12 and 1 Kings 1 and 2* (SBT 2/9, 1968) 8. Cf. W. Brueggemann, "On Coping with Curse: A Study of 2 Sam 16:5-14," *CBQ* 36 (1974) 175, 180.

[3]J. Wellhausen, *Die Composition des Hexateuchs und der historischen Bücher des Alten Testaments* (4th ed.; Berlin, 1963) 256.

[4]L. Rost, "Die Überlieferung von der Thronnachfolge Davids" (1926) *Das kleine Credo und andere Studien zum Alten Testament* (Heidelberg, 1965) 214-15.

[5]G. von Rad, "Der Anfang der Geschichtsschreibung im alten Israel" (1944) *Gesammelte Studien zum Alten Testament* (München, 1958) 148ff. E. T. in *The Problem of the Hexateuch and Other Essays* (New York, 1966) 166ff.

[6]C. Conroy, *Absalom Absalom! Narrative and Language in 2 Sam 13-20* (AnBib 81, 1978) 1.

[7]D. M. Gunn, *The Story of King David: Genre and Interpretation* (JSOT SupS 6, 1978) 67.

As for the boundaries of the SN, the most-discussed portion of the narrative in recent times is chaps. 2:8-4:12 (or 5:3).[8] Such scholars as Segal,[9] Schulte,[10] and Gunn[11] may be mentioned.

Another main issue is the theme of the SN. The following types represent many different scholarly opinions. The first type is represented by L. Rost, who asserts Solomon's succession of David's throne as the central theme of the whole narrative.[12] This well-known view interprets the theme in terms of the question "Who shall sit upon the throne of David?" as given in the final section (1 Kgs 1:20) of the SN. This view, which sees in all of the preceding chapters "the steady elimination of the alternative possibilities,"[13] was followed by von Rad and many others during the 1940s and 1950s.

The second type can be seen in Flanagan[14] on the one hand and in Delekat,[15] Würthwein,[16] and Langlamet[17] on the other. Their views are in common with each other insofar as they deny a unified political theme as proposed by Rost, but they still find themes of a political nature.

For instance, Flanagan distinguishes between the theme of David's legitimation of the earlier stratum seen in 2 Samuel 9-10, 13-20, and that of Solomon's succession in the later redactional addition in chaps. 11-12 and 1 Kings 1-2.[18] On the other hand, Delekat, Würthwein, and Langlamet in their respective ways see anti-Davidic and -Solomonic tendencies behind the present form of the narrative.

Cf. G. P. Ridout, *Prose Compositional Techniques in the Succession Narrative (2 Sam. 7, 9-20; 1 Kings 1-2)* (Berkeley Diss.; The Graduate Theological Union, 1971). See also T. N. D. Mettinger, *King and Messiah* (CB OTS 8, 1976) 31, 55.

[8]2 Sam 21:1-14 is sometimes referred. E.g., J. A. Soggin, *Introduction to the Old Testament*, (Philadelphia, 1976) 192-93 and Mettinger, *King and Messiah*, 31. Cf., however, L. Rost, *Das kleine Credo*, 192-93.

[9]M. H. Segal, "The Composition of the Books of Samuel," *JQR* 55 (1964-65) 323.

[10]H. Schulte, *Die Entstehung der Geschichtsschreibung im Alten Israel*, (BZAW 128, 1972) 142, 166.

[11]D. M. Gunn, "David and the Gift of the Kingdom (2 Sam 2-4, 9-20, 1 Kgs 1-2)," *Semeia* 3 (1975) 14, where more supporting names are listed. Attention should, however, be paid to Rendtorff, "Beobachtungen zur altisraelitischen Geschichtsschreibung anhand der Geschichte vom Aufstieg Davids," *Probleme biblischer Theologie. Festschrift von Rad* (München, 1971) 428-39, because he does not go beyond the identification of the author of 2 Sam 3:6-4:12 as belonging to the same group as the one of the SN (cf. ibid., 432).

[12]L. Rost, *Das kleine Credo*, 194ff., esp. 195 and 234.

[13]R. N. Whybray, *The Succession Narrative*, 21.

[14]J. W. Flanagan, "Court History or Succession Document? A Study of 2 Samuel 9-20 and 1 Kgs 1-2," *JBL* 91 (1972) 172-81.

[15]L. Delekat, "Tendenz und Theologie der David-Salomo-Erzählung," *Das ferne und nahe Wort. Festschrift L. Rost* (BZAW 105, 1967) 26-36.

[16]E. Würthwein, *Die Erzählung von der Thronfolge Davids. Theologische oder politische Geschichtsschreibung?* (Zürich, 1974).

[17]F. Langlamet, "Pour ou contre Salomon? La rédaction prosalomonienne de I Rois, I-II," *RB* 83 (1976) 321-79, 481-528.

[18]Cf. n. 14 and also J. Blenkinsopp, "Theme and Motif in the Succession History (2 Sam. xi 2ff) and the Yahwist Corpus," *Volume du Congrès, Genève, 1965*, (VTSup 15, 1966) 47.

A third type, which is a more radical departure from the second type, can be seen in Blenkinsopp. His approach is radical because the politically oriented theme advocated by those of the first and second types recedes into the background. Blenkinsopp detects one and the same theme recurring in the four portions of (a) 2 Sam 11:2-27 and 12:15b-25, (b) chaps. 13-14, (c) chaps. 15-20 and (d) 1 Kings 1-2, that is to say, the theme of "sin externalized in a sexual form which leads to death,"[19] and insists on the affinity in pattern and motif with the Yahwistic legends.[20] To some extent, several works of Brueggemann may also be viewed in this context.[21]

The fourth type may be seen in Carlson,[22] Schulte, and others.[23] Here the theme of the SN is said to have no connection with the succession question. Carlson, dissolving the corpus of the SN, distinguishes one section on "David under the Blessing" in 2 Samuel 2-7 and another section on "David under the Curse" in 2 Samuel 9-24. On the other hand, Schulte maintains the formal entity of the SN but includes 2 Samuel 2-4 and 1 Kings 1-2,[24] and changes the description from "The Succession Narrative" to "The Stories of David" (*Die David-Geschichten*),[25] which contains stories of the royal family of David[26] with David and Joab as the two main characters.[27]

Gunn in his most recent work adopts a similar viewpoint, in that he denies a unilateral "succession" theme. He retains a middle-of-the-road viewpoint, however, by saying that "the . . . story is a coherent . . . story of accession, rebellion and succession,"[28] and characterizes the "Story of King David" (2 Sam 2:1-5:3, or chaps. 9-20, and 1 Kgs 1-2) as "a story told for the purpose of serious entertainment."[29]

II. THE METHODOLOGY TO BE USED

There are many approaches to the synchronic and literary structural study of the SN. First of all, there is a linguistic and analytical approach

---

[19] Ibid., 48.

[20] Although his presentation in the most recent book (cf. n. 7) is put in more balanced and larger context, Gunn in his earlier article (n. 11) seems more positive to find the theme of giving and grasping frequently seen in the traditional oral tales of the SN.

[21] W. Brueggemann, "On Trust and Freedom. A Study of Faith in the Succession Narrative," *Int* 26 (1972) 3-19, where an emphasis is put in trust and abandonment (pp. 13, 16-17), whereas in *CBQ* 36 (1974) 180, he emphasizes, "Yahweh's governance of men's actions and destinies."

[22] R. A. Carlson, *David, the Chosen King: A Traditio-Historical Approach to the Second Book of Samuel* (Stockholm, 1964).

[23] J. J. Jackson, "David's Throne: Patterns in the Succession Story," *Canadian Journal of Theology* 11 (1965) 183-95.

[24] H. Schulte, *Die Entstehung der Geschichtsschreibung*, 142 and 169.

[25] Ibid., 138.

[26] Ibid., 176 and 180.

[27] Ibid., 180, cf. 141ff.

[28] D. N. Gunn, *The Story of King David*, 69, cf. 14.

[29] Ibid., 62.

carried out by W. Richter and his disciples. In the studies of the SN, a certain similarity with this method can be seen in Conroy's treatment of "the text as language system" in *Absalom, Absalom!*, though the latter is much more influenced by the approach of Alonso-Schökel.[30] It should be said that minute and detailed linguistic analysis does not always succeed in providing a synthetic and total grasp of a literary work.

Secondly, there is the structuralistic approach in which emphasis is placed on narrative patterns and motifs. Examples may be seen in Blenkinsopp and some of the works of Gunn. The patterns they use are more related to the deep structure level and tend to be too general to provide understanding of a particular literary work.

Thirdly, there is an attempt to find an overall symmetrical structure based upon corresponding themes.[31] In most cases, however, this can only be obtained by an arbitrary selection of particular themes.

In contrast to the three approaches above, both Ridout's rhetorical criticism and Conroy's narrative analysis seem more cogent in the sense that literary analysis proceeds in agreement with the form and style of a particular literary work, though there are many differences from our understanding of the structure of the SN, as is seen below.

The methodology taken here for the analysis of the literary structure is the same as that used for the analysis of the Book of Ruth.[32] This is based upon the recognition of the fact that language (and a linguistic work) comprises two totally distinct aspects of diachronism and synchronism and that literary-structural analysis should correspond to the synchronic aspect of a literary work and should be dealt with prior to the diachronic aspect.[33]

A linguistic, or literary, work synthesizes such levels as paragraph, sentence, and word level besides the levels below the word level. Opposing the view that a sentence is the basic unit for understanding a literary work, the Japanese sentence psychologist Kanji Hatano argues that a paragraph, the unit composed of sentence(s), is a thought unit, whereas a sentence, the unit which goes into the making of a paragraph, is a meaning unit. A word is to be seen as the constitutive element of sentence and/or paragraph.

If this basic orientation is followed, a literary work is seen as being composed of a series of paragraphs. Thus, the first step of our attempt to clarify a particular literary work starts with the analysis of a paragraph and the structure and texture inherent in it.

For this type of analysis, special significance is given to micro-contextual narrative patterns,[34] various types of repetition of words and

---

[30]W. Richter, *Exegese als Literaturwissenschaft: Entwurf einer alttestamentlichen Literatur-theorie und Methodologie* (Göttingen, 1971). As for the sentence division, we follow the principle of Richter.

[31]Flanagan, *JBL* 91 (1972) 177-81.

[32]"The Book of Ruth—Its Literary Structure and Theme," *AJBI* 4 (1978) 3-22.

[33]This is an essential thesis of F. de Saussure, *Cours de linguistique générale* (3d ed.; Paris, 1931).

[34]Cf. Conroy, *Absalom Absalom*, 93-95.

sentences constituting inclusio, chiasmus, or concentric structure. According to our paragraph theory, each key word/phrase, motif, and theological key phrase[35] should be seen, understood, and interpreted in accordance to its location in the context of the total structural complex, so as to avoid both subjective judgments and overemphasis on a particular passage.

III. LITERARY-STRUCTURAL ANALYSIS OF THE SUCCESSION NARRATIVE

1. 2 Samuel 15-20

(a) 15:1-17:29 and 19:9-20:22

In his recent monograph, Conroy sees the dominant narrative pattern of chaps. 15-20 as follows:[36]

A	Rebellion breaks out	15:1-12
B	The king's flight: meeting scenes	15:13-16:14
C	Clash of counselors	16:15-17:23
C′	Clash of armies	17:24-19:9
B′	The king's return: meeting scenes	19:9-41
A′	The king returns to Jerusalem, and the final stirrings of rebellion are crushed	19:42-20:22

The majority of scholars recognize the correspondence between the scene of David's flight and David's return (Conroy's B and B′). So let us, first of all, examine the sections from our structural viewpoint.

In 15:19-22 Ittai the Gittite appears. Responding to David's twice repeated command, "Return (שׁוב)" (vv. 19, 20), he affirms that he will remain with David with the repeated phrase, יהיה שׁם (vv. 21, 22). This dialogue demonstrates Ittai's loyalty.

After an interlude-like procession of penance in v. 23 the scene of the obedience to David of Zadok and Abiathar is introduced. David's command, "Carry back the ark of God (השׁב את ארון האלהים)" (v. 25) is executed in v. 29: "So Zadok and Abiathar carried back the ark of God (וישׁב צדוק ואביתר את־ארון האלהים)." Then comes the scene of David's prayer to defeat Ahithophel's counsel and his meeting with Hushai at the hilltop worshiping place (vv. 31-36), after the second interlude of the procession of penance (v. 30). Verse 37a concludes the scene, with Hushai's going to Jerusalem.

Thus, the structure of 15:19-37a may be said to be centered around a pair of persons loyal to David, plus David's prayer for the defeat of Ahithophel's counsel, and the appearance of Hushai as the means for causing that defeat.

This structure largely corresponds to 15:37b-16:15, within the framework of the similar passages of 15:37b and 16:15:

---

[35] In the study of the SN, for instance, 2 Sam 11:27, 12:24, and 17:14 are taken up by L. Rost, *Das kleine Credo*, 234-35, and significantly discussed by von Rad, *The Problem of the Hexateuch*, 181-87.

[36] Conroy, *Absalom Absalom*, 89.

15:37b   "And Absalom came to Jerusalem"

16:15   "And Absalom . . . came to Jerusalem and Ahithophel with him."

David meets here again with a pair of persons. One is Ziba (16:1-4) and the other Shimei (vv. 5-14). The latter's furious curse bracketed with a double inclusio is contrasted with David's prohibition of Abishai's killing Shimei, which is also bracketed with an inclusio.

(Shimei's curse)

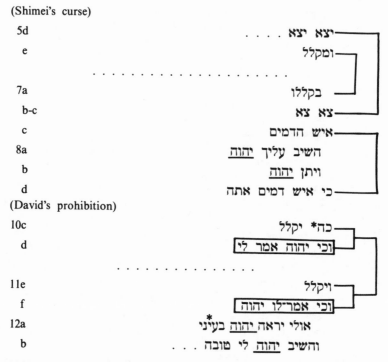

5d	יצא יצא . . . .
e	ומקלל
7a	בקללו
b-c	צא צא
c	איש הדמים
8a	השיב עליך יהוה
b	ויתן יהוה
d	כי איש דמים אתה

(David's prohibition)

10c	כה* יקלל
d	וכי יהוה אמר לי
11e	ויקלל
f	וכי אמר־לו יהוה
12a	אולי יראה יהוה בעי*ני
b	והשיב יהוה לי טובה . . .

YHWH's name (as mentioned twice in Shimei's curse) is parallel to the two occurrences of YHWH's name in David's trustful resignation. Then comes the scene of the defeat of Ahithophel's counsel by means of Hushai (16:16-17:23).

A few explanatory words should be given for the structural correspondence between 15:19-37a and 15:37b-17:23(29). In 15:19ff. we see two loyal and sincere persons with a sincere prayer. How do we judge the persons appearing in 15:37bff., particularly Ziba? Ridout clearly argues that "he (Meribbaal) rather than Ziba is the sincere party,"[37] comparing Meribbaal's words and deeds in 19:25ff. with those of Ziba in 16:1-4. Furthermore, Hushai appears as a figure who pretends himself loyal to Absalom in 16:16ff. in contrast to 15:31ff..

---

[37] Ridout, *Prose Compositional Techniques*, 166.

The structure of 16:16-17:23 may be seen as follows:

16:16-19	Hushai's pretended loyalty to Absalom	a
16:20-23	Ahithophel's counsel (vv. 20b, 23a, b), like a divine oracle	b
17:1-4	Ahithophel's counsel of killing the king alone and saving all the people	c
17:5-10	Hushai's refutation of Ahithophel's good counsel based upon an unreal fact	d

7b   לא טובה העצה אשר־יעץ אחיתפל . . .

8b   אתה ידעת את־אביך ואת־אנשיו
c   כי גברים המה

like a bear robbed of her cubs

10b   כי ידע כל־ישראל
10c   כי גבור אביך ובני־חיל אשר אתו

17:11-14b	Hushai's counsel of total annihilation	c'
17:14c-d	YHWH's ordination of the defeat of Ahithophel's counsel	b'

ויהוה צוה להפר את־עצת אחיתפל הטובה
לבעבור הביא יהוה אל־אבשלום את־הרעה

17:15-21(23)	Hushai's loyalty to David and Ahithophel's suicide	a'

It is to be noted that Hushai's strong argument based upon unreal facts occupies the center of the concentric structure of this section. It is thus seen that a pair of insincere and disloyal persons with a pretended argument is contrasted to those of 15:19-37a.

This section is concluded with mention of the formation of the battle front with the information of Amasa's being appointed as commander (17:25), which is bracketed by the double inclusio:

17:24a	ודוד בא מחנימה	a
b	ואבשלם עבר את־הירדן	b
25	Amasa appointed commander	c
26a	ויחן ישראל ואבשלם ארץ הגלעד	b'
27a	ויהי כבוא דוד מחנימה	a'

This portion centers around the two sincere characters in 15:19-37a(B_1) with an introductory note about the "passing" of David's party in 15:18(A) in the scene of David's flight. Parallel to this is the section about the two sincere figures, Meribbaal and Barzillai in 19:25-39 (B_1') with a concluding note of the "passing" of David's party in 19:40-41 (A'). It is also easy to see the correspondence between the portion centered around the two insincere figures in 15:37b-17:23(B_2) and that portion in which the same characters reappear on the scene (19:16a-24)(B_2').

Therefore 15:18-19:41 may be construed as forming a concentric structure centered around 18:1-19:9:

15:18	The passing of David's party	A
15:19-37b	David's meeting with a pair of loyal and sincere persons (Ittai and Zadok) with David's sincere prayer for the defeat of Ahithophel's counsel	B_1
15:37b-17:23	David's meeting with a pair of the insincere and disloyal persons (Ziba and Shimei) with the report of the defeat of Ahithophel's counsel by means of Hushai's pretended loyalty	B_2
17:24-29	Formation of the front: Amasa as commander	B_3
18:1-19:9	David's reign in exile (to be discussed in detail below)	C
19:10-16b	Discord between the tribes of Israel and the tribe of Judah, Amasa as commander	B_3'
19:16c-24	David's meeting with Ziba and Shimei	B_2'
19:25-39	David's meeting with a pair of sincere persons (Meribbaal and Barzillai)	B_1'
19:40-41	The passing of David's party	A'

19:42-44 may be construed as an introduction to Sheba's rebellion of chap. 20,[38] which is put in correspondence with Absalom's rebellion against David in 15:1-17. Both sections form the framework of 15:18-19:41. The correspondence of these first and last sections may be confirmed by David's word that "Sheba, the son of Bichri, will do us more harm than Absalom" (20:6).

(b) 18:1-19:9

18:1-19:9 is most appropriately placed at the summit portion of the large complex of chaps. 15-20 with regard to both content and form. It is located at the turning point from David's retreat and resignation to his return and restoration. An elevated tension sustains in full the contrasts about the fate of Absalom.

This section may be analyzed in structure as follows: 18:1-4c(A) tells how David, as the supreme commander, organizes three army divisions respectively under the commands of Joab, Abishai, and Ittai (vv. 1-2d) and sits enthroned at the gate (v. 4c). Between the scenes of David's reigning figure lies an incongruous episode that David's will to go out (יצא אצא) (v. 2f) is countered by the people's flat prohibition, "You shall not go out" (לא תצא) (v. 3b). This section corresponds to 19:6-9(A') telling of the king's public reappearance at the gate after Joab's stern remonstration against David, which is parallel to the people's confrontation with the king (vv. 2-3). Here in A' there are contrasts in much sharper form than in A between love and hate, life and death, one (rebellious son) and all (the other loyal veterans) (v. 7).

18:4d-17(18) (B) tells of Absalom's death in the midst of David's deep concern over him. As is shown in the structural analysis (Chart One), the repeated personal requests of the king over his "young man Absalom"

---

[38]Cf. H. W. Hertzberg, *Die Samuelbücher* (ATD 10, 1965) 303.

(vv. 5c, 12f) to the three army commanders (vv. 5a-b, 12d-e), just before the whole army marches off (vv. 4d, 6a), and just after the chief of the rebellion is caught in the tree branches, express a satiric irony. An ironic contrast is also shown between David's personal anxiety over Absalom and the large number of victims in the fierce battles. This personal anxiety of "the king" is put in a sharp contrast to the figure of the reigning king as seen in A.

Section B corresponds to B' (19:1-5) telling of the king's outburst of grief over his son at the roof-chamber of the gate:

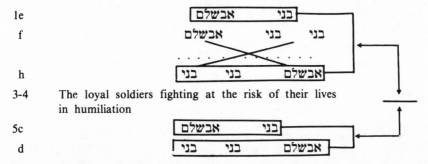

1e	אבשלם בני
f	בני בני אבשלם
h	אבשלם בני בני
3-4	The loyal soldiers fighting at the risk of their lives in humiliation
5c	אבשלם בני
d	אבשלם בני בני

Here in B' (19:1-5), too, the king laments exclusively as a father of a son in complete negligence of the loyal soldiers who fought at the risk of their lives. B' corresponds perfectly to B in this sense and is put in a sharp contrast to A'.

Chart One: 18:4d-17(18)

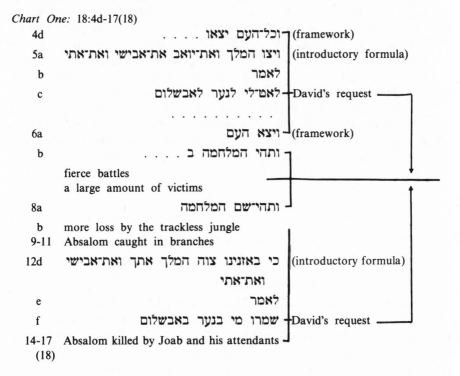

4d	וכל־העם יצאו	(framework)
5a	ויצו המלך ואת־יואב את־אבישי ואת־אתי	(introductory formula)
b	לאמר	
c	לאט־לי לנער לאבשלום	David's request
	. . . .	
6a	ויצא העם	(framework)
b	ותהי המלחמה ב	
	fierce battles	
	a large amount of victims	
8a	ותהי־שם המלחמה	
b	more loss by the trackless jungle	
9-11	Absalom caught in branches	
12d	כי באזנינו צוה המלך אתך ואת־אבישי	(introductory formula)
	ואת־אתי	
e	לאמר	
f	שמרו מי בנער באבשלום	David's request
14-17	Absalom killed by Joab and his attendants	
(18)		

As is seen above, 18:1-19:9 in itself is composed of a concentric structure:

18:1-4	David's reign at the gate. The paragraph contains the scene of the tension between the king and the people.	A
18:4d-17(18)	The king's anxiety over the fate of Absalom. The paragraph is composed of contrasts between the king's most private concern and the battle and victims of the royal army in public.	B
18:19-32	The news reaches the king at the gate. The structural features will be seen below.	C
19:1-5	The king's outburst of grief over his son's death is contrasted to the scene in which the triumph and return of the soldiers are turned into humiliation.	B'
19:6-9	The king's reappearance in reign at the gate. The paragraph contains the scene showing the tension between the king and Joab.	A'

We detect two features: (1) that A-A' and B-B' are in correspondence in structure, and (2) that each paragraph is, in turn, charged with a contrast in tension. The same characteristic feature can be detected in the central paragraph, too. Here in 18:19-32 (C) are three paragraphs, vv. 19-23, 24-27, and 28-32. The first and last paragraphs constitute a parallel in the sense that both refer to two messengers. The first paragraph (18:19-23) tells of the news of Absalom's death carried by two messengers. Ahimaaz' hasty suggestion of carrying the good tidings that "YHWH has delivered him from the power of his enemies" (v. 19) is contrasted to Joab's deliberate judgment that "the king's son is dead." This story is developed in the tension between hastiness and tardiness as well as in the contrast between good tidings and bad, between the king's enemy and the king's son, as is seen in a structural analysis (Chart Two).

The two messengers' reports to the king in the third paragraph (18:28-32) are parallel in structure between Ahimaaz' report in vv. 28-30 and the Cushite's report in vv. 31-32, both of which are centered around almost the same sentence expressing solely the king's deep anxiety over Absalom (vv. 29b, 32b) (Chart Three).

Chart Two: 18:19-23

19b	(Ahimaaz)	ארוצה נא ←
c		ואבשרה המלך
d		כי־שפטו יהוה מיד איביו ←
20	(Joab)	
b		לא איש בשרה אתה היום הזה ⌐
d		והיום הזה לא תבשר ⌐
e		כי־על־בֵן בן־המלך מת ←

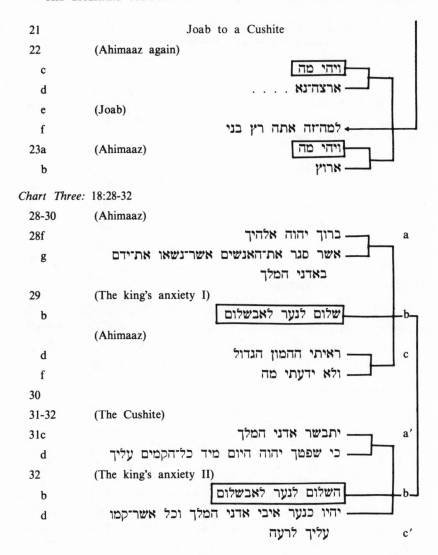

21   Joab to a Cushite

22   (Ahimaaz again)

c   ויהי מה

d   . . . . ארצה־נא

e   (Joab)

f   למה־זה אתה רץ בני

23a   (Ahimaaz)   ויהי מה

b   ארוץ

Chart Three: 18:28-32

28-30   (Ahimaaz)

28f   ברוך יהוה אלהיך   a

g   אשר סגר את־האנשים אשר־נשאו את־ידם

                                    באדני המלך

29   (The king's anxiety I)

b   שלום לנער לאבשלום   b

        (Ahimaaz)

d   ראיתי ההמון הגדול   c

f   ולא ידעתי מה

30

31-32   (The Cushite)

31c   יתבשר אדני המלך   a'

d   כי שפטך יהוה היום מיד כל־הקמים עליך

32   (The king's anxiety II)

b   השלום לנער לאבשלום   b

d   יהיו כנער איבי אדני המלך וכל אשר־קמו

                                   עליך לרעה   c'

The implication of Absalom as the king's "enemy" both at first (v. 28g) and at last (v. 32d) forms an inclusio in the last paragraph. The tidings from the battlefront that the king's enemies are destroyed are in sharp contrast to David's sole concern for the safety of his young son. It may be certain that the author is not so much interested to give a mere historiographical report of a simple fact of Absalom's death and David's grief as to display through literary skills and elaborations the ambivalences in character. David is displayed in ambivalence between being a reigning sovereign and an exiled fugitive, between being a public figure and a private father, between being an institutional-political head and a personal family head. Ambivalence turns out to be irony in the various phases.

The passage in 18:24-27 contains one of the most salient cases of irony.[39] It is ironical because the reader already knows what David does not yet know. So it is a comedy for the reader, while the story is a tragedy for the hero. Suspense grows as to how he will react when he really knows of his son's death. David alone expects good tidings up until the near end in spite of the fact that the approach of messengers one after another should reveal the king's expectation to be in vain, as is shown in the structural analysis below:

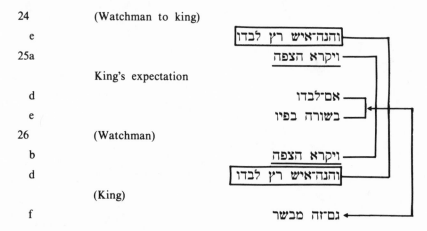

24	(Watchman to king)	
e		והנה־איש רץ לבדו
25a		ויקרא הצפה
	King's expectation	
d		אם־לבדו
e		בשורה בפיו
26	(Watchman)	
b		ויקרא הצפה
d		והנה־איש רץ לבדו
	(King)	
f		גם־זה מבשר

2. 2 Samuel 10-14

Other sections should necessarily be discussed more briefly.

In regard to chaps. 10-13, the first question to be asked is as to whether the narrative of chaps. 13-14 should continue to chaps. 15ff. Charles Conroy, in his recent work, for example, takes chaps. 13-20 as a unit and discusses the relationship between chaps. 13-14 and 15-20.[40]

It is, however, my contention that chaps. 13-14 should rather be dealt together with chaps. 11-12 both structurally and thematically. Our structural analysis shows that there repeatedly is found the same composition of the concentric structure with the sharp contrast and ambivalence at the central and chiastic point, which is generally expressed in two sentences put side by side. This particular structure is seen in 13:1-22, 23-37(38) and 11:1-12:31, as is seen below.

Thematically to be considered is the fact that adultery and murder committed by the father David in chaps. 11-12 are repeated by his sons, Amnon and Absalom.

10:1-14(15-19d), 19e may be construed as an introduction to the larger complexes of chaps. 11-12 and 13-14.

(a) 13:1-22

---

[39]Cf. Ridout, *Prose Compositional Techniques*, 102.

[40]Conroy, *Absalom Absalom*, 92-93.

Ridout gives a neat rhetorical analysis of 13:1-22.[41] Here is an alternative literary-structural analysis proposed with due consideration of Jonadab's counsel and its execution as well as of the repeated sentences (14a, 16a) as inclusios (Chart Four).

Chart Four: 13:1-22

A 1-4   Amnon is in love with his half-sister, Tamar.

1b	‏ולאבשלום בן־דוד . . . .‏	(a)
c	‏ושמה תמר‏	
d	‏ואהבה אמנון בן־דוד‏	(b)
2a	‏ויצר לאמנון להתחלות בעבור תמר אחתו‏	
	‏. . . . .‏	(c)
3a	‏ולאמנון רע‏	(a′)
b	‏ושמו יונדב . . . .‏	
c	‏ויונדב איש חכם מאד‏	(c′)
4e	‏את־תמר אחות אבשלם אחי אני אהב‏	(b′)

B 5-11a   Jonadab's counsel and its execution

5a	‏שכב . . . .‏	a
b	‏והתחל‏	
c	‏ובא אביך לראותך‏	b
d	‏ואמרת אליו‏	c
e	‏תבא נא תמר אחותי‏	d
f	‏ותברני לחם‏	e
g	‏ועשתה לעיני את־הבריה‏	
h	‏למען אשר אראה ואכלתי מידה‏	f
6	(execution I)	
a	‏וישכב‏	a′
b	‏ויתחל‏	
c	‏ויבא המלך לראתו‏	b′
d	‏ויאמר אמנון אל־המלך‏	c′
e	‏תבוא־נא תמר אחתי‏	d
f	‏ותלבב לעיני שתי לבבות‏	e′
g	‏ואברה מידה‏	f′

---

[41] Ridout, "The Rape of Tamar. A Rhetorical Analysis of 2 Sam 13:1-22," *Rhetorical Criticism* (eds. J. J. Jackson & M. Kessler; Pennsylvania, 1974) 75-84. Cf. Ridout, *Prose Compositional Techniques*, 50-56, 90-94, 110-12, etc. Cf. also Conroy, *Absalom Absalom*, 19-20.

7-11a   (execution II with elaboration)

7c	לכי נא בית אמנון אחיך	d'
d	ועשי־לו הבריה	e'
8e	ותלבב לעיניו	e"
9c	וימאן לאכל	
10b	הביאי הבריה החדר	
c	ואברה מידך	f"
e	ותבא לאמנון אחיה החדרה	
11a	ותגש אליו לאכל	

C 11b-14   Amnon's forceful action and Tamar's resistance

11b	ויחזק־בה	
c	ויאמר לה	
d	בואי	(imperat)
e	שכבי עמי אחותי	(imperat)
12-13	Tamar's persuasion	
14a	ולא אבה לשמע בקולה	
b	ויחזק ממנה	
c	ויענה	
d	וישכב אתה	

D 15a-b   Love turns to hate

15a	וישנאה אמנון	(a)
	שנאה	(b)
	גדולה מאד	(c)
b	כי גדולה	(c')
	ושנאה	(b')
	אשר שנאה	(a')
	מאהבה אשר אהבה	

C' 15c-17 Amnon's forceful action and Tamar's leaving

15d	קומי	(imperat)
e	לכי	(imperat)
16a-b	Tamar's persuasion	
c	ולא אבה לשמע לה	
17c	שלחו־נא	(imperat)
d	ונעל	(imperat)

B′ 18-19   Result of Jonadab's counsel
A′ 20-22   Absalom hates Amnon

Our literary-structural analysis reveals that the two sentences with the key words, that is, "to love" and "to hate" (vv. 15a, b), bracketed by almost the same sentence (vv. 14a, 16c) accompanying a pair of the same words or form, constitute a climactic and chiastic turning point of the concentric structure of this paragraph (D). Unsearchable psychological ambivalence between love and hate occupies the center of this section.

(b) 13:23a-38b

13:23a-38b are also composed in a concentric structure with a depiction at the climax of the contrast between Absalom's flight and the other princes' return (v. 34a and v. 34d),[42] as is seen below (Chart Five):

Chart Five: 13:23a-38b

A   23a-29b Absalom's plan to murder Amnon, its execution and his
                  flight

23a   לכל־בני המלך . . . .

25e   ויפצר־בו

27a   ויפצר־בו אבשלום

b   ואת כל־בני המלך . . . . . .

28a   ויצו אבשלום

29b   כאשר צוה אבשלום

c   וינם

B   30-31   Confusion of the royal court and mourning
C   32-33   Jonadab's cool judgment expressed to the king

32c-d   אל . . . . . את כל־הנערים בני־המלך המיתו

33a, c   אל . . . . . כל־בני המלך מתו

D   34a-d   Absalom's flight and the other princes' return

34a   ויברח אבשלום

b   וישא הנער הצפה את־עינו

c   וירא

d   והנה עם־רב הלכים מדרך . . . .

C′   35a-36b Jonadab to the king

35b   והנה בני־המלך באו

36b   והנה בני־המלך באו

---

[42] Adoption of the longer text based upon the LXX and others may not be necessary from the literary-structural viewpoint. Cf. *Preliminary and Interim Report on the Hebrew Old Testament Text Project* (Stuttgart, 1976) 235-37.

B′ 36c-e A national mourning
A′ 37-38b Absalom's flight

 37a   ‏וַאבשלום ברח‏‎

 b   ‏גשור . . . . . וילך‏

 38a   ‏ואבשלום ברח‏

 b   ‏וילך גשור‏

   It is easy to notice that the plot of this section is parallel with that of
18:1-19:9 in the sense that a story is told in such a way that David does not
know what the reader knows.

   (c) 13:38c-14:33

   This section also constitutes a concentric structure with a double
depiction at the climactic portion of the contrast between David's granting
Absalom's return to Jerusalem and yet not granting him an audience
(14:23c vs. 24c, e; 28a vs. b). The double depiction functions as an inclusio
of the statement of the beauty of Absalom and his daughter (vv. 25-27),
which provides an additional tension to the climactic portion,[43] as is seen in
the structural analysis (Chart Six):

Chart Six: 13:38c-14:33

A 13:38c-14:20 David's inclination to Absalom and Joab's device
B 14:21-23b   Joab goes to Geshur to bring back Absalom
C 14:23c-28   Absalom returns to Jerusalem but is not allowed to see
         the king's face

 23c   ‏ויבא את־אבשלום ירושלם‏

 24b   ‏יסב אל־ביתו‏ (command)

 c   ‏ופני לא יראה‏

 d   ‏ויסב אבשלום אל־ביתו‏ (execution)

 e   ‏ופני המלך לא ראה‏

 25-27   Absalom's physical charm and that of his children

 25a   ‏איש יפה‏ . . . . .

 27c   ‏אשה יפת מראה‏

 28a   ‏וישב אבשלום בירושלם‏

 b   ‏ופני המלך לא ראה‏

B′ 14:29-32   Absalom's protest to Joab as to why he came back from
         Geshur
A′ 14:33   David meets Absalom

   (d) Chaps. 11-12

   Ridout finds here a concentric structure as follows:[44]

---

[43] Even though vv. 25-27 should be regarded as a later addition, it does not have a serious
effect upon our structural analysis.

[44] Ridout, *Prose Compositional Techniques*, 63-64.

A. David sends Joab and all Israel against Rabbah; David remains in Jerusalem (11:1).
B. David has intercourse with Bathsheba, and she becomes pregnant (11:2-5).
C. Uriah is killed at David's will (11:6-17).
D. The message comes to David; he replies

אל־ירע בעיניך את־הדבר הזה (11:18-25).

    E. David takes Uriah's wife as his own, and she bears a son (11:26-27a).

D'. וירע הדבר אשר־עשה דוד בעיני יהוה.

    Yahweh sends a message by Nathan (11:27b-12:15a).
C'. The son dies; it is Yahweh's will (12:15b-23).
B'. David has intercourse with Bathsheba; she becomes pregnant and bears a son (12:24-25).
A'. Joab takes part of Rabbah. He sends for David to come and take the city. David and all the army then return to Jerusalem (12:26-31).

In the correspondences between A and A', B and B', we are in accord with Ridout. In C-D-E-D'-C', however, we have a different analysis. Viewed from both content and form, 11:6-13 and vv. 14-24 make a respective paragraph (C and D), because, in the former section, the phrase "going down to (his) house" is repeated five times (vv. 8, 9, 10, 10, 13) but not thereafter, and because the sentence that "Uriah the Hittite was slain also" is repeated three times (vv. 17, 21, 24) in the latter section (vv. 14-24). Verses 6-13(C) depict a series of conversations between David and Uriah, whereas vv. 14-24(D) depict a battle report.

Verses 25-27(E) constitute a climactic section which shows how the feelings of David and of YHWH are in sharp contrast:

25c   אל־ירע בעיניך את־הדבר הזה

27f   וירע הדבר אשר־עשה דוד בעיני יהוה

Section D (vv. 14-24), telling of a report of Uriah's death in battle, corresponds to 12:15b-20 (D'), which depicts a report of the death of David's son (cf. vv. 18, 18, 18, 19, 19).[45]

12:21-23(C'), depicting a conversation between David and his attendants, corresponds to C(11:6-13) so far as both sections deal with ascetic practices.

The structure of chaps. 11-12 may therefore be seen as follows:

A   11:1   Joab and his army are sent against Rabbah.
B   11:2-5   David's adultery with Bathsheba.

---

[45] As some scholars suspect its originality (e.g., Würthwein, *Die Erzählung von der Thronfolge Davids*, 23-24), 12:1-15a seems difficult to be placed appropriately in the structural context.

C	11:6-13	Uriah does not obey David because of his ascetism.
D	11:14-24	Report of Uriah's death in battle.
E	11:25-27	David's attitude is contrasted to YHWH's attitude.
D'	12:15b-20	Report of the death of David's son.
C'	12:21-23	David explains his ascetic practice.
B'	12:24-25	David's marriage to Bathsheba.
A'	12:26-31	Rabbah is besieged and taken by David.

(e) Chap. 10, with comments on chap. 2

As for chap. 10, vv. 1-5 may be analysed structurally as follows:

(David's intention)

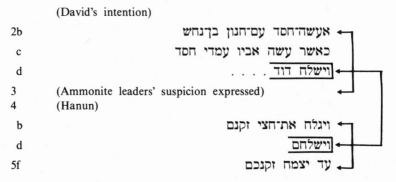

2b		אעשה־חסד עם־חנון בן־נחש
c		כאשר עשה אביו עמדי חסד
d		וישלח דוד . . . .
3	(Ammonite leaders' suspicion expressed)	
4	(Hanun)	
b		ויגלח את־חצי זקנם
d		וישלחם
5f		עד יצמח זקנכם

The cause of war between the Ammonites and David is depicted in the sentences placed around the two axes, to send forth and to send back. Around each axislike sentence are placed sentences of contrast, of good intention, and of bad suspicion in the first case, and of shaving off of beards and of growing beards in the second.

Verses 6-14[46] (+ 19b), except for vv. 15-19a, which belong to a different literary stratum, contain these elements: the dispatch of armies (vv. 6-7) in the parallel sentences, וישלחו בני עמון and וישלח את־יואב (vv. 6c-7b); in the formation of the front (vv. 8-11) in the parallel sentences, ויערכו מלחמה (v. 8b) and ויערך לקראת . . . (repeated in v. 9d and v. 10b); the flight of the Ammonites and their allies (vv. 13-14c) with an inclusio, וינסו מפני . . . (vv. 13b, 14c), and the return of the armies also with an inclusio, ויבא/ויבאו (v. 14d and f). Joab's speech (vv. 11-12) precedes vv. 13-14.

The process depicted in chap. 10 of the dispatch of troops, the formation of the front, confrontation, flight, and return is seen to be parallel with chap. 2 (2:8, 9, 10b, 12 on the dispatch of troops; vv. 13-16 on the formation of the front; vv. 17-28 on the pursuit of the fleeing enemy; vv. 29-32 on the return of the armies).

Our assumption is that chap. 10 constitutes an introduction to chaps. 11-12 and 13-14, whereas chap. 2 is an introduction to chaps. 3-4 and 9. It

---

[46]For a different judgment, Gunn, *The Story of King David*, 65, who follows Rost at this point.

is interesting to note that each larger complex of the SN, except for the epilogue of 1 Kings 1-2, is introduced by a narrative of either internal or external war.

	(Introduction: Narrative of War)		(Main Body: Episode[s])	(Conclusion)
Part III	15:1-17	+	15:18-19:41	(+ 19:42-20:22)
Part II	10:1-14, 19b	+	11-14	
Part I	2:8-32	+	3-4 and 9	

3. 2 Samuel 3, 4, and 9

(a) Chap. 3

   (1) Verses 1-6a

As is shown in the structural analysis below, the list of Daivd's sons born in Hebron, which is bracketed by an inclusio, is once more bracketed by another inclusio:

1a   ותהי המלחמה ארכה בין בית שאול ובין בית דוד ─────┐

2a   וילדו לדוד בנים בחברון ─┐   │

           List of the name of the sons of David   │   │

5b   אלה ילדו לדוד בחברון ─┘   │

6a   ויהי בהיות המלחמה בין בית שאול ובין בית דוד ─────┘

   (2) Verses 6b-39

Following this paragraph, which is usually regarded as deuteronomistic, a sentence starting with *waw* + a personal name, which may be construed as a trait of the writer of the SN, constitutes a paragraph integral to the SN.

The basic structure of 3:6bff. may be construed as follows:

A   6b-11,   A conflict between Abner and Ishbaal, set
    exc. 10   between sentences telling of Abner's strength
               (v. 6b) and Ishbaal's weakness (v. 11).

B   12a-21f   The covenant concluded between Abner and
               David

    12e   (Abner)   כרתה בריתך אתי ─┐

    13c   (David)   אני אכרת אתך ברית ─┘

       13d-19 may be secondary

    21e   ויכרתו אתך ברית ─┘

C   21g-h   David sends Abner back in safety

    21g   וישלח דוד את־אבנר

    h | וילך בשלום |─┐

D   22a-c   Abner is no longer there when Joab comes
               back from a raid

22a		והנה עבדי דוד ויואב בא מהגדוד
b		וׁשלל רב עמם הביאו
c		ואבנר איננו עם־דוד בחברון
C′ 22d-e	David sends Abner back in safety	
d		כי שלחו
e		וילך בשלום
B′ 23-25	Joab's suspicion about Abner	
23d		בא־אבנר בן־נר אל־המלך
e		וישלחהו
f		וילך בשלום
24d		והנה־בא אבנר אליך
e		למה־זה שלחתו
f		וילך הלוך
25b		כי לפתתך בא
c		ולדעת . . . .
d		ולדעת . . . .
A′ 26-39	A conflict between David and Joab after Abner was slain by Joab.	

This particular type of concentric structure is widely seen in the complexes of the SN and particularly in 13:23-38. In D, the incongruous actions of the two parties are depicted side by side, which heightens the suspense of the narrative. Furthermore, the depiction and the style of B′ (vv. 23-25) remind us of those in 10:1-5.

(b) Chap. 4

The literary structure of chap. 4 (except for vv. 2d-4) may also be construed as a concentric structure with antithetical sentences at the climactic paragraph.

The structure may be viewed as follows:

| A | 1 | Abner dies in Hebron |
| B | 2a-d, 5a-8a | Ishbosheth's head is carried to David by two servants who killed their master. |

2a-d		בענה . . . רכב בני רמון הבארתי . . .
		c b a
5a		וילכו בני רמון הבארתי רכב ובענה
		a b c
b		ויבאו
c		והוא שכב . . .
6b		ויכהו

(framework)

c   Rechab and Baanah escaped
7b   . . . ‏והוא־שכב‏
c   ‏ויכהו‏
g   ‏וילכו‏—(framework)—
8a   . . . ‏ויבאו את־ראש איש־בשת‏
C   8b-11c   The two men are reprimanded by
                David
8c (R. & B.)   ‏אשר . . . הנה־ראש איש־בשת‏
               ‏בקש את־נפשך‏
d   . . . . ‏נקמות . . . ויתן יהוה‏
9 (David)
c   ‏חי־יהוה אשר־פדה את־נפשי מכל־צרה‏
11b   . . . . ‏ועתה הלוא אבקש‏
B'   12a-d   The two men are punished
     12e-f   The head of Ishbosheth is buried in
                Abner's tomb in Hebron.

(c) Chap. 9

As seen above, chaps. 2-4, exclusive of a few passages and sections, represent a certain homogeneous character. These chapters are concerned with the fate of the house of Saul and its relation to David, and this subject is depicted in connection with certain concrete characters, such as Abner, Ishbosheth (Ishbaal), and some minor characters on the one hand, and Joab, David, and some other minor figures on the other.

This consideration with some others leads us to take chap. 9 as a direct sequel to these chapters. Historical notes (5:1-3; 6-9 [10]), lists (5:4-5, 13-16; 8:15-18), annals (5:17-6:1; 8:1-14) and a religious story on the royal theology (chap. 7) are not in accord with the literary characteristics of chaps. 2-4.

As for chap. 6, it is generally accepted that it is a sequel to 1 Sam 4:1-7:1 and a conclusion of the story of the Ark. Rost, however, extracts vv. 16, 20-23 for the point of departure of the SN and interprets these verses as telling of "the childlessness of the inborn Empress Dowager."[47]

According to our literary-structural analysis,[48] it is difficult to extract v. 16 from the immediate context of vv. 13-19. It is also difficult to

---

[47] Rost, *Die kleine Credo*, 213. Gunn touches on some possibilities to connect 5:1-3 with the story of Michal's childlessness of chap. 6 (ibid., 73-74) and to interpret them as telling of the rejoicing scene at the coronation of David in Hebron.

[48] A structural analysis of 6:13-23 is as follows:

13a   . . . ‏ויהי כי צעדו נשאי ארון יהוה‏
b   ‏ויזבח שור ומריא‏ ———

understand that particular verse referring to the childlessness of Michal (v. 23) as belonging to the succession theme. Verse 23 should be construed as referring to the motif of curse, since it is put in contrast to v. 20a referring to that of blessing.

There seems no positive reason to think that the Michal story should be included in the SN. Even if it should, it would certainly not constitute the beginning of the SN.

The structure of chap. 9 may be construed as follows:

A	1	David's intention to favor the remnant of the house of Saul

1c	ואעשה עמו חסד בעבור יהונתן	a

B	2-5	David asks Ziba about Mephibosheth

3c	ואעשה עמו חסד אלהים	a

14a	ודוד מכרכר . . . . . . לפני יהוה
b	ודוד חגור אפוד בד
15a	ודוד וכל בית ישראל מעלים את־ארון יהוה
16a	והיה ארון יהוה בא . . . . . .
b	ומיכל בת־שאול נשקפה
c	ותרא את־המלך דוד מפזז ומכרכר . . .
d	ותבז לו בלבה
17a	ויבאו את־ארון יהוה
c	ויעל דוד עלות . . . והשלמים
18a	ויכל דוד מהעלות העולה והשלמים
b	ויברך את־העם . . . .
19a	ויחלק לכל־העם . . . .
b	וילך כל־העם . . . .
20a	וישב דוד לברך את־ביתו — David's blessing
b	ותצא מיכל בת־שאול לקראת דוד
c	(M. to D.) ותאמר
d	מה־נכבד היום מלך ישראל . . . — King's shame
21a	(D. to M.)
b	לפני יהוה אשר . . — David's protestation
e	ושחקתי לפני יהוה
22a	ונקלתי עוד מזאת
b	והייתי שפל בעיני
c	ועם־האמהות . . . . אכבדה — King's shame
23	ולמיכל בת־שאול לא־היה לה ילד . . . — Michal's curse

C   6-8   David's favor expressed to Mephibosheth

7c   כי עשה אעשה עמך חסד בעבור יהונתן אביך   a

7e   ואתה תאכל לחם על־שלחני תמיד   b

B'   9-11c   David's question to Ziba

10d   ומפיבשת בן־אדניך יאכל תמיד לחם

על־שלחני   b

A'   11d-13   David's favor executed

11d   ומפיבשת אכל על־שלחני ─────── b ┐

12c   (Ziba's family serves Mephibosheth)

13a   ומפיבשת ישב בירושלם ─── ┤ b ┘

b   כי על־שלחן המלך תמיד הוא אכל ───

c   A note of his lameness is related to an
inserted note of 4:4.

This is certainly not the same type of concentric structure as those which
we have seen so far in the SN. Noticeable in this structure is an alternation
of one motif-sentence repeated three times in the first part with another
motif-sentence, which is, in turn, repeated four times in the second.

This particular structure can, however, be detected in the essential part
of the epilogue of the whole SN, that is to say, 1 Kgs 1, 2:1-2a, 10 and 12,
which will be discussed in the next section.

IV. EPILOGUE

Instead of drawing conclusions on all the important subjects with
regard to the SN, which may require more than one section, we would
close with some remarks on the theme of what is usually designated as the
Succession Narrative in terms of the literary-structural analysis of 1 Kings
1-2 and in view of its total context.

1. 1 Kgs 1:1-2:12

This section may be analysed as follows (Chart Seven):

Chart Seven: 1 Kgs 1:1-2:12
1:1-4   David's advanced age and impotence
1:5-10   Adonijah's usurpation

5c   אני אמלך   A

7-8   supporters and opponents

9a   ויזבח אדניהו   B

b   those invited and those not invited   C

ויקרא . . . . ┐

10   לא קרא   . . . . ┘

1:11-21   Nathan's counsel and its execution
            (Nathan to Bathsheba)

11d	כי מלך אדניהו בן־חגית	A′
e	ואדנינו דוד לא ידע	
13d	הלא־אתה אדני המלך	
e	נשבעת לאמתך	
f	לאמר	
g	כי־שלמה בנך ימלך אחרי	d_1
h	והוא ישב על־כסאי	d_2

            (Bathsheba to David)

17b	אדני אתה נשבעת ביהוה אלהיך לאמתך	
c	כי־שלמה בנך ימלך אחרי	d_1
d	והוא ישב על־כסאי	d_2
18a	ועתה הנה אדניה מלך	
b	ואתה אדני המלך לא ידעת	
19a	ויזבח	B′
b	ויקרא	

       those invited and those not invited   C′

c	לא קרא	
20d	מי ישב על־כסא אדני המלך אחריו	D

1:22-27   Nathan's direct advice to David

24d	אדניהו ימלך אחרי	A′
25b	ויזבח	B′
c	ויקרא	C′
26	לא קרא	
27c	מי ישב על־כסא אדני־המלך אחריו	D

1:28-31   David's sworn decision

29c	חי־יהוה אשר־פדה את־נפשי מכל־צרה	
30a	כי כאשר נשבעתי לך ביהוה אלהי ישראל	
b	לאמר	
c	כי־שלמה בנך ימלך אחרי	d_1
d	וחוא ישב על־כסאי תחתי	d_2
e	כי כן אעשה היום הזה	

1:32-37   David's concrete directives

33b	קחו	aa
c	והרכבתם את־שלמה . . . על־הפרדה	bb
d	והורדתם אתו אל־גחון	cc

34a		ומשח אתו	dd
b		ותקעתם בשופר	ee
c		ואמרתם	ff
d		יחי המלך שלמה	
35a		ועליתם אחריו	gg
c		וישב על־כסאי	d_2
d		והוא ימלך תחתי	d_1
36	Jubilation (Benaiah)		hh
1:38-40	Execution of David's directives		
38a		וירד	aa'(cc')
b		וירכבו את־שלמה על־פרדת המלך דוד	bb'
c		וילכו אתו על־גחון	cc'
39a		ויקח	(aa')
b		וימשח את־שלמה	dd'
c		ויתקעו בשופר	ee'
d		ויאמרו כל־העם	ff'
e		יחי המלך שלמה	
40a		ויעלו כל־העם אחריו	gg'
b-c	Jubilation (people)		hh'
1:41-53	Jonathan's report		
41c-e	Noise in the city		(framework)
43d		אדנינו המלך־דוד המליך את שלמה	d_1
44a		וישלח אתו־המלך את	aa'
	cf. 38a		
b		וירכבו אתו על פרדת המלך	bb'
45a		וימשחו אתו . . . בגחון	cc' + dd'
b		ויעלו משם שמחים	(gg' + hh')
46		וגם ישב שלמה על כסא המלוכה	d_2
47-48	Jubilation (David)		hh'
49	Dispersion		
50-53	Adonijah's flight		
2:1-2a, 10, 12	David's death and Solomon's enthronement		
12a		ושלמה ישב על־כסא דוד אביו	d_2'

The structure of the epilogue of the SN may be summarized as follows:

[A]   1:1-4   David's advanced age
[B]   1:5-27   Adonijah's usurpation is countered by Nathan and Bathsheba. Adonijah's usurpation motifs (A-B-C) are repeated three times; in the last two cases the counter-

                      motif (D) is with the other motifs.

[C]   1:28-31   David's basic decision—climax—

[B]'   1:32-53   Execution of David's concrete directives are also repeated three times (aa--hh)

[A]'   2:1-12   David's death

Here in the epilogue appears the alternation of a set of motifs repeated three times in the first part with another set of motifs repeated three times. In these characteristics the passage of 1 Kgs 1:1-2:12 is parallel in structure with 2 Samuel 9.

It is furthermore to be noted that the response formulated in two sentences (d_1 and d_2) to the counter-motif formulated in a question (D) appears in three paragraphs in the middle sections ([B]-[C]-[B]'), except for the first and the last paragraphs, where the variation of d_2 is used for the closing sentence of the epilogue.

Salient features in the epilogue are the recapitulations of the motifs appearing in the preceding chapters. The depiction of David's advanced age and sexual impotence (1 Kgs 1:1-4) is set in ironical contrast to his vigor and sexual potency (2 Sam 11:2-5). Adonijah's preparation of rebel forces (1 Kgs 1:5) and his sacrificing (1 Kgs 1:9, etc.) are parallel with those of Absalom's rebellion (2 Sam 15:1 and 12). A note about Adonijah's handsome appearance (1 Kgs 1:6) is also parallel to that of Absalom in 2 Sam 14:25. Adonijah's expectation of good tidings in 1 Kgs 1:42 reminds us of that of King David in 2 Sam 18:25, 26, and 27. It may not be a mere coincidence that we have a perfectly identical sentence here in the climactic portion of the epilogue as well as in the first section of the SN, that is to say, 1 Kgs 1:29 and 2 Sam 4:9:

חי־יהוה אשר־פדה את־נפשי מכל־צרה.

It may be equally significant that David's oath to Bathsheba of the succession of Solomon by YHWH is formulated in the following style:

כי כאשר נשבעתי לך ביהוה אלהי ישראל

כי כן אעשה היום הזה   (1 Kgs 1:30).

This is parallel to Abner's oath of the establishment of David's kingship similarly formulated in the following style:

כי כאשר נשבע יהוה לדוד

כי כן אעשה־לו   (2 Sam 3:9).

Thus, we do not follow the opinion that 1 Kings 1-2 should be taken as a separate stratum from the SN portions of 2 Samuel.[49] We agree with the opinion that a coherent story is found in 2 Samuel 2-4, 9-20 and 1 Kgs 1-2.

---

[49]Cf. Conroy, *Absalom Absalom*, 2, n. 9.

2. Some Remarks on the Theme of the SN

The view represented by Rost and followed by others, that Solomon's succession to David's throne is the central theme of the SN, is based upon the argument that the author's intention is clearly expressed in the repetition of the same passage in the last two chapters (1 Kings 1-2) and that these chapters should be the clue for the understanding of the whole.[50]

This is, however, difficult to sustain, viewed from our literary-structural analysis. The question as to "who shall sit on the throne of my lord the king after him" is raised and answered repeatedly by the sentence, "Solomon shall reign after me, and he shall sit on my throne" and the like, only in this last complex and not at all in the preceding complexes. Solomon's succession is the theme only of the last two chapters. It is nothing more or less than a report of the factual process.[51]

Recently, the question has been raised as to the intention of the story. Delekat detects here, for instance, the intention of scandalizing Solomon's reign and of shaking of the people's loyalty to it.[52] In view of the fact that the author criticises Adonijah as he who "exalted himself" (1 Kgs 1:5a) and, at the same time, reports in a dispassionate attitude that Solomon's succession was decided by David in a close confinement at the royal chamber, we assume that the author maintains a somewhat aloof attitude towards political affairs.[53] He is rather interested in depicting ambivalence and tension in subtlety between the private and the public-political realms[54] throughout the four larger complexes of the SN. Parts One (2 Samuel 2-4 and 9) and Four (1 Kings 1-2) are usually construed as describing exclusively political affairs. The former depicts the most significant political event in the first half of David's public life in his acquisition of the kingdom of Israel by covenant through Abner's intrigue. This happens, however, after he had a serious personal conflict with Ishbaal in terms of very private behavior. Part Four describes the most significant political event in the last half of David's public life, that is, Solomon's succession. This was done, however, through David's decision disclosed to Bathsheba in a close confinement in court after Nathan's counter-intrigue and deceit.

On the other hand, Part Two (2 Samuel 10, 11-12, 13-14) is usually construed as depicting the most private affairs of a father and his children.[55]

---

[50] Rost, *Das kleine Credo*, 195. Cf. Whybray, *The Succession Narrative*, 19-21.

[51] Gunn, *The Story of King David*, 82-84.

[52] Delekat, "Tendenz und Theologie der David-Salomo-Erzählung," 30-31.

[53] H. J. Hermisson, "Weisheit und Geschichte," *Probleme Biblischer Theologie* (München, 1971) 148, n. 16. Schulte assumes that Jonathan ben Abiathar, the author, takes the neutral position between the Saulide clans and the Davidic family (*Die Entstehung der Geschichtsschreibung*, 175).

[54] Gunn also pays due attention to the theme with somewhat different emphasis, especially as the complex interaction of husband/father and acquirer of kingdom/dynastic founder (cf. *The Story of King David*, 88-94).

[55] Hermisson cogently points out the laissez-faireism of David to his children and its historical consequence as an important theme of the SN beside the political theme (cf.

These are, however, related respectively to later political events. Ambivalence and the contradictory processes of the private and the public-political culminate in Part Three (2 Samuel 15-20), as has already been discussed.

To sum up, we may state that the SN is a story of King David, his acquisition of the kingdom, maintenance of it, and provision for succession to it.[56] We grant that the SN is historiography, and not a mere story of art and entertainment, or of moral teaching in the sense that von Rad argues, in quoting from E. Schwartz that "genuinely historical writing which faithfully represents its own era always and invariably grows out of the political life of the day, whatever shape or form that may be."[57] The author's unparalleled literary genius manifests itself in his articulation of political affairs in an intricate interrelationship to private affairs. This historical writing depicted in a series of a concentric structures is an eloquent representation of a contradictory process in full tension between the external national expansion in a relatively short period as the result of successful wars and the internal insecurity with massive problems and conflicts in a period of uncertainty shortly after Solomon's succession.[58]

"*Weisheit und Geschichte,*" 143).

[56] Schulte designates the SN as "die David-Geschichten" (e.g., *Die Entstehung der Geschichtsschreibung*, 180) in the sense that it is a story of a royal family with David and Joab as its chief characters.

[57] Von Rad, *The Problem of the Hexateuch*, 167.

[58] Our literary-structural analysis does not justify the assertion that 2 Sam 11:27, 12:24, and 17:14 represent significant interpretative clues to the theological approach of the whole narrative. "Theological judgment concerning God and his relationship to the events" (von Rad, ibid., 148) are expressed more indirectly in the real historical context of "a succession of occurrences in which the chain of inherent cause and effect is firmly knit up" (von Rad, ibid., 201).

A Theologian of the Solomonic Era?
A Plea for the Yahwist

WERNER H. SCHMIDT
University of Marburg

Once a bright spot of Old Testament research, source criticism is at the present time threatened with the loss of its general acceptance, not only in its methods but also in its results. One often senses a certain uneasiness about it. Not only is the dating of the Yahwist questionable, his existence itself is disputed. My doctoral advisor, Rolf Rendtorff, at the Congress for Old Testament Study in Edinburgh in 1974, sought to prove, from a "consistent tradition-historical assessment," that the document hypothesis, particularly the assumption of the Yahwist, was a wrong manner of research.[1] He later fully confirmed this view. To the critical observer "the document theory and particularly the image of the Yahwist it now offers" presents itself "in many respects as a frankly anachronistic undertaking with great methodological problems. The presupposition of 'sources' in the sense of the document hypothesis is no longer able to make any further contribution to the understanding of the formation of the Pentateuch."[2]

In view of such a judgment, it becomes apparent how uncertain our knowledge is and how unconvincing the arguments generally are. The

---

*This article has also appeared in German under the title: "Ein Theologe in salomonischen Zeit? —Plädoyer für Jahwisten," *BZ* 25 (1981) 82-102.

[1] R. Rendtorff, "Der 'Jahwist' als Theologe? Zum Dilemma der Pentateuchkritik," *Congress Volume, Edinburgh, 1974* (VTSup 28, 1975) 158-66.

[2] R. Rendtorff, *Das Überlieferungsgeschichtliche Problem des Pentateuch* (BZAW 147, 1977) esp. 148. Rendtorff finds no continuity between the blocks of tradition (promise to the Fathers, Exodus, Sinai) in the older, predeuteronomistic as well as prepriestly texts. This book caused a lively echo; cf. the different opinions of R. N. Whybray ("Response to Professor Rendtorff," *JSOT* 3 [1977] 11-14); J. van Seters ("The Yahwist as Theologian? A Response," ibid., 15-19); N. E. Wagner ("A Response to Professor R. Rendtorff," ibid., 20-27); G. E. Coats ("The Yahwist as Theologian? A Critical Reflection," ibid., 28-32); and H. H. Schmid ("In Search of New Approaches in Pentateuchal Research," ibid., 33-42). Also cf. the comprehensive discussion of F. Langlamet, "Review of R. Rendtorff, *Das Überlieferungsgeschichtliche Problem des Pentateuch*," *RB* 84 (1977) 609-22; E. Otto, "Stehen wir vor einem Umbruch in der Pentateuchkritik?" *VF* 22/1 (1977) 82-97; W. McKane, "Review of R. Rendtorff, *Das Überlieferungsgeschichtliche Problem des Pentateuch*," *VT* 28 (1978) 371-82; E. Zenger, "Wo steht die Pentateuchforschung heute? Ein kritischer Bericht über zwei wichtige neuere Publikationen," *BZ* 24 (1980) 101-16; also H. Seebass, "Zur geistigen Welt des sog. Jahwisten," *Biblische Notizen* 4 (1977) 39-47.

document hypothesis formulated its answer from the discovery of the literary disunity of the Pentateuch. Is this actually explicable without source criticism? Since the basics are disputed, it is advisable to begin with the plain and simple, the obvious and fundamental. In doing this it is necessary to recall familiar material. Source criticism begins with Genesis. Allow me to begin with Exodus.

I

In the form of a comprehensive discourse, Exodus 6 confirms and supports what Exodus 3 relates in the framework of a colorful scene—the call of Moses. Both reports, however, have so many common features, such as—among others—the recollection of the God of Abraham, the hearing of the laments of Israel, and the promise of deliverance, that in essential points they present parallel reports which seem to have once existed independently. Since oral tradition tends to connect traditions with each other, to blend them together and to create a balance between them, it is a more precise procedure to rely on tradition already fixed in writing in which the independence of the reports could have been more easily preserved. Moreover, at least the theologically reflective style of Exodus 6 suggests that the written text as it stands shows the existence of a special connection of Exod 6:2ff. with Exod 2:23-25 and Genesis 17 which is not to be found in Exodus 3ff.

What one may recognize on the larger scale by a comparison of Exodus 3 and 6 can be found on a smaller scale within Exodus 3, namely, *doublets*. It is twice related that God sees the misery of the oppressed, hears Israel's cry for help and will set the people free (vv. 7f., 9f.). Nonetheless, these two parallel discourses of God are characteristically different and have their own respective profiles of expression. In the one (v. 7f.) the savior is Yahweh himself, in the other (v. 9f.) Moses is the savior.

These doublets strikingly correspond to a further criterion: the *change of God's names*, "Elohim" and "Yahweh". Certainly, objections will be raised again and again against this criterion, which since the 18th century has formed the basis for true criticism of the Pentateuch as well as for source criticism. Cannot the change be explained on purely stylistic grounds? Or is a different subject presented—is "Elohim" perhaps the universal God and "Yahweh" the God of the people? Is "Yahweh" alone God's name and "Elohim" only a designation for God? Already in 1952 at the Congress in Copenhagen, de Vaux came to grips with, and carefully considered, such objections and came to this conclusion: The criterion of the divine names remains valid, but it should not be applied mechanically, or as a matter of course.[3] Even if one does not dispute that "Yahweh" alone

---

[3] R. de Vaux, "A propos du second centenaire d'Astruc. Réflexions sur l'état actuel de la critique du Pentateuque" (1953), *Bible et Orient* (Paris, 1967) 50. Cf. C. Westermann, *Genesis* (BKAT 1/1, 1974) 767ff., and H. C. Schmitt, *Die nichtpriesterliche Josephsgeschichte* (BZAW 154, 1980) 22f.

is God's name and understands "Elohim" only as a designation for God, this differentiation does not explain why both, particularly as subject of the sentence, are used alternately, even where a change is unnecessary. Exod 3:4 reads:

Yahweh saw that he (Moses) had left the path to look about and *God* (Elohim) called to him . . . and said, "Moses, Moses!"

According to this, both halves of the sentence have the same subject. This change from "Yahweh" to "Elohim" is not necessary and thus is so surprising and has such a troublesome effect that other textual witnesses eliminate it in different ways. The Samaritan links v. 4a and v. 4b by writing Elohim in both cases; the Septuagint, on the other hand, accommodates v. 4b and v. 4a by writing "Kyrios" twice. Finally, the Vulgate omits the designation for God in v. 4b altogether. The dissimilarity of the revisions betrays that the objectionable Massoretic version is the older and the original. Moreover, the striking exchange of "Elohim" and "Yahweh" corresponds to these previously mentioned doublets and other irregularities, so that literary analysis of Exodus 3 produces two textual levels which at times are understandable in themselves and therefore most likely existed independently at one time.[4] Consequently *three* different reports of the call of Moses exist: the Yahwistic and Elohistic in Exodus 3, the Priestly writer in Exodus 6.

As the existing text in these chapters leads to differentiation of literary units, so other texts also necessitate such analysis. Let me refer in passing to a few examples which are representative of others.

Jacob, after the revelation in the night, twice proclaims the holiness of the place to which he unsuspectingly climbed: "Surely *Yahweh* is in this place and I did not know it!" (Gen 28:16); and again, "How fearful is this place; it is nothing other than the house of *God*" (28:17). Again both criteria, doubling as well as the change of God's names, coincide,[5] and, if one carries the analysis further, one finds cross-references for both strands in other texts.[6] Without source criticism this fact would be incomprehensible.

What one may observe in the individual texts[7] becomes, incidentally, recognizable in larger sections as well. Why does the story of the threat to,

---

[4]The analysis of Exodus 3 is, in essentials, unanimous; cf. in particular W. H. Schmidt, *Exodus* (BKAT 2/2, 1977) 106ff. The dependancy of one text upon the other (E upon J or vice-versa) cannot be shown.

[5]Cf. Gen 28:12//13. Thus it does not suffice to conclude with H. H. Schmid (*Der sogenannte Jahwist: Beobachtungen und Fragen zur Pentateuchforschung* [Zürich, 1976]), "The change of אלהים and יהוה has nothing to do with the Elohist and Yahwist, but rather with the difference between the cultic legend and its (Yahwistic) interpretation" (120f.). Also, in Gen 28:11ff., it remains of little probability that E is dependent upon J or J upon E; v. 21b appears to belong to the redaction (R^JE).

[6]Cf. Gen 31:31; 35:3, 7 with 28:18, 20 (E) and 12:3 with 28:14 (J).

[7]Let us remember the change of God's name in the birth story in Gen 29:31ff., "Yahweh

and preservation of, the ancestress Sarah see her savior in Yahweh in one instance, and Elohim in another?[8] Or why should the creation of man be narrated again in Genesis 2 in a characteristically different sequence of events after it has just been reported in Genesis 1 in theologically well-considered words? These and other cases from Genesis 6-8 onwards to well into the book of Exodus (Exodus 14) are explained more easily if, instead of an oral tradition which has preserved certain irregularities, the possibility of later connections between different passages or even—due to existing cross-references—a series of passages is considered.[9]

II

To be sure, there is a problem concealed in this conclusion. Are the individual passages revealed through literary analysis connected, and how may these existing connections be recognized?

The previously mentioned occasional cross-references are helpful. The phenomenon in which one earlier perceived the unity of the work—the *language*—is diminished as a criterion for differentiation.[10] Likewise a characteristic style, as the more recent deuteronomistic or Priestly literature shows, does not occur in the older literature. Its language, therefore shows even less independence since, to a great degree, it is stamped by the tradition. Nonetheless, the language argument within the Yahwistic stratum is not completely invalidated. It is hardly by chance that in completely different blocks of tradition from the narrative of the Tower of Babel through the call of Moses to the Sinai pericope, the revelation of Yahweh is repeatedly designated as *yārad*, "descended."[11] In this we find a theological intention expressed at the same time. God does not dwell on earth, not even on Mount Sinai, but rather descends.

Similar *stylistic elements* occur here and there. We have here just one example from two different areas of tradition; the polytheistically misunderstood appearance of the three men to Abraham is at once interpreted by a sort of title showing the sense of faith in Yahweh: "Yahweh appeared to

---

opened Leah's womb" (29:31ff.), but to Rachel "God denied the fruit of the womb" (30:2; cf. vv. 17ff., 22), similarly 30:23//24.

[8]Cf. Gen 12:10ff. (esp. v. 17; also 26:1ff.) with 20:1ff.

[9]In the above-mentioned paper of Rendtorff (n. 2) the actual impetus for source criticism, doublings such as the change of God's names, remains unfortunately disregarded. On the contrary, this article leaves unanswered the question which Rendtorff rightly raised: How did the individual stories or the blocks of tradition grow together into one literary work?

[10]Cf. reservations against the older lists of H. Holzinger et al. in M. Noth (*Überlieferungsgeschichte des Pentateuch* [Stuttgart, 1948] 21), "Even the examination of language and style is hardly of decisive help in the analysis of the old Pentateuch material."

[11]Gen 11:5, 7; 18:21; Exod 3:8; 19:11, 18, 20; 34:5, etc. Also the expression for the petition used in the plague stories appears to be typical for J (Gen 25:21; Exod 8:4f., 24, etc.). Or the concept *môledet* "kinship" which is known from the command to Abraham is repeated frequently in J (Gen 11:28; 12:1; 31:3; Num 10:30, etc.; but Gen 31:13 [E]).

him by the 'terebinth' of Mamre" (Gen 18:1). It is almost a verbatim (וירא
אליו ב) similarity with the beginning of the scene in which Yahweh reveals
himself in the bush: "The angel of Yahweh appeared to him in the fire of
flame" (Exod 3:2a). The introduction of the angel is to preserve God's
transcendence and freedom. Man does not draw near to the divine, as the
bush story originally related (cf. Exod 3:1, 2b, 3), but rather God turns to
man on his own initiative here, and in Gen 16:7, etc., in the form of the
messenger. In both cases (Gen 18:1; Exod 3:2a) older traditions are
evidently being corrected. Thus, one has to recognize in these sentences the
work of the Yahwist who here, as elsewhere, has similarly revised the given
tradition.

These few by no means complete proofs[12] show that in the Yahwistic
stratum, too, various connections are to be discovered.

III

Beyond these individual references is there a *composition* to be seen
which expresses the theological intent of the Yahwist? As far as we can see
at present, Rendtorff was correct in his judgment, "A theological conception which embraces the *entire* Pentateuch and can be shown convincingly
to be that of the Yahwist, is apparently not to be seen."[13] One may still
easily recognize three overlapping areas of tradition, namely, in the early
history ("Urgeschichte"), the history of the Fathers, and the cluster of the
plague stories. These three circles do not stand isolated next to one
another; there are definitely connections.

(a) It is striking that the *word* of Yahweh already carries a significant
meaning in the creation story. It brings tension into the narrative and
carries further the process of the action. After the creation of man (Gen
2:7) Yahweh tests his work and decides, "It is not good that man is alone"
(2:18). That after the animals man finally finds the "helper fit for him," the
appropriate "other" in woman, he himself confirms with his word (2:23)
and testifies to the success of the divine work of creation. This creation
story is interwoven with the paradise story, which again opens with the
word of Yahweh that all the trees of the garden are available to man with
one exception. This puts a decision before man (2:16f.). As he uses his
freedom and disobeys the creator, the punishing word of God creates the
present reality of man and with it the dividedness of existence. This curse
(3:14ff.) is probably the formulation of the Yahwist himself.[14]

---

[12]Let us mention a further connection between disparate areas: the threatening of Pharaoh,
"On the day on which you see my face you will die" (Exod 10:28) is reminiscent of the
construction of God's threat in the introduction to the paradise story, "On the day on which
you eat of it, you must die" (Gen 2:17). It is hardly coincidental that in both cases it is a
matter of verbatim speech which the Yahwist probably formed himself.

[13]*Das Überlieferungsgeschichtliche Problem des Pentateuch*, 108.

[14]Cf. W. H. Schmidt, *Die Schöpfungsgeschichte der Priesterschrift* (WMANT 17; 2d ed.,

Certainly a methodological as well as material problem arises here. How much did the Yahwist participate in this narrative? Did he only pass on the given material or did he engage in editing and supplementing? To what degree is he—there is a great difference between the two—a "collector" and to what degree the "author" himself?[15] One may ascribe that section of the text to the Yahwist which : (a) so far as it is recognizable, is not given through the tradition, (b) combines different, originally independent narratives or common details of the tradition, and finally (c) sheds new light, that is, gives a particular meaning to the text.

Such a case lies before us. The lamentation over the king of Tyre in Ezek 28:11ff. takes up a tradition of man in the garden which, despite essential variances, agrees with Genesis 3 in several details. Here we find a traditio-historical connection, of whatever kind it may have been. Now the version of Ezekiel 28 only reports the banishment; it knows nothing of the curse. Moreover, this connects Genesis 3 with Genesis 4 linguistically as well as subjectively, and maintains room, as it were, for the coming events in which, in Gen 3:17ff. only the field—the working space of man—is cursed, not man himself. The murderer first encounters the curse (4:11). Finally, let us explain the addition of the curse. The Yahwist wished to stress more strongly how evil—hostility, pain, and toil—came into the world which Yahweh had created. It, too, is the product of the word of Yahweh, not, however, of the caring, but rather of the punishing creator who nonetheless does not abandon his concern and care (3:21).

The same goes for the words of Yahweh in the Cain narrative (particularly 4:6f., 11).[16] In general it would be possible to analyze the agreement of the originally quite different traditions of Genesis 3 and 4 in their text and structure,[17] as reflecting the manner of work of the Yahwist.[18] The Cain story is connected with Genesis 2f. not only through a similar structure—gracious care of God, guilt of man, punishment but

---

1967; 3d ed., 1973) 214ff.; taken up by W. Schottroff, *Der altisraelitische Fluchspruch* (WMANT 30, 1969) 89ff., 143ff.; O. H. Steck, *Die Paradieserzählung* (Neukirchen-Vluyn, 1970) 55; C. Westermann, *Genesis*, 349f., 363; P. Weimar, *Untersuchungen zur Redaktionsgeschichte des Pentateuch* (BZAW 146, 1977) 125ff.

[15]As a rule one has only minimally assessed the personal part of the Yahwist in the formation of his material; cf. Rendtorff, *Das Überlieferungsgeschichtliche Problem des Pentateuch*, 98ff.

[16]Cf. finally I. von Loewenclau, "Genesis IV, 6-7—eine jahwistische Erweiterung?" *Congress Volume, Göttingen, 1977* (VTSup 29, 1978) 177-88, esp. 182ff.; W. Dietrich, "'Wo ist dein Bruder?'. Zu Tradition und Intention von Genesis 4," *Beiträge zur Alttestamentlichen Theologie. Festschrift W. Zimmerli* (eds. H. Donner et al.; Göttingen, 1977) 94-111, esp. 98ff. The Yahwist has also contributed to the formation of Gen 4:13ff.

[17]Cf. W. M. Clark, "The Flood and the Structure of the Pre-patriarchal History,"*ZAW* 83 (1971) 184-211, esp. 195ff.; C. Westermann, *Genesis*, 412f.; Dietrich, "'Wo ist dein Bruder?'" 98ff.

[18]Therewith this possibility remains, at least methodologically to be considered: Did Genesis 3 and 4 grow together, perhaps, already before the Yahwist—in oral tradition?

gracious preservation[19]—but also in that it clearly presents an augmentation: man, disobedient to God to begin with—and therefore no longer in harmony with his "other", the woman (3:16b over against 2:23f.)—becomes his brother's murderer.

The tradition of the great flood again makes it apparent that the Yahwist interprets the story material he has received by adding God's word and thereby gives it a new meaning. Two words of Yahweh give, beyond the old oriental tradition, a reasonable foundation to the destructive event:

"The product of man's heart is evil from youth"
(8:21 after the traditional ending of 8:20; cf. 6:5f.).[20]

Does not God speak here from experience which he had with man according to Genesis 3 and especially 4?[21] Thus, the catastrophe which occurred in the flood is not blind fate, but is punishment for human sin, the result of the wicked will of the creature. Even though the punishment brought about no improvement and man remained essentially unchanged (8:21), God promises to preserve the earth. Thus, according to the Yahwistic description, God's word does not create the world (as according to Genesis 1 [P]; Pss 33:6, 9; 148:5, etc.), but it does create the realities of human life (Gen 2:18; 3:14ff.; 11:7) and maintains the earth in the rhythm of summer and winter, day and night (8:22).

With the exception of this promise (8:21f.) the words of Yahweh in the early history have a threatening or punishing character throughout. In that segment of the flood story (8:20) one hears echoes of the old oriental tradition according to which the flood brings early history to an end. Nonetheless, the results of sin and punishment do not cease (Genesis 11).[22] On the contrary, this traditional conception of the specific Israelitic understanding of history is superimposed. This understanding sees the era of the Fathers as closing the early period with the call of Abraham.

(b) Early history, with its curses,[23] finds its goal in the far-reaching promise of blessing to Abraham, Gen 12:1-3.[24] Humanity needs the salva-

---

[19]E. Zenger, *Die Sinaitheophanie: Untersuchungen zum jahwistischen und elohistischen Geschichtswerk* (Würzburg, 1971) 139, etc.

[20]Cf. R. Rendtorff, "Gen 8, 21 und die Urgeschichte des Jahwisten" (1961) *Gesammelte Studien zum Alten Testament* (München, 1975) 188-97. In the framework of early history the "leading theological reflections are expressed in important points in the form of speeches by Yahweh, as also in other material of the Yahwist. . . . The characteristics of the Yahwist begin with the speech of Yahweh in 8:21" (188).

[21]Accordingly, there exists between the verses of Gen 4:6f., "and the framework of the great flood formulated by the Yahwist, a direct connection whose statement of the human heart is already prepared in them" (I. von Loewenclau, "Genesis IV,6-7—eine jahwistische Erweiterung?" 188).

[22]For an attempt to ascertain a section of J also in Genesis 11, cf. K. Seybold, "Der Turmbau zu Babel," *VT* 26 (1976) 453-79, esp. 475ff.

[23]Gen 3:14, 17; 4:11; 9:25; cf. 5:29.

[24]Cf. only the resumption of the catchword אדמה "earth" (important for Gen 2:5-3:23; 4:11, etc.) in 12:3. The connection "all tribes of the earth" also occurs in Amos 3:2.

tion offered in Abraham. "The so-called early history explains from the beginning why all the tribes of the earth need blessing."[25] According to almost unanimous interpretation, this word is not given in the tradition but rather is formulated independently by the Yahwistic narrator under the influence of elements of tradition and programmatically imposed upon the history of the Fathers. It broadly overlaps the situation of Abraham (v. 1) in which it proclaims a great future for him and his descendants (v. 2). Abraham is to receive a blessing and pass it on. Included are the families of those who, "of all tribes of the earth" (v. 3), do not respond to him disdainfully but who accept him. This word has rightfully found particular consideration in exegesis since it has decisive meaning for the composition of the Yahwistic writing of history. It stands on the watershed between early history and the history of the Fathers and proclaims, beyond both, the national history, "I will make you a great people."[26]

This word of blessing is renewed to Jacob; he will, like Abraham, become a blessing "for all the tribes of the earth" (23:14).[27] Then, it fades out of the picture;[28] the promise of divine guidance dominates in the

---

[25]H. W. Wolff, "Das Kerygma des Jahwisten" (1964) Gesammelte Studien zum Alten Testament (2d ed.; München, 1973) 345-73, esp. 359; O. H. Steck, "Genesis 12,1-3 und die Urgeschichte des Jahwisten," Probleme biblischer Theologie. Festschrift G. von Rad (ed. H. W. Wolff; München, 1971) 535-54; L. Schmidt, "Überlegungen zum Jahwisten,"EvT 37 (1977) 230-47, esp. 236ff.; E. Ruprecht, "Vorgegebene Tradition und theologische Gestaltung in Genesis XII 1-3,"VT 29 (1979) 171-88, 444-64.

[26]According to considerations of J. van Seters (Abraham in History and Tradition [New Haven/London, 1975] 271ff.), H. H. Schmid (Der sogenannte Jahwist, 129ff.) et al., H. C. Schmitt (Die nichtpriesterliche Josephsgeschichte, 111f., 170ff.) denies Gen 12:1-3 to the Yahwist on the basis of linguistic observations and the history of ideas. He claims a later Yahwistic level for Gen 12:1-3 and even for Gen 2-11* (116f.). In another connection and with another verb (שׂים instead of עשׂה)—therefore quite independent of the Yahwist—the phrase "make a great nation" (Gen 12:2; cf. 18:18) also occurs in the Elohist (Gen 21:28; 46:3).

[27]In modified form and apparently outside the original Yahwistic composition, Gen 22:18 and 26:4 take up the promise. The blessing (ברך hitp. instead of ni.) goes, instead of to Abraham or Jacob, to the "seed"; and the recipients are not "all the tribes of the land, that is, earth" (כל משׁפחת האדמה) but rather "all the peoples of the earth"(כל גוי הארץ). Moreover Gen 22:15-18, introduced by "The angel of Yahweh called a second time," is a perceptible addition "which clearly goes beyond the story of the sacrifice of Isaac" (R. Rendtorff, Das Überlieferungsgeschichtliche Problem des Pentateuch, 59). Gen 26:4 stands outside the connection of the story. Rendtorff also recognized a more recent development (43f.) and a later stage of editing (151) in the formulation of 22:18; 26:4. Thus his observations here correspond with the results of source criticism. Accordingly H. Gunkel (Genesis [HKAT 1/1; 3d ed.; 1910] XCII) et al., also saw more recent additions in the promise speeches in Gen 18:18; 28:14. Finally H. C. Schmitt (Die nichtpriesterliche Josephsgeschichte, 102ff. and lit.) ascribed, too, a later Yahwistic editing. How then could the mentioned linguistic differences within the promise speeches be explained? Gen 12:3 and 28:14 are clearly different from 22:18 and 26:4; the disputed verse 18:18 assumes an "intermediate stage" (Rendtorff, Das Überlieferungsgeschichtliche Problem des Pentateuch, 43; cf. L. Schmidt, "De Deo": Studien zur Literarkritik und Theologie des Buches Jona, Gespräche zwischen Abraham und Jahwe in Gen 18:22ff. und von Hi 1 [BZAW 143, 1976] 136ff.).

[28]Cf., however, Gen 12:3a with 27:29; Num 24:9; also Exod 12:32.

subsequent story of the Fathers (see below). Thus the promise to the Fathers will no longer be referred to specifically. Yet no less a person than the Pharaoh himself must admit that "The people of the Israelites are too many and too mighty for us" (Exod 1:9). Beyond the simple meaning of the comparison of the size of different peoples,[29] the insight of the Pharaoh, in connection with the Yahwistic history, gains a deeper, specifically theological meaning; the Pharaoh himself confirms that the promise of multiplication is being realized or has already been realized.

As with the later Priestly writer (Exod 1:7 [P]) and also the Elohist (Gen 46:3; 50:20; Exod 1:20 [E]), the emergence of Israel as a nation in Egypt has already been accomplished for the Yahwist (1:9, 11f.[J]). Apparently he is in agreement with the tradition he received because it already relates that *Israel* languished in Egypt. At this point critical current historians register reservations; was there really "Israel" already in this early period, what did it look like, what was the group which was oppressed and liberated? As thoroughgoing as the differences are, both historically and thematically, between Genesis and the book of Exodus— family history here, national history with Moses as mediator there—one still sees connections on this point in the source materials.[30] In addition, a major theme of Exodus 3 is prepared already within the Yahwistic narrative. If Moses should give the elders of Israel the information, "Yahweh, the God of your Fathers, has appeared to me" (3:16), then this identity of Yahweh with the God of the Fathers has already been expressed in the word of the revelation to Jacob: "I am Yahweh, the God of your father Abraham and the God of Isaac" (Gen 28:13; cf. 32:10). Consequently, in the framework of the Yahwistic narrative, one may see an arc from the curse of early history to the blessing of Genesis 12; and a further arc leads from the promise to the Fathers to the beginning of the Exodus and story of Moses.

(c) The intention of the Yahwist emerges clearly again in the immediately connected textual areas. He strikes a third great arc from Exodus

---

[29] A similar statement—perhaps formulated in accord with Exod 1:9—gives the Moabite king in Num 22:6 (J). In both cases Israel is not called גוי as in Gen 12:2; 18:18 but עם; with this Exod 1:9 points ahead to 3:7. The same change of term occurs in the Elohist; cf. Gen 46:3 with 50:20; Exod 1:20. Is a certain design concealed in this change? Does גוי over against עם "kinship" have more the political-national aspect of the people in mind (L. Schmidt, *EvT* 37 [1977] 236f., 244; E. Ruprecht, *VT* 29 [1979] 444f.)? Yet this assumption remains uncertain. Cf. A. R. Hulst, "Volk," *Theologisches Handwörterbuch zum Alten Testament* 2 (eds. E. Jenni and C. Westermann; München/Zürich, 1976) 290-325, esp. 310f.

[30] The promise of increase is fulfilled; the promise of land is yet to be fulfilled. However the Yahwistic presentation of the call of Moses (Exod 3:8, 17) with the verb העלה "to lead up"—namely from Egypt to Palestine (Gen 13:1 etc.)—seems to be only indirectly or implicitly reminiscent of the annexation of the land. The statement of the goal of "a good land flowing with milk and honey," including the enumeration of the peoples, belongs as one long assumed to a later (deuteronomistic) redaction, cf. finally W. H. Schmidt, *Exodus*, 135ff. This is important for the conversation with H. H. Schmid (*Der sogenannte Jahwist*, 29f.) and R. Rendtorff (*Das Überlieferungsgeschichtliche Problem des Pentateuch*, 66ff., 111).

5-14, from the oppression of Israel to the Exodus, in which he gives the plague stories circulating among the people their own profile. The theme, which turns on the relationship of the Egyptians to Yahweh, opens with the question which provokes Yahweh (5:2),

"Who is Yahweh that I should obey his command to let Israel go? I do not know Yahweh!"

The following events will force Pharaoh to "recognize" Yahweh as the true God (7:17; 8:6, 18; cf. 10:2, etc.).[31] Pharaoh recognizes Yahweh in that he confesses his guilt (9:27; 10:16) and implores Moses to intercede with Yahweh (8:4, 24; 9:28; 10:17). As the good and evil of humanity is decided in its relationship to Abraham, so may Pharaoh participate in Israel's blessing (cf. 12:32), if he does not remain stubborn. Thus he must see and experience the superiority of Yahweh in his own decline.

These references to the overlapping connections may suffice. Where and to what degree one may recognize a continuity between the Sinai pericope and the book of Numbers can remain open.[32]

IV

Do we dare, upon this, posit a *determination of age* for the Yahwistic stratum? Every attempt at dating presupposes not only the differentiation of the Yahwist from the remaining source material, the Priestly writing and the Elohist, but also the removal of the redaction stratum, be it the Yahwistic-Elohistic, the deuteronomistic, or another redaction. Already in Genesis the name "Yahweh" occurs as a name for God in an editorial section; a widely accepted example is found in Gen 22:15ff.[33] In the light of this situation and the current multitude of opinions on the source material,

---

[31]The formulations of knowledge are also denied to be Yahwistic; so H. Schulte, *Die Entstehung der Geschichtsschreibung im Alten Israel* (BZAW 128, 1972) 68f.; H. C. Schmitt, *Die nichtpriesterliche Josephsgeschichte*, 124. Is it possible, however, to extricate the statements of knowledge from the connection (existing since Exod 5:2) without destroying the unity? How is the freer form explained over against the later occurrence (W. Zimmerli, *Gottes Offenbarung. Gesammelte Aufsätze zum Alten Testament* [München, 1963] 61ff.)? In addition, the theme of "knowledge" affects the Yahwist since Gen 2:9, 17; particularly 3:5, 7; also 12:11; 28:16; Num 16:28, 30; 24:16, etc. Similar constructions can arise therein. Of course, certain knowledge formulations such as Exod 10:2 or 9:14 may be redactional additions.

[32]A Yahwistic participation in the literary-critically difficult Sinai pericope occurs in any case in Exodus 19, perhaps in Exodus 34. After the departure from Sinai, Num 10:29f. is clearly connected to Gen 12:1, 7 (J). Observations on the Yahwist in V. Fritz, *Israel in der Wüste: Traditionsgeschichtliche Untersuchung der Wüstenüberlieferung des Jahwisten* (Marburger Theologische Studien 7, 1970); on Numbers 22-24, see L. Schmidt, "Die alttestamentliche Bileamüberlieferung,"*BZ* 23 (1979) 234-61; idem, "Bileam," *Theologische Realenzyklopädie* 6 (1980) 635-39.

[33]Cf. n. 27. Thus there was doubtless a redaction which used the name Yahweh. However, its scope remains disputed.

it is advisable to pay greater attention to the work of the redactor(s) in analysis of the Pentateuch. To be sure, the differentiation of the redaction strata is by no means easy and has been proposed in a reasonable and convincing manner only in exceptional cases. As difficult as this undertaking may be, it is still essentially important, even indispensable. Not only the correct estimation of the age, but also the understanding of the theological intention of the Yahwist depends on the precise assignment of the existing text to this source material. It is fundamentally a methodological inadequacy and places the results of research in question from the very beginning if one ignores this differentiation from the start.[34]

More recently, F. V. Winnet, J. van Seters, H. H. Schmid and H. Vorländer,[35] among others, have set a late date for the Yahwist, perhaps in the time of the exile. Even R. Rendtorff stated decisively that there is "not a single clear piece of evidence for the dating of the Yahwist in the time of the great Davidic-Solomonic kingdom."[36] In the light of these present tendencies one can stress even more than did H. Gunkel or M. Noth[37] the uncertainty regarding the precise dating of a single source. Yet this caution did not prevent M. Noth from concluding, "As far as I can see, there is nothing in the original existence of the J narrative that compels one by its style to place it under the Davidic-Solomonic Era."[38] Despite all the recent dispute on this subject, is this restrictive judgment not right?

The Yahwistic work contains some, as it were, "classic" references to the Davidic-Solomonic Era.[39] Let us choose just one of the usual arguments. Israel must have recognized quite early the danger which threatened it through the sexual behavior common to its Canaanite surroundings. The rules limiting its people's behavior in the area of that which is ethical and permissible differentiate Israel from its environment: "Such a thing is not done in Israel," or "Folly in Israel."[40] In narratives, too (Genesis 19, 34;

---

[34]Cf. H. Vorländer, *Die Entstehungszeit des jehowistischen Geschichtswerks* (Frankfurt a.M./Bern, 1978) 17: "Die an sich notwendige zeitliche und sachliche Differenzierung zwischen J, E und R^JE soll zunächst ausser Acht bleiben." Also H. H. Schmid (*Der sogenannte Jahwist*) in the execution of his textual analysis lets the differences he mentions (p. 10) be missed (cf. n. 30).

[35]Further representatives in Vorländer, *Die Entstehungszeit des jehowistischen Geschichtswerks*, 285 n. 1; H. C. Schmitt, *Die nichtpriesterliche Josephsgeschichte*, 189; cf. O. Kaiser *Einleitung in das Alte Testament* (4th ed.; Gütersloh, 1978) § 8; A. de Pury, "Review of T. L. Thompson, *The Historicity of the Patriarchal Narratives* (BZAW 133, 1974) and J. van Seters, *Abraham in History and Tradition* (New Haven/London, 1975)," *RB* 85 (1978) 589-618, esp. 603ff.

[36]*Das Überlieferungsgeschichtliche Problem des Pentateuch*, 169, n. 33.

[37]"The question of the age of J and E is extraordinarily difficult" (H. Gunkel, *Genesis*, LXXXVIII); cf. M. Noth, *Überlieferungsgeschichte des Pentateuch*, 248.

[38]*Überlieferungsgeschichte des Pentateuch*, 249.

[39]Cf., e.g. H. -P. Müller, *Ursprünge und Strukturen alttestamentlicher Eschatologie* (BZAW 109, 1969) 52ff.

[40]2 Sam 13:12; Gen 34:7; Judg 20:6; 19:23f., etc.; cf. Leviticus 18.

cf. 26:10), this difference plays an important role. According to Gen 9:22ff., the curse is uttered because of the dishonorable behavior of "Ham, the Father of Canaan": "Cursed is Canaan, a slave of slaves he shall be to his brothers!"; or else, expressly related to Shem, "Canaan shall be his slave!" (9:25f.). This servanthood of Canaan probably had in view the newly formed balance of power resulting from David's rule. From various irregularities in the text one again has the impression that it may be possible to determine a given tradition in the Yahwistic revision.[41]

As in this case, other texts point to the early period of the kings, be it to Saul (Num 24:7) or still more to David himself ("the star of Jacob," Num 24:17; cf. 24:6ff.), be it to the predominance over Canaan (Gen 9:26; 12:6), Edom (25:23; also 27:37, 40a;[42] Num 24:18) and Moab (24:17; cf. 2 Sam 8, 2, 13f.). Generally, the blessing of Isaac upon Jacob sums it up: "Peoples will serve you and nations will bow down before you" (Gen 27:29a). As the servanthood of Canaan was the result of a curse in the early period after the flood (9:25f.), the dependency of the peoples here appears as the result of a word of blessing in the age of the Fathers.

The series of references to the early period of the kings could be expanded. Some scholars claimed to have found, in addition, several references to the formation of the state.[43] Only after the annexation of the Canaanite city-states were the material prerequisites for the recording of comprehensive data made available in Israel; there may have been in the Jerusalem court a school of scribes at which officials were educated. Through international relations there came about the participation of Israel in the international development of its day and its literary as well as cultural possibilities.[44] From this the association with wisdom thought and language becomes understandable in the Yahwistic work.[45]

---

[41]Cf. in particular L. Rost, "Noah der Weinbauer: Bemerkungen zu Genesis 9, 18ff." (1953), *Das kleine Credo* (Heidelberg, 1965) 44-53; W. Schottroff, *Der altisraelitische Fluchspruch*, 148ff. (lit.); also O. H. Steck, "Genesis 12, 1-3 und die Urgeschichte des Jahwisten," 537f. H. Vorländer (*Die Enststehungszeit des jehowistischen Geschichtswerks*, 301) remains barely convincing.

[42]Gen. 27:40b, which looks ahead to the liberation of Edom, is (despite 1 Kgs 11:14ff.) probably an addition, as the introduction ("and it shall be, when") already appears to betray. Then, to the contrary, the announcement of the subjugation of Edom (Gen 27:40a) reaches back into the older time of the kings (cf. 2 Kgs 8:20ff.).

[43]Cf., e.g., W. Brueggemann, "David and his Theologian," *CBQ* 30 (1968) 156-81; W. von Soden, "Verschlüsselte Kritik an Salomo in der Urgeschichte des Jahwisten?" *WO* 7 (1973/74) 228-40; K. Seybold, *VT* 26 (1976) 468f.; F. Crüsemann, *Der Widerstand gegen das Königtum* (WMANT 49, 1978) 167ff. Cf. n. 29 and n. 51.

[44]J. Hempel, *Geschichten und Geschichte im Alten Testament bis zur persischen Zeit* (Gütersloh, 1964) 189f. On the other hand one could also ask: Did the radical changes of the early age of kings—similar to the later Exile—stimulate the attempt to establish in writing the past which was threatened with being lost?

[45]Even in critical reservations toward the reports in 1 Kings 3 and 5 one could consider as "historically correct" that in Solomon's "era the prerequisites for Israel's encounter with

I would like to add just one argument that struck me in my own work on the book of Exodus[46] and which may perhaps make possible a more precise dating. In Exod 1:11 the Yahwistic history describes the compulsory service of Israel in Egypt with the words, "They built the store-cities of Pithom and Raamses." It is hardly by chance that the pertinent concept סֵבֶל, מַס appears in a similar way in the description of Solomon's building work.[47] Indeed, in this connection (1 Kgs 9:19) this phrase which is rare in the Old Testament, (וַיִּבֶן עָרֵי מִסְכְּנוֹת) ("they built the store-cities") appears again, verbatim. This parallel is certainly not to be related to the reference to the late books of Chronicles in which one encounters this phrase more often, because the Chronicler chiefly writes (2 Chr 8:4, 6; then also 17:12, etc.) in immediate connection with 1 Kings 9. Thus this discovery in no way speaks in favour of the origin of the Yahwist in exilic-postexilic times.[48] On the contrary, the deuteronomistic history appears to incorporate in 1 Kgs 9:15ff. an old account, perhaps even "an official report."[49] Thus, in all likelihood, the circumstances of his time, in which the people—be they aliens (9:20ff.) or even Israelites themselves (5:27; cf. 12:4ff.)—were forced to do construction work, served the Yahwist as an example for the description of the situation of his time. This need not mean that the core of the tradition of Exod 1:11 is unhistorical, since the known correspondence from the time of Ramesses II testifies that "Hebrews" (ᶜpr) were put to "pulling stone,"[50] that is, to construction work. Certainly the Yahwistic narration places the memory of the compulsory service in a broader historical-theological connection; the measures of the Egyptians were intended to "oppress" Israel. To all appearances the circumstances contemporary to the Yahwist serve on one hand as an illustration of the past, and on the other hand the past may serve the present as an unspoken admonition. What is happening today in Israel took place at that time in the foreign land. In any case the Book of the Covenant contains a commandment suitable to this situation: "You shall not wrong a stranger or oppress him, for you were strangers in the land of Egypt" (Exod 22:20; cf. 2:22 [J]).

---

international wisdom and its cultivation in the court of Jerusalem existed on a large scale for the first time and that education was advanced by Solomon" (E. Würthwein, *Das Erste Buch der Könige. Kapitel 1-16* [ATD 11/1, 1977] 48; further lit. by H. C. Schmitt, *Die nicht-priesterliche Josephsgeschichte*, 160ff.). After the title of Prov 1:1, the striking and therefore reliable report of Prov 25:1 that "the men of Hezekiah" collected the proverbs likewise presumes that there were wisdom sayings already in the earlier time of the kings.

[46] *Exodus*, 39f.

[47] 1 Kgs 5:28f.; 9:15; 11:28, etc.

[48] Against H. Vorländer, *Die Entstehungszeit des jehowistischen Geschichtswerks*, 307.

[49] E. Würthwein, *Das Erste Buch der Könige. Kapitel 1-16*, 110, similarly M. Noth (*Könige* 1 [BKAT 9/1, 1968] 212, 225).

[50] G. Posener, "Textes égyptiens," *Le problème des Ḫabiru* (ed. J. Bottéro; Cahier de la Société Asiatique 12, 1954) no. 187-88; K. Galling, ed., *Textbuch zur Geschichte Israels* (2d ed.; Tübingen, 1968) no. 12.

V

If these references to his times are recognized correctly, the Yahwist's narrative looks back to the golden age of David and therefore must have been composed in the building period of *Solomon's reign*. Thus, at least a generation remains for the admission and revised interpretation of the Kings tradition[51] which appears occasionally in the Yahwistic history. Clear references to later events apparently do not occur in Yahwistic history. If one looks back from the late to the early period, one may say that in it we find neither the results of the destruction of Jerusalem in 587 and the Babylonian exile nor the centralization of the cult through the reforms of King Josiah in 621 B.C. Not only are the obviously different holy places such as Bethel and Mamre presupposed, but even the classification of the cult personnel into priests and Levites, as they obviously are in the postdeuteronomic literature (Ezekiel, P, Chronicles), is still lacking. It is profitable to remember the judgment of H. Gunkel:

"The literary prophecy is characterized by the prophecy of the fall of Israel, by the struggle against foreign gods and against the holy places of Israel, and by the rejection of sacrifice and worship habits. Precisely the characteristics of the 'prophets' do not occur in the tales of J and E. J, in Genesis, generally thinks of no other gods than Yahweh . . . and the establishing of many alters and holy places by the Fathers rings quite differently from the passionate struggle of the prophets against worship at even these places. . . . Consequently one must decide in essence that the collection falls before the great literary prophecy."[52]

The Yahwistic history does not even know of the great threat of the Assyrians.[53] The neighboring peoples, on the other hand, play a greater role. They were significant for Israel throughout the era of David-Solomon, for example, the Philistines (Genesis 26; cf. 2 Sam 5:17ff.). Even in the references to the close relationship of the Fathers to the Aramaeans (Genesis 29ff.; particularly 31:44ff.), the danger which they later created for the northern kingdom is not indicated.

Thus the Yahwistic history clearly contains a series of references to the Davidic-Solomonic era but not to the later epochs. Does not this textual circumstance require an explanation if one puts the origin of this work as from one century to five hundred years later? These dates, of course, provide only the *terminus ante quem non*. What additional evidence could require us to reach a more detailed conclusion? References to contem-

---

[51]Cf. particularly on Gen 12:2f.: O. H. Steck, "Genesis 12, 1-3 und die Urgeschichte des Jahwisten," 551, n. 70, and H. C. Schmitt, *Die nichtpriesterliche Josephsgeschichte*, 171, also n. 29.

[52]H. Gunkel, *Genesis*, XCI.

[53]The Yahwistic section of the table of peoples (Gen 10:8ff.), which is hardly free of later expansion, mentions also Assur. Yet the text remains difficult to date.

porary times are most nearly independent of the views of the observer and therefore constitute "objective" and clear arguments for dating. On the other hand, linguistic grounds do not, as a rule, possess the same power to convince except in the case of *typical* deuteronomistic or Priestly forms of expression. Against the current tendency to designate certain concepts of the Yahwistic Pentateuch stratum as deuteronomistic and therefore late, we must maintain that the language must actually be proved as "deuteronomistic." Thus frequently occurring combinations of words carry more weight than single words. This question does not need to be pursued further here since each text for earlier or later language really must be examined for itself.

Arguments from *the history of ideas* are really compelling in only a few cases. How do we know what the tenth or ninth century could think and express? In this respect a sure criterion for differentiation is hardly available to us.[54] Let us touch upon just two thematic areas.

Does it not sound somewhat suspicious when the Yahwistic history employs the theme *"creation"* so resoundingly? "The creation faith undoubtedly belongs to an advanced stage of development of the Israelite religion which is distinguished by the exile."[55] Certainly creation stories are hardly to be found in the oldest traditions of Israel from the early nomadic past, while they strikingly increase in the exilic-postexilic period (Genesis 1 [P], Deutero-Isaiah, Job, etc.). But, precisely in the Jerusalem of David's time, a noteworthy, not at all doubtful testimony appears: the scene in which Abraham receives from Melchizedek the blessing of "El Elyon, the creator of heaven and earth" (Gen 14:13ff.). Even the proclamation of the consecration of the Temple (1 Kgs 8:12), which can be reconstructed only through the help of the LXX, has a creation story. Do individual Psalms and wisdom traditions also reach far back (Pss 24:2; 19A; Prov 14:31, etc.)? In any case, no serious objection exists to dating Gen 2:4bff. in the early time of the kings, especially since the text appears to accept a description of the watering of the desert which is indigenous to Palestine.

Next to the theme of "creation," the *historical-relatedness* of Old Testament faith and thought is considered to be late in the form in which it already appears in the Yahwistic work, having originated through the radical upheaval of the exile.[56] Nevertheless, not only do meager reports of historical events arise in the early period (Judges 9; 1 Kings 12); we have also the cluster of stories of David's ascension (1 Samuel 16ff.) and the tightly knit story of David's succession to the throne (2 Samuel 9-20; 1 Kings 1f.). Certainly the precise extent of these stories will be determined

---

[54]This applies in corresponding ways for similarities in structure, insofar as the agreement cannot be convincingly demonstrated.

[55]H. Vorländer, *Die Entstehungszeit des jehowistischen Geschichtswerks*, 294.

[56]H. H. Schmid, *Der sogenannte Jahwist*, 174ff.

differently, and it is also disputed whether they were not originally "profane": whether the scattered theological judgments (as 2 Sam 17:14) belong to a more recent—but perhaps only a little more recent—stratum of interpretation. Yet there can be no doubt concerning the existence of historical reports in the early time of kings, so on the basis of these reports of events at the court the comprehensive retrospect of the Yahwist in the more distant past is conceivable. In addition, certain relationships between the different outlines appear to exist. These will be mentioned later.

That the later literature does not quote the Yahwistic text is no surprise. The Priestly writing itself, which evidently presupposes the Yahwistic-Elohistic work, including the oral tradition, shows very little literal agreement with it. Meanwhile, with the two older source materials on the one side and the deuteronomistic and Priestly writings on the other, only the books of the prophets are preserved as greater literary works. Apparently the prophets took up an essentially oral tradition (Hosea 12[57]; Isa 1:7, 9, etc.) which was much richer in variations than what was in the Pentateuch. Above all, however, the prophets interact more independently with their traditions and revised and re-created them for their own purposes. Thus the evidence allows little more than the judgment that the early traditions were not as fundamental for the prophets, especially those of the 8th and 7th centuries, as they now appear in the Pentateuch.

VI

If one asks about the theological intentions of the Yahwist, it is not enough, strictly speaking, simply to retell the story or stories he has passed on. One must bring out his characteristics over against the given tradition precisely in the composition as well as in the augmentation of it. This requires a comprehensive so-called redaction-historical groundwork which until now has only been done here and there. Thus only few points are mentioned which can surely be supplemented.

To begin at once, we hear a characteristic note in the description of the creation of man "from the dust of the earth" (Gen 2:7). The Yahwist probably added the word "dust," because (1) it is in addition to the description of the origin of the animals (2:19), (2) it is certainly not the usual term for the soft malleable material of the potter (cf. Jer 18:3f.), and (3) it points from the creation story to the paradise story, with which it was hardly connected originally. The origin of man from the "dust" allows one to consider man's future from the very beginning. The origin corresponds to the end. "You are dust and to dust you shall return" (Gen 3:19; cf. Ps 104:29, etc.). It is characteristic of "living things" to go to the end of life.

---

[57]Hos 12:14, a text whose "authenticity" is not undisputed, is reminiscent of Exod 3:8, 16f. (J): As Moses had to announce the "leading up" (הֶעֱלָה) as a deed of Yahweh, so Yahweh, according to Hos 12:14, led "Israel up through a prophet." On the other hand, for the Elohist the liberation (הוֹצִיא) is a deed of Moses.

The Yahwist does not conceive—unlike the later tradition—of an immortality of man in paradise.[58]

This creature has the freedom of his own behavior (Gen 2:15, 19f.), but uses it for evil and disobedience, so that God comes to the judgment—formulated by the Yahwist himself and mentioned above—that: "The product of the human heart is evil from youth" (8:21; 6:5). Noah, the exception in the midst of the *massa perditionis* occasioned by the flood, was judged in the popular tradition as "righteous" (Ezek 14:14, 20; Gen 6:9 [P]), while the Yahwist understands this special position as proof of the grace of God: "Noah found grace in the eyes of Yahweh" (Gen 6:8; cf. 18:3; 19:19) and was "seen as righteous" (7:1).

Expressions occur here and there in the Yahwistic work which correspond to this critical judgment that evil is rooted in the human heart. Man does not even succeed in "mastering sin" (Gen 4:7). In a verse which anticipates Genesis 18f. (13:13; cf. 18:20), it says, "The people of Sodom were wicked and sinned greatly against Yahweh." Similarly the Pharaoh, "who hardened his heart" (7:11; 8:28, etc.), confessed, "This time I have sinned; Yahweh is in the right but I and my people are in the wrong" (Exod 9:27; cf. 10:16f.; Num 22:34; Gen 38:26). The Yahwist gave the wilderness traditon "a new meaning to the degree that he depicted the stay of Israel in the wilderness as a time of disobedience and apostasy from Yahweh. . . . The whole migration of Israel through the wilderness now appears as a questioning of the exodus as the decisive redemptive act of God."[59] The main figures themselves, such as Abraham (Gen 12:10ff.), Jacob (27:30), or Moses (Exod 2:11ff.), in no way appear favorable and virtuous. Even if in these cases the Yahwist largely maintains the tradition he received, one is able to see the theological freedom of the Yahwist in contrast with the differently constructed Elohistic parallels which partially correct or eliminate the objectionable elements of the story (Gen 20:5, 12; 21:11f.[E]). Yahweh does not only work with but also in spite of man. Cannot the older wisdom ask whether man stands pure before God (Prov 20:9; 16:2; 21:2)?

An astounding concentration of theological expressions are found throughout the entire work. Yahweh gives the rain (Gen 2:5; 7:4; cf. 19:24), the rhythm of seed and harvest (8:22), bread (Exod 16:4; Num 11:18; cf. Exod 15:25a). "The change of the seasons, the growing and dying of nature, the ever renewed fruitfulness of the earth, are based exclusively on Yahweh's promise. He alone guarantees all of this. It requires no cultic guarantee and is not an event of mythological background."[60] Yahweh

---

[58]The threat (2:17) does not run, "You will become mortal," but rather "die"—a punishment which God later did not carry out, as he preserved the murderer from the death penalty (4:13ff.). Also, death was not yet seen as a punishment for sin (Rom 6:23; cf. 5:12) but rather as the end of weariness (Gen 3:19). Immortality appears only as an impossibility for humanity (3:22; cf. 6:3).

[59]V. Fritz, *Israel in der Wüste*, 136.

[60]R. Rendtorff, "Gen 8, 21 und die Urgeschichte des Jahwisten," 196.

cares for man (Gen 2:8f.; 15, 18ff.), even for the disobedient (3:21; 4:15) and sets free from need (16:7a, 11ff.; 26:22; 29:32f.; Exod 3:8, etc.). "Is the arm of Yahweh too short?" (Num 11:23; cf. Gen 18:14). The cursing of Canaan causes the judgment of Shem, but the blessing—actually contrary to the sense of the sequence of events—applies not to Shem, but to the God of Shem, Yahweh (9:25f.). The complete differentiation of God and man, unspoken here, will later be expressed openly. On the other hand, we are not unprepared for the discourse within the Yahwistic work in which Moses contrasts divine and human action in the salvation of the persecuted ones at the sea (Exod 14:13f.): "See the help of Yahweh! Yahweh will fight for you, and you only need be still." In this concentration on Yahweh, who has created good and evil (Gen 6:7; 12:17; 19:24; 38:7, 10; Exod 7:17, etc.), is hidden the exclusive demand of faith, the first commandment. To what degree can there be coincidence at all (Gen 27:20; 29:31)? Yahweh himself opens the mouth of the ass (Num 22:28) and the eyes of Balaam (22:31). So it comes as no surprise that the blessing, originally a powerful, immediately effective word of man, is understood as a matter "before God" (Gen 27:7, after v. 4) and finally as the deed of Yahweh himself (30:27, 30) which opens the future (12:2f.).

With such a pointed theology the Yahwistic work is certainly not intended to serve as legitimation of the Davidic-Solomonic kingdom even though, or precisely because, it has this situation in view.[61] Does not the Yahwistic outline already contain a critical undertone in the promise to Abraham, "I will make your name great" (Gen 12:3)? It is God's response to the attempt of the nations to "make a great name" for themselves (11:4). Beyond this, God's gift stands in contrast to the famous "names" which the king receives (1 Kgs 1:47; 2 Sam 7:9; Ps 72:17). More striking is a correspondence with the stories of David which are stamped by a similar realistic view of man. The story of the rise of David apparently begins with the confession that Yahweh was "with" David (1 Sam 16:18), reechoes this motif (17:37; 18:12, 14, 28) and concludes with it (2 Sam 5:10).[62] Even this promise of divine presence, "I am with you," is stamped upon the Isaac, Jacob, and Joseph story as presented by the Yahwist.[63] Thus history is the

---

[61]L. Schmidt (EvT 37 [1977] 230-47, esp. 240, 247) seems to exaggerate: In the great kingdom of David-Solomon "all of the history from Abraham on has come to its God-willed goal" for the Yahwist; even when L. Schmidt stresses "that this kingdom owes its existence exclusively to Yahweh." Similarly, F. Crüsemann (Der Widerstand gegen das Königtum, 168, 179): "The Davidic-Solomonic kingdom and the great empire created by him is considered by J as salvation-historical creations (heilsgeschichtliche Setzungen) of Yahweh." Are we not warned to hold reservations by the fact that the Yahwist speaks of this "goal" only most indirectly? He does not glorify his present, but rather presents the past. Abraham, Jacob, or Moses are the central figures, but not David, and Jerusalem plays (despite Genesis 14) no role in the course of history.

[62]Cf. also 7:3, 8f.; 1 Sam 10:7.

[63]Gen 26:3, 28; 28:15; 31:3; also 39:2f., 21, 23. The story of Joseph, at times understood literary-critically as an indivisible piece, is now again more strongly drawn into the source

fulfillment of the promise of God's presence; the good which we see is here thanks to God's guidance and his protection. Through Yahweh's "being with" one can understand the success of the Davidic-Solomonic era and even ascribe it not to human proficiency but rather to God's "faithfulness" (cf. Gen 32:11). The Yahwist appears to indicate and implicitly to criticise that self-understanding which Amos (6:13) expresses in the quotation, "Have we not taken Karnaim by our strength?" Thus M. L. Henry has correctly seen in this presentation of history "a hybris-prohibiting regulation in the age of the founding of the kingdom."[64]

Do the promises passed on by the Yahwist extend to the Davidic-Solomonic period? He hardly speaks of a hope which extends into his time. Yet the blessing over "all the tribes of the earth" (Gen 12:3) is certainly not merely present tense. Likewise, this intentionally universal formulation is hardly comprehensible if the blessing consists exclusively of "the rich fruitfulness given by Yahweh."[65] Does not the Pharaoh's recognition of Yahweh's dominance mean more (Exod 5:2, etc.; cf. 12:32)?

Even though the Yahwist himself had no far-reaching hope, he at any rate awakened hope that the promise that Israel would become a blessing to the nations would later be carried further and actualized (cf. Isa 19:24f.; Zech 8:13). Even the paradise story holds room for some kind of hope. Certainly the garden of Eden remains closed to man (Gen 3:24), but what is "no longer" becomes in the prophetic expectation a "not yet," hope for a world without bloodshed, for peace in creation as it once was in Genesis 2 but was lost by man. This hope, expressed in Isa 11:6ff. and passed on (Isa 65:25), limits the curse upon the snake found in the Yahwistic work but does not lift it completely. The enmity between man and snake will no longer exist (Isa 11:8, over against Gen 3:15); only its mode of life remains unchanged:

The wolf and the lamb will feed together, the lion shall eat straw like the ox, but dust shall be the serpent's food.

What more can a literary work do than to stir to reflection and awaken hope?

---

criticism of the Pentateuch. Cf. H. Seebass, *Geschichtliche Zeit und theonome Tradition in der Joseph-Erzählung* (Gütersloh, 1978); H. C. Schmitt, *Die nichtpriesterliche Josephsgeschichte.*

[64] M. -L. Henry, *Jahwist und Priesterschrift* (Stuttgart, 1960) 15ff. This conclusion has been repeated several times, e.g., by H. W. Wolff, "Das Kerygma des Jahwisten," 369f.; V. Fritz, *Israel in der Wüste*, 122.

[65] Cf. L. Schmidt, *EvT* 37 (1977) 245.

Compact and Kingship:
Stimuli for Hebrew Covenant Thinking

DENNIS J. MCCARTHY, S.J.
Pontifical Biblical Institute, Rome

When Yahwist religion takes on reality for us in the biblical record it is covenantal. As understood here this means not the natural, inevitable religion inherited by tribe, city, or other social group, nor mere overwhelming awe before the numinous, but rather a personal and social commitment to the God who presented himself. The old Sinai traditions of a self-presentation of and response to the deity, though rather simple in content, were complicated as ritual: the people (a mix of races and nation, not a community with its religion given in the nature of things) met God and proclaimed allegiance to him with word, sacrifice, and sacred meal. This is already covenant, but the representation of covenant(-making) moved from cultic and rather undefined tradition, as in Exod 24:1, 9-11 and 4b, 5-6, 8,[1] to the elaborate deuteronomic treaty covenant with introduction, detailed obligations, and conditional blessings and curse.[2] Thus biblical covenant may be described as a single species expressed in variant forms, not a unique form. Here Dr. Jörn Halbe (in a personal communication) raises a pertinent question: given the development, how are we to picture the transitions in concrete historical terms?

This paper argues that qualities of Hebrew monarchy, especially that monarchy as presented in the era of transition from loose tribal life to royal nation state, are one plausible stimulus to the development. I say "stimulus" because, if it is hardly possible to show that one thing was the model or the logically necessary antecedent for the other, the likeness of certain

---

[1] Source analysis according to W. H. Schmidt, *Alttestamentlicher Glaube in seiner Geschichte* (Neukirchener Studienbücher 6; 3d ed., 1979) 45-47.

[2] So, covenant is not a late (deuteronomic) idea, apparently without antecedents (*contra* L. Perlitt, *Bundestheologie im Alten Testament* [WMANT 36, 1969]); nor is covenant a misnomer implying relationship for what shoud be (usually one sided) "duty" (*contra* E. Kutsch, *Verheissung und Gesetz* [BZAW 131, 1973]). Discussed in D. J. McCarthy, "*bᵉrît* and Covenant in Old Testament History and Theology," *Bib* 53 (1972) 110-21; *Treaty and Covenant* (AnBib 21A; 2d ed., 1978) 16-24, 277-93 (and accepted, e.g., by B. Childs, *Introduction to the Old Testament as Scripture* [London, 1979] 44), and M. Weinfeld, "ברית," *TWAT* 1 (1970-73) 781-808; J. Barr ("Some Semantic Notes on the Covenant," *Beiträge zur alttestamentlichen Theologie. Festschrift W. Zimmerli* [eds. H. Donner et al.; Göttingen, 1977] 23-38), though unwontedly diffident, cannot quite agree with Perlitt and Kutsch.

aspects of covenant making and kingship to the classic deuteronomic religious covenant is so close that it is unrealistic to separate them entirely. It is common that a highly visible fact stimulates parallels. For example, writing has been "re-invented" more than once not because someone learned an older system but because he was stirred to invention by seeing it in use. In modern times secular ritual from freemasonry to communist weddings is shaped by the stimulus of church rites. In old Israel, memory of kingship encouraged priestly anointing in later times, and one may suppose that the inviolability of the Holy of Holies in the Canaanite-style Temple affected ideas about the complete otherness of the divine.

The key elements in the influence of the early monarchical era on covenant thinking are (1) formal compacts used to structure societies, and (2) the special sanctity of the kingship.[3] I use "compact" (as a temporary measure for the argument) to avoid fixed concepts or genres implied by usual words like "contract," "treaty," or "covenant." It refers to deliberately created, enduring social structures (often not yet defined in a technical terminology) as opposed to casual and transitory meetings and combinations on the one hand and on the other to natural social forms not defined by a more or less free choice, like family or class.

Such structures are needed because there will be friction when social units accepted without reflection like the independent clan or village meet each other. The new social factor met needs to be integrated, its relation to the familiar defined, for mere contact with the alien, even without competition, arouses suspicion which must be allayed.[4] It is this definition which I am calling "compact." This is the way mankind regularly expands natural groupings. The jealously independent Greek states tried to organize themselves by a system of oaths fixing rights and duties, Roman law dealt with graded rights and duties with its allies, Herodotus testifies to rites for

---

[3]Redaction analysis questions the historicity of much in the early monarchical story, assigning it to exilic editors, Dtr[P] and Dtr[N] (T. Veijola, *Die ewige Dynastie* [Helsinki, 1975] and *Das Königtum in der Beurteilung der deuteronomistischen Historiographie* [Helsinki, 1977], with full bibliographies). However, techniques like repetition here point to unity, not "sources," and limit the value of the analysis (R. Carlson, "Élie à Horeb; I Rois xviii-xix," *VT* 19 [1969] 416-39; "Élisée—le successeur d'Élie: II Rois ii, 1-25," *VT* 20 [1970] 385-405; D. M. Gunn, *The Story of King David. Genre and Interpretation* [JSOT SupS 6, 1978] 24-26). Gunn (ibid.) cites oral story-telling techniques and artistic construction to argue an interest in the story for its own sake without historical referents. This confuses the artistic "syntax" used to *tell* a story with its *content*. Art, oral or written (on writing art in 2 Samuel see C. Conroy, *Absalom! Absalom!* [AnBib 81, 1978]), is quite compatible with serious history, as the tradition from Herodotus to Churchill attests (some discussion of this problem in J. Levenson, "1 Samuel 25 as Literature and as History," *CBQ* 40 [1978] 11-28). In any case, our argument is based on customs and ideas older than Israel itself and tales do record real social forms, if not always events; see S. De Vries' review of H. Schulte, *Die Entstehung der Geschichtsschreibung im Alten Israel* (BZAW 128, 1972) in *BO* 31 (1974) 100-101.

[4]George Eliot's *Silas Marner* (Chap. 1) describes from personal experience the friction the alien brings to a pre-industrial hamlet. "Alien" includes unfamiliar, remote "family" (Jacob-Laban) or the alienated "natural unity" (Jacob-Esau [David-Israel?]).

compacts among Arabs, Scythians, and Persians.[5] Ancient Germans organized an artificial "family" in the chief's *comitatus*, which still echoed in the feudal oath, an essential tie among the fragmented societies of Europe's Dark Ages.[6] Among Amerinds the legendary Hiawatha united by compact five warring Iroquois tribes into a power lasting for centuries.[7]

The records also confirm the making of compacts in the ancient Near East. In the 3rd millennium Sumerian cities and Semitic Ebla made pacts. In the early 2nd millennium the Shemshara and Mari tablets show rulers dealing with alien tribes by compact. Chiefs in Syro-Palestine "do good" (technical treaty language!) to the Egyptian Sinuhe in ways like later bedouin covenant and ancient treaty making.[8] Late in the 2nd millennium there are compacts (or references to them) from Alalakh, Ugarit, Hatti, Assyria, Babylonia, and Egypt.[9] These compacts could be formal treaties, or they might have other forms. They all witness to the need to stabilize relations among diverse social units. The need and answer continued, though for later times evidence is spotty but plentiful enough. The Egyptian Wenamon's troubles in 12th-century Phoenicia are those of the stranger in a society where he has no agreed position. Later evidence comes from Assyria, Syria, and the Bible itself, as well as the classical data noted.[10]

The compact, then, meeting a primary social need, is a widespread instrument. The formalities vary but in the ancient Near Eastern and Mediterranean worlds the data cited give special importance to the oath: invocation of the gods or self-imprecation. Thus, the compact was protected by the gods as distinguished from the contract protected by mere human witnesses. Such compacts covered everything from complex perma-

---

[5]General Data: M. Weinfeld, "Covenant Terminology in the Ancient Near East and Its Influence in the West," *JAOS* 93 (1973) 190-99; McCarthy, *Treaty and Covenant*, 105, and "Ebla, ὅρκια τέμνειν, *ṭb, šlm*: Addenda to *Treaty and Covenant²*," *Bib* 60 (1979) 249-50; Greece: C. M. Bowra, *Periclean-Athens* (Harmondsworth, 1974) 86 (Original, 1971); Rome: *Kleine Pauly, s.v. foedus,* and *The Oxford Classical Dictionary, s.v. socii* (bibliography); Arabs, Scythians: Herodotus, *Historiae*, 1.74; 4.70; Persians: ibid., 3.8, and Xenophon, *Anabasis*, 2.2,9 (discussed in D. J. McCarthy, "Further Notes on the Symbolism of Blood and Sacrifice," *JBL* 92 [1973] 207-208).

[6]Tacitus, *Germania*, 13-14; the *Chanson du Guillaume* illustrates the medieval sequel: unsworn knights may not join Lord Vivien even for safety against the common paynim enemy, so inconceivable is unity apart from family or pact!

[7]See *Encyclopedia Americana, s.vv.* Hiawatha, Iroquois. Further useful facts (not the often dated interpretations) under "Brotherhood (Artificial)," Hastings, *Encyclopedia of Religion and Ethics.*

[8]For *ṭôbâ,* cognates and parallels: McCarthy, *Treaty and Covenant*, 171; *Bib* 60, 250-51 (bibliography). Hebrew טוב ("good treatment," Gen 26:29) may have preceded more abstract טובה introduced from treaty usage, but David already uses טובה in an annalistic report (2 Sam 2:6). For Sinuhe, see *ANET*, 19; D. J. McCarthy, "Semitic 'Good' in an Egyptian Text," *BASOR* (in press).

[9]References: McCarthy, *Treaty and Covenant*, chaps. 2-8; *Bib* 60, 248-49.

[10]For Wenamon, see *ANET*, 29; the rest, McCarthy, *Treaty and Covenant*, Chap. 6, and pp. 383-89 (and cf. n. 5, above).

nent treaty organizations to problems of small trade. The biblical "covenant report," used regularly to describe compact making, gives an excellent picture of what was concretely involved. It notes: (1) negotiations based on existing contacts; (2) clearer definition of the relation; (3) symbolic affirmation; (4) notice of covenant making (oath); (5) association with a shrine.[11] So the situation: strangers in contact mean conflict (e.g., Abimelech's men attack Isaac's, or Abraham's: Gen 26:20; 21:25) or tension (e.g., will good will continue?: Gen 21:23; 26:29). The situation is resolved by clear definition of obligations (often customary). Further, men need to signify assent, or who is to know of it? Hence the reports record symbol(ic actions) and oath (normally with נשבע or כרת ברית). Then, the compact must be remembered if it is to define a lasting relationship. Hence the association with shrines, focal points for traditions. All this is very important: a social need so strong as to develop a sturdy literary genre and a focus of tradition to maintain it. Rarely do we find a *Sitz im Leben* so clearly the real source of a genre. It is also very old, older than J and E.[12] This is something basic, a real response to a real need.

Moreover, the tradition was still alive at the beginning of monarchy. Joshua 8 shows genre and setting in full before deuteronomistic hands had touched the text,[13] and the hoary tale in 2 Sam 21:1-14 shows the old tradition working under the first kings. Then, there is the conspiracy between Abimelech and the lords of Shechem. Surely it meant a compact dividing the spoils of the plot, the powers of the king, and the privileges of his new subjects. Such cabals are truly social situations requiring definition. Rebels do not expose themselves without reassurances. It requires a compact, a ברית, to bring palace guards over to revolution (2 Kgs 11:4), and Abimelech too must have had a compact with his minions: it is not for nothing that they are associated with Baal- or El-Berith. Again, it matters not what comes from story teller, what from event. Either way, the story reveals the realities of its milieu.[14] Again, the citizens of Jabesh-gilead seek to resolve a conflict with Ammonite Nahash by compact. He is willing, if they mark themselves his subjects by an enduring sign of humiliation (1 Sam 11:12a).

---

[11] References: McCarthy, *Treaty and Covenant*, 18-22. The genre declines later, naturally, as the nation states learned to regulate social friction by means other than *ad hoc* compacts.

[12] Found in J (Gen 21:25-26, 28-31; 26:26-31; 31:*44-32:3) and E (Gen 21:22-24, 27, 32; 31:*44-32:3) and so from older common tradition. J. van Seters (*Abraham in History and Tradition* [New Haven, 1975] 190): the Abraham stories reflect late claims to Philistia, but see H. Cazelles' critique in *VT* 28 (1978) 241-45.

[13] J. Blenkinsopp (*Gibeon and Israel: The Role of Gibeon and the Gibeonites in the Political and Religious History of Early Israel* [SOTS MS 2, 1972]: Chap. 2 a *Forschungsbericht*); J. Halbe ("Gibeon und Israel: Art, Veränderung und Ort der Deutung ihres Verhältnisses in Jos ix," *VT* 25 [1975] 613-41; and B. Halpern ("Gibeon: Israelite Diplomacy in the Conquest Era," *CBQ* 27 [1975] 303-15) agree on a solid pre-deuteronomistic basis in Joshua 8.

[14] See R. Boling, *Judges* (AB 6A, 1975) 170; full discussion in P. Kalluveetil, *Declaration Formulae in Old Testament Secular Covenants* (PBI Diss., 1980) 60, 86-87.

These examples already involve kings, and David, seeking kingship in Israel (2 Sam 2:5-6), congratulates the Jabeshites on their fidelity (חסד) to Saul. Noting that he too is now a king, he offers them solid relations, טובה. Thus, he neatly hints at protection for the exposed city in return for חסד. An offer of a compact is part of the power game. When disillusioned with his protégé Ishbaal, Abner offers to deal with David (כרת ברית: 2 Sam 2:12). Details are murky, but at least Abner is to bring the northern tribes over to David (3:17-19) in return for a favored position in the new situation. He eats at the royal table (3:20), a possible covenant rite, and he departs with "peace" (בשלום: 3:21), a covenant word. Probably he was offered the supreme command, to judge by the general Joab's murderous reaction and the parallel case of Amasa (3:27; 20:10-11a). Surely the family feud over Asahel's death had a role in Abner's case, but just as surely a hardened soldier-plotter did not simply give himself up to David and his men. He had a position as military leader to bargain for new power by compact, and he surely did so—until Joab altered things irregularly but drastically. Still the ברית arranged by Abner betwen Israel and David (3:21) was ratified when the northern tribes did accept David as king (5:3).[15] This is explicitly connected with the LORD's promise that David shall rule and protect Israel (n.b.: the heart of compact, status and duties, granted by the LORD himself: 2 Sam 5:2b) already cited by Abner (3:9b, 18b). We are already in touch with the sacral, but our present concern is the importance of compacts in the society where monarchy began, especially any relation of king and compact. So, for the moment, we pass on to more political evidence, David's apparent compacts creating vassals as described in the style of ancient royal records: 2 Sam 8:2, 6; 10:19.[16]

Finally, monarchy began in the Hebrew Heroic Age (see n. 16). This provides a setting emphasizing personal loyalty, the formation of heroic friendships and so of faithful groups of retainers. So, we have David's friendship with Jonathan.[17] Based on affection (1 Sam 18:1), it becomes a ברית (18:3; 20:8, etc.) in which Jonathan arms his friends (shades of Achilles and Patroclus and the "gold giver" chiefs of Nordic saga!), and each is sworn to protect the other in all things (20:42). David carries out the obligation with Jonathan's crippled son Mephibaal (2 Samuel 9; but see 19:25-31). Thus the compact of heroic friendship. Saul took the classic means to engage a loyal group: grant of land in return for service, the way of generous kings (1 Sam 8:11-12:14; 22:7).

---

[15]*If* a story teller's addition (see Gunn, *King David*, 70-76, with bibliography), 5:3 imitates reality: see the parallel annalistic report in 2:4b-7 and David, Joab, and Abner, typical figures from a heroic age like the monarchy's beginnings (full discussion in H. M. Chadwick and N. K. Chadwick, *The Growth of Literature* 2 [Cambridge, 1936] 629-82).

[16]Parallels in McCarthy, *Treaty and Covenant*, 161; *Bib* 60, 253.

[17]J. Thompson ("The Significance of the Word *love* in the David—Jonathan Narratives in I Samuel," *VT* 24 [1974] 334-38; P. Ackroyd ("The verb love—ᵓĀHĒB in the David-Jonathan Narratives—A Footnote," *VT* 25 [1975] 213-14): 1 Samuel 17-20 articulates the transition

Thus the society of the early monarchy was quite familiar with formal compacts, public, (Gibeon, Abimelech, Jabesh-gilead and Nahash, David and Israel), personal (David and Jonathan, Saul and his retainers) secret (David's dealings with Jabesh-gilead and Abner will surely have been *sub rosa*), as a structuring factor. Furthermore, it is tied to the actual institution of monarchy. One element which might stimulate thought about religious covenant is clearly in evidence.

For the other element, the special sanctity of the king, we have the anointing. Samuel's anointing of Saul (1 Sam 9:16; 10:1) and of David (16:1-13) are usually held to be later accretions,[18] but the notices of the elders of Judah and of Israel anointing David king are dry annalistic reports of events (2 Sam 2:4; 5:3). Moreover, they report something probably very old in itself, for anointing to kingship was not normal ancient usage. It is documented only for Hittite kings. Egyptians used it to rub a bit of Pharaoh's numinous power into officials, not on Pharaoh himself. Later non-Israelite powers seem not to have had the rite. That is, there were no contemporary potentates, Hittite or Assyrian kings or, after the 12th century B.C., Egyptian governors, whose anointing one could imitate. Why then anoint a "king like all the nations?"[19] Surely it was

---

from personal attachment to recognition of David as the LORD's chosen by the use of אהב (and contrary קשׁר). D. Jobling (*The Sense of Biblical Narrative: Three Structural Analyses of the Old Testament* [JSOT SupS 7, 1978] 4-25) explains more fully how Jonathan's story with its compact(s) mediates theologically the transfer of Saul's kingship to David. This is correct, but a little oversimplified: Jonathan does *not* simply cede his succession rights in taking David as a follower (H. J. Stoebe, *Das erste Buch Samuelis* [KAT 8/1, 1973] 348), nor does heroic gift necessarily pass from lower to higher person (see next paragraph in the text and the story of Sinuhe: n. 8). Jobling does show well the complex dialectic of such narrative: the symbolic transfer of rights *is* complex in a story of much time and many vicissitudes. So, after 18:1-5 David is properly Jonathan's עבד (20:5) who bows to his lord (20:41), though David's future greatness is accepted (20:12-17): "thesis" and "antithesis" are finally *aufgehoben*! Earlier reflection had already given the simple tales of Jonathan's exploits (14:*4-14) an all-Israel Holy War dimension: F. Schicklberger,"Jonatans Heldentat: Textlinguistische Beobachtungen zu I Sam xiv, 1-23a," *VT* 24 (1974) 324-33. These sample moves from story to reflection on its meaning are analogous to the process from the fact of kingship to conceptualizations of covenant.

[18] See the commentaries and T. N. D. Mettinger (*King and Messiah: The Civil and Sacral Legitimation of Israelite Kings* [CB OTS 8, 1976] 174-79, 309): the story of Saul's anointing imitates David's, itself old but not original, and so is an early tale influenced by prophetic ideas, as often held; L. Schmidt, *Menschlicher Erfolg und Jahwes Initiativ* (WMANT 38, 1970) 58-102; B. C. Birch, *The Rise of the Israelite Monarchy: The Growth and Development of I Samuel 7-15* (SBL DS 27, 1976) 35-37, 39; V. Fritz, "Die Deutungen des Königtums Sauls in der Überlieferung seiner Entstehung 1 Sam 9-11," *ZAW* 88 (1976) 346-62. Z. Weisman ("Anointing as a Motif in the Making of a Charismatic King," *Bib* 57 [1976] 378-98) uses typology to separate anointing as civil acceptance (old in Israel) from that of giving "divinity" (e.g., 2 Sam 10:1) which may reflect prophetic and/or "magic" ideas (not necessarily old). However, Habel's basic study ("The Form and Significance of the Call Narratives," *ZAW* 77 [1965] 297-323) finds the divine call for various offices pre-prophetic; see also W. Richter, *Die sogenannten vorprophetischen Berufsgeschichte* (FRLANT 101, 1970) 29, 51, 55.

[19] 1 Sam 8:5, 20—old whatever the context's date, for here Israel seeks to oppose 11th-10th century Philistine unity with the only form of centralized society it knew.

because the obsequious Canaanite princelings seen in the Amarna letters had imitated their Egyptian masters. They sought power, and anointing gave it to Pharaoh's officials. They may well even have sought the very infusion of the numinous. It suited kings who had special religious duties anyway.[20] And, once a rite has been introduced it remains. Canaanite kings after the decline of Egyptian hegemony will still have been anointed. When the Hebrews imitated these nations they made a king by anointing—and stressed his religious powers. It may be that these later Canaanite monarchies were practical oligarchies, the king barely *primus inter pares*.[21] No matter: typically in such situations it was the religious role which remained to the king. Thus the βασιλεύς and the *rex* remained religious figures in Greece and Rome long after the states had become "republics." The Canaanite king, whatever his political power, would be a religious figure.

Further, we do not merely argue by analogy to the religious office of the Hebrew king. He acted as one empowered by the divine. David brought the ancient palladium, the Ark,[22] to Jerusalem. The king, that is, commanded an object of worship which held its power even beyond political barriers (1 Kgs 12:26-33). The Temple contributed to this: even its ruins attracted non-Judean pilgrims (Jer 41:4-5). But then, the king had created this focal point, seen to its design and building, and maintained it.[23] Thus, he produced massive results in the religious sphere.

---

[20]Egyptian influence and sacral anointing: R. de Vaux, "Le roi d'Israël: vassal de Yahvé," *Mélanges Eugène, Cardinal Tisserant* 1 (Vatican City, 1964) 119-33. Mettinger (*King and Messiah*, 185-232) rightly criticizes de Vaux, over-influenced by the vassal treaty genre, for insisting that anointing made a subordinate king; rather it created an official. Mettinger also treats early anointing as secular (cf. E. Kutsch, *Salbung als Rechtsakt in Alten Testament und im Alten Orient* [BZAW 87, 1963]) with a development to a sacral meaning, but his development has occurred by Rehoboam's time, quite early enough to be a royal element influencing covenant thought. Mettinger also doubts Egyptian influence on the concept as opposed to mere external imitation of the rite. Indeed, without contemporary texts that say so, one cannot prove that ideas were assimilated, but surely strange rites communicated awe, if not understanding, and this is what is in question here, and what Canaanite princelings hankered for. As for secularity, did the relatively undifferentiated 11th-10th century Hebrew society feel any crucial rite as "purely civil"? H. Seebass ("Zur Teilung der Herrschaft Salomos nach 1 Reg 11:29-39," *ZAW* 88 [1976] 361-76) emphasizes the early need for sacral confirmation; surely parvenu kings would press all symbols of authority like anointing: cf. T. Ishida, *The Royal Dynasties in Ancient Israel* (BZAW 142 [1977] 75-77).

One might also note holiness given by the divine spirit (1 Sam 11:6 [and 10:6, 10?]), but the former old tradition is *ad hoc*, showing Saul a fit successor to the judges at the moment, and the latter may not be positive value. The "secondhand" charism of the Davidic dynasty which forms Nathan's promise was more effective (hinted at by David's non-ecstatic spirit, 1 Sam 16:13: a power lived, not exhausted in an energy outburst?).

[21]R. de Vaux, *Historie ancienne d'Israël: Les Origines* (Paris, 1971) 137; J. Gray, "Canaanite Kingship in Theory and Practice," *VT* 2 (1952) 193-220; "Sacral Kingship in Ugarit," *Ugaritica* 6 (1969) 298-302.

[22]Num 10:35-36; H.-J. Zobel, "אֲרוֹן," TWAT 1 (1970-73) 391-404.

[23]2 Samuel 6; 1 Kgs 5:15-7:51; 2 Kgs 12:4-15; 23:3-7; and the great legend of David in 1 Chronicles 23-28, a hierophile source!

Nor was he merely a patron, not directly part of the sacral. Taking over a pre-Israelite model for the great shrine, along with its sacrificial rites and its psalmody, he emphasized the intrinsically religious role of the king. The psalms make him God's "son" empowered to rule nations (Pss 2:7b-8; 89:28). So close to the numinous was he that his maintenance of social order was coincident with the maintenance of the natural order of crops and life (Psalm 72). Naturally, such a figure and his family served as priests (2 Sam 8:18b) and offered sacrifice (2 Sam 24:25; 1 Kgs 8:64). His own family apart, the king made and unmade priests: Solomon removed Abiathar with his priestly lineage for the parvenu Zadok.[24] Even the apostate Ahaz has his way with so holy a thing as sacrifice (2 Kgs 16:10-16). This was anathema to late Aaronid orthodoxy, but when kings still were objects of hope and necessary leaders they could not avoid the religious character of their office.

The case of the Gibeonites in 2 Samuel 21 points this up admirably. With its blood guilt, curse, and expiation it is the very stuff of religion, the numinous at work and the problem of dealing with it. Here no one turns to priest or elder or seer, functionaries of the religious society some suppose to have run parallel to the political kingdom.[25] Israel as a people is involved in the religious guilt of a violated oath, and the king presides, turns to the oracle, receives an answer, and acts to turn away the curse. He is supreme agent in most urgent religious matters. The arcane (to us) ideas of Psalm 72 take on sharper outlines. Keeping order in society and nature involves mysterious and often harsh realities. The sacral twines the spheres together and a king must know how to act where they mix. There is no pre-established harmony keeping two orders flowing parallel. One must recognize the impingement of the numinous on both and have the power to meet it as needed. This belonged to that figure of awe, the king, whom one did not even lightly touch (1 Sam 24:4; 28:9; 2 Sam 1:14, 16; 19:22). Indeed, he was "like a מַלְאַךְ אֱלֹהִים," the embodiment of the divine power to discern good and evil (2 Sam 14:17, 20; 19:28). Perhaps a bit of this is *Hofstil* (cf. 1 Sam 29:9), but solid reality stands behind it. The king was expected to give judgments of more than human wisdom.[26] So Absalom based his

---

[24]On the early monarchical organization: T. N. D. Mettinger, *Solomonic State Officials* (CB OTS 5, 1971); on priests especially: E. von Nordheim, "König und Tempel. Der Hintergrund des Tempelverbotes in 2 Samuel vii," *VT* 27 (1977) 434-53. Of course conflicts arose between kings and priests (e.g. 2 Kgs 12:13-16); the kings selected among men who had their own priestly traditions, and history shows opposition between civil and priestly traditions almost inevitable. Each makes absolute claims in separate but overlapping spheres, and overlapping absolutes mean conflict.

[25]So M. Noth, "The Laws in the Pentateuch," *The Laws in the Pentateuch and Other Studies* (Edinburgh/London, 1966) 28-49 (German original, 1940).

[26]N. W. Porteous, "Royal Wisdom," *Wisdom in Israel and Ancient Near East* (VTSup 3, 1955) 247-49; right judgment is divine: Psalm 82; the מַלְאָךְ is the *alter ego* of his principle: R. Fischer, "מַלְאָךְ," *Theolgisches Handwörterbuch zum Alten Testament* 1 (eds. E. Jenni and C. Westerman; München/Zürich, 1971) 907.

rebellion in part on the need for a true royal judge, and the tradition made Solomon wisest of judges. Even the Chronicler has Jehoshaphat extending the judicial system (2 Chr 19:8-11), though he himself knew only priests or elders as judges in a hierocratic society. All the more significant that the tradition of a special royal power of judgment persisted through changes which had diminished royalty's prestige.

Hebrew kings, then, were as much involved in the sacral as in compacts. This mere juxtaposition in a conspicuous figure might suffice to turn thought toward a connection between the compact and the sacral and so provide the stimulus toward the development of the classic deuteronomic treaty covenant we seek. However, this remains a suggestion. Is it expressed concretely? Or, can we find an explicit tie between royal compact and sacrality, an adumbration at least of the ultimate deuteronomic expression of the covenant with God?

One must note points which raise problems, if not insuperable objections. Hebrew kingship was sacral, but with limitations. As a novelty, not a timeless, unquestioned customary institution "come down from heaven," the people who sought it for their defense would pay for it, but, as its (partial) source, they would have their say in it. Hence, the need for acceptance of the king, apparently by acclamation vividly illustrated by its refusal to Rehoboam.[27] The king, the defender of the people, must accept the definition they gave his power. One cannot isolate this from the משפט המלכה of Saul (1 Sam 10:25) with its properties associated with compacts and other *res juridica*: it was a written instrument and it was deposited in a holy place. Its contents remain unstated, but we can deduce something of their character from the demands made on Rehoboam and especially from the משפט המלך quoted in 1 Sam 8:11-17. Samuel's speech in chap. 8 is heavy with irony, but irony must travesty reality, not deny it.[28] The king must have the right to levies, the power to tax, punish, and reward if he is to do his job, organize and defend a people against the modern organization of Philistia; 22:7 indicates Saul's acting accordingly. Kings may demand too much and no one likes taxes, even necessary defense taxes, especially when they seem to succeed and the enemy threat recedes, let

---

[27]1 Kings 12: discussed in A. Malamat, "Organs of Statecraft in the Israelite Monarchy" (1965) *BAR* 3 (1970) 163-96; M. Weinfeld, "King-People Relationship in the Light of 1 Kings 12," *Lešonénu* 36 (1971) 1-13 (Hebrew, with unpaged English summary), and "The Loyalty Oath in the Ancient Near East," *UF* 8 (1976) 379-414. The latter offers valuable observations and comparative texts, but without good distinction of genres: the ancient treaty/convenant was a genre unto itself *externally* like a "decree (grant)" plus a "loyalty oath," but *separate* decrees or oaths are different genres from this, not to be called covenants. Note also I. Plein ("Erwägungen zur Überlieferung von 1 Reg 11:26-14:20," *ZAW* 78 [1966] 10): Israel, rejecting Rehoboam, formally rejected a covenant.

[28]Stoebe, *Das erste Buch Samuelis*, 186-87; R. E. Clements ("The Deuteronomistic Interpretation of the Founding of the Monarchy in I Sam viii," *VT* 24 [1974] 398-410) defends the antiquity of the basic ideas in 8:11-17 without distinguishing fact and polemic.

alone those which seem only to augment royal pomp. Hence, the irony in describing the king's *necessary* powers. Nor were these all the king's powers. How much was spelled out in documents we cannot tell. Any society must leave much to customary definition, or "the world itself could not contain the books that should be written" trying to create instruments to record them.

What we have so far may properly be labelled compact: status (kingship) with defined duties and privileges regarding another party (the people), but it is all secular. Has not the royal compact actually put a further distance between the king and the sacred? Not entirely. The duty of military service continues old Hebrew tradition with a religious tone: going to war for the people was to act for the LORD (Judges 5; 1 Samuel 15; and cf. David's use of the priestly oracle in 2 Samuel 5), and this was now the business of the king. A self-evident result of the situation demanding a king, it may not have called attention to itself. Still, it is a link joining royal compact with a religious tradition. Further, the ברית making David king over Israel is tied to a divine oath (5:2b-3 and 3:18: אמר; 3:9: נשבע). The ברית must have defined usual mutual obligations, service from the subjects and defense by the monarch, but it has a basis in a divine word. With no record of this word itself one may always think the reference is later Davidic propaganda, but already when Israel accepted him David's success had demonstrated his blessing, divine choice, and this in the mode of early thought is merely made explicit as the effect of power, the LORD's word. This ברית had a strong religious element.

Further, we are seeking a stimulus to thought, and the novelty of kingship, the introduction of a strange institution, would call attention to it and invite reaction and reflection. Ways and fields of action become custom are so habitual as not to raise questions. Who asks why we keep to the right (or left) of the road? So, novelty can be a stimulus. So, also, ideals set before the king were perhaps more important from our point of view than what they did. Ideals are already things of the mind and will, not mere externals, and so that step to stimulating new thinking. Now, the ideal king had pledged himself to foster justice and put down the wicked (Psalm 101),[29] to guard the poor, the defenceless, to be the security for those the economic and social order by-passed (Ps 72:4, 12-14). All this merely echoes the proclaimed concerns of ancient kings in general,[30] but the Hebrew king was doing something the others were not in any clear way. He was making himself *especially* responsible for duties which *religious* direction imposed on every Hebrew: direct help for the indigent: Exod 22:21; 23:6; Lev 25:35; Deut 15:7-8; regular provision for the dispossessed: Lev 19:9-10; 23:22; Deut 24:19-22 (the gleaning restrictions); protection for the

---

[29]H. Kenik, "Code of Conduct for a King: Psalm 101," *JBL* 95 (1976) 391-403.

[30]J. Eaton, *Kingship and the Psalms* (SBT 2/32, 1975) 135: references to the ideal from Hammurabi to Jeremiah.

classless: Exod 22:21, 22; 23:9; Lev 19:33-34; Deut 24:14. These are ancient ideals carried through the whole Torah tradition and always valid, only needing application to new circumstances, as the gleaning laws in Deuteronomy and Leviticus protect the classless in what has become an agricultural community. Thus, the king took over ideals making him the Yahwist *en grand*. He did not merely judge others, he was to embody Torah, that basic element in Hebrew self-identity.[31] Thus, he was a highly visible figure calling attention to obedience freely given, not subjection through fear or habit, that is, the moral element present in all religion but especially Hebrew religion with its emphasis on the correlation between status and performance.

Further, comparison of Psalm 101 with the entrance liturgies, Psalms 15 and 24, reveals a society much like those based on compacts.[32] The would-be worshipper may join the congregation if he keeps his community obligations: status, fellowship in worship, comes in return for stipulated performance. Now, though we have no ancient "entrance liturgies" especially for kings, for whom would they have been so appropriate? In fact, an ancient hymn does tell us that he, who had consciously undertaken to embody the community's basic ideals, was received by God when he lived out his undertaking (Ps 18:21-27). Surely the first *full* realization of the relationship of status in the community to performance sanctioned by God came in regard to the highly visible kings. So, the rejections in Kings are not all arbitrary *ex post facto* judgment but sharper statements of a fact first vaguely intuited: the king was responsible before God for self and people (2 Sam 12:1-13; Psalm 72).

The claims made here about Hebrew kingship do draw on psalms and Torah in what may be late expressions, but I do not think this invalidates the claims. Dating psalms is indeed tricky, and if there is anything like a consensus, it puts the royal psalms late, a consequence of and not a stimulus to change in covenant thought. I myself doubt that anyone hymned kingship as it failed, but be this as it may, Psalms 18 and 72 with their ancient ideas are about enough to make our case. Further, whatever the date of particular expressions of Torah or the royal ideal, the content we are using, concern for justice, protection for the weak, the sacrality of royalty, is as old as Yahwism and older than Hebrew monarchy. Nor need we be hesitant about particulars. There are conceptual correspondences we have noted between the "coronation pledge" in Psalm 101 and the ancient Psalm 18. Then, too, Psalm 101 uses wisdom, a timeless idiom known in Israel before the kings. If Psalm 101 itself is not early, its ideas and language show continuity with old material.[33]

---

[31]J. Halbe (*Das Privilegrecht Jahwes* [FRLANT 114, 1975]) shows how ancient in Israel was cultic proclamation of obligations: they were known and accepted.

[32]Kenik, *JBL* 95, 396 with n. 19.

Further, it appears from the beginning that the dependence of the
king's special status, even his life, on his observance of the ideals he
espoused was to be enforced by the LORD. The evidence begins with
Nathan's dynastic promise (2 Sam 7:1-17). For our purposes we need not
choose any as the original form of the promise from the infinite variety
proposed.[34] All reconstructions seem to admit a promise giving the
Davidides special status. Dating is more important, but no real problem.
There is a consensus, if not unanimity, for an early date. Indeed, the idea
should come from the early days when the Davidids were pressing a claim
to "rebel" Israel, not from a later time when the division of the kingdoms
was a pragmatically accepted fact and which would not allow much scope
for the complex development evident in the present 2 Samuel 7. The claim
that the promise is Josianic founders on the text's nondeuteronomistic
language, as does the idea that it is an exilic construct to reassure the
people after the implimentation of the unconditional deuteronomic covenant. Anyway, the idea misreads the deuteronomic covenant which always
allows and even quietly urges repentance and return.[35]

Further, a prophetic support for the new dynasty is proper to the
times. Prophecy was old, as the Mari texts show, and it is no accident that
it appears in the Bible at the beginning of the royal era (1 Samuel 10), for it
was undergoing a renaissance in the general cultural milieu of the time.
Prophets were accepted forces in courts at Byblos, at Hamath, in Tyre and
Israel, in later Philistia and throughout Phoenicia and Transjordania (Jer
27:2, 9: Tyre, Edom, Moab, Ammon).[36] At least until the penetration of

---

[33]Kenik, ibid., 399-402; for the antiquity of Psalm 18, F. M. Cross and D. N. Freedman, "A
Royal Psalm of Thanksgiving: II Sam 22 = Psalm 18," *JBL* 72 (1953) 16-20. For wisdom, note
the Succoth lad writing for Gideon (Judg 8:14) and the abecedary from a 12th century
Israelite settlement (M. Kochavi, "An Ostracon from the Period of the Judges from ᶜIzbet
Sartah," *Tel Aviv* 4 [1977] 1-13): scribal schools, primary but not unique carriers of wisdom,
taught writing in early Israelite times. Wisdom was not necessarily for the "intellectual"—see a
farmer's wisdom (Isa 28:23-29), and the proverbs, fables, etc., indigenous to peasant culture as
that of modern African agriculturalists or of 19th century Sicilian peasants illustrated in
G. Verga's novel, *I Malavoglia*. R. N. Whybray discusses the ubiquity of wisdom in this
volume: "Wisdom Literature in the Reigns of David and Solomon."

[34]T. Veijola, *Das ewige Dynastie*, 68-79 (bibliography). Some important analyses: L. Rost
(1926)—7:1-4a, 11b, 16 original; S. Herrmann (1953/54)— an early, unitary *Königsnovelle* on
the Egyptian model; Veijola himself—two old oracles: vv. 1a, 2-5, 7 and vv. 8a, 9, 10, 12, 14, 15,
17 combined in Dtr[G] into a divine guarantee of Solomon's succession; Mettinger, *King and
Messiah*, 48-63—a Solomonic: vv. 1a, 2-7, 12-14a, 17, and a dynastic promise: vv. 3, 8, 11b,
14b-15, *16, 18-22a, 27-29, from "shortly after the death of Solomon." F. M. Cross (*Canaanite
Myth and Hebrew Epic* [Cambridge, MA/London, 1973] 241-65) takes 2 Samuel 7 as
deuteronomistic but it has no significant amount of the school's language (see the forthcoming
PBI Diss. by Sr. Alice Laffey, R. S. M.).

[35]D. J. McCarthy, "The Wrath of Yahweh and the Structural Unity of the Deuteronomistic
History," *Essays in Old Testament Ethics: J. P. Hyatt in Memoriam* (eds. J. L. Crenshaw and
J. T. Willis; New York, 1974) 97-110; "2 Kgs 13:4-6," *Bib* 54 (1973) 409-10.

[36]For Mari: H. Huffmon, "Prophecy in the Mari Letters" (1968) *BAR* 3 (1970) 199-224;
W. L. Moran, "New Evidence from Mari on the History of Prophecy," *Bib* 50 (1969) 15-56;

Hellenism prophetism was a normal working factor in ancient Near Eastern politics. Surely the new Hebrew monarchy looked to the recognized instrument for support. Then, David's response to the oracle (7:28, generally accepted as old) speaks of הטובה הזאת, that is, covenanted relationship (see above, n. 9, for the language). The technical language of compact is applied to the Davidic office.

Our next step involves another prophetic intervention, 2 Sam 12:1-7a, 13-15a (at least, concisely formulated in traditional style, unexpected and against the king, without deuteronomistic language, these verses are old, whatever may have been added to them).[37] The promise turns out not to be quite so unconditional as usually claimed. Like all relations that were created by it, it had its limits, its definition, spelled out by custom, not by stipulation. It often must be so. A thing is so well understood that it needs no explicit definition, or it cannot support one: "friends" carefully defining the limits of their friendship make a contract, not friendship. Or, the definition is too long and complex for formal expression. At any rate, David is not left free, the LORD's protected no matter what he does. He is bound by the usages of his people and of mankind. No adultery, no murder! David was to be the ideal king, the model of justice and mercy, whether this was made explicit or left implicit. Oppressing the weaker, he went directly against the key points in the ideal. He must pay for this, though repentance mitigates the penalty. Mitigation or not, we now have the element balancing the Davidic status: performance. Only the promise plus the condemnation in chap. 12 gives the full picture. There is no really unconditional relation; there is promise of favor within the framework of fundamental customary responsibilities. The Davidic "promise" turns out to be very like a compact involving the LORD and a family, with obligations on both sides. This is not yet the expressly conditional form with spelled-out obligations of the treaty covenant, but there is more than the mere juxtaposition of religion and compact in the person of the king with which we began. The two elements are intertwined so that one practically is the other: David is the LORD's chosen, holy, but his performance must match his status, protecting and observing the "law," the ideals the hymns proclaim and the All Holy sanctions.

An explicit link between religion, compact, and king is finally found in the so-called Last Words of David (2 Sam 23:1b-7). Heavy, sententious gnomic poetry like this is typical of heroic and post-heroic society like the

---

for Byblos, the Wenamon story, *ANET*, 26; Hamath, the Zakir inscription, *ANET*, 655; Tyre and contemporary Israel: Jezebel and her rivals, 1 Kings 18-19; Philistia, the local *muḫḫû* who urged submission to Assyria and saved his lord: J. Gray, "The Period and Office of Isaiah in the Light of a New Assyrian Tablet," *ExpTim* 63 (1951-53) 263-65. An exhaustive study of non-Israelite prophecy: L. Ramlot, "Prophétisme," *DBSup* 8 (1972) 812-903.

[37] For the antiquity of the heart of 2 Samuel 12 see Rost, n. 35, and the general arguments in n. 3.

ages of David and Solomon.[38] The style is heavy with images and tropes.
It opens straightforwardly: the king is the mouthpiece of the LORD (vv. 1b-
3a). A pair of simple proverbs follows (v. 3b), but the king's relation to
nature, civil order assuring natural order, is put metaphorically. Then the
contrast between just king and worthless men (Belial, v. 6) hints at diverse
fates for good and bad kings (vv. 5-7). The hint is broad enough, but still it
is partly figurative and so subject to various interpretations. Still, do the
contrasting figures not remind one of the contrasting blessings and curses
formulated in the treaty covenant? Behind the dense expression is all that
concerns us: the king is sacred for he is the voice of the LORD, he has
numinous attributes, for his justice means order and plenty in the land, but
most of all his status, his success or failure and with him that of the people,
is tied to performance, ruling justly. We have the sacred and something
very like the two elements of the compact, and the set-up is explicitly called
a ברית at last (23:5b).

Our final evidence is Samuel's reconciliation speech concluding the
introduction of monarchy (1 Samuel 12), and it may be the most important
of all. The speech is usually dismissed as deuteronomistic, but careful
reading shows that the Deuteronomist built his scenes (Samuel's vindi-
cation, vv. 1-5; paranesis, vv. 6-15; reconciliation, vv. 16-25) around a core
of older material. This includes (1) the confession-vindication liturgy in
vv. 2-5 (probably); (2) the introductory legal adjuration in v. 7abA
(probably); (3) and argument from history justifying the LORD's actions:
v. 8a, bC—"going into Egypt" is a formula available to any biblical writer,
and מקום for the Land, not the Temple is not deuteronomistic usage;
vv. 9b-11a—the list of enemies and of judges is not that of the deuteronomistic Book of Judges; v. 12—the reason for needing a king is not of this
same book; (4) some form of grant of a king—v. 13 may not be a

---

[38]The poem is gnomic both because it is aphoristic and because it is very intricate, with a
weighty series of synonymous parallelisms (vv. 1b-3), synthetic parallelism (v. 4), interwoven
synthetic (v. 5a-bAB)-synonymous (v. 5bA-B)-synthetic (v. 5bAB-C) parallelisms within an
inclusion (v. 5a=bD) containing the climax: David's ברית, and another interweaving of
antithetic parallelism (vv. 6a-b7a)—synonymous parallelism (v. 7aA-B)—synthetic parallelism
(v. 7a-b) to contrast with the climax in v. 5 and the metaphor in v. 4. Further, the image of
growing things links the final three, more complex sections (v. 4: דשא מארץ; v. 5b: יצמיח;
v. 6: קוץ [v. 7a: עץ?]). On gnomic form and milieu: Chadwick and Chadwick, *Growth of
Literature* 1, 377-403. So "baroque" form argues for antiquity as well as for lateness, while the
gnomic is ancient wisdom suited to the age (*contra* common opinion summarized in
S. Mowinckel, " 'Die Letzten Worte Davids:' II Sam 23:1-7," *ZAW* 45 [1927] 30-58). As for
language, see "late" נאם in the ancient Balaam oracles, and, while ברית עולם may be a P
phrase (Mettinger, *King and Messiah*, 257, 279-80); in P it refers to the patriarchal not the
Davidic covenant. In any case, the phrase is too little used to provide a solid basis for
comparative dating. H. N. Richardson ("The Last Words of David: Some Notes on II Samuel
23:1-7," *JBL* 90 [1971] 257-66) and D. N. Freedman ("II Samuel 23:4," *JBL* 90 [1971] 339-40)
show the ancient language and syntax of the poem's original form. A study of content and
structure without reference to the Gnomic: T. N. D. Mettinger, " 'The Last Words of David:'
A Study of Structure and Meaning in II Samuel 23:1-7," *SEÅ* 41-42 (1976-77) 147-56.

particularly old expression, but vv. 14-15 show that it gives the substance of what did stand here;[39] (5) a blessing and curse in vv. 14-15—v. 14 is not corrupt or an example of aposiopesis, for v. 14b is a complete apodosis: "you and the king who reigns over you will truly be the LORD's," the greatest blessing imaginable; (6) the miracle and the people's repentance in vv. *16-20 (and elements in vv. 21-25 less important for us).

The confession-vindication need not concern us in detail, but note that it does make kingship a part of the ongoing institutions of Hebrew society, the successor to the judgeship introduced with solemn liturgical form. The rest of the old material is very significant. The summons in v. 7abA puts us in an official context. We have a historical introduction, to keep the legal flavor, perhaps "plea." We have a grant clause. We have a blessing and a curse conditioned on fidelity. Even the repentance scene fits well with all this. It is a sort of "enabling act" making the sinful people parties to a compact with the holy God. For a sinful partner-to-be repentance is the equivalent to ratification in normal biblical covenant usage.[40] If there were a proper stipulation instead of a grant (remember, grants are *not* covenants), the text would have the form of a full treaty covenant. As it is, we are but a step away in this old royal material.

As for dating, we begin by noting that the present text is pre-deuteronomistic precisely because it is *not quite* deuteronomistic. Its language is *almost* deuteronomistic, an all-important point. So firm a style as the deuteronomistic knows exactly how to express things. There are no near misses. A phrase not *exactly* deuteronomistic must simply be non-deuteronomistic, for example, "dwell in safety (v. 11b: בטח)" for deuteronomistic "quiet (שקט)," "*making* a people for Yourself (v. 22b)" for deuteronomistic "be a people . . .," or מקום for "land" (v. 8b) and not deuteronomistic "Temple." Such material, then, cannot be dismissed simply as deuteronomistic.

---

[39]Verses 14-15 refer expressly back to *king and people* (v. 13), now a God-granted unity. The presence of a king is no more a sin but part of God's plan for the people: see D. J. McCarthy, "The Inauguration of Monarchy in Israel: A Form-Critical Study of 1 Sam 8-12," *Int* 27 (1973) 401-12 (bibliography); "The Wrath of Yahweh and the Structural Unity of the Deuteronomistic History," 97-110. For the apodosis in v. 14: אתם . . . אחר יהוה, "be in the retinue of, truly belong to," see McCarthy, *Treaty and Covenant*, 215 with n. 10 (bibliography). All this departs from the commonplace that 1 Samuel 12 is anti-monarchical (e.g., T. Veijola, *Das Königtum*, 83-99—bibliography). For the positive attitude of 1 Samuel 12: McCarthy, *Treaty and Covenant*, 206-21; *Int* 27, 401-12; Jobling, *Sense of Biblical Narrative*, 5, 17; J. R. Vannoy, *Covenant Renewal at Gilgal* (Cherry Hill, NJ, 1978), good synthesis and philology, too insistent on detailed historicity; A. D. H. Hayes, "The Rise of the Israelite Monarchy," *ZAW* 90 (1978) 1-20, but thinks the chapter deuteronomistic; Z. Ben-Barak, "The Mizpah Covenant (1 Sam 10:25)—The Source of the Israelite Monarchic Covenant," *ZAW* 91 (1979) 30-43, but elicits more detail than the text will bear.

[40]For the doctrine, see, e.g., Deut 4:29-31; 30. Exodus 32-34 shows it in action: the repentant people are receptive and so ratify covenant as it is promulgated; see McCarthy, *Treaty and Covenant*, 126-29, 216-17, 298 (bibliography).

The text as a whole, then, is pre-deuteronomistic (and pre-deuteronomic: the language is no more deuteronomic than it is deuteronomistic). Why pre- and not post-deuteronomic? A major reason is the link of such material (other examples Exod 19:3b-8; 23:20-33; Josh 24:2-24, [28]) to the "pre-writing" prophets recognized by classic source criticism.[41] But, we need not and should not stop with the text in itself, old as it may be. Its core fragments go back even farther: old legal formulae uncharacteristic of later practice, a variant tradition of the judges era naming a forgotten hero, Bedan, an affirmation of belonging to a retinue not normal to later times, and all this in a cultic-*cum*-juridical context. Here are links with very old forms, tales, and institutions. Is it presumptuous to suggest that some of this nucleus goes back to the beginnings of monarchy? After all, they had their משפט המלך/המלכה (1 Sam 8:11; 10:25) and ברית (2 Sam 5:3; 23:5): king, people, and God in 1 Samuel 12, are involved in compacts with some feature of the treaty covenant. This links with notices in 2 Kgs 11:17: the priest makes a covenant between God, king, and people, and in 2 Kgs 23:3: the king himelf makes the covenant. King, people, and covenant were a full part of the liturgy.

Here was a carrier and adapter of the traditions, with new coronations, new circumstances, new and more adequate expressions of the royal office in relation to God and people were worked out. This assumes a sacral renewal or at least reiteration of the royal covenant at normal coronations in Judah and, surely, Israel (1 Kings 12 points to covenant as an essential part of legitimation in the north). Renewal is explicit in one crisis: restoration of David's dynasty after Athaliah's attempt at usurpation (2 Kings 11). Surely it was needed in other crises with less obvious priestly involvement when ceremonies receive less attention, for example, the palace intrigues with murder of the reigning monarch frustrated by the עם הארץ insisting on dynastic continuity (2 Kgs 12:20; 14:19-21; 21:23-24). However, as long as monarchy as such retains its "charism," the mystique it can certainly hold, *any* royal death is a crisis. There is a chance of an interregnum, with the danger that, the keystone gone, the arch of society will topple, and with it, in the ancient world at least, the very order of nature. Hence, the high probability that all coronations renewed or reiterated covenant to show that the crisis was met and normal order assured.[42]

---

[41] For the pre-/proto-deuteronomistic style leading to the "almost deuteronom(ist)ic" concept: C. Brekelmans, "Éléments deutéronomiques dans le Pentateuque,' *RechBib* 8 (1967) 77-91; applied in detail to 1 Samuel 12 in McCarthy, *Treaty and Covenant*, 206-13. For the pre-, not post-deuteronomistic nature of this vigorous, original style: J. Muilenburg, "The Form Structure of the Covenantal Formulations," *VT* 9 (1959) 346-51.

[42] Other evidence for repetition of royal covenant: a covenant specifically with Hezekiah and so not simply the dynastic promise continued, with Jehu (argued by P. Kalluveetil, *Declaration Formulae*, 190, 195-235). Royal covenant renewal in general: G. Fohrer, "Der Vertrag zwischen König und Volk in Israel," *ZAW* 71 (1959) 1-22; G. von Rad, "The Royal Ritual in Judah," *The Problem of the Hexateuch and Other Essays*, (New York, 1966) 222-31 (German original, 1948).

But, even granting, solely for the sake of argument, that covenant renewal or reiteration was rare, the liturgy is a key. The special nearness of the king to God, his status and responsibilities, that is, a *de facto* compact, were kept to the fore from of old in the Temple liturgy where royalty was the object of song, where it controlled, directed, and presided from Solomon to Josiah. This is enough. The liturgy is not dumbshow. It must be meaningful to evoke a reaction, and this demands response to problems and new situations. So, the Temple liturgy reflected especially in the Psalms celebrated the king's, the Temple's (Zion) and the people's relation to God with continuity, true, but not in stasis. There was development as circumstances altered and understanding changed and deepened.

Perhaps we have met our aim? Compact and holiness came together in the king and stimulated development of a religion expressed in covenant terms. The Bible even adumbrates this when Isa 55:3 extends the Davidic covenant to the whole people,[43] expressing actual intellectual development (though it would not recognize this terminology) as well as stating a theological idea. The development may be summarized. (1) Hebrew kingship began in a society familiar with compacts, the beginnings of kingship actually being associated with them. (2) The king was a sacred figure in whom the compactual and the sacral met *de facto*. (3) Nathan's promise and judgment oracle (2 Sam 7:12) express this early, practically defining a compact giving the king status before God based on responsibility before God, and 2 Sam 23:5 actually speaks of a royal ברית. (4) All Hebrews must observe certain ideals of conduct if they as individuals are to belong to the religious community, but the king's observance affects the very community itself (Psalm 72). This is a key: the king manifests in himself the more or less explicit ideals of the community and the relation between them and his status and the community's. If he lives them, he and the people are God's community, otherwise not. All the features of Hebrew covenantal religion are highly visible in this if one looked at it. (5) The king's and people's tie to the LORD was early expressed in a compact with most of the elements of the full treaty covenant (core of 1 Samuel 12). (6) The tie was continually re-expressed in a developing liturgy. (7) This material is explored and developed in pre-deuteronomic circles. (8) Ur-deuteronomy finally expresses the relationship to God in the full treaty covenant form. The obligations emphasized for the king and his status near to God really involve the whole people. The status is theirs if they choose, for the obligations, the honorable and honored definitions of a life specially related to God, are theirs too. The logic of the development is clear, and there is concrete evidence supporting each step in it. The royal association of compact and sacrality does seem to have stimulated the growth of the concept of covenant religion.

---

[43]O. Eissfeldt, "The Promise of Grace to David in Isaiah 55:1-5," *Israel's Prophetic Heritage. Essays in Honor of J. Muilenburg* (eds. B. W. Anderson and W. Harrelson [New York, 1962]) 196-207.

A final note about dates: the long-continued working of the royal stimulus prohibits fixing *a* date for its effect. The basic elements, compact and sacral kingship, antedate Israel itself, but their direct, combined influence on Hebrew religious thought hardly preceded their actual presence and impact together in the king. They *need* not have been so visible as to have marked effect under David and Solomon. Still, the problem in the history of ideas remains. Covenant did change in its form of presentation. Change implies stimulus. It suffices that key points (for example, Davidic promise and responsibility, psalmody) come enough before the "pre-writing" prophets to allow the two influences to fuse in the pre-deuteronomic texts. If everything is late (deuteronomic, exilic), there is no time or mechanism to explain change. On the other hand, the story of kingship provides time and stimulus for development to pre-deuteronomistic passages, to Urdeuteronomy and the Deuteronomistic History. Tying biblical matters to more particular times (and places) than this is often imprudent. The relative chronology is meaningful, the data are insufficient for more precision.[44]

---

[44] J. Levenson, "The Davidic Covenant in Modern Interpretation," *CBQ* 41 (1979) 205-19, unavailable for this paper, though wrongly connecting treaty covenant and Sinai, grant and covenant, properly separates Davidic from Sinaitic covenant: one did not grow from or into the expression of the other but did affect the other as diverse theologies will. Hence our insistence on stimulus, influence without identification or derivation.

Zion in the Theology of the Davidic-Solomonic Empire

J. J. M. ROBERTS
Princeton Theological Seminary

I wish to thank Prince Mikasa, The Society for Old Testament Studies in Japan, and the Medical Tribune Japan for their gracious hospitality and for the kind invitation to participate in this symposium. I am particularly pleased with the chance to read a paper at this meeting because of the opportunity it affords me to make up what I have long felt to be a deficiency in my earlier study on the Zion tradition. My *JBL* article of 1973 was largely a negative critique of other scholars' attempts to find a suitable *Sitz im Leben* for the Zion tradition.[1] I basically accepted Rohland's analysis of that tradition, and, while I did give positive arguments for dating its formation to the period of the Davidic-Solomonic empire, I did not offer my own positive analysis of the tradition. It is to that task this paper is dedicated.

Ideally, the study of any aspect of the theology of the Davidic-Solomonic era should be limited to texts written in that period. Unfortunately, the nature of our sources for the glorification of Zion precludes such a direct approach. The prose sources from this era have been reedited at a later period, and it is often difficult in the key passages to separate the early material from the later editing. Moreover, the prose sources have relatively little to say on the topic. The far richer poetic sources, on the other hand, often lack the historical specificity that makes it possible to date the prose sources, and, as a consequence, there is even less agreement about the dating of the relevant poetic texts. Therefore, it is necessary to approach the problem obliquely. I will begin with a composite picture of the Zion tradition drawn from texts of varied date. Then, following an analysis of its main features, I will attempt to show which of these features can be dated to the Davidic-Solomonic period.

THE ZION TRADITION

The main features of the Zion tradition may be schematically represented in the following outline:

---

[1] J. J. M. Roberts, "The Davidic Origin of the Zion Tradition," *JBL* 92 (1973) 329-44.

  I. Yahweh is the great king.

 II. He chose Jerusalem for his dwelling place.

    A. Yahweh's choice has implications for Zion's topography.

       1. It is on a high mountain.

       2. It is watered by the river of paradise.

    B. Yahweh's choice has implications for Zion's security.

       1. Yahweh protects it from his enemies:

          a. The unruly powers of chaos, and

          b. The enemy kings.

       2. At Yahweh's rebuke:

          a. The enemy is undone,

          b. War is brought to an end,

          c. And plunder is taken.

       3. The nations acknowledge Yahweh's suzerainty.

    C. Yahweh's choice has implications for Zion's inhabitants.

       1. They share in the blessings of God's presence.

       2. But they must be fit to live in his presence.

ANALYSIS

Yahweh is the great king

One of the two fundamental conceptions of the Zion tradition is that Yahweh is the great king. Ps 48:3 actually refers to God as מלך רב,[2] while Ps 46:5 designates him עליון, a title synonymous to מלך גדול in Ps 47:3. Both terms imply that Yahweh is king not just over Israel but over the other gods and their nations as well.[3] The development of this conception requires some discussion.

That Yahweh was praised as king in Israel prior to the monarchic period seems certain. Exod 15:18 explicitly says, "Yahweh will reign for ever and ever," and the work of Albright, Cross, Freedman, and David Robertson should have established beyond reasonable doubt the antiquity of the old poem that this verse concludes.[4] If one rejects their early dating,

---

[2]Malamat, in his essay in this volume, has suggested that this title refers to Solomon, the builder of Jerusalem, but, while I recognize the Ugaritic and Aramaic antecedents for מלך רב, I am not convinced that as a Hebrew title it is more archaic than מלך גדול or that it refers to the human king. Both Ugarit and the Aramean area were under strong cultural influence from Mesopotamia, so their usage could be due to the influence of the Akkadian title *šarru rabû*, attested as early as the Old Babylonian period for the king of Aleppo and widely used in the last half of the second millennium B.C. (M.-J. Seux, *Épithètes royales akkadiennes et sumériennes* [Paris, 1967] 298-300. מלך גדול is the Hebrew counterpart of מלך רב, but it can be very early. Psalm 48 is probably no earlier than the late eighth century, while Psalm 47 appears to be Solomonic. Moreover, the parallels in the Psalms point to מלך רב as a divine title.

[3]This is explicit in Psalm 47, but it is also clear from Ps 97:9, where עליון is construed exactly as מלך גדול in Ps 47:3. See my article, "The Religio-Political Setting of Psalm 47," *BASOR* 221 (1976) 129-32.

[4]W. F. Albright, *Yahweh and the Gods of Canaan* (Garden City, 1968); F. M. Cross, Jr. and D. N. Freedman, *Studies in Ancient Yahwistic Poetry* (Baltimore, 1950); Cross, "The

one must at least answer their arguments, which, as far as I am aware, no one has bothered to do.[5] Stig Norin's recent book, *Er spaltete das Meer*, is one of the very few European works I have seen which seriously grapples with the issue, and he concludes that the original Song of the Sea was contemporary with or at most a century younger than the event it portrays.[6] For Norin that original song included vv. 3, 6-7a, 9, 7b, 10-13, 15ab, 16a, and 17-18.[7] His reasons for the numerous deletions are in general no more convincing than his attempt to derive *leviathan* and *tanin* from the Egyptian *apophis* monster,[8] but Norin's acceptance of an early date for the kernel of the song, including v. 18, points up the force of the typological argument, at least with regard to this poem. I am also convinced of the premonarchic date of Num 23:21 and Deut 33:5, two other texts which refer to Yahweh as king, but here the evidence is less overwhelming. Robertson's purely linguistic criteria do not speak to the date of these texts.

The major argument against such an early designation of Yahweh as king has been the conception that kingship was foreign to Israelite experience and that a people would only choose its religious metaphors from the range of their own culture's fundamental structures of reality. Behind this argument lies the conceptual model of Israel as uncultured Bedouins from the desert for whom Canaanite culture and institutions were a brand new experience, but that model is outdated, to say the least.[9] Whatever one's view of the conquest/settlement, nearly everyone today agrees that much, if not most, of later Israel was already in Canaan when Moses' group arrived. Moreover, it is difficult to assign such a cultural blank even to the group that left Egypt with Moses. Canaanite culture and religion had already made great inroads in Egypt, particularly in the delta region where the Israelites were settled,[10] and one can hardly see how they could be

---

Song of Miriam," *JNES* 14 (1955) 237-50; idem, "Song of the Sea and Canaanite Myth," *JTC* 5 (1968) 1-25; idem, *Canaanite Myth and Hebrew Epic* (Cambridge, MA/London, 1973); Freedman, *Prolegomenon to G. B. Gray's The Forms of Hebrew Poetry* (New York, 1971); idem, "Divine Names and Titles in Early Hebrew Poetry," *Magnalia Dei: The Mighty Acts of God. Essays on the Bible and Archaeology in Memory of G. E. Wright* (eds. F. M. Cross et al.; Garden City, 1976) 55-102; D. A. Robertson, *Linguistic Evidence in Dating Early Hebrew Poetry* (SBL DS 3, 1972).

[5]D. W. Goodwin's book, *Text Restoration Methods in Contemporary U. S. A. Biblical Scholarship* (Naples, 1969), is only an apparent exception. It was dated before it appeared and was thoroughly demolished in a devastating response by Cross and Freedman ("Some Observations on Early Hebrew," *Bib* 53 [1972] 413-20).

[6]Norin, *Er spaltete das Meer* (CB OTS 9, 1977) 92-93.

[7]Ibid., 103.

[8]Ibid., 42-75.

[9]See most recently N. K. Gottwald, *The Tribes of Yahweh* (Maryknoll, 1979). One does not have to accept all of Gottwald's views to see that he has established this point, a point which everyone should have already known, but which many ignored in their treatment of Israelite religion.

[10]R. de Vaux, *The Early History of Israel* (Philadelphia, 1978) 117-19; W. Helck, *Die Beziehungen Ägyptens zu Vorderasien im 3. und 2. Jahrtausend v. Chr.* (2d ed.; Wiesbaden, 1971) 446-73.

unaffected by it. In Canaanite religion, as throughout the Near East, the gods were arranged in political hierarchies with a divine king. Thus Israel would have been familiar with such religious use of royal language from the cultural environment they shared with their neighbors, and it would be very strange if that environment left no imprint on Israel's own religious language.

Furthermore, the late development of the monarchy in Israel appears to reflect a conscious rejection of political structures that had been experienced as oppressive, and in the context of such a political decision the metaphor of Yahweh as king could function polemically against human kingship. If Deut 33:4-5 is premonarchical, it suggests that this conception of Israel's political structure as a confederation of tribes under Yahweh as king originated in the Mosaic covenant:

> Moses commanded for us torah
> A possession of the assembly of Jacob.
> Then (Yahweh) became king in Yeshurun
> When the leaders of the people gathered together,
> The assembly of the tribes of Israel.[11]

In other words, this community of newly liberated slaves took the metaphor of God as king, known from their environment, and introduced it into their political structure as part of their conscious rejection of human kingship.

The recognition of Yahweh as king, however, meant that two important theological problems would have to be faced. The first concerned Yahweh's relationship to the other members of the Canaanite pantheon. In Canaanite mythology Baal was the king of the gods, while El was the titular head of the pantheon. Where was Yahweh to fit into this preexisting pattern of divine rule? It appears that Israel identified Yahweh and El without any serious difficulty, but Baal presented more of a problem. The course eventually chosen was simply to replace Baal with Yahweh. One can already see the process at work in Exodus 15, where the poet uses the pattern of the Baal myth in structuring his poem.[12] It is more blatant in Psalm 29, where an original hmyn to Baal has been adapted by the simple expedient of replacing the name Baal with the name Yahweh.[13] The process eventually results in Yahweh despoiling Baal of all his mythology that was compatible with Israel's God.

The same problem was presented in a slightly different form by those members of the pantheon who were also national gods of the rival

---

[11]Following P. D. Miller's translation (*The Divine Warrior in Early Israel* [Cambridge, 1973] 82).

[12]Cross, *Canaanite Myth and Hebrew Epic*, 112-44.

[13]Ibid., 152, and earlier bibliography cited there. More recently, A. Fitzgerald, "A Note on Psalm 29," *BASOR* 215 (1974) 61-63.

neighboring states. To some extent Yahweh's struggle with Baal was an in-house quarrel. In the process of replacing Baal, Yahweh was identified with him often enough to create religious confusion. Their conflict was basically a religious conflict, not just the ideological reflection of political conflict, though that was also involved. Yahweh's position vis-à-vis the national gods of her neighbors, however, was a different matter. Here there was no question of identification or replacement. Here the conflict was to a large extent the reflex of political conflict. How then was Yahweh's relationship to these deities to be understood?

Deut 32:8 presents an early attempt to resolve this question:

> When Elyon allotted the nations as an inheritance,
> When he parcelled out the sons of men,
> He established the boundaries of the peoples
> According to the number of the sons of El.
> Yahweh's portion is his people,
> Jacob his allotted inheritance.[14]

According to this text the national gods have a legitimate function within their own assigned territory, similar to Yahweh's function within Israel. Jephthah enunciated this point of view when he asked the king of Moab,[15] "Do you not take possession of that which Chemosh your god gives you as a possession? All that Yahweh our God has given us as a possession we will take in possession" (Judg 11:24). This legitimate sphere of hegemony was assigned to the national gods by a higher deity, however, Elyon, the Most High. One must ask whether the poet intended to distinguish between him and Yahweh. Eissfeldt thought that he did.[16] It is just possible that at one point in Israel's theological reflection Yahweh, though king, was assigned a subservient position vis-à-vis Elyon, much as Baal, though king, was ranked under El. I am not convinced, however. The identification of El, Elyon, and Yahweh took place very early,[17] and I think the poet is stressing rather Israel's special privilege. The other nations were parcelled out to various gods, but the suzerain himself chose to keep Israel and rule her directly.

---

[14]For the discussion of the text and date of this passage, see my earlier study, *JBL* 92 (1973) 339-40, nn. 69-72.

[15]The text has "king of the Ammonites," but it is questionable whether Jephthah would have characterized the Moabite god as the god of the Ammonite king, *contra* Boling (*Judges* [AB 6A, 1975] 201-204). The compositional history of this piece is rather complicated, however, and the last word has certainly not been written.

[16]"El and Yahweh," *JSS* 1 (1956) 29-30 = *Kleine Schriften* 3 (Tübingen, 1966) 390.

[17]El and Elyon (Num 24:16) and Yahweh and El (Num 23:8) are equated in the Balaam oracles, and Yahweh and Elyon are identified in Ps 47:3 (cf. *BASOR* 221 [1976] 129-32; *JBL* 92 [1973] 340, n. 72).

The same motif is picked up in Psalm 82 and given a new twist.[18] In this text from the Elohistic Psalter, God stands in the council of El giving judgment against the gods. He accuses them of judging unjustly, of showing partiality to the wicked, of failing to acknowledge his order to vindicate the poor and orphan, the needy and oppressed. As a result the foundations of the earth were endangered. Therefore, despite the fact that the gods were divine, the sons of Elyon, nonetheless they are condemned to die like mere mortals. The text then ends with a prayer to God to rise and execute this judgment. The closest extrabiblical parallel to this text is the Assyrian text that tells of Marduk's trial before Ashur, a text that von Soden has convincingly interpreted as a propaganda piece to justify Sennacherib's sack of Babylon.[19] Psalm 82 may be interpreted along similar lines. Though the national gods had once been assigned the task of ruling their respective nations, they had botched the job, and now Yahweh was to remove them and rule their nations directly. Such a text can best be understood as an oracle justifying and encouraging David's imperial wars.

Yahweh's status as king undoubtedly took on new significance as a result of David's conquests. They demonstrated Yahweh's kingship in the same way that Ishtar's position in the pantheon was established by Sargon's conquests, in the same way that the ascendancy of Marduk was correlated with the political ascendancy of Babylon, and in the same way that Ashur's supremacy was demonstrated by the success of Assyrian arms.[20] Moreover, they established Yahweh as the great king. He was no longer just the king of Israel; he was now suzerain over the whole earth with vassal states who actually acknowledged his suzerainty. This situation is reflected in Psalm 47,[21] and it is the necessary background for Ps 2:1-3:

Why do the nations rage
And the peoples vainly scheme,
Kings of the earth plot together
And rulers take council together
Against Yahweh and against his anointed (saying):
"Let us break his bonds.
Let us cast off his yoke ropes."
. . .

This is the speech of rebellious vassals, and the necessary conceptual background for such speech is an ideology of Yahweh's suzerainty. In the

---

[18]See *JBL* 92 (1973) 340-42. I agree with most of the conclusions of H.-W. Jüngling, *Der Tod der Götter* (Stuttgarter Bibelstudien 38, 1968), but we part company on the date and *Sitz im Leben* of Psalm 82.

[19]W. von Soden, "Gibt es ein Zeugnis, dass die Babylonier an Marduks Wiederauferstehung glaubten?" *ZA* NS 16-17 (1952-55) 130-66; "Ein neues Bruchstück des assyrischen Kommentars zum Marduk-Ordal," *ZA* NS 18-19, (1957-59) 224-34.

[20]*JBL* 92 (1973) 341.

[21]*BASOR* 221 (1976) 129-32.

ancient Near East such ideologies were normally rooted in political realities if not of the present, then of some more favored time in the past. They were seldom spun out of whole cloth or simply borrowed from another culture without reference to the political realities in the target culture.

The second theological problem inherent in the conception of Yahweh as king arose with the institution of human kingship. How is the human king related to the divine suzerain? Once Israel overcame her earlier reluctance to accept a human monarch, she settled the problem along the same lines followed in Assyria and Babylon. The real king was the deity; the human king was just his representative or regent, elected by the deity to carry out his earthly tasks.[22] One even reads of the gods making an oath to the king.[23] The tradition of Yahweh's choice of David and his house, therefore, is not completely unparalleled, although one can hardly cite a parallel where such a tradition has had the same impact on later developments as the covenant with David did in later Israelite history.

Yahweh chose Jerusalem for his dwelling place

The second fundamental conception of the Zion tradition is that Yahweh chose Jerusalem for his dwelling place. This is explicitly stated in Ps 78:68 and 132:13, but it is implicit in the Zion songs' affirmations that Zion is God's city (Pss 46:5; 48:2-3, 8-9; 87:2), that he resides within her (Pss 46:6; 48:4), and that his covert or lair is within her (Ps 76:3). This last reference could refer to the tent sanctuary or temple in Jerusalem, though that is not certain. Israelite religious poetry moves easily back and forth between a specific reference to the temple and a more general reference to the city as a whole. Thus Yahweh founds his sanctuary like the earth and builds it like the heavens (Ps 78:69), but he also founds Zion (Pss 48:9; 87:1, 5) and builds Jerusalem (Ps 102:17; cf. Pss 51:20; 147:2).

Topography

From these two fundamental conceptions of the Zion tradition several subsidiary motifs follow. Since Zion was the abode of Yahweh, the divine

---

[22]In the Assyrian enthronement ritual the kingship of Ashur is significantly proclaimed prior to the crowning of the human king (K. F. Müller, *Das assyrische Ritual* 1 [MVAG 41/3, 1937] 8-9, line 29). The Babylonian view is well reflected in the prologue to the Code of Hammurabi, i 1-52, v 14-24.

[23]Thus Marduk claims to have made a covenant with the future king of Babylon who will destroy Elam (*anākuma . . . ittišu salmāku*) in the Marduk prophecy text (R. Borger, "Gott Marduk und Gott-König Šulgi als Propheten," *BO* 28 [1971] 11, 17, iii 21'-22'). Note also K2401 ii 10'-32', which records an oracle of Ashur promising salvation to Esarhaddon, and which refers to the tablet containing the oracle as "the sworn tablet of Ashur" (*ṭup-pi a-de-e an-ni-u šá* ᵈ*Aš-šur*, S. A. Strong, "On Some Oracles to Esarhaddon and Ashurbanipal," *Beiträge zur Assyriologie* 2 [1894] 639, obv. ii 27; the complete text is translated in H. B. Huffmon's forthcoming volume on prophecy.).

king, any of the language used to describe the abode of the comparable Canaanite deities whom Yahweh had despoiled could now be transferred to Zion.

THE HIGH MOUNTAIN

West Semitic deities were generally conceived of as having their abode upon high mountains, and Yahweh appears to have been no exception. His original mountain abode seems to have been Mt. Sinai/Horeb, the mountain of God (Exod 3:1; 18:5; 24:13; Num 10:33) which he left (Deut 33:2; Judg 5:4; Hab 3:3) to take up his abode in Canaan (Exod 15:17; Ps 78:54). At first it would appear that the central hill country as a whole was thought of as his holy mountain (Ps 78:54),[24] but with David's transfer of the ark to Jerusalem, Mt. Zion became Yahweh's chosen mountain (Ps 78:68-69). Since Yahweh had replaced Baal as king of the gods, it was possible to identify Mt. Zion with Baal's famous Mt. Zaphon (Ps 48:3).[25] Even when this precise identification is not made, however, Mt. Zion is constantly thought of as a high mountain appropriate for the dwelling of the divine king.[26]

At this point it is worth noting that there is no necessary contrast, at least in the early material, between the deity residing in heaven and the deity residing on his mountain.[27] By definition the top of the sacred mountain reached into heaven, as is clear from Isa 14:13-14, where "to sit enthroned on the mount of assembly, on the heights of Zaphon" is equivalent with scaling heaven, putting one's throne above the stars of El, and rising above the clouds. One should also observe that the traditions about Yahweh's giving the law at Mt. Sinai sometimes describe him as speaking from heaven, sometimes as speaking from the mountain without any apparent distinction in meaning (Exod 19:18-19; 20:22). The deuteronomistic theologians introduced a distinction with their name theology, but that distinction seems relatively late. One should not read the deuteronomistic contrast into every poetic passage where Yahweh is said to have done something from heaven, particularly if the same piece speaks of God as living in Zion or acting from Zion.

THE RIVER

The standard epithet for El's abode in the Ugaritic texts is *mbk nhrm qrb apq thmtm*, "at the sources of the two rivers midst the streams of the

---

[24]D. N. Freedman, however, would take this as a reference to the wilderness mountain sanctuary ("Early Israelite History in the Light of Early Israelite Poetry," *Unity and Diversity* [eds. H. Goedicke and J. J. M. Roberts; Baltimore/London, 1975] 8-9).

[25]For the rendering of צפון as a proper name for a mountain, see the discussion in *JBL* 92 (1973) 334-35 and Roberts, "*Ṣāpôn* in Job 26, 7," *Bib* 56 (1975) 554-57.

[26]Pss 2:6; 68:17; 87:1; 99:9; Isa 2:2; 27:13; 66:20; Ezek 40:2; Zech 14:10; etc.

[27]See the fine discussion by Mettinger in his article in this volume.

two seas."[28] Since Yahweh was identified with El, it is not surprising that the watery nature of his abode also makes its imprint on the Zion tradition. Ps 46:3 speaks of a river whose streams make glad the city of God. This motif plays a major role in late prophetic descriptions of the new Jerusalem (Ezek 47:1-12; Joel 4:18; Zech 14:8), and it also occurs in a rather peculiar form in Isaiah 33, a text that may be Isaianic.[29] In the context of his description of a redeemed Jerusalem the prophet says in vv. 21-23a:

> But there Yahweh will be majestic
> For us a reservoir[30] of rivers,
> Of streams broad and wide.
> No galley with oars will travel it.
> No mighty ship will cross it.
> For Yahweh is our judge,
> Yahweh is our lawgiver,
> Yahweh is our king.
> He will save us.
> Its rigging will hang loose;
> They cannot hold the mast in place,
> They cannot spread the sail.

The references in both Psalm 46 and Isaiah 33 are tantalizing because it is not quite clear syntactically what Yahweh's relation to this river or reservoir of rivers is. Is Yahweh himself the stream? It is evident from Jer 2:13 and 17:12-13 that Yahweh could be described metaphorically as a spring of living waters. Whether the orignal motif had already been so transformed in Psalm 46, it is at least clear in the later texts that the source of the stream is found in the very presence of God. One may be dealing with a very early transformation of a geographical feature into a religious metaphor about the source of life.

One other feature about El's abode seems to be reflected in Ezekiel's description of Tyre's abode in the garden of God. Tyre is described as "on the holy mountain of God, in the midst of the stones of fire" (Ezek 28:14-16). The precise meaning of the term "stones of fire" is still debated, but some have seen its background in the incident in the Baal epic where a fire burns in Baal's new palace to melt down the silver and gold needed for the building. Nothing appears to be made of this motif in the Zion songs, but

---

[28] *CTA* 2 iii 4; 3 E v 14-15; 4 iv 21-22; 5 vi 2*-1*; 6 i 33-34; 17 vi 47-48; cf. the only slightly variant form found in *Ugaritica* 5 (1968) no. 7 (RS 24.244) 3: *mbk nhrm. b^cdt. thmtm,* "at the sources of the two rivers, at the gathering of the two seas."

[29] Most recent studies date the piece to the postexilic period, but I hope to show in a forthcoming article that the Isaianic attribution given by many of the older scholars (e.g., S. R. Driver, *An Introduction to the Literature of the Old Testament* [New York, 1912] 225) is more credible.

[30] Reading *miqwē-m* with W. H. Irwin, *Isaiah 28-33: Translation with Philological Notes* (BibOr 30, 1977) 158-59.

one wonders whether Isaiah's references to Yahweh "who has a fire in Zion and a furnace in Jerusalem" (31:9), who is "a devouring fire, a perpetual burning" (33:14), and who threatens to purify Jerusalem by smelting (1:25), may not have their background in such a mythological setting.[31]

Security

Another consequence of Yahweh's living in Jerusalem is the absolute security his presence provides. With Yahweh in it the city cannot be shaken (Ps 46:7). He is its stronghold (Pss 46:8; 48:4), and he is more than a match for any hostile power.

THE ENEMY

These hostile powers are sometimes described under the mythological imagery of the unruly sea (Ps 46:2-4), sometimes more historically as hostile kings or nations (Pss 46:7; 48:5-7; 76:6-8), and sometimes the two merge into one (Isa 17:12-14). The mythological imagery of the unruly sea was undoubtedly borrowed from the Canaanite myth of Baal's struggle with Prince Yamm, but there has been no consensus on the source of the imagery for the hostile nations.[32] In my earlier study I rejected any possibility of finding its antecedents in the Baal myth and argued for its derivation from some historical incident early in the history of the united monarchy.[33] Though I still think historical events helped shape the motif, I am now convinced that there are also mythological antecedents. *CTA* 4 vii 30-37 seems to refer to an attempt to storm Baal's mountain after he has established his palace there, an attempt, one should note, that Baal turns back by the thunder of his voice:

Baal gives forth his holy voice
Baal discharges the utterance of his lips
His holy voice convulses the earth, . . . the
     mountains quake,
     A-tremble are . . .
East and west, earth's high places reel,
Baal's enemies take to the woods,
Hadd's foes to the sides of the mountain.[34]

The gory picture of Anat's slaughter of the people of the seashore and of the sunrise may refer to the same enemies (*CTA* 3 B ii 3-39). *CTA* 3 D iii 43-iv 47 may even contain a reference to a successful assault against Baal's mountain that temporarily drove Baal from Zaphon.

---

[31]Other passages, however, associate Yahweh's fire with storm imagery (29:6; 30:27-30).
[32]*JBL* 92 (1973) 337-39.
[33]Ibid., 337-39, 343-44.
[34]Following Ginsberg's translation, *ANET* (2d ed. Princeton, 1955) 135.

Perhaps one should also discuss Ps 48:8 under this rubric. After describing the panic of the enemy kings the psalmist adds, "With an east wind you smashed the ships of Tarshish." In the context of an attack on Jerusalem this is a rather strange statement. Nevertheless, the "ships of Tarshish" reappear as a metaphor for human arrogance in Isaiah's magnificent portrayal of Yahweh's solitary exaltation (2:16), a portrayal with strong mythological overtones. One should also note the image of the stately ship in Isa 33:21, where it clearly stands for powers hostile to Yahweh's well-watered Jerusalem. Moreover, the ship there is also disabled, if not smashed, by the wreckage of its tackle. The continuity of the metaphor and the difficulty of explaining it from Israelite historical experience suggests that it too may be derived from Canaanite tradition, perhaps a seaborne assault on Baal's abode. Where, after all, did the "men of the seashore" in the Baal epic come from?

YAHWEH'S REBUKE

As in the Baal epic, Yahweh turns back these hostile forces by his thunderous rebuke (Pss 46:7; 76:7, 9).[35] But, from where does Yahweh thunder? The verse transmitted in both Amos 1:2 and Joel 4:16 has Yahweh roar from Zion, but Ps 76:9 says he makes his judgment heard from heaven. Nonetheless, there is probably no difference intended in Psalm 76, since that Psalm has already described Yahweh as having his lair in Zion. The temple mount and heaven are probably also equivalent in Psalm 18, where Yahweh utters his voice from "his temple" (v. 7), "in heaven" (v. 14), and sends help from "the heights" (v. 17)—the same term that Ps 78:69 uses to describe how Yahweh built his sanctuary and that Isa 33:5 parallels with Zion. Ps 48:6 suggests that the enemy is turned back by visual phenomena,[36] and this is followed by the verse that tells of the east wind wrecking the ships of Tarshish. All these clues taken together suggest that the original phenomenon behind the mythological pattern in its original setting was the experience of a sudden thunderstorm sweeping down over the Mediterranean from the heights of the Jebel Aqra. This was given a mythological transformation in the Baal epic, and it received a further historical transformation when it was taken up in Israel and applied to Jerusalem.

---

[35]Cf. Ps 2:4-5; Isa 17:13; 29:6; 31:4-5; 33:3.

[36]Ps 48:6 does not specify what "they saw," but its structural correspondance to Yahweh's "rebuke" in the parallel passages suggests the visual counterpart to Yahweh's "roar." His "roar" appears to be drawn from thunderstorm imagery, so the visual phenomena implied should also be understood from that same background: lightening, etc. This is strongly suggested by Ps 50:2, "From Zion, the perfection of beauty, Yahweh shines forth. Our God comes and will not be silent; a fire devours before him, and around him a tempest rages." Isa 29:6 also portrays Yahweh's sudden intervention in the imagery of the thunderstorm with both the loud thunder, קוֹל גָּדוֹל, and the devouring fire, לֶהַב אֵשׁ אוֹכֵלָה.

The defeat of Yahweh's enemies has several results. In the first place the weapons of war are shattered and peace is established in the earth (Ps 46:10; 76:4, 9). There may be Canaanite antecedents for this theme in Baal's command to Anat to banish war from the earth, if the relevant Ugaritic lines have been correctly understood (*CTA* 3 C iii 10-15; D iv 51-54, 71-75). Another result of Yahweh's victory is the collection of a vast amount of booty. This may be referred to in the very difficult lines of Ps 76:5-6,[37] and it is very clear in some of the later texts (Isa 33:4, 23; Ezek 39:9-10; Zech 14:14). Finally, the nations must acknowledge Yahweh's sovereignty and honor him with praise and tribute. Ps 76:11-13 gives much fuller expression to this motif than Psalms 46 and 48, which are satisfied with vague statements about Yahweh's exaltation among the nations.[38] The motif finds its most elaborate expression in Zech 14:16-19.

Implications for Zion's inhabitants

The fact that Yahweh lives in Zion has at least three implications for the human inhabitants of Jerusalem. These implications are not spelled out in the Songs of Zion, but they do appear in other texts that are heavily dependent on the Zion tradition. In the first place, only those who meet God's righteous standards can live in his presence (Isa 33:13-16; Ps 24:3-4). One of the duties of God's regent, the human king, was "to cut off the doers of iniquity from the city of Yahweh" (Ps 101:8). In the second place, the inhabitants, and especially the king, have the duty of building God's city. The texts normally speak of God doing the building or they express it in the passive, but it is clear from Hag 1:2-11 that God expected help from his human agents. Ps 78:69 says that God built his sanctuary like the heavens, but Solomon was the human agent in that construction, and he claims as much in 1 Kgs 8:13, "I have indeed built a princely house for you, a place for you to dwell forever."[39] Finally, those inhabitants who are fit to live with God will rejoice in the security and abundant life that Yahweh's presence brings.[40]

---

[37]The verb אשתוללו points in that direction.

[38]I read v. 11 as follows:

כי חמת אדם תודך
שארית חמת תחגך

Surely the fortress (?) of Edom will praise you.
The remnant of Hamath will celebrate your festival.

[39]Thus Micah is actually criticizing the Zion tradition from within that tradition when he attacks all of Jerusalem's leaders for exercising their legitimate functions in the wrong way and includes the line "who build Zion with blood and Jerusalem with wrongdoing" (3:10).

[40]Pss 48:12-14; 132:13-18; 133:3; 147:13; Isa 33:17-24.

DATE

It should be clear from the preceding analysis of the Zion tradition that all that was required for its crystallization was the belief that Yahweh, the suzerain, had chosen to make his dwelling in Zion. Once that step had been taken, the glorification of Zion with motifs drawn from Canaanite mythology about the abode of the great gods would follow as a matter of course. Historical events might shape the use of these motifs, but the historical events themselves could also be shaped by the pattern of the myth. Given this situation, what can one say about the historical development of the tradition?

First, its crystallization point must still be sought in the Davidic-Solomonic era. Most of my earlier arguments against the wholesale adoption of a prepackaged Jebusite tradition remain valid, but the beginning of the tradition must have followed shortly on David's movement of the ark to Jerusalem. That act presupposes oracular approval. One did not set up sanctuaries in antiquity without the prior approval of the deity to be housed in the sanctuary, and Jerusalem had no ancient Yahwistic tradition to commend it. Whether that move was originally conceived of as a permanent move, it is clear that David's desire to build a temple implied the establishment of Yahweh's permanent residence in Jerusalem, and that step, which marked a major departure from Israel's past religious practice, certainly required divine validation. In the Israelite tradition that validation came in the form of an oracle that coordinated Yahweh's choice of David with his choice of Jerusalem (2 Sam 7; Pss 78:68; 132:10-18). Whatever the precise date at which these texts were written, there is no reason to doubt the original linkage of the choice of David and the choice of Jerusalem. This pattern is also found outside Israel, in the prologue to the Code of Hammurabi, for instance, where the divine election of Hammurabi and his capital city Babylon are coordinated. But, if the two were originally linked, the tradition of Yahweh's election of Jerusalem cannot postdate David's reign, because the tradition of Yahweh's election of David certainly comes from David's own time. It was a necessary part of his struggle for legitimation in view of his suspiciously irregular succession to the throne, and it is paralleled by numerous examples from Mesopotamia, where a king often refers to his divine election. Solomon no doubt cultivated David's religious propaganda for his own purposes, but there is no compelling reason to make him the creator of these traditions. I doubt that there are many examples, if any, where one can show that a Near Eastern king created a tradition of divine election for his predecessor on the throne.

But, if it is clear that the necessary crystallization point for the development of the Zion tradition existed from the time of David's later years, it is also clear that many of the motifs in its later elaboration are also attested as early as Solomon's reign. Psalm 68 would appear to be from that period. Its mention of the temple in v. 30 dates it after Solomon's construction of that edifice, but other indications in the text make it difficult to see a *terminus ad quem* later than Solomon. The poem contains a number of archaic linguistic features such as the use of זו or זה as a relative (vv. 9, 29; cf. Exod 15:17). Many of its formulas have their closest parallels in the old poetry: v. 2 is parallel to the old formula in Num 10:35, vv. 8-10 have their closest parallel in Judg 5:4-5, and vv. 34-35, which speak of God as riding in the heavens, are closely paralleled in Deut 33:26. Psalm 68 also has many more contacts with the Baal myth than one might expect in a later work. Verses 21b-24 are very difficult to interpret, but they seem to speak of Yahweh's power over Mot, his smiting of his enemies, his conquest of Yamm, and his wading in the gore of his slain foes:

> From Yahweh the lord is the escape from death.
> Surely God smote the head of his enemies,
> He split[41] the crown of him who walked in sin.
> The Lord said, "I will repulse the Serpent,[42]
> I will muzzle the depths of the Sea."
> So that your foot plunged in blood,
> the tongue of your dogs had their share of the enemy.[43]

One should note, also, that this passage is followed by a victory processional of the divine king. The description of that cultic procession in vv. 25-28, with its mention of the princes of Zebulon and Naptali as well as Benjamin and Judah, would also suggest a period before the northern tribes split off from the south. The religious and political rivalry between Jerusalem and the Aramean territory, expressed in the motif of Mt. Bashan's jealously toward Mt. Zion, would also be easier to explain against the background of David's Aramean conquests than at any later period. The parallel usage of ישׁב and שׁכן to describe the nature of Yahweh's abiding on his mountain is the same as the usage found in the old poetic fragment from the book of Yashar embedded in Solomon's prayer of dedication of the temple (1 Kgs 8:12-13). It is clearly a predeuteronomistic usage and also antedates the later technical distinction between ישׁב and שׁכן exploited by the P tradition.[44]

Of course, all these bits and pieces help in dating the Psalm only if the Psalm is, in fact, a literary unit. If Albright's thesis that Psalm 68 is simply a series of incipits were correct,[45] one could not argue from material in one verse of the Psalm for the date of any other verse. Albright's view is unconvincing, however. Although I do not understand much of the Psalm

---

[41]Reading the verb שׁער, "to split," following Dahood, *The Psalms* 2 (AB 17, 1968) 144.

[42]Attaching the *mem* to the end of אדני as an enclitic with Dahood, *The Psalms* 2, 145, but reading אשׁיב as the hiphil of שׁוב.

[43]Following Dahood, *The Psalms* 2, 145-46.

[44]See the discussion of these terms in Cross, *Canaanite Myth and Hebrew Epic*, 97, n. 24.

[45]W. F. Albright, "A Catalogue of Early Hebrew Lyric Poems (Psalm LXVIII)," *HUCA* 23 (1950-51) 1-39.

and certainly cannot at this point reconstruct an orderly whole with a nice progression of thought throughout the Psalm, there are large blocks where there are more logical connections than one would expect in a random collection of incipits. Verses 16-17, even taken by themselves, are long for an incipit, but it is possible that v. 15 is connected (Ṣalmon could be the name for the Jebel Druze) and vv. 18-19, with the triumphant entrance into the sanctuary, perhaps even the transfer of the sanctuary from Sinai to Jerusalem, could also be a continuation of the same thought. Verse 19c, "In the presence of God no rebel can dwell," picks up the same theme as v. 7. Verses 22-24 also appear to be connected and may lead into the description of the processional in vv. 25-28. Verses 29-33 appear to be connected by the theme of the tribute of the foreign nations. One should also note that it is not easy to follow the logical progression in Judges 5 or in long Mesopotamian hymns.

If one accepts this dating for Psalm 68, one already has the motif of Yahweh choosing Mount Zion as the high mountain on which he desires to dwell and where his temple in Jerusalem is to stand (vv. 16-17, 30). The poem also tells of his victory over the mythological powers as well as over the enemy kings, and it mentions Yahweh's thunder against his foes, as well as the plunder which results from the flight of the enemy. Finally, it mentions the tribute of the nations and Yahweh's exaltation in the world.

The oldest of the Zion songs, Psalm 76, may also date this early. It coordinates Judah and Israel in a way compatible with a date in the united monarchy, in contrast with the Judean orientation of Psalm 48, and it breathes the same air of imperialism that one finds in Psalms 47, 68, and 82. There is a certain resemblance to Psalm 2, but one should note that Psalm 76 does not characterize the enemy kings as Yahweh's vassals until after the battle. In effect, it is his victory which establishes his rule as in Psalm 68. In both Psalms 68 and 76 there seem to be reflexes of David's imperial wars, suggesting that the tradition is shaped by both the mythological pattern and the actual course of history. I take Ps 76:4 to reflect David's defeat of the Philistines in the vicinity of Jerusalem, and vv. 10-13 I see as rooted in his imperial wars against Aram and Edom.

The Zion tradition is certainly older than Isaiah, whose message is permeated by it. In his inaugural vision he saw Yahweh as the king sitting enthroned upon a high and lofty throne in the temple (Isa 6:1). For him Yahweh dwelt on Mount Zion (8:18; 12:6), and his conception of Yahweh's plan to save Jerusalem through purging (1:25), when it is spelled out in detail, involves an adaptation of the assault of the nations motif (10:16-17; 14:24-25; 17:12-14; 29:1-8; 31:8-9; 33:1-24). Isaiah appears to innovate in making Yahweh fight against Jerusalem before saving it (29:1-4)—an innovation that is further developed in Zechariah 12 and 14—but otherwise he appears to stay very much within the contours of the tradition. There are good reasons for connecting both Isaiah 33 and Psalm 48, which have striking contacts with each other, with the Assyrian crisis of Hezekiah's time, and specifically with Sennacherib's failure to take Jerusalem. This must have given added weight to the Zion tradition, but since both Psalm 48 and Isaiah 33 treat the freshly experienced deliverance (Psalm 48) or the soon-to-be-expected deliverance (Isaiah 33) as a new realization or confirmation of an old tradition—"As we had heard, so now we have seen" (Ps 48:9; cf. Isa 33:3-5)—it is clear that that event did not create the tradition. The Zion tradition, in fact, probably shaped Israel's perception of that event and no doubt heightened its miraculous quality.

CONCLUSION

The fundamental point necessary for the formation of the Zion tradition was the belief that Yahweh had chosen Jerusalem as his permanent abode. That dogma could not date much later than David's decision to move the ark to Jerusalem, and certainly not later than the decision to build the temple there. Once this dogma was accepted, it brought in its wake the glorification of Jerusalem, with mythological traditions associated with the abode of those gods with whom Yahweh was identified or whom he had displaced. Some of these traditions had points of contact with Israel's historical experience in the period of David's imperial wars, and the precise form the Zion tradition took was probably due to the mutual influence of myth and history. Certainly the political ascendancy of Jerusalem in the imperial period had a great deal to do with both the imperial conception of Yahweh's suzerainty and the glorification of his capital. The Zion tradition was basically fixed by the end of this period. It was reinforced by Jerusalem's deliverance from Sennacherib, though the interpretation of that event was largely colored by the preexisting Zion tradition; however, about this time the first major innovations in the tradition were introduced by Isaiah and Micah. Working from within the tradition, they introduced the notion of Yahweh's fighting against Zion, in order through judgment to realize the ideals embodied in the tradition.

YHWH SABAOTH—The Heavenly King on the Cherubim Throne

TRYGGVE N. D. METTINGER
University of Lund

A treatment of the divine designation צבאות יהוה (YHWH Sabaoth) might seem out of place within the framework of this symposium, given the distribution of the term in the texts.[1] Of its 285 occurrences, only 11 are to be found in the books of Samuel, 5 in the books of Kings. The majority of references are found in the prophetic literature, primarily in Isaiah (62 instances, 56 of which are found in Isaiah 1-39) and Jeremiah (82 instances), as well as in certain of the postexilic prophets: Haggai (14 instances), Zechariah (53), and Malachi (24). Nonetheless, the question may be asked whether this term did not play a very important role during the Solomonic era.

Scholarly literature is replete with varying, often incompatible interpretations of the designation, "YHWH Sabaoth." Here I need give no introductory survey of the state of scholarship: that need has been competently met by R. Schmitt.[2] Still, it will be worth our while to note the types of methodological approach which have been used in the study of the problem.

(1) The usual procedure has been to start with the use of צבא in texts where it is not connected with the divine designation. Depending on which usage has been made the focus of attention, the divine designation has been understood in differing ways. Thus, צבאות has been taken to refer to the (earthly) armies of Israel. This interpretation is defined more precisely by J. Maier: in his view, the divine designation involves a dual number and refers to the popular militias (*Heerbanne*) of Judah and the Northern Kingdom of Israel as they were united under the double monarchy of David.[3] Other scholars have taken as their starting point the usage of צבא

---

[1]For the distribution, see F. Baumgärtel, "Zu den Gottesnamen in den Büchern Jeremia und Ezechiel," *Verbannung und Heimkehr. Festschrift W. Rudolph* (ed. A. Kuschke; Tübingen, 1961) 1-29. My study has also benefitted from the surveys of B. Wiklander, "Material för diskussionen om tolkningen av *JHWH ṣᵉbaʾôt*" (unpublished material, brought together for the Swedish Bible Commission).

[2]R. Schmitt, *Zelt und Lade* (Gütersloh, 1972) 145-59.

[3]J. Maier, *Das altisraelitische Ladeheiligtum* (BZAW 93, 1965) 50-51.

to refer to a host of cosmic and heavenly powers. The rather special, unusual usage of צבא to express a totality (Gen 2:1; Isa 34:2) has led Wambacq to conclude that צבאות in the divine designation gradually came to denote "la totalité des créatures."[4]

(2) A second type of approach has found its starting point in syntactic and morphological considerations relating to the divine designation. For Arnold, "the pertinent and decisive facts are, first, צבאות is *indeterminate*; and second, the word is an *adjectival genitive*." The sense is thus not "*Yahwe of the Armies*, whether Israelitish or celestial." The designation is rather to be understood as "*Yahwe Militant*."[5] Eissfeldt adopted this line of approach, his primary contribution being the theory that the plural צבאות is an abstract plural, "Mächtigkeit," used as a personal designation to mean "Mächtiger." He showed, too, that this interpretation is quite compatible with the statement that YHWH "sits enthroned on the cherubim."[6] Tsevat, too, proceeds on the basis of syntactic considerations.[7] In his view, it is highly improbable that יהוה צבאות represents a construct relation, since personal names govern a genitive only where there is a special need of overdetermination. According to Tsevat, we are rather to understand the divine designation either as made up of noun plus appositive (YHWH, the צבאות), or as a noun sentence (YHWH is צבאות). In both cases, an identity is affirmed between YHWH and צבאות. Semantically, צבאות in the name bears "the common and general denotation 'armies'." Just as King Joash could address the prophet Elisha, "My father, my father, Israel's corps of chariots and its horses" (2 Kgs 13:14), so "the people called its God 'Armies' (plural of extention and importance)," writes Tsevat.[8] An alternative interpretation of the syntax has been maintained during recent decades by certain American scholars (F. M. Cross and others). They see in יהוה צבאות an example of verb + object: "He who creates armies." On the basis of mythological parallels, צבאות is then understood as "the hosts of heaven."[9]

(3) Rather than begin with philological questions, J. P. Ross[10] took as his starting point a study of the content of the statements made in those texts which he judged to be the oldest, namely, those of Samuel and

[4]B. N. Wambacq, *L'épithète divine Jahvé S^{e}ba$^{\text{?}}$ôt* (Bruges, 1947) 276.

[5]W. R. Arnold, *Ephod and Ark* (Cambridge, MA, 1917) 142-43.

[6]O. Eissfeldt, "Jahwe Zebaoth" (1950) *Kleine Schriften* 3 (Tübingen, 1966) 102-23. A criticism of Eissfeldt is found in W. Kessler, "Aus welchen Gründen wird die Bezeichnung 'Jahwe Zebaoth' in den späteren Zeit gemieden?" *Gottes ist der Orient. Festschrift O. Eissfeldt* (ed. A. Lehmann; Berlin, 1959) 79-83.

[7]M. Tsevat, "Studies in the Book of Samuel, 4," *HUCA* 36 (1965) 49-58. A critique of Tsevat is found in P. D. Miller, *The Divine Warrior in Early Israel* (HSM 5, 1973) 256f.
[8]*HUCA* 36 (1965) 55.

[9]See, in particular, F. M. Cross, *Canaanite Myth and Hebrew Epic* (Cambridge, MA, 1973) 65-75. Cross was criticized by Tsevat, *HUCA* 36 (1965) 54, n. 28.

[10]J. P. Ross, "Jahweh S^{e}bā$^{\text{?}}$ôṯ in Samuel and Kings," *VT* 17 (1967) 76-92.

Psalms. He found that the contexts in which Sabaoth occurs in these books are predominantly royal. With regard to the semantic problem, he found himself compelled to posit a gulf between, on the one hand, the divine designation with its royal connotations and, on the other hand, the root *ṣ-b-ʾ* in isolation from the divine name as it appears in military terms: the noun meaning "army" and the verb meaning "to serve in an army." For this reason Ross weighs the possibility of distinguishing the divine designation from the well-known root *ṣ-b-ʾ*.[11] Maag, too, emphasizes the occurrences in the books of Samuel, above all those instances in which the worship of YHWH Sabaoth is assigned to pre-monarchic Shiloh (1 Sam 1:3, 11; 4:4). His investigation, however, is marked by a history-of-religion type approach. According to Maag, the name originated in a situation characterized by the meeting between the YHWH-faith of the Hebrew tribes and Canaanite polytheism; it is seen to constitute evidence that this meeting at certain times was marked by integration: צבאות denotes "die depotenzierten mythischen Naturmächte Kanaans," accomodated to YHWH.[12]

When one considers how varying and mutually contradictory these interpretations are, one is tempted to agree with von Rad when he asks if the attempt to define the meaning of the divine title is "due to the false supposition that an element of cultic epiklesis as old as this is in all circumstances capable of rational explanation."[13] The evident disagreement between scholars is at any rate a testimony to the difficulty of the navigation problem which here confronts us: in analyzing the Sabaoth problem, how is one to decide in which direction to proceed, so that the peril of hidden rocks is avoided by giving due attention to the buoys which indeed are to be found in the texts themselves?

CONTEXTUALIZATION

Modern linguistics has for decades stressed the importance of context for semantic analysis (Firth and others).[14] A contextualization can be conducted on two levels. (a) The attempt can be made to establish the situational context of the word in question (Firth). Here one deals with the cultural context; the pursuit involves essentially what Gunkel called *Sitz im Leben*.[15] (b) On the level of language, the word's lexical environment can be analyzed. The word is then studied in collocation with other words on the syntagmatic level of speech.

---

[11]Ibid., 78-79, 89, 92.

[12]V. Maag, "Jahwäs Heerscharen," *STU* 20 (1950) 27-52, quotation from p. 50.

[13]G. von Rad, *Old Testament Theology* 1 (Edinburgh/London, 1962) 19.

[14]For good surveys, see H. Geckeler, *Strukturelle Semantik und Wortfeldtheorie* (München, 1971) 48-58 and J. Lyons, *Semantics* 2 (Cambridge, 1977) 607-13.

[15]This was seen by J. F. A. Sawyer, "Context of Situation and Sitz im Leben," *Proceedings of the University of Newcastle upon Tyne Philosophical Society* 1/11 (1967).

Here I shall make my *first* task that of attempting to establish a situational context which to a great extent left its stamp on the connotations borne by the divine designation of our discussion. By connotations, I mean here semantic overtones, supplementary values. On this matter, scholarly endeavors concerned with this designation have hitherto been confined to impulsive beginnings never carried through in any deliberate or systematic way.[16] My *second* task will be to attempt to define more closely the semantic content of יהוה צבאות. My *third* task will be to check the conclusions on these two points by using the traditions of Shiloh as a touchstone. I shall then, finally, discuss the transference of the divine designation from Shiloh to the cultic milieu of Jerusalem.

Even a precursory overview of the material indicates a strong linkage between the designation יהוה צבאות on the one hand and Zion, with the temple, on the other. Isaiah's temple vision is an eloquent witness to such a connection (Isa 6:3, 5). YHWH Sabaoth is explicitly called השכן בהר ציון, "he who dwells on Mount Zion" (Isa 8:18). The Isaiah Apocalypse tells how YHWH Sabaoth establishes his royal sway on Zion (Isa 24:23) and later describes the banquet he holds on this mountain (25:6). Connected with this latter notion is the portrayal of how the nations will go up to YHWH Sabaoth on Zion (Zech 14:16-17), bringing gifts (Isa 18:7). The link between YHWH Sabaoth and Zion finds further support in the occurrence of the designation in the Hymns of Zion (Pss 46:8, 12; 48:9; 84:2, 4, 9, 13). Here Jerusalem is called "the city of YHWH Sabaoth" (Ps 48:9), just as the city in a different context is called "the mountain of YHWH Sabaoth" (Zech 8:3).

We can however, define the link with Zion and the temple even more precisely. As W. Richter has pointed out, among others, fixed formulas often provide valuable aid in establishing *Sitz im Leben*.[17] Of those formulas where the divine designation is an element,[18] two in particular have been utilized for this purpose: כה אמר יהוה צבאות, "thus says YHWH Sabaoth," and יהוה צבאות ישב הכרבים, "YHWH Sabaoth, who is enthroned on the cherubim": the messenger and the cherubim formulas. Baumgärtel made an attempt to interpret the messenger formula as an ancient priestly oracular formula closely connected with the ark and to link the Sabaoth designation via the messenger formula to the institution of the priestly oracle.[19] The distribution of the designation and of the messenger formula, however, witnesses against the supposition that the two were originally linked.[20] There is, to be sure, a connection with the ark (1 Sam

---

[16]See the studies by Eissfeldt (n. 6), Baumgärtel (n. 1), and Ross (n.10), mentioned above.

[17]W. Richter, *Exegese als Literaturwissenschaft* (Göttingen, 1971) 101, 117.

[18]For statistics on the various formulas see F. Baumgärtel, "Zu den Gottesnamen," 1-29.

[19]Baumgärtel, "Zu den Gottesnamen," 20-24.

[20]H. W. Wolff, *Dodekapropheton 2: Joel und Amos* (BKAT 14/2, 1969) 166.

4:4; 2 Sam 6:2, 18; 7:8, 26, 27; Ps 24:10); but this connection is of an indirect nature, as we shall see.

If the messenger formula provides little help, the clues given by the cherubim formula are so much the more valuable. It is the great merit of Eissfeldt that he introduced the cherubim formula into the discussion of the Sabaoth problem.[21] It is probable, as Eissfeldt maintains, that ישב הכרבים never existed independently, but that from the beginning it was connected with יהוה צבאות. The link between the two is supported by 1 Sam 4:4, 2 Sam 6:2, and Isa 37:16. The texts in which the cherubim formula occurs by itself without יהוה צבאות are insufficient evidence for an originally independent existence of the formula in question. 1 Chr 13:6 is no more than a parallel to 2 Sam 6:2, and one, moreover, where the text is in some disorder. Nor can 2 Kgs 19:15 be ascribed any evidential value here, since the text is a parallel to Isa 37:16, in which יהוה צבאות does occur. Admittedly, the cherubim formula occurs independently in Ps 80:2, but the continuation of the Psalm shows יהוה צבאות playing an important role (vv. 5, 8, 15, 20). Ps 99:1 remains, but even together with LXX Dan 3:55 it cannot offset the texts which attest a connection between the cherubim formula and יהוה צבאות.[22]

With regard to the concrete background of the cherubim formula, the art of the ancient Near East is very instructive. In pictorial art, the cherubim are portrayed as winged sphinxes with human heads. They are seen performing two different functions: that of guardians beside a tree of life (cf. Gen 3:24; Ezek 41:17-19), as well as that of important elements in a throne contrivance.[23] Three archaeological discoveries deserve mention in this context because of their origin and date. Ahiram's sarcophagus from Byblos shows a king or a god on his cherubim throne (fig. 1).[24] In an excavation level from the end of the Late Bronze Age, an ivory plaque 26 cm. long was found at Megiddo showing a prince on his cherubim throne (fig.2).[25] The same site has yielded an ivory mode of a cherubim throne a few

---

[21]Eissfeldt, *Kleine Schriften* 3, 116-21.

[22]Thus, I am not convinced by the remarks made by R. Smend (*Jahwekrieg und Stämmebund* [FRLANT 84, 1963] 59-60) and J. Jeremias ("Lade und Zion," *Probleme biblischer Theologie. Festschrift G. von Rad* [ed. H. W. Wolff; München, 1971] 183-98, 188 n. 18), who argue against a connection between the Sabaoth designation and the cherubim formula.

[23]On cherubim thrones see H. Schmidt, "Kerubenthron und Lade," *Eucharisterion* . . . *H. Gunkel* (ed. H. Schmidt; FRLANT 19/1, 1923) 120-44; R. de Vaux, "Les chérubins et l'arche d'alliance" (1960-61) *Bible et Orient* (Paris, 1967) 231-59; J. Maier, *Vom Kultus zur Gnosis* (Kairos Religionswissenschaftliche Studien 1, 1964) 64-86; O. Keel, *Jahwe-Visionen und Siegelkunst* (SBS 84/85, 1977) 15-45; P. Welten, "Mischwesen," *Biblisches Reallexikon* (ed. K. Galling; 2d ed.; Tübingen, 1977) 224-27; M. Görg, "Keruben in Jerusalem," *Biblische Notizen* 4 (1977) 13-24, and M. Haran, *Temples and Temple-Service in Ancient Israel* (Oxford, 1978) 246-59. See also below n. 28 and n. 96.

[24]See the publication by P. Montet, *Byblos et l'Egypte. Texte* (Paris, 1928) 215-38; *Atlas* (Paris, 1929) pl. CXXVIII-CXLI.

[25]See the publication by G. Loud, *The Megiddo Ivories* (OIP 52, 1939) pl. 4, 2a, and 2b.

Fig. 1. Relief on Ahiram's sarcophagus. Byblos. Drawing by Andrzej Szlagor.

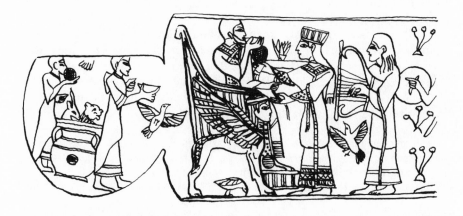

Fig. 2. Ivory plaque from Megiddo. Drawing by Andrzej Szlagor.

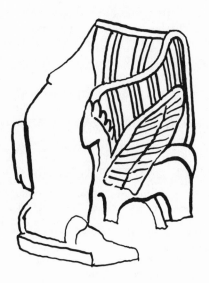

Fig. 3. Ivory model of a cherubim throne. Megiddo. Drawing by Andrzej Szlagor.

centimeters in size (fig. 3).[26] These thrones are supported (and guarded?) by two cherubim. The outer wings can be clearly seen; the inner appear to meet under the throne.

These discoveries illustrate the function of the cherubim in Solomon's temple. According to 1 Kgs 6:23-28, Solomon had two cherubim made. They were placed parallel to each other, their faces turned towards the temple entrance (cf. 2 Chr 3:13). The total height of the two cherubim was 10 cubits, i.e., no less than 4.3 m. Their outer wings touched the walls of the inner chamber, while their inner wings met.

> He put the cherubim in the innermost part of the house; and the wings of the cherubim were spread out so that a wing of the one touched the one wall, and a wing of the other touched the other wall; their other wings touched [נגע] each other in the middle of the house (1 Kgs 6:27).

According to 2 Chr 3:12, the inner wings were in contact (דבק) with each other (cf. also Ezek 1:11; 3:13). Hence, it is difficult to avoid the conclusion that the inner pair of wings met horizontally (cf. Ezek 1:23: ישרות) and formed the throne seat.[27] Thus, in the Jerusalem temple, the cherubim formed a throne. But, for human eyes, this throne was empty. God was enthroned in invisible majesty above the meeting wings of the two cherubim.[28]

A reminiscence of the notion of God's enthronement is still to be found in priestly statements concerning the epiphany of the divine כבוד, "glory", over the ark and the כפרת, "mercy seat" (Exod 25:22; Lev 16:2; Num 7:89). This, however, must not induce us to conclude that the כפרת was analogous to the cherubim throne.[29] The כפרת is situated *beneath* the wings of the cherubim (Exod 25:20; 37:9), like the ark in Solomon's temple (1 Kgs 8:7). And, just as the ark serves as a footstool in the throne contrivance of the temple (cf. 1 Chr 28:2; Ps 132:7), it is possible that the

---

[26]See G. Loud, ibid., pl. 4, 3.

[27]See esp. M. Haran, "The Ark and the Cherubim," *IEJ* 9 (1959) 30-38, 89-94, esp. 35-36. On the technical details (measurements, etc.) see J. Maier, *Vom Kultus zur Gnosis*, 73-86. I personally believe that the ark served as the footstool of the cherubim throne (cf. Ps 132:7; 1 Chr 28:2). As for 1 Kgs 8:7, where the cherubim have the function of sheltering the ark, this seems to be influenced by the P concept in Exod 25:20. Note the P influence in 1 Kgs 8:11, and compare E. Würthwein, *Das Erste Buch der Könige. Kapitel 1-16* (ATD 11/1, 1977) 87.

[28]On the idea of the aniconic god, see T. Mettinger, "The Veto on Images and the Aniconic God in Ancient Israel," *Religious Symbols and Their Functions* (ed. H. Biezais; Scripta Instituti Donneriani Aboensis 10, Stockholm, 1979) 15-29. On the problem of a cherubim throne at Shiloh, see below. As for the cherubim throne in Solomon's temple, note the possibility of influence from Tyrian iconographic tradition, 1 Kgs 5:15-26; 7:13-14; see H. Seyrig, "Antiquités syriennes," *Syria* 36 (1959) 38-89, esp. 51-52, and compare O. Keel, *Jahwe-Visionen und Siegelkunst*, 30.

[29]Contra M. Haran, *Temples and Temple-Service*, 254 bottom, but note what he says on p. 252f.

term כפרת is to be understood on the basis of an Egyptian term for "footstool" (kp rdwy).[30]

Our observations to this point lead us to an important conclusion: the divine designation of יהוה צבאות had its *Sitz im Leben* in the milieu of the Solomonic temple.[31] Around the cherubim throne and the ark a theological complex of ideas takes form in the Jerusalem cultic tradition, having at its center the notion of God as king.[32] It is against this background that we are to understand a number of texts in which this notion of God as king is linked with the temple or Zion. "A glorious throne set on high from the beginning is the place of our sanctuary," Jer 17:12 reads (cf. Jer 3:16-17; 14:21; Ezek 43:7). Jeremiah asks, "Is the Lord not in Zion? Is her king not in her?" (Jer 8:19). Even though a number of witnesses to this linkage are from the period of the exile, such texts as Isaiah 6 and Mic 4:7 demonstrate that we are dealing with traditional material of an older era.[33]

The temple on Zion is the Lord's היכל, his palace.[34] On the immense cherubim throne in the inmost shrine, God sits enthroned as king. Thus Solomon says at the dedication of the temple (1 Kgs 8:13):

בנה בניתי בית זבל לך
מכון לשבתך עולמים

I have built a royal house for thee,
An established place for thy throne for ever.[35]

The divine designation יהוה צבאות is to be understood as a functional element in the structural context of the conception of the Lord as king. Hence, the divine designation associated with the cherubim throne occurs in a number of contexts in which God is depicted in royal categories. In Jeremiah we three times encounter the stock phrase: נאם המלך יהוה צבאות

---

[30]M. Görg, "Eine neue Deutung für kápporæt," *ZAW* 89 (1977) 115-18. For a different interpretation see G. Gerleman in his forthcoming Franz Delitzsch-Vorlesungen. That the ark was placed parallel with the cherubim is due to the fact that ark and cherubim were originally independent of each other. The ark was not originally made to be placed under the cherubim.

[31]On the original *Sitz im Leben* in the cult of Shiloh, see below.

[32]See esp. A. Alt, "Gedanken über das Königtum Jahwes" (1945) *Kleine Schriften* 1 (München, 1953) 345-57. In the Sabaoth studies, esp. Eissfeldt (n. 6 above) and Ross (n. 10 above) have moved in this direction, but the full implications of this *Sitz im Leben* do not seem to have been elaborated.

[33]Other passages that testify to the same connection are Isa 33:20-22; 52:7-10; Zeph 3:14-15; Zech 14:8-9; Psalms 74, 146, 149.

[34] On היכל, see M. Ottosson, *TWAT* 2 (1977) 408-15.

[35]Translation following J. Gray, *I & II Kings* (2d ed.; London, 1970) 212. I thus understand Heb בית זבל in the light of Ugaritic zbl bᶜl arṣ, "the Prince, Lord of Earth," zbl bᶜl, "Prince Baal," and kht zbl, "throne of princeship." On the root z-b-l, see M. Held ("The Root zbl/sbl in Akkadian, Ugaritic and Biblical Hebrew," *JAOS* 88 [1968] 90-96) and J. Gamberoni ("זבל," *TWAT* 2 [1977] 531-34). On the *Tempelweihspruch*, see M. Görg ("Die Gattung des sogenannten Tempelweihspruchs," *UF* 6 [1974] 55-63).

שמו, "says the King, whose name is YHWH Sabaoth" (Jer 46:18; 48:15; 51:57). Apart from such standard expressions, we find in free, nonformulaic usage as well occurrences of this divine designation where royal associations are present, especially in Psalms and Isaiah. In Ps 89:9, the designation occurs in a context which describes God as king, sitting on his throne (v. 15), surrounded by his divine council (vv. 6-8). Ps 24:10 speaks of YHWH Sabaoth as "the King of glory" (cf. Ps 84:4). In Ps 48:9, עיר יהוה צבאות, "the city of YHWH Sabaoth," forms a parallel to קרית מלך רב, "the city of the great King" (v. 3). That both instances of יהוה צבאות in Isaiah 6 are to be seen against a royal background is made explicitly clear when the prophet says: "Woe is me! . . . For my eyes have seen the King, YHWH Sabaoth" (v. 5; cf. v. 3). The occurrence of the designation in the prayer of Hezekiah may also be of interest. The prayer begins with the address: "O YHWH Sabaoth, God of Israel, who art enthroned above the cherubim, thou art the God, thou alone, of all the kingdoms of the earth" (Isa 37:16). It is at least possible that the choice of words reflects a deliberate contrast between the great king of Assyria and YHWH Sabaoth (cf. Isa 36:4, 13).

In Isaiah, the Lord's divine planning plays a significant role. The terminology involved is יעץ and עצה, "plan," "purpose," a terminology which is also used in connection with the messianic king (Isa 9:5; 11:2). Pregnant statements about God's planning are to be found in, among other texts, Isa 14:24-27. Here the divine designation is יהוה צבאות: "For YHWH Sabaoth has purposed (יעץ) and who will annul it?" (v. 27; cf. v. 24). Isa 19:12 speaks of "what YHWH Sabaoth has purposed against Egypt" (cf. 19:17; 23:9). Finally, in Isa 28:29 we meet the statement: "This also comes from YHWH Sabaoth; he is wonderful in counsel (הפליא עצה), and excellent in wisdom." Thus, if the messianic king is פלא יועץ, "Wonderful Counsellor" (Isa 9:5), this is much more true of the supreme king, YHWH Sabaoth. Hence, it is against the background of the notion of YHWH Sabaoth as king that we are to understand the statements as to his purposing and planning. The same background presumably lies behind the statement in Jer 11:20 that YHWH Sabaoth is שפט צדק בחן כליות, the one "who judges righteously, who tries the heart and the mind" (cf. Jer 20:12). It is worth noting that the prophet has probably appropriated phrases from the language of the cult (cf. Pss 7:10; 26:2). In Mal 1:14, too, YHWH Sabaoth is spoken of as a king: "for I am a great King, says YHWH Sabaoth." Finally, the prophetic hope finds expression in statements as to how YHWH Sabaoth assumes royal power on Zion (Isa 24:23), makes a royal banquet for all nations (Isa 25:6), and receives in his capital those who come up "to worship the King, YHWH Sabaoth (להשתחות למלך יהוה צבאות)" (Zech 14:16-17).

We have now established the situational context, the *Sitz im Leben*, for the designation יהוה צבאות. It is used in the Jerusalem cult, and refers to the God who sits invisible on the immense cherubim throne in the most sacred chamber of the Solomonic temple. This explains the important role which the conception of God as king plays in the Sabaoth texts. Understandable, too, is the high frequency with which this divine designation occurs in Isaiah, a prophet with profound roots in the Jerusalem cultic tradition.

THE TEMPLE: HEAVEN ON EARTH

Let us remain, however, a while longer in the temple. I take as a starting point for the next stage in our investigation the sculptured scene from the Neo-Babylonian king Nabuapaliddina's tablet in the temple of the Sun god in Sippar (fig. 4, from the 9th century B.C., a copy of an older original), a scene to which Metzger has drawn attention, though without going into its implications for YHWH Sabaoth.[36] In the right of the picture we see the solar deity Shamash sitting on his throne, which is placed on a stylized cosmic mountain. Beneath the canopy we see the symbols of the three celestial deities, Sin, Shamash, and Ishtar. Under the throne are a number of wavy lines, at the bottom of which we see a base. Clearly the wavy lines represent the celestial ocean. Indeed, an inscription above the canopy states explicitly that Sin, Shamash, and Ishtar are situated "above the ocean." Beneath the heavenly ocean is a slab which, like the biblical רקיע, the "firmament," divides the waters above from those beneath (Gen 1:7). Four stars have been placed upon this "firmament" (cf. Gen 1:14-19). This part of the depiction is a striking illustration of the statement in Ps 29:10 as to how God sits enthroned above the heavenly ocean:

יהוה למבול ישב
וישב יהוה מלך לעולם

The Lord sits enthroned over the flood;
the Lord sits enthroned as king for ever.[37]

Let us now consider the left part of the relief. Here the king is shown being presented before the god; an inscription beneath the relief informs us that it is the priest Nabunadinshum who is leading in King Nabuapaliddina. A goddess completes the procession. It does not approach the deity himself directly; rather, the deity is represented by a cultic table with the sun's disc, representing the solar god Shamash. The scene takes place in the temple. Here it is important to observe that the wavy lines extend over the entire breadth of the picture, thus indicating that both scenes—the presentation scene and the throne scene—take place above the celestial sea. The picture

---

[36]See the publication by L. W. King, *Babylonian Boundary Stones and Memorial Tablets* (London, 1912), text in transliteration pp. 120-27, plates no. XCVIII-CII. Discussion in M. Metzger, "Himmlische und irdische Wohnstatt Jahwes," *UF* 2 (1970) 139-58, esp. 141-44.

[37]For the construction ישב למבול, cf. ישב לכסא in Ps 9:5 and cf. Isa 3:26 and 47:1. On מבול see J. Begrich, "Mabbūl" (1928) *Gesammelte Studien zum Alten Testament* (München, 1964) 39-54.

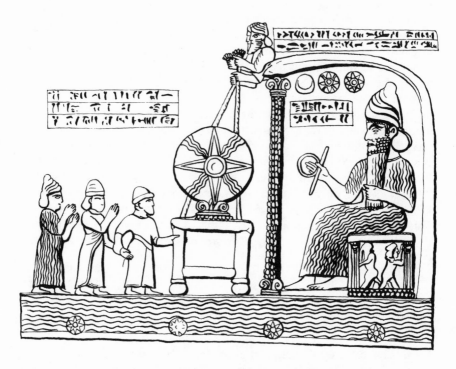

Fig. 4. Presentation scene and throne scene on Nabuapaliddina's tablet in the temple of
Shamash at Sippar. Drawing by Andrzej Szlagor.

is a striking illustration of the mythical concept of space: the temple is the place where heaven and earth meet, or heaven on earth.[38]

As a witness to the temple's heavenly associations, this relief is by no means isolated. As we know, there is a good deal of other evidence from Mesopotamia.[39] In Egypt we encounter an expression of the same basic view in the phrase ʿ3wy pt, "doors of heaven," used to mean "shrine."[40] The temple in Heliopolis could be denoted as pt n kmt, "Egypt's heaven"; Karnak was called pt ḥr s3 t3, "heaven on earth."[41] The heavenly symbolism could be brought out by architectural and ornamental means.[42] Similar phenomena can be found on Phoenician and Canaanite soil. A temple precinct in Sidon was thus called šamem romim, "high heaven."[43]

That the Jerusalem cultic tradition, too, was profoundly influenced by this mythical concept of space is evident from the well-known associations between the temple and Zion on the one hand and the Zaphon-mountain on the other.[44] It is instructive to compare the statement in Isa 14:13-14:

> You said in your heart
> 'I will ascend to heaven;
> above the stars of God
> I will set my throne on high;
> I will sit on the mount of the assembly (בהר מועד)
> in the far north (better: on the heights of Zaphon, בירכתי צפון)
> I will ascend above the heights of the clouds,
> I will make myself like the Most High.'

with the statement about Zion in Ps 48:2-3:

> His holy mountain, beautiful in elevation,
> is the joy of all the earth,

---

[38]This was beautifully demonstrated by Metzger, *UF* 2 (1970) 143-44.

[39]See the references in G. W. Ahlström, "Heaven on Earth—at Hazor and Arad," *Religious Syncretism in Antiquity* (ed. B. A. Pearson; Missoula, 1975) 67-83, esp. 67-68 and in G. Widengren, "Aspetti simbolici dei templi e luoghi di culto del Vicino Oriente antico," *Numen* 7 (1960) 1-25.

[40]See J. Černý, "Note on ʿ3wy-pt, 'Shrine'," *JEA* 34 (1948) 120; and E. Brovarski, "The Doors of Heaven," *Or* 46 (1977) 107-15. I am indebted to Professor G. W. Ahlström for the reference to Brovarski.

[41]See Erman and Grapow, "pt," *Wörterbuch der ägyptischen Sprache* 1 (Leipzig, 1926) 491.

[42]See H. Brunner, "Die Sonnenbahn in ägyptischen Tempeln," *Archäologie und Altes Testament. Festschrift K. Galling* (ed. A. Kuschke; Tübingen, 1970) 27-34. On the cosmic symbolism of Egyptian temples see also W. Spiegelberg, "Die Auffassung des Tempels als Himmel," *Zeitschrift für ägyptische Sprache* 53 (1917) 98-101.

[43]See Eusebius, *Praep. evangelica* (ed. K. Mras; Berlin, 1954) I 10.9 and *KAI* 15, 1. A general discussion of the symbolism of the sanctuary in the ancient Near East is found in J. Hofer, *Zur Phänomenologie des Sakralraumes und sein Symbolismus im Alten Orient* (Wien Diss., 1970).

[44]On these problems, see esp. R. E. Clements, *God and Temple* (Oxford, 1965) 40-78; H. Ringgren, *Israelite Religion* (London, 1969) 156-66; R. J. Clifford, *The Cosmic Mountain*

Mount Zion, in the far north [better: on the heights of Zaphon],
the city of the great King.[45]

The same conception of the temple as founded on the cosmic mountain
finds expression in the statement in *m. Yoma* 5:2 about the holy rock,
שתיה, situated beneath the ark in the most sacred chamber.[46]

This classical temple theology does not distinguish terrestrial from
celestial; such a distinction is first drawn when this mythical concept of
space breaks down and is replaced by the kind of thinking in terms of
analogy evidenced in P, where we find the tabernacle constructed according
to a heavenly "pattern." This explains how the statement that "the Lord
roars from Zion, and utters his voice from Jerusalem" (Amos 1:2; Joel
4:16) can be expressed in a variant form by which the roaring comes "from
on high" and "from his holy habitation" (Jer 25:30).[47] The theophany can
occur from heaven (e.g., Ps 18:10), but also from Zion (Ps 50:2:
מציון מכלל יפי אלהים הופיע). It is therefore not surprising that one and
the same text can localize God both in the sanctuary (קדש) on Zion and in
heaven (שמי קדשו, Ps 20:3, 7), just as Ezekiel speaks in the same breath of
how heaven opened (1:1) and how the cloud and the fire came from צפון
(1:4).

Indeed, the temple throne itself has heavenly associations. The cherubim are no doubt to be regarded as a tangible representation of God's
heavenly chariot of clouds (cf. Deut 33:26; 2 Sam 22:11 = Ps 18:11; Isa
19:1; Pss 68:5, 34; 104:3). The heavenly associations of the throne are
particularly clear in Ezek 1:22-28. Over the heads of the living creatures—
which are comparable to the cherubim (Ezek 10:15, 20)—there is a רקיע, a
"firmament" (1:22). This firmament appears like קרח (1:22), a word which,
on the basis of the LXX, has often been translated here as "crystal", but
which nonetheless should probably be rendered "ice"—its usual meaning
(cf. Job 6:16; 37:10)[48]—and be regarded as representing the sea, now
pacified forever. The throne foundation here is thus the same as in Ps 29:10
(cf. Rev 15:2; 21:1).

We can summarize what has been said in two points. (1) The divine
designation יהוה צבאות had, at least during the period of the older mon-

---

in Canaan and the Old Testament (HSM 4, 1972); and S. Talmon, "הר," *TWAT* 2 (1977) 459-
83, esp. 470-78.

[45] I connect the end of v. 2 with v. 3.

[46] According to Josephus, *Bell. Jud.* 5.5.4 (= V 212-214) the veil of the second temple was
given a cosmic symbolism; cf. also 5.5.5 (= V 216-217), Cf. Wis 18:24 for the information
about the cosmic symbolism attached to the priestly robe. Also, the zodiacs of the synagogues
may have such a symbolism. On these, see R. Hachlili, "The Zodiac in Synagogue," *Ariel* 47
(1978) 58-70. I am indebted to Mr. Krister Brandt of the Swedish Bible Commission for these
references.

[47] For other examples see Metzger, *UF* 2 (1970) 139-40. Note in this connection also the
remarks made by J. Maier, *Vom Kultus zur Gnosis*, 101.

[48] Keel, *Jahwe-Visionen und Siegelkunst*, 254. For an abundance of iconographic material
for the study of Ezekiel 1, see Keel, ibid., 125-273.

archy, its formative *Sitz im Leben* in the context of the temple cult.[49] (2) In the milieu of the temple, the Jerusalem cultic tradition was cultivated.[50] For our purposes, two of its conceptions are of special importance: (a) the Lord is king, and (b) the temple is his royal abode, being situated where heaven and earth meet.[51] The designation יהוה צבאות is to be understood as a functional element within the framework of this complex of ideas.

THE SEMANTIC FORCE OF צבאות

We proceed now with the more strictly linguistic problems. The difficulties confronting us are apparent: it is clear both that this divine designation functions as a personal name, and that the linguistic status of names involves a history of controversy. J. Lyons maintains that names may have reference but not sense, even though certain names can be said to have a symbolic, etymological, or translational meaning.[52] On the basis of our study so far, we are entitled to say that this particular designation has its reference in the heavenly king on his cherubim throne. This is what the term denotes. Our concern now is the term's semantic content in a narrower sense; here we must limit our pursuit to the term's etymological meaning.

In my view, there is no reason to deny the relation between the designation יהוה צבאות and the well known root *ṣ-b-ʾ*.[53] For the inventory of the philological material which follows, our observations as to the situational context of the designation יהוה צבאות have provided us with a clue to pursue. Our question must be: do words based on this root occur in a sense which shows both royal and celestial associations?

The heavenly king, like earthly kings, has his divine court or council. Among the various terms in Hebrew for the divine council we may mention בני אלים, "sons of gods", עדת אל, "the divine council", סוד קדשים, "the council of the holy ones", etc.[54] But one in particular attracts our attention: צבא.[55] The texts which must be mentioned in this context are the following.

---

[49] The low frequency of the designation in deuteronomistic literature and its total absence in Ezekiel are discussed at the end of this paper.

[50] For a comprehensive survey of this tradition and for the relevant scholarly literature, see O. H. Steck, *Friedensvorstellungen im alten Jerusalem* (Theologische Studien 111, 1972) 13-25.

[51] Note also the pentagram as a possible expression of the cosmic symbolism of the temple; see M. Ottosson, "Hexagrammet och pentagrammet i främreorientalisk kontext," *SEÅ* 36 (1971) 46-76, esp. 72-73.

[52] J. Lyons, *Semantics* 1 (Cambridge, 1977) 215-23, esp. 219, 223. On "sense"- "reference'", see ibid., 174-206.

[53] Contrast Ross, *VT* 17 (1967) 76-92. On the biradical basis *ṣb*, see J. A. Thompson, "Expansions of the *ṣb* Root," *AJBA* 2/1 (1972) 187-96.

[54] On the divine council, see esp. P. D. Miller, *Divine Warrior in Early Israel* and H. J. Fabry, "סוד. Der himmlische Thronrat als ekklesiologisches Modell," *Bausteine Biblischer Theologie. Festschrift G. J. Botterweck* (BBB 50, 1977) 99-126.

[55] The connection between YHWH Sabaoth and the divine council was often stressed in older literature. See the fine studies of O. Borchert, "Der Gottesname Jahwe Zebaoth,"

1 Kgs 22:19-23 (2 Chr 18:18-22). Here it is narrated how Micaiah ben Imlah has had a vision: "I saw the Lord sitting on his throne, and all the host of heaven [וכל צבא השמים] standing beside him on his right hand and on his left" (v. 19). In what follows, the deliberations of the heavenly council are depicted. The result is that the spirit is sent to be a lying spirit in the mouth of all the prophets consulted by Israel's king.

Ps 103:19-22. The scene is again royal: "The Lord has established his throne in the heavens" (v. 19). The heavenly throng is exhorted to bless him. The following terms are included in the enumeration of that throng: מלאכיו, "his messengers"; גברי כח, "mighty ones"; כל צבאיו, "all his hosts"; and, parallel to the latter, משרתיו, "his ministers."

Ps 148:1-5. In this Psalm, which shares motifs with the *YHWH-mālak* Psalms, God's entourage is again exhorted to praise him. The exhortation is directed to "all his messengers" (מלאכיו), "all his host" (Ketib: צבאו; Qere: צבאיו), "sun and moon" and "all you shining stars."

Dan 8:10-13. The passage speaks of the little horn which grows great, even up to "the host of heaven," indeed, up to "the Prince of the host" (שר הצבא). Here the connection between the host and the sanctuary in vv. 11-13 should be noted, a connection which surprises little when seen in the light of the characteristic features of the temple theology.

Other texts. In Daniel 8, the heavenly host has military characteristics. The same is true of Josh 5:13-15, where we meet the commander of the heavenly host with a drawn sword in his hand. To the same category belong Isa 13:4; 40:26; and 45:12, which speak of the celestial host and of its divine commander.[56] The two latter references contain astral allusions; so also do Ps 33:6 and Neh 9:6.

The usage of צבא to refer to the divine council is not particularly frequent. The probable explanation for this lies in the penetration of the astral cult from the eighth century on. In the texts which express a criticism of this development, the phrase צבא השמים is often used for the object of the cult.[57] As a result, צבא as a term for God's council becomes a loaded word in the late pre-exilic period. Against this background, what is surprising is rather that the Deuteronomists did not replace כל צבא השמים as a term for the council in the vision of Micaiah ben Imlah.

We have now seen how one usage of the noun צבא corresponds closely with the basic connotations of the divine designation יהוה צבאות. Our next question is then if this divine designation occurs in passages in

---

Theologische Studien und Kritiken 69 (1896) 619-42 and G. Westphal, "צבא השמים," *Orientalische Studien. Festschrift Th. Nöldeke* 2 (ed. C. Bezold; Giessen, 1906) 719-28. In spite of V. Maag's contribution (*STU* 20 [1950] 27-52), which takes up this theme from a new point of departure, this interpretation has not received due attention in more recent discussion.

[56]Cf. P. D. Miller, *Divine Warrior in Early Israel*, 136-37 and 139-40, and the literature he mentions.

[57]Deut 4:19; 17:3; 2 Kgs 17:16; 21:3, 5; 23:4-5; Jer 8:2; 19:13; Zeph 1:5; 2 Chr 33:3-5. On this cult, see M. Weinfeld, "The Worship of Molech and of the Queen of Heaven," *UF* 4 (1972) 133-54.

which the divine council plays a role. Evidence does exist, though it is limited.

Ps 89:6-19. In this hymn, the view of the Lord as king plays a significant role (see especially vv. 15-16, 19). Just as the Davidic king is "the highest of the kings on earth" (v. 28), so the Lord is the supreme king in the divine council, here denoted as קהל קדשים ,בני אלים, and קדשים סוד (vv. 6-9). In v. 7, God is identified as יהוה, but in v. 9 this is further specified as יהוה צבאות. It seems reasonable to assume that the choice of this divine designation is conditioned by the context: the portrayal of the divine council in vv. 6-8 naturally carries with it the divine designation יהוה צבאות as a corollary.

Isaiah 6. In this passage, God is presented as sitting on his throne in the temple (v. 1), surrounded by the seraphim (v. 2). Just as the sons of God in Ps 29:1-2 give voice to their praise of the heavenly king, so the seraphim here sing their trishagion (v. 3). When God raises the questions "Who will go for *us*?" (v. 8), the plural contains an allusion to the deliberations of the divine council (cf. Gen 1:26; 3:22; 11:7[58]). The divine designation יהוה צבאות occurs twice in this passage: in the trishagion of the seraphim in v. 3; and in Isaiah's cry in v. 5, "Woe is me! . . . For my eyes have seen the King, YHWH Sabaoth!"

1 Kgs 18:15 and 2 Kgs 3:14. In these two texts, the prophets Elijah and Elisha speak of how they "stand before YHWH Sabaoth" (עמד לפני פ'). The same statement is made without צבאות in 1 Kgs 17:1 and 2 Kgs 5:16. The more complete divine designation seems to have been chosen in order to emphasize the contrast with an earthly king. At the same time, however, allusions to a heavenly council do seem to be present. The Hebrew expression עמד לפני פ' is a close parallel to the Akkadian *izuzzu ina/ana pān N.N.* and means roughly "serve as a courtier for N.N."[59] In several texts, the verb עמד is used with a preposition to refer to serving in the celestial court.[60] In Jer 23:18, 22, it is used of prophets who "stood in the council of the Lord," thereby functioning as co-opted members in the divine council, deriving directives for their ministry in this way (cf. Jer 15:19). When we now meet the expression "to stand before YHWH Sabaoth," it seems suitable to interpret it on the basis of the notion of the prophets as co-opted members of the heavenly assembly.

Zechariah 1-8. In these chapters, the divine designation יהוה צבאות occurs with an unusual frequency: there are no fewer than 44 occurrences, 15 of which are free, nonformulaic.[61] It is generally recognized that the Jerusalem cultic tradition plays an important role in this block of text.

---

[58]On these passages in Genesis, see now P. D. Miller, *Genesis 1-11. Studies in Structure and Theme* (JSOT SupS 8, 1978) 9-26.

[59]Gen 41:46; Deut 1:38; 1 Sam 16:21-22; 1 Kgs 1:2; 12:6; Jer 52:12; Dan 1:5.

[60]1 Kgs 22:19; Isa 6:2; Jer 23:18,22; Zech 3:4; 4:14; 6:5; cf. Luke 1:19.

[61]I must here correct Baumgärtel ("Zu den Gottesnamen," 6), who gives the number 11.

Similarly, the notion of a divine council can here be seen (particularly 1:7-15; 3:1-10; 6:1-8).[62] The frequency with which our divine designation occurs in these chapters ought to be viewed in the light of the traditio-historical anchoring. The designation is closely connected with Jerusalem-Zion-the temple.[63] It occurs as well in connection with the court. As supreme Head of the divine council, God dispatches his messengers (2:12, 13, 15; 4:9; 6:15). Such a מלאך addresses God as יהוה צבאות (1:12), and introduces a citation of the divine message with the formula: "Thus says YHWH Sabaoth" (3:6-7).

We have thus made three observations: (1) The divine designation of our study has its formative *Sitz im Leben* in the context of the temple cult, and refers to the heavenly king on his cherubim throne in the temple. (2) The noun צבא is attested in a usage referring to the divine council which gathers about the heavenly king. (3) יהוה צבאות occurs in passages where the divine council is part of the associative field.[64] There appears, then, to be some probability in favor of the conclusion that the element צבאות in this designation alludes to the heavenly council, the צבא around the heavenly king. The noun, used in this sense, is the etymon for the divine designation of our discussion.

This is a diachronic observation which, however, is not without relevance from the synchronic point of view. In this particular divine designation, we have an unusually clear case of semantic motivation. It is transparent, self-explanatory, like German "Handschuh," as opposed to English "glove."[65] For reasons discussed by Sawyer in a noteworthy article, we must take etymological motivation into account in Hebrew as an important factor, in that the "root-meaning" may produce a kind of transparency.[66] In spite of James Barr's well-known warning for "the root fallacy,"[67] we must, in my view, be aware that this etymological "root-meaning" might at any time be actualized in the divine designation יהוה צבאות. I am inclined to think that certain instances in Zechariah 1-8 can be seen in this perspective. At the same time we must note that the use of this designation formulaically with כה אמר, נאם, etc. is generally conventional, with very little semantic motivation.

---

[62]Chr. Jeremias, *Die Nachtgesichte des Sacharja* (FRLANT 117, 1977) 110-55, 201-25.

[63]In free usage in Zech 7:3; 8:3, 9, 21-22, and in formulaic speech in Zech 1:14, 17; 8:2.

[64]I have borrowed the term "associative field" from J. F. A. Sawyer, *Semantics in Biblical Research* (SBT 2/24, 1972) 30. Sawyer discriminates between "associative field," comprising "all the words associated in any way with a particular term," and "lexical field" or "group," which "consists only of words very closely related to one another" (p. 30).

[65]On semantic motivation, see S. Ullmann, *The Principles of Semantics* (Glasgow University Publications 84; 2d ed.; 1957, reprinted 1967) 83-92.

[66]J. F. A. Sawyer, "Root-Meanings in Hebrew," *JSS* 12 (1967) 37-50. See also his *Semantics in Biblical Research*, 50. Cf. J. Barr, "The Image of God in the Book of Genesis: A Study in Terminology," *BJRL* 51 (1968) 17-19.

[67]J. Barr, *The Semantics of Biblical Language* (Oxford, 1961, reprinted 1969) 100-106, 159-60.

The allusion to the heavenly host allows this designation to be used with connotations of both war and peace. Just as the heavenly host in 1 Kgs 22:19 appears like an administration involved in a cabinet meeting, so the divine designation can have associations of peace. And, just as the heavenly host can appear as an army on the field of battle, so the designation can also be used with overtones of war. Readily apparent instances of the latter are those texts in which the designation is part of a play on words with military connotations: 1 Sam 17:45 יהוה צבאות אלהי מערכות ישראל), Isa 13:4 (יהוה צבאות מפקד צבא מלחמה), Isa 29:6 (note vv. 7-8), and Isa 31:4 (כן ירד יהוה צבאות לצבא). Indeed, the martial character of YHWH Sabaoth is well attested.[68]

The syntax of the designation must be evaluated on the basis of the insight that the short form יהוה צבאות is the oldest, and that the form יהוה אלהי (ה)צבאות is secondary.[69] The views that we, in יהוה צבאות, are dealing with a verb + object, with a noun clause, or with a noun + appositive carry with them considerable difficulties.[70] The designation is to

---

[68]See e.g., 1 Sam 4:4; Isa 10:23; 13:13; 14:24-27; 19:16; 22:5; 24:21-23; Jer 32:18; 50:25; Nah 2:14; 3:5; Pss 24:8, 10; 46:8, 12 and 59:6.

[69]See the discussion in M. Löhr, *Untersuchungen zum Buch Amos* (BZAW 4, 1901) 57-59; W. R. Arnold, *Ephod and Ark*, 144-46; H. W. Wolff, *Dodekapropheton* 2, 332-34. The arguments adduced by Maag (*STU* 20 [1950] 27-29) cannot prove that the long form is the more original one.

[70]To these theories the following must be said:
(1) As for the theory that we have to do with a verb in the causative stem + an object, note the following points: (a) There are no other examples in Hebrew of a causative of the verb היה. (b) It is difficult to find examples of יהוה apt to demonstrate that the name has a verbal force. Already in the Song of Debora יהוה is used as a normal proper name. (c) The long form יהוה is probably secondary over against the short יהו. What was formerly taken to be the earliest example of the long form, viz., the Moabite stone lines 17-18, is to be analyzed as יהו + suffix as is demonstrated by line 12. In recent research the lengthening into יהוה is placed in the deuteronomic era. See L. Delekat, "Yáho-Yahwáe und die alttestamentlichen Gottesnamenkorrekturen," *Tradition und Glaube. Festschrift K. G. Kuhn* (eds. J. Jeremias et al.; Göttingen, 1971) 23-75, esp. 65-70; M. Rose, *Jahwe* (Theologische Studien 122, 1978) 34, 39; and S. Norin, "Jô-Namen und Jᵉhô-Namen," *VT* 29 (1979) 87-97. Note in this connection Num 13:16 (Dtr?) with the change from הושע into יהושע, and cf. Ps 81:6 (also with Dtr affinities) with יוסף lengthened into יהוסף. As Rose points out, an etymological connection with the verb היה/הוי, "to be," is not thereby precluded; but this association is nevertheless more easily understood as due to a process of interpretation (pp. 30-34). This development is not attested except in Exodus 3, which is a passage with deuteronomistic features, and Hos 1:9. Note in this connection the links between Exod 3:15 and Hos 12:6. The protodeuteronomic stream of tradition thus comes to the fore.
(2) The theory of a nominal clause (Tsevat) finds an obvious difficulty in our conclusion that the divine designation contains an allusion to the heavenly council. If this is correct, there can be no question of an identity between יהוה and צבאות. On Tsevat's theory, see also above n. 7.
(3) The theory of a noun + apposition argued by Eissfeldt (*Kleine Schriften* 3, 110-13) is based on two presuppositions. Eissfeldt assumes a semantic development in צבא— "Masse," "Wucht," "Schwere," Macht"—that is merely postulated and is not attested by the evidence. And Eissfeldt holds that צבאות is originally an abstract plural, a supposition neither proved nor necessary.

be analyzed as a construct relation. The fact that we are then dealing with a case of overdetermination has been thought to be a difficulty for such an interpretation;[71] in this particular case, however, there are several conceivable explanations. (a) יהוה could be thought to have weakened to an appellative with the non-specific sense "God." This would be similar to the use of Akkadian ištaru (ištartu) in the sense of "goddess." This explanation is less likely. (b) The various local cults in pre-monarchic times stressed different aspects of YHWH (cf. 1 Sam 1:3; 2 Sam 15:7).[72] The designation יהוה צבאות would then have been created to indicate what was, for the cult in Shiloh, the essential aspect (1 Sam 1:3, 11). (c) Specially worthy of attention is the possibility that YHWH has been introduced into what was originally an אל צבאות designation (see below).[73]

The interpretation which sees a construct relation is the least problematic. The divine designation then means "YHWH of hosts." The absence of the definite article with the nomen rectum has analogies in בעל ברית (Judg 8:33; 9:4) and בעל זבוב (2 Kgs 1:2, 3, 6, 16).

SHILOH

There is some evidence for the worship of YHWH Sabaoth in pre-monarchic times. In the ark traditions, the designation occurs at two critical transitional points: when the ark leaves Shiloh (1 Sam 4:4) and when it reaches Jerusalem (2 Sam 6:2; cf. v 18). It is probable that the designation here serves the purpose of emphasizing a continuity between Solomon's temple and the sanctuary at Shiloh (cf. Jer 7:10-14; Ps 78:59-72). If the texts in the ark traditions are to be understood from the perspective of the Solomonic temple, and their evidential value for the cult at Shiloh is thus problematic,[74] the occurrences in 1 Sam 1:3, 11 still remain; as evidence for a worship of YHWH Sabaoth already at Shiloh, they are more difficult to dispose of.[75] Our present task is thus to test our earlier conclusions on the basis of the fragile material for the cult in Shiloh. Our concern here is not only the specific question whether or not a cherubim

---

[71]In spite of G. R. Driver's list of examples ("Reflections on Recent Articles," JBL 73 [1954] 125-36, esp. 125-28), Tsevat (HUCA 36 [1965] 51-54) saw a difficulty and argued that there was no need to determine YHWH. Note, however, the case of šamaš līmīma below, n. 109.

[72]Cf. A. Bertholet, Götterspaltung und Göttervereinigung (Sammlung gemeinverständlicher Vorträge 164; Tübingen, 1933) 4-5.

[73]C. Steuernagel, "Jahwe, der Gott Israels," Studien zur semitischen Philologie und Religionsgeschichte. Festschrift J. Wellhausen (ed. K. Marti; BZAW 27, 1914) 329-49, esp. 344.

[74]On the ark traditions, see most recently A. F. Campbell, "Yahweh and the Ark: A Case Study in Narrative," JBL 98 (1979) 31-43 with lit. J. Maier (Das altisraelitische Ladeheiligtum, 50-60) and F. Stolz (Jahwes und Israels Kriege [ATANT 60, 1972] 45-60) especially take the references to a cult of YHWH Sabaoth at Shilo as retrojections of later, Jerusalemite realities.

[75]On the problem of Shiloh and Jerusalem, see O. Eissfeldt, "Silo und Jerusalem" (1957) Kleine Schriften 3, 417-25 and E. Otto, "Silo und Jerusalem," TZ 32 (1976) 65-77.

throne existed there, but also the larger question: did the cult at Shiloh provide a situational context similar to that in Jerusalem, i.e., with the notion of the Lord as king surrounded by his celestial court?

One indication that the Lord was thought of as king at Shiloh can be found in the תרועה cry connected with the ark (1 Sam 4:5-6; cf. 2 Sam 6:15).[76] Another is found in a pair of personal names. Among the priests at Nob (who stemmed from Shiloh) was a certain אחימלך (1 Sam 22:9, 20) with a theophoric name speaking of God as king.[77] The name איכבוד (1 Sam 4:21-22) should also be mentioned here. To be sure, v. 22 is possibly secondary: the fact remains that a name with the element כבוד occurs among the priestly clan at Shiloh.[78] This onomastic element probably is to be explained on the basis of notions of the Lord as king; its ultimate explanation must be based on El's royal כבוד (Pss 19:2; 29:1-3, 9; cf. Pss 24:7; 97:6; Isa 6:3). The predication of YHWH as האלהים הקדוש, "the Holy God" (1 Sam 6:20), belongs to the same complex of ideas.[79]

We cannot overlook the possibility of Canaanite affiliations in the case of the Israelite cult at Shiloh. The site flourished already during MB II; it was inhabited both during LB II and Iron I.[80] The feast with a dance in the vineyards (Judg 21:19-23) shows characteristics of the Canaanite vintage festival (cf. Judg 9:27). Shiloh had the only sanctuary which the OT designates as היכל (1 Sam 1:9; 3:3)[81] apart, of course, from the Jerusalem temple itself. Leaving aside the question of origin, this cult building at Shiloh can only be understood against the background of Canaanite culture.

Now the Ugaritic texts demonstrate that the notion of a celestial court was very much alive in the Canaanite milieu.[82] According to G. W. Ahlström, the LB II temple of area C at Hazor seems to supply an interesting archaeological illustration of this. In the cult niche of this sanctuary a basalt statue (ca. 40 cm. high) was found, with a cup in his

---

[76]Cf. Num 23:21; Pss 47:6; 89:16 and, for the verb הריע, 1 Sam 10:24; Pss 47:2; 98:6. See P. Humbert, La "Terouᶜa" (Neuchatel, 1946) 30-35 and E. Lipiński, La royauté de Yahwé dans la poésie et le culte de l'Ancien Testament (Brussel, 1965) 352-54.

[77]M. Noth, Die israelitischen Personennamen (BWANT 3/10, 1928) 66-75. See also E. Lipiński, La royauté de Yahwé, 428-30.

[78]On names of the type I-chabod, see J. J. Stamm, "Hebräische Ersatznamen," Studies in Honor of B. Landsberger (AS 16, 1965) 413-24, esp. 416.

[79]Cf. H.-P. Müller, "קדש heilig," Theologisches Handwörterbuch zum Alten Testament 2 (eds. Jenni and Westermann; München/Zürich, 1976) 589-609, esp. 598.

[80]See M.-L. Buhl and S. Holm-Nielsen, Shiloh (Publications of the National Museum; Arch.-Hist. Series 1/12; Copenhagen, 1969). Note also S. Holm-Nielsen, "Shiloh," IDBSup, 822-23.

[81]Haran's idea (Temples and Temple-Service, 198-202) that the description of the sanctuary in P reflects conditions at Shiloh is worth considering; but we should not follow Haran when he argues that there was no solid structure at Shiloh. He is much too cavalier in his handling of such evidence as 1 Sam 1:9, 24; 3:15; 4:18.

[82]See n. 54 above.

right hand and an engraved moon crescent on his chest; behind this were ten stelae in a slightly curved row.[83] Ahlström has suggested that we are to understand the cult niche as "nothing other than a divine assembly."[84] This interpretation is one possibility among others. Another possible case is the mysterious טבור הארץ (Judg 9:37), which could be an indication of omphalos conceptions at the pre-Israelite Shechem.[85] In the case of Bethel, we can point to Jacob's dream and his words: "How awesome is this place! This is none other than the house of God, and this is the gate of heaven" (Gen 28:17).[86]

The fragile mosaic of materials thus seems to form a pattern. Among the priests at Shiloh the notion of the Lord as king seems to have been current.[87] And, such a notion has as its natural corollary the idea of a divine council, a linkage which is quite natural in a formerly Canaanite milieu.[88]

The designation יהוה צבאות originated in connection with the meeting of religions in Canaan.[89] It is here interesting to observe that there are certain indications that the designation is to be seen in connection with the El qualitites of YHWH.

(a) El's power over fertility is well known. He bestows fecundity on Danel and Keret, and is called *bny bnwt*, "Creator of Creatures," and *ab adm*, "Father of Mankind."[90] Hannah's prayer to YHWH Sabaoth for a son (1 Sam 1:11) can be seen in this perspective. (b) The child she bears

---

[83]Y. Yadin et al., *Hazor* 1 (Jerusalem, 1958) pl. XXVIII-XXXI and pp. 87-89.

[84]G. W. Ahlström, "Heaven on Earth—at Hazor and Arad," (above n. 39) 79.

[85]G. R. H. Wright, "The Mythology of Pre-Israelite Shechem," *VT* 20 (1970) 75-82, and S. Terrien, "The Omphalos Myth and Hebrew Religion," *VT* 20 (1970) 315-38. See also the literature mentioned above in n. 44, esp. S. Talmon (*TWAT* 2, 471-73), who questions the omphalos interpretation of Judg 9:37.

[86]K. Jaroš, *Die Stellung des Elohisten zur kanaanäischen Religion* (Orbis Biblicus et Orientalis 4, 1974) 179-96. Cf. also C. Houtman, "What Did Jacob See in His Dream at Bethel?" *VT* 27 (1977) 337-51.

[87]That the Lord was conceived of as king already in premonarchic times in ancient Israel is continually questioned by certain scholars; see most recently F. Crüsemann, *Der Widerstand gegen das Königtum* (WMANT 49, 1978) 76-78. This position is untenable, see A. Alt, "Gedanken über das Königtum Jahwes" (1945) *Kleine Schriften* 1 (München, 1953) 345-57; W. H. Schmidt, *Köngtum Gottes in Ugarit und Israel* (BZAW 80, 1961) 76-79; E. Lipiński, *La royauté de Yahwé*, 428-30; and F. M. Cross, *Canaanite Myth and Hebrew Epic*, 99 n. 30. Thus, the position of T. Ishida (*The Royal Dynasties in Ancient Israel* [BZAW 142, 1977] 37-39) is basically sound.

[88]The statement that the אהל מועד was at Shiloh (Josh 18:1; 19:51; 1 Sam 2:22) could be interesting in this context. R. J. Clifford ("The Tent of El and the Israelite Tent of Meeting," *CBQ* 33 [1971] 221-27) is inclined to believe that Heb. אהל מועד originally meant "tent of meeting (of the divine assembly)," cf. Ugaritic *phr m^cd* (p. 225).

[89]This aspect was stressed by V. Maag, *STU* 20 (1950) 27-52. See also F. M. Cross, *Canaanite Myth and Hebrew Epic*, 65-75.

[90]On El and the procreative powers, see M. H. Pope, *El in the Ugaritic Texts* (VTSup 2, 1955) 47-48.

receives a name compounded with אל, namely, שמואל; furthermore, El names are current among Samuel's ancestors (1 Sam 1:1; note the app.). (c) Baal reveals himself in the storm theophany, El, by way of contrast, through his word or decree, e.g., through a dream or visitation.[91] When God speaks to Samuel, he reveals himself at night in the temple at Shiloh (1 Samuel 3). (d) El is king of the gods, chief of the pantheon.[92] Corresponding to this are the unmistakable references to the divine council in the designation יהוה צבאות.

Thus, the material, though fragile, does seem to indicate that the designation יהוה צבאות was used at the היכל of Shiloh in a context which reminds us in many ways of the one we later meet at Solomon's temple: in connection with the ark, notions were cultivated of the Lord as king, as a holy God (קדוש) with royal "glory" (כבוד). I find it difficult to explain this as anachronistic *Rückprojektionen* of conditions prevailing at Solomon's temple.

Was there even a cherubim throne at Shiloh? The existence of such a throne would suit admirably the El qualities of YHWH. Among Punic materials (a stele from Hadrumetum-Sousse, fig. 5,[93] and scarabs from Sardinia,[94] as well as others) there can be found iconographic representations of a male god with beard, sitting on a throne of cherubim, his right hand raised in a gesture of greeting or blessing. The god is dressed in a long ceremonial garment; on his head is a conical crown. Above is a winged solar disc. These reliefs, as Culican and Cross have pointed out,[95] carry further the iconographic tradition from older Canaanite representations of El, sitting on a throne (fig. 6).[96] Admittedly, the Ugaritic El stela lacks cherubim bearing the throne; still, they have the most important characteristics in common, showing that we are dealing with an iconographic tradition to be traced to El, not Baal.[97] This seems to imply that the

---

[91] F. M. Cross, *Canaanite Myth and Hebrew Epic*, 177-86.

[92] See n. 54 above.

[93] P. Cintas, "Le sanctuaire punique de Sousse," *Revue Africaine* 91 (1947) 1-80 and fig. 48-49; A. M. Bisi, *Le stele puniche* (Studi Semitici 27, 1967) 91-103 and fig. 56; O. Keel, *The Symbolism of the Biblical World* (New York, 1978) no. 236.

[94] W. Culican, "Melqart Representations on Phoenician Seals," *Abr Nahrain* 2 (1960) 41-54, esp. 44-49; and idem. "The Iconography of Some Phoenician Seals and Seal Impressions," *AJBA* 1/1 (1968) 50-103, esp. 57-73, note p. 60 n. 52.

[95] W. Culican, *AJBA* 1/1 (1968) 63, and F. M. Cross, *Canaanite Myth and Hebrew Epic*, 35-36.

[96] Representations of El are probably to be found (a) on the so-called stela of El, published by C. F. A. Schaeffer, "Les fouilles de Ras Shamra-Ugarit," *Syria* 18 (1937) 125-54, esp. 128-34 and pl. XVII; cf. *ANEP*, no. 493 and Keel, *The Symbolism of the Biblical World*, no. 283. The other probable case (b) is a figurine of an aging god, seated (on a missing throne) and with his right hand raised; see C. F. A. Schaeffer, "Nouveaux témoignages du culte de El et de Baal," *Syria* 43 (1966) 1-19, pl. II and fig. 3. Cf. *ANEP*, no. 826 and Keel, *The Symbolism of the Biblical World*, no. 284. For a list of Phoenician cherubim thrones, see H. Seyrig, *Syria* 36 (1959) 51-52.

[97] On the iconography connected with Baal see A. Vanel, *L'iconographie du dieu de l'orage* (Cahiers de la Revue Biblique 3, 1965) esp. 119-30.

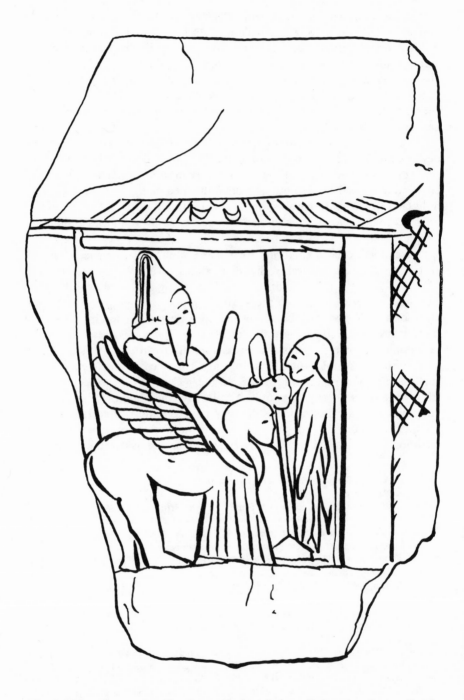

Fig. 5. Male god on a cherubim throne. Punic stela from Hadrumetum-Sousse. Drawing by Andrzej Szlagor.

Fig. 6. El-stela from Ugarit. Drawing by Andrzej Szlagor.

designation יֹשֵׁב הַכְּרֻבִים ought to be understood on the basis of El's iconographic tradition, not as a Baal epithet analogous to *rkb ʿrpt*, "driver of the clouds."

Thus, the results of our look at Shiloh's cultic traditions and at El's iconography make it reasonable to suppose that both the complete divine designation יהוה צבאות יֹשֵׁב הַכְּרֻבִים and a corresponding throne of cherubim existed already at Shiloh. As Cross has observed, the texts permit us to suspect as well a competition between this cherubim iconography, cultivated at Shiloh, and the bull iconography of Bethel.[98]

Our analysis lends increased probability to the old supposition that the original designation was אֵל צבאות.[99] This solves the syntactic problem, and is supported by the El affiliations of YHWH at Shiloh. Such a designation fits in beautifully with a number of epithets formed by combining אֵל with a feminine plural: אֵל דֵּעוֹת, "God of knowledge" (1 Sam 2:3!); אֵל נְקָמוֹת, "God of vengeance" (Ps 94:1); and אֵל גְּמֻלוֹת, "God of recompense" (Jer 51:56). If we are thus to assume an original אֵל צבאות, this designation and (אֵל) עֶלְיוֹן served as twin titles for YHWH as the supreme Head of the divine assembly.[100] The question must then be put whether יהוה צבאות represents an adaptation of a pre-Israelite, Canaanite title. Does the Ugaritic material perhaps support such a conclusion?

Two items in the Ugaritic material need to be mentioned in this context. First, we have a *ṣbu špš*,[101] which has been interpreted as a "heavenly host of the sun."[102] Second, we have a deity *ršp ṣbi*,[103] a name which has been interpreted as "Reshep the soldier," or "Reshep of the army"; Liverani links it to the interpretation of יהוה צבאות.[104] But, neither piece of evidence seems to offer a passable path to an understanding of our Israelite designation. Among the occurrences of Ugaritic *ṣ-b-ʾ* which Whitaker lists in his concordance,[105] we find both the Ugaritic word for

---

[98]F. M. Cross, *Canaanite Myth and Hebrew Epic*, 198-215. Cf. B. Halpern, "Levitical Participation in the Reform Cult of Jeroboam I," *JBL* 95 (1976) 31-42.

[99]See above, n. 73.

[100]What would seem to point to the worship of El Elyon at Shiloh is (a) the name of the priest, עֵלִי, and (b) the massoretic עֶלְי(וֹ)ן in 1 Sam 2:10, which is probably a corruption of עֵלִי, cf. Ps 18:14. See above all H. S. Nyberg, "Studien zum Religionskampf im Alten Testament," *ARW* 35 (1938) 329-87. Note that עֶלְיוֹן appears in parallelism with אֵל (Num 24:16; Pss 57:3; 73:11; 78:17-18; 107:11; cf. Gen 14:19-22 and Ps 78:35). The designation has to do with the idea of God as king (Pss 9:3; 47:3; 97:9) and occurs in connection with the divine assembly (Deut 32:8; Pss 82:6; 97:9; Isa 14:14).

[101]References below in n. 107.

[102]J. Gray, *The Legacy of Canaan* (VTSup 5, 2d ed.; 1965) 188. Gray expresses himself with due caution. Cf. below n. 107.

[103]*KTU*, 1.91.15 (= *CUL*, 2004.15).

[104]M. Liverani, "La preistoria dell'epiteto 'Yahweh ṣĕbāʾōt'," *AION* 17 (1967) 331-34 (not seen; known to me from J. A. Soggin's summary in *ZAW* 80 [1968] 99). A similar understanding of *ršp ṣbi* seems to be presupposed by P. D. Miller, *The Divine Warrior in Early Israel*, 21.

[105]*CUL*, 535.

"host," "army," "soldier,"[106] and a word of a different homonymic root corresponding to the Arabic *ḍabaʾa*, "to hide." This Ugaritic root is used of the sunset, where *ṣbu špš* at times is parallel with *ʿrb špš*.[107] The combination thus means, not "the host of the sun," but "the sunset." In my view, an interpretation of *ršp ṣbi* along similar lines should be considered. In one text speaking of the sunset, Reship is called the "door-keeper" (*ṯgr*) of the Sun.[108] We must therefore reckon with the possibility that *ršp ṣbi* may mean "Reshep of the sunset."

When all is said and done, there is to my knowledge nothing in the Ugaritic material known to date which indicates a technical use of *ṣbu* to mean a celestial host, comparable with the Hebrew צבא השמים. The view that the Sabaoth designation should be traced to a pre-Israelite title can therefore not be supported. By all appearances, it is a genuinely Israelite creation, originating in a milieu where the El qualities of YHWH played an important role.[109] A reminder that these El qualities of YHWH have deep roots in the soil of Canaan is to be found in the fact that in Philo Byblius El is depicted as a deity that has a host that assists him in battle; he has σύμμαχοι, "allies" (10.18 and 20). Here, Philo Byblius sems to take us back to an early stage of the tradition behind the Ugaritic texts[110] to a stage where the martial features of El are still prominent.

*

Regardless of when our divine designation came to be used in Jerusalem,[111] we must suppose that in any case it played a central role in the

---

[106]This is found in *KTU*, 4.40, lines 1, 7, 10 (= *CUL*, 79[83] lines 1, 7, 10), *KTU*, 1.3.II.22 (= *CUL*, 3 [ʿnt].2.22), *KTU*, 1.7.5 (= *CUL*, 7.1[131].5), and in *CUL*, 14[KRT].2 lines 86, 88 and 14 [KRT].4 lines 176, 177, 178.

[107]*KTU*, 1.15.V.19 (= *CUL*, 15 [128].5.19), where the spelling is *ṣbia*, *KTU* 1.87.51 (= *CUL*, APP. II [173]51), *KTU*, 1.41.47 (= *CUL*, 35 [3].47), and in line 53 of the last mentioned text without *ʿrb špš*. Note also *ṣba rbt špš*, KTU, 1.16.I.36-37 (= *CUL*, 16.1[125].36) and *ṣbi nrt ilm špš*, *KTU*, 1.19.IV.47 (= *CUL*, 19 [1 AQHT].4.209). The correct etymology was suggested by J. Gray, *The KRT Text in the Literature of Ras Shamra* (2d ed.; Leiden, 1964) 63. See also *UT*, Glossary no. 2138.

[108]*KTU*, 1.78.3-4 (= *CUL*, 143.3-4). That the designation *ršp ṣbi* can be brought into connection with this seems to have been overlooked in previous research. On Reshep, see D. Conrad, "Der Gott Reschef," *ZAW* 83 (1971) 157-83, esp. 169-71 and W. J. Fulco, *The Canaanite God Rešep* (AOS 8, 1976) esp. 36-44.

[109]A Canaanite formation that deserves to be mentioned as an interesting analogue is *ᵈšamaš līmīma*, "der Sonne der Tausende," in *EA* 205:6. On the implications of the proclamation of the divine name יהוה צבאות over the ark in 2 Sam 6:2; cf. K. Galling, "Die Ausrufung des Namens als Rechtsakt in Israel," *TLZ* 81 (1956) 65-70, esp. 68-69; Eissfeldt, *Kleine Schriften* 3, 417-25, esp. 422f. and Clements, *God and Temple*, 33.

[110]See P. D. Miller, "El the Warrior," *HTR* 60 (1967) 411-31, and idem, *The Divine Warrior in Early Israel*, 48-63.

[111]It could have been brought to Judah already by Abiathar (1 Sam 21:2-10; 22:6-23). On David's early connections with Shiloh, see E. Otto, *TZ* 32 (1976) 65-77. An alternative is that it came to Judah in connection with the transfer of the ark to Jerusalem. The distribution of

cult at Solomon's temple. Indeed, the site of the temple was pointed out by a representative of the heavenly host (2 Sam 24:14-25; cf. 1 Chr 21:16). *The central cultic object of the temple was the enormous cherubim throne with the ark as its footstool.* Of all the Israelite designations for their deity, צבאות יהוה is *the one peculiarly associated with the cherubim throne* in the temple. Thus at the latest during Solomon's reign, but possibly already earlier צבאות יהוה played a central role as the designation of the God of the dynasty and empire. With regard to the question of the significance of the innovation, I must here content myself with a few suggestions. Eissfeldt and J. J. M. Roberts have focused attention on the empire's need for ideological legitimation. The emphasis on the predication of YHWH as king and on the imperial God's older identification with the supreme head of the pantheon served, among other purposes, that of providing imperial politics with an ideological superstructure: in this way was maintained "Yahweh's divine right to grant world dominion to his earthly regent in Jerusalem."[112] The combination of the temple and the royal palace within a common encompassing wall on Zion (1 Kgs 7:12)[113] suggests an ideological link between the heavenly sovereign on the temple's throne of cherubim and the Davidic king in the palace. The king functions within the framework of the world-wide dominion of YHWH Sabaoth, exercising power delegated by the supreme Head of the divine council. Though in its present form quite a late text, Psalm 89 gives very pregnant expression to the basic view which must have been official already during the Solomonic era. That which is said about the earthly king in vv. 20-28 corresponds with what is said about the heavenly in vv. 6-19.[114] God presides over his heavenly council as צבאות יהוה (vv. 6-9). He has subdued the sea and Rahab (vv. 10-11). The imperial dominion of the Davidic king on earth appears as a reflection of God's cosmic supremacy. God has "set his hand on the sea and his right hand on the rivers" (v. 26), and made him עליון למלכי ארץ, "the highest of the kings of the earth" (v. 28).

יהוה צבאות in 1-2 Samuel is as follows: 1 Sam 1:3, 11, belonging to the Samuel traditions; 1 Sam 4:4; 2 Sam 6:2, 18, belonging to the ark traditions; 1 Sam 15:2; 17:45, belonging to the History of David's Rise (?), see T. Mettinger, *King and Messiah* (CB OTS 8, 1976) 33-35; 2 Sam 5:10; 7:8, 27, belonging to the History of David's Rise, see Mettinger, ibid., 41-45, 48-63; and 2 Sam 7:26, deuteronomistic (Mettinger, ibid., 51). Note the use of the *Beistandsformel* in connection with יהוה צבאות in 2 Sam 5:10 and Ps 46:8, 12. On this formula, see esp. H. D. Preuss, ". . . ich will mit dir sein," *ZAW* 80 (1968) 139-73, esp. 155f.

[112]Eissfeldt, "Jahwes Königsprädizierung als Verklärung nationalpolitischer Ansprüche Israels" (1972) *Kleine Schriften* 5 (Tübingen, 1973) 216-21; and J. J. M. Roberts, "The Davidic Origin of the Zion Tradition," *JBL* 92 (1973) 329-44, quotation above from p. 340. See also T. Ishida's well-informed chapter on "The Concentration of the Religio-National Traditions" in his *The Royal Dynasties,* 136-50.

[113]Cf. N. Poulssen, *König und Tempel im Glaubenszeugnis des Alten Testaments* (SBM 3, 1967) 11-26.

[114]T. Mettinger, *King and Messiah,* 254-56, 262-64.

It would be tempting to discuss here the use of יהוה צבאות in statements about the day of the Lord[115] and in creation hymns.[116] Such matters will have to be deferred. Some concluding reflections on the general distribution of this divine designation are not, however, to be avoided. How are we to explain the fact that the designation is so strikingly infrequent in the Deuteronomistic Historical Work? And, how are we to account for its total absence in Ezekiel, an absence the more remarkable when we recall Ezekiel's deep roots in the temple traditions—after all, the notion of a throne plays a central role in his thinking—and the high frequency with which we encounter the designation in the roughly contemporary Jeremiah?[117]

If the designation is as closely associated with the temple theology and with notions of God's presence as I have sought to establish, it is obvious that changes in the view of the temple may have influenced the use of this particular designation. It is well known that, in late preexilic times, certain circles abandoned the old theology of divine presence, replacing it with conceptions which emphasized rather the divine transcendence. Thus, in the deuteronomistic tradition, the name-theology comes to play a key role. Cherubim are never mentioned in Deuteronomy, and the ark has been reduced to a container for the law tablets (Deut 10:1-5). And, in the Deuteronomistic Historical Work, it is no longer יהוה צבאות who is enthroned in the temple. The place once occupied by this designation is now taken by God's שם, his name.[118] This explains why our divine designation is so rare in 1-2 Kings. In the priestly tradition which has been preserved in the Priestly Code, we meet an epiphany theology in which כבוד plays a significant role.[119] This provides the basis for an explanation of the absence of our divine designation in Ezekiel. On the linguistic level, אדני יהוה has come to serve the purpose once served by יהוה צבאות in certain formulas.[120] On the level of theological conceptions, on the other hand, כבוד has come to occupy the place in Ezekiel where we would have expected to find יהוה צבאות in the temple,[121] more specifically, above the

---

[115]As occurrences to be studied in that connection one can mention: Isa 2:12; 13:4, 13; 18:7; 22:5, 12, 14; 24:23; 31:4; Jer 46:10; 50:25; Zech 14:16-17, 21.

[116]Cf. Isa 51:15; 54:5; Jer 10:16; 31:35; 32:18 (cf. v. 17); 50:34; 51:19; Amos 4:13; 9:5. See J. L. Crenshaw, "YHWH Ṣᵉbaʾôt Šᵉmô. A Form Critical Analysis," ZAW 81 (1969) 156-75.

[117]See Baumgärtel, "Zu den Gottesnamen," 1-3.

[118]Cf. F. Dumermuth, "Zur deuteronomischen Kulttheologie," ZAW 70 (1958) 59-98, esp. 70-79. Note also Görg's observation in Biblische Notizen 4 (1977) 21. Note also the use of צבא to denote the object of the astral worship, condemned by the Deuteronomists (n. 57 above); and cf. W. Kessler, "Aus welchen Gründen," 81. As for the high frequency of the divine designation in Jeremiah, note that Jeremiah does not mention the reform of Josiah! For a fine discussion of the name theology and the new concept of the divine abode, see M. Weinfeld, Deuteronomy and the Deuteronomic School (Oxford, 1972) 191-209.

[119]E.g., Exod 16:10; 29:43; Num 14:10; 16:19; 17:7; 20:6; and, without kābôd, Exod 25:22; Num 7:89.

[120]See Baumgärtel, "Zu den Gottesnamen," 1-3.

[121]Ezek 8:4; 11:23; 43:4-5; 44:4.

cherubim.[122] Thus we see how שם and כבוד have dethroned יהוה צבאות from its place in the temple of Solomon.[123]

Translated by Stephen Westerholm.

POSTSCRIPT

Note also J. J. M. Roberts' study of the Zion tradition in the present volume. In my monograph, *The Dethronement of Sabaoth—Studies in the Shem and Kabod Theologies* (CB OTS 18, 1982), I discuss the "Name" and the "Glory" and their relation to the Sabaoth designation.

---

[122]Ezek 1:28; 9:3; 10:4, 18, 19; 11:22.

[123]A problem that remains to be explained is the low frequency in the Psalms, only 15 occurrences in 8 different psalms, mostly Hymns of Zion (Pss 24:10; 46:8, 12; 48:9; 59:6; 69:7; 80:5, 8, 15, 20; 84:2, 4, 9, 13; 89:9). On Sabaoth in post-biblical literature, see F. T. Fallon, *The Enthronement of Sabaoth* (Nag Hammadi Studies 10, 1978).

Female Cult Figurines in Late Canaan and Early Israel: Archaeological Evidence

MIRIAM TADMOR
Israel Museum, Jerusalem

It is a well-known fact, but nonetheless one still worth repeating, that our knowledge of religious and cultural life in Canaan is limited mainly to the second millennium B.C. One may of course assume the existence of Canaanite culture from at least the beginning of the third millennium. However, the artistic achievements of the Canaanites in the third millennium still remain basically unknown—either buried in the lower layers of the major mounds, or destroyed by inhabitants of later ages and obliterated. It is therefore to the second millennium that the student of history and archaeology turns when looking for his evidence. This—as is also well known—was the period of increasing literacy, which to date has been documented by the Ras Shamra literary texts, the Taanach and Amarna correspondence and, more recently, by the significant though scanty cuneiform tablets from Hazor and Aphek. The contacts of Canaan with the surrounding countries were close and numerous. They leave no doubt that Canaan of the second millennium was an integral part of the highly developed and multifaceted cultural and political mosaic spreading from Mesopotamia to Egypt and to Mycenae in Greece. Furthermore, the subtle and intricate contacts with the biblical world of the first millennium indicate that the Canaanite culture must be regarded as the native substratum upon which the Israelite culture of the first millennium was to be superimposed.

The schism and the contrast between the two are repeatedly emphasized in the Bible whereas biblical scholarship has also stressed the influence of Canaanite culture and religion upon the Hebrews. However, it is mainly through growing archaeological evidence that we can gain an insight into the otherwise obscure layers of daily life, burial customs and cultic practices. A detailed study of the structural and artistic elements unearthed in excavations has ascertained not only the differences; in many cases this study has revealed the elements of continuity and influence which were insistently interwoven in the fabric of the younger culture.

The Bible itself focuses attention on Canaanite religion. It naturally followed, therefore, that biblical archaeology had been concentrating its research on the same matters: temples, high places and tombs were among the favored targets for excavations. And, indeed, these structures as well as the assemblages of the artifacts they contained, furnish highly illuminating information on Canaanite cult practices. Representational art is of special significance in this context, the easiest to grasp, most readily interpreted. Luckily, Canaan of the second millennium has left numerous remains of representational art, which must once have been abundant. The existence of zoomorphic representations can be traced almost from the beginning of the millennium, either as elements of decoration or, as zoomorphic vessels, in the round. Anthropomorphic images, appearing mostly in small sculpture, soon followed in their wake. Both zoomorphic and anthropomorphic images must have become exceedingly popular during the centuries, whether locally made or imported. For the modern scholar anthropomorphic elements commonly constitute the very basis for the inclusion of an object in the category of "ceremonial" or "cult" objects.

Special attention has been devoted to one class of anthropomorphic cult objects, namely, the female figurines made mostly of clay, making their first appearance in Canaan sometime towards the middle of the millennium and becoming abundant in the third quarter. They are of small dimensions, usually made by pressing a lump of clay into an open mold, and therefore have been termed either "plaque" or "relief" figurines. The image of a naked woman appears on them in high-relief, virtually three dimensional, backed by a clay plaque, usually some 12-20 cm in length.

As of the early decades of this century, scholars of Bible and biblical archaeology have been dealing with this genre of Canaanite art. It was interpreted in the light of biblical literature and rapidly became known as "Astarte figurines." It was W. F. Albright who in several studies contributed most significantly to the subject. He first discussed the topic in his "Archaeology and the Bible," later devoted to it a separate study and finally returned to it in his latest monograph on Tell Beit Mirsim in the Iron Age period.[1] He was followed by James B. Pritchard, whose "Palestinian figurines in Relation to Certain Goddesses known through Literature" of 1943, is in fact the latest extensive study published on the subject of the relief-plaques.

The growing bulk of material accumulated during last decades justifies a renewed analysis of the so-called Astarte figurines—this most significant group among the cult objects of the period—according to strict stylistic and comparative criteria.

In order to properly interpret these Late Bronze plaque-figurines, we shall digress and investigate a distinct group of female figurines of a type

---

[1]E. Pilz, "Die weiblichen Gottheiten Kanaans," *ZDPV* 47 (1924) 129-68; V. Müller, *Frühe Plastik in Griechenland und Vorderasien* (Berlin, 1924); W. F. Albright, *The Archaeology of Palestine and the Bible* (New York, 1932-33) 95-98; "Astarte Plaques and Figurines from Tell Beit Mirsim," *Mèlanges Syriens Offerts à Monsieur Renè Dussaud* 1 (Paris, 1939) 109-17; W. F. Albright et al., *The Excavations of Tell Beit Mirsim* 3: *The Iron Age* (AASOR 21-22, 1943) 25-26; and also, W. F. Albright, *Archaeology and the Religion of Israel* (Baltimore, 1942) 114-15.

Pl. 1.

hitherto unattested in Canaanite sites, which was unearthed only recently in the cemetery of Deir el-Balaḥ, south of Gaza. One such figurine was found in the excavations of the Hebrew University (pl. 1), associated with the anthropoid sarcophagi burials, and therefore, stratigraphically, it belongs to the Late Bronze period, most probably to the thirteenth century B.C. Other figurines published here were in all likelihood also found in the Deir el-Balah cemetery and stylistically form a coherent group.

One of the figurines, Israel Museum no. 70.113.459, will be described in detail. It is 17 cm long and 6 cm wide. A figure of a young woman, in fact a girl (pl. 2), is carved in the whitish stone, wearing a heavy wig and

Pl. 2.

Pl. 2a.

nude but for her necklace. She is depicted in a completely frontal pose with arms stretched alongside the body, and with straight legs. The eyes are closed, her hands and her feet are exaggerated in length. Also, there is a slenderness of the body and a clear elongation of arms and legs. This peculiarity, characteristic of the whole group, can be regarded as a convention employed by the sculptors to depict the youthfulness of the girl. The body of the girl is covered with red paint, but for the wig, necklace and the pubic triangle, which are painted in black.

The plaque is rectangular with a flat back and slightly rounded head. Its surface was decorated with black and red stripes which have faded but are clearly visible. The bottom of the plaque is shaped like a low footrest, the feet are extended along this footrest without falling sideways. Red and black vertical stripes decorate also the outer surface of the footrest. The plaque itself is unexpectedly thick (2 cm), forming a disproportionally heavy base for the slender figure resting upon it.

The fragmentary stone figurine found in the excavations at Deir el-Balaḥ[2] (pl. 1) is larger, but otherwise identical with the previously described one (l. 11.5 cm; w. 8.03 cm). The same elongation of legs, feet and palms, and a striking similarity in the treatment of the body and in the shape of the plaque. The stylistic characteristics of nudity, frontality and plaque conformation can be distinguished in all the other statuettes in this group, irrespective of their artistic quality. We can trace them in a slightly laiger limestone statuette (l. 19.5 cm) and in another (l. 20.5 cm, pl. 3) somewhat inferior in artistic quality.[3] Again we see an outstretched nude girl in a completely frontal pose, with a long wig, elongated arms and legs and enlarged hands and feet. The plaque, though somewhat narrower, is identical to that of the previous statuette, including the footrest. An additional figurine of the same group, the one made of clay (B109, pl. 4), is of special significance for our discussion, since it must have been cast in an open mold, in a technique typical both of the Egyptian and of the Canaanite plaque-figurines of the Late Bronze period. Further, in distinction from the wigs which we have seen in the previous stone statuettes, this girl has a hairdo of a type which we shall later see in other typical Canaanite figurines. But, in all other details of pose, elongation of arms and contours of the plaque, she clearly belongs in the category of our statuettes.[4]

The stylistic affinities of the Deir el-Balaḥ statuettes with contemporary Egyptian small sculpture leave no doubt that they were either of Egyptian manufacture, imported from Egypt, or that they were locally made in strongly Egyptianizing style. Thus, they belong to a large group of artifacts

---

[2]I am grateful to Prof. Trude Dothan of the Hebrew University of Jerusalem for her permission to publish this figurine here.

[3]The statuette belongs to the R. Hecht Collection, Haifa (no. H-499). I am grateful to Dr. Hecht for his permission to study and publish the figurines in his collection.

[4]From the collection of Mr. A. Spaer, Jerusalem, published here with his kind permission.

deposited with the anthropoid sarcophagi which, likewise, are either of Egyptian origin or heavily Egyptianizing; it should be repeated here that the sarcophagi themselves, though locally made, are in Egyptian style and have close parallels in similar clay coffins in Egypt.[5]

The Deir el-Balaḥ statuettes discussed here belong to a well-defined group of Egyptian small sculptures, depicting people lying on beds, which was popular in Egypt during the New Kingdom. Both men[6] and women may be depicted in such manner, sometimes women with children or nursing an infant (see below) or couples in erotic postures.[7] In this broad category of "people lying on beds," there is a special group of the so-called concubine figurines, depicting a young woman lying in a frontal pose on a bed[8]; it is to this special group that our Deir el-Balaḥ statuettes belong. The following figurines, similar to our figurines, will add some details which do not appear in the Deir el-Balaḥ group and will exemplify a more realistic approach, mainly in the depiction of the bed.

A figurine of unknown provenance, NM80, now in the National Museum of Stockholm, is the closest to our Deir el-Balaḥ group.[9] The figure of the girl is indeed almost identical with ours but for the more elaborate wig. The stone is finely ground, similar to the stone in our statuettes. Likewise, the bed is rectangular, with a low footrest. There is one significant addition: the head of the girl rests on a pillow, indicated on the plaque by incisions and oval in shape when viewed from above.

A further example is another figurine, made of clay with painted surface, now in Munich (pl. 5).[10] Here the woman is depicted holding a baby to her breast. But for this detail, the relief-figurine stylistically resembles our Deir el-Balaḥ group in the long wig, the frontal pose and in the contours of the plaque. The most striking feature is the up-curving footrest support, elevated very high in contrast to the head, which is low in this as in previous figurines. The realistic additions of four rather massive legs which supported the horizontal surface leave no doubt that the plaque was indeed intended to represent a bed (pl. 5a).

---

[5]T. Dothan, *Excavations at the Cemetery of Deir el-Balah* (Qedem 10, 1979).

[6]MFA 1971.292, published by W. K. Simpson, "Century Two: Collecting Egyptian and Near Eastern Art for the Boston Museum," *Apollo* 98 (1973) 250-57 and private communication (8 February 1979).

[7]Brooklyn Museum nos. 60.181, 16.103, 16.104 and 37.590 (Private communication of Dr. B. V. Bothmer on 8 March 1973). I am grateful to Dr. Bothmer for several references to various collections.

[8]Cf. U. Hölscher, *The Excavations of Medinet Habu* 5 (Chicago, 1954) 11, fig. 12; W. M. Petrie, *Illahun, Kahun and Gurob* (London, 1891) 22, pl. XXVII, 12.

[9]NM 80 was described in Cat. *5000 år egyptisk Konst*, National Museum, no. 94 (1961). I am grateful to Dr. B. Peterson, Director of Egyptian Antiquities in the Medelhausmuseet for his help and permission.

[10]Published here through the kindness of Dr. D. Wildung, Director of the Staatliche Sammlung Ägyptischer Kunst, Munich. Cf. *Staatliche Sammlung Ägyptischer Kunst* (München, 1976) 115: Ägyptische Sammlung 413.

Pl. 3.

Pl. 3a.

Pl. 4.

These few statuettes may be taken as representative of the whole category of small sculptures depicting girls lying on beds. The dual components are the plaque meant to represent the bed, and the human figure in relief. The figure follows somewhat strict stylistic conventions. It is invariably nude and depicted frontally; the position of the hands may vary, but not that of the legs and feet. And, indeed, the straight feet indicate a supine position; when the ancient sculptor sought to portray a figure standing upright, he employed the convention of both feet turned sidewise or in opposite directions.

In contrast to the rigid portrayal of the human figure, we distinguish a pronounced variety in the representation of the bed, from a detailed realism to an almost geometric abstraction of a rectangular plaque, the most persistent element being that of the footrest. It is interesting to note that the Deir el-Balaḥ group uses this most advanced form of stylistic "shorthand" in which nothing but the plaque and the footrest are employed, a "pars-pro-toto" device standing for a bed with all its details.

One other feature must be mentioned, namely, the total absence of any divine symbolism. And, indeed, the reclining figures seem to be representations of human beings. Their consistent association with burials, so clearly demonstrated also by their presence in the Deir el-Balaḥ cemetery, permits the assumption that they were in some way connected with funerary practices and customs.[11]

The stylistic criteria which we defined for the Deir el-Balaḥ group, both the shape of the plaque and the pose of the figure, as well as the absence of divine symbolism, must be considered when an analysis of some contemporary Canaanite "Astarte" relief-figurines is attempted. Earlier research focused mainly on the position of the hands and the coiffure of the female figure: whether or not it was a "Hathor wig." I believe that if we broaden our criteria to include both the plaque and the figure, a close stylistic affinity will be discerned between the statuettes of "women lying on beds" and a certain group of Canaanite figurines; this similarity may eventually shed some new light on the significance of these Canaanite figurines and on their function. We shall therefore proceed to the so-called Astarte figurines of Late Bronze Canaan and compare them to the stone figurines of girls lying on beds from Deir el-Balaḥ, this in spite of the difference of materials and the rather poor quality of the clay plaques created by the Canaanite artisans. Let us bear in mind that these were not individually made objects carved in stone, but rather reproduced mechanically by casting to meet the great popular demand.

The Canaanite clay figurines, like the Deir el-Balaḥ ones, are a representation of a nude female figure projecting from a plaque in a full

---

[11]W. K. Simpson suggested that the plaque in MFA 1971.292 represents a funerary bed, see above n. 6.

Pl. 5.

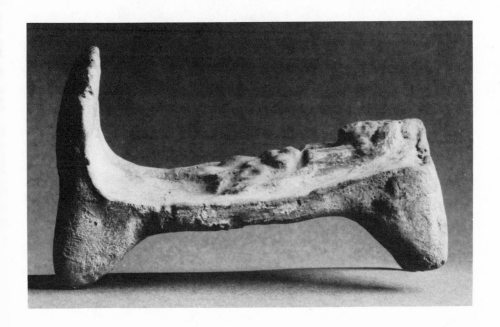

Pl. 5a.

Pl. 6.

Pl. 6a.

Pl. 7.

Pl. 7a.

frontal position (pls. 6,7).[12] The arms are stretched alongside the body. Both arms and legs are elongated, the head and feet disproportionately large. The feet continue the line of the body, held closely together without turning sidewise. In contrast to the Egyptian figurines, the coiffure in the Canaanite clay plaques is realistic; the hair, low on the forehead, sometimes falls in two long tresses on the shoulders.

The plaque is rounded on top and curves upwards at the feet, in a manner reminiscent of the other group. It is this feature that we consider the key towards the correct interpretation of the whole figurine. What we see here must, by analogy with the previously discussed group, be interpreted as representation of a figure lying on a bed. The plaque was intended to represent the bed and therefore the figurine has to be kept in a horizontal not vertical position. This will explain the fact that little effort was ever expended by the artisan on the back of the plaque, which was mostly left unfinished. It will also explain the up-curving end, which is usually slanting and could thus not serve as base on which the figurine could stand.[13]

The figurine will serve as a representative example of this specific type of Canaanite plaques. In spite of the obvious aesthetic differences, all the cardinal stylistic features which we observed in the Deir el-Balaḥ and related Egyptian statuettes are repeated in all the figurines of this group: nudity, frontality, frequent elongation of body and limbs and exaggeration of palms and feet; as mentioned above, in contrast to the wig, we see in the Canaanite figurines mostly a natural, non-conventionalized hairdo. The red paint, which seems to have covered all figurines is still preserved in some. The plaques are rounded on top and curve diagonally up at the base so that the feet of the reclining women are pressed against the bed footrest. We have observed that the position of the hands varies and seems not to have been of prime iconographic importance in this class of figurines (cf. the plaque from Tel Zeror in pl. 9). A representation of a woman nursing an infant seems to have been especially meaningful: it has been found in Late Bronze Beth-Shean and in a Persian period temple at Makmish, near Tel Mikhal on the Mediterranean shores.[14]

---

[12]This figurine, 56-1424, found at Tel Masad, belongs to the collections of the Israel Department of Antiquities and Museums and is exhibited in the Israel Museum. It has previously been published in Hebrew by N. Tzori, "Cult Figurines in the Eastern Plain of Esdraelon and Beth-Shean," *Eretz-Israel* 5 (1958) 52-55, pl. 7, 1. The other clay plaque-figurines are published here with the kind permission of Dr. R. Hecht (pls. 7,10-12, respectively).

[13]E. Douglas Van-Buren, *Clay Figurines of Babylonia and Assyria* (New York, 1930) XLIII. Mrs. Van-Buren, who recognized this difficulty when dealing with Mesopotamian figurines, concluded that the plaques must have been "intended to be laid on a flat surface, or at least to be propped up against a shelf or wall."

[14]A. Rowe, *The Four Canaanite Temples of Beth-Shan* (Philadelphia, 1940) pl. LXVIII, 4; N. Avigad, "Excavations at Makmish, 1958, Preliminary Report," *IEJ* 10 (1960) 90-96, pl. 11, C; "Makmish," *EAEHL* 3 (1977) 769.

When dealing with the Deir el-Balaḥ group we have pointed out the variants in the rendering of the beds and the frequent stylistic "shorthand," resulting in the omission of one or of several component details. When casting his figures in clay, the Canaanite sculptor never employed the realistic style; his was rather a conventionalized schematic approach using different means in representing the bed. The side view of the figurine in pl. 8 reveals that the plaque is "hammock"-shaped. And, indeed, this unusual feature induced the late J. Leibovitch of the Israel Department of Antiquities, to remark on the similarity of this to the Egyptian "concubine figurines."[15]

An additional device can also be observed, namely, a frame-like line which encloses the body of the woman, separating it from the edges of the plaque (cf. pl. 11). That this frame is intentional and of iconographic significance, is exemplified in another figurine (below, pl. 12), where it is thickest at the base, suggesting a foot support upon which both feet are spread, and repeating the shape of the plaque itself. This feature can best be observed in the figurine from Tel Zeror (pl. 9),[16] covered by red paint, which depicts a woman holding her hands to her breasts. The plaque is disproportionately thick, a feature we have already observed in other figurines. What was a dividing frame-line in the former figurine, becomes here a virtual ledge, projecting from the surface of the plaque, a three-dimensional foot support. Such ledge-like foot supports appear also in Mesopotamian and Syrian plaque-figurines and are frequently depicted in other Canaanite figurines. Good examples have been unearthed in the excavations of Lachish and Tell Beit-Mirsim. All stratified Canaanite figurines are of the Late Bronze period.[17]

I would like to submit that the Canaanite plaque-figurines which we have followed untill now form a separate, distinct and coherent group. By comparison to similar Egyptian figurines of the period, including the Deir el-Balaḥ finds, we have interpreted these Canaanite clay plaque-figurines as also depicting women lying on beds. We have found support for our thesis in certain features of the female figure as well as in the shape of the plaque, viewed by us as a distinct iconographic element. Due to the absence of any divine elements in the depiction of the human figure, we are led to conclude that—like the Egyptian "women lying on beds"—these could also be human rather than divine images. We shall note that in contrast to the Egyptian representations in the New Kingdom period, the Canaanite

---

[15]IDAM 52-706, published by L. Y. Rachmani, "A Lion-Faced Figurine from Bet-Sheʾan," ꜥAtiqot 2 (1959) 184-85, pl. XXIV, 1-2. I believe that the disfiguration of the face and the resemblance to a lion are accidental, due to technical difficulties when pulling the figurine out of the mold. No other Canaanite plaque figurine is lion-faced.

[16]K. Ohata, Tel Zeror 2 (Tokyo, 1967) 28 and pl. XLVII, 1-2; 66-357.

[17]W. F. Albright, "Astarte Plaques and Figurines from Tell Beit-Mirsim," Mèlanges Syriens 111, pl. A, 2; p. 116, fig. 1 b-c; O. Tufnell, Lachish 4 (London, 1958) 90 and pl. 49:1, 3 and 5.

Pl. 8.

Pl. 8a.

Pl. 9.

figurines depict female figures only; in this the Canaanite iconography closely resembles the slightly earlier Syrian plaque-figurines of the second millennium.

The characteristics of this group will become even more apparent when compared to a different type of clay plaque figurines, found both in Canaan and in Egypt. An outstanding example of the latter is the figurine in pl. 10, now in the Hecht Collection (H726; l. 12.5 cm). The image is of a nude woman, as in the previous group, but here she is wearing a typical Hathor wig, with the well-known characteristic ringlets. Her arms are bent, each holding a long stemmed flower; the legs are separated, the feet turned outwards. The image stands on a short ground line and together with the two flower stalks an almost continuous frame is created, surrounding the human figure. Of special significance is the shape of the plaque: in contradistinction to the plaques in the previous group, here it is flat, of uniform thickness, and lacks the up-curving base.

The turned-out feet are a convention common both in Late Bronze Canaan and in New Kingdom Egypt to represent an upright position. The straight, uncurved plaque cannot indicate a bed and should be interpreted in the commonly accepted manner, as a mere background for the image depicted in relief. And, most significantly, we must note here the persistent presence of divine attributes, such as the Hathor wig and flower stalks; alternatively, the woman may also be holding snakes in her hands.

Female images of this type are frequently encountered in clay and, unlike the recumbent figures, they also appear in metal. They join a group of images of standing women incised in gold jewelry, especially in amulets.[18]

A female figure standing on a lion or a horse is a variant, belonging to the same group: a recently found gold-leaf plaque from the Canaanite temple at Lachish, depicting a most elaborate image in strongly Egyptianizing style, is the latest addition to the latter category.[19]

We have concluded that the reclining figures of the first group, devoid of any divine attributes, were most probably images of mortals. The presence of Hathor wigs, flower stalks or snakes and animal pedestals clearly points to the divine character of the female images of the second group. Do we indeed have here a representation of Astarte, as commonly accepted and as implied by the popular name "Astarte plaque"?

---

[18] A. Rowe, *The Four Canaanite Temples of Beth-Shan* (London, 1940) pl. 68 A:5; O. Negbi, *Canaanite Gods in Metal* (London, 1976) pls. 39, 48, 53. Similar figurines made of glass: D. Barag, "Mesopotamian Core-Formed Glass Vessels (1500-500 B.C.E.)," *Glass and Glassmaking in Ancient Mesopotamia* (eds. A. L. Oppenheim et al.; London, 1970) 188, fig. 98; H. Kühne, "Bemerkungen zu einige Glasreliefs der 2. Jahrtausend v. Ch. aus Syrien und Palästina," *ZA* 59 (1969) 299-318.

[19] D. Ussishkin, "Excavations at Lachish 1973-1977, Preliminary Report," *Tel Aviv* 5 (1978) 21 and pl. 8; Ch. Clamer, "A Gold Plaque from Tel Lachish," *Tel-Aviv* 7 (1980) 152-62; S. Ben-Arie and G. Edelstein, "Akko, Tombs Near the Persian Garden," *ᶜAtiqot* 12 (1977) 29, 37, fig. 15 and pl. V.

Pl. 10.

Pl. 10a.

We must advocate caution even in this case and emphasize the uncertainty of identification. Two examples will suffice to illustrate the reasons for this hesitation. Of all the shrines excavated to date in Israel, none merits this appellation more than the seaside site at Nahariyah, of the Middle Bronze Age II.[20] Indeed, I. Ben-Dor suggested that it was dedicated to Aṯirat-of-the-Sea. Whether this can be accepted or not, at Nahariyah we have a unique case of a temple in which over twenty female figurines, mostly made of silver, were found, but, surprisingly, no two of them are iconographically identical; each figure is different and the well-known image carved in a stone-mold differs from all the actual figurines found in the temple.

An Egyptian stele from the Winchester Collection is brought here as our second example.[21] The image belongs stylistically to our second group of standing female figures with Hathor wigs and flowers. The hieroglyphic inscription Qudshu-ᶜAstarte-ᶜAnath appends all three names to a single image.

Thus, in the Nahariyah temple we encounter a diversity, where uniformity of image might have been expected; on the other hand, in the Egyptian stele we are confronted with a standardized single image, used for the depiction of several deities. Clearly, the art of Canaan in the late second millennium, with its conventional, standardized repertoire, does not easily offer the means for clear-cut definitions and identifications. Therefore, for the time being we shall only define the images of the second group as representing a divinity of the Canaanite or Egyptian pantheon, without further identification, in contrast to the seemingly human character of the women lying on beds, of the first group.

It is commonly accepted that mold-made plaque-figurines originated in Mesopotamia and Iran at the end of the third millennium. They are also attested in Syrian sites of the second millennium;[22] Riis, in his study, cites numerous such figurines. Indeed, some close comparisons to the figurines

---

[20]I. Ben-Dor, "A Middle Bronze Age Temple at Nahariya," *Quarterly of the Department of Antiquities of Palestine* 14 (1950) 1-43; M. Dothan, "The Excavations at Nahariya," *IEJ* 6 (1956) 14-25; "Nahariya," *EAEHL* 3 (1977) 908-12; "Sanctuaries along the Coast of Canaan in the MB Period: Nahariyah," *Temples and High Places in Biblical Times* (ed. A. Biran; Jerusalem, 1981) 74-81.

[21]I. E. S. Edwards, "A Relief of Qudshu-Astarte-Anath in the Winchester College Collection," *JNES* 14 (1955) 49-51, pl. III; I. V. Bogoslovskaya and E. S. Bogoslovsky, "The Syro-Palestinian Goddess Qudshu in Ancient Egypt," *Palestinskij Sbornik* 26 (89) Moskwa, 1978) 140-64 (Russian); cf. also M. Th. Barrelet, *Syria* 35 (1958) 27ff.

[22]P. J. Riis, "The Syrian Astarte Plaques and their Western Connections," *Berytus* 9 (1948-49) 69-90; R. Ghirshman, *Tchoga Zanbil* (Dur Untash) I, Memoirs Délégation Archeologique en Iran, XXXIX (Paris, 1966) pl. LXXI: G.T.Z. 664; M. G. Stève and H. Gasche, *L'Acropole de Suse*, Nouvelles Fouilles (Rapport Preliminaire), Memoirs Délégation Archeologique en Iran, XLVI (Paris-Leiden, 1971) 46, 47; pl. 1:7-15, especially no. 10; R. Hachmann, *Kamid el-Loz 1966/67*, Saarbrücker Beiträge zur Altertumskunde 4 (Bonn, 1970) pls.1: 1a, b; 8:1-3; 17:10.

of our first group can be brought forward. We observe in these figurines the same type of plaque with the raised foot support, the same frontal pose of the human figure and the extended feet continuing the line of the body. Sometimes the foot support is in the shape of a separate ledge, projecting from the plaque itself, exactly as in some Canaanite figurines mentioned above. Nudity and elongation of limbs also persist in the figures in the Syrian plaque-figurines of this genre. The position of both hands may differ. A later development here, seen already in the Late Bronze and Early Iron Ages in Canaan, is the representation of a woman holding her breasts. Some figurines of the same type, most probably of Syrian or Lebanese provenance, now form part of private collections in Israel. The few published here will prove that we can trace in them all the above-mentioned details, including the realistic representation of coiffure and the emphasis in the representation of the foot support (pls. 11,12).

The use of molds for small terra-cotta sculpture spread from the East and in the Orientalizing period reached Greece, which adopted the plaque-figurines and the representation of the female figure depicted in high relief.[23] One significant characteristic of the East Mediterranean female figurine was destined to undergo a thorough change here: the figurine is no longer nude, but is now clothed in a high-waisted dress with flat drapery and embroidery. In this form the plaque-figurine, which became popular throughout Greece and the islands, appears also in Neirab and in other Syrian sites in the late Iron Age and subsequent periods.[24]

Several clay plaque-figurines, encountered in Punic sites, indicate that this genre traveled still further west. A figurine from the acropolis on the island of Ibiza in Spain (6th-5th centuries B.C.) registers all the stylistic criteria which we have itemized. No different is a figurine from Carthage, with the same configuration of plaque and female figure, depicted in high relief, in complete frontality, with both arms alongside the body and with the feet resting on a footrest.[25]

We venture to suggest that these stylistic characteristics, defined in small sculpture, may also be found in the lids and in the life-sized figures appearing on the lids of stone sarcophagi of the 6th-5th centuries B.C. Whether at Sidon or in Sicily,[26] the shape of the lid and the raised footrest are strongly reminiscent of the plaque in our small size clay figurines; the draped figure depicted frontally with the feet resting on a raised support closely follows these of the small size versions. Moreover, we may also suggest that some figurines, placed in funerary stelae, also belong to the

---

[23] J. Boardman, *Pre-Classical* (Harmondsworth, 1967) 87-88.

[24] See n. 21 above.

[25] A. Parrot, M. H. Chéhab and S. Moscati, *Les Phéniciens* (Gallimard, 1975) 247, fig. 283; 159, fig. 164 (nécropole de Douimès, c. sixth century).

[26] See above, n. 25, p. 102, fig. 106 (Sidon, fourth cent.) and p. 207, fig. 227 (Pizzo Cannita, sixth-fifth cent.).

Pl. 11.

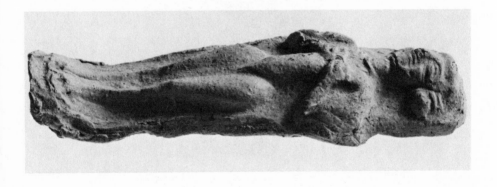

Pl. 11a.

Pl. 12.

Pl. 12a.

category of our figurines. The representations within the stelae vary considerably: it may be an image of a deity, a banquet or male and female figures. It seems to us that when a female figure is depicted on a plaque within a stele, it should be interpreted as a representation of a woman lying on a bed, analogous to our plaque figurines.[27]

We have been following the plaque-figurines depicting women in horizontal position in their development through a millennium, from their homeland in Mesopotamia and Iran, to the eastern shores of the Mediterranean and to Egypt and finally to their later manifestations further west. We shall devote some of our concluding remarks to the identification of the plaque-figurines depicting reclining women. Already Perrot and Chipiez, in discussing the figurines in their "History of Art in Phoenicia and its Dependencies" in 1885, wrote that "it is often difficult to distinguish between gods and mortals. Our chief aid is first the absence of those attributes and symbolic animals which are reserved for gods and goddesses; secondly, iconic statues are always standing" (vol II, p. 27). Later research often associated the nude female figure with fruitfulness and fertility. Once the term "Astarte figurines" had been coined, the identification became popularly known and the divine connotation widely accepted for all types of the clay plaque-figurines of Late Bronze Canaan. Still, Pritchard in his study of Palestinian figurines emphasized that "there is no direct evidence connecting the nude female figure represented upon the plaques and figurines of Palestine with any of the prominent goddesses" (p. 86). He debated whether some images represent the goddess herself, a prostitute of the cult of the goddess, or a talisman employed in sympathetic magic to stimulate the reproductive processes of nature. Others, he thought, "seem to be associated with the process of child-bearing" (p. 87).

Our stylistic investigation, which included both the plaque and the figure on it, has led us to deduce two main categories of Canaanite plaque-figurines: those standing erect, furnished with divine symbols, and others persistently devoid of any symbols, which we interpreted as lying on beds. A detailed comparative study resulted in a comparison of the latter with the Egyptian and Egyptianizing statuettes which were found in the cemetery of Deir el-Balaḥ. We have seen that several strikingly similar stylistic features could still be discerned both in small and life-sized sculpture in the Phoenician and Punic cemeteries some thousand years later.

We therefore propose that the Late Bronze Canaanite plaque-figurines of women lying on beds, though undoubtedly deriving from various religious contexts, are to be regarded chiefly as objects associated with mortuary beliefs and funerary practices, frequently found in tombs. We

---

[27]See above, n. 25, p. 203, fig. 222 and p. 204, fig. 223 (Motya, *tophet*, sixth-fifth cent.); W. Culican, "A Terracotta Shrine from Achzib," *ZDPV* 92 (1976) 47-53; For latest extensive discussion on models of shrines, see S. S. Weinberg, "A Moabite Shrine Group," *Muse* 12 (1978) 30-48.

have repeatedly emphasized that the shape of the plaque, interpreted by us as the representation of a bed, was the most persistent stylistic element; indeed, in spite of the wide geographic diffusion, it hardly changed during the centuries. No funerary representations have been preserved in Canaanite art, and the identification of the plaque as a funerary bed would be speculative; still, it should be considered. We might also add the similarity of our figurines to the Egyptian ushabti plaques[28] as well as the static pose of the female figure and the serenity of expression as further elements favoring our suggestion that these plaque-figurines were in fact anthropomorphic objects connected with mortuary beliefs, ex voto offerings to the dead; the fact that they are being found also in private dwellings, indicates their role also as talismans or amulets protecting the living.

Finally, we shall turn now to Israel in the period of the Judges and in the times of the Monarchy to see whether the female plaque-figurines were accepted there.

The images of women, standing upright and bearing symbols of Canaanite religion, so common in the Late Bronze Age, are not encountered among the finds of the Early Iron Age, the period of the Judges; they seem to have been discontinued from the era of the Israelite conquest on. In contrast, the figurines of women lying on beds, devoid of any symbols, continue into the closing centuries of the second millennium into the Early Iron Age. An 11th-century plaque-figurine found in the excavations at Tel Zeror is one example;[29] A group of Early Iron Age plaque-figurines found at Tell Beit-Mirsim prompted W. F. Albright[30] to engage in a lengthy discussion on the identity of these figurines. He designated the Late Bronze Age female figure, with arms hanging by her sides, as a *dea nuda* and pointed out that the female plaque figurines of that period were "all of religious or magical character" and "representations of known images of the Syrian goddess."

When discussing the Early Iron Age figurines of Stratum B, he concluded that they depict a naked woman in process of accouchement and that "it is most unlikely that our figure represents the *dea Syria* in any of her aspects, since there is an entire absence of any cult symbolism." In keeping with the stylistic criteria we have set out in our analysis, we must rather point out the similarity of these Early Iron Age plaque-figurines to those of the Late Bronze Age. There is considerable degree of crudeness and deterioration but certainly no major change in style, no inclusion or omittance of divine attributes.

It is still impossible to determine on stratigraphic grounds how long these figurines persisted. Like several groups of small metal sculptures,[31]

---

[28]Cf. H. G. May, *Material Remains of the Megiddo Cult* (Chicago, 1935) 31.

[29]See above, n. 16, pl. XLVII, 3.

[30]*Archaeology of Palestine and the Bible* (New York, 1932-33) 109.

[31]O. Negbi, "The Continuity of the Canaanite Bronze Work of the Late Bronze Age into Early Iron Age," *Tel Aviv* 1 (1974) 159-72.

they seem to have been a remnant of Canaanite tradition, still present in the early strata of the Iron Age and subsequently discontinued. Plaque-figurines are generally absent from Iron Age II sites in Judah in the period of the United Monarchy and later. The hundreds of Iron Age tombs excavated in Judean sites produced no plaque-figurines. They contained numerous pottery vessels and some metal objects, but no plaque-figurines, in fact, hardly any object from the realm of representational art.

In the Northern Israel the situation seems to have been somewhat different. Occurences of several plaque-figurines at Hazor and in sites like Megiddo, Beth-Shean, Tell el-Farᶜah (N) or Taanach,[32] indicate that this genre continued to exist, if only sporadically, in the North, also in the time of the Monarchy. The imagery is somewhat different now: the figurines depict mostly a woman holding a round object over her breast, a theme common in the Phoenician repertoire. The geographic distribution also suggests Phoenician influence: the figurines are attested mostly in sites where Phoenician influence would most strongly be expected.

The later occurrences of plaque-figurines in sites like Ashdod or the temple at Makmish[33] (of the Persian Period), must be viewed in the context of the spread of the Greco-Phoenician art which was noted above. Likewise, the "Pillar Astarte" figurines, which appear towards the end of the Monarchy, can in no way be regarded as direct descendants of our plaque-figurines in Judah. Stylistically they belong to the category of sculpture in the round. Appearing after a lapse of several centuries, they were rather a throwback to the Phoenician figurines common at that time and further proof of the spread of Phoenician styles in Judah in the last centuries before the destruction.

In conclusion, we have discussed the plaque-figurines in the period of their *floruit* in the Canaanite society of the Late Bronze Age and divided this category of small sculptures into two distinct groups. By stylistic comparison with contemporary statuettes, recently found at Deir el-Balaḥ, we have interpreted one group as depicting women lying on beds, possibly to be included in the realm of objects with funerary connotations. The fact that these plaque-figurines ceased to be produced in the time of the United Monarchy[34]—the Davidic-Solomonic period—seems to be of considerable

---

[32] Y. Yadin et al., *Hazor* 2 (Jerusalem, 1960) pl. CXCV:7, 8, pl. 103:1, 2; H. G. May, *Material Remains of the Megiddo Cult* (Chicago, 1935) 31, pls. XXVII-XXXI; A. Rowe, *The Four Canaanite Temples of Beth-Shan* (London, 1940) pl. 35:19, 26; R. de Vaux, "Les Fouilles de Tell el-Farᶜah près Naplouse," *RB* 64 (1957) 579, pl. XI:1-4; P. W. Lapp, "The 1963 Excavations at Taᶜannek," *BASOR* 173 (1964) 39-41; A. M. Bisi, "Les Déesse au Tympenon de la Mesopotamie à Carthage," *Assyriological Miscellanies* 1 (Copenhagen, 1980) 57-78.

[33] M. Dothan, "Ashdod II-III," ᶜ*Atiqot* 9-10 (1971) 128; for Makmish, see above, n. 14. The figurines of Makmish are made by hollow casting, not by pressing a lump of clay into an open mold.

[34] Cf. Albright's statement in discussing the figurines of Stratum A: "Astarte Plaques and Figurines from Tell Beit Mirsim," *Mèlanges Syriens* 120.

significance, possibly reflecting a change in mortuary beliefs, which from that time on became dissociated from the earlier Canaanite traditions.[35]

[35]I am fully aware that the conclusions of this study, rooted in the disciplines of archaeology and art history, bear upon the questions of religious beliefs and practices of the Canaanites as well as those of the Israelites. It is hoped that an inquiry into these complex matters, which could not have been dealt with here, will be undertaken in the future. I am grateful to Prof. F. M. Cross for having read the manuscript and for his valuable comments. A short study on the Late Bronze Canaanite plaque figurines has been published in the Aharoni volume, *Eretz Israel* 15 (Jerusalem, 1981) 79-84 (Hebrew).

Solomon's Succession to the Throne of David—A Political Analysis

Tomoo Ishida
University of Tsukuba, Japan

Recent studies have raised a question about a longstanding thesis of Leonhard Rost concerning the "Succession Narrative," the core of which comprises 2 Samuel 9-20 and 1 Kings 1-2.[1] As a result, the consensus on the unity, boundaries, purpose, date, and literary genre of the narrative, which had been once established among the majority of scholars, has been lost again.[2] Some scholars have discarded even the very name "Succession Narrative" for the literary complex.[3]

I am of the opinion, however, that the thesis of Rost is still valid as a working hypothesis. I regard this literary complex, without discussing its

---

[1] L. Rost, "Die Überlieferung von der Thronnachfolge Davids" (1926) *Das kleine Credo und andere Studien zum Alten Testament* (Heidelberg, 1965) 119-253. Despite criticisms, the thesis of Rost is still held by many scholars as a working hypothesis, e.g., R. N. Whybray, *The Succession Narrative: A Study of II Sam. 9-20 and I Kings 1 and 2* (SBT 2/9, 1968); G. Fohrer, *Introduction to the Old Testament* (London, 1970) 222; J. A. Soggin, *Introduction to the Old Testament* (London, 1976) 192-93; T. N. D. Mettinger, *King and Messiah: The Civil and Sacral Legitimation of the Israelite Kings* (CB OTS 8, 1976) 27-32; J. Gray, *I & II Kings* (3d ed.; London, 1977) 14-22.

[2] Critical opinions on the thesis of Rost are given from the various points of view in the following studies: R. A. Carlson, *David, the Chosen King: A Traditio-Historical Approach to the Second Book of Samuel* (Stockholm, 1964); J. Blenkinsopp, "Theme and Motif in the Succession History (2 Sam XI 2ff.) and the Yahwist Corpus," *Volume du Congrès, Genève, 1965* (VTSup 15, 1966) 44-57; L. Delekat, "Tendenz und Theologie der David-Salomo-Erzählung," *Das ferne und nahe Wort, Festschrift L. Rost* (BZAW 105, 1967) 26-36; H. Schulte, *Die Entstehung der Geschichtsschreibung im alten Israel* (BZAW 128, 1972) 138-80; J. W. Flanagan, "Court History or Succession Document? A Study of 2 Samuel 9-20 and 1 Kings 1-2," *JBL* 91 (1972) 172-81; E. Würthwein, *Die Erzählung von der Thronfolge Davids. Theologische oder politische Geschichtsschreibung?* (Theologische Studien 115, 1974); idem, *Das Erste Buch der Könige, Kapitel 1-16* (ATD 11/1, 1977) 1-28; T. Veijola, *Die ewige Dynastie: David und die Entstehung seiner Dynastie nach der deuteronomistischen Darstellung* (Helsinki, 1975); F. Langlamet, "Review of Würthwein (1974) and Veijola (1975)," *RB* 83 (1976) 114-37; idem, "Pour ou contre Salomon? La rédaction prosalomonienne de I Rois, I-II," *RB* 83 (1976) 321-79, 481-528; idem, "Absalom et les concubines de son père. Recherches sur II Sam., XVI. 21-22," *RB* 84 (1977) 161-209; D. M. Gunn, *The Story of King David. Genre and Interpretation* (JSOT SupS 6, 1978).

[3] E.g., "die David-Geschichten" (Schulte), "the Court History of David" (Flanagan), "the Story of King David" (Gunn).

exact boundaries for the present, as a narrative composed with the definite
purpose of defending the legitimacy of Solomon's kingship. It is not the
purpose of the present paper to argue for the thesis by a re-examination of
the literary-critical or redaction-critical problems. I fully recognize these
problems as being important, but I also have a feeling that a rehashing of
the argument without employing a new approach is liable to prove endless.
In view of this, I will attempt in the present paper to limit myself to making
a political analysis of the structure of the power struggle in the narrative.
Whatever genres it may belong to, it is difficult to deny that the theme of
the narrative is highly political in one sense or another.[4] Accordingly, if a
political analysis of the narrative shows a coherent outline, it seems
possible to conclude that the narrative as a whole was composed from a
certain political standpoint.

I

I will begin with an analysis of the political situation in the last days of
David, as described in 1 Kings 1-2. The narrative tells us that, at that time,
the leading courtiers were divided into two parties revolving about the two
rival candidates for the royal throne: Adonijah the son of Haggith and
Solomon the son of Bathsheba. The former was supported by Joab,
commander-in-chief of the army, and Abiathar the priest, while the latter
was backed by Zadok the priest, Nathan the prophet, Benaiah, the leader
of the royal bodyguard called the "Cherethites and the Pelethites," and
David's heroes (1:7-8, 10; cf. 1:19, 25-26, 32, 38, 44; 2:22, 28).[5]

What was the root cause of the antagonism between the two parties?
Some scholars have suggested that it was a conflict between Yahwism
and the Jebusite-Canaanite religion, represented by Abiathar and Zadok
respectively.[6] It is not easy to accept this view, however, since there is no
clear evidence for the Jebusite origin of Solomon's supporters. As is well
known, Zadok's origins have been a vexing question, but, so far as I know,
arguments for his Jebusite origin rely solely on indirect or circumstantial
evidence.[7] Even if he had been a Jebusite priest, it seems misleading to

---

[4]Gunn (*The Story of King David*, 21) maintains that "if there is clearly an area in which the
author has little interest (or knowledge?) it is that of the political undercurrents of the reign."
But, at the same time, he (ibid., 89) defines the story "as one of accession, rebellion and
succession." Are these themes not political?

[5]In addition, "Shimei and Rei" are found among Solomon's supporters (1 Kgs 1:8).
However, we do not know exactly who or what they were. Since no mention is made about
them elsewhere, we cannot assume anything about their roles in the struggle for the throne of
David; for various conjectural readings see M. Noth, *Könige* 1 (BKAT 9/1, 1968) 16-17; Gray,
I & II Kings, 79.

[6]G. W. Ahlström, "Der Prophet Nathan und der Tempelbau," *VT* 11 (1961) 113-27.

[7]For a summary of various views of Zadok's Jebusite and other origins, see A. Cody, *A
History of Old Testament Priesthood* (AnBib 35, 1969) 88-93; the Jebusite hypothesis was
defended most recently by A. Tsukimoto, "Der Mensch ist geworden wie unsereiner," *AJBI* 5
(1979) 29-31.

consider him the leader of Solomon's party. The fact that Abiathar, the rival of Zadok, was not put to death but just banished from Jerusalem after the establishment of Solomon's kingship would seem to show that both the priests played rather a secondary role in the struggle for the throne of David from the political point of view. On the contrary, Nathan must be regarded as the ideologue of Solomon's party. I will deal with this problem at the end of the paper. Although no information is available at all about his provenance, there is no reason to doubt that Nathan was a prophet of Yahweh.

It is clear that Uriah the Hittite, Bathsheba's former husband, was a foreigner, but I am sceptical about the view that he was of Jebusite stock.[8] In any case, Bathsheba herself seems to have been the daughter of Eliam, the son of Ahithophel of Gilo (2 Sam 11:3; 23:34) in the mountains of Judah (Josh 15:51). By contrast, we are well informed about the origins of Benaiah and David's heroes. Benaiah came from Kabzeel, or Jekabzeel, one of the towns of Judah in the Negev (2 Sam 23:20; cf. Josh 15:21; 1 Chr 11:22; Neh 11:25), and David's heroes were mostly from Judah and Benjamin, though some of them were from the mountains of Ephraim, on the east side of the Jordan, or some foreign countries (2 Sam 23:8-39; 1 Chr 11:10-47).[9] As these data show, Solomon's supporters were mixed in their provenance and ethnic origins, but the Judahites and Israelites clearly accounted for the great majority of them. Therefore, I can hardly assume that they were adherents of the Jebusite-Canaanite religion.

It has been observed that Adonijah and his supporters were men who had held positions at the court already in the days of David's reign at Hebron, whereas the members of Solomon's party appeared for the first time after David transferred his capital from Hebron to Jerusalem.[10] It is interesting to note that members of these rival parties were opposed to each other in contesting for the same positions, i.e., Adonijah vs. Solomon for the royal throne, Haggith vs. Bathsheba as the mother of the heir apparent, Abiathar vs. Zadok as the chief priest, and Joab vs. Benaiah as the commander of the army. Judging from the fact that Solomon replaced Joab by Benaiah as the commander of the army, and Abiathar by Zadok as the chief priest, after the purge of his opponents (1 Kgs 2:35), it is legitimate to assume that both Benaiah and Zadok were upstarts. The conflict seems to have been caused by the newcomers' challenge to the old authority.

An exception to the above analysis is presented by David's heroes. They were, for the most part, soldiers who had followed David since the

---

[8] Against B. Maisler (Mazar), "The Scribe of King David and the Problem of the High Officials in the Ancient Kingdom of Israel" (1946-47) *Canaan and Israel* (Jerusalem, 1974) 210 (Hebrew). I can hardly accept the view that the Jebusites are to be regarded as a branch of the Hittites; see T. Ishida, "The Structure and Historical Implications of the Lists of Pre-Israelite Nations," *Bib* 60 (1979) 461-90.

[9] Cf. B. Mazar, "The Military Élite of King David," *VT* 13 (1963) 310-20.

[10] See T. Ishida, *The Royal Dynasties in Ancient Israel* (BZAW 142, 1977) 157-58.

days of his wandering in the wilderness (1 Sam 22:1-2; 1 Chr 12:8, 16), like Joab and Abiathar, or the days of his staying at Ziklag (1 Chr 12:1, 20). Nevertheless, they did not join Adonijah's party together with Joab and Abiathar but took sides with Solomon. Although the reason for their associating themselves with Solomon's party is not stated explicitly, it is possible to assume that animosity towards Joab had been growing among them, as their importance had been diminishing with the establishment of the national army under Joab.[11]

There is reason to believe that the rivalry between Joab and Benaiah originated with the situation in which the latter was appointed to be leader of the royal bodyguard (2 Sam 23:23). Although Benaiah is mentioned as "over the Cherethites and the Pelethites" in the first list of David's high officials (8:18), I am inclined to assume that his appointment was actually made some time after Sheba's revolt. Otherwise, it is extremely difficult to explain the reason for his absence at the time of both Absalom's and Sheba's revolts, in both of which the Cherethites and the Pelethites served as foreign mercenaries loyal to David (15:18; 20:7). The leaders of David's army at the time of Absalom's rebellion were Joab, Abishai, and Ittai (18:1, 12), and those during Sheba's revolt were Joab and Abishai (20:6-7, 10b). It is clear that Joab and Abishai, the sons of Zeruiah, held the first and second places, respectively, in the hierarchy of David's army after Sheba's revolt had been suppressed. Oddly enough, however, while Joab regained the position of commander-in-chief of the army, Abishai disappeared from the scene forever. Instead, Benaiah ranked next to Joab as the leader of the Cherethites and the Pelethites (20:23b). Owing to lack of information, we do not know anything certain about Abishai's final fate. It is unlikely, however, that Abishai, the commander of David's heroes (23:19), was opposed to Joab, his brother, in the struggle for the throne of David, since he had always served David as Joab's right-hand man from the days of the cave of Adullam up to Sheba's revolt. Perhaps, Abishai died a natural death after Sheba's revolt, and in his place Benaiah became a military leader, sharing with Joab the exercise of power in the kingdom. It is not difficult to imagine that Joab felt uneasy about Benaiah from the beginning. Probably, Benaiah's appointment was backed by a circle which was interested in checking the growing power of Joab at the court. I will deal with this assumption later.

In the narrative, Nathan says to Bathsheba: "Have you heard that Adonijah the son of Haggith has become king?" (1 Kgs 1:11; cf. 1:13, 24-25), and Bathsheba to David: "And now, behold, Adonijah is king" (1:18). Despite these words, it is fairly evident that Adonijah had no intention to raise the standard of a *coup d'état* at the feast at En Rogel (1:9). As David was near death (1:1-4), and Adonijah was expected to become David's successor by everybody but Solomon's supporters (2:15,

---

[11]Cf. Mazar, *VT* 13 (1963) 320.

22), he had no reason to be in a hurry to usurp the throne. Moreover, it seems that David himself had given Adonijah his tacit approval (cf. 1:16).[12] Therefore, the feast which Adonijah gave at En Rogel was nothing but another demonstration of his intention to be king as the legitimate successor to David, just as was his preparation of "chariots and horsemen, and fifty men to run before him" (1:5).

Under these circumstances, it is more conceivable that Nathan fabricated a *coup d'état* on the part of Adonijah to furnish a pretext for extracting from David the designation of Solomon as his successor. At the same time, by taking advantage of the dotage of David, Nathan succeeded in inducing him to believe that he had once pledged himself to designate Solomon as his successor (1:13, 17, 30; cf. 1:24). When Bathsheba says: "And now, my lord the king, the eyes of all Israel are upon you, to tell them who shall sit on the throne of my lord the king after him" (1:20), and Nathan adds: "You have not told your servants who should sit on the throne of my lord the king after him" (1:27), their words betray that David's pledge to Solomon was a fabrication. Evidently, there was neither pledge nor designation, but the indecision of a senile king who was vaguely expecting that the eldest son would be designated as his successor. If Solomon's supporters had stood idle, Adonijah would have been king. The narrative clearly tells us that the one who changed the current was not Adonijah but Solomon. In other words, Solomon gained his designation as David's successor by challenging the existing order supported by the regime, whose nominal ruler was doting David, and whose strong-man was Joab, commander-in-chief of the army.

II

Royal lineage and divine election served as the fundamental principles for the legitimation of kingship in the ancient Near East, including Israel.[13] Both principles can be found also in the narrative in 1 Kings 1-2 for legitimizing the kingship of Solomon. It is striking, however, that the fact that Solomon sat upon the throne of David is repeatedly told by either the narrator (2:12), Solomon himself (2:24; cf. 2:33, 45) or David (1:30, 35, 48; cf. 1:13, 17; 2:4), while the divine approval of Solomon's kingship is mentioned just a few times in an indirect way, i.e., in a prayer of Benaiah (1:36-37; cf. 1:47) and confirmation by David (1:48) and Adonijah (2:15). This phenomenon has nothing to do with the so-called non-charismatic character of Solomon's kingship.[14] The divine legitimation of his kingship

---

[12]Cf. Gray, *I & II Kings*, 81.

[13]See Ishida, *The Royal Dynasties in Ancient Israel*, 6-25.

[14]Against A. Alt, "Die Staatenbildung der Israeliten in Palästina" (1930) *Kleine Schriften* 2 (München, 1953) 61-62 = "The Formation of the Israelite State in Palestine," *Essays on Old Testament History and Religion* (Oxford, 1966) 233; idem, "Das Königtum in den Reichen Israel und Juda" (1951) *Kleine Schriften* 2, 120-21 = "The Monarchy in the Kingdom of Israel and Judah," *Essays*, 245; cf. also J. Bright, *A History of Israel* (2d ed.; London, 1972) 206.

is dealt with in 1 Kings 3. In this narrative, the emphasis on the throne of David on which Solomon sat derived from certain problems with which our narrator was concerned.

Undoubtedly, our narrator knew that Solomon had actually usurped the throne of David by a court intrigue, though he described it with ingenious obscurity. However, I can hardly agree with the view that he composed the narrative with the intention of denouncing either Solomon or the dynasty of David, let alone monarchy as such.[15] From his point of view, in spite of the intrigue and usurpation, Solomon is the legitimate king. The court intrigue by which Solomon outmaneuvered Adonijah and seized the throne of David reminds us of the story of Jacob in Genesis 27.[16] By exploiting the blindness of his old father, Jacob snatched away the blessing of Isaac, his father, from Esau, his elder brother, with a trick devised by Rebecca, his mother. Although the acts of Jacob and Rebecca were clearly immoral, the narrator, who was interested in Jacob's fate, does not mind telling the story. What he was most concerned with was not a moral judgment on Jacob's acts but the fact that the blessing of Isaac was diverted from Esau to Jacob, the ancestor of the people of Israel. The same spirit seems to be found in the narrative of the court intrigue which set Solomon on the throne. What was important for our narrator was not the process by which Solomon established his kingship but its establishment. Therefore he could insist without embarrassment that it came "from Yahweh" (2:15). This does not mean that he did not care about the defense of the legitimacy of Solomon's kingship. On the contrary, he was very sensitive about it, since when Solomon's kingship was established it had neither popular support nor the consent of the majority of senior officials but only the backing of his faction which consisted of part of the courtiers and professional soldiers. The styles of royal legitimation correspond to the situations in which the kingship is established. If Solomon had been a genuine usurper from another house than the Davidides or an Absalom who had seized the throne of his father by force with popular support, our narrator could have simply underlined the divine election. But the situation was more complicated. Solomon gained designation as the successor from his father, but he gained it by a court intrigue. Under these circumstances, the regime of Solomon had to lay emphasis first on the continuity of the dynasty, since the "throne of David" was the sole foundation of his kingship when it was established. At the same time, it was necessary to legitimize the drastic measure which Solomon's supporters took to secure the kingship for him, for Solomon became king contrary to general expectation (cf. 2:15).

---

[15]Against Delekat, "Tendenz und Theologie der David-Salomo-Erzählung," 26-36; Würthwein, *Die Erzählung von der Thronfolge Davids*; Langlamet, *RB* 83 (1976) 321-79, 481-528.

[16]Cf. Mettinger, *King and Messiah*, 29; H. Hagan, "Deception as Motif and Theme in 2 Sm 9-20; 1 Kgs 1-2," *Bib* 60 (1979) 302.

In my opinion, these two elements of the Solomonic legitimation are blended in the words of congratulation offered by Benaiah (1:37) and David's servants (1:47): "May your God make the name of Solomon more famous than yours, and make his throne greater than your throne." I have tried to explain these words elsewhere as a blessing to David, symbolizing a dynastic growth.[17] This interpretation seems correct but insufficient. I am now inclining to think that these words imply not only the growth of the Davidic dynasty but also a real wish on the part of Solomon's supporters that the name and throne of Solomon should literally become superior to those of David. This wish originated in their judgment that the regime of David had long been deteriorating and had to be taken over by Solomon, even though this meant resorting to a court intrigue, in order to establish the dynasty of David in the true sense.

III

It has been noted that the figure of David as described in the Succession Narrative presents a striking contrast to that in the History of David's Rise.[18] In the latter, he is described as a blessed person chosen by Yahweh as king, while David in the former is an object of scandal and a man of indecision and finally a dotard. Scholars have puzzled over the intention of the narrator of the Succession Narrative who persistently discloses the weak points of David and his decadence. The answers propounded to the question differ mainly according to the way the critics define the purpose of the narrative. From my viewpoint of finding a Solomonic legitimation in it, I am convinced that the purpose of the description of David's shortcomings in the Succession Narrative can be elucidated solely from the political standpoint of those with a critical attitude towards the regime of David, who assisted Solomon in establishing his kingship.

It is important to note that the criticism is leveled against David not as a private person but as a king.[19] For instance, David is described with much sympathy when he, as a father, weeps over the death of his rebellious son (2 Sam 19:1 = EB 18:33). But, what the narrator intends to show by this moving description is that David is disqualified from being king in the sense of a military leader, as Joab's remonstrance indicates (19:6-8 = EB 19:5-7). This is a typical example of a description of David's disqualification to be king, in which Joab's influence over the regime increases in inverse proportion to the decline of David's control over the kingship. I am

---

[17]Ishida, *The Royal Dynasties in Ancient Israel*, 105-106.

[18]According to Carlson (*David, the Chosen King*), in 2 Samuel 2-7 David is described as a person under the blessing, while in 2 Samuel 9-24 he is described as a man under the curse.

[19]K. R. R. Gros Louis ("The Difficulty of Ruling Well: King David of Israel," *Semeia* 8 [1977] 15-33) finds in the narrative many conflicts between David's personal desires and his public obligations as king.

of the opinion that the key to understanding the purpose of the narrator of the Succession Narrative lies in this interrelation between David and Joab.[20]

When the people of Israel demanded that Samuel install a king over them, they expected the king to be שׁופט (i.e., the ruler and supreme judge) as well as the war-leader of the kingdom (1 Sam 8:20; cf. 8:5; 12:12; Ps 72). These two functions were regarded as the fundamental duties of a king in the ancient Near East.[21] David, while he was still competent to perform the task of being ruler and supreme judge of the kingdom, is mentioned in the first list of his high officials as follows: "So David reigned over all Israel; and David administered justice and equity to all his people" (2 Sam 8:15). By contrast, he puts on a very poor performance or gets just failing marks for this duty in the Succession Narrative.

David betrayed the people's confidence in him as a just judge by his adultery with Bathsheba and his murder of Uriah the Hittite, her husband, to cover up his crime (11:2-27). It was Joab who first learned the secret from David (11:14-21). We do not know how the affair came to Nathan's knowledge. It is possible to assume that, by informing Nathan of the fact, Joab vindicated himself in the matter of Uriah's death in battle. In the disclosure of the affair through Nathan's prophetic reproach (12:7-15), David was disgraced, but Joab escaped from having his reputation ruined as the commander of the army.

No action was taken by David as a judge concerning Amnon's rape of Tamar. "When King David heard of all these things, he was very angry; but he did nothing to harm Amnon, his son, for he loved him, because he was his firstborn" (13:21, LXX). This unjust treatment of the affair caused Absalom, Tamar's brother, to kill Amnon in revenge. This time David once again did nothing but weep with his sons and all his servants (13:36). Moreover, in the stories of Amnon's rape of Tamar and Absalom's revenge on Amnon, by stupidly granting the respective requests of Amnon and Absalom without penetrating into their hearts (13:6-7, 26-27; cf. 15:7-9), David indirectly helped them to realize their evil designs. These mistakes also call into question his competence as a wise ruler.

Though David wanted to pardon Absalom, he hesitated to take any initiative towards healing the breach between himself and Absalom. In the meantime, Joab took an active hand in the problem by sending a woman of Tekoa to David. We are not explicitly told the reason for Joab's intervention. But the conversation between David and the woman from

---

[20]Schulte (*Die Entstehung der Geschichtsschreibung*, 141-43) has pointed out that Joab dominates the narrative from the beginning to the end.

[21]See H. Frankfort, *Kingship and the Gods* (Chicago, 1948) 51-60; T. Jacobsen, "Early Political Development in Mesopotamia" (1957) *Toward the Image of Tammuz and Other Essays on Mesopotamian History and Culture* (ed. W. L. Moran; Harvard Semitic Series 21, 1970) 154; idem, "Ancient Mesopotamian Religion: The Central Concerns" (1963) *Toward the Image of Tammuz*, 43.

Tekoa indicates that Joab was concerned about the problem of the royal succession. Since Absalom was the first candidate for the throne at that time, we can assume that Joab also expected Absalom to become king in the future. It is quite possible, therefore, that by mediating a settlement between David and Absalom, Joab wanted to place Absalom under an obligation to himself and to exert influence on him when he should become king. However, contrary to his expectation, Absalom kept aloof from Joab (cf. 1 Kgs 2:28b), and appointed Amasa commander of the army instead of Joab (2 Sam 17:25). Absalom undoubtedly felt much more at ease with Amasa than with Joab, since the former was much less brilliant than the latter (cf. 20:4-5). But, this appointment proved fatal to Absalom. He was not only defeated at the battle in the forest of Ephraim (18:6-8) but also killed by Joab (18:9-15), who was a man of vengeful character (cf. 3:27). In any case, as the woman from Tekoa told David, "in order to change the course of affairs," Joab intervened in the problem and succeeded in reconciling David with Absalom (14:33). The fact that the course of events was determined not by David but by Joab testifies to the existence of a situation in which David was not active enough to exercise the office of ruler, while Joab actually conducted the affairs of state.

According to the Succession Narrative, the direct cause of Absalom's rebellion was David's negligence in his duty as the supreme judge of the kingdom. Absalom said to any person who "had a suit to come before the king for judgment. . . . See, your claims are good and right; but there is no man deputed by the king to hear you. . . . Oh that I were judge in the land! Then every man with a suit or cause might come to me, and I would give him justice" (15:2-4). By these words, "Absalom stole the hearts of the men of Israel" (15:6), and succeeded in rising in revolt with them against the regime of David. Then, the people dethroned David and elevated Absalom to the position of king (cf. 15:10, 19:10-11 = EB 19:9-10). This episode is one of the clearest pieces of evidence for David's disqualification for the office of ruler.

Simply because of Absalom's death, David was restored to the throne, contrary to the people's original intention (cf. 19:23 = EB 19:22). David tried to save a difficult situation after the rebellion but eventually sowed the seeds of new trouble. Resenting David's one-sided dealing with the tribe of Judah (19:42-44 = EB 19:41-43), the northern tribes decided to dissolve their covenant with David, according to which he had reigned over them (5:1-3), by the instigation of Sheba, the son of Bichri (20:1-2). By calling Sheba "a worthless fellow" (20:1), the narrator shows his pro-Davidic stance, but he does not hesitate to tell about David's mismanagement of the affair. After Absalom's defeat, David appointed Amasa commander of the army in place of Joab (19:14 = EB 19:13). Although this change was made to appease the people of Judah who had taken part in Absalom's rebellion,[22]

---

[22] Although there are some scholars who maintain that Judah was not involved in the

it was clearly an unjust action, for Amasa had served as the commander of
the rebel army, while Joab had rendered the most distinguished service to
David in suppressing the rebellion, though he had killed Absalom in
disobedience to David's order. To make matters worse, Amasa was an
incompetent commander. He was not able to call up the people of Judah in
time to quell Sheba's revolt. David was obliged to ask Abishai and his
soldiers, among whom Joab was included, to deal with the trouble. While
going on an expedition against Sheba, Joab assassinated Amasa and seized
command of the expeditionary force. When Joab returned triumphant
from the campaign, David was compelled to restore him to the command
of the army. The unmistakable message of the story is that David was only
a nominal ruler, and Joab had become the strong-man holding sway over
the kingdom.

Also in the performance of his duty as the war-leader of the kingdom,
David in the Succession Narrative is a thoroughly incompetent person.
During the Ammonite war David committed adultery with Bathsheba. His
behaviour is described in sharp contrast to that of Uriah the Hittite, who
refused to go down to his house because of his strict self-control (11:11). It
is clear that the story implicitly accuses David of negligence in his duty as
the war-leader by his adultery with Bathsheba and murder of Uriah during
the war.[23] Moreover, Joab's urging to David to capture the city of Rabbath
Ammon himself, "lest I take the city, and it be called by my name" (12:28),
shows that the war was virtually conducted by Joab under the nominal
supervision of David.

In the battle against Absalom, David first tried to assume his responsibility as war-leader by mustering the men who were with him (18:1). But
being dissuaded by the people from going out with them, he easily
conceded and said to them: "Whatever seems best to you I will do" (18:4).
These words are nothing but a dereliction of his duty as war-leader. In
addition, he could not restrain himself from giving such an order, improper
to troops going to the front, as to deal gently with Absalom, the leader of
the enemy (18:5). Judging from the consequences, it is likely that Joab
prevented David from going into battle. David's leniency towards Absalom
must have been an obstacle to Joab, who had determined to eliminate
Absalom, most probably since Absalom had appointed Amasa commander
of the army instead of Joab. He ignored David's command and killed
Absalom. As for the story of David as a father in a frenzy of grief at the
death of his rebellious son, I have already dealt with the narrator's
intention. In fact, no one can deny that the episode tells us that the real
commander in the battle against Absalom was not David but Joab.

---

rebellion, we can hardly explain the situation by that assumption; see Ishida, *The Royal
Dynasties in Ancient Israel*, 69-70, n. 61.

[23]It is probable that Uriah kept continence in accordance with the obligations of cleanliness
which the holy war imposed on him, see R. de Vaux, *Ancient Israel* (London, 1961) 258-59,
263.

In the campaign against Sheba the son of Bichri, Joab murdered Amasa, the commander of the army appointed by David, and usurped the position of commander of the expeditionary force. So, David could not help giving his consent to Joab's self-appointment as commander of the army. As I have suggested above, if Benaiah was appointed commander of the royal bodyguard at the same time, this appointment was made, most probably, with the intention of counterbalancing Joab's growing power. Those who were loyal to the dynasty of David must have been alarmed at Joab's self-appointment as commander of the army and David's impotent rule. In any case, there is no reason to doubt that Joab was then at the zenith of his power. It cannot be an accident that David as the ruler of the land is omitted from the second list of his high officials (20:23-26), which is placed immediately after the story of Joab's victorious campaign against Sheba. There are three such lists; two of David's high officials and one of Solomon's. Except for the second list of David's, either David or Solomon is mentioned at the top of the list as the ruler reigning over all Israel (2 Sam 8:15 = 1 Chr 18:14; 1 Kgs 4:1).[24] Accordingly, we may assume that by omitting David's name from it, the second list of David's high officials tells us, though implicitly, that the *de facto* ruler was then Joab, who ranked at the top of the list (2 Sam 20:23a).

IV

The episode concerning Abishag the Shunamite (1 Kgs 1:1-4) tells us that David had lost his physical strength, especially his virility, in his last days. This story adds another proof of his disqualification as king.[25] However, in the present context, it rather serves as an introduction to the narrative of the intrigue, by which Solomon gained David's designation as his successor. Although the narrator was concerned with the problem of succession, he took care not to mention it explicitly. In this way, he skillfully provided a reason for the intrigue. According to his analysis, the *de facto* ruler of the regime was Joab; accordingly, if Joab had succeeded in making Adonijah king, the latter would have been the former's puppet, just like Eshbaal, who was placed on the throne of Abner, the commander of Saul's army (2 Sam 2:8-9). In his opinion, this was the sort of usurpation to be prevented. However, David became not only too senile to bring the ambitions of Joab and Adonijah under his control but also to decide upon his successor by himself. Under these circumstances, it was legitimate, so asserts the narrator, to take all possible steps to interfere with the plan of Joab and Adonijah. This was the reason for the intrigue by which Solomon's supporters secured his designation as the heir apparent by turning the tables on Adonijah's party at the last moment.

---

[24]Mettinger, (*Solomonic State Officials* [CB OTS 5, 1971] 7, n. 4) regards 2 Sam 8:15 as editorial. He seems right from the stylistic point of view. However, I cannot but find in this verse an intentional addition of the author of the narrative to the original list.

[25]See Gray, *I & II Kings*, 77.

Some scholars have argued that the story of Solomon's purge of his opponents (1 Kgs 2:13-46) must be regarded as anti-Solomonic.[26] The argument seems to miss the point. Though gaining the upper hand, Solomon could not eliminate his opponents immediately after his accession. This fact shows that Solomon's rule was still shaky at first. In other words, Joab continued to have influence with the courtiers and the people. However, since the aim of Solomon's *coup d'état* was to remove Joab's influence over the regime, Solomon had to get rid of Joab by any possible means. Therefore, exploiting Adonijah's request for the hand of Abishag as a sign of a conspiracy,[27] on this pretext Solomon ordered Benaiah to execute Adonijah and Joab. The charge of the murder of Abner and Amasa brought against Joab, and the declaration of the removal of the guilt of the blood which Joab shed from Solomon's regime and the dynasty of David (2:31-33), finally make it clear that the target of Solomon's party was Joab's downfall.

Solomon restricted himself to banishing Abiathar the priest from Jerusalem to Anathoth, his home village. This fact indicates that Abiathar did not play a significant role in the struggle for the throne from the political point of view. By contrast, Shimei was to be put to death, on any pretext, in order to establish firmly the dynasty of David. Ever since David had taken over Saul's kingship, the house of Saul had continued to lay claim to the kingship even after David had become the king of Israel. Ziba's words about Meribbaal's expectation of the restoration of Saul's kingship (2 Sam 16:3), Shimei's curse on David (16:5-8) and Sheba's revolt (20:1-2) show that David had not succeeded in silencing that claim by the end of his reign. By the execution of Shimei, Solomon demonstrated that this latent claim of Saul's house to the kingship was rejected for good. The execution of Shimei, together with that of Joab, must be regarded not as a token of Solomon's coldblooded character but as one of his political achievements in a matter which David had left unfinished.

V

I have no intention to deal in detail in this paper with the questions of the boundaries, date, and author of the Succession Narrative. It seems necessary, however, to make some provisional remarks about these questions in order to complete my analysis. Since the relationship between David and Joab and the way of dealing with the claim of Saul's house to the kingship may be regarded as the main and second themes, respectively, the story of the beginning of David's kingdom of Judah, established by

---

[26]Delekat, "Tendenz und Theologie der David-Salomo-Erzählung," 27; Noth, *Könige* 1, 32-41; Würthwein, *Die Erzählung von der Thronfolge Davids*, 11-17; idem, *Das Erste Buch der Könige*, 21-27; Langlamet, *RB* 83 (1976) 330-37.

[27]For monarchical legitimacy by the acquisition of the previous king's harem, see Ishida, *The Royal Dynasties in Ancient Israel*, 74.

taking over Saul's kingship, and the conflict between David and Eshbaal, culminating in Joab's assassination of Abner and David's curse on Joab in 2 Samuel 2-3, seems the most suitable beginning to the narrative.[28] By the same reasoning, I am inclined to find the concluding remark in the words: "So the kingdom was established in the hand of Solomon," placed after the execution of Shimei (1 Kgs 2:46b), rather than in the similar words in 1 Kgs 2:12.

The date of composition could not be as late as the second half of Solomon's reign. For the regime of Solomon must have felt it necessary to make this sort of legitimation only in its early years. Besides, the narrator's candid attitude towards the disgraceful conduct of the members of David's house, such as David's adultery, his murder of Uriah or Amnon's rape of Tamar, would also indicate the same early years. It appears that these scandals were still too fresh in the memory of the general public to be concealed, when it was composed.

I am convinced that the author of the Succession Narrative was one of the supporters of Solomon. Judging from Nathan's role as the driving force of Solomon's party in the court intrigue, one of Nathan's followers may be a likely candidate for author. An examination of the roles which Nathan played in the Succession Narrative also confirms that he was the ideologue of the movement for establishing Solomon's regime. Apart from the episode of the court intrigue (1 Kings 1), he appears only twice in the Succession Narrative, viz., in his prophecy about the perpetuation of David's dynasty (2 Sam 7) and in his prophetic verdict on David's sins of adultery and murder (12:1-25). It is important to note that both episodes are directly connected with the claim of Solomon's party that the name and throne of Solomon were superior to those of David. In the prophecy, it is expressed as a prediction about the builder of the Temple: "He shall build a house for my name" (7:13a). This is nothing but a declaration that Solomon did in fact build the Temple which David had failed to build. In the verdict, Solomon loved by Yahweh (12:24-25) presents a striking contrast to David under Yahweh's curse (11:27; 12:10-11). Yahweh's curse brought on by David's adultery with Bathsheba and his murder of Uriah no longer has any unfavourable influence upon Solomon's birth to David and Bathsheba. This was a sin to be redeemed by David himself, involving the life of the first son of David and Bathsheba. From the above I conclude that Nathan was a prophet who, being disappointed in David, placed his hopes in young Solomon to restore the rule of the dynasty of David with justice and equity over the kingdoms of Israel and Judah.[29]

---

[28]Cf. Schulte, *Die Entstehung der Geschichtsschreibung*, 140-41, 165.

[29]It is worth comparing this attitude of Nathan towards David with that of Samuel, who regretted having made Saul king (1 Sam 15:10-35) and that of Ahijah the Shilonite, who predicted the downfall of Jeroboam whom he had helped to the throne (1 Kgs 14:6-16).

A Political Look at the Kingdom of David and Solomon and Its Relations with Egypt

ABRAHAM MALAMAT
The Hebrew University, Jerusalem

I

The kingdom of David and Solomon achieved the status of an intermediate power between Mesopotamia and Anatolia on the north, and Egypt on the south, constituting a prime political and economic factor in Hither Asia.[1] It was a "great" or "major power" in its day, to use terms of modern political science, a highly effective analytical tool (and one which I shall often utilize here) in scanning events of the remote past. Neither before nor after were the Israelites capable of consolidating and maintaining a sovereign entity of such significant strength and size. After Solomon's death, the kingdoms of Judah and Israel were merely "small powers" or "weak states" in the hierarchy of the international system, and their combined strength, even when acting in concert as under Ahab and Jehoshaphat, hardly matched that of the United Monarchy.

Unfortunately, the available source material on David and Solomon is entirely lopsided, and in delving into the unique status of their kingdom and its impact on the Near Eastern scene, we are confronted by a serious methodological drawback. The relative abundance of biblical material is left unsustained, by a total lack of contemporaneous external sources. Yet the possibilities for balanced, controlled research here are thereby drastically curtailed, confined to internal historical evidence. The outstanding and predominant nature of the United Monarchy clearly calls for a

---

[1] For the author's earlier treatments of the policies of David and Solomon, see "Aspects of the Foreign Policies of David and Solomon," *JNES* 22 (1963) 1-17; "The Kingdom of David and Solomon in its Contact with Egypt and Aram Naharaim" (1958) *BAR* 2 (1964) 89-98. On this period in general, see J. Bright, *A History of Israel* (2nd ed.; London, 1972) 190-224; J. A. Soggin, "The Davidic-Solomonic Kingdom," *Israelite and Judaean History* (eds. J. H. Hayes and J. M. Miller; London, 1977) 332-80; B. Mazar, "The Era of David and Solomon," *The Age of the Monarchies: Political History. The World History of the Jewish People* 4/1 (ed. A. Malamat; Jerusalem, 1979) 76-100; D. N. Freedman, "The Age of David and Solomon," *The World History of the Jewish People* 4/1, 101-25; S. Herrmann, *Geschichte Israels* (2nd ed.; München, 1980) 185-233.

broader, far more comprehensive historical perspective than that presented by the biblical canvas. For the Bible is, so to speak, myopic and simply inadequate for a proper grasp of the full significance of David and Solomon's kingdom in its "global" context. Moreover, the reliability of the relevant biblical sources themselves can be questioned: how far do they reflect historical reality and to what extent do they incorporate later literary efforts glorifying David and Solomon.

Nevertheless, the Bible is studded with numerous signposts pointing to the true status of this kingdom on the international scene. Not the least of these is the titulary applied to Solomon, which seems to parallel the Akkadian *šarru rabû*, "imperatore" (to which we shall return later).[2] Typical indicators, besides David's actual extensive military conquests, are scattered throughout the Second Book of Samuel and First Kings (and, of course, the parallel passages in Chronicles), attesting to the contacts maintained by David and especially Solomon with other countries, some of them quite remote. This material would put Israel as an integral factor in the contemporaneous fabric of the ancient Near East, and provide a more adequate picture of this kingdom and its international impact.

Leaving aside the two outstanding points of contact for the moment, Egypt and Syria, what is the evidence of Israel's variegated web of foreign relations?

(1) First of all, the intensive relations between David/Solomon and Hiram, king of Tyre, generated by mutual interests in various spheres.[3]

(2) Solomon's economic ties with the land of Que, in southern Anatolia, from whence he imported horses (1 Kgs 10:28-29).[4]

(3) The expeditions down the Red Sea to Ophir (1 Kgs 9:28; 10:11), and the enigmatic "ships of Tarshish" (1 Kgs 10:22; or, according to the suspect reading in 2 Chr 9:21, "ships travelling to Tarshish"), in this context apparently not to be associated with the western Mediterranean.[5] The apes and baboons (not peacocks!), the "*almug* wood which has not been seen [in Jerusalem] to this day" (1 Kgs 10:11-12), the perfumes and spices from Sheba, the precious stones and the huge quantities of gold, all

---

[2]See below, p. 197.

[3]See, in the present volume, H. Donner, "The Interdependence of Internal Affairs and Foreign Policy during the Davidic-Solomonic Period (with Special Regard to the Phoenician Coast)." See also G. Bunnens, "Commerce et diplomatie phéniciens au temps de Hiram Ier de Tyr," *JESHO* 19 (1976) 1-31.

[4]On this obscure passage in 1 Kgs 10:28-29 see, in the present volume, Y. Ikeda, "Solomon's Trade in Horses and Chariots in its International Setting."

[5]For the biblical Tarshish as a location in the western Mediterranean (most likely Spain), only from the 8th century B.C. on, see e.g., K. Galling, "Der Weg der Phöniker nach Tarsis in literarischer und archäologischer Sicht," *ZDPV* 88 (1972) 1-18, 140-81. For "Tarshish ships" as a particular type of large, sea-going vessel, see below, p. 201. For a recent note on Tarshish, cf. S. B. Hoenig, "Tarshish," *JQR* 69 (1979) 181f.

must have aroused intense amazement among the people of Israel.[6] This was clearly a bolstering of Solomon's prestige, with status symbols imitative of the luxuries and exotica wrested from the four corners of the earth by the monarchs of Egypt and Assyria.

(4) Finally, the intriguing tale of the Queen of Sheba, in southwestern Arabia (1 Kgs 10:1-13).[7] Solomon was impressed by the "gifts" he had received in accord with diplomatic decorum; the Queen for her part was overwhelmed by Solomon's statesmanship and grandeur and largesse. Actually, a strictly political-economic understanding is reflected here, though we can only ponder what Solomon would have had to offer in trade. Logically, it may well have been finished products, in any event, high-value, low-bulk goods of some sort.

These innovative enterprises are clear traits of imperial stature,[8] of a "great power" seeking to expand its political-economic frontiers far beyond its own actual borders. Solomon's role in the international power game was no less potent than that of his predecessor, but it assumed a new dimension. His policies reflect a decided shift of emphasis in foreign affairs from the military sphere to the economic. Entering the realm of long-distance trade, Solomon initiated a north-south political-commercial axis embracing Tyre-Israel-Sheba, with branches across the Mediterranean and Red Seas.

II

Actually, the unprecedented expansion of the United Monarchy, territorial and economic, was a natural outcome of the geo-political situation prevailing at that time. For centuries, the region of Syria and Palestine had been caught between Egyptian ambitions and those of Mitanni and especially, later, the Hittites. In modern political terms, it had been in the clutches of a long-standing "bipolar" power structure. The collapse of this constellation led to a political vacuum in the Syro-Palestinian sphere—till the resurgence of Egypt, toward the end of Solomon's reign, and the rise of Assyria, several decades later. This rare moment of calm, free of all "super-

---

[6]For תכי as "baboon" (supposedly derived from *[t-3] ky[t], rather than the traditional "peacocks", see W. F. Albright, *Archaeology and the Religion of Israel* (2nd ed. Baltimore, 1946) 212, n. 16. For אלגמ/אלגמם trees, cf. A. Malamat, "Campaigns to the Mediterranean by Iahdunlim and Other Early Mesopotamian Rulers," *Studies in Honor of B. Landsberger* (AS 16, 1965) 367-69; J. C. Greenfield and M. Mayrhofer, "The ʾalgummīn/ʾalmuggīm-Problem reexamined," *Hebräische Wortforschung. Festschrift W. Baumgartner* (VTSup 16, 1967) 86-89. For luxury commodities coming from Ophir and Sheba, see now M. Elat, *Economic Relations in the Lands of the Bible* (Jerusalem, 1977) 192-96 (Hebrew).

[7]For the legendary overtones in the Queen of Sheba episode, see J. Gray, *I & II Kings* (2nd ed.: London, 1970) 257ff.; M. Noth, *Könige* 1 (BKAT 9/1, 1968) 223ff.; E. Würthwein, *Das Erste Buch der Könige, Kapitel 1-16* (ATD 11/1, 1977) 119ff. Despite its late literary character, the episode surely reflects the geo-economic reality of a Solomonic context.

[8]Cf. J. Kegler, *Politisches Geschehen und theologisches Verstehen* (Stuttgart, 1977) esp. 212ff.

power" interference, provided a unique opportunity for the one nation in
this region which would most successfully exploit the interlude, and who
would thus gain hegemony over what was normally a buffer region. Of the
nations living between the Nile and the Euphrates and now seeking to
assert themselves were, foremost, Tyre on the coast, Aram in the north,
and Israel to the south. In Machiavellian phraseology, the *occasione* was
there, but who was the ruler possessing the *virtu*?

It was David who ultimately fulfilled this destiny. His deep historical
perception of current trends was combined with a marked capacity for
decision-making—outstanding qualities which enabled him to overcome all
rivalry in the fateful intra-regional struggles. In bringing his national goals
to realization, David was driven by universal motivations which have
steered all great political figures to success: attainment of security, attainment of power, and attainment of glory. Applying what we today would
call a "grand strategy,"[9] David built up an empire by a process both
gradual and fascinating. David's grand strategy reflects decisive planning
and well-defined, specific aims, and a long-range perspective. These dominant traits enable us to perceive five major phases on his path to empire;
they can be likened to five concentric rings in progression: (1) tribal
kingdom; (2) national kingdom; (3) consolidated territorial state; (4) multi-
national state; (5) empire (see figure).

Phase one: Tribal kingdom. Using Hebron as an initial springboard,
David was crowned king over the "House of Judah" with the support of his
seasoned "troop" (Hebrew *gĕdūd*) and probably with Philistine consent.
This early period was exploited intensively in the military sphere—for
instance, for the conquest of Jerusalem,[10] as well as for laying diplomatic
foundations—such as David's marriage to Maacah, daughter of Talmai,
king of Geshur, the future mother of Absalom (2 Sam 3:3). This alliance
with the petty kingdom of Geshur, far to the north in the Gaulan—and
possibly the ties with the kings of Ammon (inferred from 2 Sam 10:2) and
Moab (inferred from 1 Sam 22:34 and, more deviously, 14:47)—enabled
David to outflank the northern tribes of Israel, and thus facilitate achievement of his second phase.

Phase two: National kingdom. The most far-reaching political act to
take place at Hebron was the alliance between David and the northern

---

[9]This concept, elaborated in recent years by political and military analysts, covers economic,
and even psychological, aspects no less than military and political facets. See, e.g., B. H.
Liddell-Hart, *Strategy* (2nd ed.; New York, 1967) 335f. ("the term 'grand strategy' serves to
bring out the sense of 'policy execution'").

[10]B. Mazar, "David's Reign in Hebron and the Conquest of Jerusalem," *In the Time of the
Harvest. Essays in Honor of A. H. Silver* (ed. D. J. Silver; New York, 1963) 235-44, would
place David's capture of Jerusalem at the very beginning of this period, but the shift of the
capital of Israel only much later, in David's eighth regnal year. Cf. also N. L. Tidwell, "The
Philistine Incursions into the Valley of Rephaim" (ed. J. A. Emerton; VTSup 30 [1979])
190-212.

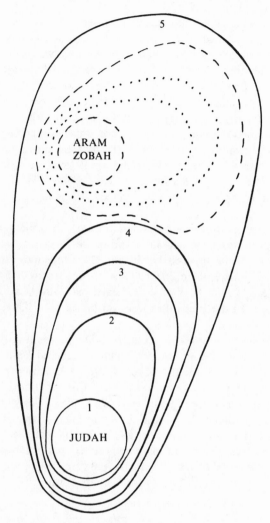

The Growth of the Empire of David and Solomon (schematic). 1. Tribal Kingdom; 2. National Kingdom; 3. Consolidated Territorial State; 4. Multi-National State; 5. Empire.

tribes of Israel. After the abortive negotiations with Abner, but only following the elimination of Eshbaal, Saul's successor, the elders of the northern tribes came forth to recognize David at Hebron as king over all Israel. The covenant formalizing this recognition sheds light upon the circumstances underlying the split of the United Monarchy after Solomon's death, when the northern tribes once again regarded themselves as free agents to negotiate.[11]

---

[11]Cf. A. Malamat, "Organs of Statecraft in the Israelite Monarchy" (1965) *BAR* 3 (1970) 163-98, esp. 168-70.

Since Alt's basic study of the formation of the United Monarchy, this union of Israel and Judah has most often been understood as a *Personalunion* under one crown.[12] Yet this term, current as it is, is essentially misleading. Terminology often being more than what meets the eye, it would be more appropriate to define the relationship as a *Realunion*.[13] And what is the essential difference? In contrast to a *Personalunion*, the *Realunion* is not incidental but results from the reciprocal will of two political entities to join together (as did David and the northern elders). Whereas in a *Personalunion* two or more international legal entities (or "personalities") remain separate in both internal and external affairs, a *Realunion* is internally composite, but a single legal entity in its external aspect. This latter entity finds full expression, *inter alia*, in a united army and a unified foreign policy. Such indeed was the case of the United Monarchy.

Phase three: Consolidated territorial state. The emergence of a Pan-Israelite bloc, upsetting the balance of power in Palestine, inevitably led to military confrontation between David and the Philistines, hitherto uncontested masters of the region. This was well perceived by the biblical historiographer: "When the Philistines heard that David had been anointed king over Israel, all the Philistines went up in search of David . . ." (2 Sam 5:17).

In the ensuing series of encounters, David eventually grasped the initiative, and though he seems not to have conquered Philistia proper, he did break the Philistine might once and for all. This certainly isolated Philistia and prevented her free access to the Canaanite areas to the north, and to her sources of metal, especially iron, presumably in the Succoth region of Transjordan.[14] Foremost, however, David thus brought about an entirely new political order, for, as Alt has noted, the Philistines had regarded themselves as the legitimate heirs to Egyptian rule in Canaan, and upon their defeat this legacy was to pass to the Israelites, at least nominally.[15] In fact, David had to impose his control over the remaining

---

[12]A. Alt, "Die Staatenbildung der Israeliten in Palästina" (1925) *Kleine Schriften* 2 (München, 1953) 1-65, esp. 45ff. For the continued use of this concept, cf. the studies noted in n. 1, above. See also G. Buccellati, *Cities and Nations of Ancient Syria* (Studi Semitici 26, 1967) 148ff.

[13]For the *Personalunion* and *Realunion*, respectively, from a political and legalistic point of view, see G. Jellinek, *Allgemeine Staatslehre* (3rd ed.; Bad Homburg, 1960) 750ff.; L. Oppenheim, *International Law* 1 (ed. H. Lauterpacht; 8th ed.; London, 1955) 171f.; J. Crawford, *The Creation of States in International Law* (Oxford, 1979) 290f.

[14]For copper and iron ore slag in that region, see N. Glueck, *The River Jordan* (New York, 1968) 119; and cf. 1 Kgs 7:45f. Cf. M. Har-El, "The Valley of the Craftsmen (Geʾ Haḥarašim)," *PEQ* 109 (1977) 75-86, esp. 81ff., who assumes that Philistine smithing, which he locates in the Sharon plain, was based on raw materials from the vicinity of Succoth.

[15]A. Alt, "Das Grossreich Davids" (1950) *Kleine Schriften* 2, 68f.; A. Malamat, *BAR* 2, 95.

Canaanite areas (cf. the list of alien enclaves, in Judges 1)—foremost of which were the city-states of the Sharon plain and the Jezreel valley.[16]

The kingdom of Israel at this stage might be characterized in modern international law as a sort of "successor state" to the Philistines. This notion of "succession of states"[17] can provide a new perspective in understanding the "special" relations of David and Solomon with the kingdom of Tyre, which seems to have superseded the ties between Philistia and the Phoenician coast. Solomon's commercial enterprises with the land of Que, too, were apparently based on earlier, established ties between the Anatolian coast and the Sea-Peoples, including the Philistines. Furthermore, mercenary troops were drafted into David's ranks from among the Philistines— the Cheretites and Pelethites, and a contingent of Gittites (2 Sam 15:18). David must have taken over the potent Philistine chariotry too (cf. 1 Sam 13:5; 2 Sam 1:6), as well as that of the Canaanite enclaves, for otherwise the later Israelite successes against the "mechanized" Aramean forces would be rather difficult to account for.[18] The Philistine monopoly of metal manufacture (cf. 1 Sam 13:19-20) must also have fallen into Israelite hands.

In this phase, the kingdom of Israel exceeded the confines of its own national state, having become a consolidated territorial state by incorporating the Canaanite city-states and considerable tracts peopled by remnants of the erstwhile gentile population (e.g., 2 Sam 24:7; 1 Kgs 9:20).

Phase four: Multinational state. Having broken through the western flank of the belt of hostility surrounding Israel, David could now turn to the long-standing foes on his eastern and southern perimeter: Edom, Moab and Ammon. The actual order of their conquest and incorporation[19] —whether as a vassal state (Moab; 2 Sam 8:2), a province (Edom; 2 Sam 8:14) or annexed outright (Ammon; 2 Sam 12:30)—is unclear, but a sort of "domino theory" most probably came into play here, that is, the fall of the one led to the fall of the next, and so forth. In conducting these campaigns, David had not merely a political aim, but primarily economic-exploitative

---

[16]The destruction layers at such sites as Tell Qasile (level X; see A. Mazar, "Qasile, Tell," *EAEHL* 4 [1977] 966) and Megiddo (level VI A; see Y. Yadin, "Megiddo," *EAEHL* 3 [1977] 851) would seem to reflect David's heavy arm.

[17]On this doctrine see, e.g., L. Oppenheim, *International Law* 1, 156ff.; and recently "Ch. 28: State Succesion" in I. Brownlie, *Principles of Public International Law* (2nd ed.; Oxford, 1973) 631ff.; G. von Glahn, *Law Among Nations* (4th ed.; New York/London, 1981) 119ff.

[18]For the existence of chariotry, however modest, in David's army, see Y. Yadin, *The Art of Warfare in Biblical Lands* 2 (Jerusalem/Ramat Gan, 1963) 285 (where 2 Sam 8:3-4 is cited as a basis), and cf. now C. Hauer, "The Economics of National Security in Solomonic Israel," *JSOT* 18 (1980) 63ff. Y. Ikeda regards the chariotry of this period primarily as a prestige symbol, its military value having been overrated in modern scholarship (see above, n. 4).

[19]On the varying degree of dependence of these states, see A. Malamat, "The Monarchy of David and Solomon—The Rise of a Power," *Thirty Years of Archaeology in Eretz-Israel, 1948-78. The 35th Archaeological Convention of the Israel Exploration Society* (Jerusalem, 1981) esp. 194-96 (Hebrew).

designs, gaining not only control of the "King's Highway" but also direct access to the Red Sea as a bonus.

This cumulative expansion of Israel dwarfed every previous political entity established in the Palestinian sphere, even exceeding the extent of the Egyptian province in the second millennium B.C.

Phase five: Empire. Coeval with the growth of David's kingdom, a political bloc arose in Syria under the leadership of Hadadezer, king of Aram-Zobah, also attaining "great power" status. Following the principle of "competitive exclusion,"[20] it was inevitable that these two up-and-coming rivals should clash, for they had gobbled up all the independent territories situated between them. The vast power accumulated by Israel and the Arameans on the eve of their final contest predicated that absolute hegemony over the entire region of Syria-Palestine would fall to the winner. David's triple victory thus assured him mastery over the entire kingdom of Hadadezer as far as the Euphrates River (as we have shown elsewhere in detail).[21] This unprecedented territorial expansion of the kingdom of Israel can better be comprehended by assuming that Aram-Zobah already comprised a comprehensive states-system. In the vanquishing of their overlord, these territories passed to David *en bloc*, with all their components more or less intact. It was this legacy which facilitated David's acquisition of empire.

By modern definition, the kingdom of David and Solomon—a highly complex political conglomerate with Judah at its nucleus—was a supernational system of political and economic domination by a center over a periphery, in other words, indeed a true empire.[22]

How does the Bible grasp this new status? David and Solomon are referred to by such obvious phrases as king "over Judah," "over all Israel and Judah," "over all Israel," "over Israel," and twice, David "King of Israel" (2 Sam 6:20 and 2 Chr 8:11). But the Bible goes much further, graphically, at least concerning Solomon: "Solomon ruled over all the kingdoms from the Euphrates, the (sic!) land of the Philistines and to the border of Egypt; they brought tribute and served Solomon all the days of his life. . . . For he had dominion over all the region west of the Euphrates from Tiphsah to Gaza, over all the kings west of the Euphrates" (1 Kgs 4:21, 24 [MT 5:1, 4]). Then this passage continues: ושלום היה לו מכל עבריו מסביב, "and he had peace on all sides round about him"—a *"pax Salomonica,"* so to speak. On a more hyperbolic plane, one of the two

---

[20]This concept has been borrowed by political scientists from the realm of biology; see R. L. Caneiro, "Political Expansion as an Expression of the Principle of Competitive Exclusion," *Origins of the State* (eds. R. Cohen and E. R. Service; Philadelphia, 1978) 205ff., esp. 208f.

[21]*JNES* 22 (1963), 1 ff.

[22]For various definitions of "empire," in the context of antiquity, see now "Ch. 1: Introduction" in *Imperialism in the Ancient World* (eds. P. D. A. Garnsey and C. R. Whittaker; Cambridge, 1978); and *Power and Propaganda. A Symposium on Ancient Empires* (ed. M. T. Larsen; Copenhagen, 1979), esp. 21-33 (S. N. Eisenstadt) and 90ff. (M. T. Larsen).

Psalms actually dedicated to Solomon poeticizes: "May he have dominion from sea to sea, from the River to the ends of the earth. . . . May the kings of Tarshish and of the isles render him tribute, may the kings of Sheba and Seba bring gifts. May all kings fall down before him, all nations serve him" (Ps 72:1, 8, 10-11).[23]

Is such magnitude ever channeled into a specific, grandiose titulary? There appears to be a particular biblical expression befitting this majesty —*melek rab*—associated with Solomon in both of its two occurrences: one possibly relates to the builder of Jerusalem in all its splendour, while the other definitely refers to the builder of the Temple. Ps 48:2 (MT 48:3), glorifies: קרית מלך רב, "the city of the great king." Now, regardless of whether this king is heavenly (as is usually held) or earthly, the imagery here is of a mortal ruler. In the second instance, an Aramaic passage in Ezra (5:11) retrospectively refers to ומלך לישראל רב בנהי ושכללה, "a great king of Israel built it and completed it." This latter instance certainly reflects the parallel Akkadian title *šarru rabû*, "great king," "emperor." Elsewhere in the Bible the expression *melek gadol*, also translating into English as "great king," is applied either to God or to the king of Assyria,[24] and the *melek yareb* in Hosea (5:13; 10:6) refers to the Assyrian king alone. But, interestingly, both Ugaritic and Early Aramaic (e.g., the Sefire inscriptions) use the term *mlk rb*. We can thus assume that the usage *melek rab* in the Bible represents a stylistic stratum different from that of *melek gadol*, which latter is strictly a Hebrew loan-translation of *šarru rabû* (and note *melek gadol* in Hebrew script upon a Nimrud ivory of the late eighth century B.C.)[25]

In other words, a title applied (albeit retrospectively) to Solomon, alone of all the Israelite kings, evokes a particular category of major potentate, the "overlord," which later history was to call "emperor." That this title was no empty shell is shown by Solomon's marriage to Pharaoh's daughter, further confirmation of the image of Israel as an empire. With this happy event we enter into a discussion of Solomon's relations with Egypt, and his activities within the traditional Egyptian sphere of influence.

---

[23]B. Mazar relates this psalm to the days of an assumed coregency of David and Solomon, on the basis of its superscription (and final verse); B. Mazar, "The Phoenicians and Eastern Shore of the Mediterranean Sea," (1965) *Cities and Districts in Eretz-Israel* (Jerusalem, 1975) 262 (Hebrew). For such a coregency, cf. recently T. Ishida, *The Royal Dynasties in Ancient Israel* (BZAW 142, 1977) 153f., 170; E. Ball, "The Co-Regency of David and Solomon," *VT* 27 (1977) 268-79 (who suggests that this institution was introduced into Israel under Egyptian influence).

[24]It is also applied to Sihon, king of the Amorites, and Og, king of Bashan (in Ps 136:17-19; and cf. Ps 135:10-11), but only poetically, as is obvious from the context.

[25]On *šarru rabû*, see M. J. Seux, *Épithètes royales akkadiennes et sumériennes* (Paris, 1967) 298ff. For its West-Semitic and biblical equivalents, cf. J. C. Greenfield, "Some Aspects of Treaty Terminology in the Bible," *Fourth World Congress of Jewish Studies* 1 (Jerusalem, 1967) 118f., who already pointed out that מלך גדול is "a sure calque on *š. r.*" For the Nimrud inscription, see A. Millard, "Alphabetic Incriptions on Ivories from Nimrud," *Iraq* 24 (1962), 45ff.

III

Royal diplomatic marriages, as a means of cementing international relations and a practical alternative to warfare, were a cornerstone of Solomon's foreign policy. Solomon thus long anticipated the apt Habsburg witticism: *Bella gerant alii! tu, felix Austria, nube!* "Let others fight wars! Thou, O happy Austria, marry!" The full significance of Solomon's marriage with Pharaoh's daughter eluded the biblical historiographer, who failed even to mention the name of the Pharaoh, let alone that of the bride. Indeed, the event was entirely unique in both Israelite and Egyptian annals. Solomon's various other political marriages were with states of the second rank (Moab, Ammon, Edom, or the Phoenician coastal cities and the Neo-Hittite kingdoms). From ancient Near Eastern records in general—and especially those from the Amarna Letters down to Herodotus—it is now clear that Egyptian kings rarely, if ever, married off their daughters to foreign potentates, whom they apparently regarded as inferior.[26] Of this fact, too, the biblical historiographer appeared to be ignorant.

In the book of Kings (with parallels in Chronicles), Pharaoh's daughter is mentioned in no less than five unrelated contexts, most of them likely of a pre-deuteronomic layer. Though this would lend historical credibility to the marriage, the Bible has neglected to disclose the motivations underlying this unusual event. Since the extant Egyptian records contain no trace of it whatsoever, we must construct a rational scenario if we are to arrive at a plausible historical assessment. The Israelite kingdom at this time was of a magnitude never before seen upon Egypt's eastern doorstep. Moreover, until midway through Solomon's reign, Egypt was split into two political units, the kings of the relatively weak twenty-first dynasty (1070-945 B.C.), with their capital at Tanis, ruling the north, and the theocracy at Thebes, firmly entrenched in the south. The outline which follows is a restatement, up-dated and revised, of a hypothesis which I put forth some years ago.[27]

(1) The data in the Bible would place the marriage with Pharaoh's daughter early in Solomon's reign. Thus, the campaign to Gezer by Solomon's future father-in-law—most likely Siamun, penultimate king of the twenty-first dynasty (ca. 978-960 B.C.)—must have taken place at the very beginning of (or just prior to?) Solomon's reign as sole ruler (ca. 967/66 B.C.).[28]

(2) The conquest of Gezer (now attested also by archaeological evidence)[29] on the northern border of Philistia was part of an Egyptian

---

[26]Cf. A. Malamat, *BAR* 2, 91f.; and see most recently A. R. Schulman, "Diplomatic Marriage in the Egyptian New Kingdom," *JNES* 38 (1979) 177-93; "Königstochter," *LÄ* 3/21 (1979) 659-61.

[27]*JNES* 22 (1963) 10ff.; and see there for further details and bibliographical references.

[28]For a most recent review, see A. R. Green, "Solomon and Siamun: A Synchronism between Dynastic Israel and the Twenty-First Dynasty of Egypt," *JBL* 97 (1978) 353-67.

[29]W. G. Dever, ("Further Excavations at Gezer, 1967-71," *BA* 34 [1971] 110) assumes "Post-Philistine/Pre-Solomonic ... Stratum 7 was brought to a violent end in the mid-10th century B.C." (at least in area 1 there); cf. also ibid., 130; Dever et al., *Gezer* 1 (Jerusalem,

attempt to recover the southern coast of Palestine and part of the Shephelah, lost to Egypt some two centuries before. Pharaoh surely did not undertake an entire campaign against Gezer solely in order to hand this fortress over to Solomon (1 Kgs 9:16), as a token of friendship. Historically, such an act would hardly be comprehensible.

(3) This conquest of Gezer, lying on the main road to Jerusalem, presented a direct threat to Israel. Pharaoh's ultimate goal may well have been the very capital of the kingdom of Israel (as it was in Shishak's campaign, some forty years later), in an attempt to topple the Israelite dynasty in the opportune moment following David's demise. It would have thus restored Egyptian hegemony over the Land of Canaan.

(4) This Pharaoh, however, certainly underestimated Israelite potential. Since Solomon had secured his kingdom internally, having eliminated all domestic opposition, he could have concentrated his strength against the invader, and thus no doubt turned Pharaoh from his aggressive intentions in favour of rapprochement. In other words, a diplomatic course proved a more desirable alternative than stark confrontation.

(5) A treaty, to which Solomon was at least an equal party, encompassed territorial concessions to Israel. This treaty, ratified (so to speak) by the marriage to Pharaoh's daughter, involved the transfer of Gezer, under the guise of a dowry, probably only part of Solomon's gains in Philistia at this time. Much later, after the rise of Shishak, Solomon may well have extended his control even further into Philistia, strengthening his position in the face of a new Egyptian threat.

And, finally (6), the previous assumption leads us to a true understanding of the borders of the Kingdom of Israel. Returning to the passage in 1 Kgs 4:21 and 24 (MT 5:1, 4), we read that "Solomon ruled over all the kingdoms from the Euphrates, the (sic!) land of the Philistines and unto the border of Egypt. . . . For he had dominion over all the region west of the Euphrates (MT ʿeber hannahar) from Tiphsah unto Gaza." Philistia is mentioned here as a separate, distinct unit *under* Israelite control—if we follow the Massoretic text as it stands (the standard English translations insert "to" or "unto" the land of the Philistines, following the parallel passage in 2 Chr 9:26). With this expansion to the southwest, the United Monarchy arrived at its fullest extent—not under David but as a result of Solomon's own political achievements.

This picture leaves many secondary questions unanswered, some of them quite intriguing. For example, why does the Bible make no mention of a Philistine amongst Solomon's numerous foreign wives? Could Pharaoh's daughter—daughter of the traditional suzerain over the southern coastal plain—have also "represented" Philistia, so to speak?

In any event, the above scenario has met with varying degrees of approval. Most recently, Manfred Görg has adopted its general aspect in his forthcoming book *Die Tochter Pharaos*, where he holds that the episode of Solomon and Pharaoh nurtured the story in the book of Exodus, on the Israelites in Egypt. Both stories involve an unnamed Pharaoh and a daughter. To paraphrase Görg, in Exodus is there not a Pharaoh who prevents the Israelites from leaving Egypt but then allows them to go, only to relent again and pursue them? Is this not like Siamun in the days of Solomon, who threatens Israel—only later to make peace, who takes Gezer and then presents it to Solomon? Furthermore, in both stories the role of Pharaoh's daughter is a positive one, beneficial to Israel.[30]

Many scholars, however, assume that Siamun was favorably disposed toward Israel in the first place, that his campaign to Philistia, (still under Egyptian hegemony) was merely a police action, or was limited to punishing a rebellious Gezer alone. It may also have been intended to eliminate Philistia from trade with Tyre.[31] Handing Gezer over to Solomon was a small price to pay for maintaining friendly ties with Israel. But whether Siamun's initial intentions were hostile or friendly, the fact remains that the marriage inaugurated an Egyptian-Israelite *détente* which lasted some twenty years—until the twenty-first dynasty was superseded by Shishak (ca. 945 B.C.).

What impact did these new relations have upon either party? What did Egypt receive in tangible exchange for her concessions? And what mutual interests evolved, if any? On these points we can only speculate, for even the circumstantial evidence is rather motley.[32]

One service Solomon could have rendered Siamun was political support for his dynasty. Libyan elements—settled in Egypt some two centuries, much in the manner of the "Sea-Peoples"—gradually had come to the fore within the Egyptian army, occupying even top command positions. Foremost amongst their leaders were the grandfather and the father of Shishak, the future Pharaoh, as well as Shishak himself, and all three bore the title

---

[30]Pending publication of M. Görg's book, cf. his article "Ausweisung oder Befreiung," *Kairos* NF 20 (1978) 272-80.

[31]Thus recently A. Green, *JBL* 97, 365; for a similar view, see K. A. Kitchen, *The Third Intermediate Period in Egypt* (Warminster, 1973) 281f. On the other hand, S. Yeivin, "Did the Kingdoms of Israel Have a Maritime Policy?" *JQR* 50 (1960) 193ff., supposes that Siamun's campaign sought to counter an Israelite-Phoenician threat to the Egyptian monopoly over trade to the South.

[32]For Egyptian influence of Israel in the administrative and literary spheres, outside our present scope, see now T. N. D. Mettinger, *Solomonic State Officials* (CB OTS 5, 1971); D. B. Redford, "The Taxation System of Solomon," *Studies in Relations between Palestine and Egypt during the First Millennium B.C.* (eds. J. W. Wevers and D. B. Redford; Toronto, 1972) 141-56; and E. W. Heaton, *Solomon's New Men* (London, 1974). A. R. Green, "Israelite Influence at Shishak's Court?" *BASOR* 233 (1979) 59-62, speculates on Israelite influence on Shishak's administration.

"Great Chief of the Me" (or "Meshwesh"), the latter being the name of a major Libyan people.[33] This faction, which was already seeking to topple the twenty-first dynasty, may well have held more than mere ties of tradition with the Philistines, harking back to the days of Ramesses III when their forefathers shared a common cause against Egypt.[34] Siamun may have sought in Solomon a means of neutralizing this potential threat in Philistia.

Another advantage undoubtedly sought by Siamun was a share in Solomon's international trade, or at least a "right-of-way" for his own agents and goods into Asia. This was apparently vital to him, for access to and from Nubia was currently controlled by the rival authorities in Thebes and was thus denied to him. Concerning possible trade with Israel, a clouded passage in I Kgs 10:28-29 (and the parallels in 2 Chr 1:16-17 and 9:28) may indicate that Solomon imported Egyptian chariots and teams. In general, however, Siamun's expectations were thwarted. Not only did Solomon exclude Egypt from his commercial ventures, but he even set up a rival cartel, bypassing the traditional Egyptian monopoly over raw materials precious metals, and exotica coming from Africa.

The major motive for Solomon's entry into the Red Sea trade—like his direct horse-trading with Que—was to obtain luxury goods straight from their source, eliminating the middleman, but such activities called for a maritime lore not available amongst the Israelites themselves, and hence Solomon sought the cooperation of Hiram of Tyre. Their Red Sea enterprises, based on Ezion-Geber,[35] must have been highly lucrative, despite adverse conditions of navigation in those waters. The Red Sea is known proverbially for its ever-changing winds and currents, "uncharted" islets and hidden reefs—dangers vividly illustrated by the ancient Egyptian *Tale of the Shipwrecked Sailor* (and cf. 1 Kgs 22:49). In the first book of Kings, Solomon's Red Sea ventures are noted in three instances (1 Kgs 9:26-29; 10:11-12, 22, with significant variants in the parallel passages in 2 Chr 8:17-18, 9:10-11, 21); two of these mention Ophir as the destination, while the third merely notes the use of "ships of Tarshish," presumably large "freighters" (like the "Byblos" and "Coptos" ships used by the early Egyptian voyagers to the Land of Punt). The goods brought back by

---

[33]On the Libyans in general and the Meshwesh in particular, see W. Hölscher, *Libyer und Ägypter* (Glückstadt, 1937); "Libyen, Libyer," *LÄ* 3/23 (1979) 1015-33. For the forebears of Shishak, to five or six generations, bearing the title "Great Chief of the Me(shwesh)", see Kitchen, *The Third Intermediate Period*, 285, and n. 244.

[34]See W. F. Edgerton and J. A. Wilson, *Historical Records of Ramses III* (Chicago, 1936) 20ff., 35, 44-47, 146f.; A. Gardiner, *Ancient Egyptian Onomastica* (Oxford, 1947) 119ff.; Cf. *LÄ* 3/23 (1979) 1022. For similarities in weapons (long sword) between the Meshwesh and the Philistines, cf. K. Zibelius, *Afrikanische Orts-und Völkernamen . . .* (Wiesbaden, 1972) 131.

[35]Solomon's hold over this port would indicate that an Edomite attempt to regain independence after the return of Hadad the Edomite from Egyptian exile, was abortive; see 1 Kgs 11:14-22. For a recent study of this episode, see J. R. Bartlett, "An Adversary against Solomon, Hadad the Edomite," *ZAW* 88 (1976) 205-26.

Solomon's agents were gold, silver, ivory, "ᵓalgum" or (preferably) "ᵓalmug" wood, precious stones, monkeys, and baboons.[36]

This entire enterprise indeed recalls the Egyptian expeditions to Punt, from the time of Sahure (ca. 25th century B.C.) down to Ramesses III (12th century B.C.).[37] The products brought back by the expedition of Queen Hatshepsut in the fifteenth century B.C. included virtually all those sought by Solomon, and many more—incense and incense trees, and such exotic animals as giraffes. Hatshepsut's reliefs at Deir el-Bahri are also indicative of the sort of goods probably offered by Solomon in Ophir: bead necklaces, weapons, jewelry and the like—the usual trinkets palmed off on primitive peoples in trade throughout history.[38]

Where are these lands to be located? The animals, trees, and products of Punt would all point to the northern coast of Somalia, between Djibouti and Cape Guardafui, and though opinions are divided widely, it is here that the "emporium" of Ophir is preferably to be sought.[39] The fascinating *Periplus of the Erythrean* (or Red) *Sea*, from the first century A.D. describes this coast, as well as the Arabian coast opposite and the Red Sea in general. This seaman's manual lists in detail the many ports of call and their imports and exports, on the Somali coast, often the very sort of goods as at Punt and Ophir.[40] The latter name is noteworthy among the sons of Joktan in the Table of Nations in Gen 10:26-30, which reads almost like a periplus of Arabia for ships and "ships of the desert." In this same Table, the two names Sheba and Havilah, "brothers" of Ophir, also occur amongst the sons of Cush; in other words, geographically they lay across the Red Sea as well, in Africa. In any event, the Joktan list in the Table of

---

[36]On Tarshish, see above, n. 5 and on "Tarshish" and "Byblos" ships see T. Säve-Söderbergh, *The Navy of the Eighteenth Egyptian Dynasty* (Uppsala, 1946) 47ff.; on baboons and אלמג/אלמג, see above, n. 6.

[37]For the more recent literature on Punt, see R. Herzog, *Punt* (Glückstadt, 1968), and the important review article by K. A. Kitchen, "Punt and How to Get There," *Or* 40 (1971) 184-207; A.Théodoridès, "Les escales de la route égyptienne de la côte de Somalie," *Recueils de la Société Jean Bodin* 32 (1974) 51-64; and W. W. Müller's brief summary, "Das Puntproblem," Pauly-Wissowa, *Realenzyklopädie der classischen Altertumswissenschaft Sup* 15 (Stuttgart, 1978) 739ff. For the occurrences of Punt in the Egyptian texts, see now Zibelius, *Afrikanische Orts-und Völkernamen*, 114ff. For a Red Sea port of departure for voyages to Punt, at Wadi Gawasis east of Coptos, as indicated by inscriptions found there, see A. M. A. H. Sayed, "Discovery of the Site of the Twelfth Dynasty Port at Wadi Gawasis on the Red Sea Shore," *Revue d'égyptologie* 29 (1977) 139-78; "The Recently Discovered Port on the Red Sea Shore," *JEA* 64 (1978) 69-71.

[38]For Queen Hatshepsut's Punt expedition, see E. Naville, *The Temple of Deir el Bahari III* (London, 1894) pls. 64-76; for the Egyptian goods offered at Punt, see p. 14 there. The most recent summary concerning this expedition is S. Ratié, *La Reine Hatchepsout. Sources et problèmes* (Leiden, 1981) 141-61.

[39]For the various hypotheses of the location of Ophir (the three main locations being South Arabia, India, and Somalia), see recently G. Ryckmans, "Ophir," *DBSup* 6 (1960) 744-51; R. Hanslik, "Ophir," Pauly-Wissowa, *Realenzyklopädie der classischen Altertumswissenschaft Sup* 12 (1970) 969-80.

[40]See, still, W. H. Schoff, *The Periplus of the Erythraean Sea* (New York, 1912; reprinted New Delhi, 1974) esp. 24ff. and 75ff.

Nations may well stem from Solomonic times, when the South Arabian sphere, including the Horn of Africa, was just coming into the Israelite scope of awareness.[41]

The advent of the twenty-second dynasty in Egypt, in the person of Shishak, brought Israel's brief "flirt" with Egypt to an abrupt end. Shishak's agressive policy soon reunited Egypt and apparently even regained Nubia.[42] We can arrive at a date for this turning-point by reference to an event much later in Shishak's reign, his campaign to Palestine, singularly documented not only in the Bible but also in his monumental inscription at Karnak and by a fragmentary Egyptian stele found at Megiddo. On the basis of other evidence from Egypt, it can be inferred that the campaign took place around Shishak's 21st year, shortly before his death. According to 1 Kgs 14:25 (2 Chr 12:2), the invasion occurred in the fifth year of Rehoboam, Solomon's successor. Reckoning backward, Shishak must have reigned for about sixteen years coeval with Solomon, placing his accession in Solomon's 24th year or thereabouts (ca. 945 B.C.).[43]

We can note here only a few repercussions of this new Egyptian policy, concerning the second half of Solomon's reign. Shortly after Solomon's 24th year (cf. 1 Kgs 6:1, 37-38; 7:1; 9:10, 24), Jeroboam led a rebellion against him and upon its failure was forced to flee to Shishak (cf. 1 Kgs 11:26-28, 40). One wonders what connection the new Pharaoh Shishak may have had with these events. Either Jeroboam, an Ephraimite, deemed that a new dynasty in Egypt antagonistic to Solomon bettered his chances of success, or Shishak himself was inciting anti-Davidic elements, especially in the embittered northern Israel.[44]

Solomon also built a network of strategic fortresses after his 24th year—at Hazor and Megiddo in the north, and at Gezer, Beth-horon, Baalath, and Tamar in the south (1 Kgs 9:15-18), and perhaps also at Ashdod, where recently a "Solomonic" gate has apparently been uncovered.[45] This new measure was certainly in response to internal unrest, as well as in anticipation of external threats, foremost from Egypt. But, these activities forced Solomon to increase the burden of taxation and the corvée, especially in the north—the major factor ultimately leading to the schism of the United Monarchy after his death. Solomon thus also fell

---

[41]Cf. C. Westermann, *Genesis 1-11* (*BKAT* 1/1, 1974) 704.

[42]On Shishak's foreign policy, see now Kitchen, *The Third Intermediate Period*, 292ff. On his possible domination of Nubia, which would have opened trade southward, cf. ibid., 293 and n. 284 (as well as below). Mention of Cushites (i.e., Nubians) in 2 Chr 12:3, alongside Libyans and Sukki, among Shishak's troops invading Palestine, may also be relevant.

[43]See, in short, Malamat, *BAR* 2, 94; and now a résumé of the chronological problematics, by A. Green, *JBL* 97 (1978) 353-67, with detailed bibliographical references.

[44]Cf. A. Malamat, *BAR* 3, 192f. For a different explanation of Jeroboam's rebellion, relating it to the sale of Cabul (i.e., of "northern" lands by Solomon), see B. Halpern, "Sectionalism and the Schism," *JBL* 93 (1974) 524ff.

[45]For Hazor, Megiddo, and Gezer, see Y. Yadin, "The Archaeological Sources for the Period of the Monarchy," *The Age of the Monarchies: Culture and Society. The World*

deeper into debt with Tyre, which he placated with territorial concessions in the Cabul region of western Galilee (also around his 24th year; 1 Kgs 9:10ff).

The visit of the Queen of Sheba, too, must have taken place after Solomon's 24th year—a fact generally overlooked—for Solomon feted the queen in his already-completed palace (cf. 1 Kgs 10:4ff.). She came not only to conclude commercial ties and thus secure her hold over trade with South Arabia, which Solomon has long been circumventing, for both she and Solomon, we can assume, foresaw the restoration of Egyptian trade in the Red Sea under the forceful Shishak and would have sought to counter this threat. That Shishak did have his eye on Israelite Red Sea connection is quite apparent from his side-thrust through the southern Negev, possibly toward Ezion-Geber, during his campaign, years later.[46]

In conclusion, the age of David and Solomon was indeed a unique chapter in Israelite history, and especially concerning relations with Egypt. It was the only point in history that the Holy Land ever attained primary status in international politics.

History of the Jewish People 4/2 (ed. A. Malamat; Jerusalem, 1979) 190, 195f., 208f. For the gate at Ashdod, see M. Dothan, "Ashdod," *EAEHL* 1 (1975) 114; and idem, "*Ashdod VI*," ʿ*Atiqot* 14 (in press); for a post-Solomonic ascription of the Ashdod gate, see Y. Yadin, *The World History of the Jewish People* 4/2, 217f., 229.

[46]For the inclusion of Ezion-Geber amongst the sites in the Negev listed by Shishak, see B. Mazar, "The Campaign of Pharaoh Shishak to Palestine," *Volume du Congrès, Strasbourg, 1956* (VTSup 4, 1957) 57-66; Y. Aharoni, *The Land of the Bible* (London, 1967) 283-90. The reading of this toponym is questioned, however, by Kitchen, *The Third Intermediate Period,* 439 and n. 87.

The Interdependence of Internal Affairs and Foreign Policy during the Davidic-Solomonic Period (with Special Regard to the Phoenician Coast)

HERBERT DONNER
University of Tübingen

"Nicht jedem Menschen bekommt es, ein reicher Erbe zu sein. Auch Salomo ist der Gefahr erlegen. Die Luft, die er in der Jugend einsog, war der schwüle Dunstkreis üppigen Hoflebens. Ein grosser Erzieher seiner Söhne war David nie gewesen. Wo sollte dem Knaben und Jüngling inmitten des weichlichen Hof- und Haremlebens und später des Ränkespiels um die Thronfolge der Sinn für Pflicht und Lebensernst geweckt werden? Er sieht nur die Ungebundenheit des Herrschers und der Seinen und die Annehmlichkeiten des Regierens. Brechen im Vater nur vereinzelt sultanische Neigungen durch, so ersteht im Sohne ein richtiger Sultan, wenn auch durchaus nicht einer der schlimmsten."[1]

These fine sentences are to be found in R. Kittel, *Gestalten und Gedanken in Israel, Geschichte eines Volkes in Charakterbildern* (Leipzig, 2nd ed., n.d.) p. 160. They describe the basic features which characterize the portrait of Solomon to the present day, even though Old Testament studies since Kittel have brought into consideration other aspects at many particular points. The sentences describe the atmosphere which we ascribe to "Solomon in all his glory":[2] his court had in it something of the courts of

---

[1] "It is not every man's good fortune, to be a wealthy heir. Even Solomon was a prey to danger. The air which he breathed in his youth was the heady atmosphere of the exalted palace life. David was never a good educator of his sons. How could a sense of duty and responsibility be aroused in a boy and youth surrounded by the enervating life of palace and harem and later by the intrigues for the succession to the throne? He sees only the independence of the ruler and his court and the comforts which belong to him who rules. While the tendencies of a sultan break through only on occasions in the father, the son is a real sultan, although indeed not one of the worst of them." For the translation of this article from German into English I am obliged to my colleague Professor Dr. Eric Osborn, Melbourne (Australia).

[2] Matt 6:29.

Italian princes at the time of the Renaissance and of the Versailles of Louis XIV. He himself had the qualities of an Ottoman Padischah of the 18th century.

One must not continually attack this portrait. It has no point, because this is the way in which at least 2,000 years of Jewish, Christian, and Moslem thought about Solomon have established the characteristics of the son of David's later years. That does not, of course, release the historian from his obligation to examine continually the sources of the Solomonic period and to relate their claims with the results which have come from new scientific questions and insights. The historical Solomon, who emerges from this process, has his own right and his own standing alongside that of the tradition.

It is in this area that I wish to make a modest contribution. It is concerned exclusively with the interdependence of internal affairs and foreign policy during the Davidic-Solomonic period. At any rate, it is obvious that one cannot confine one's interests to Solomon alone, for he certainly cannot be understood apart from what his father began and built up. The period of the two kings became the unique epoch in the life of ancient Israel, in which the state rose to the status of an empire.[3] Under David and Solomon, for the first time, one can properly speak of internal affairs and foreign policy and of their mutual interaction. It was David and Solomon, and not Saul, who, each in his own way, first established and consolidated the state from within; they were the first to appear as performers in the international concerto of Near Eastern powers. One could indeed suppose that the two things go together, even if the texts did not make it evident.[4] Because every aspect can hardly be dealt with here, we shall discuss only the problem of the relation of the empire to the Phoenician coastal cities, especially to the city-state of Tyre.[5]

At first sight everything appears to be straightforward. King Hiram of Tyre on his own initiative entered into relations with David and sent him building materials and craftsmen for woodwork and stonemasonry (2 Sam 5:11). The territory of David's empire stretched along the Phoenician coast to the area of Sidon (2 Sam 24:5-7). The good relations between Tyre and Israel continued under Solomon: there was a trade-agreement, according to

---

[3] See A. Alt, "Das Grossreich Davids" (1950) *Kleine Schriften* 2 (München, 1953) 66-75.

[4] On the definition of the term "political," see G. E. Mendenhall, "The Relation of the Individual to Political Society in Ancient Israel," *Biblical Studies in Memory of H. C. Alleman* (eds. J. M. Myers et al.; New York, 1960) 89-108, esp. 89-91. On the problems of foreign policy, see A. Malamat, "Aspects of the Foreign Policies of David and Solomon," *JNES* 22 (1963) 1-8; idem, "The Kingdom of David and Solomon in its Contact with Egypt and Aram Naharaim" (1958) *BAR* 2 (1964) 89-98.

[5] Cf. F. C. Fensham, "The Treaty between the Israelites and Tyrians," *Congress Volume, Rome, 1968* (VTSup 17, 1969) 71-87; H. J. Katzenstein, *The History of Tyre. From the Beginning of the Second Millennium B.C.E. until the Fall of the Neo-Babylonian Empire in 538 B.C.E.* (Jerusalem, 1973); S. Moscati, *The World of the Phoenicians* (London, 1973) esp. 31ff.

which Hiram sent timber to Solomon and received in return natural produce for the needs of his palace (1 Kgs 5:15-26). Further, Hiram provided laborers for the building of the temple in Jerusalem (1 Kgs 5:32) and took part in Solomon's trade expeditions to Ophir and Tarshish with his ships and sailors (1 Kgs 9:26-28; 10:11, 22). For reasons which are not completely clear, Solomon gave over to Hiram 20 villages in the district of Galilee in return for remuneration (1 Kgs 9:10-14).

These items of information are of different kinds and certainly of different value. If at first one takes them at their face value, a clear or at least rather convincing picture of the reign of Solomon emerges: the relations to the trading center of Tyre indicate the political weakness in external affairs of the Solomonic empire, or even the dependence of Solomon on the king of Tyre. That is clear from 1 Kgs 9:10-14. The text runs as follows: "(10) And it came to pass at the end of twenty years, wherein Solomon had built the two houses, the house of Yahweh and the king's house, (11) now Hiram the king of Tyre had furnished Solomon with cedar-trees and fir-trees, and with gold, according to all his desire, that then King Solomon gave Hiram twenty cities in the land of Galilee. (12) And Hiram came out from Tyre to see the cities which Solomon had given him; and they pleased him not. (13) And he said, What cities are these which thou hast given me, my brother? And he called them the land of Cabul unto this day. (14) And Hiram sent to the king sixscore talents of gold."[6] In this text the verses 10-11a can be regarded as secondary to the report beginning in v. 11b with אז "then";[7] that is, the chronology is uncertain, and the motive for the transfer of territory—a kind of compensation for goods and services,[8] perhaps indeed in the sense of a state bankruptcy[9]—must be excluded. It may also be further asked, whether vv. 12-13—the aetiology of the name "land of Cabul"—should be deleted as an addition and the twenty villages should be located in eastern Upper Galilee.[10] In favor of this is the break between v. 13 and v. 14; against it is the factor that one cannot understand two things: 1) that the king of Tyre would have been at all interested in Israelite villages (belonging to Naphtali

---

[6]On analysis and historical evaluation, see M. Noth, *Könige* 1 (BKAT 9/1, 1968) 209-12; Y. Aharoni, "The Land of Kabul," *Western Galilee* (Haifa, 1961) 171-78 (Hebrew); idem, "Mount Carmel as Border," *Archäologie und Altes Testament. Festschrift K. Galling* (ed. K. Kuschke; Tübingen, 1970) 4f.; J. Kegler, *Politisches Geschehen und theologisches Verstehen* (Stuttgart, 1977) 215f.

[7]The chronological statement of 20 years after having begun to build the temple and the palace may be based on an addition of the numbers mentioned in 1 Kgs 6:38b and 7:1. But perhaps the whole reign of Solomon (40 years according to 1 Kgs 11:42) has simply been halved; cf. M. Noth, *Könige* 1, 209. Verse 11a depends almost word for word on the deuteronomistic text of 1 Kgs 5:24.

[8]Y. Aharoni, "Mount Carmel as Border," 4f.

[9]J. A. Soggin, "The Davidic-Solomonic Kingdom," *Israelite and Judaean History* (eds. J. H. Hayes and J. M. Miller; London, 1977) 375.

[10]As proposed by M. Noth, *Könige* 1, 210f.

or Asher) in the mountains, and 2) that Solomon was in the position to transfer these villages or indeed to sell them. But if one takes "Cabul" seriously,[11] then one is concerned with the plain of Acco, which is bordered by Mount Carmel in the south. Phoenician interests in this area are understandable much earlier, and in the plain of Acco there existed, from of old, predominantly if not exclusively Canaanite villages.[12] These Solomon could not indeed sell, but he could transfer the political authority over them in exchange for concessions, perhaps even financial concessions. The plain of Acco is not to be found in the list of the Solomonic districts (1 Kgs 4:7-19): perhaps an indication that the territorial transfer took place relatively early in the reign of Solomon.[13] According to Fl. Josephus, *Bell. Jud.* 3.3.1 (§ 38) χαβουλων = Cabul was still the border between Jewish Galilee and the Hellenistic city of Acco/Ptolemais in the Hellenistic-Roman period.[14] Here possibly the territorial relations have been preserved which had been laid down in the Solomonic period. In any case, it is clear that the transfer of a whole district was no triumph for Solomon's foreign policy. But, Hiram's activities in Solomon's commercial expeditions and in the construction of the temple also betray the dependence of Israel on Tyre, for in both cases Solomon was plainly not in the position, to do without the Phoenician "know-how." Similarly, one can also interpret in the sense of dependence the agreement of 1 Kgs 5:15-26,[15] which has been certainly worked over by a deuteronomist, even if the report is not of purely deuteronomistic origin.

That is all easily understood, for the empire under Solomon entered on a new, second stage of its existence. During the time of David, at least up to the rebellions of the northern tribes (2 Sam 15:1-6; 20), new territories were constantly annexed to the Palestinian nucleus, under different legal conditions, in apparently rapid succession: one conquest and subjection produced another.[16] The empire, as a result of its inner dynamic, was involved in constant growth, facilitated by the fact that David had abandoned the principle of a national state. The aggressive policy in external affairs had, without question, the primacy. After it followed, as a reaction, what was at first indeed a modest internal consolidation and organization. When Solomon ascended to the throne, the process of

---

[11]Kābūl, about 15 km eastsoutheast of Acco, at the edge of the mountains of Lower Galilee.

[12]Kabul as a frontier town of the tribe of Asher (Josh 19:37) is a factor only in the theoretical geography of the tribes of Israel!

[13]Cf. A. Alt, "Israls Gaue unter Salomo" (1913) *Kleine Schriften* 2 (München, 1953) 84f.; "Galiläische Probleme" (1937-40) *Kleine Schriften* 2, 363-374.

[14]Cf. Josephus, *Bell. Jud.* 2.18.9; *Ant.* 8.5.3; *Vita* 43-44; *Con.Ap.* 1.17.

[15]Cf. M. Noth, *Könige* 1, 88-92.

[16]Philistines: 2 Sam 8:1 (vassaldom); Canaanites: indirectly from 1 Kgs 4:7-19; 2 Sam 21:1-10; Judg 1:21-33; Ammonites: 2 Sam 10:1-11:1, 16-27 and 12:26-31 (personal union); Moabites: 2 Sam 8:2 (vassaldom); Edomites: 2 Sam 8:13f. (province); Aram-Ṣōbā and Aram-Damascus: 2 Sam 8:2-12 (provinces).

growth of the empire had come to an end, the dynamic had disappeared, the offensive was over. It was now necessary to preserve and consolidate as far as possible the existing conditions, to go over to the defensive, to organize and to amalgamate. That Solomon certainly achieved—so far as we can see—with considerable success: the establishment of districts mainly for the purpose of levying taxes (1 Kgs 4:7-19; 9:19),[17] the reorganization of the military forces (1 Kgs 5:8; 9:19, 22; 10:26), the fortification program (1 Kgs 9:15-18),[18] forced labor (1 Kgs 5:27ff.; 9:15ff.; 11:26),[19] and joined to all this the development of trade and commerce, the erection of new buildings, the development of Jerusalem as a cultural center. In a word, the internal affairs now had primacy; they prescribed the area of action. This was bound to produce external political reactions, either that the distant provinces of the empire tried, with some success, to regain their political independence, or that neighboring powers gained influence and expended at Israel's expense. An example of the first was to be seen in the Syrians of Damascus (1 Kgs 11:23-25)[20] and the Edomites (1 Kgs 11:14-22),[21] and an example of the second in the Phoenicians of Tyre. Hiram of Tyre did not need to fight for freedom or to become independent; he was already free and independent. But, he could draw from the new situation political and commercial advantages, and he did not hesitate to do so.

But, if the thesis of the interdependence of internal affairs and foreign policy, in the sense of action and reaction, be correct, and if it be also the case that the relationship at the time of Solomon was the reverse of that at the time of David, then certain questions arise concerning David's dealings with the Phoenician coastal cities. Did he conquer them? We hear nothing of a campaign. Could Hiram of Tyre be a special case rather like Tōʿī of Hamath in Middle Syria, who of his own free will accepted subjection and entered into the first stage of vassaldom?[22]

The sources are not very helpful in solving these questions. There are only two references which concern David's relations to the Phoenician coast: 2 Sam 5:11 and 2 Sam 24:5-7. Both are problematic. 2 Sam 24:5-7 describes the journey of Joab and the military census-officials to carry out the population census which David had ordered. The badly preserved text

---

[17]Cf. A. Alt, *Kleine Schriften* 2, 76-89; G. E. Wright, "The Provinces of Solomon," *Eretz-Israel* 8 (1967) 58-68; Y. Aharoni, "The Solomonic Districts," *Tel Aviv* 3 (1976) 5-15; T. N. D. Mettinger, *Solomonic State Officials* (CB OTS 5, 1971) 111-27.

[18]Cf. M. Gichon, "The Defences of the Solomonic Kingdom," *PEQ* 95 (1963) 113ff.

[19]Cf. I. Mendelsohn, "State Slavery in Ancient Palestine," *BASOR* 85 (1942) 14-17; idem, *Slavery in the Ancient Near East* (New York, 1949); idem, "On Corvée Labor in Ancient Canaan and Israel," *BASOR* 167 (1962) 31-35; A. F. Rainey, "Compulsory Labour Gangs in Ancient Israel," *IEJ* 20 (1970) 191-202; T. N. D. Mettinger, *Solomonic State Officials*, 128-39.

[20]Perhaps in the Syrians of Aram-Ṣōbā too: 1 Kgs 11:25 LXX.

[21]Cf. J. R. Bartlett, "An Adversary against Solomon, Hadad the Edomite," *ZAW* 88 (1976) 205-26.

[22]On the stages of vassaldom, exemplified with the expansion of the Neo-Assyrian empire, see H. Donner, *Israel unter den Völkern* (VTSup 11, 1964) 2f.

runs as follows: "(5) And they passed over the Jordan, and encamped in Aroer, on the right side of the city that is in the middle of the valley; Gad and unto Ya‘zēr. (6) Then they came to Gilead, and to the land of Taḥtīm Ḥādšī; and they came to Dan . . . , and round about to Sidon. (7) Then they came to the stronghold of Tyre, and to all the cities of the Hivites and of the Canaanites, and they went out to the southern desert of Judah unto Beersheba." This text is certainly not preserved intact; the ancient versions vary widely. The attempts at reconstruction are based primarily on the Lucian recension of the Septuagint which P. de Lagarde has set out in his edition of the Septuagint. Of course one can never be sure whether one is dealing with the first corrections of an incomprehensible *Vorlage* or not. In v. 5 the LXX^L καὶ ἐξῆζαν ἀπὸ κτλ. points to מערוער (ויסעו) ויחלו ומן־העיר אשר בתוך הנחל "they began (set out?) from Aroer and from the city that is in the middle of the valley";[23] afterwards one should perhaps read (אל־הגדי). The expression ארץ תחתים חדשי in v. 6 is completely enigmatic: Vulgate "in terram inferiorem Hodsi" paraphrases the Masoretic text, the Septugint includes every erroneous possibility,[24] and the LXX^L reads χεττιειμ Καδης, thereby appearing to have read or corrected ארץ החתים קדשה. The possibility that the famous Kadesh on the Orontes (Tall Nabī Mind) is meant cannot be excluded, although this site is located far from the other cities and territories; but, also Kedesh in Naphtali (Josh 19:37; modern Qadas) deserves consideration.[25] The meaningless word-sequence יען וסביב is according to the Septuagint καὶ ἐκύκλωσαν (Vulgata: circumeuntesque) to be reconstructed in the following way: ומדן סבבו "and from Dan they turned (to Sidon)" or—following a proposal of A. Klostermann—ועין ויסבו "and to ‘Iyyōn, then they turned (to Sidon)."[26] The deviations of the Septuagint in v. 7 appear to presuppose no other text besides that which we have.

However, the question remains, how one should interpret the passage apart from its corruption? It is customarily considered as a reliable source for the extension of the Davidic empire.[27] The first scholar who raised

---

[23]Cf. Deut 2:36; Josh 13:9, 16.

[24]LXX: καὶ εἰς γῆν θαβάσων ἥ ἐστιν Αδασαι. Cod. Alexandrinus reads εθαων instead of θαβασων; ἥ ἐστιν is lacking in Alexandrinus, and more than three quarters of the minusculi have καὶ εἰς ἔσθων καὶ εἰς instead of ἥ ἐστιν. Finally, Αδασαι appears in the Cod. Vaticanus as Ναδασαι, certainly a mistake in writing (dittography ἥ ἐστιν (ν)αδασαι).

[25]Therefore A. Klostermann proposed (ם)נפתלי קדשה; others (for instance Grätz, Budde) תחת חרמון. Cf. P. W. Skehan, "Joab's Census: How far North (2 Sam 24,6)?" *CBQ* 31 (1969) 42-49.

[26]Cf. 1 Kgs 15:20; 2 Kgs 15:29.

[27]Cf. K. Elliger, "Die Nordgrenze des Reiches Davids," *PJ* 32 (1936) 65; M. Noth, *Geschichte Israels* (7th ed.; Göttingen, 1970) 176f.; Y. Aharoni, *The Land of the Bible* (London, 1966) 71, 264f.; Z. Kallai, *The Tribes of Israel: A Study in the Historical Geography of the Bible* (Jerusalem, 1967) 32-35 (Hebrew); B. Oded, *The Political Status of Israelite Transjordan during the Period of the Monarchy* (Haifa, 1968) 28-31 (Hebrew); M. Ottosson, *Gilead. Tradition and History* (CB OTS 3, 1969) 213f., 218; S. Herrmann, *Geschichte Israels in alttestamentlicher Zeit* (München, 1973) 202.

difficulties concerning it was M. Wüst.[28] We shall take up his observations and develop them a little further. 2 Sam 24:1-9 tells of the population census, instigated by Yahweh and commanded by David. A census must be taken of the people (הָעָם vv. 2,4), namely, "Israel and Judah" (v. 1), that is, the population of the Palestinian nucleus, of the northern and southern kingdoms. For this purpose David sends Joab and the officers with the instruction "to go to and fro (שׁוּט v. 2) through all tribes of Israel from Dan to Beersheba." By this the ethnographic and geographical scope is precisely delineated: the population of the kingdoms of Israel and Judah, not that of the outlying provinces of the Davidic empire! The carrying out of this command is reported in v. 8: וַיָּשֻׁטוּ "they went to and fro, they traversed." But, what, according to vv. 5-7, do the officials actually do? They do not indeed traverse the territory of the Israelite tribes, but they set out on a route-march along the eastern and northern borders of the kingdom. Thereby they include areas in the population census which plainly did never belong to Israel and Judah: Sidon (v. 6) and Tyre (v. 7), that is, the southern part of the Phoenician coast. If one excludes vv. 5-7 as an addition (they are lacking in the parallel narrative of 1 Chronicles 21),[29] then v. 8 runs on smoothly from v. 4. There are not only literary reasons, but also grounds of content which point to vv. 5-7 as an editorial comment. It is easy to show that the description of the march along the borders is nothing more than the product of scribal speculation and combination on the basis of particular geographical texts of the Old Testament, above all Joshua 13 and Joshua 19. Already the "city that is in the middle of the valley" (v. 5) suggests that we are not dealing with an authentic source from the time of David, for there is no such city; it is a phantom. It owes its literary existence in the description of the southern border of the tribe of Reuben (Josh 13:16) to a learned redactor with an inclination to geographical combinations. He had before him Num 21:13, 15, 28 and Num 22:36, and he tried to make some sense of the evidence of these verses.[30] All the other references which speak of the "city that is in the middle of the valley" stand in literary dependence on Josh 13:16[31]—including 2 Sam 24:5 and, indeed, all the more so as, with one exception,[32] the "city that is in the middle of the valley" always occurs together with Aroer (Ḫirbat ᶜАrāᶜir on

---

[28] M. Wüst, *Untersuchungen zu den siedlungsgeographischen Texten des Alten Testaments. I. Ostjordanland*, (BTAVO B/9, 1975) 142f.

[29] There are two possibilities: (1) The Chronicler omitted these verses, because he did not understand them or took them as unimportant. Cf. M. Noth, *Überlieferungsgeschichtliche Studien* 1 (Tübingen 1943, reprint 1963) 137, n. 2; W. Rudolph, *Chronikbücher* (HAT 21, 1955) 142; W. Fuss, "II Samuel 24," *ZAW* 74 (1962) 151f.; Th. Willi, *Die Chronik als Auslegung* (FRLANT 106, 1972) 99. (2) The verses did not exist in the Chronicler's *Vorlage*. Cf. M. Wüst, *Untersuchungen*, 143.

[30] Proved by M. Wüst, *Untersuchungen*, 133-41.

[31] Deut 2:36; 3:16; Josh 12:2; 13:9.

[32] Deut 3:16.

the Wādi Sēl el-Mōğib). Further the contiguity and continuity of Gad, Ya‘zēr and Gilead in vv. 5-6 depend plainly on Num 32:1 and Josh 13:25.[33] Kedesh in Naphtali, if one should read and think so in v. 6, occurs in Josh 19:37; ארץ החתים is found in Josh 1:4 as a general description of the land of the Canaanites, but can also be applied to the northern region.[34] Sidon and Tyre are placed in this order (from north to south!) in Josh 19:28-29 in the description of the west border of the tribe of Asher: here is not implied that the Phoenician cities belonged to the theoretical tribal area of Asher, but that the border of Asher ran through the eastern hinterland of the coastal cities. The expression מבצר־צר "stronghold, fortress of Tyre" occurs only in Josh 19:29 and 2 Sam 24:7! The redactor, who took his position from Joshua 19, believed that he should interpret the description of the border in the sense of extension of the Davidic empire. For the rest, namely, the Palestinian nucleus, he used only the general descriptions "all the cities of the Hivites and of the Canaanites" and "to the southern desert of Judah unto Beersheba" (v. 7), the latter with reference back to v. 2. So, 2 Sam 24:5-7 is a learned editorial comment which obtains the route of the census-officials on the basis of already existing quasi-canonical scriptural references; it is therefore no reliable source for the extension of the Davidic dominion, and certainly not over the Phoenician coast.

But what are we to say about 2 Sam 5:11? The text runs: "Hiram king of Tyre sent messengers to David as well as cedar-wood, carpenters and stone-masons, so that they might build a house for David (or: and they built a house for David)." Which house? Of course the palace which also is mentioned in 2 Sam 7:2 (בית ארזים) and 20:3 (ביתו)[35]—and certainly not the temple, of which the whole tradition speaks unambiguously that Solomon first built it.[36] Hiram of Tyre provided building materials and craftsmen, just as he later did for Solomon in the building of the temple (1 Kgs 5:15-26, 32). Now we cannot overlook—although it has always been overlooked—the fact that the isolated reference of 2 Sam 5:11 has striking similarities with the "Solomon texts." The introductory formula וישלח חירם מלך־צר מלאכים אל־דוד "Hiram king of Tyre sent messengers to David" corresponds almost word for word with 1 Kgs 5:15 וישלח חירם מלך־צור את־עבדיו אל־שלמה "Hiram king of Tyre sent his servants to Solomon." Indeed, this is the beginning of the section concerning the establishment of diplomatic relations and of a trade agreement between Hiram and Solomon, which has been strongly edited along deuteronomistic lines, if not wholly written by a deuteronomist.[37] In 1 Kgs 5:17 David is

---

[33] M. Wüst, Untersuchungen, 143, n. 474 and p. 166.

[34] The expression is lacking in LXX[BAL] and in the parallel reference of Deut 11:24.

[35] Cf. perhaps 2 Sam 5:9b. The buildings ascribed to David in later texts of the Old Testament do not come into question here: Neh 3:16, 19, 25; Cant 4:4.

[36] On the possible pre-Solomonic history of the Temple of Jerusalem, see K. Rupprecht, Der Tempel von Jerusalem. Gründung Salomos oder jebusitisches Erbe? (BZAW 144, 1977).

[37] Cf. M. Noth, Könige 1, 88ff.

excused for not having already begun the building of the temple (לבנות בית
לשם יהוה; cf. v. 19): his intentions were good, but his many wars and
campaigns left him no time for their fulfilment. In this connection should
not also the temple be understood in 2 Sam 5:11? We do not know. Also,
what Hiram sent to David with his messengers appears almost word for
word again with reference to Solomon: עצי ארזים "cedar-wood" (1 Kgs
5:20, 22, 24; 9:11);[38] חרשי עץ "carpenters" and חרשי אבן קיר "stone-
masons" reflect 1 Kgs 5:32 ויפסלו בני שלמה ובני חירם והגבלים
ויכינו העצים והאבנים לבנות הבית "Solomon's builders and Hiram's
builders and the people of Byblos did fashion them (i.e., the blocks of stone)
and prepared the logs and the stones, in order to build the house (= the
temple)." The concluding formula לבנות הבית sounds very similar to 2 Sam
5:11 ויבנו בית לדוד—except that, if the temple be meant, nothing came of it.
If the temple were meant, that would explain the use of חרשים "artisans"
instead of בנים "builders" (1 Kgs 5:32):[39] because בנים "those building,
builders" could have implied that something actually had been built. But, it
is of course possible that David's palace and not the temple is intended. In
any case the following conclusion is highly probable: 2 Sam 5:11 stands in
literary dependence on 1 Kgs 5:15-26, 32 (and 9:11?). It is the note of a
deuteronomistic or post-deuteronomistic redactor, who backdated to the
time of David the connections between Tyre and Israel on the basis of 1 Kgs
5:15-26.

From all this we may draw the following conclusions: if 2 Sam 5:11 and
2 Sam 24:5-7 be late redacted texts, then they cannot be taken into account
as authentic sources for the situation in the time of David. But, then there is
in the whole tradition no evidence whatever that David had anything to do
with Tyre and the Phoenician coast as far as Sidon. No one should be
surprised at this, for it fits perfectly with the picture which we gained above
of the interdependence of internal affairs and foreign policy in the Davidic-
Solomonic period: an interdependence which may be clearly understood
through the concept of action and reaction. Tyre entered the political
horizon of Israel definitely for the first time during the second stage of the
empire; and indeed this happened as a reaction to the primacy given to
internal affairs under Solomon. At the time of David these relations,
political relations and not mere cognizance, did not yet exist; had they done
so, David must have conquered the Phoenician coastal cities or at least made
them vassals. But, where do we find that written? The possibility is suggested
that David dealt with the Phoenician coast during the stage of the expansion
of the empire just as, centuries later, the overlords of the Neo-Assyrian
empire did, namely, according to the principle: if not really necessary, do not
touch! Leave things as they are! Handle with kid-gloves! The kings of the
Phoenician coast would also have followed a policy of wise passivity, so as not

---

[38] According to 2 Kgs 5:20 ארזים only, but cf. LXX ξύλα = עצים.
[39] On חרשי עץ cf. 2 Kgs 12:12; Isa 44:13; 1 Chr 14:1; on חרשי אבן קיר cf. Exod 28:11;
1 Chr 22:15.

to attract the attention of the lion of Judah at the wrong time. David and the Phoenician coast? A peaceful, independent coexistence. Solomon and the Phoenician coast? Relations, trade, and dependence.

Solomon's Trade in Horses and Chariots in Its International Setting

YUTAKA IKEDA

The Hebrew University, Jerusalem

One of the most significant biblical passages describing the broad extent of Israel's international relations in the time of Solomon is in 1 Kgs 10:28-29 (= 2 Chr 1:16-17); it says that Solomon purchased horses from Egypt and Que (i.e., Cilicia in the southeast of Anatolia) and chariots from Egypt. Yet, with the difficulty of believing that Egypt had ever exported horses, most of the commentators have tried to correct the text, and the majority (following H. Winckler[1]) tend to take *Miṣrayim* in verse 28 as a corrupted form of an original *Muṣri*, a land which is supposedly to be sought in the Taurus region of Anatolia.[2] There are those who go even further and apply the same correction to verse 29, and thus Solomon imported not only horses but also chariots from Anatolia, not Egypt.[3] Still, (as has been demonstrated by H. Tadmor[4]) the theory of an "Anatolian *Muṣri*" is now hardly to be maintained.[5] Indeed, in spite of frequent

---

[1] *Alttestamentliche Untersuchungen* (Leipzig, 1892) 172f.

[2] A. Šanda, *Die Bücher der Könige* (EHAT 9/1, 1911) 292; J. A. Montgomery and H. S. Gehman, *The Books of Kings* (ICC, 1951) 227; M. Noth, *Könige* 1 (BKAT 9/1, 1963) 202, 234ff.; J. Gray, *I & II Kings* (2d ed.; London, 1970) 264, 269; S. Herrmann, *Geschichte Israels in alttestamentlicher Zeit* (München, 1973) 221 and n. 14; H. J. Katzenstein, *The History of Tyre* (Jerusalem, 1973) 113f.; A. D. Crown, "Once Again 1 Kings 10:26-29," *Abr Nahrain* 15 (1974/75) 35; M. Elat, *Economic Relations in the Lands of the Bible c.1000-589* B.C. (Jerusalem, 1977) 200f. (Hebrew); B. Peckham, "Israel and Phoenicia," *Magnalia Dei: The Mighty Acts of God. Essays on the Bible and Archaeology in Memory of G. E. Wright* (eds. F. M. Cross *et al.*; Garden City, 1976) 242, n. 59.

[3] Šanda, Montgomery and Gehman, Gray, Crown (above n. 2) and for the similar apprehension by Mowinckel and others, see also below n. 6.

[4] "Que and Muṣri," *IEJ* 11 (1961) 141-50. Cf. also P. Garelli, "Nouveau coup d'oeil sur Muṣur,' *Hommage à A. Dupont-Sommer* (Paris, 1971) 37ff.; K. A. Kitchen, *The Third Intermediate Period in Egypt (1100-650* B.C.) (Oxford, 1973) 325, n. 454; J. A. Soggin, "The Davidic-Solomonic Kingdom," *Israelite and Judaean History* (eds. J. H. Hayes and J. M. Miller; London, 1977) 374; N. Naʾaman, "Two Notes on the Monolith Inscription of Shalmaneser III from Kurkh," *Tel Aviv* 3 (1976) 100, n. 24; idem, "Looking for KTK," *WO* 9 (1978) 225f.

[5] The possibility that *Muṣur* in the inscriptions of Esarhaddon (R. Borger, *Die Inschriften Asarhaddons Königs von Assyrien* [AfO Beiheft 9, 1956] 112:15) is to be located in the vicinity of Tyre has been suggested (Naʾaman, *WO* 9 [1978] 225f.). It may be noted, however, that the

proposals of textual emendation,[6] historical problems related to the above passages are yet to be fully discussed.[7] It is the purpose of this paper to reconsider the issue of Solomon's trade in horses and chariots and to view the background of the international relations of his age.

I

First, it should be remembered that horses and chariots had been known to the land of Canaan long before the time of Solomon. It was indeed through Canaan that horses and chariots were introduced into Egypt toward the end of the Hyksos period.[8] Thuthmose III claims that he captured 924 chariots and 2,238 horses in the battle of Megiddo, against

---

geographical terms such as *Muṣur* and *Meluḫḫa* are used rather loosely in this text (A. L. Oppenheim, *ANET*, 292b, n. 1). Otherwise *Muṣur* is used only for Egypt in the text; it is by no means improbable that by *Muṣur* in the passage under the present discussion (line 15) is concerned with a general description of the broad extent of the Egyptian influence (KUR *Muṣur*), under which was also found the city of Tyre whose ruler Baʾlu is indeed said to have "put his trust in his friend Tirhakah, king of Kûsu (Nubia)" (line 12); cf. the translation of the text by *ARAB* 2 § 556. One cannot take *Mṣr* in the Sefire inscriptions (J. A. Fitzmyer, *The Aramaic Inscriptions of Sefîre*, [BibOr 19, 1967] 12:5) as an evidence for Anatolian Muṣri, either, for it may most reasonably be understood as a personal name (see the context there: "with Mṣr and *his* sons"). Cf. M. Noth, "Der historische Hintergrund der Inschriften von Sefîre," *ZDPV* 77 (1961) 131, n. 38; E. Lipiński, *Studies in Aramaic Inscriptions and Onomastics* 1 (Leuven, 1975) 25; Naʾaman, *WO* 9 (1978) 225f. But, cf. also the view that *mṣr* in the Sefire inscriptions is to be taken as a loan from the Akkadian *miṣru* "boundary," which has been suggested by H. Tadmor ("Notes to the Beginning Lines of the Aramaic Treaty from Sefire," *Sefer Shmuel Yeivin* [Jerusalem, 1970] 397-404 [Hebrew]) and followed by S. A. Kaufman, *The Akkadian Influences on Aramaic* (AS 19, 1974) 72f., and cf. also 154, n. 73. I am grateful to Prof. H. Tadmor for his critical comments on this as well as other problems dealt with in this paper.

[6]S. Mowinckel proposed to reread *mimiṣrayim* to *lᵉmiṣrayim* "to Egypt (from Que)" both in verse 28 and verse 29 ("Drive and/or Ride in O.T.," *VT* 19 [1962] 282, n. 11). The suggestion has been repeated recently by Elat, though he tends to understand *miṣrayim* in verse 28 as referring to an Anatolian-Muṣri (see above n. 2). For the same rereading in verse 28, see also K. Galling, apud J. Fichtner, *Das erste Buch von den Königen* (Stuttgart 1964) 174f. On the other hand, W. F. Albright suggested to delete *mimiṣrayim* in verse 28 as dittography ("Review of J. A. Montgomery and H. S. Gehman, *Kings*," *JBL* 71 [1952] 249), a suggestion followed by J. Bright, *A History of Israel* (2d ed.; London 1972) 212; J. M. Myers, *II Chronicles* (AB 13, 1965) 4f.; cf. also the translation of the verses in *JB*.

[7]But, see Naʾaman, *Tel Aviv* 3 (1976) 100f. and n. 24.

[8]Cf. J. H. Breasted, *A History of Egypt* (New York, 1909) 222; H. von Deines, "Die Nachrichten über das Pferd und den Wagen in den ägyptischen Texten," *MIO* 1 (1953) 6; H. Ranke and P. Thomsen, "Pferd," *RLV* 10 (1927/28) 113; A. Kammenhuber, *Hippologica Hethitica* (Wiesbaden, 1961) 9. Cf. also Y. Yadin, *The Art of Warfare in Biblical Lands* (Jerusalem/Ramat-Gan, 1963) 86ff.; W. Nagel, *Der mesopotamische Streitwagen und seine Entwicklungen im ostmediterranen Bereich* (Berlin, 1966) 36ff.; A. Kempinski, "סוס," *EncBib* 5 (1968) 1005-8 (Hebrew).

the Canaanite princes (1490 B.C.),[9] while his son Amenhotep II returned home with 820 horses and 730 chariots as booty from his campaign against Canaan.[10] Both the Egyptian words for "horses" (*śśm.t* and *ibr*) and the one for "chariot" (*mrkbt*) are Semitic loanwords,[11] and the Egyptians' protecting deities of chariots and chariot-horses are the Canaanite Anath and Astarte.[12] The chariots of Canaanite princes in the period of the Judges are well attested by both textual and archaeological evidence,[13] while the presence of a chariot repair workshop at Jaffa is noted in Papyrus Anastasi I (from the end of the 13th century B.C.).[14] It is argued whether Israel had a chariot unit in its armies when David fought against the Aramaeans, who were well equipped with many chariots.[15] However, there is reason to assume that when the Canaanite regions were brought under David's rule, all the professional personnel among the indigenous peoples were also

---

[9]J. A. Wilson, *ANET*, 237. Cf. Breasted, *A History of Egypt*, 289ff.; W. Helck, *Die Beziehungen Ägyptens zur Vorderasien im 3. und 2. Jahrtausend v. Chr.* (Wiesbaden, 1962) 138; A. Malamat, "Origins and Formative Period," *A History of the Jewish People* (ed. H. H. Ben-Sasson; London, 1976) 13ff. and more recently, A. Spalinger, "A New Reference to an Egyptian Campaign of Thutmose III in Asia," *JNES* 37 (1978) 35-41.

[10]*ANET*, 246b and see also n. 29 for a variation. In another year the king of Egypt is said to have captured 1,632 chariots from the princes of Retenu, i.e., Syria-Palestine (*ANET*, 247b). On the land Retenu, see more recently S. Ahituv, *The Egyptian Topographical Lists Relating to the History of Palestine in the Biblical Period* (Hebrew Univ. Diss. 1979) 196ff. (Hebrew).

[11]J. Yoyotte, "Cheval," *DCÉ* (1959) 51; Helck, *Beziehungen*, 393f. On *ibr* "stallion" (Heb. אביר) cf. Erman and Grapow, "ibr," *Wörterbuch der ägyptischen Sprache* 1 (Leipzig 1926) 63 and also A. Salonen, *Hippologica Accadica* (Helsinki, 1955) 14. For another important Egyptian term for chariot, *wrr.t*, which is probably a Hurrian loan, cf. von Deines, *MIO* 1 (1953) 11f.; W. Helck and E. Otto, *Kleines Wörterbuch der Aegyptologie* (2d ed., Wiesbaden 1970) 407.

[12]Von Deines, *MIO* 1 (1953) 12.

[13]Judges 4-5. On the Song of Deborah and the Canaan-Israel war described there, cf. more recently Z. Kallai, "Judah and Israel: A Study in Israelite Historiography," *IEJ* 28 (1978) 251ff.; Y. Ikeda, "The Song of Deborah and the Tribes of Israel," *Studies in the Bible and the Hebrew Language Offered to Meir Wallenstein* (ed. Ch. Rabin; Jerusalem, 1979) 65ff. (Hebrew) and the references there, and for the date of the Song of Deborah see also D. N. Freedman, "Early Israelite Poetry and Historical Reconstruction," *Symposia. Celebrating the Seventy-Fifth Anniversary of the Founding of the American Schools of Oriental Research [1900-1975]* (ed. F. M. Cross; Cambridge, MA, 1979) 85ff. On the chariot scenes depicted on the ivory plaques found in Megiddo, see Yadin, *The Art of Warfare*, 242f. and also ibid., 255. For other related archaeological evidences cf. F. James, "Chariot Fittings from Late Bronze Age Beth Shan," *Archaeology in the Levant. Essays for K. Kenyon* (eds. P. R. S. Moorey and P. J. Parr; Warminster, 1978) 103, 107, 109.

[14]*ANET*, 478a.

[15]2 Sam 8:4 says: "David hamstrung all the chariot teams, keeping only a hundred of them," which has been taken as a proof that Israel did not have a chariot unit in its armies in the days of David, see, e.g., S. R. Driver, *Deuteronomy* (ICC 1896) 211; R. de Vaux, *Ancient Israel* (1961) 222; Mowinckel, *VT* 12 (1962) 282; Bright, *A History of Israel*, 209, but for the opposite opinion, see Yadin, *The Art of Warfare*, 285; E. Oren, "The Beginning of the Chariot-Force in the Kingdom of David," *Ma'arachôt* 247/248 (1975) 57ff. (Hebrew), and also Malamat in this volume.

integrated into the complex of the new Israelite society, including the chariot craftsmen. In fact, in dividing his kingdom into 12 administrative districts, Solomon not only partly followed the division of the former Canaanite territory but also appointed members of Canaanite families, apparently with long administrative experience, as the governors (niṣabīm) over some of the districts, among which was the non-Canaanite hill-country of Ephraim (1 Kgs 4:7-19).[16] Significantly, one of the main tasks placed upon them was to provide fodder for the horses of the royal stables: "The regional governors, each for a month in turn, supplied provisions for King Solomon and for all who came to his table; they never fell short in their deliveries. They provided also barley and straw, each according to his duty, for the horses and horse-chariots,[17] where it was required" (1 Kgs 4:27-28 [NEB]; MT 5:7-8).[18]

Thus, Israel in the time of Solomon surely had the capability of chariot production, as well as an agricultural basis sufficient to maintain quite a number of horses in its land; it is even not difficult to assume that Israel then had its own chariot factory. The question, therefore, is if Solomon nevertheless purchased chariots and horses abroad, and what his motives were.

II

There is no doubt that Solomon made an effort to reinforce the army of his kingdom,[19] but it is also true that Israel had enjoyed an unusually

---

[16]On this issue see especially A. Alt, "Israels Gaue unter Salomo" (1913) Kleine Schriften 2 (München, 1953) 76-89; Y. Aharoni, "נציב," EncBib 5 (1968) 914-16 (Hebrew); idem, The Land of the Bible (London, 1966) 277-80; B. Mazar, "The Scribe of King David, and the Problem of the High Officials in the Ancient Kingdom of Israel" (1946/47) Canaan and Israel (Jerusalem, 1974) 208ff. (Hebrew); idem, "The Cities of Territory of Dan," IEJ 10 (1960) 65-77; idem, "Dor and Reḥob in an Egyptian Topographical List" (1963) Cities and Districts in Eretz-Israel (Jerusalem, 1975) 154ff. (Hebrew); W. F. Albright, "The Administrative Divisions of Israel and Judah," JPOS 5 (1925) 17ff., and see also de Vaux, Ancient Israel, 133f.; G. E. Wright, "The Provinces of Solomon," Eretz-Israel 8 (1967) 58ff.; Noth, Könige 1, 66-75; T. N. D. Mettinger, Solomonic State Officials: A Study of the Civil Government Officials of the Israelite Monarchy (CB OTS 5, 1971) 111ff.; D. B. Redford, "Studies in Relations between Palestine and Egypt during the First Millennium B.C. 1. The Taxation System of Solomon," Studies on the Ancient Palestine World. Presented to Prof. F. V. Winnett (eds. J. W. Wevers and D. B. Redford; Toronto/Buffalo, 1972) 141-56; J. Bright, "The Organization and Administration of the Israelite Empire," Magnalia Dei, 198ff.

[17]For rekeš as chariot-horse, cf. also Mic 1:13; Esth 8:10, and see Gray, I & II Kings, 144.

[18]For the Akkadian equivalent for straw (tibnu) and the Assyrian government tax on straw, šibšu, see J. N. Postgate, Taxation and Conscription in the Assyrian Empire (Rome, 1974) 186-89; cf. also W. von Soden, "šibšu," AHw Lief. 13 (1976) 1227f.; Montgomery and Gehman, Kings, 127. For the corn taxes imposed upon the province of Samaria (ŠE nusaḫe ša KUR Samirnaya) by the Assyrian administration (ABL 1201:4-5), see Postgate, Taxation, 182. It is also worth noting that Obadiah, "the master of palace," was sent out by King Ahab during the draught to find forage for his horses, mules, and livestock (1 Kgs 18:5).

[19]King Solomon is said to have possessed one thousand and four hundred chariots, twelve thousand horses (1 Kgs 10:26) and forty (four [?]—see, e.g., JB) thousand stalls (4:26). Cf.

long period of peace in the reign of Solomon and indeed it is the intention
of the books of Kings to present Solomon as a man of peace, in contrast to
the image of David, his predecessor (1 Kgs 4:20; 5:5, 16-18). In fact, the
account of Solomon's import of chariots and horses is given in a literary
context whose main theme is to display his glory and great wealth (1 Kgs
10:23; cf. also 3:13)—not just in "quantity" but, more important, in
"quality."

Solomon's "Tarshish fleet"[20] returned from the land of Ophir once
every three years with great cargos of gold, silver, and ivory—precious
materials used, among other things, for the ornamentation of his palace,
the "Forest of Lebanon"; Solomon also made 300 golden shields for honor-
ific use, as well as a "great ivory throne" magnificently plated with refined
gold (1 Kgs 10:14-21).[21] But, of special significance are the exotic animals
brought for the king from the south, such as apes and baboons (1 Kgs
10:22; cf. also 4:33).[22] Solomon's "zoological interest" is indeed in line with
what we know of the Assyrian kings of the 12th-9th centuries B.C. Tiglath-
pileser I (1115-1077 B.C.) recounts that he "formed the herds of horses,
oxen, (and) asses" as well as those of "*nayalu*-deer, *ayalu*-deer, gazelles,
and ibex."[23] But, it is the author of the "Broken Obelisk," apparently
Ashur-bel-kala, the son of the former (1074-1057 B.C.), who boasts of his
collection of luxurious animals; he not only bred various kinds of wild
animals, but especially "dispatched merchants" to acquire rare animals,
including dromedaries, which he "bred, (and) displayed herds of them to
the people of his land"; the Assyrian king—the account of the "Broken
Obelisk" continues—received from the king of Egypt "a large female ape, a
crocodile (and) a 'river-man,' beasts of the Great Sea," which were also
displayed to the people of Assyria.[24] No less competitive were the succeed-

---

de Vaux, *Ancient Israel*, 222f. and more recently F. M. Cross, *Canaanite Myth and Hebrew
Epic: Essays in the History of the Religion of Israel* (Cambridge, MA/London, 1973) 239f.
For the descriptions of enforcing military power in the extra-biblical royal inscriptions see
below n. 23.

[20]For Solomon's "Tarshish-fleet," see below, n. 111.

[21]See also 1 Kgs 7:2ff.; Isa 22:8 (the "House of Forest"). Cf. Noth, *Könige* 1, 134-38;
Mongomery and Gehman, *Kings*, 219ff.

[22]For the translation of *tukkiyîm* as "baboons" (*NEB*; *JB*) rather than the older "peacocks"
see W. F. Albright, "Ivory and Apes of Ophir," *AJSL* 37 (1921) 144. Cf. also Montgomery
and Gehman, *Kings*, 224f.; Noth, *Könige* 1, 205; Gray, *I & II Kings*, 236f., 268.

[23]*ARI* 2 § 46. Concerning the reinforcement of his military forces, Tiglath-pileser I is saying:
"I had in harness for the forces of my land more chariots and teams of horses than ever
before" (*ARI* 2 § 48). Likewise, Adad-nirari II boasts of his effort in multiplying horses for his
army: "I hitched up more teams of horses than ever before for the forces of my land" (*ARI* 2
§ 435). For the similar expression see also the Phoenician inscription from Karatepe where
Azitawada, king of Adana, says: "I added horse to horse, shield to shield, and army to army"
(F. Rosenthal, *ANET*, 653). For the more recent translation of this bilingual text—particularly
that on the hieroglyphic Luwian part—see J. D. Hawkins and A. Morpurgo-Davies, "On the
Problem Karatepe: The Hieroglyphic Text," *AnSt* 28 (1978) 114ff.

[24]*ARI* 2 § 247. For the view to ascribe the authorship of the "Broken Obelisk" to Ashur-bel-
kala, see K. Jaritz, "The Problem of the 'Broken Obelisk'," *JSS* 4 (1959) 204-15; E. Weidner,

ing Assyrian kings, who presented themselves as the possessors of rare, costly animals. Adad-nirari II (911-891 B.C.) says of his collection of "lions, wild bulls, elephants, *ayalu*-deer, ibex, wild asses, deer (and) ostriches" in Ashur,[25] that he added "a large female ape (and) a small female ape" sent by the inhabitants of Bit-Adini, who appreciated the "taste" of their suzerain.[26] Just as enthusiastically, Ashurnasirpal II (883-859 B.C.) too describes his rich collection of wild animals: "I formed herds of wild bulls, elephants, lions, ostriches, male apes, female apes, wild asses, deer, *ayalu*-deer, female bears, leopards, *senkurru*, *tušēnu*, beasts of mountain (and) plain, all of them in my city Calah; I displayed (them) to all the people of my land."[27]

Among the list of the large cargos which Solomon's merchants brought from the Red Sea was the rare *ʾalmuggîm*-wood,[28] which Solomon used so lavishly for the furnishings of the Temple and his palace that the later historian saw fit to add a note: "No such *almuggim*-wood has ever been imported or even seen since that time" (1 Kgs 10:11-12).[29] In Eccl 2:4-6 King Solomon is represented as saying: "I . . . planted vineyards for myself; I made myself gardens and parks, and planted in them all kinds of fruit trees. I made myself pools from which to water the forest of growing trees." Indeed, Solomon's "botanical interest" (1 Kgs 5:13) is another important element in the depiction of the king, which goes handsomely with the descriptions in the inscriptions of the Assyrian kings of his age. Tiglath-pileser I says: "I took cedar,[30] box-tree, Kanish oak from the lands

---

"Die Annalen des Königs Assurbelkala von Assyrien," *AfO* 6 (1930) 87; H. Tadmor, *IEJ* 11 (1961) 146, n. 19; R. Borger, *Einleitung in die assyrischen Köngsinschriften* 1 (Leiden, 1961) 135, 138-42; J. A. Brinkman, *A Political History of Post-Kassite Babylonia 1158-722 B.C.* (An Or 43, 1968) 337, 383; *ARI* 2 § 227; A. K. Grayson, *Assyrian and Babylonian Chronicles* (New York, 1975) 208f.

[25]*ARI* 2 § 436, and see also above n. 23.

[26]*ARI* 2 § 426. A "large female ape" is also mentioned in the inscriptions of Ashurnasirpal II in connection with the tribute from the king of Pattin (*ARI* 2 § 583) and with that from the princes of the Phoenician coast (*ARI* 2 § 586). On monkeys as pets in the ancient Near East, see R. D. Barnett, "Monkey Business," in *The Gaster Festschrift* (*JANES* 5, 1973) 1-5. Cf. also Ch. Rabin *et al.*, "קוֹף," *EncBib* 7 (1976) 104-7 (Hebrew).

[27]*ARI* 2 § 598.

[28]But, in 2 Chr 2:7 *ʾalgummîm* is associated with Lebanon. For the problem of the origin of the wood see Albright, *AJSL* 37 (1921) 145; N. H. Tur-Sinai, "אלמגים, אלגומים," in *EncBib* 1 (1950) 360-61 (Hebrew), but also J. C. Greenfield and M. Mayrhofer, "The algummim/almuggim-Problem Reexamined," *Hebräische Wortforschung. Festschrift W. Baumgartner* (VTSup 16, 1967) 83-89.

[29]For the description of Solomon's lavish use of cedar in 1 Kgs 10:27 see below, and on cedar and other trees in Lebanon see the references in the following note.

[30]For the literary *topos* "cutting cedar in Lebanon" in the royal inscriptions of Mesopotamia see A. Malamat, "Campaigns to the Mediterranean by Iahdunlim and Other Early Mesopotamian Rulers," *Studies in Honor of B. Landsberger* (AS 16, 1965) 365ff. and more recently Y. Ikeda, "Hermon, Sirion and Senir," *AJBI* 4 (1978) 33ff. See also H. Tadmor, "The Decline of Empires in Western Asia ca. 1200 B.C.E.," *Symposia* (ed. F. M. Cross; Cambridge, MA, 1979) 8.

over which I had gained dominion—such trees which none among previous kings, my forefathers, had ever planted—and I planted (them) in the orchards of my land. I took rare orchard fruit which is not found in my land (and therewith) filled the orchards of Assyria."[31] It is once again Ashurnasirpal II who, unable to concede to his predecessors, boasts of his own enormous "botanical" collection, in the so-called Banquet Stele:

(I collected and planted in my garden) from the countries through which I marched and the mountains which I crossed, the trees (and plants raised from) wherever I discovered[32] . . . (a long list of trees). . . . The canal crashed from above into the gardens. Fragrance pervades the walkways. Streams of water (as numerous) as the stars of heaven flow into the pleasure garden (*kiri ṣīḫate*). Pomegranates like grapevines . . . in the garden . . . [I], Ashurnasirpal, in the delightful garden (*kiri rīšate*) pick fruit like a mouse.[33]

Likewise, fine chariots and horses were the items most sought by all the princes of the ancient Near East and were among the most desirable gifts to be expected. When his sister Giluhepa married Amenhotep III (ca. 1380 B.C.), Tushratta of Mitanni sent "four good horses who can run fast and a chariot made entirely of gold (*gabba hurāṣu*)," as a part of dowry (*EA* 22: 1-4).[34] Ashuruballit of Assyria sent to Amenhotep IV (Akhenaton) a fine chariot and two horses (*EA* 7:58), while on another occasion he wrote to the Egyptian king: "I am sending you a fine royal chariot (*narkabta banīta ša šarrūti*) that I drive (myself) and two white horses that I likewise drive (myself)" (*EA* 16:9-11).[35]

Admittedly, the prime function of these costly ornamental chariots was for the display of princes' glory and status in processions and cere-monies, not for the battlefield. Thus, Tushratta clearly distinguishes be-tween the chariot taken as booty in the war against the land of Hatti and other fine chariots, which he specifies "as gift to my brother," although both were sent to the Egyptian king on the same occasion (*EA* 17:36-40). In the Epic of Gilgamesh, the goddess Ishtar says to the royally atired Gilgamesh: "I will harness for thee a chariot of lapis lazuli and gold, whose wheels are gold and whose horns are brass. . . . In the fragrance of cedars thou shalt enter our house. When our house thou enterest, threshold (and)

---

[31] *ARI* 2 § 47.

[32] D. J. Wiseman, "A New Stele of Assur-Naṣir-Pal II," *Iraq* 14 (1952) 32:40ff. For the translation of the text see Oppenheim, *ANET*, 559.

[33] J. N. Postgate, *The Governor's Palace Archive* (Hertford, 1973) 239. For the translation see *ARI* 2 § 678; cf. also "*ṣīḫtu*," *CAD* Ṣ, 186b.

[34] For the translation of the text cf. "*banû*," *CAD* B, 82a. Cf. also Helck, *Beziehungen*, 441f. and also *EA* 19:84; "*maršu*," *CAD* M/1, 296.

[35] Cf. "*ṣamādu*," *CAD* Ṣ, 91b and B. Meissner, *Assyriologische Studien* (MVAG 18, 1913) 3. According to *EA* 266:26-33, Tagu, prince of Gath-Carmel, apparently sent a chariot with all its appurtenances to the king of Egypt (see N. Naʾaman, "*ašītu* (SG.) and *ašâtu* (PL.)—Strap and Reins," *JCS* 29 [1977] 238).

dais shall kiss thy feet! Humbled before thee shall be kings, lords and princes!"[36] And in the story of the Poor Man of Nippur, who borrowed a chariot of the king for the payment of one mina of gold a day, in order to proceed on the street of Nippur toward the temple of Enlil, it is repeatedly stated that a new chariot is "the mark of noblemen" (narkabtu eššu simat rabūte).[37] The private chariots with teams of horses, belonging to Nur-Adad, a prince of Hanigalbat, are designated as the most precious treasures of his palace, "befitting his royalty" (simat šarrūtīšu) along with his gold throne, polished gold dishes, gold tent and other items, in the inscriptions of Adad-nirari II,[38] while the same attribute (simat šarrūtīšu) is applied by the scribes of Ashurnasirpal II to the splendid objects sent as tribute from Sangara, king of Carchemish, among which were a great amount of silver, a gold ring, a gold bracelet, furniture of box-wood, and, in particular, a "chariot of polished (gold)."[39]

The inscriptions of Ashurbanipal (668-631 B.C.) recount how the Assyrian king had mercy upon Necho (I), prince of Sais in the Delta of Egypt, "clad him in a garment with multicolored trimmings, placed a golden chain on him (as the) insignia of his kingship (simat šarrūtīšu), put golden rings on his hands" and gave him a gold-mounted dagger as well as "chariots, horses and mules as means of transportation (befitting) his position as ruler" (ina rukūb bēlūtīšu).[40] Quite understandably, the private Prunkwagen of vassal kings or provincial governors, that is, their display chariot (narkabtu šarrūtīšu)[41] and their ornamental light chariot drawn by men (ša šadādi šarrūtīšu[42] or ša šadādi rukūb bēlūtīšu)[43] would become a

---

[36]ANET, 83f. "ṣamādu," CAD Ṣ, 91a.

[37]O. R. Gurney, "The Poor Man of Nippur," AnSt 6 (1956) 154:81, 83. Cf. A. L. Oppenheim, Ancient Mesopotamia (Chicago/London, 1964) 274; "narkabtu(m)," AHw 2 (1972) 747.

[38]J. Seidmann, Die Inschriften Adadnirâris II (MAOG 9/3, 1935) 24:71; ARI 2 § 429.

[39]E. Budge and L. W. King, Annals of the Kings of Assyria (London, 1902) 367: III 68; ARI 2 § 584.

[40]M. Streck, Assurbanipal und die letzten assyrischen Könige bis zum Untergang Nineveh's 2 (VAB 7, 1916) 14:II 8-14. For the translation see ANET, 259a; ARAB 2 §§ 774, 905. On Necho I see more recently Kitchen, The Third Intermediate Period, 145f. Cf. also "rukūbu(m)," AHw 2 (1972) 994a. For the similar rukūb šarrūti, cf. J. V. Kinnier Wilson, The Nimrud Wine Lists. A Study of Men and Administration at the Assyrian Capital in the Eighth Century B.C. (Hertford, 1972) 53.

[41]The attribute is used for the chariot of the king of Urartu in inscriptions of Tiglath-pileser III (H. Tadmor, Inscriptions of Tiglath-pileser III [forthcoming] Ann. 17:12'. For the older translation of the text see P. Rost, Die Keilschrifttexte Tiglat-Pilesers III [Leipzig, 1893] 14:69. Cf. also "narkabtu(m)," AHw 2 [1972] 747a).

[42]Tadmor, Inscriptions of Tiglath-pileser III, Ann. 17:12'.

[43]See, e.g., E. Weidner, "Assyrische Beschreibungen der Kriegs-Reliefs Aššurbânaplis," AfO 8 (1932/33) 196: 19. Cf. also what is told in ND 421: "Let them quickly cover that drawing-chariot (giš mugirri[š]a giš šadādi) with silver" (Postgate, The Governor's Palace Archive, no. 191). On ša šadādi cf. also A. Salonen, Die Landfahrzeuge des Alten Mesopotamien (Helsinki, 1951) 64ff. and "šadādu(m)," AHw Lief. 12 (1974) 1121a.

"tribute chariot" for their suzerain. In fact, in a letter found at Tell Halaf, Adad-nirari III (810-783 B.C.) demands that Adiyabu, prince of Guzana, send him 40 minas of gold, saying: "Put the gold in your (own) chariot!"[44] And in a Kuyunjik Letter (K 1044=ABL 241) we read of a provisional governor's readiness to appear before his lord, apparently Sargon II (721-705 B.C.), together with his chariot: "When the king goes to Babylon, I shall come for an audience with the king (ana šulme ša šarri) with one chariot."[45]

Sharing the splendid, flowery atmosphere of life and literature which commonly prevailed in the courts of the great kings of his age, the writer of the life of King Solomon made a special effort to present him as the greatest among the rulers of the entire world. Thus, one reads in 1 Kgs 10:25: "The whole world sought audience of Solomon to hear the wisdom God had implanted in his heart and each would bring his own present: gold vessels, silver vessels, robes, armor, spices, horses and mules;[46] and this went on year after year"[47] (cf. also 1 Kgs 5:1, 14, but especially the stately visit to Solomon paid by the queen of Sheba, in 1 Kgs 10:1-10),[48] and further in verse 27: "The king made silver as common in Jerusalem as stone, and cedar as plentiful as sycamore fig in the Shephelah." Hence, the image of King Solomon—the very wealthy, extravagant "collector," more than a mere builder of strong military forces—must have been the original literary intention of the account in the middle verse (verse 26): "(and) Solomon collected (waye³esōf) chariots and horses," a part of which he kept with care "at hand"[49] in Jerusalem.

It should also be noted that, while the Hebrew term rekeb is repeatedly used in the general description of Solomon's chariot collection in verse 26, we find that the chariots which are said to have been imported from Egypt, in the coming passage (verse 29), are called merkābāh, an indication that the specific use of the latter term, at least in this context, should not be ignored.[50] As a matter of fact, the use of the term merkābāh as a royal display chariot is attested in the Bible more than once. According to the "Manner of the King," the merkābāh was the mark of royalty par excel-

---

[44]E. Weidner, Die Keilschrifttexte vom Tell Halaf. 1. Das Archiv des Mannu-ki-Aššur (AfO Beiheft 6, 1967) 16. Cf. Postgate, Taxation, 128.

[45]ABL, 241 rev. 16'-19'. See W. J. Martin, Tribut und Tributleistungen bei den Assyrern (StOr 8/1, 1936) 34-38; Postgate, Taxation, 126. For Sargon II's Babylonian campaign see Grayson, Assyrian and Babylonian Chronicles, 273f. and the references there.

[46]For horses and mules as precious belongings "befitting PN's royalty," see also the citation from the inscriptions of Ashurbanipal below and n. 54.

[47]For the similar literary expression, see, e.g., R. Borger, Asarhaddon, 47:63-64: "Year after year, without cease, he (Na³id-Marduk) came to Nineveh with his heavy gifts and kissed my feet." For the translation see Postgate, Taxation, 126; cf. ARAB 2 § 510.

[48]On the verses see Noth, Könige 1, 223-27. For the queen of Sheba and the later traditions related to her see J. B. Pritchard, ed., Solomon & Sheba (New York, 1974).

[49]Lit. "with the king."

[50]But there are also cases where רכב is used in connection with dignity and display; cf. 1 Kgs 1:5; 2 Kgs 5:9; Jer 17:25, 22:4; Isa 66:20.

lence (1 Sam 8:11). Thus, when Absalom attempted to ascend the throne in place of David, he "procured a *merkābāh* and horses, with fifty men to run ahead of him," in order to flaunt his dignity (2 Sam 15:1). Shebnah, master of the palace (*ʾašer ʿal habbayit*) in the time of Hezekiah, is condemned by the prophet Isaiah for misuse of his official authority, having hewn for himself a magnificent tomb, so that when he would die, he would be buried with his costly chariots, of which he had so boasted as his special "honor" (*merkᵉbōt kᵉbôdekā*; Isa 22:18).[51] As to the Egyptian chariots, one may recall the verse on *merkᵉbōt parʿōh*, "Pharaoh's chariots," in the archaic Song of the Sea (Exod 15:3-4).[52] But, it is in the Joseph story that we find the most impressive description of the *merkābāh* as an Egyptian royal display chariot: "Pharaoh took the ring from his hand and put it on Joseph's. He clothed him in fine linen and put a gold chain around his neck. He made him ride in the best *merkābāh* he had after his own,[53] and they cried before him 'Abrek.' This is the way he was made governor of the whole land of Egypt" (Gen 41:42-43 [*JB*])—a description whose literary style is indeed similar to that of the above-mentioned Mesopotamian texts, among others, the inscriptions of Ashurbanipal.[54]

From the foregoing it is not difficult to assume that the *merkābāh*, which Solomon especially imported from Egypt, was first and foremost for ceremonial and processional use, as once suggested by Tadmor.[55] Richly ornamented Egyptian chariots, especially those mounted with gold and silver, are known from textual as well as archaeological evidence.[56] Amenhotep IV sent to Burnaburiash of Babylonia two *šuššūgu*-wood chariots plated with gold (*EA* 14 col. 2:15-16),[57] while Papyrus Anastasi IV

---

[51]It is worthwhile noting that the king of Egypt often gave a chariot as a sign of his speical favor to his subject who would order before his death to draw a picture of the chariot on the wall of his tomb with an inscripton such as: "The chariot, which His Majesty granted as a special gift" (von Deines, *MIO* 1 [1953] 15). On the attribute אשר על הבית cf. Mettinger, *Solomonic State Officials*, 70ff.; S. Yeivin, "פקידות," *EncBib* 6 (1971) 547ff. (Hebrew).

[52]On the Song of the Sea see especially F. M. Cross, *Canaanite Myth and Hebrew Epic*, 121-44, and for the date of the poem cf. also more recently, Freedman, "Early Israelite Poetry and Historical Reconstruction," 85ff.

[53]More literary: "his second best chariot (מרכבת המשנה אשר־לו), see *JB*; *HALAT*, 614. Cf. also another view to translate such as "his viceroy's chariot" (*NEB*) or "the chariot of his second-in-command" (E. A. Speiser, *Genesis* [AB 1, 1964] 311). For the feasible connection of "Abrek" with Eg. *ʾbrk* "Attention," not with Heb. √ברך see T. O. Lambdin, "Egyptian Loan Words in the Old Testament," *JAOS* 73 (1953) 146; Speiser, *Genesis*, 311, 314. *NEB* attempts to translate: "Make way!" For the Egyptian setting of the episode see Speiser, *Genesis*, 316f.

[54]Oppenheim, *ANET*, 295a, n. 8. Prof. A. Malamat kindly informed me on "a mare of Pharaoh's chariots" depicted in Song of Songs, which is traditionally ascribed to Solomon (1:9)—though the term for chariot here is רכב, not מרכבה.

[55]H. Tadmor, "The Period of the First Temple, the Babylonian Exile and the Restoration," *History of the Jewish People* 1 (ed. H. H. Ben-Sasson; Tel Aviv, 1969) 105 (Hebrew) = *A History of the Jewish People* (London, 1976) 104.

[56]Cf. von Deines, *MIO* 1 (1953) 13; Helck, *Beziehungen*, 440-42; Yadin, *The Art of Warfare*, 186-93, 210-17; James, "Chariot Fittings from Late Bronze Age Beth Shan," 113-14.

[57]For the *šuššūgu*-wood cf. "*šaššūgu, šuššūg/qu*," *AHw* Lief. 13 (1976) 1198b.

presents a description of Pharaoh's chariots, which were ornamented with gold and ivory, and whose body was made of "*brry*-wood more resplendent than lapis lazuli" (16:7-10).[58] Solomon is said to have paid 600 shekels of silver for each chariot from Egypt (1 Kgs 10:29). The above-mentioned "golden chariot" of Tushratta of Mitanni was made of 320 shekels of gold (*EA* 22:3). Egypt's need to import much of her lumber for chariots[59] was possibly among the factors for the high price of the Egyptian products. Still, it should not be overlooked that indigenous hard wood of the "Nubian acacia" had long been used in Egypt, especially for ships and chariots, as well as for coffins.[60] In fact, the main body of the large gold-mounted chariots, of Queen Hatshepsut (early 15th century B.C.) was made of "Nubian acacia."[61] Furthermore, according to Papyrus Anastasi III (6:7-8), of the 13th century B.C., an ordinary chariot together with its pole cost eight *deben* in Egypt, that is, 64 shekels (of silver);[62] while a boundary-stone inscription from the time of Marduk-nadin-ahhe (1098-1081 B.C.) relates the price of a chariot with its furnishings in Babylonia in that period: 100 (shekels) of silver (see below, Comparative Table).[63] Thus, proportionately the price of the Egyptian chariots given in 1 Kgs 10:29 is very high. At the same time, there is no doubt that the price of chariots varied according to the type and the period of purchase. It is therefore most plausible that "600 shekels" was the "highest price" ever put to an Egyptian chariot in the time of Solomon—another effort of the biblical writer to display Solomon's extravagance as distinctly as possible.

The number of chariots which Solomon imported from Egypt is not given; but it is quite probable that Israelite orders for new chariots, "marks of noblemen," were received by the chariot factories in Egypt more than once during the long peaceful period of Solomon's reign, for he had indeed

---

[58]R. Caminos, *Late-Egyptian Miscellanies* (London, 1954) 201. Cf. also Erman and Grapow, "*brri*," *Wörterbuch der ägyptischen Sprache*, 446.

[59]Indeed, various kinds of wood were needed to make a chariot according to the different functions of its parts. See Helck and Otto, "Wagen," *Kleines Wörterbuch*, 407f.; von Deines, *MIO* 1 (1953) 12f. Cf. also W. F. Albright, *Archaeology and the Religion of Israel* (5th ed.; Baltimore, 1969) 213, n. 24.

[60]It is also to be noted that in the 18th Dynasty pines from North Palestine (*Pinus halepensis*) was well used for chariot building. Cf. Ch. Müller, "Holz und Holzverarbeitung," *LÄ* 2 (1977) 1265-68; Helck and Otto, "Wagen," *Kleines Wörterbuch*, 408; von Deines, *MIO* 1 (1953) 12.

[61]Von Deines, *MIO* 1 (1953) 13.

[62]A chariot-pole cost 3 *deben* (of silver), and a chariot itself 5 *deben* (Caminos, *Late-Egyptian Miscellanies*, 34). Since the 18th Dynasty 1 *deben* (= 10 ḳd.t) of Egypt was accounted as 91 gr, while 1 shekel of Canaan weighed 11.39 gr. Cf. Helck and Otto, "Masse und Gewichte," *Kleines Wörterbuch*, 218; "Wagen," ibid., 408; E. S. Hartum, "מידות ומשקלות," *EncBib* 4 (1970) 867, 877 (Hebrew). On Papyrus Anastasi III cf. also Sir A. H. Gardiner, "The Delta Residence of the Ramessides," *JEA* 5 (1918) 184.

[63]L. W. King, *Babylonian Boundary Stones and Memorial Tablets in the British Museum* (London, 1912) 39:15. On the verse cf. also W. von Soden, "Zum akkadischen Wörterbuch," *Or* NS 24 (1955) 140. On Marduk-nadin-ahhe see Grayson, *Assyrian and Babylonian Chronicles*, 225; Brinkman, *A Political History of Post-Kassite Babylonia*, 42f., 119-30, 330-33, 679-767.

COMPARATIVE TABLE

Prices of Chariots and Horses in the Second and First Millennia B.C.

	Price in silver shekels	Market	Dating	Source
Chariots	64	Egypt	13th century B.C.	Pap. Anastasi III, 6:7-8
	100	Babylonia	Marduk-nadin-ahhe (1098-1081 B.C.)	BBSt 39, 15
	600	Egypt	Solomon (967-928 B.C.)	1 Kgs 10:29
Horses	300	Qatna	Ishme-Dagan (1780 B.C.)	ARM 5, 20:18ff.
	30	Nuzi	15th century B.C.	Chiera, JEN 515:3
	200	Carchemish	14th-13th centuries B.C.	PRU 3, 16:180
	30 (mare)	Ugarit	14th-13th centuries B.C.	PRU 6, 7B:12
	35 (mare)	Ugarit	14th-13th centuries B.C.	UT 1127:6
	20 (chariot horse)	Anatolia	14th-13th centuries B.C.	HL § 180
	15 (one-year-old filly)	Anatolia	14th-13th centuries B.C.	HL § 180
	14 (un-broken horse)	Anatolia	14th-13th centuries B.C.	HL § 180
	10 (one-year-old colt)	Anatolia	14th-13th centuries B.C.	HL § 180
	4 (weaned colt, filly)	Anatolia	14th-13th centuries B.C.	HL § 181
	50 (mare)	Babylonia	Marduk-nadin-ahhe (1098-1081 B.C.)	BBSt 39, 16
	150	Egypt	Solomon (967-928 B.C.)	1 Kgs 10:29
	230	Babylonia	Nabonidus (555-539 B.C.)	GCCI 1, 269:1-2
	88 (?)	Syria	Seleucus Nicator (312-281 B.C.)	CT IV, 29d, 1ff.

established good diplomatic relations with Egypt.[64] Various national celebrations such as the Jubilee and the feast of New Year's Day were no doubt the most favorable occasions for Solomon and other princes to buy new chariots from Egypt, as one may readily assume from the case of the Egyptian kings themselves. Indeed, in Papyrus Bologna 1094, a scribe of the armoury of Pharaoh speaks to his disciple: "Further, apply yourself to causing to be executed the commissions of the second Jubilee with the utmost zeal and the firmness of brass, and to causing the chariots of the second Jubilee to be made."[65] In Papyrus Anastasi III, we read: "The carpenters are working on the chariots of Pharaoh which have been in their hands for the feast of New Year's Day, keeping up with their companions. . . . Likewise, the coppersmiths are working on the chariot which they bid be done anew."[66]

III

As seen above, it is the general opinion that Cilicia was Israel's sole source of horses in the days of Solomon. True, the first kings of the 18th Dynasty, to whom horses had been introduced not long before, resorted to booty and tributes as the main supply of horses, as well as of chariots.[67] Still, it should be emphasized that horses soon acclimatized in Egypt, and the land of the Delta—in particular the region of Pithom—provided vast, grassy pasturages suitable for breeding large herds of horses in Egypt;[68] and Per-Ramesses (mentioned along with Pithom as a "store-city" in Exod 1:11) was one of the royal residences where Ramesses II (1304-1237 B.C.) built "great stables."[69] Even so, the Egyptians by no means ceased to seek fine horses from abroad.[70] But, this was not an Egyptian peculiarity, for it was

---

[64]Solomon married a daughter of the Egyptian king, apparently Siamun, and received from him the city of Gezer as a dowry (1 Kgs 3:1, 9:16). On this issue see especially A. Malamat, "Aspects of the Foreign Policies of David and Solomon," *JNES* 22 (1963) 10-17; idem, "The Kingdom of David and Solomon and the First Treaty with Egypt," *Bitzaron* 1 (1979) 12ff. (Hebrew); cf. also R. J. Williams, "The Egyptians," *Peoples of Old Testament Times* (ed. D. J. Wiseman; Oxford, 1973) 92-93; Kitchen, *The Third Intermediate Period*, 280-83, but see also H. D. Lance, "Solomon, Siamun, and the Double Ax," *Magnalia Dei*, 209-23. For the general character of Solomon's diplomacy see also Cross, *Canaanite Myth and Hebrew Epic*, 240.

[65]Caminos, *Late-Egyptian Miscellanies*, 15:4, 3-5.

[66]Caminos, *Late-Egyptian Miscellanies*, 105f.: 1, 2-3.

[67]Cf. Helck, *Beziehungen*, 441f.

[68]Yoyotte, "Cheval," *DCÉ*, 52. See also K. W. Butzer, "Delta," *LÄ* 1 (1975) 1048f.; H. Kees, *Ancient Egypt. A Cultural Topography* (Chicago/London, 1971) 29f.

[69]Caminos, *Late-Egyptian Miscellanies*, 11f. For Per-Rameses see more recently M. Gitton "Ramesès," *DBSup* 9 (1979) 1117-21. On Pithom see S. Aḥituv, "פתם," *EncBib* 6 (1971) 639-41 (Hebrew).

[70]Papyrus Anastasi IV 17, 8-9 recounts on "horse-teams and fine young steeds of Sangar, top stallions of Hatti and cows of Alashia. . . ." (Caminos, *Late-Egyptian Miscellanies*, 201). Cf. also Helck, *Beziehungen*, 394; J. M. Sasson, "Canaanite Maritime Involvement in the Second Millennium B.C.," *JAOS* 86 (1961) 132. For the Anatolian horses see also below and nn. 90-92.

a common policy amongst all rulers of the ancient Near East, and even the Hitite kings—whose land was bountiful with Anatolian horses—were no exception to this. Thus, we witness that Hattusili III asks Kadashman-Enlil II (1279-1265 B.C.) of Babylonia to send him young stallions who are strong enough to withstand the cold of the Anatolian plateau (*KBo* I, 10, rev. 62-65):[71]

> Send me [hor]ses, (indeed send me) young stallions! The stallions which thy father [sent me and those] which my brother sent me so far were good but have become stunted (lit.: short); full-grown horses [can't hold out (?) here]. (Indeed,) the cold is very severe [in the land of Ha]tti and full-grown horses do not live to old age. So send me, [my brother, fine] young stallions (which can become acclimatized)! There are (already) many stunted horses in my country.[72]

In fact, the receipt of the finest horses brought from abroad, in the royal stables of the New Kingdom, whether as a gift or tribute, made the land of the Nile renowned for its own splendid steeds.[73] Thus, the king of Alashia (Cyprus) in the El-Amarna period imported two horses from Egypt, together with a gold-mounted chariot (*EA* 32:21-22).[74] The horses sent by Ramesses II to Hattusili III must also have been the finest amongst the "home-bred" horses of Egypt.[75] In the 1st millennium B.C. we learn that Sargon II received as a gift from Shilkani, king of Egypt (716 B.C.), "twelve big Egyptian horses, their like not to be found in Assyria,"[76] and "big

---

[71]For the reading of the text and its translation cf. F. Sommer, *OLZ* 42 (1939) 627f. (critical reviews of H. A. Potratz, *Das Pferd in der Frühzeit*); D. D. Luckenbill, "Hittite Treaties and Letters," *AJSL* 32 (1921) 205; "*balāṭu*," *CAD* B, 56; "*kurrû*," *CAD* K, 565b; "*mūru*," *CAD* M/2, 229b. On the historical background of the letter, see J. M. Munn-Rankin, "Assyrian Military Power 1300-1200 B.C.," *CAH* 2/2 (1975) 282-84; E. Cassin, "Babylonien unter den Kassiten und das mittlere assyrische Reich," *Die altorientalischen Reiche II: Das Ende des 2. Jahrtausends* (Fischer Weltgeschichte 3, 1966) 52f. For the chronological and other problems of the letter cf. also E. Edel, "Die Abfassungzeit des Briefes KBo I 10 (Hattušil-Kadašman-Ellil) und seine Bedeutung für die Chronologie Rameses II," *JCS* 12 (1958) 130-33; M. B. Rowton, "Comparative Chronology at the Time of Dynasty XIX," *JNES* 19 (1960) 16ff.; B. Meissner, "Sychronismen," *OLZ* 20 (1917) 225ff.; cf. further B. Landsberger, *Samʾal* (Ankara, 1948) 106f., n. 251; A. L. Oppenheim, *Letters from Mesopotamia* (Chicago, 1967) 139-46.

[72]For the purchase of fine young steeds from Babylonia by the king of Egypt see above n. 70. As to the definition of stallion by the Hittite Laws see below n. 92.

[73]Yoyotte, "Cheval," *DCÉ, 52*.

[74]Cf. "*šuhītu*," *AHw* Lief. 14 (1977) 1261b; "*kitû*," *CAD* K, 474a.

[75]*KUB* III 27 Rs.17.

[76]Weidner, "Šilka(he)ne, Könige von Muṣri, ein Zeitgenosse Sargons II," *AfO* 14 (1941) 44f.; H. Tadmor, "The Campaigns of Sargon II of Assur: A Chronological-Historical Study," *JCS* 12 (1958) 78:10-11; idem, "Philistia under Assyrian Rule," *BA* 29 (1966) 92. Egyptian horses are probably mentioned also in the inscriptions of Tiglath-pileser III (Tadmor, *Inscriptions of Tiglath-pileser III*, Summ. 8:7′; Summ. 9:8; the texts were first published by D. J. Wiseman, *Iraq* 13 [1951] 23; *Iraq* 18 [1956] 125). On the issue of the Egyptian horses see also Naʾaman, *Tel Aviv* 3 (1976) 100, n. 24.

horses" are also found in Ashurbanipal's list of booty taken from Egypt.[77] Moreover (as has been fully discussed recently by J. N. Postgate), the horses of the land of Kusû (*sīsê* [kur]*Kusaya*), i.e., "Nubian" horses, were the best horses sought by the Neo-Assyrian kings, except for "Mesaean" horses, whose origin was in the Iranian uplands.[78] The Nubian horses were classified by the Assyrians for the yoke (*ša nīri*).[79] Similarly, in the Annals of Sargon II we read of "large Egyptian horses broken to the yoke" (*sīsê* [kur]*Muṣuri ṣimitti nīri rabūte*).[80] Thus, the horses of the land of the Nile were especially suitable as chariot horses.

It is not certain whether Nubia in the time of Solomon was already known for its own fine horses, for both horses and chariots had apparently been introduced into Nubia not long before.[81] Neither are we certain that the horses which Solomon imported from Egypt were indeed of extraordinary size, as attested in later sources. Although the Anatolian horses are merely said to have been purchased by the king's traders "against equivalent" (*bim^eḥīr*; 1 Kgs 10:28),[82] the purchase price of the Egyptian horses is given: 150 shekels per horse (verse 29). Higher prices are recorded in the extra-biblical sources: 300 shekels in a Mari document,[83] 200 shekels in a Ugaritic text,[84] and 230 shekels (for a horse "of best quality"—*muḫḫu ina sīsê*) in a document from the time of Nabonidus (548 B.C.).[85] Yet, 150

---

[77]"*sīsê rabūti*," Streck, *Assurbanipal* 2, 16:II 40. For the translation see *ARAB* 2 § 778, and also Oppenheim, *ANET*, 259b, who translates there: "fine horses" (cf. on this also Weidner, *AfO* 14 [1941] 44).

[78]Postgate, *Taxation*, 11f. and see Na³aman, *Tel Aviv* 3 (1976) 101, n. 24. On the biblical כוש, cf. Y. Liver, "כוש," *EncBib* 4 (1970) 65-70 (Hebrew); *HALAT*, 445.

[79]Postgate, *Taxation*, 13; cf. "*nīru*," *AHw* 2 (1972) 794a. A Nimrud Letter (ND 2765) from the date between 720-715 B.C. informs that the emissaries of Egypt, Gaza, Judah, Moab, and Ammon arrived in Calah with 45 horses as their tribute contributions, but, interesting enough, 24 out of these horses were brought by the Gazan emissary (Postgate, *Taxation*, 117f.; Tadmor, *BA* 29 [1966] 92f.; M. Cogan, *Imperialism and Religion: Assyria, Judah and Israel in the Eighth and Seventh Centuries B.C.E.* [SBL MS 19, 1974] 118). In the light of the strong connections between Gaza and Egypt, both geographically and politically, it is not difficult to assume that the Gazan prince had kept not a few fine "Egyptian horses" in his land.

[80]A. G. Lie, *The Inscriptions of Sargon II, King of Assyria. Part I: The Annals* (Paris, 1929) 80:17. "*ṣibtu*," *CAD* Ṣ, 166b.

[81]Yoyotte, "Cheval," *DCÉ*, 52.

[82]Heb. מחיר is generally taken as derived from Akk. *maḫīru* "market place, price equivalent, rate, purchase" (*CAD* M/1, 92ff.; *AHw* 2 [1972] 583a; cf. *HALAT*, 539), while B. Landsberger ("Akkadisch-Hebräische Wortgleichungen," *Hebräische Wortforschung. Festschrift W. Baumgartner* [VTSup 16, 1967] 184f., n. 2) tends to see a closer connection with Akk. *me/iḫru* and with the older *meḫertu/miḫirtu* "equivalent" (*CAD* M/2, 50, 54f.; *AHw* 2 [1972] 640; cf., e.g., *ana meḫrišu nadānu* "to lend out xxx against corresponding commodity," A. Goetze, *The Laws of Eshnunna* [AASOR 31, 1956] 64f., cf. also 111f.; "*miḫru*," *CAD* M/2, 58a). Cf. the translations: "at a price" (*RSV*), "at a fixed price" (*JB*; Montgomery and Gehman), "by purchase" (*NEB*), "at a certain price" (Gray), "at the prevailing price" (Myers), "at a market price" (Rudolph), "on payment" (Noth).

[83]G. Dossin, *ARM* 5 (1952) 37, no. 20: 18ff.

[84]J. Nougayrol, *PRU* 3 (1959) 41:5-7.

[85]Lit. "3 5/6 minas": R. P. Dougherty, *Goucher College Cuneiform Inscriptions 1: Archives*

shekels is very high indeed, when compared with 30 shekels in a Nuzi text[86] or in a Ugaritic text (for a mare),[87] with 35 shekels (for a mare) in another Ugaritic text which deals with the transaction of two mares for 70 shekels of silver,[88] and with the purchase price for a mare, given in an almost contemporary source from Babylonia: "six mares (SAL+ḪÚB ANŠE. KUR.RA) for 300 silver," i.e., 50 (shekels) silver per mare.[89] The Hittite Laws, though not commercial texts, give not only much lower prices but, significantly enough, separate prices for various types of horses in Anatolia of the Imperial Period (§§180-181):[90] 20 shekels (of silver) for a "horse of harnessing" (ANŠE.KUR.RA turiyawaš, i.e., "chariot horse"); 15 shekels for one-year-old filly; 14 shekels for a "horse of grazing" (ANŠE.KUR.RA uešiyawaš, i.e., probably, horse that has not yet been broken in);[91] 10

---

from Erech, Time of Nebuchadrezzar and Nabonidus (New Haven, 1933) no. 269. For the meaning of ruḫḫu in NB texts see "ippatu," CAD I/J, 164b; "ruḫḫu," AHw 2 (1972) 993b. In this case, the horse was bought by two payments: First 2 minas and three months later 1 5/6 minas. See also W. H. Dubberstein, "Comparative Prices in Later Babylonia," AJSL 56 (1939) 32.

[86]D. Cross, Movable Property in the Nuzi Documents (AOS 10, 1937) 23, and cf. also 22: "It is evident . . . that unlike the age of cattle and asses, age of horses was not of particular moment in these transactions." Cf. also F. R. Steele, Nuzi Real Estate Transactions (AOS 25, 1943) 34.

[87]J. Nougayrol, PRU 6 (1970) 10 7B:10-12.

[88]UT 1127:6. For the commodity prices in Ugarit see more recently M. Heltzer, Goods, Prices and the Organization in Ugarit (Wiesbaden, 1978) and also R. R. Stieglitz, "Commodity Prices at Ugarit," JAOS 99 (1979) 16.

[89]King, Babylonian Boundary Stones and Memorial Tablets in the British Museum, 39, 1.16. Cf. B. Meissner, Warenpreise in Babylonien (Berlin, 1936) 34, but his reading rak-kab (ibid., n. 4) should be corrected to SAL+ḪÚB (A. L. Oppenheim, "The Archives of the Palace of Mari. A Review Article," JNES 11 [1952] 135; "anātu," CAD A/2, 482). [1(?)] 1/3 minas and 8 shekels (=88 [?] shekels) silver is given as the price of one horse in a text from the time of Seleucus I Nicator in the year 305 B.C. (CT IV, 29d [88-5-12, 514]); see Meissner, Warenpreise, 17; J. Kohler and A. Ungnad, Hundert ausgewählte Rechtsurkunden aus der Spätzeit des babylonischen Schrifttums von Xerxes bis Mithridates II (485-93 v. Chr.) (Leipzig, 1911) 62 no. 91.

[90]For the texts see J. Friedrich, Die Hethitische Gesetze (Leiden, 1959) 79, 81; G. P. Carratelli, Le Leggi Ittite (Roma, 1964) 164, 166. O. R. Gurney assumes that the prices of commodities "may be intended as maximum prices, which should not be exceeded; but as approximations they no doubt present a fairly accurate picture of economic conditions" (The Hittites [revised ed., Harmondsworth, 1962] 92). Putting separate prices according to the different types of horses is another indication to the rich soil of Anatolia for horse breeding (cf. above n. 86 for a different situation in the sources of Mesopotamia); cf. Heltzer, Goods, Prices and the Organization in Ugarit, 100. For the Hittite text for horse training (the "Kikkuri-text") see Kammenhuber, Hippologica Hethitica, 40ff. and for a fragmentary text in Hittite on merchants dealing with various goods and commodities among them horses and mules, see H. J. Hoffner, Jr., "A Hittite Text in Epic Style about Merchants," JCS 22 (1968) 34-45. Thanks are due to Dr. G. Kellerman for her valuable comments on the related issue.

[91]See H. G. Güterbock, JCS 15 (1961) 78 (critical reviews of Friedrich, Die Hethitischen Gesetze).

shekels for a one-year-old colt; 4 shekels for a weaned colt, filly (see above, Comparative Table).[92]

It seems, therefore, that 150 shekels stated in 1 Kgs 10:29 was not a price for an ordinary horse, but that for one of high quality—apparently a chariot-horse especially trained for use in stately processions. In the ancient Near East, fine chariots as royal gifts were always sent together with their fine teams (see above). Equally, as we know from the examples of the king of Alashia, costly ornamental chariots were certainly ordered from Egypt along with matched teams of horses, by foreign clients, among whom was the king of Israel. Hence, Solomon did import horses from Egypt (cf. Deut 17:16; Isa 31:1).[93]

IV

According to the account in 1 Kgs 10:29, some of the horses and chariots were apparently resold to "all the kings of the Hittites and to the kings of Aram $b^e y\bar{a}d\bar{a}m$," that is, through Solomon's traders (verse 28: $s\bar{o}h^er\hat{e}$ hamelek). By the "Hittites" here are meant no doubt those states in North Syria in which the so-called Neo-Hittite culture flourished after the fall of the Hittite Empire, toward the end of the 2nd millennium B.C. Yet it was only in the 9th century B.C. that the Neo-Hittite culture (which expressed itself most prominently by use of hieroglyphic Luwian for royal inscriptions) became dominant in considerable parts of North Syria; thus, the people of Syria in the time of Solomon could have witnessed the existence of but few "Neo-Hittie" states, such as Gurgum, Carchemish and Til-Barsip.[94] The princes of these states may have bought Egyptian display-

---

[92] The Hittite Laws § 178 (*ANET*, 195-96) states that the prices of stallion and mare, he-ass and she-ass are "the same," but does not give the actual prices. For the discussion on this paragraph, see Güterbock, *JCS* 15 (1961) 77-78. As to stallion cf. the definition given in the Hittite Laws § 58: "If anyone steals a stallion—if it is a weanling, it is not a stallion; if it is a yearling, it is not a stallion; if it is a two-year-old, that is a stallion" (A. Goetze, *ANET*, 192). It may be added that in the Hittite Laws § 180 (*ANET*, 196) the price of mule is given as 1 mina of silver, i.e., 40 shekels of silver (not 60 shekels as in other parts of the ancient Near East; see H. Otten, "Zum hethitischen Gewichtssystem," *AfO* 17 [1954/56] 128-31).

[93] Cf. W. Rudolph, *Chronikbücher* (HAT 21, 1955) 198; E. L. Curtis, *The Book of Chronicles* (ICC, 1910) 319; Driver, *Deuteronomy*, 211, and cf. M. Weinfeld, *Deuteronomy and the Deuteronomic School* (Oxford, 1972) 281, 364, 368f.; Cross, *Canaanite Myth and Hebrew Epic*, 221, n. 9, 240.

[94] On the Neo-Hittite states, see J. D. Hawkins, "Assyrians and Hittites," *Iraq* 36 (1974) 69-75, and cf. E. Laroche, "Hieroglyphen, hethitische," *RLA* 4 (1972-75) 394ff. For the new proposal to read the early dynastic name of Gurgum as *Laramas*, see now J. D. Hawkins and A. Morpurgo-Davies, *AnSt* 28 (1978) 105. For the problem of the Neo-Hittite culture in Til-Barsip and its relations with the Aramaean state Bit-Adini, see D. Ussishkin, "Was Bit-Adini a Neo-Hittite or Aramaean State?" *Or* NS 40 (1970) 431ff.; Y. Ikeda, *The Kingdom of Hamath and its Relations with Aram and Israel* (Hebrew Univ. Diss., 1977) 86-96 (Hebrew); idem, "Royal Cities and Fortified Cities," *Iraq* 41 (1979) 77-79. On the period when the Neo-Hittite states arose as the heirs of the Hittites see more recently, Tadmor, "The Decline of Empires in Western Asia ca. 1200 B.C.E.," 1f.

chariots and teams through the king of Israel, who played a role of middleman, but it seems unlikely that they purchased Anatolian horses by these same means, for they were situated close to the sources of horses in the Taurus and thus they could obtain them more readily and more directly than could Solomon. Among others, the land of Gurgum[95] was located next to the land of Tabal, which occupied an important part of the Taurus region and was famous for its horse rearing. Ashurbanipal imposed upon Mugallu, king of Tabal, a yearly tribute of "big horses,"[96] and, indeed, a cuneiform text from Kuyunjik (K 286 = *ADD*, 698) reports on the arrival of 589 (!) horses sent by Mugallu by two shipments, in 651 B.C.[97]

On the other hand, Carchemish, on the west bank of the Euphrates, had long been known as a center of the international trade between Anatolia and Mesopotamia and, in fact, its rulers played the role of middlemen for the horse trade. In a Mari Letter, a prince of Carchemish writes in reply to an order from the king of Mari that due to the lack of "white horses" in stock, he would send him "red-brown (i.e., sorrel) horses" from the region of Harsamna[98] in Anatolia.[99] That the court of the king of Carchemish was deeply engaged in the horse trade is also attested in a legal document from Ras Shamra.[100] Because of the strategic importance of Carchemish in international trade, Tiglath-pileser I built two colonies, Pitru and Mutkinu, on either bank of the Euphrates near Carchemish, in order to keep this Neo-Hittite state under Assyrian control.[101] Yet, it is not certain that Carchemish of that period was still especially important in the international horse trade; Tiglath-pileser I is said to have imposed upon Ini-Teshub of Carchemish "tax, tribute and impost consisting of cedar beams;"[102] but there is no indication of Carchemish's special connection with Anatolian horses at that period. Concerning the land of Nairi, in the

---

[95]On this geographic name see Ikeda, *Iraq* 41 (1979) 81, n. 46.

[96]*ARAB* 2 § 981. Togarma in Anatolia was also known for its horses (Ezek 27:14). For the Hittite equivalent *Takarma* cf. G. F. del Monte and J. Tischler, *Die Orts- und Gewässernamen der hethitischen Texte* (Répertoire géographique des textes cunéiformes 6, 1978) 383f. On the purchase of "top stallions of Hatti" by the Egyptians see above n. 70, while Herodotus reports that "360 white horses, one for each day in the year" were sent from the province of Cilicia as a yearly tribute to King Darius (III 90).

[97]F. M. Fales, "Notes on Some Nineveh Horse Lists," *Assur* 1/3 (1974) 14 and 15, n. 4.

[98]For this toponym see H. Otten, "*Haršumna*," *RLA* 4 (1972-75) 126; del Monte and Tischler, *Orts- und Gewässernamen*, 91. On the horses of various colors see Fales, *Assur* 1/3 (1974) 1-8.

[99]G. Dossin, "Aplahanda, roi de Carkémiš," *RA* 35 (1938) 120. See also E. Weidner, "Weisse Pferde im Alten Orient," *BO* 9 (1952) 157-59; J.-R. Kupper, "Northern Mesopotamia and Syria," *CAH* 2/1 (1963) 18.

[100]Nougayrol, *PRU* 3 (1959) 41 and nn. 1-2.

[101]*ARAB* 1 § 603. Cf. Ikeda, *Iraq* 41 (1979) 75f. and n. 4.

[102]*ARI* 2 §§ 82, 95. On the conquest of Carchemish by Tiglath-pileser I, see Hawkins, *Iraq* 36 (1974) 70 and more recently Tadmor, "The Decline of Empires in Western Asia ca. 1200 B.C.E.," 11.

Van region, it is emphasized that Tiglath-pileser I received "teams of horses in harness," as tribute.[103]

The Assyrians, however, could not hold the trade route between East and West via Carchemish under their control for long, because of strong Aramaean pressure. Indeed, Tiglath-pileser I himself admits that he had to cross the Euphrates twenty-eight times (twice in a single year!) in pursuit of the Aramaeans.[104] The struggle with the Aramaeans continued and the Assyrian dominion over the trade route along the Euphrates further deteriorated in the time of Tiglath-pileser's successors.[105] In fact, the two Assyrian colonies built by Tiglath-pileser I near Carchemish fell into the hands of an Aramaean king during the reign of Ashur-rabi II (1013-973 B.C.), a contemporary of David—an incident which cut Assyria's vital link with the West.[106] Carchemish regarded the Aramaean conquest of the Assyrian colonies in a more serious light than the other states, for it was now forced to face the direct Aramaean threat not merely to its economic interests in the international context, but to its very existence as an independent, non-Aramaean state. Further, Carchemish experienced an internal change, with the downfall of the Ura-Tarhunda dynasty and the rise of the Suhi dynasty, toward the mid-10th century B.C., the struggle between the descendants of the two dynasties continuing for several generations.[107]

It seems, therefore, that Carchemish in the time of Solomon suffered political instability due to both internal and external pressures. The situation no doubt brought about the decline of Carchemish as a center of international trade, on the one hand, and the rise of Que in the Adana plain, as an important center for the products of the Anatolian highlands, on the other hand. This must have been the main reason that Solomon's traders came to the market at Que in seeking to purchase good Anatolian horses,[108] and not

---

[103]*ARI* 2 § 80.

[104]*ARI* 2 § 97. Cf. A. Malamat, "The Aramaeans," *Peoples of Old Testament Times* (ed. D. J. Wiseman; Oxford, 1973) 135-37; Liverani, "The Amorites," *Peoples of Old Testament Times*, 119; Ikeda, *AJBI* 4 (1978) 34, n. 17, and more recently Tadmor, "The Decline of Empires in Western Asia ca. 1200 B.C.E.," 12.

[105]Cf. R. Labat, "Assyrien und seine Nachbarländer (Babylonien, Elam, Iran) von 1000 bis 617 v. Chr. / Das neubabylonische Reich bis 539 v. Chr.," *Die altorientalischen Reich* 3: *Die erste Hälfte des 1. Jahrtausends* (Fischer Weltgeschichte 4, 1967) 9, 11; G. Roux, *Ancient Iraq* (Bungay, 1964) 253f.

[106]See above n. 97 and cf. also Malamat, "The Aramaeans," 138.

[107]See Hawkins, *Iraq* 36 (1974) 72. The problems of the struggles between the two dynasties of Carchemish is to be discussed in detail by Prof. R. Stefanini in his forthcoming article "La restaurazione di Katuwa." For the Suhi dynasty as well as the early hieroglyphic Luwian inscriptions from Carchemish see also H. G. Güterbock, "Carchemish," *JNES* 13 (1954) 102ff.; D. Ussishkin, "Observations on Some Monuments from Carchemish," *JNES* 26 (1967) 87ff.; Sir M. E. L. Mallowan, "Carchemish," *AnSt* 22 (1972) 63ff.; J. D. Hawkins, "Building Inscriptions of Carchemish. The Wall of Sculpture and Great Staircase," *AnSt* 22 (1972) 87ff.

[108]On the land of Que, see A. Goetze, "Cilicians," *JCS* 16 (1962) 48-58; J. Bing, *A History*

to Carchemish, even though relations between Solomon and the princes in
the Euphrates region are indicated in the Bible (1 Kgs 5:4).[109]

V

How, then, were the Anatolian horses transported to Israel? Some
scholars (following the LXX) emending $b^e y\bar{a}d\bar{a}m$ in 1 Kgs 10:29 to $bayy\bar{a}m$
assume that Solomon's merchants brought horses from Que "by sea."[110]
However, while there is no special reason for the above emendation,
according to its context 1 Kgs 10:29 should be related to the shipment of
Egyptian chariots and teams to the kings of North Syria, not of Anatolian
horses (see above). True, it is known that there was cooperation between
Solomon and Hiram of Tyre in connection with trade on the Red Sea
(1 Kgs 9:26-28; 10:11, 22), but there is no evidence that such joint ventures
were also undertaken in the Mediterranean.[111] Rather, there are indications
that the Phoenicians managed to keep Solomon and his agents out of the
Mediterranean trade which, along with the export of timber from
Lebanon,[112] had traditionally been the monopoly of the Phoenicians. In
fact, even Solomon's request that his men should work alongside the
Phoenicians on the slopes of Mount Lebanon was rejected by Hiram, who
insisted that the entire procedure, from cutting the timber to its transportation to the final destination on the Jaffa coast, should be carried out

---

of Cilicia during the Assyrian Period (Indiana Univ. Diss., 1969, Ann Arbor, 1973); W. W.
Hallo, The Ancient Near East (New York/Chicago, 1971) 110; N. Naʾaman, "קוה,
קואʾ" EncBib 7 (1976) 87-93 (Hebrew). Cf. also J. D. Hawkins, "Ḫilakku," RLA 4 (1972-75)
402f.; on the cities of Que see also Ikeda, Iraq 41 (1979) 76, nn. 8-9.

[109]On the apparently later insertion of the term עבר הנהר, see Noth, Könige 1, 75f., but cf.
also J. J. Finkelstein, "Mesopotamia," JNES 21 (1962) 84 and n. 36; Malamat, JNES 22
(1963) 1, n. 2.

[110]E.g. Katzenstein, The History of Tyre, 114; Elat, Economic Relations, 198; Crown, Abr
Naharain 15 (1974/75) 37. Gray tends to understand the Greek rendering as meaning "of the
west" (I & II Kings, 269).

[111]In the later biblical sources the terms "Tarshish" and "Tarshish-fleet" are used in
connection with a certain land on the Mediterranean coast. Yet, Solomon's "Tarshish-
fleet" had nothing to do with the Mediterranean but with the land of Ophir in the
south. King Jehoshaphat also built a "Tarshish-fleet" to sail "to Ophir for gold, but his ship
never reached there; it wrecked at Ezion-Geber" (1 Kgs 22:48: 2 Chr 20:36-38). A voyage
around the horn of Africa was quite unlikely in that day. According to Albright, tarshîsh
meant "refinery" in Phoenician, and Ezion-geber "was then presumably a tarshîsh something
like Phoenician stations with the same name in Sardinia and Spain" (Archaeology and the
Religion of Israel, 133-34), while H. Gaubert (Solomon the Magnificient [New York, 1970]
112) assumes that any ocean-going vessel was called a "ship of Tarshish, even when it was of
other trading routes than those to Spain." Cf. Noth, Könige 1, 233; Gaubert, Solomon the
Magnificient, 102; G. F. Bass, A History of Seafaring Based on Underwater Archaeology
(New York, 1972) 38; Myers, II Chronicles, 55.

[112]See the Story of Wen-amun (ANET, 25ff.), and cf. also S. Yeivin, "Did the Kingdom of
Israel Have a Maritime Policy?" JQR 50 (1959/60) 193f.; M. Chehab, "Relation entre l'Égypt
et la Phénicie des origines à Oun-Amon," The Role of the Phoenicians in the Interactions of
Mediterranean Civilization (Beirut, 1968) 1ff.; Peckham, "Israel and Phoenicia," 229.

entirely by Phoenicians (1 Kgs 5:20-23).[113] It can also be added that Tell Abu Hawam, on Acre Bay, which could have served as one of the country's few doors to the western sea from its conquest by David on,[114] apparently came under Tyrian rule when Solomon ceded Western Galilee, included twenty towns, to the king of Tyre as partial payment of his debt (1 Kgs 9:11-13).[115] The fact of undisputed Tyrian domination over the western coast of Israel, on the one hand, and the apparent emphasis of the biblical account of the strength of Solomon's merchants in the horse trade, on the other hand, may lead us to another possibility as well: the overland transportation of horses.

The feasibility of overland transportation of animals, however, depends upon geopolitical as well as pasturage conditions along the route. Inland Syria along the Orontes was under the control of the kingdom of Hamath in the time of David and Solomon.[116] It is of special significance

---

[113]According to 2 Chr 2:15 the timbers from Lebanon were transported "in rafts by sea to Jaffa (Joppa)"; but there it is probably meant the coast of Jaffa, not the city of Jaffa itself, for the latter in this period seems to have remained under the control of the Philistines (cf. Josh 19:46). It is plausible that either Tell Qasile or Tell Kudadi at the mouth of the Yarkon, or both of them, was used for landing the timbers from Lebanon to be then sent to Jerusalem (M. Broshi, "יָפֹוא, יפו," *EncBib* 3 [1958] 741 [Hebrew]). On the excavations at Tell Kudadi see N. Avigad, "Kudadi, Tell," *EAEHL* 3 (1977) 720, and on those at Tell Qasile, T. Dothan and I. Dunayevsky, A. Mazar, "Qasile, Tell," *EAEHL* 4 (1978) 963-75.

[114]B. Mazar, "Stratification of Tell Abu Huwâm on the Bay of Acre," *BASOR* 124 (1951) 21-25; E. Anati, "Abu Hawam, Tell," *EAEHL* 1 (1975) 9-12; P. J. Riis, *Sukas. The North-East Sanctuary and the First Settling of Greeks in Syria and Palestine* 1 (København, 1970) 152; D. L. Saltz, *Greek Geometric Pottery in the East: The Chronological Implications* (Harvard Univ. Diss., 1978) 165-68.

[115]Aharoni, *The Land of the Bible*, 277; Y. Aharoni and M. Avi-Yonah, *The MacMillan Bible Atlas* (New York/London, 1968) 72. The presence of the adverb זָא as an archival quotation formula in 1 Kgs 9:11b indicates the secondary character of the literary connection between the account on the land transaction and the note on the years which were needed for the construction of the temple and the king's palace in the preceding passage see J. A. Montgomery, "Archival Data in the Book of Kings," *JBL* 53 (1934) 46-52; Montgomery and Gehman, *Kings*, 204; Noth, *Könige* 1, 206f. On the formula in the book of Kings cf. also M. Cogan and H. Tadmor, "Ahaz and Tiglath-pileser in the Book of Kings: Historiographic Considerations," *Bib* 60 (1979) 491-508.

[116]For the geopolitical situation in the regions of the Amanus and the Amuq plain in this period, see the present writer's discussion in *The Kingdom of Hamath and its Relations with Aram and Israel*, 121ff. In the Late Bronze Age, Ugarit (Ras Shamra) played an important role as a port to connect the inland Syria with the Mediterranean world, but after its destruction by the Sea Peoples (ca. 1200 B.C.) Ugarit was never rebuilt; instead, a new port was founded in the nearby site: Al-Mina at the mouth of the Orontes. Yet, the settlement of Al-Mina was first established in the 9th century B.C., corresponding to the building of Tell Ta'yinat on the Orontes bend, which is presumably to be identified with Kulania, the royal city of Unqi/Pattin (cf. Ikeda, *Iraq* 41 [1979] 76), and not before (J. du Plat Taylor, "The Cypriot and Syrian Pottery from Al Mina, Syria," *Iraq* 21 [1959] 91, which revised the former dating of the levels of the site by Sir C. L. Wooley, *A Forgotten Kingdom* [New York, 1968] 165ff.; Riis, *Sūkās*, 142f., 152f.; Saltz, *Greek Geometric Pottery*, 39ff. Cf. also D. Ussishkin, "Building IV in Hamath and the Temples of Solomon and Tell Tayanat," *IEJ* 16 [1966] 104ff.). The settlement of Sukas south of Jabla, on the other hand, existed already in the 10th

that the trade route running through the heart of Hamath was blessed with abundant pasturage and corn lands, which could have provided good relay stations for animal transportation. The vast marshy depression along the middle Orontes provided an ideal setting for horses. The last king of Ugarit must have owed much to this land on his eastern border, in keeping his 2,000 horses alive (*UT* 1012:22-25).[117] It was certainly for the same motive that Ashurnasirpal II chose Aribua, the fortified city of Lubarna, king of Pattin, in this part of the land as a new Assyrian base; indeed, the Assyrian king is said to have "reaped the barley (*šeᵓum*) and straw (*tibni*) of the land of Luhute," the northern province of Hamath, and "stored (them) inside," i.e., in the silos of Aribua, in order to feed the Assyrian horses and other pack-animals and to serve as a relay station for the horses on their way to Assyria as tribute from the rulers of the West (cf. "barley and straw," in 1 Kgs 5:8).[118] Furthermore, according to Strabo, Seleucus Nicator (312-218 B.C.) built a stud-farm in the town of Apamea (modern Qalaat el-Mudiq, ca. 40 km. northwest of Hama), which at one time contained 30,000 mares and 3,000 stallions[119] (see above, Comparative Table, for the price of a horse in this late period).

Places suitable for feeding horses were also to be found in the southern Hamath region. Already in the 2nd millennium B.C., Qatna (modern Mishrefe, southeast of Hama) was known for its export of local horses to Mesopotamia.[120] On the other hand, a Nimrud document from early in the second half of the 8th century B.C. (ND 2766) relates that the Assyrian administration, apparently by agreement with the king of Hamath, would station horses and other pack-animals in the towns of Qidisi and Rabla

---

century B.C., and the archaeological evidences attest distinct cultural links between Sukas and the settlement at Hama on the east (biblical Hamath-Rabbah, see Ikeda, *Iraq* 41 [1979] 82f.) late in the 9th and also in the 8th centuries B.C. Thus, it seems probable that the port of Sukas acted as the important entrance to the Mediterranean for the kingdom of Hamath of this period (Riis, *Sūkās*, 148ff., 156; idem, "The First Greeks in Phoenicia and their Settlement at Sukas," *Ugaritica* 4 [Paris, 1969] 449f.). In fact, the kings of Usnu (probably Tell Daruk southeast of Sukas) and Sianu (Tell Sianu east of Jabla) were the important allies of Irhuleni, king of Hamath, in his war against Shalmaneser III in middle of the 9th century (*ARAB* 1 § 611) to be annexed to the kingdom of Hamath during the 8th century B.C. (Tadmor, *Inscriptions of Tiglath-pileser III*, Ann. 19; Summ. 5 II 16-24. Cf. Rost, *Die Keilschrifttexte Tiglat-Pilesers III*, 24, 85). Still, there is no evidence that Sukas was indeed used as Hamath's port in the 10th century B.C.

[117]M. C. Astour, "New Evidence on the Last Days of Ugarit," *AJA* 69 (1965) 257. On the historical setting of this text see also more recently Tadmor, "The Decline of Empires in Western Asia ca. 1200 B.C.E.," 6.

[118]*ARI* 2 § 585. On Aribua see H. Tadmor, "Assyria and the West: The Ninth Century and Its Aftermath," *Unity and Diversity* (ed. H. Goedicke and J. J. M. Roberts; Baltimore/London, 1975) 37f.; Naᵓaman, *WO* 9 (1978) 231-32. For Aribua's attribute: "a fortified city of PN," see Ikeda, *Iraq* 41 (1979) 76.

[119]H. L. Jones, *The Geography of Strabo* 7 (London/Cambridge, 1930) 251.

[120]Dossin, *ARM* 5 (1952) 37, no. 20.

(Ribla)[121] in the northern Biqa[c].[122] Another Nimrud administrative text (ND 2437) mentions the towns of Laba³u (biblical Lebo-Hamath) and Hiesa in the province of Zobah (Ṣubate), in connection with the harvesting of corn to feed the animals in that part of Hamath.[123] Some of these settlements were among "the ten fortified towns in the desert"[124] which were built by the Assyrians and acted (as Postgate has rightly assumed) as granaries, as well as local centers of administration.[125] After David defeated the king of Zobah, Israel and Hamath established good diplomatic relations: "When Toi king of Hamath heard that David had defeated the entire army of Hadadezer, he sent his son Joram to King David to greet him and to congratulate him on defeating Hadadezer in battle, for Hadadezer had been at war with Toi; and he brought with him vessels of silver, gold, and copper" (2 Sam 8:9-10). It is not implausible (as assumed by A. Malamat) to see a certain Israelite influence on internal affairs in Hamath, in the fact that Toi's son is denoted by a name having distinctly Israelite theophoric element (Joram) alongside the more original form (Hadoram; 1 Chr 18:10).[126] But, it seems that, in the following period, Israel's influence in the north significantly increased. Through diplomatic, if not military pressure, Solomon surely obtained considerable concessions from the king of Hamath, and was thus able to build Israelite bases in the land of Hamath, especially in the southern part, for we read in 2 Chr 8:3-4 that Solomon "went to Hamath-Zobah and took it, and built Tadmor in the desert and all the store-cities which he built in Hamath."[127]

---

[121]The text was published by H. W. F Saggs (*Iraq* 25 [1963] 79f.) but the reading [uru]*Qi-di-si* in the place of [uru]*Kin-di-si* has been proposed by B. Oded ("Two Assyrian References to the Town of Qadesh on the Orontes," *IEJ* 14 [1964] 272-73; idem, "קדש על הארנת," *EncBib* 7 [1976] 43-44 [Hebrew]), followed by M. Weippert ("Menahem von Israel und seine Zeitgenossen in einer Steleninschrift des assyrischen Königs Tiglathpileser III. aus dem Iran," *ZDPV* 89 [1973] 45, n. 72. See also "*madbaru*," *CAD* M/1, 12b; "*qabaltu*[*m*]," *AHw* 2 [1972] 886a). On Ribla see "רבלה," *EncBib* 7 (1976) 320-21 (Hebrew).

[122]As can be understood from ND 2647, "pack-animal" ([anše]*aṣappu*) must have included horses; thus, Saggs translated it "the horse train" (*Iraq* 17 [1955] 136; idem, *Iraq* 25 [1963] 79). Cf. Postgate, *Taxation*, 397; *CAD* M/1, 12b; "*aṣappu*," *AHw* 1 (1965) 77b. ND 2766 refers to a man by the name [m]*A-i-ni-ili* who is probably to be identified with Eni-ilu, king of Hamath, contemporary of Tiglath-pileser III (K. L. Tallqvist, *Assyrian Personal Names* [Helsingfors, 1914] 74a), cf. Saggs, *Iraq* 17 (1955) 71, 80. Pack-animals of Hamath ([kur]*Hamate*) are mentioned in ND 2495:15-16 (Postgate, *Taxation*, 381).

[123]Saggs, *Iraq* 17 (1955) 139f. Hiesa is also mentioned in *ABL*, 414 together with Zobah. Cf. B. Oded, "Observations on Methods of Assyrian Rule in Transjordania after the Palestinian Campaign of Tiglath-pileser III," *JNES* 29 (1970) 183, n. 45, 185. For the reading of ND 2437:31-33 and its translation, see Kinnier Wilson, *The Nimrud Wine Lists*, 9.

[124]"10 URU.MEŠ É.BÀD ina mad-bar," ND 2437: rev.37 (Postgate, *Taxation*, 382). For the similar expressions see ND 2766: rev.13' and ND 2495:10-14 (see above nn. 121-22).

[125]Postgate, *Taxation*, 193, 397.

[126]Malamat, *JNES* 22 (1963) 6f. Cf. B. Mazar, "The Aramean Empire and its Relations with Israel" (1962) *BAR* 2 (1964) 132; Y. Ikeda, "תעי," *EncBib* 8 (forthcoming) (Hebrew).

[127]Qerê reads Tadmor in 1 Kgs 9:18 in place of Tamar, but it may be that the account's

These store-cities (ʿarê hamisk^enôt)[128] in Hamath were no doubt strategic bases for Solomon's traders in connection with their northern trade, and they must have served, like the later Assyrian "towns in the desert," as local centers for storage of official grain supplies. Yet, apparently the most significant role was for the trade in horses from Que, the Israelite store-cities in Hamath serving not merely as relay stations between Anatolia and Israel; the Anatolian horses were kept and reared there until required by the central administration (in analogy with the pack-animals bred in the Assyrian provinces). We believe that Solomon's trade in Anatolian horses was carried out with the full cooperation of the king of Hamath, most likely as a mutual enterprise, though the main initiative was retained by Solomon. It is by no means improbable that some of the Anatolian horses were resold to other states which had no means of obtaining fine Anatolian horses other than through Solomon's agents and their partners in Hamath.

In sum, we have sought to present here the special achievement attained by Solomon in the international relations of his age, an achievement too significant to be treated simply as a private enterprise in horses and chariots. Indeed, Solomon opened a "window" for the international trade, through which contemporaneous cultural "trade winds" could breeze in and out, conveying innumerable cargos of costly goods and commodities, together with their cultural tastes, among the royal courts of the day.

---

context is a little different from that of 2 Chr 8:3 (see Myers, *II Chronicles*, 48). On the usage of עַל חֹזָק, see also 2 Chr 27:5 (cf. P. Welten, *Geschichte und Geschichtsdarstellung in den Chronikbüchern* [Neukirchen-Vluyn, 1973] 36, 51; *HALAT*, 290). The province of Zobah stretched approximately east of the northern Anti-Lebanon toward Tadmor (see M. Noth, "Das Reich von Hamath als Grenznachbar des Reiches Israel," *PJ* 33 [1937] 42). For the different opinion see E. Forrer, *Die Provinzeinteilung des assyrischen Reiches* (Leipzig, 1920) 62.

[128] For מִסְכְּנוֹת, a loan-word from Akk. *maškattu/maškantu*, pl. *maškanātu* ("deposit, storehouse") *CAD* M/1, 375; "*maškanu(m),*"*AHw* 2 (1972) 626-27, see B. Mazar, "מִסְכְּנוֹת, עָרֵי מִסְכְּנוֹת," *EncBib* 5 (1968) 165-67 (Hebrew); *HALAT*, 573.

Traditional Institutions and the Monarchy: Social and Political Tensions in the Time of David and Solomon

HAYIM TADMOR

The Hebrew University, Jerusalem

Historical periods are usually named for the monarchs who left an imprint upon them. A case in point is the present symposium, which is entitlted "The Age of David and Solomon." Indeed, our primary sources, the Court History presented in 2 Samuel and 1 Kings 1-2, center around the figures of these kings and the destiny of their immediate families.[1] This is especially true of the age of Solomon. Whereas in the history of David's reign one still finds some expression of the role of the people, in the record of Solomon's reign one encounters an account written within the circles of *ḥokmah*, which extolls the Divine Wisdom of the king, his riches and attainment.[2] These accounts provide very little in the nature of the historiography.

It is only natural, as a consequence, that modern biblical scholarship has devoted most of its efforts to the literary analyses of these court histories and to the classification of the religious phenomena intrinsic to them. Only later, did questions of social organization, political ideology, and the actual organs of statecraft come to the fore.

---

[1] On the ideology and date of these court histories we should note the recent studies of R. N. Whybray, *The Succession Narrative* (SBT 2/9, 1968); E. Würthwein, *Die Erzählung von der Thronfolge Davids. Theologische oder politische Geschichtsschreibung?* (Theologische Studien 115, 1974); T. Veijola, *Die ewige Dynastie* (Helsinki, 1975) and especially T. N. D. Mettinger, *King and Messiah: The Civil and Sacral Legitimation of the Israelite Kings* (CB OTS 8, 1976) 27-63, with fuller critical remarks on previous studies, especially those of Veijola. Cf. also T. Ishida, "Solomon's Succession to the Throne of David—A Political Analysis" in the present volume. D. M. Gunn, *The Story of King David: Genre and Interpretation* (JSOT SupS 6, 1978), was not available to me at the time this paper was prepared for publication.

[2] Cf. M. Noth, "Die Bewährung von Salomos 'Göttlicher Weissheit'," *Wisdom in Israel and in the Ancient Near East* (VTSup 3, 1960) 225-37; R. B. Y. Scott, "Solomon and the Beginnings of Wisdom," (VTSup 3, 1960) 262-79; (but cf. J. Liver, "The Book of the Acts of Solomon," *Bib* 48 [1967] 75-101); R. N. Whybray, *The Intellectual Tradition in the Old Testament* (BZAW 135, 1974).

Apart from the prolonged delay in dealing directly with historical, political, or social issues, there was still another primary emphasis in modern scholarship. In large part, the sources, themselves molded the interest of scholars and directed them to the subject of kingship, its ideology, and institutions. Thus, the role of the people, a powerful, though silent partner, has been largely bypassed, even in the most scholarly treatments.[3] Here, we will direct our attention precisely to the role of the people, and its traditional political institutions, in a modest attempt to achieve a measure of balance in our comprehension of a formative epoch in biblical history.

In the pre-monarchial period, the Elders—the heads of the local communities—were the people's source of authority in everyday matters.[4] They were the ones who judged the people and who held the powers of leadership. So, for example, the Elders of Gilead appealed to Jephthah, the leader of an armed band, and appointed him "commander over all the inhabitants of Gilead" in their war and struggle against Ammonite domination (Judg 11:8). Similarly, the Elders of Israel were the ones who approached David in Hebron, and who offered him the kingship of Israel, after he had already ruled over Judah for some years (2 Sam 5:1-3).[5] We are concerned, then, with an institution which possessed authority and which was empowered (and perhaps obligated) to select the leaders in times of crisis.

The role of the Elders during David's reign will be discussed in due course, and we shall see that it was decisive. After the division of the United Kingdom, however, the Elders are mentioned only infrequently. Only in a time of national emergency do we hear of an appeal to "the Elders of the land." This was during Ahab's reign, when the Elders were required to decide whether or not to yield to Ben-Hadad, king of Aram (1 Kgs 20:7). In Judah, too, the Elders are mentioned only in connection with a crisis; King Josiah thus gathers the Elders of Judah in Jerusalem and "all the people, young and old" (2 Kgs 23:2) for a ceremony enacting the covenant which underlay his religious reform.

---

[3]Therefore, of special significance are the following studies: Mettinger, *King and Messiah* (CB OTS 8); T. Ishida, *The Royal Dynasties in Ancient Israel: A Study on the Formation and Development of Royal-Dynastic Ideology* (BZAW 142, 1977), and especially, F. Crüsemann, *Der Widerstand gegen das Königtum: Die antiköniglichen Texte des Alten Testamentes und der Kampf um den frühen israelitischen Staat* (WMANT 49, 1978).

[4]See, in general, J. L. McKenzie, "The Elders in the Old Testament," *Studia Biblica et Orientalia* 1 (AnBib 10, 1959) 388-406; on the relationship between the Elders and the Urban Leadership, see H. Reviv, "The Structure of Society," *The Age of the Monarchies: Culture and Society. The World History of the Jewish People* 4/2 (ed. A. Malamat; Jerusalem, 1979) 131-36.

[5]Cf. Mettinger, *King and Messiah*, 114-15, 138-39. On the duration of David's reign in Hebron, cf. B. Mazar, "David's Reign in Hebron and the Conquest of Jerusalem," *In the Time of Harvest, Essays in Honor of A. H. Silver*, (ed. D. J. Silver; New York, 1963) 235-44.

One might go so far as to state that the authority of the Elders was weakened to the degree that the king's power increased. This was true, in particular, of their main field of activity: adjudication. One example of this is the affair of Naboth the Jezreelite, in which the king's command overrules legal integrity and a serious misjudgment results (1 Kgs 21:8-13).

However, on a number of major occasions, it was not the Elders but the "people" as a whole that selected the leader or elected the king. Several terms are used to denote the entire people as the bearer of political, military, or ceremonial authority. The most common are ישראל, "Israel," כל ישראל, "all Israel," עם ישראל, "the people of Israel,"[6] or, in an abbreviated form, העם, "the people." These terms denote the totality of the tribes or any part thereof, representative of the whole. Certain documents employ the term עדה, "assembly" (of the people), which is believed to be an ancient term. Others, especially later sources, refer to the assembly as קהל, "congregation."[7]

A key term illustrating the political institutions in the pre-monarchial period and especially the account of Absalom's rebellion is איש ישראל, "the men of Israel." I attmepted to clarify the meaning of this term in an earlier study,[8] the main points of which are summarized here.

After Gideon's victory over the Midianites, he is offered dynastic chieftainship by איש ישראל: "Rule over us, you, your son, your grandson as well" (Judg 8:22). Likewise, it is the name given to the select body that decides to go to war against the tribe of Benjamin: "ten men to a hundred, a hundred to a thousand and a thousand to the ten thousand" (Judg 20:10).[9] It was thus the army of Israel or, in actual fact, the few that were called to arms, who offered Gideon the dynastic chieftainship on behalf of all Israel.

The most prominent appearance of איש ישראל, however, is in the account of David's war with Absalom. When David is told that "the loyalty of the men of Israel has veered toward Absalom" (2 Sam 15:13), he speedily leaves Jerusalem and escapes across the Jordan. His army, defined

---

[6]See recently T. Ishida, "The Leaders of the Tribal Leagues 'Israel' in the Pre-Monarchic Period," *RB* 80 (1973) 514-30.

[7]Cf., e.g., B. Luther, "*Kāhāl* und ᶜ*Ēdāh*, als Hilfsmittle der Quellenscheidung im Priesterkodex und in der Chronik," *ZAW* 56 (1928) 44-63; and R. Gordis, "Democratic Origins in Ancient Israel: The Biblical ᶜ*Ēdah*," *Alexander Marx Jubilee Volume*, English Section (New York, 1950) 369-88. A case for the antiquity of the term עדה as against קהל has been put recently by A. Hurvitz, "Linguistic Observations on the Biblical Usage of the Priestly Term ᶜ*Edah*," *Tarbiz* 40 (1970/71) 261-67 (Hebrew). Cf. also, J. Milgrom, "Priestly Terminology and the Political Social Structure of the Pre-Monarchic Israel," *JQR* NS 69 (1978) 65-76.

[8]H. Tadmor, " 'The People' and the Kingship in Ancient Israel: The Role of the Political Institutions in the Biblical Period," *Cahiers d'histoire mondiale — Journal of World History* 11 (1968) 46-68 (Reprinted in: *Jewish Society through the Ages*, [ed. H. H. Ben-Sasson and S. Ettinger: London, 1971]. Also in Russian translation in; *Sozialnaya jizn i sozialnye zennosti evreiskovo naroda* [Tel Aviv, 1977] 57-91).

[9]Cf. Crüsemann, *Widerstand*, 42-44.

throughout the story as "the servants of David," confronts Absalom's
army, which is called "Israel" or "the people of Israel" (2 Sam 18:7).[10]

It is clear that "men of Israel" and "Israel" must, in all the instances
quoted above, mean "Israel-at-arms."[11] Some scholars have suggested that
these terms designate the heads of clans and tribal chiefs,[12] but this view is
unlikely. In my opinion, the heads of clans and tribes are the Elders.
Whereas איש ישראל represents the structure of the tribe or tribes from the
standpoint of military organization, the Elders seem to represent the tribal
notables, those of a high familial-social status. They are the ones who
represent the existing leadership of the tribe, of the family, and later of the
city as well.[13] They "sit at the gate" as the supreme judicial authority. The
people, as a whole, assemble at times of crisis, such as war or election of
the leader, while the Elders' activity is continuous. This type of self-
government, often termed "primitive democracy," is reminiscent of similar
structures in other societies at early stages of their development.[14] The men-
at-arms constituted the sole source of authority. When assembled, they
were empowered to decide on war and peace and to choose a leader in
times of emergency.

If historical analogues are desired, we may perhaps adduce one such
comparison from a kin-related society at a similar stage of development—
the Amorites on the Middle Euphrates, best attested in the Mari documents of the 18th century B.C. These documents contain a letter concerning
the men of the city of Qa, which was the vassal-city of the king of Mari.
The city of Qa swore allegiance to the king of Mari while he was in conflict
with King Hammurabi of Babylon:

> In connection with the matter of the men of Qa and the people of the city of
> Qa—I heard as follows: 'Provisions are required for ten days and they will
> march to the aid of Hammurabi'. Thus did I hear and I wrote to Yamruṣ-El

---

[10]Ibid., 94-100.

[11]Tadmor, *Cahiers d'histoire mondiale* 11 (1968) 50-51.

[12]E. S. J. Grintz, "The Treaty of Joshua with the Gibeonites," *JAOS* 86 (1966) 119.

[13]See, most recently, H. Reviv, "The Structure of Society," *The World History of the Jewish People* 4/2, 127-29.

[14]For comparative evidence, mainly for Mesopotamia, see the pioneer studies of Th. Jacobsen, "Primitive Demoncracy in Ancient Mesopotamia," *JNES* 2 (1943) 159-72; "Early Political Development in Mesopotamia," *ZA* 18 (1957) 91-140 = *Towards the Image of Tammuz* (ed. W. L. Moran; Cambridge, MA, 1970) 132-72 and I. M. Diakonoff, "Gosudarst-vennyi Stroi Drevneishevo Shumera," *Vestnik Drevnei Istorii* (1952/2) 13-37; idem, "The Rise of the Despotic State in Ancient Mesopotamia," *Ancient Mesopotamia* (ed. I. M. Diakonoff; Moscow, 1969) 173-203. Cf. also S. Evans, "Ancient Mesopotamian Assemblies," *JAOS* 78 (1958) 1-11. Contrast, however, the relatively late origin of the "popular assembly" in ancient Greece: J. A. O. Larsen, *Representative Government in Greek and Roman History* (Berkeley/Los Angeles, 1955) 14-21. Thus, in Athens, the council of the few—mainly nobles and former magistrates—preceded the popular council which represented the entire citizen body (ibid., 18).

and to the Elders of Qa (*šībut* URU *Qa*) and to the men of Qa. And they assembled here, two hundred first-rank warriors (*ṣābum qaqqadātim*) from the men of Qa, and in their assembly (*ina puḥrišunu*) I thus addressed them: "What is the reasoning of yours? Where are you heading? You say: 'We are the servants of Zimri-Lim', but now you have taken a decision of your own to go to the aid of Hammurabi!"[15]

Three authorities are mentioned in this letter: Yamruṣ-El, the local suzerain; the Elders; and the "Men of Qa." But, the ultimate authority for decsions on waging war, in this context, obviously was the assembly of the two hundred selected warriors and not the Elders, who on another occasion[16] appear as a delegation to Zimri-Lim in negotiations of some sort.[17]

To return to ancient Israel, and to our first example, the Elders were the ones who negotiated with Jephthah on the terms of his appointment as military leader of Gilead, but it was the people who made him head and commander (Judg 11:11). The subsequent solemn agreement before Yahweh at Mizpah was the natural culmination of this process.

In exactly the same way, David, king of Judah, was crowned king of all Israel. The Elders negotiate with him at Hebron, he concludes a treaty with them before Yahweh, and they anoint him king over all Israel (2 Sam 5:3).

The details of Absalom's coronation in Hebron are not related in 2 Samuel 15; all we are told about (v. 10) is the ceremony of blowing the horn, followed by the acclamation: "Absalom is king." Apparently, however, there was a public ceremony of anointment, involving the people as a body. This we learn from 2 Sam 19:10-11:

All the people throughout all the tribes of Israel were arguing (וַיְהִי כָל־הָעָם נָדוֹן בְּכָל־שִׁבְטֵי יִשְׂרָאֵל): Some said: "The king saved us from the hands of our enemies, and he delivered us from the hands of the Philistines; and just now he had to flee the country because of Absalom. But Absalom, whom we anointed over us has died in battle: why then do you sit idle instead of escorting the king back?" (New JPSV).

The word נָדוֹן translated by "were arguing" is unique in its root דון in the present participle of the *Nifᶜal*. Could it be a technical term for the official deliberations of the people convened in the assembly? If so, we might have here a description of the discussions at the tribal assemblies which took

---

[15]C. Jean, *ARM* 2 (1951) no. 75:1-21.

[16]Ibid., no. 95.

[17]A similar situation seems to have existed in the same period in lower Kurdistan, in a Hurrian milieu. A letter from Shemshara—ancient Shushara—written by Shamshi-Adad I, king of Assyria, to the local king, his vassal, shows that the institution of the Elders played a leading role in connection with the military affairs alongside the army itself, serving under the king. J. Laessøe, *The Shemshāra Tablets* (Arkaelogisk-Kunsthistoriske Meddeleser Det Kongelige Danske Videnskabernes Selskab, 4/3, 1959) 47-51.

place, more or less simultaneously, after Absalom's death. Left without a
king—with Absalom dead and David a fugitive—the people in the various
tribal territories addressed their leaders in the second person plural.
Effectively their appeal meant: "Why are you inactive in restoring David to
his throne?" Again, two bodies seem to be involved: the assemblies of the
people and the leaders, most probably the local chieftains, i.e., the Elders.

The next extraordinary assembly of all Israel was convened at Shechem, to negotiate with Rehoboam before his coronation (1 Kings 12).
Here it is "all Israel" that come to crown the new king, not just the "men of
Israel," since this was not a case of war. When Rehoboam rejects their
terms, it is "the people" who proclaim secession, and it is they who later
invite Jeroboam to be their king. The terms איש ישראל no longer occur
as a synonym for "Israel-at-arms."

In the Northern Kingdom, however, where royal dynasties rose and
fell quite frequently, the new king was usually appointed by the army,
which, in spite of its obviously limited numbers, is customarily referred to
as "Israel," "all Israel" or just "the people." Thus, Nadab, Jeroboam's
successor, is killed in a military camp, while he and "all Israel" are
besieging the Philistine city of Gibbethon (1 Kgs 15:27). The same body of
warriors undoubtedly acclaimed his murderer Baasha as the new king of
Israel. One generation later Omri, the founder of a new dynasty, was
crowned by "all Israel," again in a military camp (1 Kgs 16:16).[18]

One should not assume, of course, that "all" Israel were actually
besieging the Philstines at Gibbethon. The besieging force must have been
only a part of the army, perhaps a fraction of "Israel-at-arms." It was
representative enough, however, to be acknowledged as the legal, constitutional body.

In later practice, the actual power to decide which of the military
commanders should be crowned king was invested solely in the commaders
themselves. Nevertheless, even in later times the political fiction persisted.
This select circle of officers was required to claim that it was, indeed, the
"people of Israel." This was especially true when the king, coming from
their midst was nominated by a prophet. So it was in the case of Jehu, who
was nominated by Elisha's emissary at a military camp in Ramot Gilead
and who was immediately acclaimed by his fellow commanders (2 Kgs
9:1-13).[19] However, as important as the role of the pre-literary prophet was
in shaping public opinion in Israel, this subject is beyond the scope of the
present discussion.

---

[18]Tadmor, *Cahier d'histoire mondiale* 11 (1968) 62-64; J. A. Soggin, *Das Königtum in Israel*
(BZAW 104, 1967) 88-103; and especially: Ishida, *The Royal Dynasties*, 171-72.

[19]On the anointing of Jehu by a prophet and the exclamation "יחי המלך," see Mettinger,
King and Messiah, 117, 131, 193; Z. Weisman, "Anointing as a Motif in the Making of the
Charismatic King," *Bib* 47 (1976) 383.

What gave the army and its officers the right to claim that they were acting on behalf of "all Israel"? The answer lies, I believe, in the close connection between the structure of the army and the tribal-familial pattern in early Israel.

Under the customary recruitment system, the military unit was identical with the kinship unit, or ʾeleph, a word which means both "sub-tribe" or "clan," as well as "thousand." The people of Israel were called to arms by their "clans" אלפים, and therefore the large-scale organization of the army was based on the tribal-territorial units.[20] This would explain the traditional formulation whereby the army consisted of 12 units corresponding to the 12 tribes in the cases of war involving the whole of Israel. Our example is Ahithophel's advice to Absalom: "Let me pick twelve thousand men (שנים־עשר אלף איש) and set out tonight in pursuit of David" (2 Sam 17:1). The implication here is that the war against David should encompass all of Israel-at-arms—one ʾeleph from each tribe. It is therefore not surprising that the Elders, the tribal-territorial chieftains, are also involved in military matters.

There are several cases that testify to this organization of the army into tribal-territorial units: איש אפרים, the "men of Ephraim" assembled to assist Jephthah are simply the army of Ephraim. Likewise, איש יהודה, the "men of Judah" is clearly the tribal-territorial body of Judah, assembled in war. After the defeat of Absalom, David negotiates with the Elders of Judah and the "men of Judah," a point which we shall discuss further. Similarly, the rebellion of Sheba is ignited by a conflict between the "men of Judah" and the rest of Israel. Again, it is the "men of Judah" whom David enlists to fight Sheba.

It should be noted that, when the text speaks of Judah in contradistinction with the rest of Israel, the term "men of Israel" should mean, specifically, the "army of the ten tribes."[21] In the account of Absalom's rebellion, however, the terms undoubtedly denotes the people of Israel as a whole, including Judah.[22]

Having commented on the key terms of the social structure of early Israel, which, as we have seen, was intimately interwoven with the military structure, we now proceed to examine the several rebellions which occurred during the reigns of David and Solomon. These were occasions on which the authority of the popular institutions clashed with that of the monarchy, creating and reinforcing tensions that finally culminated in the schism and the division of Israel.

---

[20]Cf. G. E. Mendenhall, "The Census Lists of Numbers 1 and 26," *JBL* 52 (1958) 52-66; J. Liver, "משפחה," *EncBib* 5 (1968) 583-84 (Hebrew).

[21]Cf. Crüsemann, *Widerstand*, 95-103.

[22]On this well-known dichotomy, see most recently, Z. Kallai, "Judah and Israel—a Study in Israelite Historiography," *IEJ* 28 (1978) 251-61. For early Israel cf. also Ishida, *RB* 80 (1973) 530.

There were three rebellions. The first—Absalom's—shook the reign of David, then already an aging monarch, and forced him to flee Jerusalem and jeopardize his life. The second, the rebellion of Sheba ben Bichri, an offshoot of the first, challenged the very legitimacy of David's rule over the ten tribes of Israel. The third rebellion, known as Jeroboam's revolt (a misnomer, as we shall see), split the United Kingdom of Israel and left David's grandson as the king of one tribe (or one and a half tribes), with Jeroboam as the first king of the confederacy of the "ten tribes of Israel." In trying to determine the causes of these rebellions, the social forces that shaped them, and the ideology of their perpetrators, one is hampered by the fact that the sources present a rather one-sided view of the events. Absalom's revolt is related in the context of David's Court History, which centers on the biographical sequence which depicts David as the tragic hero and Absalom as an equally tragic antihero. A similar juxtaposition occurs later, with Rehoboam as being the tragicomic hero, as against Jeroboam, his mischievous counterpart. Moreover, while David's court history is closer to the time of the events, and hence of high validity as a historical source, the account of Jeroboam's rise to power and the division of the kingdom is the product of a complex editorial redaction (rather biased, at that). As a result, very little of the possible original account has survived.

Who were then the powers who backed Absalom, the ambitious and arrogant crown prince, in his attempt to wrest the throne from his father? It is paradoxical that Absalom was supported by the traditional institutions of Israel, whereas David was left only with his courtiers, his bodyguard, and mercenaries. In other words, the army of Israel and its officers did not remain loyal to the king. When David reached Gilead and found refuge and support with families related to the Benjaminites, he was obliged to recruit a new army. Even so, as we have noted, the historiographer refrained from calling these new recruits an "army," referring to them rather as "David's servants," עבדי דוד (2 Sam 18:6).

When Absalom enters Jerusalem, "all the people, the men of Israel," accompany him (2 Sam 16:15), and they, as well as the Elders of Israel, assume the function of a consultative body to the king. The Elders and the king accept Ahithophel's advice to pursue David forthwith, but the assembly of the "men of Israel" rejects it, accepting instead the conspiratorial counsel of Hushai the Archite (2 Sam 17:3) intended to thwart the counsel of Ahithophel.[23]

---

[23]On the "Counsel of Ahithophel" see W. McKane, *Prophets and Wise Men* (SBT 44, 1965) 55-58; W. M. W. Roth, "A Study of the Classical Hebrew Verb *śkl*," *VT* 18 (1968) 71; cf. also the recent and highly critical studies of F. Langlamet, "Ahitofel et Houshaï. Rédaction prosalomonienne en 2 S 15-17?" *Studies in Bible and the Ancient Near East. Presented to S. E. Loewenstamm* (ed. Y. Avishur and J. Blau; Jerusalem, 1978) 57-88 and "Absalom et les concubines de son père," *RB* 84 (1977) 161-209.

All of this is entirely new. Never before, either in the times of Saul or in those of David, (and never thereafter), do we find the people-at-arms and the Elders acting in a consultative capacity to the king. In times of anarchy, as after the death of Saul and the assassination of his son Eshba^cal, the Elders of Israel appear as a source of authority, but they never function in coexistence with royalty. No royal power in the ancient Near East would willingly consent to be limited by a council of Elders or an assembly of warriors. How, then, can one explain Absalom's surrender to the popular institutions? It could hardly be rooted in his upbringing as a royal prince and heir-apparent to the throne, nor does it accord well with his arrogant personality.

This may be the key to our question. The traditional institutions abandoned David and backed Absalom, presumably, because the young prince promised them privileges that they had never possessed under the monarchy.[24] In other words, the traditional leadership, snubbed by David, now found a fitting moment to retrieve the power that they had lost long before, at the dawn of the monarchical regime. Their success, however, was ephemeral and doomed to failure: The age of constitutional monarchies never arrived in antiquity. Despite this, their failure did not affect the ability of the traditional institutions to act during subsequent crises, namely, during the rebellions of Sheba and Jeroboam.

We must now comment on the role of the tribe of Judah, a point that has been much debated by scholars.[25] As far as we can ascertain, Judah and its traditional leadership played a major role in Absalom's conspiracy and rebellion. His kingship was proclaimed at Hebron, the sacred city of Judah. His commander-in-chief was Amasa, one of his cousins, a Judahite, as was his advisor, Ahithophel of Gilo. The latter, I believe, was Bath-Sheba's grandfather, who sought revenge for his granddaughter's disgrace. (Bath-Sheba was the daughter of Eliam [2 Sam 11:3], who may be identified with Eliam son of Ahithophel the Gilonite, one of David's "thirty mighty men" [1 Sam 23:24]).

It would seem that this central role of Judah in the rebellion was the main cause for David's attitude toward that tribe after Absalom's death. The tribes of Israel represented by their traditional institutions, began to negotiate with David, with an eye to restoring him to the throne. While negotiations were underway, David contacted the Elders of Judah, through Zadok and Abiathar the priests, suggesting that they should not be "the last to bring back the king." Appealing to them in the words, "You are my

---

[24] Tadmor, *Cahiers d'histoire mondiale* 11 (1968) 54.
[25] E.g., A. Alt, "Die Staatenbildung der Israeliten in Palästina" (1930) *Kleine Schriften* 2 (München, 1953) 56-58; M. Noth, *Geschichte Israels* (2d ed.; Göttingen, 1954) 184-85 = *The History of Israel* (2d ed.; London, 1960) 201. More recently: Soggin, *Das Königtum in Israel*, 75; M. Garsiel, *The Kingdom of David* (Tel Aviv, 1975) 132-40 (Hebrew); Ishida, *The Royal Dynasties*, 69, and especially Crüsemann, *Widerstand*, 95-98.

kinsmen, my own flesh and blood!" (2 Sam 19:13), he clearly hinted at the advantages awaiting them as his preferred tribe ("Why should you be the last to escort the king back?"). Furthermore, he also offered a crowning concession: the appointment of Amasa, Absalom's commander, as his own commander-in-chief (v. 14). "So (David) swayed the hearts of all the men of Judah as one man" (v. 15).

Was this indeed just a matter of prestige? I believe it is more probable that David promised the Judahites certain advantages, perhaps preference in the nomination of officials and stewards or alleviation of forced labor requirements. It should be noted that the list of David's ministers after the revolts of Absalom and Sheba ben Bichri (2 Sam 20:23ff.), which includes Benaiah ben Jehoiada (the commander of the mercenaries) in the second place, after Joab, also includes, for the first time, Adoniram אֲשֶׁר עַל הַמַּס "in charge of the levy." Although all our information about the levy of forced labor comes from the reign of Solomon, it is clear from this list that the institution of the מַס, which was new in Israel, had been introduced in David's era after Absalom's revolt.[26]

Let us examine David's relationship with the tribe of Judah more closely. We stand at a crucial juncture in the reign of David, perhaps even more crucial than the rebellion itself. All of his life, from the very beginnings of his activities, David had taken special pains to consolidate his kingship outside the scope of narrow tribal interests. He established his capital at Jerusalem, a city which he himself had captured and which lay outside the tribal realms, ideally located, at the borderline between Judah and Israel. If the Elders of Israel indeed posed any conditions during their negotiations with David at Hebron (2 Sam 5:3), these were probably in the nature of precautions, limiting the privileges of Judah and its preferred status in the new state structure. The Israelites were concerned, and probably rightly so, lest David, as king of Judah, give preference in all respects to his own tribe, whether of his own accord or because forced to do so. In fact, as far as we can ascertain from the sources, David showed no special favor to the traditional institutions of Judah during the whole period from the capture of Jerusalem up to Absalom's revolt (probably the major part of his reign). On the contrary, he created a ramified bureau-cratic system, a well-developed class of stewards whose power derived from the king himself and not from any local, tribal-territorial factors.

The king was now cut off from the people by a strong bureaucracy which, though impartially inclined to the various tribes, gave much cause

---

[26]On the institutions of the מַס and סֵבֶל under the Unified Monarchy, see I. Mendelsohn, "On Corvée Labor in Ancient Israel," *BASOR* 167 (1961) 31-35; M. Held, "The Root *ZBL/SBL* in Akkadian, Ugaritic and Biblical Hebrew," *JAOS* 88 (1968) 90-96; A. F. Rainey, "Compulsory Labour Gangs in Ancient Israel," *IEJ* 20 (1970) 191-202; T. N. D. Mettinger, *Solomonic State Officials* (CB OTS 5, 1971) 128-39. Cf. now A. Soggin, "Compulsory Labor under David and Solomon" in the present volume.

for unrest and anger in that it prevented people from reaching the king (the supreme judge) as easily as they had expected. Essentially, this is the main reason that the biblical narrator gives for Absalom's revolt. The young prince promised the people that, once on the throne, he would not emulate his father's example—his house would be open to all those demanding justice (2 Sam 15:1-6).

The people of Judah and its tribal institutions no doubt found much cause for disappointment in the reign of David—up until Absalom's revolt. Their hope for special status had not materialized. In fact, Jerusalem had supplanted Hebron as the capital. Now, after the rebellion had been quelled David again took stock of the situation and realized that he could not reign as king over the United Monarchy unless he used Judah as a power base. The preferred status of Judah was immediately brought out in the crossing of the Jordan at Gilgal, a place fraught with historical memories.[27] It was the "men of Judah" who "escorted the king across" (2 Sam 20:41). Against the complaints of the "men of Israel" addressed to David: "Why did our kinsmen, the men of Judah, steal you away, and escort the king and his family across the Jordan . . . ," they replied: "Because the king is our relative!" (vv. 42-43). The unity of the tribes of Israel and of the United Monarchy had thus been shaken; it had been put to the test. The foundation was thus laid for the second rebellious outburst during the reign of David—the revolt of Sheba ben Bichri.

The slogan of this new revolt (2 Sam 20:1) was

We have no portion in David,
No share in Jesse's son!
Every man to his tents, O Israel.

The words "portion" (חלק) and "share" (נחלה)—the accepted terms for inheritance in the agrarian society—are highly significant. They lie at the very heart of the traditional tribal terminology, as do perhaps the words "We have ten shares in the king" occurring in the retort of the "men of Israel" to the "men of Judah" (v. 44). (The term "tent" is also archaic, referring perhaps to the make-up of a military camp.)[28] The biblical narrator proceeds with his story: ". . . all the men of Israel left David and followed Sheba . . . but the men of Judah accompanied their king from the Jordan to Jerusalem" (2 Sam 20:2).

---

[27]Mettinger, *King and Messiah*, 119, considers this ceremony at Gilgal as the second "coronation" of David. Note, however, the sequence of events in 2 Sam 19:10, representing, as the narrator has put it, the popular attitude: (a) David has "left the country" (= West of Jordan). His reign, thus, came to an end. (b) Absalom—now the legal king—was killed. (c) Hence, David should be invited to return and resume his office. The legal implications of this rather unique, constitutional situation are still to be considered.

[28]On this slogan and the terms "tents" and "portion and inheritance," see A. Malamat, "Organs of Statecraft in the Early Israelite Monarchy," *BA* 28 (1965) 39-40.

He does not tell us, however, anything that might shed light on the political program of David's new adversary. It is very questionable whether Sheba himself intended to assume the throne or to crown a Saulite prince over the northern tribes. This latter possibility, might have eventuated in any case, because at that stage, only a descendant of Saul had a real claim to the throne of Israel. However, it seems that the rebels had no immediate candidate for kingship. Thus, the rejection of "Jesse's son" inaugurated an interregnum of an indefinite period during which "the men of Israel" would naturally constitute the sole source of authority.

David realized in no time that this extraordinary situation was far more dangerous than Absalom's revolt had been: his very right to rule the ten tribes of Israel was now being denied and his kingship, as king of Israel and Judah, was thus put to a severe test. He had two alternatives: He could either suppress the revolt immediately, with the help of his professional army—the "mighty men" and the Cherethites and the Pelethites—the mercenaries, or he could appeal to the army of Judah. He chose the latter alternative, but it failed. Amasa, the commander-in-chief, was unable to muster the men of Judah within three days as he had been commanded, and he was ultimately assassinated. David had no choice but to recapture the kingship with the aid of his professional soldiers. Sheba and his associates fled to Abel of Beth-maacah, far off in Upper Galilee, the city was besieged, Sheba was killed. Thus came an end to the first abortive revolt, which challenged the legitimacy of the Davidic dynasty to rule over Israel (2 Sam 20:4-22).[29]

The sources leave us no details as to what happened after these events. It is a reasonable assumption that the king's power was now reinforced with regard to the status of his elite troops, the only one that had not betrayed him during Absalom's revolt, and had just save him again. As we have alrealy stated, Benaiah, the commander of the Cherethites and Pelethites, was now elevated to second position, after Joab the commander. During Solomon's reign he even inherited the latter's position (1 Kgs 4:4).

We now turn to the third revolt that shook the United Monarchy, that of Jeroboam. At this point, however, the questoin arises as to just what is implied by the term "revolt." Is it the abortive rebellion indicated by the words וירם יד במלך "... he raised his hand against the king" (1 Kgs 11:26)? That rebellion occured during Solomon's lifetime, culminating in the flight of Jeroboam to Egypt. Or, should the term be extended also to the people's assembly at Shechem, convened after Solomon's death, which proclaimed the secession from the house of David and finally elected Jeroboam as king? Moreover, there appears to be no immediate connection between Jeroboam's abortive rebellion and his coronation at Shechem. Each of these was an independent event, and should therefore be considered separately from the others.

---

[29]Cf. Crüsemann, *Widerstand*, 108-11.

Let us first consider the biblical account of that abortive rebellion:

And Jeroboam son of Nebat, and Ephrathite of Zeredah, the son of a widow whose name was Zeruah, was in Solomon's service; he raised his hand against the king. The circumstances under which he raised his hand against the king were as follows: Solomon built Millo, and repaired the breach of the city of his father David. This man Jeroboam was an able man (גבור חיל): and when Solomon saw that the young man was a capable worker he appointed him over all the levy of the house of Joseph (לכל־סבל בית יוסף) (1 Kgs 11:26-28).

At this point the reader is faced with a frustrating interruption: the account breaks off at the very moment the rebellion should be described. Instead, we have the story of Ahijah the Shilonite and the rending of Jeroboam's garment, which is a separate literary unit, and which originates, no doubt, in prophetic (Northern?) circles.[30] Clearly, the meeting of Jeroboam and Ahijah is not a rebellious act; it is certainly not what the biblical narrator would call "raising a hand against the king." Hence, the story is incomplete; it is completed in the Septuagint, which presents, though in the following chapter, a detailed and an entirely different narration of the events. However, this, so-called Second Account of the Septuagint, in its version of Jeroboam's rebellion,[31] far from solving the problem, raises new and graver difficulties.

It relates that Jeroboam (son of Sareisa, a harlot!), Solomon's "lash-master" (ἄρχων σκυτάλης), built the city of Sareira (=Zeredah, MT) for his king. He possessed 300 chariots, rebelled, and escaped to Shishak king of Egypt. After Solomon's death, he returned, fortified his native town, and gathered the tribes of Israel at Shechem. Only there did he receive the prophecy that the kingdom was to be rent from the house of David, and moreover, he received it not from Ahijah the Shilonite but from Shemaᶜiah, the Judahite prophet.

Is there any kernel of historical truth in this story? Could it contain an authentic, ancient tradition on the accession of Jeroboam? These problems were much debated and scholars are still divided on them. Some accept the historicity in the LXX or, at least, certain elements in it. Others consider it a late midrash in the sytle of Chronicles, not to be regarded as an independent, and equally valid source.[32] Strictly on historical grounds,

---

[30]See A. Caquot, "Ahiyya de Silo et Jéroboam 1ᵉʳ," *Semitica* 11 (1961) 17-27; M. A. Cohen, "The Role of the Shilonite Priesthood in the United Monarchy of Ancient Israel," *HUCA* 36 (1965) 59-98.

[31]It is marked as 1 Kgs 12:24ᵃ⁻ᶻ in Swete's edition of the LXX. See also A. G. Brooke, N. McLean and H. St. J. Thackeray, *The Old Testament in Greek* II, Pt. II (Cambridge, 1920) 255-58.

[32]See, e.g., E. Meyer, *Die Israeliten und ihre Nachbarstämme* (Halle a/S, 1906), 363-70; J. Skinner, *I and II Kings* (Century Bible, n.d.) 443-46; J. A. Montgomery and H. S. Gehman, *The Books of Kings* (ICC, 1951) 251-54. More recently: D. Debus, *Die Sünde Jeroboams* (Göttingen, 1967) 68-80; H. Seebass, "Zur Königserhebung Jeroboams I," *VT* 17 (1967) 325-

without commenting here upon the validity of each of the details in the account of the LXX, I would tend to follow the latter approach.

To come back to Jeroboam's abortive rebellion; the question is: What is the meaning of "raised" (הרים) his hand against the king? The answer is not unequivocal, as this is the sole occurrence of the phrase in the Bible. "To lift up one's hand" (whether the Hebrew verb used is נשא or הרים) never has a negative connotation; the expression sometimes denotes an oath, and so sometimes the actual, physical raising of the hand. The idiom used to denote infliction of harm is usually "to lay a hand on . . ." (שלח יד ב. . .). However, the very same idiom ("raised his hand"), though with the verb הרים, "raise," instead of נשא, "lift up," appears in the story of Sheba ben Bichri (2 Sam 20:21), and there the context makes the intention unambiguous: he stood up against the king in public, committing an act of mutiny (20:1). Hence, one is obliged to put a similar interpretation on Jeroboam's act. He challenged the king and issued some proclamation against him, possibly quite an extreme one. Perhaps, like Sheba ben Bichri, he publicly defied the king.[33] Nevertheless, just as Sheba did not proclaim himself king, it does not seem that Jeroboam's raising his hand against Solomon was an attempt to crown himself king. Such attempts are usually preceded by conspiracy, like that of Absalom or of subsequent conspirators in the Kingdom of Israel; indeed, the term קשר, "to conspire, conspiracy" is current in contemporary texts.[34] On the other hand, the term מרד, "revolt," was not yet in use; it first appears in narrative and historical texts of the eighth century, or perhaps slightly earlier.[35] In the literature of the tenth century, however, it is unattested. The term for rebellion, at this stage is, "to raise one's hand against the king," which does not recur in later times.

The next crucial event is the assembly at Shechem after Solomon's death. The text reads: "Rehoboam went to Shechem, for all Israel had come to Shechem to acclaim him king" (1 Kgs 12:1).

33; D. W. Gooding, "Text and Midrash in the Third Book of Reigns," *Textus* 7 (1969) 11-12; and especially, R. P. Gordon, "The Second Septuagint Account of Jeroboam: History or Midrash?," *VT* 25 (1975) 368-93 with a bibliographic survey in notes 4-8.

[33]Crüsemann, *Widerstand*, 120.

[34]E.g., 1 Sam 22:8, 13; 2 Sam 15:12, 31. It is the common term for the historical narratives and in the editorial framework in Kings: e.g., 1 Kgs 16:16; 2 Kgs 9:14; 10:9; 11:14; 12:21.

[35]E.g., Gen 14:4; Josh 22:22, 29; Isa 36:5; 2 Kgs 18:7; 24:20. Later instances (not before the eighth century) of rebellion are defined by the verb פשע, literally "to transgress," i.e., to break the loyalty oath. The verb denotes the rebellion of a vassal king or vassal state against their overlord, e.g., Mesha against Ahab (2 Kgs 3:5), Edom against Israel (2 Kgs 8:22). Similarly, violations of the Covenant by Israel are often defined as "transgressions" by the prophets, e.g., Isa 1:2; Hos 8:1; Jer 33:8. In the same manner, the division of the Kingdom is described by the deuteronomic editor of 1 Kings 12, in terms of פשע: "So Israel revolted against the house of David (ויפשעו ישראל בבית דוד) until this day" (1 Kgs 12:19).

I cannot concur with the often repeated suggestion[36] that the assembly was convened in order to renew the covenant with Rehoboam, to confirm his kingship, nor with the more extreme view[37] that every king in Judah and Israel obtained—upon accession to the throne—the people's confirmation or renewed the covenant with them. The conclusion of a covenant between the king and the people is actually mentioned only twice in the history of the united and the divided Monarchy: once, at the founding of the Davidic dynasty, when David—already king of Judah—was crowned at Hebron as king of all Israel (2 Sam 5:1-3), and again, at the restoration of the dynasty, when the infant Jehoash was crowned after the Davidides had been almost decimated by Athaliah (2 Kgs 11:7). Both cases were exceptional, since they both signified the beginning of a dynasty. We have no evidence, I submit, that a renewal of the covenant was necessary when the crown passed in the normal manner from father to son, or that the people, through the act of acclaiming יְחִי הַמֶּלֶךְ "long live the king!" were inevitably supposed to confirm the royal heir upon accession to the throne.

Still, the assembly at Shechem—an ancient hallowed site of pre-monarchic Israel[38]—reflects, no doubt, a grave emergency. The very fact that it was convened is evidence of deep unrest and ferment among the people. I would therefore tend to see in Rehoboam's pilgrimage to Shechem an expression of goodwill on his part, an act of appeasement in an attempt to calm the growing dissatisfaction. Those assembled at Shechem—"all Israel," "all the people," or "the congregation"—most probably the Elders and notables of the Northern Tribes[39]—were willing to remain loyal to the house of David and to acknowledge Rehoboam as king. There is no allusion in 1 Kings 12 that the assembly intended to displace the Davidites, still less to establish a new dynasty. All we can conclude

---

[36]See G. Fohrer, "Der Vertrag zwischen König und Volk in Israel," *ZAW* 71 (1959) 8; Malamat, *BA* 28 (1965) 36; Mettinger, *King and Messiah*, 139-40.

[37]See Fohrer, *ZAW* 71 (1959) 9-17. Mettinger, however, postulates the existence of the Covenant only for the Davidides, suggesting that "the royal Covenant (in Judah) was normally renewed at every new investiture," *King and Messiah*, 150, and in detail, ibid., 141ff.

[38]See in general: E. Nielsen, *Shechem: A Traditio-Historical Investigation* (Copenhagen, 1955), and more recently, G. E. Wright, *Shechem—The Biography of a Biblical City* (New York, 1965) 9-23; H. J. Kraus, *Worship in Israel* (English Translation of *Gottesdienst in Israel*, 2d ed.; 1962) (Oxford, 1966) 134-46; B. Mazar, "The 'Place of Shechem'—An Israelite Sacred Area" (1973) *Canaan and Israel* (Jerusalem, 1974) 144-51 (Hebrew); M. Haran, *Temple and Temple Service in Ancient Israel* (Oxford, 1978) 48-52.

[39]It is also probable, that despite the all-inclusive language of the text, i.e., "all Israel," "the people," the assembly did not include the tribe of Judah and its traditional leadership. Judah, apparently, enjoyed certain privileges during Solomon's reign, perhaps in the area of taxation. In spite of some cogent arguments to the adverse, there is still no conclusive evidence that Judah was included in the Solomonic system of twelve districts. On that question see W. F. Albright, *Archaeology and the Religion of Israel* (Baltimore, 1942) 141; Alt, "Israels Gaue unter Salomo" (1913) *Kleine Schriften* 2, 89; Y. Aharoni, *The Land of the Bible* (London, 1966) 279; Mettinger, *Solomonic State Officials*, 121-23.

from this source is that the coronation of Rehoboam was subject to a condition, politely but firmly phrased—and which stands in stark contrast to Rehobam's arrogant reply—that he should proclaim a reform alleviating the burden of the corvée:[40]

הקל מעבדת אביך הקשה ומעלו הכבד
אשר־נתן עלינו ונעבדך

Lighten the harsh labour and the heavy yoke which your father laid on us and we will serve you (1 Kgs 12:4).

The progression from grievances aired at Shechem to the next historical development was only natural. The spokesmen for the traditional institutions snubbed by Rehoboam, had proclaimed the very slogan which characterized the situation during the rebellion of Sheba ben Bichri: if the tribal balance is to be violated and Judah is to receive preferred treatment, there could be no further place for a monarchy uniting all the tribes of Israel under the house of David. Let "Jesse's son" continue to rule over its home region of Judah; northern Israel, for its part, is free of any obligation and is entitled to choose another king. As we have noted above, had David not suppressed Sheba's revolt rapidly, it is quite possible that then, too, an alternative king would have been elected after a period of interregnum.[41] Perhaps the outcome of the events at Shechem would have been different, had Rehoboam resorted to military force and immediately suppressed the rebellion. Instead, however, he dispatched his minister, Adoram in charge of the levy, as a mediator, to negotiate concessions. But he underestimated the people's reaction to this mission, headed by this most hated of his ministers. The stoning of Adoram and Rehoboam's flight to Jerusalem epitomize the open schism which ensued.

The precise period of time that elapsed between Rehoboam's flight to Jerusalem and Jeroboam's coronation—the final act of schism—is not known. Neither is Jeroboam's part in the events clear. According to one

---

[40]In this connection a few additional points should be made: (a) the advice of Rehoboam's old courtiers ("If you will be a servant to those people today and serve them, and if you respond to them with kind words, they will be your servants always," 1 Kgs 12:7) speaks—obviously—of temporary and tactical concessions to the people's demands, and not of a binding covenant that should be reaffirmed; (b) the reform in the corvée-burden that Rehoboam was asked to make could be compared to the enactments of *mīšarum* and *andurārum* of the Old Babylonian kings proclaimed upon thier accession to the throne; see Tadmor, *Cahiers d'histoire mondiale* 11 (1968) 57. Cf. also M. Weinfeld, "The Counsel of the Elders of Rehoboam," *Lĕšonénu* 36 (1972) 3-11 (Hebrew). On the *mīšarum* enactments see B. Landsberger, "Die babylonische Termini für Gesetz und Recht," *Symbolae ad iura orientis antiqui pertinenta Paolo Koschaker didicatae* (Leiden, 1938) 219-34; ;F. R. Kraus, "Ein Edikt des Königs Samsu-iluna von Babylon," *Studies in Honor of Benno Landsberger* (AS 16, 1965) 225-31; J. J. Finkelstein, "Some New *Misharum* Material and Its Implications," ibid., 233-46.

[41]Tadmor, *Cahiers d'histoire mondiale* 11 (1968) 56; Crüsemann, *Widerstand*, 107.

version he was a party to the negotiations, together with the people.[42] According to another, which is apparently to be preferred, he was summoned before the congregation only after the schism.[43] There is no doubt, however, that Jeroboam was the natural candidate and that the crown would be offered to him. He was the only person who had defied Solomon and had gained the prophet's support as Yahweh's chosen king.

And yet, the overriding factor in Jeroboam's favour was, I believe, the ideology for which he stood, of which his sons, Nadab and Abijah, were living symbols. They bore the same names as the sons of Aaron, Nadab and Abihu, who had forfeited their lives by offering "Before the Lord alien fire" (Lev 10:1).[44] It seems that Jeroboam was opposed to the house of David not merely on the social issue—the corvée—but that his profound distaste for Jerusalem, for its cult and its prevalent traditions was rooted in an alternative religio-cultic conception. The reform that he instituted, undoubtedly with the full knowledge and consent of the popular institutions that had raised him to the throne, was also intended to eliminate the special cultic privileges of Jerusalem and its priests. To this end, the most ancient symbols were chosen. No longer is Yahweh portrayed as "sitting upon the *cherubim*," as in Jerusalem, but rather is Yahweh "standing by the calf," the very symbol that Aaron had fashioned in the desert.[45] Apparently there existed another version of the story of the Golden Calf, which was sympathetic to Aaron and which was probably current among the northern tribes. The existence of that version is masked behind the words, "This is your God, O Israel, who brought you up from

---

[42] 1 Kgs 12:2-3a, the reference to Jeroboam in v. 12 (omitted in the LXX) and 2 Chr 10:1-3. Cf. the commentaries, esp. Montgomery and Gehman, *Kings*, 248; M. Noth, *Könige* 1 (BKAT 9/1, 1968) 271ff.; J. Gray, *I and II Kings* (3d ed; London, 1977) 299ff. Cf., however, D. W. Gooding, "The Septuagint's Rival Versions of Jeroboam's Rise to Power," *VT* 17 (1967) 173-85, who prefers the version of the MT to that of the LXX.

[43] 1 Kgs 12:20 with the LXX of 1 Kgs 12:2-3, 12, preferred by the majority of the critics; see the preceding note and more recently R. W. Klein, "Jeroboam's Rise to Power," *JBL* 89 (1970) 217-18; idem, "Once more 'Jeroboam's Rise to Power,'" *JBL* 92 (1973) 582-84; but see D. W. Gooding's response: "Jeroboam's Rise to Power: A Rejoinder," *JBL* 91 (1972) 529-33. See also the comments of Crüsemann, *Widerstand*, 112.

[44] G. R. Gradwohl, "Das 'Fremde Feuer' von Nadab und Abihu," *ZAW* 75 (1963) 288-96; A. Aberbach and L. Smolar, "Aaron, Jeroboam and the Golden Calves," *JBL* 86 (1967) 134, 139.

[45] On the calf as symbol—though not the representative—of Yahweh, see O. Eissfeldt, "Lade und Stier," *ZAW* 58 (1930/41) 190-215. The view that the calf (a derogatory term for young bull?) was the "pedestal" upon which Yahweh was believed to be enthroned had been suggested by K. M. Obbink "Yahwebilder," *ZAW* 47 (1929) 264-74. It was accepted by W. F. Albright, *From the Stone Age to Christianity* (Baltimore, 1940) 229; idem, *Yahweh and the Gods of Canaan* (London, 1968) 172, by R. de Vaux, "Le schisme religieux de Jéroboam 1er," *Biblica et Orientalia. R. P. Vosté dedicata* (Rome, 1943) 77-83 (= *Bible et Orient* [Paris, 1967] 155-57), and by several other authorities. A different point of view is expressed by M. Weippert, "Gott und Stier," *ZDPV* 77 (1961) 102-7, and by Kraus, *Worship in Israel*, 29; however their critique of Obbink's thesis is not very convincing.

the land of Egypt . . ." (1 Kgs 12:28//Exod 32:8). It was later reworked as a polemical passage in Exodus 32 and turned against Jeroboam and his cultic innovations.[46] The utterly negative view of the Deuteronomist, who characterizes Jeroboam as the archetype of all the royal offenders of the Northern Kingdom, reflects, after all, a historical truth, once we regard it as a mirror-image of reality.

Jeroboam's other reforms betray a similar tendency: archaization, the elimination of the remnants of those religious and administrative institutions introduced by David and Solomon, and the establishment of separate cultic centers served by priestly families.[47]

To conclude: The process that we have attempted to describe indicates, in brief, that Israel could no longer return to non-monarchial self-rule. During Absalom's revolt the traditional bodies had tried to regain some measure of authority, alongside the king. In the subsequent two crises there was even an explicit attempt to abolish the house of David in order to elect a new king. It was no longer possible to revert to the traditional, tribal ideology according to which Yahweh himself was regarded as the actual king of Israel.[48] Jeroboam ascended to power on the waves of the anti-Davidite movement. The traditional bodies, which had abolished the covenant with the house of David, did not claim power for themselves; on the contrary, it is doubtful whether their king Jeroboam (who was perhaps also their leader) shared any of his powers with them, as Absalom had promised, and even tried to do. But, there can hardly be any doubt of Jeroboam's connection with the pre-monarchial order and its symbols. This connection, however, is not embodied in the granting of authority to the traditional organs of self-government, but rather in the revival of the ancient cultic symbolism, whose very archaism is indicative of the people's yearning for the older popular institutions that had led to the coronation of Jeroboam. Yet, Jeroboam's kingdom inherited the bulk of Solomon's domain, and as well all its inner order of things. The hands of the clock of history, to use a cliché, could not be turned back. The monarchial order gained power, and all that the traditional institutions of self-government could do was, occasionally, to depose the current dynasty and crown a new king, but even this usually happened only in times of crisis, in war or after a military defeat.[49]

---

[46]See W. Beyerlin, *Origins and History of the Oldest Sinaitic Tradition* (Oxford, 1965) 126-33; F. M. Cross, *Canaanite Myth and Hebrew Epic* (Cambridge, MA/London, 1973) 198-200; B. Halpern, "Levitical Participation in the Reform Cult of Jeroboam I," *JBL* 95 (1976) 31-42.

[47]See S. Talmon, "Divergences in Calendar-Reckoning in Ephraim and Judah," *VT* 8 (1958) 48-58; Cross, *Canaanite Myth and Hebrew Epic*, 199. Cf. also in general, J. Bright, *A History of Israel* (2d ed.; London, 1972) 234; Tadmor, "The Period of he First Temple, the Babylonian Exile and the Resotration," *A History of the Jewish People* (ed. H. H. Ben-Sasson; London, 1976) 115-16.

[48]M. Buber, *Kingship of God* (London, 1967) 59ff.

[49]Tadmor, *Cahiers d'histoire mondiale* 11 (1968) 62-65; Ishida, *The Royal Dynasties*, 171ff.

It would be wrong, however, to claim that these traditional organs of self-government were ever totally eclipsed. They should rather be described as dormant during the period of the monarchy. The proof of this lies in the fact that when the monarchy and its institutions came to an end with the exile to Babylon, the traditional institutions, and particularly the Elders, reappeared in all their vigor and once again assumed their historical role.[50] This state of affairs was essentially characteristic of the Jewish diaspora, from the Babylonian Exile until almost modern times.

---

[50]Cf. H. C. M. Vogt, *Studien zur nachexilischen Gemeinde in Esra-Nehemia* (Werl, 1966) 76-105; I. Eph^{c}al, "The Western Minorities in Babylonia in the 6th-5th Centuries B.C.: Maintenance and Cohesion," *Or* NS 47 (1978) 79.

Compulsory Labor under
David and Solomon*

J. Alberto Soggin,
University of Rome

1. This paper deals with an important aspect of Israelite society during the United Kingdom under David and Solomon: compulsory labor. Important because it appears as a major source of unrest first and of rebellion later, and, therefore, eventually one of the main reasons for the decay and the disruption after Solomon's death of the kingdom founded by David. I shall refrain for the time being from the use of other expressions such as "forced labor," "*corvée*," and the like, as the exact rendering of the pertinent Hebrew terminology will be one of the subjects of this paper. One characteristic element we may, however, already take for granted: the involuntary aspect of the labor thus exacted. We are dealing here with a type of work which was performed by the individual not to earn his living, nor for reasons felt to be of public service. We deal with work to which individuals and communities alike were unrelated and had to be, therefore, forced, because its aims were unimportant or even unknown to them.

In the course of the paper we shall deal first with the relevant texts and the terminology therein; we shall then examine the nature of compulsory labor in Israel and try, finally, to offer a general evaluation of the phenomenon.

2. The following texts appear relevant to our subject; they can be divided into three groups, according to the terminology they use.

(a) 2 Sam 20:24; 1 Kgs 4:6; 5:27-28 // 2 Chr 2:16-17; 1 Kgs 19:15, 20-22 // 2 Chr 8:8-10; 1 Kgs 12:18 // 2 Chr 10:18. Here we find either the term מַס or the expression מַס עֹובֵד. They have been examined in detail by I. Mendelsohn, T. N. D. Mettinger, and I. Riesner.[1] The Septuagint (LXX) translates normally with φόρος, a word related to taxation in general; only in 1 Kgs 9:15, 20-22 (LXX^B: 10:22a-c) we have προνομή, a term which is connected with military requisition.

---

[1] I. Mendelsohn, "State Slavery in Ancient Palestine," *BASOR* 85 (1942) 14-27; idem, *Slavery in the Ancient Near East* (New York, 1949) 97-99; idem, "On Corvée Labor in Ancient Canaan and Israel," *BASOR* 167 (1962) 31-35; idem, "מס," *EncBib* 5 (1968) 51-55 (Hebrew); T. N. D. Mettinger, *Solomonic State Officials* (CB OTS 5, 1971) 128-39; I. Riesner, *Der Stamm* עבד *im Alten Testament* (BZAW 149, 1979) 138-42.

* For reading and correcting my English manuscript, I wish to thank the Rev. and Mrs. Edward A. Bishop, of the Methodist Church of Rome.

(b) 1 Kgs 5:29; 2 Chr 2:1, 17 use the expression סָבָל נוֹשֵׂא) and 1 Kgs 11:28 the word סֵבֶל, both studied in detail by Mettinger.[2] The LXX translates here literally. The first word indicates the person engaged in the work, the second refers to the category or to the status. The word *sablum* appears already in the texts of Mari as West-Semitic and also refers to the category. The Akkadian verb *zabālu* is normally used for the concept in general; also in Hebrew the root *zbl* can be used, although rarely, in this sense. But, certainly *sbl* and *zbl* were practically homophonic.[3] Also the word מְלָאכָה is used in 1 Sam 8:16; 1 Kgs 5:30; 9:23 and 11:28; it usually means "work" in general and is here used, therefore, in a specialized way.

(c) A third type of workmen is found in the expression עַבְדֵי שְׁלֹמֹה, 1 Kgs 9:27 // 2 Chr 8:18 and 9:10. A similar expression appears in post-exilic times in Ezra 2:55-58 // Neh 7:57-60 and 11:3 as בְּנֵי עַבְדֵי שְׁלֹמֹה.[4]

Now the context makes it quite clear that in these texts סָבָל and סֵבֶל refer to a special category within מַס: they are, according to various translations, "hauliers" or "burden bearers," better than, more generally, "forced labor"; another category of people are called מוֹצֵב, i.e., "hewers of stone," or, better, "quarry men." As the *Good News Bible* puts it pertinently: "Solomon . . . had 80,000 men . . . quarrying stone, with 70,000 men to carry it . . . ," and these two groups formed that which the texts call מַס.

The third group is apparently of superior social standing. It refers without exception to the men engaged in Solomon's and Hiram's joint enterprises by sea. One might even question that they were assigned to compulsory labor at all, as they could easily have escaped at any of many landing places their ships had to touch in their journey. There is, therefore, hardly any reason not to consider them sailors on the king's payroll, especially as there is no sign that they should be considered as slave oarsmen.

What the expression meant in post-exilic times is still a matter of debate, but one thing is generally agreed upon, that it refers to slave families, i.e., to something probably quite different. Any connection with 1 Kgs 9:27 seems therefore unwarranted.

A summary of the whole system appears, finally, in 1 Sam 8:11-17.

3. But, what do the biblical authors mean exactly by מַס and מַס עוֹבֵד? The word *massu* without specifications appears in the Akkadian of Alalaḫ, Ugarit, and el-ʿAmarna for statutory labor[5] and is a West-Semitic loan

---

[2] Mettinger, *Solomonic State Officials*, 128-39.

[3] *AHw* 2 (1972) 999; cf. M. Held, "The Root *zbl/sbl* in Akkadian, Ugaritic and Biblical Hebrew," *JAOS* 88 (1968) 90-96.

[4] On Solomon's and Hiram's enterprises by sea, see K. Schreiden, "Les entreprises navales du roi Salomon," *Annuaire de l'Institut de Philologie et d'Histoire Orientales et Slaves* 13 (1955) 587-90.

[5] See R. de Langhe, *Les textes de Ras Shamra-Ugarit et leur rapport avec le milieu biblique de l'Ancien Testament* 2 (Louvain/ Paris, 1945) 417; W. L. Moran, "The Hebrew Language in its North-West Semitic Background," *The Bible and the Ancient Near East: Essays in Honor of W. F. Albright* (ed. G. E. Wright; London, 1961) 55-72; I. Mendelsohn, "Samuel's

word. From there it seems to have passed also into Biblical Hebrew.[6] Its origin in Syria-Palestine is therefore quite clear.[7] The expression מַס עוֹבֵד has not appeared, until now, anywhere outside of Israel.

(a) In a series of studies whose results have been widely accepted, I. Mendelsohn[8] has tried to solve the problem posed by this double terminology in Hebrew alone, by attributing to מַס the meaning of "corvée," to מַס עוֹבֵד the one of "state slavery," i.e., a permanent condition of enslavement. For the former I wish, incidentally, to use the expression of "statutory labor"; "corvée," although often[9] used as if it were synonymous, refers to the services owed to one's overlord within the feudal societies of central and western Europe during the Middle Ages. Its use here could therefore be misleading.

מַס thus refers, according to Mendelsohn, to the obligation to perform periodically certain services for one's landlord or for the state, while מַס עוֹבֵד means a perpetual condition of servitude, something similar to the sentence *ad metalla* under Roman law, if I understand him correctly. The latter thesis is presented in a variant, although less radical form by M. Noth and I. Riesner:[10] we are dealing here with the lowest form of statutory labor, whose members, although technically speaking not slaves, could be compared to them as long as their service lasted. To this type of labor the Canaanite population only are supposed to have been subjected, while the Israelites had to perform certain services periodically.

It is possible, as R. de Vaux[11] suggests, although not stated in the sources, that these services were exacted from the Israelites in lieu of taxes in money or produce. Personal labor would therefore appear as a type of contribution in kind.

(b) Professor Mendelsohn's analysis puts forward a subtle distinction. It can hardly be sustained, however, as far as I see, either philologically or sociologically. Already in 1967[12] I expressed some misgivings about it. I did not pursue the matter further in my commentary on Joshua,[13] where I simply rendered in the original French with "corvée,"

Denounciation of Kingship in the Light of the Akkadian Documents from Ugarit," *BASOR* 143 (1956) 17-23; A. F. Rainey, "Compulsory Labor Gangs in Ancient Israel," *IEJ* 20 (1970) 191-202; idem, *The El Amarna Tablets 359-379* (AOAT 8, 2d ed., 1978) 24-27.

[6] *AHw* 2 (1972) 619.

[7] A. Eben-Shoshan (המלון החדש [Jerusalem, 1973]) connects it tentatively with an Egyptian word *ms*, which over Syria-Palestine is supposed to have entered into Akkadian. But, the Egyptologists I have consulted do not accept this possibility.

[8] Mendelsohn, 1942 to 1968.

[9] E.g., by O. Eissfeldt, "The Hebrew Kingdom," *CAH* 2/2 (1975) 584 and, recently, N. K. Gottwald, *The Tribes of Yahweh* (Maryknoll, NY, 1979) 134ff., 158, 216, 483.

[10] M. Noth, *Könige* 1 (BKAT 9/1, 1968) 217; Riesner, *Der Stamm* עבד, 138ff.

[11] R. de Vaux, *Les institutions de l'Ancien Testament* 1 (Paris, 1958) 125ff., 138f., 215ff.

[12] J. A. Soggin, *Das Königtum in Israel* (BZAW 104, 1967) 86-87, n. 18.

[13] Soggin, *Joshua* (London, 1972; French original 1970) 163.

translated into English with "forced labour." I had not seen, at that time, the important article by A. Biram,[14] who questions on good grounds the theses proposed by I. Mendelsohn. Further studies on the subject, notably by A. F. Rainey,[15] have meanwhile made Mendelsohn's proposal even more doubtful. This for two reasons: (1) It forces this meaning upon other texts as well, where the expression occurs. (2) It confronts us also with a historical and sociological picture of David's and Solomon's realm which hardly makes any sense: that of entire populations reduced to *perpetual* state slavery. The Davidic-Solomonic kingdom was, further, an extremely complex entity from what we would call nowadays the constitutional point of view, and the juridical status of its populations can hardly be reduced to elementary categories such as "free Israelites" and "enslaved Canaanites"![16]

The other biblical texts I refer to are: Gen 49:15; Josh 16:10; 17:13// Judg 1:28; 1:30, 33, 35. The LXX paraphrases in the first two cases, translates with ὑπήκοος "subject to," in the third, and with φόρος in the remaining. Here מַס and מַס עוֹבֵד are thus used interchangeably for identical situations and do not presuppose the existence of any semantical difference between them. It is not pertinent to consider Gen 49:15 " . . . as a poetical exageration of Issachar's fate," or to speak of Josh 16:10 " . . . as inconsistent with the numerous statements . . . that only use *mas* . . . ";[17] to adopt such a position means simply to beg the question!

In these texts it can thus hardly be submitted that first Issachar towards the Canaanites and later the Canaanites towards the Israelites had become state slaves. It is simply stated that one group became politically subject to the other: first Issachar to the surrounding Canaanites (apparently not without material advantages, if we take the text seriously), later the Canaanites of the plains to Israel when it grew strong, whatever this new status involved juridically and practically. The biblical authors did not want in any way to express that these peoples were reduced to some kind of slavery, perpetual or temporary, although their new condition may well have included statutory labor. The LXX is therefore on the right track when it translated Josh 16:10 with "subject to." Perhaps also Gen 9:25ff., where Canaan is עֶבֶד to Shem, ought to be interpreted along these lines.

Thus, we have here a first, essentially political meaning of מַס and מַס עוֹבֵד, which appear to be synonymous expressions. This is also why most contemporary studies on slavery in the ancient Near East do not mention מַס עוֹבֵד as a special category of labor.

---

[14]A. Biram, "מס עובד," *Tarbiz* 23 (1951-52) 137-42 (Hebrew).

[15]Rainey, "מס עובד," *EncBib* 5 (1968) 55-56 (Hebrew); idem, *IEJ* 20 (1970) 191-202; idem, *The El Amarna Tablets*, 24-27.

[16]Soggin, "The Davidic-Solomonic Kingdom," *Israelite and Judaean History* (ed. J. H. Hayes and J. M. Miller; London, 1977) 378ff., and A. Malamat in this volume.

[17]Mendelsohn, *Slavery in the Ancient Near East*, 97; cf. Gottwald, *The Tribes of Yahweh*, 483f.

(c) But, there are also texts that seem to presuppose some kind of enslavement or at least a more or less permanent form of statutory labor: Exod 1:11; Deut 20:11; Isa 31:8; Prov 12:24, and Lam 1:1. In the first two cases the LXX has rendered respectively with ἔργον and φορολογητός, with φόρος in Lam 1:1, and in different, paraphrasing ways in the other cases. But, it is difficult to ascertain what the authors wanted exactly to say: we do not know how Israel looked at its own servitude in Egypt from the theoretical point of view, although the model might well have been taken, for practical purposes, from statutory labor at the time of the United Monarchy, nor do we know how Deuteronomy concretely imagined the enslaving of the Canaanites, as it probably never happened the way it was announced. Isa 31:8 and Lam 1:1 use the word for deportation *en masse*, and not for forced labor, while Prov 12:24 considers lazyness as the best road to slavery, probably by debt.

(d) A third meaning we find in Esth 10:1: here מַס is a technical term and refers to taxation within the Persian empire. A similar use for the word appears in modern Hebrew. This late, technical use of the word could explain why the LXX uses φόρος so often.

(e) The fourth meaning, the one of our texts, refers to compulsory, "statutory" labor.[18]

(f) Finally, we ought to rule out completely an ingenious proposal by D. Künstlinger.[19] According to him, עוֹבֵד should be related to אוֹבֵד, "perish," and the latter's meaning be "perpetual." This proposal would confirm, although with quite a different argument, I. Mendelsohn's theses, who, on the other hand, has not noticed it. It appears to me as artificial because of the suppsoed exchange of ע and א, which, for the roots studies, happens only here.

(g) Our contention seems confirmed, although only *e silentio*, by the use of *massu* in pre-Israelite Syria and Palestine. Therefore, the most reasonable explanation of עוֹבֵד brought forward until now seems to me still the one proposed by A. Kahana:[20] that it is simply a gloss to מַס, and, as we have seen, not always a pertinent one. Such a gloss can be reasonably explained in a time, when מַס meant either "vassallage" or simply "tax," as we have seen a few lines before about the use of φόρος by the LXX.

(h) Summing up, in the case posed by our texts we deal with statutory labor, i.e., with the obligations by members of a community to perform manual labor for public service, possibly instead of what otherwise would have been due in taxes.

(i) Such systems lend themselves to arbitrariness and abuse under the most favorable conditions of government, and we know well that the

---

[18]Mettinger, *Solomonic State Officials*, 139.

[19]D. Künstlinger, "I. עֲדֵי עוֹבֵד, II. לְמַס עוֹבֵד," *OLZ* 34 (1931) 609-12.

[20]A. Kahana, *Pêrûš madday* (Zitomir, 1904) (Hebrew). I have no access to this work and must, therefore, quote second-hand.

Davidic-Solomonic monarchy hardly ever produced such conditions. Our system seems to have pretty soon degenerated, so that people resented very much the new state of affairs. The terminology used by 1 Kgs 9:21 is very eloquent: וַיַּעֲלֵם, i.e., Solomon "made them go," cf. LXX ἀνήγαγεν "he pressed them;" and Josephus: ἐπέταξε, "he commandeered them." It states that the people were simply put to work, a fact which went against any appearance of law and order. This explains well the resentment of the North towards David first and later towards Solomon, as the North had to bear the main burden alone, as we shall see.

4. Let us now turn to the texts in detail.

(a) 2 Sam 20:24; 1 Kgs 4:6; 12:8//2 Chr 18:10 provide us with information about the names of the men in charge of the labor gangs. We cannot enter here into the problems connected with these names;[21] it is enough to state that in one case it seems to have been the same person during the reign of David and of Solomon, and that he met his death by the very people he had been overseeing. In the other case, he became eventually king of the North.

But, we obtain other, relevant information from two other groups of texts.

(b) 1 Kgs 5:27-28//2 Chr 2:16-17 state:

King Solomon raised a forced levy from the whole of Israel, amounting to 30,000 men. He sent them to Lebanon in monthly relays of 10,000 men, so that the men spent one month in Lebanon and two at home . . . (NEB).

The text in Chronicles has one, important variant reading, which we shall examine below.

(c) 1 Kgs 9:15a, 20-22 (LXX^B 10:22a-c)//2 Chr 8:8-10 inform us:

This is the record of the forced labour which King Solomon conscripted . . . (then follow the works they were used for, vv. 15b, 17-19, and the insertion about Gezer, v. 16).

(20) All survivors of the Amorites, Hittites, Perezzites, Hivites and Jebusites, who did not belong to Israel—(21) that is, their descendants who survived in the land, wherever the Israelites had been unable to annihilate them—were employed by Solomon on perpetual forced labour,[22] as they still are. (22) But Solomon put none of the Israelites to forced labour; they were fighting men, his captains and lieutenants and the commanders of chariots and of his cavalry (NEB).

The text of Chronicles is identical but for a few variant readings. Important among them is the omission of עוֹבֵד after מַס in v. 8. But, to add it here seems to me, again, to be begging the question, although it has

---

[21] Mettinger, *Solomonic State Officials*, 133.
[22] *Sic!* but see above § 3, a-b.

been done authoritatively by W. Rudolph[23] and by some other authors; as the text stands, it seems obvious that Chronicles considered מַס and מַס עֹבֵד as synonymous.

(d) The first text states explicitly that "out of the whole of Israel" (מִכָּל יִשְׂרָאֵל; the Canaanites are *not* mentioned!) Solomon recruited people to perform statutory labor, in order to complete his building projects in the capital city (the palace and the temple), and maybe also elsewhere. It is not clear to me why M. Noth[24] considers this text to be a late, post-deuteronomistic addition; it lacks, if anything else, those lexicographical features which belong to the Dtr. and its sucessors. The parallel in Chronicles, however, states that only "the alien residents (הָאֲנָשִׁים הַגֵּרִים)," after a census had been taken of them, were put to work. The Chronicler accepts here, therefore, the thesis of 1 Kgs 9:20f., according to which only the Canaanites were put to work. But, on the other hand, Josephus, *Ant.* 8.2.9 = § 58 confirms 1 Kings 5.

This text follows, although not very closely, the lists of royal officials and administrative districts and the notice about Solomon's taxation system of the North. "Israel" can mean here only the North, as 1 Kings 4 never mentions Judah (a similar district list of Judah, Josh 15:21-63, can be dated, in its older parts, not before the 9th century B.C. and belongs, as is well known, probably to the time of King Josiah).[25] It appears, therefore, quite probable that Israel only, i.e., the North, and not Judah, was subject to statutory labor, as it was announced by Samuel to Israel in 1 Sam 8:11-17. This would again account for the hostility which the North kept towards the house of David and the United Kingdom, after its first enthusiasm.

(e) The second text, which in its end clearly relates to 1 Sam 8:11-17, tells us a different story, as is well known and generally accepted nowadays,[26] with the sole exceptions of I. Mendelsohn and T. N. D. Mettinger.[27] The former's attempt to draw a distinction between מַס and מַס עֹבֵד is really an attempt to solve the problem which arises from this difference by showing that, in reality, there is no such difference, and therefore no problem at all. But there are elements which make us assign the relevant

---

[23]W. Rudolph, *Chronikbücher* (HAT 1/21, 1955) 218ff.

[24]Noth, *Könige* 1, 88, 217; the same objections in Mettinger, *Solomonic State Officials*, 135.

[25]Soggin, *Joshua*, 176ff.; cf. A. Alt, "Israels Gaue unter Salomo" (1913) *Kleine Schriften* 2 (München, 1953) 76-89; contra W. F. Albright, "The Adminstrative Divisions of Israel and Judah," *JPOS* 5 (1927) 17-54; idem, *Archaeology and the Religion of Israel* (3d ed.; Baltimore, 1953) 140-42; idem, *The Biblical Period* (3d ed.; New York/Evanston, 1963) 56-57.

[26]Cf. S. Herrmann, *Geschichte Israels in alttestamentlicher Zeit* (München, 1973) 224-25; F. Crüsemann, *Der Widerstand gegen das Königtum* (WMANT 49, 1978) 70ff.

[27]Mendelsohn, *BASOR* 85 (1942) 14-27; idem, *Slavery in the Ancient Near East*, 97-99; idem, *BASOR* 167 (1962) 31-35; idem, *EncBib* 5 (1968) 51-55; Mettinger, *Solomonic State Officials*, 134-35.

parts of this text to the Dtr. They are, first, Deut 20:11, which we have already mentioned, and which states:

> When you advance on a city and attack it, make an offer of peace. If the city accepts the offer and opens its gates to you, then all the people in it shall be put to forced labour and shall serve you" (*NEB*).

Now 1 Kgs 9:21 and its parallel show Solomon complying with this order, albeit on a national, and not only on a local basis: the Canaanite population was put to statutory labor or even enslaved, a condition apparently still lasting at the time of the writer.[28] The Israelites had to serve too, but only in the upper echelons.

Second, the stereotype list of the pre-Israelite population of Canaan is often connected with the Dtr.[29]

So T. Veijola[30] speaks of a "secondary (Dtr.) excuse of Solomon." This attempt to excuse Solomon seems a forerunner of his almost hagiographical exaltation in later times, notably by the Chronicles, where he appears only as pious, wise, and faultless!

In the LXX the text appears mainly in LXX[B], where it has been transposed to 10:22a-c.[31] Josephus seems to feel the contrast between 1 Kgs 5:27f. and 9:20f.: in *Ant.* 8.6.3 = § 160 he indicates only those Canaanites from the northern region and the Lebanon, who had not yet been subjected.

5. About the origin of the use of compulsory labor in Israel we hear only very little. 2 Sam 20:24 speaks about the man "in charge of the forced levy" among the royal officials of David as a matter of course. The title does not (yet?) appear, however, in the first list of royal officials, 8:16-18[32]. It seems, therefore, a reasonable assumption that the use of compulsory labor started some time under David and was fully developed under Solomon, who needed it most. It is also quite likely that 2 Sam 12:31 refers to the institution of statutory labor among the conquered people of Transjordan, but this text is notoriously difficult: nowadays the trend is to interpret it as statutory labor imposed, we do not know for how long, on these peoples as an extraordinary tax-collection or some other form of

---

[28] A. H. J. Gunneweg, *Geschichte Israels bis Bar Kochba* (Stuttgart, 1972) 84.

[29] So E. Würthwein, *Das Erste Buch der Könige, Kapitel 1-16* (ATD 11/1, 1977) 112-13; Gunneweg, *Geschichte Israels*, 84. But, contrast recently T. Ishida, "The Structure and Historical Implications of the Lists of Pre-Israelite Nations," *Bib* 60 (1979) 461-90.

[30] T. Veijola, *Das Königtum in der Beurteilung der deuteronomistischen Historiographie* (Helsinki, 1977) 66, n. 98.

[31] So, rightly, Mettinger, *Solomonic State Officials*, 135; cf. D. W. Gooding, "Text-Sequence and Translation-Revision in 3 Reigns IX 10-X 33," *VT* 19 (1969) 449-63; against Soggin, *Das Königtum in Israel*, 86.

[32] The title appears now on a recently discovered seal of the 7th cent. B.C., cf. N. Avigad, "The Chief of the Corvée," *IEJ* 30 (1980) 170-73.

punishment. But, one ought to remember the older renderings,[33] according to which David decimated those populations in particularily cruel ways.

But, as we saw, David did not have to look far for models. The texts of Alalaḫ, Ugarit, and el-ʿAmarna prove to us that the institution was well known and alive within the frame of the Syro-Palestinian city-state during the second half of the 2nd millennium B.C.

6. After the disruption of the United Monarchy, statutory labor is rarely mentioned. Does this mean that it withered away and was eventually suppressed? We do not know. One clear case for its existence is 1 Kgs 15:22, where Asa of Judah "summoned (הִשְׁמִיעַ) the whole of Judah, without exception (אֵין נָקִי)" for fortification works. In this case, however, we are obviously dealing with a national emergency caused by the state of war, so that it is quite possible that the summon was not felt as an authoritarian imposition from above.

7. At the beginnig of this paper I stated that forced labor in Israel was a factor of unrest, of revolt, and eventually of disruption of the United Monarchy founded by David, after Solomon's death. Most parts of 1 Kings 12 state that the negotiations between the newly appointed king Rehoboam and the popular assembly of the North revolved about one main subject: to obtain relief on this very point, and attribute to the failure of these negotiations the secession of the Northern Tribes. But, we know that already under David the North had been restless, up to the point of questioning altogether the legitimacy of the United Kingdom;[34] cf. 2 Samuel 15ff. and 20. The texts never connect these revolts with forced labor, but it does not seem foolhardy to reckon in this institution also here one of the main sources of unrest.

---

[33]S. R. Driver, *The Books of Samuel* (2d ed.; Oxford, 1913); cf. recently C. G. O'Ceallaigh ("And so David Did to All the Cities of Ammon," *VT* 12 [1962] 179-89) for the arguments pro and contra both of these renderings.

[34]Crüsemann, *Der Widerstand gegen das Königtum*, 70ff.

Monumental Architecture in Ancient Israel in the Period of the United Monarchy

WILLIAM G. DEVER

University of Arizona, Tucson

INTRODUCTION

The "United Monarchy" in ancient Israel spans barely a century, covering the reigns of the first three kings of Israel: Saul (*ca.* 1020-1000 B.C.); David (*ca.* 1000-960 B.C.); and Solomon (*ca.* 960-918 B.C.). The basic historical and chronological framework for the period is derived principally from the Hebrew Bible itself, especially the books of 1-2 Samuel and 1 Kings, together with the more or less parallel account in Chonicles.[1] These literary sources are manifestly closer to the events they purport to record, and therefore more reliable, than the Pentateuchal pre-history—though they do not, of course, by that virtue constitute modern historiography. We are dealing, rather, with "Deuteronomistic history"—a composite, heavily-editorialized work of a particular school of Israelite history-writing, the objective of which may be called prophetic or "theocratic history." From this account, however, we can abstract the main thread of a narrative concerning the chief public events which probably characterized the reigns of Saul, and particularly of David and Solomon. The account of these events is more annalistic than truly "historical," in that it is more satisfactory on the descriptive than on the explanatory level; but, it does allow us to isolate the major political, economic, social, and religious developments, and to arrange these in rough chronological sequence. The result is at least a reliable *outline* of early Monarchical history in the 10th century B.C.

There are, nevertheless, several shortcoming of this outline. First is the obvious fact that the literary source materials, together with their interpretations, originated and were perpetuated in courtly and priestly circles, and were thus "establishment-oriented." The focus is almost exclusively on public happenings, particularly large-scale political events, or on the deeds of prominent figures such as kings and prophets. Completely missing is the private history of other individuals, that is, we have nothing of such literary genres as biography, *belles lettres*, and other primary historical documents.

---

[1]For the latest scholarly discussion and full references, see J. A. Soggin, "The Davidic-Solomonic Kingdom," *Israelite and Judaean History* (eds. J. H. Hayes and J. M. Miller; Philadelphia/Westminster, 1977) 332-80.

The second problem is one that concerns us here. Is it possible to correlate the literary with the non-literary remains increasingly available, i.e., archaeological discoveries, and thus to correct and supplement the bare historical outline previously available? This general goal has been foremost in the topographical and archaeological investigation of the Holy Land for more than a century. Indeed, the quest to reconstruct from external sources a historical background for written biblical history has been partially successful for several epochs—notably the period of the Judges and the later Divided Monarchy, where archaeology has supplied numerous, surprisingly detailed data not recorded in the Bible, and moreover has provided corroboration for specific events which are mentioned. But it must be admitted that until very recently Palestinian and biblical archaeology have been surprisingly silent regarding the United Monarchy, a period which not only was truly formative for ancient Israel but also witnessed the first flourishing of the material culture and the development of monumental art and architecture, which should have left the clearest imprint on the archaeological record.

The period in question, from roughly 1000 to 900 B.C., corresponds in archaeological terms almost exactly to the "Iron IC" of Albright and most American authorities, or to the "Iron IIA" of Israeli archaeologists. The difference in terminology is more archaeological than historical, i.e., it represents the divergent views of specialists on the stratigraphic and ceramic continuity/discontinuity at several key sites[2] (fig. 1). Two observations concerning this divergence of opinion may be helpful. First, the "archaeology of Palestine" is not necessarily limited to, or even parallel with, the "History of ancient Israel," so scholarly schemes for subdivisions in these two disciplines need not correspond exactly. In particular we must not expect that various systems of biblical chronology can dictate archaeological terminology, even in the Iron Age or so-called "Israelite" period. Second, the absolute chronology of the historical events is what really matters, and that can be fixed both by internal as well as by international synchronisms. Whether we designate the United Monarchy as late Iron I or early Iron II in archaeological parlance, there can be no question that (1) in absolute chronology it is set in the 10th century B.C.; and (2) in the relative course of actual political and cultural developments in ancient Israel, this brief period is a distinct entity, set off from the tumultous, formative centuries of the period of the Judges preceding it, as well as from the largely separate histories of the states of Israel and Judah flowing from it in the 9th-7th centuries B.C.

I. SITES, DISTRIBUTION, STRATIGRAPHY

Before we can appreciate the specific, individual archaeological discoveries which illumine this period, we must characterize the chief sites and

---

[2]See, for example, Y. Aharoni and R. Amiran, "A New Scheme for the Sub-Division of the Iron Age in Palestine," *IEJ* 8 (1958) 171-84.

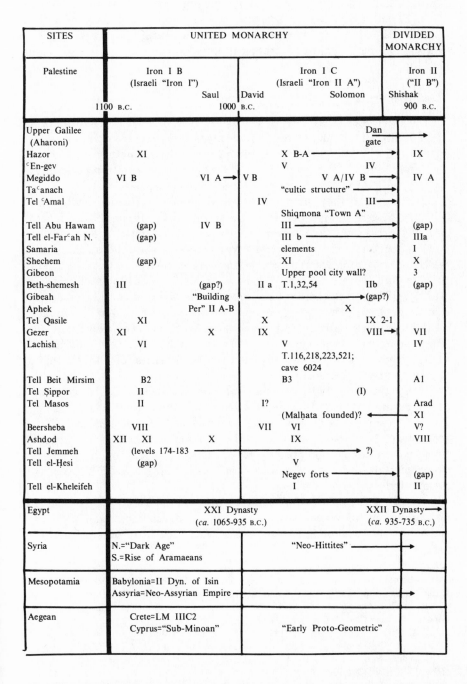

SITES	UNITED MONARCHY				DIVIDED MONARCHY
Palestine	Iron I B (Israeli "Iron I")		Iron I C (Israeli "Iron II A")		Iron II ("II B")
		Saul | David		Solomon	Shishak
	1100 B.C.	1000 B.C.			900 B.C.
Upper Galilee (Aharoni)			Dan gate	→	
Hazor	XI		X B-A ————→		IX
ʿEn-gev			V	IV	
Megiddo	VI B	VI A→ | V B	V A/IV B ——→		IV A
Taʿanach			"cultic structure" ——→		
Tel ʿAmal		IV	III→		
			Shiqmona "Town A"		
Tell Abu Hawam	(gap)	IV B	III ——————→		(gap)
Tell el-Farʿah N.	(gap)		III b ——————→		IIIa
Samaria			elements		I
Shechem	(gap)		XI		X
Gibeon			Upper pool city wall?		3
Beth-shemesh	III	(gap?)	II a T.1,32,54	IIb	(gap)
Gibeah		"Building Per" II A-B	————————→(gap?)	X	
Aphek				X	
Tel Qasile	XI	X		IX 2-1	
Gezer	XI	X	IX	VIII→	VII
Lachish	VI		V		IV
			T.116,218,223,521; cave 6024		
Tell Beit Mirsim	B2		B3		A1
Tel Ṣippor	II			(I)	
Tel Masos	II	I?			Arad XI
			(Malḥata founded)? ←		
Beersheba	VIII	VII	VI		V?
Ashdod	XII | XI	X	IX		VIII
Tell Jemmeh	(levels 174-183 —————		————→ ?)		
Tell el-Ḥesi	(gap)		V		(gap)
			Negev forts ————→		
Tell el-Kheleifeh			I		II
Egypt	XXI Dynasty (ca. 1065-935 B.C.)		XXII Dynasty——→ (ca. 935-735 B.C.)		
Syria	N.="Dark Age" S.=Rise of Aramaeans		"Neo-Hittites" ——————→		
Mesopotamia	Babylonia=II Dyn. of Isin Assyria=Neo-Assyrian Empire ———		——————————→		
Aegean	Crete=LM IIIC2 Cyprus="Sub-Minoan"		"Early Proto-Geometric"		

Fig. 1. Stratigraphic chart showing major Israelite sites of the 11th-10th centuries B.C. Arrows indicate continuity of destruction level.

their distribution, their state of excavation and publication, and the stratigraphic problems confronted in the scholarly literature.

The pertinent archaeological sites and strata known to date are so few that virtually all can be schematized in a simple stratigraphic chart (fig. 1). We shall discuss them in geographical order, moving from north to south (cf. the map, fig. 2).

A. Galilee

In Galilee, especially Upper Galilee, surface survey has revealed many small 12th-11th century Israelite settlements founded on virgin soil,[3] but many of these apparently were abandoned by the 10th century, and few of the larger, centralized towns and cities that had developed to replace them by the early Monarchy have been extensively excavated.

1. Dan, later the northernmost boundary of Israel, is to be identified with the 50-acre mound of Tell el-Qadi, on the Lebanese border. It was partially excavated by A. Biran in 1966-81 and brought to light on the south slopes a monumental three-entryway city gate and solid offsets/insets wall. The excavator dated these constructions to the time of Jeroboam I, in the late 10th century B.C., but Aharoni, on the basis of supposed parallels with Megiddo and Beersheba, has argued for a Davidic date.[4] Only the gate plan is published, but the preliminary reports suggest a 10th/9th century date. Little can be attributed to the United Monarchy, suggesting that the site attained its prominence only in the late 10th century B.C. and thereafter, when it became one of the royal sanctuaries of the Northern Kingdom under Jeroboam I.

2. At the great 180-acre mound of Hazor, in Upper Galilee near the Huleh basin (Tell el-Qedaḥ), excavated by Y. Yadin and others in 1952-58, Str. XB-A of the Upper City is securely dated to the mid-late 10th century B.C. The Israelite settlement of the period was apparently restricted to a fortified citadel comprising ca. 6.5 acres, of which only a stretch of casemate wall and a fine four-entryway gate were exposed in Area A (below and fig. 3).[5]

3. At ᶜEn-gev (Kh. el-Asheq), on the eastern shore of the Sea of Galilee, in 1961 B. Mazar and A. Biran excavated a solid city wall of Str. V and a casemate wall of Str. IV in Area I, which appear to be, respectively,

[3]Y. Aharoni, *The Settlement of the Israelite Tribes in the Upper Galilee* (Jerusalem, 1957) (Hebrew); see also idem, "New Aspects of the Israelite Occupation in the North,". *Near Eastern Archaeology in the Twentieth Century. Essays in Honor of N. Glueck* (ed. J. A. Sanders; Garden City, NY, 1970) 254-67.

[4]Cf. A. Biran, "Tel Dan," *IEJ* 22 (1972) 164-66, fig. 1; "Dan, Tel," *EAEHL* 1 (1975) 316-20; Y. Aharoni, "The Building Activities of David and Solomon," *IEJ* 24 (1974) 13-16.

[5]Y. Yadin, *Hazor, the Head of All Those Kingdoms* (London/Oxford, 1972) 135-46; "Hazor," *EAEHL* 2 (1976) 474-95.

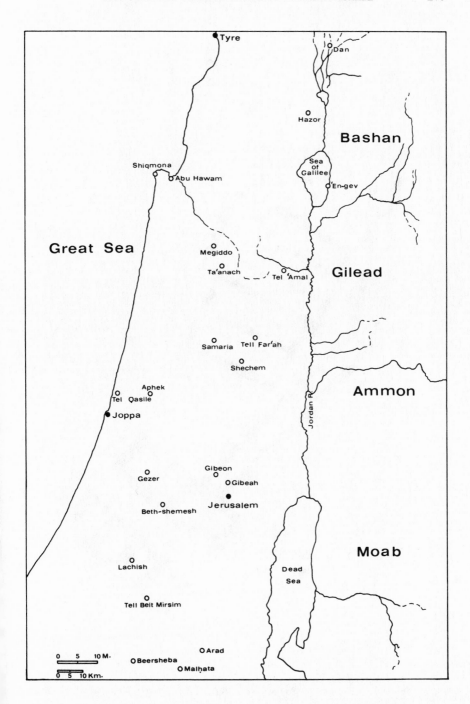

Fig. 2. Map of principal 10th century B.C. sites in ancient Israel, north of the Negev.

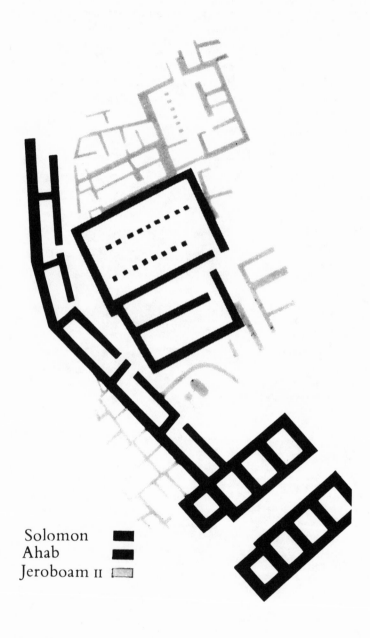

Solomon
Ahab
Jeroboam II

Fig. 3. Acropolis at Hazor (after Yadin, *Hazor: The Rediscovery of a Great City of the Bible*, p. 195).

Davidic and Solomonic. Virtually no domestic remains were investigated. The evidence indicates a small, though heavily fortified, Israelite citadel.[6]

4. At the great site of Megiddo (Tell el-Mutesellim) in the Jezreel Valley, the 1925-39 excavations of the University of Chicago under Fisher, Guy, and Loud partially cleared structures of the Davidic period (Str. VB), as well as a four-entryway city gate and a "palace" (1723) of Solomonic construction, i.e., Str. "VA/IVB," as reconstructed from the faulty Chicago stratigraphy by Albright, Wright, and others.[7] Later soundings by Y. Yadin in 1960-67 removed the so-called Solomonic stables from our consideration by dating them to Str. IVA of the 9th century B.C., but also added another large casemated residence ("Palace 6000") and definitive proof that beneath the wrongly-dated offsets/insets wall (now Str. IVA), there lay the true casemate wall going with the Str. VA/IVB Solomonic gate (below and fig. 4).[8] Archaeological investigation has thus confirmed that Megiddo was one of the most prominent Solomonic provincial administrative centers, as already suggested by I Kgs 9:15.

5. A sister site in the Jezreel Valley, Taᶜanach (Tell Taᶜannek), was excavated in 1963-68 by P. W. Lapp and revealed a "cultic structure" and a bizarre Astarte incense-stand probably of the 10th century B.C. (below).[9] But it would appear that since Taᶜanach's occupational history was complementary to that of its more powerful neighbor Megiddo, to the northwest, it was largely deserted during the Solomonic heyday of that site.

6. A minor site in the eastern Jezreel Valley, Tel ᶜAmal, near Beth-Shean was investigated in 1962-66 by G. Edelstein and S. Levy. Stratum IV-III belong apparently to the 10th century B.C., but the few small houses and other remains indicate nothing more than an Israelite village of the period.[10]

7 Toward the extreme west of the Jezreel, at the promontory of Mt. Carmel on the Bay of Acco, Shiqmona (Tell es-Samak) has been cleared by

---

[6]See preliminary reports in B. Mazar, A. Biran, M. Dothan, and I. Dunayevsky, "ᶜEin Gev: Excavations in 1961," *IEJ* 14 (1964) 1-49; B. Mazar, "ᶜEn Gev," *EAEHL* 2 (1976) 382-85.

[7]R. S. Lamon and G. M. Shipton, *Megiddo* I: *Seasons of 1925-34, Strata I-V* (Chicago, 1939); G. Loud, *Megiddo* II: *Seasons of 1935-39* (Chicago, 1948); and cf. W. F. Albright, "Review of *Megiddo* II," *AJA* 53 (1949) 213-15; G. E. Wright, "Reviews of *Megiddo* II," *BA* 13 (1950) 28-46; *JAOS* 70 (1950) 56-60.

[8]For preliminary reports, see Y. Yadin, "New Light on Solomon's Megiddo," *BA* 23 (1960) 62-68; "Megiddo of the Kings of Israel," *BA* 33 (1970) 66-96; *Hazor, Head of All Those Kingdoms*, 150-64; "Hazor," *EAEHL* 2 (1971) 848-55. The clearest published plan disentangling the 10th and 9th centuries B.C. levels is found in Y. Yadin's popular book *Hazor: The Rediscovery of a Great Citadel of the Bible* (London, 1975) 220.

[9]See preliminary reports in P. W. Lapp, "The 1963 Excavation at Taᶜannek," *BASOR* 173 (1964) 4-44; "The 1966 Excavations at Tell Taᶜannek," *BASOR* 185 (1967) 2-39; "Taanach by the Waters of Megiddo," *BA* 30 (1967) 2-27; "The 1968 Excavations at Tell Taᶜannek," *BASOR* 195 (1969) 2-49; A. E. Glock, "Taanach," *EAEHL* 4 (1978) 1139-47. On the incense stand, see below.

[10]See S. Levy and G. Edelstein, "Cinq années de fouilles à Tel ᶜAmal," *RB* 79 (1972) 325-65.

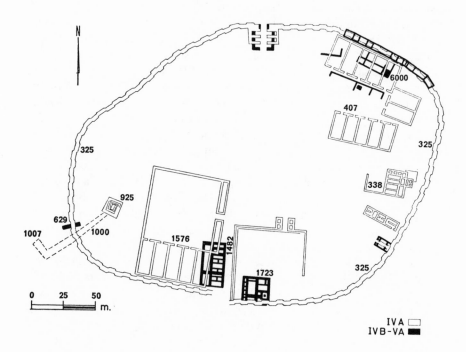

Fig. 4. Key plan of Megiddo in Str. IVA, IVB/VA (after Yadin, *Hazor, the Head of all Those Kingdoms*, p. 153, fig. 39).

J. Elgavish (1963-   ). Siqmona has produced a casemate wall and two "four-room" houses attributed by the excavator to Town A of the late 10th century B.C., but uncertain stratigraphy and lack of publication preclude our saying anything more.[11]

8. Tell Abu Hawam (identification uncertain), on the Bay of Acco near the banks of the Kishon River, is not certainly an Israelite site until Str. III (mid-late 10th century B.C.), but in the clearance of Str. IVB by R. W. Hamilton in 1932 an early "four-room" building of Israelite type was discovered.[12]

---

[11]See, provisionally, J. Elgavish, "Tel Shiqmona," *EAEHL* 4 (1978) 1101-09, esp. 1101-03 and references there to earlier preliminary reports.

[12]See R. W. Hamilton, "Excavations at Tell Abû Hawâm," *Quarterly of the Department of Antiquities in Palestine* 4 (1934) 9-10, pls. IV, VII; cf. B. Mazar, "The Stratification of Tell Abû Hawâm on the Bay of Acre," *BASOR* 124 (1954) 21-25; Y. Shiloh, "The Four-Room House: Its Situation and Function in the Israelite City," *IEJ* 20 (1970) 180-90 and fig. 1:1; for overall summary, see E. Anati, "Abu Hawam, Tell," *EAEHL* 1 (1975) 9-12.

B. Samaria

Here the Israelite occupation was evidently much more intensive, since, as Alt argued long ago, the absence of Canaanite domination in the hill country gave ready access to the incoming tribes.

1. Tirzah (Tell el-Far^cah N.), in the hills at the head of the ^cAin Far^cah, was excavated by Père R. de Vaux from 1946-60. Though one of the earliest capitals of the Northern Kingdom in the 9th century, Tirzah in the 10th century exhibits only a few "courtyard" houses of Israelite type (Str. IIIb) and was evidently little more than a small town.[13]

2. Shechem (Tell Balâṭah), one of the principal Israelite centers of the pre-monarchical period, was the focus of important American excavations led by G. E. Wright and others (1956-68), J. D. Seger (1969), and W. G. Dever (1972-73). However, the 10th century B.C. is represented only by Str. XI, which consists of some pottery and traces of a late 10th century destruction, probably attributable to Pharaoh Shishak, ca. 918 B.C., and an Iron II rebuild of Casemate Wall B near the Northwest Gate in Field IV, possibly attributable to Str. IX.[14]

3. Samaria (Sabastiyeh), as is well known from both the biblical and archaeological sources, became the capital of the newly divided Northern Kingdom only in the 9th century B.C., under the Omrides, but the work of the Joint Expedition in 1931-35 revealed a few sherds which indicate possibly a pre-Omride settlement.[15]

4. Gibeon (Tell el-Jîb) was excavated from 1956-62 by J. B. Pritchard, but the only Israelite elements which appear to be earlier than Iron II are the upper water tunnel and possibly a reuse phase of an earlier city wall.[16]

5. Gibeah (Tell el-Fûl), on the northern outskirts of Jerusalem, was sounded in 1922-23 and 1933 by W. F. Albright, who acclaimed a small tower-citadel (Fortress II) as "Saul's rude fortress."[17] The date was substantially confirmed by P. W. Lapp's salvage campaign in 1964, which dated the casemate phase much later (Period III) but clarified the existence

---

[13]See, conveniently, R. de Vaux, "El-Far^ca, Tell, North," *EAEHL* 2 (1976) 395-404 and references there to preliminary reports in *RB* (1947-1962); cf. Y. Shiloh, *IEJ* 20 (1970) 183-84 and fig. 2:8.

[14]See G. E. Wright, *Shechem, the Biography of a Biblical City* (New York, 1965) 144-45; W. G. Dever, "The MB IIC Stratification in the Northwest Gate Area at Shechem," *BASOR* 216 (1974) 44.

[15]Cf. Aharoni and Amiran, *IEJ* 8 (1958) 178-80; and G. E. Wright, "Israelite Samaria and Iron Age Chronology," *BASOR* 155 (1959) 20, 21; but K. M. Kenyon (*Bulletin of the Institute of Archaeology of the University of London* 4 [1964] 143-56) maintains an Omride date for both "Building Period" I and "Pottery Period" I.

[16]See, conveniently, J. B. Pritchard, "Gibeon," *EAEHL* 2 (1976) 446-50; and also idem, "Industry and Trade at Biblical Gibeon," *BA* 23 (1960) 23-29.

[17]See W. F. Albright, *Excavations and Results of Tell el-Fûl (Gibeah of Saul)* (AASOR 4, 1924); L. A. Sinclair, "An Archaeological Study of Gibeah (Tell el-Fûl)," *AASOR* 34/35 (1960) 5-52.

of the fort itself in "Building Period IIA-B," *ca.* 1025-950 B.C. (fig. 5).[18] Thus, the structure may be in fact Saul's early palace, but alternately it may have been a Philistine citadel. In any case its plan and contents, not yet fully published, reveal little that is distinctly Israelite, much less of "royal" dimensions.

6. Jerusalem, despite its being the Solomonic capital, has thus far revealed no trace of Iron Age remains *in situ* earlier than the 9th/8th centuries B.C. Scattered soundings throughout the past century and more systematic excavations by K. M. Kenyon in 1962-67 and by several Israeli excavators, principally B. Mazar, N. Avigad, and Y. Shiloh since 1967, have not yet reached these deep levels, or more likely have failed to recover the fragmentary remains left by frequent destructions and continuous rebuilding in later periods.[19] (On the Solomonic Temple, see below.)

C. The Shephelah and Coastal Plain

This region in general was not occupied by the Israelites until the Davidic-Solomonic period, and even then not effectively controlled.

1. Beth-shemesh (Tell er-Rumeileh), a dominant "buffer-zone" site near the mouth of the Vale of Elah, was excavated by E. Grant in 1928-33. Despite faulty stratigraphy, it has been shown that Str. IIa is probably Davidic and IIb Solomonic.[20] The principal elements which indicate the establishment of an Israelite settlement on this erstwhile Philistine site (Str. III) are an early casemate city wall, a large "residency," and a typical "four-room" structure of "Israelite" type which is possibly a granary.[21]

2. Gezer, guarding the entrance to the Ajalon Valley at the juncture of the Coastal Plain and the northern Shephelah, was excavated early in the century (1902-09) by R. A. S. Macalister. However, only the modern excavations of W. G. Dever, H. D. Lance, and others in 1964-73 clarified and correctly dated the splendid four-entryway city gate and casemate wall of Field III to the Solomonic period (Macalister's "Maccabean Castle"; below and fig. 6). It is likely that a casemate building west of the gate is a 10th-century "palace" comparable to those of Solomonic Megiddo (below). Elsewhere there are traces of 10th-century domestic structures (Str. IX-

---

[18]P. W. Lapp, "Tell el-Fûl," *BA* 28 (1965) 2-10; N. W. Lapp, "Casemate Walls in Palestine and the Late Iron II Casemate at Tell el-Fûl (Gibeah)," *BASOR* 223 (1976) 25-42; L. A. Sinclair, "Gibeah," *EAEHL* 2 (1976) 444-46.

[19]See, for instance, the survey of K. M. Kenyon (up to *ca.* 1965) in *Jerusalem: Excavating 3000 Years of History* (New York, 1967) 19-62, and on more recent excavations, *Jerusalem Revealed: Archaeology in the Holy City 1968-1974* (ed. Y. Yadin; Jerusalem, 1975).

[20]See E. Grant and G. E. Wright, *Ain Shems Excavations* IV-V (Haverford, 1938-39); cf. G. E. Wright, *JBL* 75 (1956) 202-26; "Beth-Shemesh," *EAEHL* 1 (1975) 248-53.

[21]Cf. Wright, *EAEHL* 1 (1975) 252; Y. Shiloh, *IEJ* 20 (1970) 180-83, fig. 1:5 and references there.

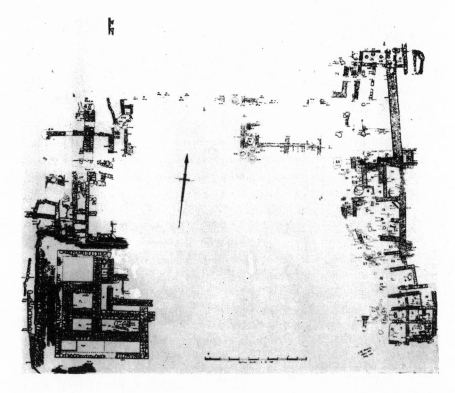

Fig. 5. Plan of the excavated remains at Gibeah, with tower of "Saul's fortress" at lower left; running north is the later Iron II casemate wall (after Lapp, *BA* 28, p. 5, fig. 3).

VIII), but it appears that Gezer was little more than an Israelite outpost after the Egyptian destruction and the Solomonic takeover.[22]

3. Aphek (Râs el-ʿAin), farther out on the Coastal Plain at the mouth of the Yarkon River, has revealed a few Israelite "four-room" houses in Str. IX of the current Israeli excavations directed by M. Kochavi and P. Beck since 1972.[23] These would appear to represent the Israelite takeover from the Philistines.

4. Tel Qasile (identification unknown), at the mouth of the Yarkon, was clearly founded by the Philistines, but the excavation of B. Mazar in 1948-50 and of A. Mazar in 1971-74 have shown that Str. X (early 10th century) exhibits several early-style "four-room" houses but is pre-Israelite.

---

[22]W. G. Dever et al., "Further Excavations at Gezer, 1967-71," *BA* 34 (1971) 94-132; "Gezer," *EAEHL* 2 (1976) 428-43; cf. also W. G. Dever, H. D. Lance, and G. E. Wright, *Gezer* I: *Preliminary Report of the 1964-66 Seasons* (Jerusalem, 1970) 31-32, 61-63; W. G. Dever, et al., *Gezer* II: *Report of the 1967-70 Seasons in Fields I and II* (Jerusalem, 1974) 59-69.

[23]M. Kochavi, "Tel Aphek, 1975," *IEJ* 26 (1976) 51-52.

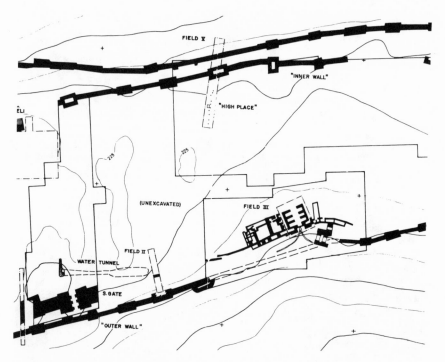

Fig. 6. Plan of Gezer, showing structures revealed by excavations of Macalister (1902-09) and Dever et al. (1964-71; after Dever et al., *Gezer* I, pl. 1).

Str. IX 2-1 above the destruction of the Philistine (Str. XII-X) temples spans the mid-late 10th century, is almost certainly Israelite, and exhibits several more developed "four-room" houses.[24]

D. Judea

Intensive surface surveys in recent years have demonstrated that the hill country south of Jerusalem was densely settled by the Israelites, beginning in the 9th/8th century and culminating in the 7th century B.C. However, the 10th century, still poorly represented, may have seen relatively spare occupation.

1. Lachish (Tell ed-Duweir) revealed little clear 10th century remains except a few tombs during the British excavation of J. Starkey in 1935-38,

---

[24]See preliminary reports in B. Mazar, "The excavations at Tell Qasîle: Preliminary Reports I-III," *IEJ* 1 (1951) 61-76, 125-40, 194-218; A. Mazar, "A Philistine Temple at Tell Qasîle," *BA* 36 (1973) 42-48; "Excavations at Tell Qasîle, 1971-72," *IEJ* 23 (1973) 65-69; "Excavations at Tell Qasîle, 1973-74," *IEJ* 25 (1975) 77-88; "Qasile, Tell," *EAEHL* 4 (1978) 968-75; cf. also T. Dothan and I. Dunayevsky, "Qasile, Tell (the earlier excavations)," *EAEHL* 4 (1978) 963-68; Y. Shiloh, *IEJ* 20 (1970) 181-83.

but Israeli excavations led by D. Ussishkin since 1973 suggest that the monumental four-entryway Iron II gate of Str. IV-III may have been established as early as Str. V of the 10th century B.C. and also proved that the monumental "Palace A" belongs to Str. V (fig. 7).[25] In addition, the "four-room" house excavated earlier (Building 1031) has been considered 10th century.[26] Finally, Y. Aharoni's 1966-68 excavations suggest that a small cult room beneath the "Solar Shrine" should be attributed to Str. V (below).[27]

2. Tell Beit Mirsim (Albright's Debir/Kiryath-Sefer) still gives us perhaps our clearest evidence of Solomonic constructions in the south in the casemate wall of Str. B₃ of Albright's 1926-32 excavations.[28]

E. The Negev

Until recently this area was thought to be sparsely settled in any period, much less under Israelite occupation.[29] However, recent Israeli exploration and several major excavations have broadened our picture and have revealed an extensive Israelite presence.

1. Iron Age Beersheba (Tell es-Seba^c), east of the modern town (fig. 8), is a small (*ca.* 3-acres) but impressive citadel, cleared almost in its entirety by Y. Aharoni in 1969-75. The major phase (Str. III-II) is 8th-7th century B.C. Str. VI, with its "four-room" house, is probably late 10th century; and Str. V, with its *glacis* or rampart, its solid offsets/insets wall,

---

[25]See D. Ussishkin, "The Destruction of Lachish by Sennacherib and the Dating of the Royal Judean Storage Jars," *Tel Aviv* 4 (1977) 28-60; "Excavations at Tel Lachish—1973-77," *Tel Aviv* 5 (1978) 1-97, esp. 27-31, 55-67, 91-93. Thus far Ussishkin attributes the founding of the gate to Level IV (9th century), but as its lowest levels may not have been reached it is our opinion that the earliest four-entryway gate may yet turn out to be 10th century in date (i.e., Str. V), like those at Hazor, Megiddo, and Gezer (and the Ashdod gate, possibly even earlier; on all, see below). A recently completed Israeli dissertation on Israelite gates also dates the Lachish gate to the 10th century; see Z. Herzog, *The City-Gate in Eretz-Israel and Its Neighboring Countries* (Tel-Aviv, 1976) xviii (Hebrew).

[26]G. E. Wright, "A Characteristic North Israelite House," *Archaeology in the Levant. Essays in Honor of K. Kenyon* (eds. P. R. S. Moorey and P. J. Parr; Warminster, 1978) 149-54. See also Y. Shiloh, *IEJ* 20 (1970) 182 and references there.

[27]Y. Aharoni, *Investigations at Lachish: The Sanctuary and the Residency (Lachish V)* (Tel Aviv, 1975) 26-32.

[28]W. F. Albright et al., *The Excavation of Tell Beit Mirsim III: The Iron Age* (AASOR 21-22, 1943) 1-19. The three-entryway East Gate was only excavated partly, and that not down to foundation levels, so Albright's supposition that it went back to Str. B₃ is less likely than the possibility of its having been built in early Str. A, i.e., 9th century B.C.

[29]On possible 10th century Israelite remains at Tell el-Ḥesi (Eglon?), see Y. Shiloh, *IEJ* 20 (1970) 181-83 (Bliss' Str. V "storehouse"); R. Amiran and J. E. Worrell, "Ḥesi, Tel," *EAEHL* 2 (1976) 514-20. Also, at Tell esh-Shariᵓa (Tel Seraᵓ), see the excavations of E. Oren in 1972-76, where VIII of the 11th century B.C. has produced an early "four-room house"; cf. E. Oren, "Esh-Shariᵓa, Tell," *EAEHL* 4 (1978) 1062-64.

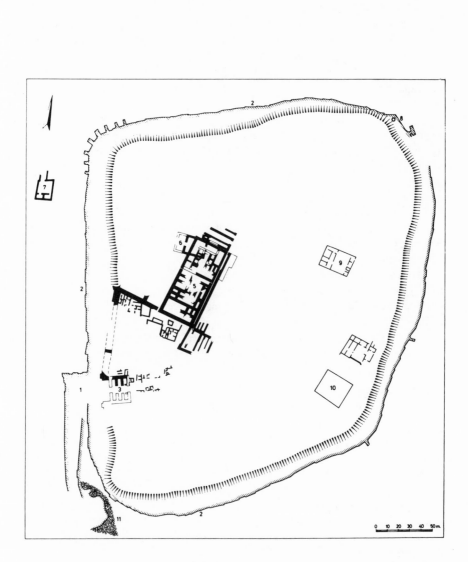

Fig. 7. Lachish: (1) The Bastion, (2) The Outer Wall, (3) The Level IV-III Inner Gate,
(4) Area S, (5) The Judean Palace-Fort, (6) The Late Bronze Age Temple, (7) The
Fosse Temple, (8) The Well, (9) The Solar Shrine, (10) The Great Shaft, (11) The
Siege Ramp (after Ussishkin, *Tel Aviv* 5, p. 4, fig. 1).

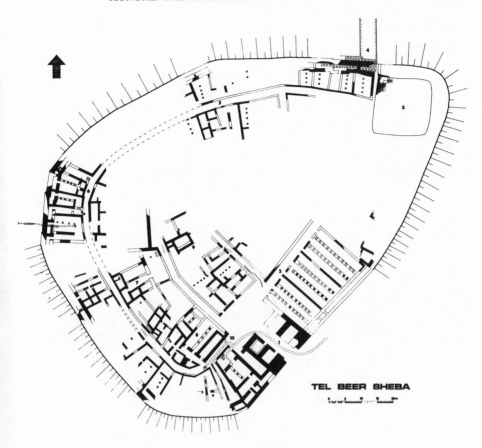

Fig. 8. General plan of Beersheba III-II (after Aharoni, *Tel Aviv* 1, fig. 1).

and its triple-entryway gate has been attributed by the excavator to the 10th century B.C. but is more likely late 9th century in date.[30]

2. To the east, Arad (Tell ʿArad) poses similar problems, though the excavation of the Iron Age acropolis in 1962-67 by Y. Aharoni suggests

---

[30]On a Solomonic date for Str. V, see Y. Aharoni, *Beer-Sheba* I: *Excavations at Tel Beer-Sheba, 1969-71 Seasons* (Tel Aviv, 1973) 5-67; "Beersheba, Tel," *EAEHL* 1 (1975) 160-68; cf. however, "Building Activities," 13-16 (= Davidic date). However, Aharoni's high dates for Beersheba (and Arad) are disputed by many scholars, including the present writer, who would attribute Str. V to the late 9th century B.C.; cf. Y. Yadin, "Beer-sheba: The High Place Destroyed by King Josiah," *BASOR* 222 (1976) 6-7, for a 9th century date for Str. V. On the most recent campaigns and the controversy over dates, see Y. Aharoni, "Excavations at Tell Beer-Sheba: Preliminary Report of the Fifth and Sixth Seasons, 1973-74," *Tel Aviv* 2 (1975) 146-68; "Tell Beer-Sheba 1975," *IEJ* 25 (1975) 169-71; and contrast Y. Yadin, *BASOR* 222 (1976) 6-7.

that the earliest casemated fort (Str. XI) and possibly the "temple/ sanctuary" (below) are 10th century in date.[31]

3. Related to the Beersheba-Arad complex are two other sites, both only partially investigaed in connection with Aharoni's Tel-Aviv project in the Negev. M. Kochavi's soundings in 1967-71 at Tel Malḥata (Tell el-Milḥ) have bared in Period 3 a solid town wall and a public building of the 10th century B.C.[32] The work of A. Kempinski and V. Fritz at nearby Tell Masos (Kh. el-Meshâsh = Hormah?) in 1972-75 have revealed several fine "four-room" houses of Israelite style in Str. II of the 11th century, continuing into Str. I, but this latter stratum seems to have ended in the early 10th century B.C.[33]

4. The Negev surveys and soundings, principally of Y. Aharoni and R. Cohen in the past decade, have placed on our map a string of more than 40 small Israelite forts throughout the Negev, many of them apparently dating only to the 10th century B.C. (fig. 9).[34]

5. Two sites founded in the 10th century B.C., but continuing in use throughout the Iron II, represent the maximum Israelite expansion in the desert. Tell el-Kheleifeh (Ezion-geber), Solomon's seaport on the Red Sea near modern Elat-Aqaba, was excavated in 1937-40 by N. Glueck. The date of the founding of the fortress and casemate enclosure of Str. I (never fully published) has been widely debated but probably is 10th century B.C.[35] The Israelite pilgrim site and fortress at Kadesh-barnea (Tell el-Qudeirat) in eastern Sinai was investigated in 1956 by M. Dothan and has been excavated further by R. Cohen in 1978-81. Building Period I, the founding

---

[31]See, provisionally, Y. Aharoni, "Arad: Its Inscriptions and Temple," *BA* 31 (1968) 2-32; "Arad: The Upper Mound," *EAEHL* 1 (1975) 82-89. However, the stratigraphy of Arad is exceedingly confused, as generally recognized, and the material remains unpublished. Most scholars would lower Aharoni's dates by at least a century. For instance, two inscribed bowls found near the altar of the small Str. X "temple" rebuild were attributed to the 9th century ("Inscriptions and Temple," 20), but F. M. Cross (anticipated by the writer) has recently dated them to the 7th century; see Cross, "Two Offering Dishes with Phoenician Inscriptions from the Sanctuary of ᶜArad," *BASOR* 235 (1979) 75-78. In our opinion, Str. X is late 9th century B.C. *at earliest*, and it is questionable where there is any appreciable 10th century occupation at Arad. On the "temple," see further below.

[32]M. Kochavi, "Malḥata, Tel," *EAEHL* 3 (1977) 772-74.

[33]See the preliminary reports of Y. Aharoni, V. Fritz, and A. Kempinski, "Excavations at Tel Masos (Khirbet El-Meshâsh), Preliminary Report of the First Season, 1972," *Tel Aviv* 1 (1974) 64-74; idem, "Second Season, 1974," *Tel Aviv* 2 (1975) 97-124; V. Fritz and A. Kempinski, "Third Season, 1975," *Tel Aviv* 4 (1977) 136-58; A. Kempinski, "Masos, Tel," *EAEHL* 3 (1977) 816-18.

[34]Y. Aharoni et al., "The Ancient Desert Agriculture of the Negev, V. An Israelite Agricultural Settlement at Ramat Maṭred," *IEJ* 10 (1960) 97-111. See now the first English survey of much of this material in R. Cohen, "The Iron Age Fortresses in the Central Negev," *BASOR* 236 (1979) 61-79. Cf. earlier, N. L. Lapp, *BASOR* 223 (1976) 27.

[35]Cf. N. Glueck, "Kheleifeh, Tell," *EAEHL* 3 (1977) 713-17 and references there.

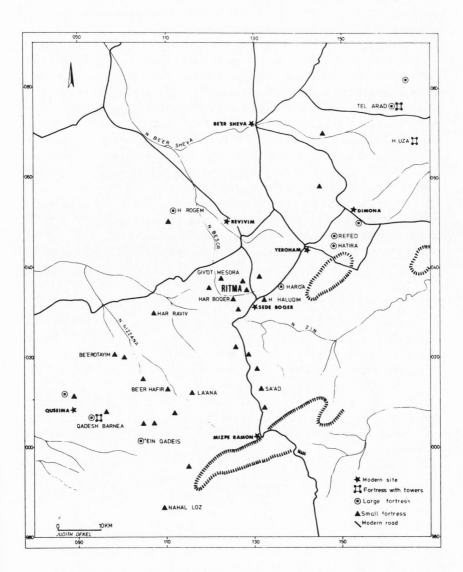

Fig. 9. Map of Israelite sites in the Negev (after Meshel, *Tel Aviv* 4, p. 111, fig. 1).

level, has barely been reached but lies below the 9th-8th century phase II building and may be 10th century in date.[36]

The above summary of known 10th century sites and their distribution is based on less systematic and thorough excavation than would be desirable. Nevertheless, the emergent picture of the Israelite occupation of Canaan in the 10th century B.C. is probably accurate in broad outline. (1) The 12th-11th century settlements of the period of the Judges were restricted by Canaanite and Philistine opposition to Upper Galilee, the Hill Country, parts of the Shephelah, and the northern Negev. For this pattern, particularly important is the new evidence of Aharoni's surveys in Galilee;[37] and especially the discovery of small early Israelite sites at ᶜAi and Kh. Raddana near Jerusalem,[38] at Izbet Sarteh near Aphek,[39] and at Tel Masos near Beersheba (above). In general these early Israelite settlements, many of which came to an end by the late 11th century B.C., tend to confirm the view of Alt and Noth on the Israelite occupation of Canaan.[40] (2) In the 10th century B.C., particularly under Solomon, there was a marked tendency toward centralization and urban development, with an accompanying increase in population, a rise in prosperity, and the development of monumental art and architecture, all reflected in the archaeological record.

II. TOWN PLANNING AND DOMESTIC BUILDINGS

Having surveyed the general early Israelite settlement pattern, the major 10th century sites, and the material safely attributable to the United Monarchy, we now turn to more detailed treatment of specific categories, first town planning and domestic buildings.

No direct archaeological evidence yet exists for centralized town planning—at least of domestic quarters—for the towns we presume were rapidly built up or first founded in the early Monarchy. This may be the case simply because there has to date been no large-scale clearance of any

---

[36]Cf. M. Dothan, "The Fortress at Kadesh-Barnea," *IEJ* 15 (1965) 134-43; R. Cohen, "Kadesh-Barnea," *IEJ* 26 (1976) 201-02; cf. also C. Myers, "Kadesh Barnea: Judah's Last Outpost,"*BA* 39 (1976) 148-51.

[37]See n. 3 above.

[38]J. A. Callaway, "The 1968-1969 ᶜAi (Et-Tell) Excavations," *BASOR* 198 (1970) 12-19; J. A. Callaway and R. E. Cooley, "A Salvage Excavation at Raddana, in Bireh," *BASOR* 201 (1971) 9-19.

[39]M. Kochavi, "An Ostracon of the Period of the Judges from ᶜIzbet Ṣarṭah," *Tel Aviv* 4 (1977) 1-13.

[40]See M. Weippert, *The Settlement of the Israelite Tribes in Palestine* (London, 1971); "The Israelite 'Conquest' and the Evidence from Transjordan," *Symposia. Celebrating the Seventy-Fifth Anniversary of the Founding of the American Schools of Oriental Research* (ed. F. M. Cross; Cambridge, MA, 1979) 15-34; and cf. the latest survey of J. M. Miller, "The Israelite Occupation of Canaan," *Israelite and Judaean History* (eds. J. H. Hayes and J. M. Miller; Philadelphia/Westminster, 1977) 213-84.

10th century site. Tirzah, although the exposure was small, did produce evidence, however, of differences between groups of "rich" and "poor" houses in *Niveau* III, which could be interpreted in terms of social stratification, if not of town planning.[41]

Elsewhere, the only Iron Age towns cleared sufficiently to present an overall picture have given us quite naturally the plan of the uppermost levels, which have not then been removed. The best recent example is the well laid-out 8th-7th century town of Beersheba III-II (fig. 8).[42] The older plans of 7th century Tell Beit Mirsim[43] or of 9th-8th century Tell en-Nasbeh (Mizpah) are also instructive.[44] However, the striking homogeneity of 10th century fortifications and their long, continuous rebuild on the same architectural plan (below) has been noted by many and had been taken as evidence for centralized town planning from the earliest stages. If this is true, then in the case of domestic architecture as well we may reasonably extrapolate from the later town plan of those sites first founded in the 10th century, such as Beersheba, for the original layout. Particularly in the case of royal, provincial administrative centers, we should expect to see evidence for crown supervision, and indeed Megiddo VA/IVB, though only partially cleared, gives us such evidence in the layout of the city defenses and the two "palaces" (below and fig. 4). It is doubtful, however, that smaller towns, or villages of lesser importance, were similarly laid out or were planned according to standardized specifications. As villages and hamlets of early Iron I grew rapidly into sizeable towns, or new settlements were planted on virgin soil due to population growth and increasing prosperity, urban development was probably difficult to control and quite haphazard.

We may not yet be able to see the overall picture of town planning, but the development of a standardized plan for *individual* structures which served many purposes is already clear in the 10th century. We refer to the well-known "four-room building," which has a long history but is first encountered in the 11th century, and then more frequently in such 10th century sites as Beth-shemesh IIa, Lachish V, Tel Qasile X, and Tell el-Hesi V, among other sites (fig. 10). This stereotyped building plan, in which a long back room and two side-rooms surround a central court (sometimes unroofed), seems to have been adapted for private dwellings, for larger public structures of various sorts, for granaries, and possibly for other uses.

---

[41]Cf. de Vaux, "El-Far°a, Tell," *EAEHL* 2 (1976) 403, although de Vaux interprets the observable differences as due to other causes, and also dates the superior construction to his "Intermediate" III-II phase, i.e., 9th century B.C.

[42]See references in n. 30 above; the Str. II plan, published widely, is the most complete.

[43]See W. F. Albright, *The Excavation of Tell Beit Mirsim* III, pls. 1, 3-7.

[44]On Tell en-Nasbeh, see C. C. McCown, *Tell en-Nasbeh* I (Berkeley, 1947), map. On the subject of Israelite town planning in general, see now Y. Shiloh, "Elements in the Development of Town Planning in the Israelite City," *IEJ* 28 (1978) 36-51, with full references and convenient illustrations.

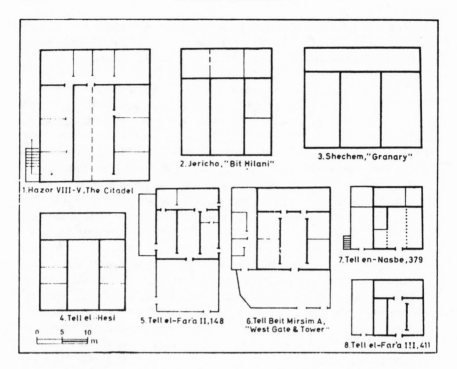

Fig. 10. Large "four-room" buildings of the Iron Age (after Shiloh, *IEJ* 20, p. 184, fig. 2).

Y. Shiloh has recently surveyed the available evidence and has concluded that the "four-room building" is a 11th-10th century Israelite innovation.[45] On the other hand, there is some evidence from two large 12th century houses of Str. XIII-XI at Gezer that the Philistines or "Sea Peoples" may have introduced the idea from the Mediterranean sphere. However, at present we cannot point conclusively to either an Aegean or to a local Canaanite background for this distinctive style of Iron Age courtyard houses, so its development may indeed be basically "Israelite."[46]

---

[45]See, conveniently, Y. Shiloh, *IEJ* 20 (1970) 180-90, and illustrations and references there; and, more recently, idem, "The Four-Room House—The Israelite Type-House?," *Eretz-Israel* 11 (1975) 277-85 (Hebrew) (English summary, *32).

[46]Dever et al., *BA* 34 (1971) 129-30. There is also new evidence of early Iron I "four-room" houses in Moab, in Transjordan and probably non-Israelite (oral communication from Prof. J. M. Miller, who will soon publish the material). Finally, the 12th century B.C. "four-room" houses at Masos are probably Israelite, but they also raise the 11th-10th century B.C. date; see V. Fritz and A. Kempinski, *Tel Aviv* 4 (1977) 138-47.

III. DEFENSE WORKS

Here we have somewhat more data, due in part to the monumental character and excellent construction of town walls and gates, which tended to survive even frequent destruction, to be rebuilt and reused for may centuries, and to leave substantial remains today. Also, the orientation of much biblical archaeology in the 20th century to "political history" has meant that most excavations at Israelite sites have concentrated on the development and destruction of fortifications (often to the exclusion of the domestic quarters).

We have already noted above the casemate or double, chambered city walls which first appear at 10th century Israelite sites. We have well-dated Solomonic casemates in Hazor X, Megiddo VA/IVB, Gezer VIII (figs. 3, 4, 6), Tell Beit Mirsim B₃, Beth-shemesh IIa (possibly Davidic), and Tel Qasile X; and, in addition, we may add the less certainly dated 10th century (?) casemates from Shiqmona, Arad XI, Tell el-Kheleifeh I, and the several Negev forts (fig. 9).[47] These distinctive double, partitioned walls were long thought to be of Syrian or Anatolian origin, but recently discovered MB IIC examples from Hazor, Taᶜanach, and Schechem demonstrate that there was a local, Canaanite tradition of casemate construction that goes back at least to the 17th century B.C.[48] The thickness of the 10th century Israelite casemates averages 1.50-2.00 m in width for each wall, or a combined width, including chambers, of 4.50-5.00 m. The walls were thus light yet strong, and the inner chambers could be used as towers; or, in peacetime, the chambers served for storage or even living quarters, as examples at many sites attest. The earliest Israelite casemates were built mostly during the Solomonic period, and indeed, with the possible exception of a solid offsets/insets wall at Beersheba V, these very distinctive casemate walls characterize that period almost exclusively. In Iron II, during the 9th-7th centuries B.C., these casemates were replaced at many sites with solid walls, but nevertheless they continued to be reused and even founded as original constructions right to the end of the Israelite Monarchy.[49]

City gates brought to light by excavations are fewer. Apart from the disputed three-entryway gates at Dan and Beersheba, which despite Aharoni are basically 9th century B.C., the typical 10th century gate is of the four-entryway type, attested thus far by striking coincidence at three of the four sites listed in 1 Kgs 9:15-17 as having been fortified by Solomon: Hazor, Megiddo, and Gezer (only Jerusalem, unexcavated at 10th century levels, is missing). The only other four-entryway gates excavated to date are (1) the

---

[47]See, conveniently, N. L. Lapp, *BASOR* 223 (1976) 25-27, and references there. Add now R. Cohen (n. 34 above).

[48]See references in W. G. Dever, *BASOR* 216 (1974) 19, n. 18.

[49]Cf. N. L. Lapp, *BASOR* 223 (1976) 27-39, with references.

massive four-entryway gate of Lachish IV-II, the ground-plan of which, when clarified, may go back to Str. V of the 10th century; and (2) the equally massive gate of Str. IX in Area M at Ashdod, which may be 11th century in date and suggests possibly a Philistine origin for these so-called Solomonic city gates (fig. 11).[50]

The story of the discovery of the nearly identical Solomonic city gates at Hazor, Megiddo, and Gezer is well known. R. A. S. Macalister had cleared the western half of the Gezer gate in 1902-09 but had termed it a "Maccabean Castle," mistakenly supposing it to be part of the citadel of Simon Maccabeus and dating it to the 2nd century B.C., and thus the Gezer gate went unnoticed for decades. In the 1920s and '30s, the Chicago excavators at Megiddo brought to light the first recognizable and datable example in Str. VA/IVB (above). The complex includes the inner four-entryway (= three-chamber) gate of fine ashlar masonry, an outer ramp and lower two-entryway gate/tower, and, as Y. Yadin later demonstrated, a connected casemate wall (figs. 4, 11).[51]

Following his 1955-58 excavations at Hazor, where a nearly identical inner gate and casemate wall was discovered in Str. X on the Acropolis (figs. 3, 11), Yadin again turned to the plan of Macalister's "Maccabean Castle" and made the brilliant suggestion that here was a hitherto unrecognized Solomonic city gate of similar type; he cited the text of 1 Kgs 9:15-17, and further suggested that all three gates "were in fact built by Solomon's architects from identical blue-prints."[52]

The subsequent excavations at Gezer, led by W. G. Dever and others in 1964-73, relocated the buried Gezer gate (Str. VIII) and completed its excavation, dating it on ceramic evidence to the 10th century B.C. and dramatically confirming both Yadin's intuition and the biblical record. The Gezer gate is even closer to the dimensions of the other two than Yadin surmised:

Detail	Megiddo	Hazor	Gezer
Length	20.3	20.3	19.0
Width	17.5	18.0	16.2
Between towers	6.5	6.1	5.5
Entrance width	4.2	4.2	4.1
Wall width	1.6	1.6	1.6
Total casemate width	(ca. 5.5)	5.4	5.4

---

[50]On the Lachish gate, see n. 25 above; on the Ashdod gate, see M. Dothan, "Ashdod," *IEJ* 22 (1972) 244; and "Ashdod," *EAEHL* 1 (1975), 109-12, where a 10th century B.C. date is argued. None of the associated material has been published, however, and the confused Ashdod statigraphy has suggested to some the possibility of an 11th century date, as early notices hinted.

[51]See references in nn. 7, 8 above.

[52]See Y. Yadin, "Solomon's City Wall and Gate at Gezer," *IEJ* 8 (1958) 80-86.

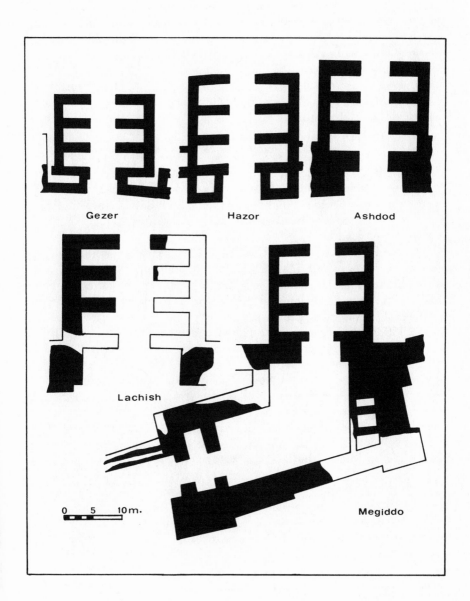

Fig. 11. City gates of the 10th century B.C. (after Herzog, *City-gate in Eretz-Israel*, p. 216, figs. 80-84).

Exactly like the Megiddo gate, the one at Gezer features fine ashlar construction, has an outer ramp and offset, two-entryway gate/tower, exhibits hinge and bolt-holes of double doors inside the threshold, and has a large drain running through the gate passageway. Moreover, like both the Megiddo and Hazor gates, it is connected to a casemate wall (figs. 6, 11). Thus, the parallels between the three Solomonic gates alluded to in 1 Kings 9 and actually uncovered by archaeology are so close that we must posit royal supervision in the construction of fortified, provincial administrative centers in the 10th century B.C.[53]

IV. OTHER "ROYAL" CONSTRUCTIONS

We turn now to a consideration of other categories of "royal" architecture. In addition to the defensive works discussed above, we possess some knowledge of other buildings at the regional administrative centers which biblical scholars have reconstructed from the Solomonic province lists in 1 Kgs 4:7-19.

Megiddo provides our most complete data (fig. 4). From the Chicago excavations we have several structures, notably Building 1482, and particularly Building 1723, probably the governor's palace. The latter is at the south of the mound just inside the city wall, a splendidly constructed building of ashlar and rubble-filled masonry similar to that of the Str. VA/IVB Solomonic gate. The enclosed compound, with its own triple-entryway gate, measures some 60 × 60 m; the main structure is 20 × 22 m and has a dozen rooms surrounding a central court, as well as a tower-staircase indicating a second floor (fig. 12). This palatial structure has properly been compared with the Assyrian-style bīt ḫilāni familiar from contemporary sites to the north—especially at Zinjirli (ancient Samᶜal in North Syria), where the 9th-8th century Hilani III and Palaces J-K of Kings Kilamua and Bar-Rakkib are extremely close (fig. 13). Comparable examples also come from Sakçegözü and Karatepe in Anatolia, Tell Tayinat in Syria, and Tell Halaf (ancient Gozan) in Mesopotamia. It seems likely that this southern structure is, in fact, the palace of Solomon's governor, Baᶜana, son of Ahilud, mentioned in 1 Kgs 4:12.[54]

In his campaigns of 1960-67, Yadin uncovered another, even larger palatial structure along the north casemate wall, in area BB just east of the gate, also attributable to Str. VA/IVB. "Palace 6000" was 21 × 28 m, built of fine ashlar masonry laid in header-stretcher fashion with field stones in the in-between stretches, like the southern "palace." The arrangement of its

[53]See references in n. 22 above; the gate plan is published in Dever, *BA* 34 (1971) 114, fig. 8, and in idem, "Gezer," *EAEHL* 2 (1976) 437.

[54]See references in nn. 7, 8 above; and add D. Ussishkin, "King Solomon's Palace and Building 1723 in Megiddo," *IEJ* 16 (1966) 174-86; "King Solomon's Palaces," *BA* 36 (1973) 78-105.

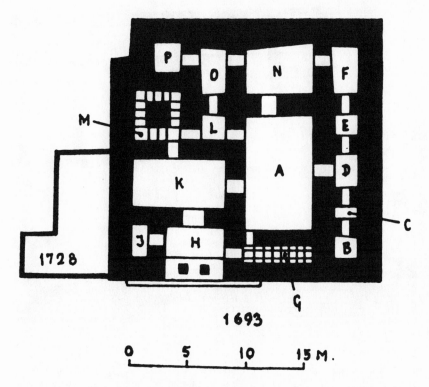

Fig. 12. A suggested reconstruction of the ground-plan of the "Palace 1723" at Megiddo (after
Ussishkin, *IEJ* 16, p. 182, fig. 4).

eight rooms around a central court also strongly suggests the North Syrian-
Anatolian *bīt ḫilāni* (figs. 4, 14).[55]

The existence of close northern parallels for both the Megiddo palaces
only reinforces the unanimous biblical witness that Solomon, having no
native Israelite tradition in art and architecture, employed artisans and
architects from Phoenicia. If we may assume that the southern, enclosed
"Palace 1723" was the district governor's residence, then the northern
"Palace 6000," like many of the other known *bīt ḫilāni*s, was probably used
as a reception-court and for other ceremonial functions (perhaps even as a
guest-residence for the King).

Another closely-comparable structure has largely escaped attention
but is probably a 10th century *bīt ḫilāni*. The casemated building immediately west of Macalister's "Maccabean Castle" is now almost certainly
Solomonic, since the recent excavations have redated the gateway to the
10th century B.C. (cf. fig. 6). This building is *ca.* 34 × 14 m, even larger

---

[55]Y. Yadin, *BA* 33 (1970) 73-74; cf. also D. Ussishkin, *BA* 36 (1973) 101-102.

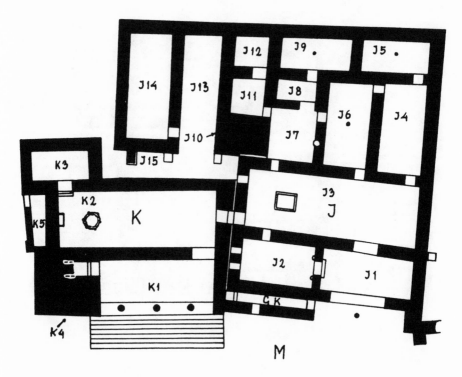

Fig. 13. Ground-plan of the 9th-8th century Palaces of Kilamua (J) and Bar-Rakkib (K)
at Zinjirli (after Ussishkin, *IEJ* 16, p. 177, fig. 1).

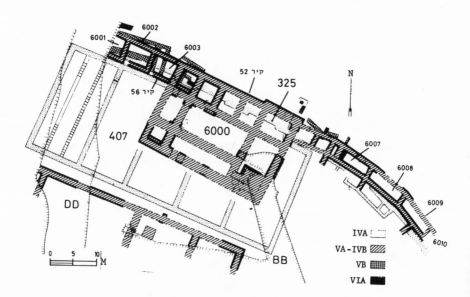

Fig. 14. "Palace 6000" at Megiddo (after Yadin, *BA* 33, p. 79, fig. 8).

than those at Megiddo; its plan is not altogether clear, but it appears to have at least 8-10 rooms surrounding a double (?) center court, and a tower-staircase at the northwest corner. Since it seems to be integral to the casemate city wall, part of this structure may be a barracks or palace guard.[56]

Finally, the "Residency" at Lachish has been shown by the latest excavations to have been founded in its first phase (Palace A) late in Str. V, and thus either late 10th or (more likely) early 9th century B.C. in date. It is also a ḥilāni-type structure ca. 32 × 32 m (fig. 7).[57]

The last category of "royal constructions" we might discuss—the so-called stables or storehouses—may be treated briefly. The latest excavation and research have shown that most of these colonnaded structures are post-10th century B.C., including the famous "Solomonic stables" at Megiddo attributed to Str. VIA/IVB, which Yadin has shown belong rather to IVA of the period of Ahab (fig. 4). The only examples that may be dated to the 10th century B.C. are those at Tell Abu Hawam IVb, Tel Qasile IX, and possibly Tell el-Ḥesi V (fig. 15). These buildings have often been interpreted as stables, particularly the ones at Megiddo, but current theory regards them as public storehouses, perhaps part of the construction of regional administrative centers under crown supervision.[58]

V. CULTIC STRUCTURES

By far the best known religious edifice of the 10th century B.C. is the famous Temple of Solomon. The design and construction of this splendid temple are elaborated in considerable detail in 1 Kings 6-8 (and reflected also in Ezekiel's vision of the restored Temple). However, thus far not a single trace of such a temple has come to light from excavations anywhere in Jerusalem. The lack of extant remains is undoubtedly due to the thorough destruction of both the Solomonic Temple by the Babylonians, as well as of the later Persian Temple on the same spot; the thorough clearance to bedrock by the Roman engineers who erected the Second Temple on the site; and finally the construction of the Dome of the Rock by the Caliph Abd el-Malik in 691 A.D. In any case, Islamic sentiment,

---

[56]W. G. Dever et al., *BA* 34 (1971) 112-16. Cf. also Y. Shiloh, *IEJ* 28 (1978) 49; D. Ussishkin, *IEJ* 16 (1966) 186.

[57]See D. Ussishkin, *Tel Aviv* 5 (1978) 28-31, 93.

[58]On Megiddo, see nn. 7, 8 above, especially Y. Yadin, *BA* 23 (1960) 67, 68. On the colonnaded structures generally as storehouses, see J. B. Pritchard, "The Megiddo Stables: A Reassessment," *Near Eastern Archaeology in the Twentieth Century. Essays in Honor of N. Glueck* (ed. J. A. Sanders; Garden City, NY, 1970) 268-76; Z. Herzog, "The Storehouses," *Beer-Sheba* I, 23-30. Against this view, cf. Y. Yadin, "The Megiddo Stables," *Magnalia Dei: The Mighty Acts of God. Essays on the Bible and Archaeology in Memory of G. E. Wright* (eds. F. M. Cross, W. E. Lemke, and P. D. Miller; Garden City, NY, 1976) 249-52; and J. S. Holladay's exhaustive treatment in *The Archaeology of Jordan. Essays in Honor of S. Horn* (forthcoming).

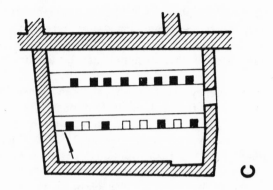

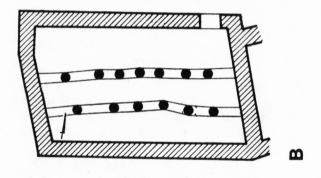

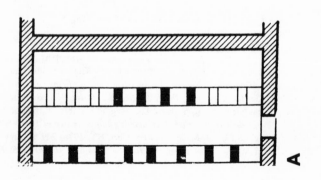

Fig. 15. Colonnaded 10th century B.C. buildings at Tel Qasile (A), Tell Abu Hawam (B), and Tell el-Ḥesi (C; after Aharoni et al., *Beer-Sheba* I, p. 24, fig. 1).

Orthodox Jewish tradition, and international law all combine to render any systematic archaeological investigation of the Temple Mount out of question.

Even in the absence of direct archaeological confirmation, we have a surprising wealth of detailed comparative data to aid in elucidating the biblical texts and in reconstructing the Temple of Solomon. First, the ground-plan of the building. The tripartite plan of the biblical description of the Solomonic Temple features three rooms arranged along a central axis: the outer *ulam* or vestibule, the central *hekal* or court, and the innermost *debir* or "Holy of Holies" (fig. 16). Until a few years ago no examples of such tripartite temples had been encountered outside the Bible, but then the University of Chicago excavations at Tell Tayinat in Syria turned up a 9th century example exceeding close to the biblical description—thus confirming the generally "Phoenician" provenance of the basic temple design, in accordance with 1 Kgs 5:8ff. Then in Yadin's 1955-58 excavations at Hazor, a local Canaanite temple of similar plan was brought to light in Area H, dating to the Late Bronze Age, *ca.* 15th-14th centuries B.C. Finally, in 1973 W. G. Dever reinvestigated part of Sellin's "Palace" near the Northwest Gate at Shechem and discerned the plan of an MB IIC tripartite temple of the 17th-16th centuries B.C., the earliest such temple yet found in Palestine (fig. 17). Mention should also be made of the Middle Bronze Age Temple in Area D of Tell Mardikh (ancient Ebla) in Syria.[59]

Second, the superstructure and decoration of the Solomonic Temple is illuminated by several archaeological discoveries of the period. (a) The distinctive, Phoenician-style "ashlar" (or finely dressed) masonary, probably laid in alternate header and stretcher fashion (1 Kgs 5:17; 7:9-12), is illustrated by the Solomonic gates at Megiddo and Hazor, as well as in the 9th century Tell Tayinat temple already discussed. (b) The twin pillars of "Jachin and Boaz" at the entrance (1 Kgs 7:15-22) are reflected in many Syro-Anatolian temples of the Late Bronze Age and Iron Age, including the example already cited from Tell Tayinat. (c) The interior walls of the Temple were panelled in cedar-wood from Lebanon (1 Kgs 6:15-18). This may presume lower stone orthostat or dados, with upper wooden panels affixed by mortise-and-tenon, a basically Syrian style of decoration which we know from the Late Bronze Area H temple at Hazor, as well as from the later Tell Tayinat temple. (d) Finally, the carved and gilded decoration of the woodwork and the entrance columns is described as featuring gourds, open flowers, lilies, palm trees, pomegranates, and network of "chain" designs (1 Kgs 6:18, 29; 7:15-22). These motifs are well illustrated by the nearly contemporary 9th-8th century Phoenician and Israelite ivory carved panels from Nimrud, Arslan-Tash, Samaria, Hazor, and elsewhere—

---

[59]On the above temples, as well as on the plans and prototypes of the Solomonic Temple in general, see W. G. Dever, *BASOR* 216 (1974) 43-52, with full references to the earlier literature.

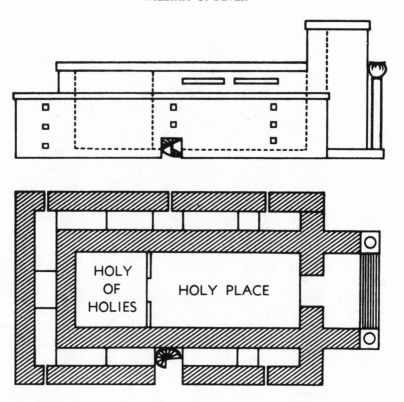

Fig. 16. Ground-plan and reconstruction of the Solomonic temple (after Corswant, 1956, in *IDB* IV, p. 537, fig. 7).

especially the palm or "palmette" design, which appears (fig. 18) not only on the ivories, but on many seals (below). This design was ultimately schematized in the "Proto-Aeolic" (or Proto-Ionic) capitals, of which more than 30 are now known from Israelite sites of the 10th-8th centuries B.C. (fig. 19).[60]

Third, the interior furnishing of the Solomonic Temple may be illustrated from archaeological finds, especially the two-winged cherubim (fig. 20) of the "Holy of Holies" (1 Kgs 6:23-28), which are now illustrated in numerous 9th-8th century ivories and in several Iron Age seal impressions. The particular expression of the cherub in the art and iconography of Israel is clearly less Assyrian and more Phoenician, combining as it does

---

[60]On the superstructure and decoration of the Solomonic Temple in general, see D. Ussishkin, *IEJ* 16 (1966) 174-86. On the "palmette design" in general, and the "Proto-Aeolic" capitals in particular, see now Y. Shiloh, "The Proto-Aeolic Capital—the Israelite 'Timorah' (Palmette) Capital," *PEQ* 109 (1977) 39-52; "New Proto-Aeolic Capitals Found in Israel," *BASOR* 222, (1976) 67-77.

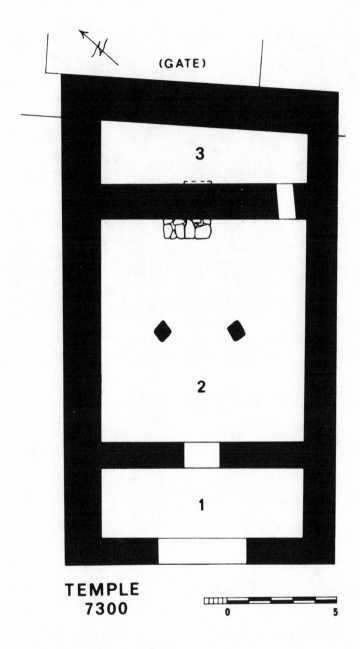

TEMPLE 7300

0   5

Fig. 17. Schematic plan of "Temple 7300" at Shechem, MB IIC (1650-1550 B.C.; after Dever, *BASOR* 216, p. 40, fig. 10).

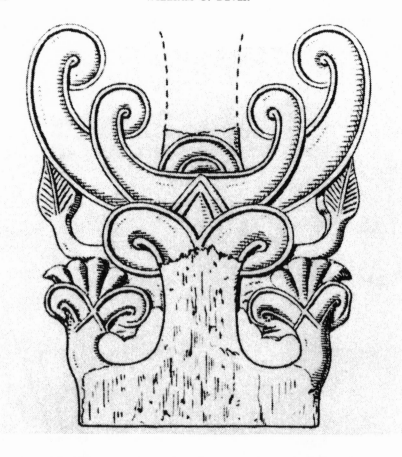

Fig. 18. "Palmette" design on ivory fom Samaria (from *Samaria-Sebaste* II, pl. XVII:4a).

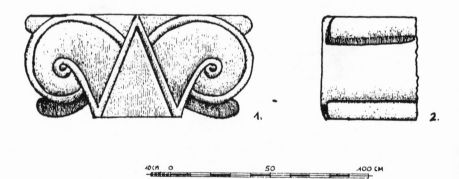

Fig. 19. Proto-Aeolic capital from Samaria (after *Samaria-Sebaste* I, p. 13, fig. 6).

Fig. 20. Cherub and "palmette" on ivory from Samaria (after *Samaria-Sebase* II, pl. V. 3a).

the characteristically mixed, bungled motifs of both Mesopotamian and Egyptian art.[61] Thus, once again the Phoenician prototypes of the Solomonic Temple are confirmed in comparative material provided by archaeology.

Fourth, the forecourt of the Temple in Jerusalem may be better understood in the light of such recent discoveries as the large "horned altar" from 8th century Beersheba, which recalls the great altar of burnt offerings in Ezekiel's description (43:13-17).[62] The 10 wheeled bronze stands and the 10 bronze lavers of the Temple forecourt described in 1 Kings are also seen in examples from earlier Phoenician art, including several which have precisely the pomegranate decoration mentioned in the Bible. Finally, the "pots, shovels, and basins" (1 Kgs 7:40, 45), which probably were used for incense and burnt offerings, have several parallels in archaeological finds of the period.[63]

Fifth, several structures related to the Solomonic Temple are mentioned in 1 Kings: the "Millo" (or "filling"); the "House of the Forest of Lebanon"; the "Hall of Pillars"; a harem for wives and concubines, and a separate residence for Solomon's Egyptian wife, Pharaoh's daughter; the "Hall of the Throne" and Solomon's own royal residence. As stated above, no actual trace of these buildings has been found or is likely to be found; but it has been persuasively argued that these several structures formed a unified complex of the type attested in the North Syrian-Anatolian bīt ḫilāni, examples of which we have already noted as parallels for the regional palaces at Solomonic Megiddo. The basic plan of the 10th century Acropolis in Jerusalem is undoubtedly seen in the 9th-8th century complexes at Tell Halaf (ancient Gozan) in Mesopotamia, at Karatepe and Sakçegözü in Anatolia, and at Tell Tayinat in Syria. But the most complete example is Hilani III and Palaces J-K at Zinjirli, ancient Samᶜal (fig. 21), the capital

---

[61]On the ivories, see the major collections of Syro-Palestinian ivories: F. Thureau-Dangin, G. A. Barrois et al., *Arslan-Tash* (Paris, 1931); G. Loud, *The Megiddo Ivories* (Chicago, 1939); J. W. and G. M. Crowfoot, *Samaria-Sebaste* II: *Early Ivories From Samaria* (London, 1938); and cf. C. Descamps de Merzenfeld, *Inventaire commenté des ivoires phéniciens apparentés découverts dans le Proche-Orient* (Paris, 1954); R. D. Barnett, *A Catalogue of the Nimrud Ivories* (London, 1957). On North Syrian and our "Phoenician" art generally, see R. D. Barnett, "The Nimrud Ivories and the Art of the Phoenicians," *Iraq* 2 (1935) 185-99; "Phoenician and Syrian Ivory Carving," *PEQ* (1939) 4-19; H. J. Kantor, "Syro-Palestinian Ivories," *JNES* 15 (1956) 153-74; I. J. Winter, "Phoenician and North Syrian Ivory Carving in Historical Context: Questions of Style and Distribution," *Iraq* 37 (1975) 1-22. On the seals, see "Siegel und Stempel," *Biblisches Reallexikon* (ed. K. Galling; 2d ed.; Tübingen, 1977) 299-307, especially Abb. 78:5-7. The older work of D. Diringer, *Le iscrizioni antico-ebraiche palestinesi* (Florence, 1934), is still useful. And see also the recent catalog of the Israel Museum, *Seals from the First Temple Period* (eds. R. Hestrin and M. Dayagi-Mendeles; Jerusalem, 1978) (Hebrew). See further Y. Shiloh, "Proto-Aeolic Capital," 41-43.

[62]See Y. Aharoni, "The Horned Altar of Beer-Sheba," *BA* 37 (1974) 2-6; and cf. Y. Yadin, *BASOR* 222 (1976) 6-7.

[63]See G. E. Wright, *Biblical Archaeology* (Philadelphia/Westminster, 1957) 141-42.

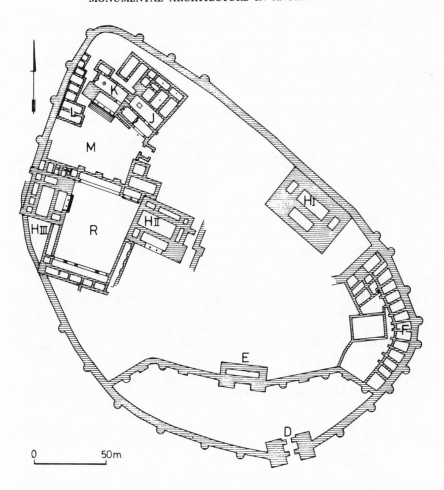

Fig. 21. Plan of the 9th-8th century Acropolis of Zinjirli (after Ussishkin, *BA* 36, p. 4, fig. 4).

of the kings of Kilamua and Bar-Rakkib. Here we see *all* the elements of Solomon's "Royal Quarter" in Jerusalem.[64] We can even illustrate details of the individual buildings and their furnishings from archaeology: the ashlar masonry (1 Kgs 7:9-10), the alternating stone/wood courses and the cedar paneling (1 Kgs 7:11-12), the throne borne on the wings of lion-cherubim (cf. 1 Kgs 6:23-28), and the portable braziers.[65]

---

[64]Cf. D. Ussishkin, *IEJ* 16 (1966) 84-89, for Iron Age parallels; and for earlier comparisons, W. G. Dever, *BASOR* 216 (1974) 48-51.

[65]Here, the older works are still useful, such as G. E. Wright, *Biblical Archaeology*, 136-45; and also P. Garber, "Reconstructing Solomon's Temple," *BA* 14 (1951) 2-24; "Reconsidering the Reconstruction of Solomon's Temple," *JBL* 77 (1958) 122-33 (with comments by W. F. Albright and G. E. Wright). See further detail in Ussishkin, *IEJ* 16 (1966) 89-91 on the

In addition to the Solomonic Temple—which was, of course, the focus
of Solomon's attempt to centralize religion in Jerusalem and thus the only
national shrine—we have some archaeololgical evidence of local Israelite
sanctuaries of the 10th century B.C.[66]

At Megiddo, the Chicago excavators foud in the courtyard of Building
2081 of Str. VA a small "cult corner" which contained among other items
two small "horned" limestone altars, chalices, and cultic stands of stone
and terra cotta.[67] A similar household shrine was found in 1968 by Aharoni
below the Persian-Hellenistic "Solar Shrine" at Lachish, "Cult Room 49,"
dating to Str. V of the 10th century (figs. 7, 22).[68] The finds were strikingly
similar to those at Megiddo: on benches around the small room were a
horned limestone altar, four ceramic incense stands, seven chalices, and
other miscellaneous pottery. Finally, Lapp found in 10th century levels at
Taᶜanach a "cultic installation" featuring a stone slab-lined basin with two
stelae or *maṣṣēbôth*; nearby were more than 100 pig astragali, a stone mold
for casting Astarte figurines, and a fantastic cult stand similar to one Sellin
had found 60 years earlier.[69]

Two larger cultic installations of the 10th century B.C. have been
interpreted as actual full-scale temples, though in both cases we should
prefer to regard them merely as local sanctuaries, no doubt Israelite, if not
truly "Yahwistic." The first is in Str. XI of the Upper City at Arad, the
basal level, where Aharoni uncovered a sanctuary of several rooms around
a central courtyard with a large fieldstone altar. At the western end was a
cella featuring two small limestone altars flanking the stepped entrance;
nearby was a well-dressed stela or *maṣṣēbāh* (fig. 23). Earlier, Aharoni had
compared the plan of the Arad structure with the Jerusalem Temple, but
later turned to the wilderness Tabernacle for a parallel.[70] But the Arad

---

Phoenician-style stone orthostat and wood paneling, the "cherub-throne," and the portable
braziers. The typical Solomonic ashlar masonry is now well known from many 10th
century B.C. sites, as for instance, the Gezer city gate; see W. G. Dever et al., *BA* 34 (1971)
cover and 112-13.

[66]See the useful essay of Y. Shiloh, "Iron Age Sanctuaries and Cult Elements in Palestine,"
*Symposia: Celebrating the Seventy-Fifth Anniversary of the Founding of the American
Schools of Oriental Research (1900-1975)* (ed. F. M. Cross; Cambridge, MA, 1979) 147-57.

[67]G. Loud, *Megiddo* II, 45-46, figs. 100-102.

[68]See n. 27. Further on the date, cf. also D. Ussishkin, *Tel Aviv* 4 (1977) 50; *Tel Aviv* 5
(1978) 92.

[69]On the "cultic installation," see P. W. Lapp, *BASOR* 173 (1964) 26-41; *BASOR* 195 (1969)
42-44; and *BA* 30 (1967) 17-24; for excellent color illustration of the cult stand, see A. E.
Glock, "Taanach," *EAEHL* 4 (1978) 1142.

[70]For the sanctuary, see Y. Aharoni, *BA* 31 (1968) 18-31; "Arad: The Upper Mound,"
EAEHL 1 (1975) 82-86. In these reports Aharoni argues that the Arad sanctuary is a full-
fledged 10th century temple of "House of Yahweh" like that of Solomon in Jerusalem. Later
he drew upon the less ambitious parallel of the wilderness Tabernacle; see Y. Aharoni, "The
Solomonic Temple, the Tabernacle, and the Arad Sanctuary," *Orient and Occident. Essays in
Honor of C. H. Gordan* (ed. H. Hoffner; AOAT 22, 1973) 1-8. On the opposing view that the
Arad sanctuary is merely a local cult installation, cf. Y. Yadin, *BASOR* 22 (1976) 7; and

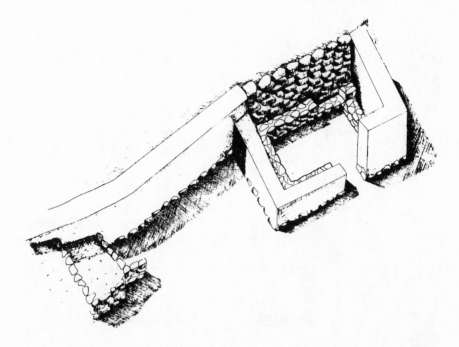

Fig. 22. "Cult Room 49" at Lachish (Str. V; after Aharoni, *Lachish* V, p. 29, fig. 7).

sanctuary need not be understood in such grandiose terms. Furthermore, the contents and the related pottery have not been published, and the stratigraphy of Str. XI has been much debated (above)—leaving both date and function of the Arad cult installation in doubt.

The rather poor Str. IX rebuild of the 10th century Philistine temple of Tel Qasile X has been attributed by the excavator to the Israelite conquerors and settlers, but it is not at all clear that the building continued to serve as a cult center at this stage of its history.[71]

CONCLUSION

With this survey of the building remains of the Davidic-Solomonic era, we come to the end of our treatment of the architecture of the period.

P. Welten, "Kulthöhe und Jahwetempel," *ZDPV* 88 (1972) 19-37. On the questionable 10th century date of Str. XI, see n. 31 above (where a date *ca.* 9th century is preferred). For even more drastic lowering of the Arad dates, cf. Y. Yadin, "A Note on the Stratigraphy of Arad," *IEJ* 15 (1965) 180. On the Solomonic Temple (though largely without reference to archaeology) see the exhaustive study of Th. A. Busink, *Der Tempel von Jerusalem, von Salomo bis Herodes* I (Leiden, 1970), especially 582-664.

[71] A. Mazar, *IEJ* 25 (1975) 86-88. Str. IX is, however, mid-late 10th century in date and probably Israelite; on the "four-room" houses of this stratum, see n. 24 above, and further T. Dothan and I. Dunayevsky, "Qasile, Tell," (the earlier excavations), *EAEHL* 4 (1978) 966-67.

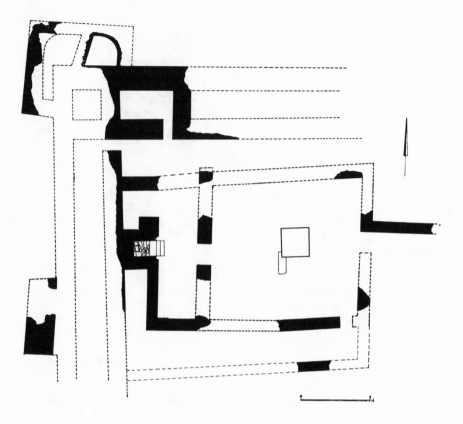

Fig. 23. Plan of the sanctuary at Arad (Str. XI; after Aharoni, *BA* 31, p. 18, fig. 12).

It must be stressed that these remains are not only the earliest evidence we possess of monumental architecture in ancient Israel, but they are among the most impressive. We can now understand the biblical tradition of 1 Kgs 10:4-5, which relates of the visit of the Queen of Sheba to view Solomon's splendid buildings in Jerusalem that she was so astonished that "there was no more spirit left in her."

Part II

Biblical Studies and the Ancient Near East

Ebla and the Old Testament

DAVID NOEL FREEDMAN
University of Michigan, Ann Arbor

On the first of October, 1975, a remarkable discovery was made near an obscure village in Northern Syria called Tell Mardikh, at a large mound or *tell*, with the same name, the site of the ancient city of Ebla. On that day an Italian team from the University of Rome, headed by Professor Paolo Matthiae, came upon a room containing the royal archive of Ebla; it consisted of about 15,000 cuneiform tablets of varying sizes and shapes, but substantially intact and undisturbed since the place was destroyed and abandoned 4,500 years ago. Unlike other major discoveries with which it might be compared, this was not an accidental find by a shepherd pursuing an errant goat into a cave, or by a camel-driver digging holes in an ancient cemetery for nitrate-rich soil.

This was a planned excavation then in its 12th annual campaign; the tablets were found exactly where they had been left, in a stratum, or level, of the mound previously identified and dated in a general way by pottery and other artifacts. Furthermore, an earlier find the year before, consisting of a small cache of 42 tablets, had alerted the excavators to the likelihood of finding more tablets in the vicinity. In fact, another room in the main courtyard of the royal palace had yielded a large collection of about a thousand tablets earlier in the 1975 season, so there was already a high pitch of excitement and expectation in the camp as the team, which included a small staff of trained personnel from the University of Rome and a more numerous group of local workmen, entered the last two weeks of the digging period. Even with this successful experience behind them, they were not at all prepared for the discovery of such a huge archive with its contents in such an excellent state of preservation.

The sheer numbers of a find of this magnitude are overwhelming, and even the most basic and simplest tasks—recording, photographing, and numbering all the items before careful removal—became an enormous burden for the overworked staff. The work could not be completed in the short time remaining, so the season was extended for two more weeks, while efforts continued to collect and organize the thousands of tablets in some systematic fashion. The object was twofold: to gather and store the tablets so that they would be safe and readily accessible for examination and study by experts, and to register the tablets and their findspots in such a way that the original scene could be reconstituted down to the last detail, so as to enable scholars to reconstruct the library with its sections and shelves and recover the order and arrangement of the tablets when the archive was in use thousands of years ago. While the bulk of the tablets could be sorted and examined in a preliminary way by the expedition's epigrapher, Professor Giovanni Pettinato, several thousand remained to be looked at when the season ended. Along with the others, these were boxed for shipment to the National Museum of Archeology at Aleppo, to await investigation and identification at a later date.

During the season which ended in October, 1976, an additional 1,600 tablets were found in other rooms associated with the palace; only a fraction of these have been examined, so we may be sure that many surprises await scholars as they undertake the painstaking and arduous task of deciphering and interpreting each tablet in turn. A preliminary reading of batches of tablets established beyond question that this was the archive of the royal palace of ancient Ebla; it consisted mainly of the economic accounts (covering trade and tribute) of the rulers of the city-state during a period of perhaps 100-150 years in the middle of the 3rd millennium B.C. While the bulk of the tablets reflected the vast trading interests and commercial activities of this prosperous kingdom, there were many others which dealt with diplomacy and foreign relations, internal and domestic affairs, cultic and cultural matters, all illustrating the many-sided character and quality of life in this teeming metropolis, direct knowledge of which was almost totally lacking before the current excavations and discoveries.

The importance of the new finds can hardly be exaggerated, not only because of the size of this practically intact archive (to which must be added the many other tablets of the same period found in other rooms in and adjoining the palace), but also because of the period to which they belong, and the place from which they came. Very little of a historical nature was known about the western part of the Fertile Crescent, including Syria and Palestine during this era, although excavations at a number of sites in this region had revealed the existence of large well-planned and heavily fortified cities, with impressive public buildings. Extensive trade between cities within and beyond this area could be demonstrated from the pottery and other artifacts found at the sites in the appropriate levels, but in the general absence of written records, the historical framework and the course of events could not be recovered or reconstructed. The newly discovered tablets have already produced an avalanche of information, with the promise of much more to come, about a world the full nature and dimensions of which could barely be perceived. What has emerged is that a complex civilization based upon a network of city-states like Ebla flourished in Syria-Palestine during the middle third of the 3rd millennium B.C.; it was just as elaborate and sophisticated as the Sumerian city-state cultures of Mesopotamia, with its centers in Kish, Uruk, Ur, and other localities of the Early Dynastic period. In other words, the "Sumerian" pattern prevailed throughout the Fertile Crescent, from the Persian Gulf to the Mediterranean and the border of Egypt; also included in the socioeconomic internation were outlying areas to the east (Elam) and north (Kanish and Hattusha), and doubtless also to the south (Arabia Felix) and the west (Alashiya = Cyprus; and other islands and coastlands of the Great Sea). Leadership and preeminence passed from one city to another as the Early Dynastic king lists indicate, but they cover only part of the territory and the period. Ebla was dominant in the west when Kish held sway in the east, but other cities, like Hamazi in Elam, or Mari and Ashur in Upper Mesopotamia, were prominent as well, and a flexible balance was achieved through treaties and trade. Adjustments could be made to reflect the realities of change. Resort to war was apparently less common than in earlier or later times. A rare instance of Ebla's involvement in a military campaign is reported in a letter from the general of the army to the king of Ebla. This man, Enna-Dagan, reports to King Ar-en-num that he has attacked the king of Mari, whose name was Iblul-il, defeated him in battle, and captured the city. The cause of the attack was an alleged breach of contract or treaty on the part of Iblul-il, probably involving the non-payment of tribute. Relations were broken off and war ensued. The issue was not finally resolved until the king of Mari was deposed and driven out and the previously-mentioned general installed as the new king of Mari. Presumably diplomatic relations more agreeable with Ebla's interests were now established, and trade and tribute restored to optimum levels. The overriding concern from the point of view of Ebla was to conclude successful commercial transactions on an international scale, and little was allowed to interfere with the maintenance of elaborate trading routes and religions throughout the Near East. This carefully controlled and promoted business activity produced a degree of prosperity rarely matched, much more rarely surpassed, in the ancient Near East, and is reflected in the great walled cities and crowded urban centers, which dotted the landscape and dominated the rural areas around and between them. In the Ebla tablets, city names famous in later times are already present and are attached to the same localities, indicating that the urban tradition was well established at that time in the 3rd millennium B.C., and that basic patterns of location and distribution were fixed. The city system did not change significantly during the millennia that followed but was worked into larger national patterns, beginning with Sargon the Great, founder of the First Dynasty of Akkad. and finally into imperial structures in the 1st millennium B.C. Suffice it to say that the tablets, when deciphered, translated, annotated, and published, will fill out the historical picture in the pre-Sargonic world with a degree of specificity not thought possible before these discoveries. The perspective is that of Northwest Syria, itself unique, while the scope is the entire Near East. The wealth of material permits the reconstruction of the whole scene of human activity: from commercial transactions to mythological speculations, from internal administrative orders and public edicts governing domestic affairs to foreign diplomatic correspondence and international trade agreements, from school texts (for example, there are small clay tablets on one side of which the instructor would write the sign or group of signs being used as models, while the students would attempt to emulate the master by copying the sign on the other side, but with varying degrees of success) to bilingual vocabulary lists, and others belonging to assorted categories of administrative documents and literary texts.

Archeological excavation has a glamorous reputation; with the many stories of high adventure and the ever-present air of expectancy as digging proceeds into unknown depths, the reputation is justified. For the most part, however, excavating is dull, tedious work, often conducted under the most trying conditions (hot, humid, semi-tropical climate; rough, frequently primitive accommodations and facilities; hard rigorous work, always exhausting and generally dangerous especially as the excavation reaches deeper and deeper levels). At Tell Mardikh living and working conditions have been fine to excellent by contrast with many other digs. The tell itself is immediately accessible from the main highway north from Damascus to Aleppo, lying about 30 miles (= 50 km.) south of the latter city, and almost 50 miles (= 80 km.) north of Hama. It rises sharply from the surrounding plain, which it dominates for miles around in all directions, although many other somewhat smaller mounds are visible from Tell Mardikh. According to the excavator, 80 sites of ancient occupation have been identified within a radius of 25 miles (= 40 km.) of the central mound, though not all were settled at the same periods. Headquarters for the expedition were set up in the village at the foot of the mound, which bears the same name, Tell Mardikh. A compound on the edge of the village nearest the mound, consisting of several dwellings opening on to a central court, was taken over. During the season, which extends from August into October, the staff lives there and works on the materials brought from the mound, including pottery and other artifacts, and the famous tablets. This is where the objects are registered, and the most important drawn, photographed, described, with the information carefully filed for later publication. The workers come mostly from the village and surrounding areas and are paid daily wages. The staff, however, is all Italian, and most of the members have worked together at Tell Mardikh for years. The chief of the mission is Paolo Matthiae, Professor of Archeology at the University of Rome, and for some time Director of the Institute of Near Eastern Studies there. His wife, Gabriella Matthiae Scandone, an Egyptologist by training has been associated with him in this enterprise from the beginning, and a small group of colleagues and students have been drawn from the University of Rome and the Institute. From the time that the site was selected and negotiations concluded with the Syrian authorities for permission to dig there, the enterprise has enjoyed the most cordial relationship with the Syrian Department of Antiquities, and there has been full cooperation in the pursuit of common objectives: the excavation of the site according to plan, the preservation of the monumental remains, the conservation of valuable objects, including statuary, figurines, pottery, and the tablets, and, finally, the essential project of publication. The excavation reports began to appear some years ago, and the first volumes of the tablets are now in process and should be in print shortly.

Typically a day on the mound begins early in the morning, at dawn or shortly thereafter, so that full advantage can be taken of the light and relative cool before the sun rises high in the heavens and the heat of the day becomes oppressive. At the start, digging is done by squares, usually five meters on a side, to provide convenient limits within which to classify building remains and objects as they are found. A small group of workmen is assigned to each square with appropriate tools: one to use a pick, another a shovel, while the remaining pair use smaller hand-tools to sift through the dirt for objects and to fill the baskets with refuse. The work is carried out under the watchful eye of the supervisor, who may be in charge of more than one square, and who makes sure that the work is done with the greatest care, so that nothing of importance is missed or accidentally broken and that the lines of walls and floors are preserved. Since archeology is a destructive science, accurate records of everything that was done and a complete description of what was found and precisely where (three coordinates are necessary to indicate the location and the depth of the object in any square) had to be made, beginning with the supervisors' daily logs, so that, theoretically at least, from the maps, pictures, objects, diaries, and descriptions, a detailed reconstruction of the site exactly as it was could be undertaken. Hence the precise techniques and careful procedures. Later, when structures and floor levels appear, the balks (as the partitions between squares, generally a meter thick to permit access, are called) may be cut through or removed in their entirety. But while they stand, and some are kept permanently, they serve as a guide and check for the excavators in the effort to determine exactly the sequence of strata, one of the prime objectives of archeological research: to determine the successive levels of occupation. By correlating strata with finds, principally pottery (which can be arranged in chronological sequence on the basis of shape, size, texture, decoration, special features like rims, handles, bases, and other criteria), it is possible to establish the occupational history of the site, and to interpret the evidence in relation to other mounds in the region, and beyond.

In practice, as the dirt is removed (and now in many modern excavations, even the dirt may be saved, or samples of it, since much can be learned from soil composition about the site and its inhabitants in different periods) the artifacts are put in numbered baskets, labeled with the site-plan coordinates for later identification and examination. So, the work proceeds through the morning, with the senior archeologists making the rounds from square to square to observe the progress of the digging and the emergence of unusual features or objects. Intrusive elements, e.g., the sudden appearance of pottery of a different period from that of the rest of the materials in an area, generally signify that a pit or foundation trench of a later period has been dug into an earlier stratum. Then it is necessary to identify the contours of the pit (often its appearance is signalled by a change in composition or density, but on occasion its outline can only be observed in the balk, where such changes can be detected more easily than in the course of digging). A mid-morning break is obligatory, at which a second breakfast is consumed, and strength and energy renewed for the second session of work on the mound. This extends on into the early afternoon, when all hands leave the mound, the staff for dinner at the camp, the workers to return to their homes. After a leisurely repast and the customary siesta, the staff resumes work in the late afternoon and evening: mostly this work is done at the camp, though return visits to the mound to check stratigraphic data and the like are occasionally required. There is no problem about this since the mound is immediately accessible. The work at the camp includes the following: examination of the day's finds and maintenance of the expedition log and registry of objects; continuing activity associated with the long-range objectives: preparation of maps and plans of the layout of the city, especially major walls and buildings and other installations; the repair and restoration of artifacts, especially pottery, most of which is found broken (except in undisturbed tombs); the analysis of epigraphic materials (i.e., the cuneiform tablets, and other inscribed objects); the examination and classification of art objects: statues, figurines, etc.

The routine is essentially unvaried, and the results for the most part are quite predictable and unexciting. Aside from dirt and stones, the chief finds are sherds of pottery, which are ubiquitous; that is the main reason pottery serves as the universal indicator of chronology. Pottery analysis and classification, together with stratigraphy, is central to the archeological enterprise, but neither is very stimulating or adventurous, however important the results obtained. The regularity of the routine is shattered occasionally by an extraordinary and unexpected discovery: sometimes it is an important epigraphic find, like a hoard of tablets, such as those found at Mari, Nuzi, and Ugarit in earlier decades of this century; sometimes it is a collection of manuscripts and fragments, such as those found at Qumran or Nag Hammadi; rarely it is the discovery of an undisturbed royal tomb with all its rich and variegated contents intact, such as the tomb of King Tutankh-amun of the 18th Dynasty of Egypt. At Tell Mardikh, the dramatic moment came with the discovery of the royal archive with its many thousands of tablets, but there was a long history of determined, painstaking effort beforehand.

Excavations at Tell Mardikh began in 1964 and continued for ten seasons (through 1973) before anything of sensational interest turned up. While the mound was occupied many times during its long history, i.e., going down through the various levels, there were occupations during the Arabic period, the Byzantine, Late Roman, Hellenistic, Persian, and the

Iron Age, the first level of truly major occupation was in the Middle Bronze Age (*ca.* 2000 to 1600 B.C.). For the first ten seasons of digging, the small staff and their workers scraped away at a series of different loci on the huge mound. Tell Mardikh covers 56 hectares (= about 140 acres), which by ancient standards would be an extremely large city. According to information provided in the tablets, the metropolitan area, or the official city-state, had a population of 260,000. The massive gateway to the city in the huge circumferential wall was located in the southeast and excavated. Other work was concentrated on the acropolis, which rises from the lower city and constitutes a separate entity (as indicated in the tablets for an earlier period), with a major share of the public buildings. Here an important temple of the Middle Bronze Age was found; it was laid out in the usual arrangement for this period, on a spacious scale, and with impressive cultic appurtenances. Among smaller finds of the Middle Bronze Age was a statue of a king of the city, Ibbit-lim, who is known from other sources to have been king of Ebla around 2000 B.C. This discovery strengthened the view of the excavator that Tell Mardikh was to be identified with ancient Ebla, a position fully confirmed by the tablets discovered later on. Another small object of importance was a fragmentary statue discovered in the 1970 campaign, and published by Matthiae in 1974, just before the first tablets came to light. While the fragment was found out of proper archeological context (i.e., in a later stratum), it was identified as Sumerian in style and workmanship, and could be dated to the "second transition period" of the Early Dynastic Age (*ca.* 27th-26th centuries B.C.). While it could not be known at the time, it is clear now that the statue belonged to the period when Ebla was at the height of its power and wealth, and when all the tablets were written and deposited in the archive.

In the eleventh season (1974), the excavators penetrated beneath the MB levels of Tell Mardikh and reached the EB city. On the acropolis a great palace complex was exposed, which extended over most of the upper mound. The walls of the great tower still stood to a height of almost 20 feet (= 6 meters), and the state of preservation was remarkable in view of the fact that the palace had finally been destroyed by fire. In one of the smaller rooms on the palace grounds (L. 2586), a cache of 42 cuneiform tablets was discovered. While a total of perhaps 15 fragmentary tablets of the Middle Bronze Age (*ca.* 2000 to 1600 B.C.). For the first ten seasons of digging, the sizeable group of tablets clearly belonged to a much earlier period, certainly in the 3rd millennium B.C. The exact date is a matter of dispute, which is not yet resolved. Originally both Matthiae and Pettinato believed that the tablets and their archeological context belonged to the age of Sargon the Great and the First Dynasty of Akkad (*ca.* 2400-2250 B.C.) and that the palace was destroyed by Naram-Sin, the grandson of Sargon. More recently, Pettinato has voiced the opinion that the tablets are older, perhaps as early as Early Dynastic II or III, but in any case pre-Sargonic. For the present, Matthiae holds firmly to the earlier opinion, chiefly on the

basis of the stratigraphy of the palace and the pottery, which according to
him is uniformly of the type assigned to EB IV A (which is dated to the
same period as the First Dynasty of Akkad).

The first group of 3rd-millennium tablets were written in the Sumerian
script, were of a type hitherto found only in Mesopotamia, and were
associated with pre-Sargonic settlements at Fara and Abu-Salabikh (modern
names). The 42 tablets consisted mainly of economic texts, dealing with
shipments of textiles, metals, and wood. One tablet was exceptional, being
a student exercise (a so-called school text) in which the names of people of
Ebla were listed. From a study of the tablets, Pettinato determined that
two languages were represented at Ebla: one was Sumerian, the basic
language of the older civilization in Mesopotamia, with which the writing
system itself was associated; the other was clearly a Semitic dialect, but its
provenience and affinities remained to be decided. The only attested
Semitic language of this early period is Akkadian, or East Semitic, and the
natural assumption was that the other language of Ebla would be a form of
Akkadian (which is the prevailing view concerning the other pre-Sargonic
tablets mentioned above). While Pettinato's natural inclination was in the
same direction, he was convinced early that the language of Ebla was not
Akkadian, but a form of West Semitic, namely paleo-Canaanite. Among
the better-known Canaanite dialects are Ugaritic (language of the tablets of
Ras Shamrah, a site not far from Ebla but on the coast of Syria; these date
from the 14th and 13th centuries B.C.), Phoenician, and Biblical Hebrew.
Even before the discovery of the great hoards of tablets in 1975, on the
basis of a preliminary analysis, Pettinato was willing to make the claim that
the Semitic language of Ebla was a form of Old Canaanite, related to
Ugaritic, and similar in many respects to Phoenician and Biblical Hebrew.
A final determination of the language-type will take protracted analysis
and debate, since Eblaite (as it may be called) does have some affinities
with Akkadian and its dialects. At the same time, it differs strikingly from
Amorite (usually regarded as a West Semitic dialect), which was at home in
the area of Mari and Haran; Eblaite also has very little in common with
Aramaic, another branch of West Semitic (parts of Ezra and Daniel in the
Old Testament are written in a dialect of Aramaic, while a few words of a
different Aramaic dialect are preserved in the New Testament). When
Pettinato presented his findings and his challenge to the scholarly world at
a conference of Assyriologists in the spring of 1975 the general response
was one of skeptical reserve. After all, 42 tablets were hardly enough to
make a linguistic judgment about the complex affinities of a very ancient
language, especially when the material was in a difficult and obscure
writing system consisting of a large number of ideograms which offer little
help in determining linguistic features. In effect, judgment was suspended
pending further analysis of the existing texts, or better still, the discovery of
more tablets. Neither Pettinato nor the scholarly world had long to wait.
The next campaign in the summer and fall of 1975 produced a huge

quantity of new tablets: about 1,000 in a courtyard room designated L. 2712, and then on October 1, the archive of 15,000 more in L. 2769, also in the courtyard adjoining the royal palace. So far as Pettinato is concerned, the new discoveries have confirmed his original hypothesis fully: the Semitic language of the tablets is western-oriented, and may be safely called paleo-Canaanite, though with its own dialectal peculiarities. This conclusion is especially interesting, since Pettinato's training is mainly in the area of Sumerian and Akkadian, rather than in West Semitic dialects; after all, he is Professor of Assyriology. Other scholars are divided in their opinions, and most are reserving judgment until a substantial number of tablets are published and more evidence of the morphology, grammar, and syntax of the language is available. This will require publication of the literary texts, which contain connected sentences and paragraphs, whereas the economic texts are mainly lists of goods, quantities, prices, and the like. For those who have dealt with the texts, it is clear that a knowledge of all Semitic languages is desirable, though not in equal proportion. Since in reading cuneiform tablets a knowledge of Akkadian and its relatives is taken for granted, and Pettinato approached the texts with the assumption that the language was an East Semitic dialect, it came as a surprise to him and to his colleagues that the key to decipherment and the solution to persistent problems lay in the West Semitic sources. Where the vocabulary can be classified geographically, i.e., where words do not belong to the common Semitic stock but can be assigned to one family or another, the West Semitic component is overwhelming, which is all the more impressive since the known vocabulary for Akkadian and its dialects is much greater than that of the West Semitic languages. Nevertheless, considering the age of the tablets, and our lack of controls for the period, arguments based upon vocabulary distribution must be treated with caution. It may well be that for this period, much of the vocabulary is common Semitic, and that it is by happenstance that words turn up in later vocabularies only in one branch or the other of the Semitic family. When it comes to verb forms, nominal forms, pronouns, and pronominal elements, prepositions, and other particles, the picture is mixed. Once again the extent of the common Semitic base in this period is uncertain, and this fact must qualify decisions about the assignment of features to one branch or another. Certain elements stand out: the laryngeals, i.e., ʾ, h, ḥ, ʿ, seem to have been lost to a considerable degree, as is true of East Semitic but not West Semitic, where they survived intact for another two thousand years. There is a problem with the writing system, which was not geared to represent all the sounds in Semitic, but the treatment resembles the way Akkadian is handled rather than the way a West Semitic language would be treated. In addition the use of the semi-vowel y is distinctive in the two branches: the y (= yod in Hebrew and West Semitic) has lost consonantal force in East Semitic, especially as the pronominal prefix to verb forms, and that is the case in Eblaite; on the contrary, in West Semitic dialects including Ugaritic,

Hebrew, and Amorite, the consonantal value is preserved intact. In the end, the best judgment about this language may be the most facile: the dialect of the tablets is Eblaite, a language peculiar to the city and its inhabitants, but very similar to the dialects of neighboring and even more distant cities, so that it and the others could be used for diplomatic exchanges, international treaties, and the like. It may ultimately be assigned a place in the spectrum of Semitic (though, for example, there is still some dispute about Ugaritic concerning to which branch it properly belongs) from east to west, and south to north, but, in the meantime, it is quite possible to read the material and to understand it without making a permanent decision about its status.

The sensational finds of the 1975 season greatly increased the quantity of written materials and extended the range of subjects covered and types of texts. The tablets themselves varied considerably in size and shape: from tiny school exercises with barely enough room for one or two signs on each side (with the master writing on one side for the student to copy on the other after study, but without being able to copy it directly) to the great economic and lexical texts; the largest so far discovered is roughly square, about 16 inches on a side (= 40 cm.) with 30 columns on each face of the tablet and about 50 entries per column, for a total of about 3,000 signs. Some tablets are rounded, while others are squared off; most are inscribed on both sides, though many have blank spaces, especially on the reverse. Many are also inscribed on the edges, usually with a brief description of the contents, or mark of classification. The tablets were filed in a vertical stance, with the inscribed edge visible so that the filing clerk could identify the tablet without actually removing it from the shelf. The general arrangement would have been similar to that of folders in filing cabinets or phonograph records in stores. In this collection, economic texts were preponderant, but a wide variety of other texts also appeared. In addition to the economic-administrative tablets, there were literary, legal, diplomatic, and religious texts including both mythic and cultic materials, royal edicts, reports of a military and political nature, and lexical texts with long lists of place names, personal names, professions and occupations, birds, beasts, and fishes, metals and other materials, and so on. The bilingual vocabularies are especially important, since they provide the basic key to the decipherment of the rest of the tablets. So far, 114 different vocabulary tablets have been found: three (A, B, C) are master tablets with lengthy lists, while most of the rest are partial copies of one or another of the three. It is assumed that the latter were prepared by student scribes as part of their training. The existence and activity of a scribal school at the royal palace has been confirmed by the presence of school tablets, the student copies of master tablets, and marginal notations by the instructors on the quality of the student's work. One mathematical text has turned up; it was composed by a visiting scholar from that center of classical Sumerian culture, the city of Kish. From the vocabulary lists, Pettinato has compiled a bilingual dictionary of more than 3,000 words in Sumerian and Eblaite. While the work of analysis has only begun, the implications for the study of both Sumerian and early Semitic are weighty. Already the Ebla lists have shed light on difficult and problematic passages in the Ugaritic texts and the Hebrew Bible (it is significant that the Book of Job, with its many strange and obscure terms and forms, has been a principal beneficiary of the preliminary examination of the texts).

The next season of digging (1976) saw the extension of excavations to the royal palace itself and involved the clearing of several rooms inside of the building for the first time. Two rooms yielded a total of about 1,600 tablets, generally of the same character and variety as the earlier materials, though closer study may turn up differences which could help to explain why these tablets were in these rooms instead of being in the main archive. In any case, the new finds show that the riches of the palace have not been exhausted, and it is reasonable to suppose that many more tablets will turn up as the excavation of the rooms of the palace continues. It may be questioned whether another great archive or, even better, the royal library itself will be uncovered. The royal library would be distinguished from the royal archive, as the Library of Congress would be distinguished from the Bureau of Records. Whereas the archive properly is filled with economic records and statistical reports, presumably the library would have a preponderance of literary texts. The palace is very large, and it will take many more seasons of digging to exhaust its rooms and stores; the possibility remains of even more startling discoveries than those which have already been made. But such speculations are for the future. Right now, the collection in hand is ample to keep Pettinato and his associates and students, and all the rest of the Sumerologists and Semitists in the scholarly world busy for many years to come.

Before proceeding to a discussion of the contents of the tablets and the picture of Ebla and its world which they present, it may be well to describe the cuneiform system of writing and to explain how scholars go about deciphering a text, identifying the language in which it is written, translating, interpreting, and comparing it with others. The actual writing technique involves the use of a stylus (at least one has turned up at Ebla: it looks like a short ball-point pen or a pencil) to make wedge-shaped characters on the soft clay, and a butt end which is used to impress circles and half-circles representing numbers. The original form of the writing was pictographic; each sign was a picture of some object and expressed an action, word or idea. Grammatical elements were not originally indicated. Because of the structural inadequacies of such a system, the original language of the oldest cuneiform tablets remains something of an enigma, although it is presumed to be Sumerian. The remote antiquity of the source materials poses an additional problem, and, finally, Sumerian is unrelated to any other known language of the world, and hence cannot be elucidated by references to related linguistic groups. By the time of the Ebla texts, the original pictures were stylized and conventionalized so that they bore little or no resemblance to the objects they were supposed to represent. At the same time, the system had been adapted for use with a second language, a form of Semitic. Whether as part of the effort to make the adaptation effective, or more likely as an inner development in the process of making Sumerian more intelligible, some signs appropriated from the common stock were used as semantic "classifiers": they were either predeterminatives or postdeterminatives, indicating that the following word or preceding term belonged to one of several categories; determinatives for "deity," "city," and "country" were the most common. An even more remarkable and revolutionary development on the road to a full alphabet occurred, which involved the use of these root-elements to represent syllables. In some cases, a sign would be placed after a word, as a phonetic complement to spell out the syllable with which the word ended; this would be a sufficient clue to the actual word meant by the scribe, since the root-element could represent more than one term out of the available vocabulary. Based on the actual pronunciation of the word in Sumerian, the sign would be given that syllabic value quite apart from any special meaning attached to the word. Signs could then be combined to produce words out of their syllabic values, which had nothing to do with the meaning of the individual signs. In this way syllabic writing became an adjunct of logographic systems, though it never replaced the older method entirely. Since the same signs could be used both as logograms and as syllables, there could be some ambiguity in reading and interpreting the material. In addition, in time, certain signs gained additional syllabic values, so that the same sign might represent a number of different syllables; contrariwise, the same sound could be indicated by a number of different signs. As a result of all this complexity and variety, reading early Sumerian and Semitic texts remains a very difficult exercise in scholarly ingenuity and wisdom. In the bilingual vocabularies, the Sumerian root-element most often is matched with the Eblaite word, which is spelled out syllabically; rarely in addition the Sumerian word will be written phonetically. There would have been no point in putting the logogram in the Semitic list, since it would just duplicate the Sumerian root-element. With respect to the Sumerian words, in some cases the sign also provided the pronunciation of the term, since its primary phonetic value was the word itself; if the person actually spoke Sumerian, he would have no difficulty pronouncing the sign. On the other hand, Sumerian may not have been in use locally, i.e., in Ebla, so there was no need to pronounce the language, except for scribes to be able to interpret the Sumerian signs. In the texts generally, there is a vast preponderance of root-elements or word signs, and a much smaller incidence of phonetic or syllabic writing.

The system of syllabic writing, which was both more useful and would ultimately be more simple (using a total of 80-90 signs to represent possible syllabic combinations, as against a logographic system which employed hundreds of signs), never completely displaced the older system, and the result was a composite, which makes for very difficult reading. The same set of signs may be used in their original character as logograms, or they may be used to represent syllabic sounds, or, as is most often the case, a mixture of both, though in general, the earlier the period the higher the proportion of logograms. At the same time, the system may be used to represent either of the two languages, Sumerian or Eblaite. With rare exceptions (e.g., when a bilingual text is offered) it is assumed that the texts are in a single language. The logograms as such do not indicate which language is intended or is being used by the scribe: only the syllabic writing (including syllabically written phonetic complements) can determine the nature of the language. Since in any given tablet 80% or more of the signs will be logograms, the determination of the identity of the language, as well as the description of verbal and nominal forms, rests upon the scattered instances of syllabic writing. While the great bulk of the Sumerian texts is predominantly logographic, sporadic syllabic writing and the use of phonetic complements help to fix the language and its forms. The Semitic texts, on the other hand, exhibit a higher proportion of syllabic writing as a rule, thus enabling scholars to identify both the language and some of its grammatical features. The language of any tablet that was written entirely in logograms could not be decided without some other indication. It could be in Sumerian, Semitic, or some other language. But, by common consent, such tablets are taken to be Sumerian; that is the simplest inference from the evidence, since so far as we know, the system of writing was devised by the Sumerians as a pictographic method of representing their language. Theoretically, it could have been used in precisely that way for any other language, but in practice use with another language required some adaptation, and the change would show up in the representation of that language. Cumbersome as it was, the system remained in use for almost 3,000 years, not finally dying out until the Seleucid Era near the end of the 1st millennium B.C., while its origins go back to the last years of the 4th millennium. It remained the special preserve of the scribal guilds, who jealously guarded their prerogatives and their secrets. Since many years were devoted to the training of scribes, and the rest of their lives were spent in polishing their skills, not only was there no need to simplify the system, but there was a positive value for the scribes in keeping it as esoteric and complicated as possible.

Since the texts consist largely of logograms, the bulk of which can be identified and interpreted, it has been possible for Pettinato and his assistants to gain a general knowledge of their contents, while leaving for later the determination of details concerning linguistic structure and grammatical relationships. The overall picture which has emerged from a survey of several thousand tablets may be described as follows. Ebla was a very substantial city-state which flourished in the Early Dynastic period (perhaps during the 27th and 26th centuries B.C.). While its immediate territory was not very large, it exercised economic power over a much larger area and claimed tribute from many cities in the region of Greater Syria and Upper Mesopotamia. Its commercial and diplomatic relations extended over the entire Fertile Crescent and beyond to Elam on the east and to Anatolia in the north. It demonstrated its military prowess in a major campaign against Iblul-il, an attested king of Mari, which resulted in the capture of the king and the conquest of the city. Mari remained a dependency of Ebla, being ruled first by a general of Ebla, Enna Dagan, and then by a royal prince, Šura-Damu, the son of Ebrium.

During the Early Dynastic period of Sumero-Semitic culture, first one city-state, then another exercised "kingship" or enjoyed preeminence over the others, according to the formulas in the Sumerian King Lists, compiled at a later age. While the dynasties are listed sequentially, it is apparent that many must have overlapped, and hence supremacy may have been less than absolute and the eminence must have been claimed by more than one city at a time. This revised picture is sustained by archeological data as well, since they show that many centers of wealth and power were spread throughout Mesopotamia and, as it turns out, Syria-Palestine also, where many large and prosperous city-states existed. Among the most prominent in the west was Ebla, while at the same time (Early Dynastic II) Kish was preeminent in the east (this would be the second dynasty of Kish, *ca.* 2700-2550 B.C.). Other important cities of the period which are mentioned in the Ebla tablets include: Adab, Akhshak, Ashur, Nineveh, Mari, Haran in Mesopotamia, while a much longer list of cities in Syria-Palestine is given. The latter include: Carchemish, Ugarit, Damascus, Aleppo, Homs, Hama, Hazor, Megiddo, Byblos, Acco, Carmel, Ashdod, Gaza, Sinai, and Jerusalem. The picture reflected in the tablets is clearly compatible with the Early Dynastic period (between E. D. II and E. D. III), and in any case must be pre-Sargonic, since Akkad is never mentioned in the texts, and the First Dynasty of Akkad instituted so many far-reaching changes in the political, social, and economic patterns of the Near East that had the texts come from that period or later, they would have reflected the changes. Since the tablets cannot be later than the period of Akkad, and can hardly have come from that period, they must be earlier.

The city-state of Ebla was the capital of a commercial empire, and its kings were successful executives of the equivalent of multinational corporations. Ebla was a manufacturing center which traded finished products (mainly textiles, but also metal-work, and other products) for raw materials with neighboring and more distant communities, reaping great wealth as the reward of aggressive business activity. They did not hesitate to use economic muscle to enhance their political power, or political pressures to strengthen their economic position, or in the end, military means to shore up either or both of the others. The tablets attest abundantly to the extraordinary range and volume of trade, and the rich rewards of vigorous and unremitting salesmanship. During the period covered by the tablets,

five kings are known to have reigned at Ebla, but only two can be proved
to have been related by blood: No. 3, Ebrium, was the father of No. 4,
Ibbi-Sipiš. Before Ebrium there were No. 1, Igriš-Ḥalam, and No. 2, Ar-en-
num, who were apparenetly not related to each other, or to any of the
following kings. The oldest son of Ibbi-Sipiš, Dubuḫu-Ada, served as
crown prince and heir apparent during the reign of his father, but never
seems to have reigned as king. In his place we have Irkab-Damu, who was
not related to the previous kings, and with him the series comes to an end.
It was during his reign that the city fell to an enemy and the palace in and
around which the tablets were discovered was destroyed. The impending
crisis may be reflected in a letter from Irkab-Damu to a man named Zizi,
the king of Hamazi (in Elam), in which he urgently requests military
assistance in the form of picked troops. The fact that Irkab-Damu would
seek help from such a remote source is an indication of the magnitude of
the crisis; it may also imply that the threat came from nearer at hand,
probably from southern Mesopotamia. Troops from Hamazi might well
distract an army coming up from the south and east, but it would appear
that the help did not materialize or was too little and too late: Ebla fell,
and never regained its former prestige and glory. Its greatest king was
Ebrium, who achieved notable successes on the diplomatic and commercial
fronts, established prosperity and security for his people during a long
stable reign, and bequeathed to his son Ibbi-Sipiš a rich and powerful state.
The latter carried on in his father's footsteps, but was unable to pass the
scepter on to his son, Dubuḫu-Ada. A partial parallel to the dynasty of
David in the Bible may be noted: like Ebrium, David was the founder of a
dynasty, who passed on to his son a rich and powerful kingdom. Solomon,
however, could not deliver his kingdom intact to his son Rehoboam.
Unlike Dubuḫu-Ada, however, Rehoboam managed to hang on to the
southern part of his father's realm, Judah, and the dynasty remained in
power for more than 300 years thereafter.

Other tablets describe the organization and administration of the city.
Alongside the king, who was the supreme authority, was the queen, who
held a position of prestige and not a little power. Her first-born son was the
crown prince, who in his majority also served as prime minister of the
realm in charge of domestic affairs. The next son (not necessarily by the
same wife; Ebrium had 38 sons by several wives) held the foreign portfolio,
and judging by the diplomatic correspondence and the number of treaties
concluded with other city-states, this was a very busy office. For administrative purposes the upper and lower cities were treated separately. There
were four administrative centers on the acropolis: the palace of the city, the
palace of the king, the stables, and the palace of the servants. The lower
city was divided into quadrants, each associated with one of the gates of
the city: (1) the Gate of the City; (2) the Gate of (the god) Dagan: he was
the chief god of Ebla, well-known from other sources including the Bible;
(3) the Gate of (the god) Rašap: another well-known Semitic deity, who

appears in the Ugaritic tablets, and in somewhat attenuated form in the Bible as the agent of pestilence and attendant of Yahweh in his heavenly court (Hab 3:5); (4) the Gate of (the god) Sipiš, the sun-god: the word is equivalent to *šemeš* = sun in Biblical Hebrew. There was a highly organized civil service, which according to information in the tablets numbered 11,000, or slightly over 4% of the total population cf 260,000. That would be equivalent to a bureaucracy of over 9,000,000 for the present population of the United States (around 220,000,000), including federal, state, and local officials.

Reference has already been made to historical data in the tablets. In particular there is an account of the campaign against Iblul-il, king of Mari, conducted by Enna-Dagan, the commanding general of the armies of Ebla. Enna-Dagan succeeded in deposing Iblul-il, and was himself installed as king of Mari, to be succeeded later by a son of King Ebrium, as the new royal family consolidated its hold on Ebla and its tributaries. In Enna-Dagan's report to King Ar-en-num, the predecessor of Ebrium, Iblul-il was called king of Mari and Ashur, another city-state, which became the capital of the kingdom of Assyria in later times. Curiously, nothing is said in the tablet about the disposition of Ashur after the overthrow of Iblul-il; Enna-Dagan and his successor, Šura-Damu, are named kings of Mari only. Another text, however, consists of a treaty between Ebla and Ashur, involving Ebrium on one side and a man named Dudiya king of Ashur. It is of the greatest interest to scholars that this king has the same name as the first king in the Assyrian King Lists. These lists were compiled almost two millennia later when Assyria was a great empire and the royal dynasts wished to trace the history of their kingdom back to its origins. Specific information was lacking about the earliest names on the list, and the first 17 are simply described as "kings who dwelt in tents." Since Hammurabi of the First Dynasty of Babylon (perhaps around 1800 B.C.) traced his ancestry back to the same kings, it was thought that this particular group was simply part of a floating tradition, and that the kings themselves were legendary figures or eponymous ancestors, whose names were those of tribes and ethnic groups who made up the kingdoms of later times. We can imagine the general surprise and consternation in scholarly circles when one of these misty monarchs has emerged into the full light of history, as signatory to a formal treaty some time in the 27th century B.C. It is as though a document signed by King Arthur, the legendary king of English tradition, were to be found linking him directly with some other historical figure or event. A firm synchronism has therefore been established between Dudiya, the first Assyrian king, and Ebrium of Ebla. It may also be possible to explain why the Assyrians traced their history and identity as a nation to this man. As we know from the other tablet, there was at least one king of Ashur before Dudiya, Iblul-il. But he was clearly not Assyrian, and that must be presumed for any other Kings of Ashur of that early period. Dudiya (= Tudiya of the Assyrian King Lists; in our tablets, *d* and $t/\underline{t}$ are not distinguished, but whereas no satisfactory etymology of the Assyrian form has been determined, the Eblaite form of the name can be interpreted on the basis of the root *dwd*, with the meaning of "beloved") was apparently the first native Assyrian to be elevated to the throne of Ashur, and even though Ashur at the time was tributary to Ebla, nevertheless in the eyes of the Assyrian chronologers and historians, the authentic history of Assyria began with Dudiya. Hence we have a rare view of a turning-point, a creative moment in the national consciousness of a people. Dudiya, the founding father, the first king of the Assyrians, has emerged from the shadows of legend into the light of history, and the later tradition can now be traced to a fixed point in time. The treaty between the two states establishes extraterritorial enclaves (though presumably not on the basis of parity) and prescribes the code of conduct for these communities in criminal and civil matters. While the terms do not constitute a law-code, it seems clear that they are drawn from such a code; it is no accident therefore that such a code has been found, though it is not yet translated. The logical connection between treaty terms and law codes can now be investigated in the light of ancient first-hand data.

Turning to the religion of Ebla, we find the typical polytheism of the ancient Near East dominant there. On the basis of its geographic position, it could have been predicted that Eblaite religion would consist of a mixture of Western and Eastern elements both as to the deities represented and the legends and myths associated with them. In agreement with much later practice, Sumerian and Semitic deities are already equated, e.g., Nergal = Rašap (both are gods of pestilence and the underworld); Utu = Sipiš (both are sun-gods); Inanna = Aštar, and Bara = Aštarta (both pairs are astral deities). The identification of Enlil the chief of the Sumerian pantheon with Dagan might have been expected, but the name Enlil is simply transcribed syllabically in the name list: *i-li-lu*. Dagan is identified as the chief god in various places (like Jupiter in the Roman period), and in one connection he is called "the Canaanite," emphasizing that this god had his beginnings in the west.

Many of the personal names preserved at Ebla provide us with information about the local contemporary religion. They normally consist of verbs or nouns combined with a theophoric element (i.e., the name of a god), as generally in the Near East and in the Bible. In addition to the gods already mentioned, we find as components in personal names the following: Adad (= Hadad the storm god whose title in later times was Baal), Malik, Ašera (= Asherah, the queen of the gods, and consort of El in later mythology), and Kamiš (= biblical Chemosh, the chief god of Moab in later times). Among the thousands of names in the tablets, note may be taken of a few:

Ana-Malik = I am (the god) Malik
Re-i-na-Adad = Adad is our shepherd

Adam-Malik = Man of Malik
Du-bù-ḫu-Malik = Feast (or sacrifice) of Malik
Eb-du-^{d}Ra-ša-ap = Servant of (the god) Rašap
I-ad-Damu = The hand of (the god) Damu (= blood).

Many names are compounded with the element *il*, which is a generic term for deity, but is also the name of the chief god of the Canaanite pantheon; together with an appropriate modifier (Shaddai), it is also the name of the patriarchal God. Among the Ebla tablets, a number of the same names are compounded with the element *-ya* as well as with the element *-il*; some of these are all but identical with biblical names in which the same phenomenon occurs: e.g., Mì-ka-ilu = Michael; Mi-ka-ya = Micaiah; Is-ra-ilu = Israel; Is-ra-ya (there is no equivalent in the Bible); En-na-ni-il and En-na-ni-ya. Whether the *-ya* component can be regarded as an abbreviated form of yahu<yahweh is much debated, and no conclusive decision can be reached. There may be no connection at all; however, the Ebla name šu-mi-a-ù = my name is Yahu, gives one pause.

The royal family were avid supporters of the official cult, and the tablets list sacrifices offered by the king, the queen, and the princes to many gods of Ebla in their separate temples. In return the religious establishment supported the royal house and contributed to its survival and success. Again, the similarity to the kingdom of David and Solomon is noteworthy. The separation of church and state, except in a formal sense, was unheard of in those days; on the contrary, it was understood that they would promote and defend each other. The king himself was the symbol of their collaboration and unity. Among the various functionaries at the shrines were two classes of prophets, called respectively *maḫḫu* and *nabiʾutum*. The latter is closely related to the terms for prophet and prophecy in the Bible (the root is the same).

Mythic materials have turned up in the tablets, including the well-known flood story, derived from Sumerian sources. In addition, there is a hymn addressed to the lord of heaven and earth, the subject of which is the creation of the world; it bears at least superficial resemblance to the first creation story in Genesis. Other texts are more obscure, but describe scenes in which the gods appear and have contact with each other.

Mention has been made of the scribal school associated with the palace and the courtyard archives. Because of the bilingual nature of the scribes' world (i.e., Sumerian and Semitic), the compilation of lists of comparable phenomena in the two languages became obligatory if not obsessional. Essential working tools, as well as an extraordinary conceptual and linguistic feat, these lists are of many different kinds, e.g., occupations, personal and place names, birds, beasts, and fishes. The geographic lists in particular have already proved invaluable in filling out the picture of the world of the ancient Near East during this period. Further analysis of the lists and especially of the relationships of the places to each other (presumably in some instances at least contiguity in the list will suggest proximity in the region as well) should enable scholars to locate many if not most of the places named with some degree of accuracy. In any case, the maps of the future for this part of the world at this time will be very different from the maps of the past.

While it is still early in the study of the tablets, some general and a few specific observations about the relationship of the tablets to the Bible (and to a lesser degree the Koran) are in order. The basic expectation that the tablets will shed light on many aspects of the Bible will certainly be fulfilled. The major addition to the existing vocabulary of West Semitic or Semitic generally is bound to be of help in elucidating the text of the Bible, especially when we consider the large number of rare and exotic words which remain to be explained. Similarly, any information about the background and setting of the biblical experience is bound to be useful and significant, though far-reaching conclusions are best avoided at this time. Of more immediate and specific value is the occurrence of the same term or name, especially of people and places. We find an extensive area of overlap between the Ebla tablets and the biblical text: among the many personal names in both the Bible and the tablets are the following: Abram, David, Esau, Ishmael, Israel, Micaiah, Michael, and Saul. We have normalized the spelling of these names to conform to the biblical pattern, but the spelling in Eblaite is so close in all cases that there can be no question of the identity of the names (in no case can we relate the persons, however). In some cases, notably that of David (which in Eblaite is spelled *da-ud-um*), the name is not known from any other source in ancient times. Such occurrences point back to a common basis in language and culture for the ancestors of the Israelites and the people at Ebla. Actually, this is no surprise, because the Bible, while not mentioning Ebla, does point to this region as the fatherland of the Israelites. The patriarchs came to Canaan from Haran, where elements of their kinship group continued to live long after Abraham and his family had departed. A bride was brought from there for Isaac, and Jacob returned to his kinsmen there when prudence called for a rapid removal from Canaan. Haran is not very far away from Ebla and is often mentioned in the Ebla texts. If an archive exists at Haran at the same level and is ever found, those tablets should contain even more specific information about the patriarchs and their forebears and have closer contacts and correlations with the Bible. As it is, Ebla draws from a common pool of terms, names, and traditions, which was also shared by the biblical people.

Place names are of great significance, especially since Ebla, being west of the Euphrates, was oriented mainly toward the west and south, and therefore its trade and other concerns overlapped heavily with the biblical territory. Many names of places in Syria and Palestine are the same as those mentioned in the Bible. Often the cities in the Ebla texts are mentioned as the receivers of shipments of goods from Ebla, or as the senders of raw materials in trade, or as the payers of tribute in precious metals (i.e., gold and silver with a ratio in value of about 1:10 in favor of gold), precious stones, or other commodities. In some cases the tablets describe the route taken by an emissary, who proceeds from one city to the next along a predetermined course. Following in his footsteps, we can locate the names geographically without question. Among the cities mentioned in the tablets are neighbors of Ebla in Syria: Aleppo, Ugarit, Hama, and Homs, and a little further south, Damascus. Moving in a westerly direction, we find very familiar names of place: among them Byblos, Sidon, Acco, Carmel, Dor, Ashdod, Gaza, Sinai. The sequence is clearly geographical in certain instances. Both Salem (cf. Gen 14:18) and Jerusalem are mentioned, indicating that they are separate cities, and not to be equated. In view of the fact that a number of the cities mentioned in the tablets were not thought to have existed in the Early Bronze Age, some reconsideration of the data seems to be in order, and perhaps some new digging at the sites or near them, because the movement of cities from one age to another is an attested phenomenon.

Most striking from the point of view of biblical studies is the occurrence of the first two of the five cities of the plain (Sodom, Gomorrah, Admah, Zeboiim, and Bela, also called Zoar in Gen 14:2) in the Ebla tablets:

Si-da-mu = Sodom
E-ma-ra = Gomorrah

It was suggested years ago by E. A. Speiser in his Anchor Bible commentary on Genesis that the narrative in Genesis 14 was based upon a cuneiform source, and in the light of the Ebla tablets that seems very likely now. In fact, it looks as though the tradition in Genesis 14 must go back to the period of the Ebla tablets or very close to it. I believe that we must project the story into pre-Sargonic times, not later than the middle of the 3rd millennium B.C. The destruction of the cities of the plain is not mentioned in the Ebla tablets; on the contrary, these are flourishing commercial centers. Only in the Bible do we have the description of their sudden and violent demise (Genesis 18-19). Since Abraham and Lot figure in both stories, it is reasonable to infer that Genesis 14 and 18-19 belong to the same time-frame, around the middle of the 3rd millennium, or somewhat later than the Ebla tablets. One possible clue to the dating of the Ebla materials in relation to the biblical tradition is to be found in a correlation of Ebla's great king, Ebrium, and an ancestor of Abraham and the Israelites whose name occurs in the genealogical lists in Genesis 10 (vv. 24-25) and Genesis 11 (vv. 14-16) as Eber. Semantically, the names are equivalent, and it is possible that Eber, who is the eponymous ancestor of the Hebrews (= ⁽ibri and ⁽ibrîm), is a reflection of the great king of the same name. Assuming that there is a connection and that the two are really the same person, we can construct a sequence of descendants of Eber leading to Abraham, in which the age of the father is given at the birth of the son. Thus, in Gen 11:16-26, we find the following:

Eber	34
Peleg	30
Reu	32
Serug	30
Nahor	29
Terah	70
Abraham	—
	225 years

That places Abraham exactly 225 years after Eber (= Ebrium?). The figures themselves are quite reasonable (except for the last), if we suppose that the son named is not necessarily the first-born (perhaps the oldest surviving, since the death rate among children was very high). In the case of Terah and Abrahaham, we seem to have an abnormally high number, and an artificial one at that. If we were to reduce the figure substantially, we would still come out with at least 175 years for the gap between Eber and Abraham (= Abram). If we go on to say that the symbolic figure of Eber is based on the real figure of Ebrium, and that whatever embellishments or modifications the transmitter of the tradition may have made, he nevertheless kept his chronology straight, the conclusion would be that if Ebrium was born around 2700 B.C. and reigned later in that century, then we should date the birth of Abraham around 2500 B.C. (perhaps as early as 2525 B.C. or as late as 2475 B.C.) and the destruction of the cities of the plain sometime during the 25th century B.C. It may be that the violent end of the cities of the plain can be associated with the historical phenomenon of the general destruction and abandonment of EB III settlements all over the area of Syria and Palestine. Whatever the correct correlation with archeological data on the one hand and historical data on the other, there is good reason to believe that Genesis 14 is based on authentic historical tradition.

In view of the evidence from Ebla and archeological excavations in the Dead Sea region, the question of the location of the cities should be reconsidered. While a number of place names appear in Genesis 14, many of them cannot be identified or located with much assurance. There are, however, two place-names that can be fixed with reasonable certainty and can provide the markers for a new search. One is the Salt Sea (= the Dead Sea) mentioned in Gen 14:3; the other is Damascus, which occurs in Gen 14:15, in connection with Abram's pursuit of the coalition of four eastern kings. The implication in the Genesis passage is that Damascus is some distance from the five cities. Between Damascus and the Dead Sea there is a great deal of distance, but at the least it might be wise to consider the eastern side of the Dead Sea rather than the southwest for the location of the cities. What remains to be done is to identify a pentapolis of Early Bronze Age cities somewhere in the vicinity of the Jordan basin, also linked with the Dead Sea. In the quest for appropriate sites, we should not neglect Bab-edh-Dhra, which is on the *lisan* or tongue of land which juts out into the Dead Sea, but from the east side. The current excavators at Bab-edh-Dhra, which was occupied for most of the Early Bronze Age, have reported that several other EB sites have been found in the vicinity of Bab-edh-Dhra, and it may be that we should look in that region (southeast quadrant of the Dead Sea littoral) for the cities of the plain.

It should be added that scholars generally have recognized that Genesis 14 is a separate unit of the book, independent of the other stories, and of the sources to which most of Genesis and the other books of the Pentateuch are assigned. Thus, Genesis 14 has never been identified with J, E, D, or P. The new evidence from Ebla tends to confirm this opinion, in the sense that the background and setting of Genesis 14 must be placed as early as the first half of the 3rd millennium, whereas the traditional sources of the Pentateuch belong to a much later date of compilation and composition. How Genesis 14 relates to the other traditions in Genesis (and we have seen that there is a correlation between Genesis 14 and some of the lists scattered in other chapters, especially Genesis 10 and 11) and especially the figure of Abram (= Abraham), who is quite different in the other narratives, remains a difficult question. At least for the present, the implication of the new finds is that we must extend the patriarchal age back into the Early Bronze Age and recognize in Abram a figure of the mid-3rd millennium B.C. Until now, most scholars have dated the patriarchs to the first half of the 2nd millennium.

In the Koran, there is a reference to three cities or communities who also suffered judgment at the hands of God (the reference to Sura 89). They are held up as an example of divine judgment in a way similar to that in which Sodom and Gomorrah have become proverbial symbols of sinful communities which suffered direct violent punishment. The three, which are to be read ᶜAd, Iram, and Thamudu, have now turned up in a slightly different form in an Ebla tablet. In the Ebla list, they are cities, probably located in Syria (it is interesting that they are linked to Damascus in Islamic tradition). Their names are slightly different, but the difference can be accounted for in a variety of ways; they are respectively: ᶜAd, Erma, and Shamutu. The first is the same; the second has a slightly different vocalization, but the consonants are the same; as to the third, in Ebla spelling, *šamutu* could also be read *thamudu* as in the Koran. It may be, however, that in the Koran the name *thamudu* intended here of the city long since lost has been assimilated to the name of the pre-Islamic Arabian tribe, which is mentioned elsewhere in the Koran. It should be noted that before the Koran and after Ebla there is no mention anywhere of these three localities.

CONCLUSION

What began as an interesting novelty, when 42 tablets were discovered at Tell Mardikh (= Ebla) in 1974, turned into an avalanche of more than

16,000 tablets in 1975. The outpouring has subsided somewhat, but still another 1,600 turned up in 1976, and there is every prospect of further discoveries in future seasons at the mound. The tablets have already revealed the existence of an ancient, complex, and sophisticated civilization dating to the mid-3rd millennium B.C. The implications of the discovery for the analysis and understanding of the early development of urban culture in the Near East and the political, social, and economic history of that period are vast but not yet precisely defined. It is safe to speak of a First Internationalism at least a millennium before the Amarna Age of the 14th century B.C., when a similar situation obtained with the discovery of the modest remains of the archive of Akhnaton the Egyptian sun-king, more than six or seven hundred years before Hammurabi and his law code, and antedating the great innovator and empire builder, Sargon of Akkad, by at least a century or two. Future excavation and examination of available materials will yield much more information, and some day a detailed picture of men grappling with the problems and possibilities of a complicated social organism and creating a new kind of urban-international culture will emerge. The main lesson is that the more deeply we probe into man's recent past (the last 5,000 years), the more modern he seems to be.

BIBLIOGRAPHY

(Compiled by M. O'Connor)

Adams, James E.
   1976   Scholars Hail Eblaite Find. *St. Louis Post-Dispatch*, 29 October 1976.
Althann, Robert, S.J.
   1978   Ugarit, Ebla, and the Old Testament. *The Bible Today*. 97: 1710-15.
Amoz, J.
   1978   Tell Mardikh, ventana abierta al tercer milenio antes de Cristo. *Mayéutica* 4: 267-75.
Andersen, F. I.
   1977   Ebla: The More We Find Out, The Less We Know. *Buried History* 13, No. 1: 6-12.
Anonymous
   1976a   15,000 Tablets in "Paleo-Canaanite." *BA* 39: 4.
   1976b   A New "Third World." *Time*, 18 October 1976.
Archi, A.
   1979   The Epigraphic Evidence from Ebla and the Old Testament. *Bib* 60: 556-66.
Baldacci, Massimo
   1979   Una probabile attestazione eblaitica dello "Spiritus Domini." *BeO* 21: 73-77.
Barstad, Hans M.
   1978   Utgravningene i Tell Mardikh/Ebla i Nordsyna. *Norsk Teologisk Tidsskrift* 1: 41-48.
Bermant, Ch., and Weitzman, M.
   1979   *Ebla: A Revelation in Archaeology*. New York: Times Books.

Biggs, Robert
1980   The Ebla Tablets: An Interim Perspective. *BA* 43: 76-88.
Cole, S. D.
1977   Polemics and Irenics. *BA* 40: 49.
Dahood, M.
1978a   Ebla, Ugarit and the Old Testament. *The Month*, August and October 1978. Translated from *La Civiltà Cattolica*, May and June 1978.
1978b   Ebla, Ugarit and the Old Testament. *Congress Volume, Göttingen, 1977. VT* Sup 29: 81-112.
Freedman, D. N.
1977a   A City Beneath the Sands. *Science Year, The World Book Science Annual: A Review of Science and Technology During the 1977 School Year*, eds. Arthur G. Tressler, *et al.* Chicago: Field Enterprises Educational Corporation.
1977b   A Letter to the Readers. *BA* 40: 2-4.
1977c   Ebla is a Four-Letter Word. *LSA Magazine*. The University of Michigan, Spring, 1977.
1978   The Real Story of the Ebla Tablets: Ebla and the Cities of the Plain. *BA* 41: 143-64.
1979   Ebla. P. 198 in *New Catholic Encyclopedia Vol. 17 Supplement*. Washington: McGraw-Hill.
Freedman, Nedezhda
1977   The Nuzi Ebla. *BA* 40: 32-33, 44.
Fronzaroli, P.
1977   West Semitic Toponymy in Northern Syria in the Third Millennium B.C. *JSS* 22: 145-66.
Garbini G.
1978   La lingua di Ebla. *La parola del passato* 33: 241-59.
Gaster, L. M.
1977   American Institute of Archaeology Report. *BA* 40:8-10.
Gelb, I. J.
1977   Thoughts about Ibla: A Preliminary Evaluation, March 1977. *Syro-Mesopotamian Studies*, 1, No. 1 (May): 3-30.
Gilbert, Glenn
1976   Syrian Finds Excite U-M Man. *Ann Arbor News*, 14 June 1976.
Gordon, C. H.
1977a   Poetic Legends and Myths from Ugarit. *Berytus* 25: 5-133.
1977b   Where is Abraham's Ur? *Biblical Archaeology Review* 3, No. 2: 20-21, 52.
LaFay, Howard
1978   Ebla: Splendor of an Unknown Empire. *National Geographic* 154: 730-59.
McCarthy, D. J.
1979   Ebla, *horkia temnein, ṭb šlm*: Addenda to *Treaty and Covenant*². *Bib* 60: 247-53.
McIntire, Carl
1977   *The Tell-Mardikh Tablets*. Collingswood, N.J.: Twentieth Century Reformation Hour (with newspaper reprints).
Magri, Edward
1977   *Ebla Finds Evaluated*. Ann Arbor News, 9 October 1977.
de Maigret, A.
1974   Tell Munbatah. Un nuovo sito nordsiriano del periodo calciforme. *OrAnt* 13: 249-98.
1976   Due punte di lancia iscritte da Tell Mardikh-Ebla. *RSO* 50: 31-41.
Maloney, Paul C.
1978   Assessing Ebla. *Biblical Archaeology Review* 4, No. 1: 4-10.
Mander, P.
1979   Presenza di scongiuri én-é-nu-ru ad Ebla. *Or* 48: 335-39.

Margalit, O.
1978   Was Ebla the Land of the Hebrews? *Beth Mikra* 23: 183-88 (Hebrew).
Matthaie, P.
1965-66 Le sculture di Tell Mardikh. *Rendiconti della Pontifica Accademia Romana di Archeologia* 38: 19-59.
1967   Les fouilles à Tell Mardikh de la Mission Archéologique en Syrie de l'Université de Rome. *RSO* 42: 19-26.
1969   Empreintes d'un cylindre paléosyrien de Tell Mardikh. *Syria* 46: 1-43.
1971   Tell Mardikh. Excavations in the Campaigns of 1967 and 1968. *Archaeology* 24: 55-61.
1974a   Tell Mardikh. Origin et développement de la grande culture urbaine de la Syrie du Nord à l'époque des royaumes amorrhéens. *Archeologia* 69: 16-31.
1974b   A Fragment of a "Second Transition Period" Statuette from Tell Mardikh. *Baghdader Mitteilungen* 7: 125-37.
1975   Ebla nel periods delle dinastie amorree e della dinastia di Akkad. Scopate archeologiche recenti a Tell Mardikh. *Or* 44: 337-60.
1976a   Il Palazzo Reale G di Ebla del Periodo Protosiriano IIA e l'architettura palatina del Vicino Oriente nel III millennio a C. *Atti del Primo Convegno Italiano de Studi sul Vicino Oriente antico.* Rome.
1976b   Ibla (Ebla) B. Archäologisch. *RLA* 4: 13-20.
1976c   Ebla in the Late Early Syrian Period: The Royal Palace and the State Archives. *BA* 39: 94-113.
1976d   Ebla à l'époque d'Akkad: archéologie et histoire. *CRAIBL* 190-215.
1976e   La scoperta del Palazzo Reale G e degli Archivi di stato di Ebla (c. 2400-2250 a C.). *La parola del passato* 168: 233-66.
1976f   La biblioteca reale di Ebla (2400-2250 av. Cr.): risultati della Missione Archeologica Italiana in Siria, 1975. *Rendiconti della Pontificia Accademia Romana di Archeologia* 48: 19-45.
1976g   Aspetti amministrativi e topografici di Ebla nel III millennio a. C. B. Considerazioni archeologiche. *RSO* 50: 1-30.
1977a   *Ebla, un impero ritrovato.* Turin: Giulio Einaudi = Matthiae 1980.
1977b   Le palais royal et les archives d'état d'Ebla protosyrienne. *Akkadica* 2: 2-19.
1977c   Tell Mardikh: The Archives and Palace. *Archaeology* 30: 244-53.
1977d   Le palais royal protosyrien d'Ebla: Nouvelles recherches archéologiques à Tell Mardikh en 1976. *CRAIBL* 148-72.
1978a   The Excavations at Tell Mardikh-Ebla and Their Historical Value. *Annali di Ebla* 1: 19-30 = Matthiae 1978b.
1978b   Gli scavi di Tell Mardikh-Ebla e il loro valore storico. *Annali di Ebla* 1: 3-14 = Matthiae 1978a.
1978c   Tell Mardikh: Ancient Ebla. *AJA* 32: 540-43.
1978d   Recherches archéologiques à Ebla, 1977: le quartier administratif du Palais Royal G. *CRAIBL* 204-36.
1978e   Preliminary Remarks on the Royal Palace of Ebla. *Syro-Mesopotamian Studies* 2: 13-40.
1980   *Ebla: An Empire Rediscovered.* Trans. Christopher Holme. Garden City, NY: Doubleday = Matthiae 1977a.
Matthiae, P., and Pettinato, G.
1972   *Il torso de Ibbit-Lim, re di Ebla.* Rome: Universita di Roma.
Matthiae, P., *et al.*
1966   *Tell Mardikh 1965. Missione Archeologica Italiana in Siria.* Rome: Istituto per Vicino Oriente.
Mazzoni, S.
1975   Tell Mardikh e una classe glittica siroanatolica del periodo Larsa. *AION* 25: 81-103.

Mikaya, A.
1978   The Politics of Ebla. *Biblical Archaeology Review* 4, No. 3: 2-6.
Millard, A. R.
1977   Les découvertes d'Ebla et l'Ancien Testament. *Hokhma* (Lausanne) 6: 55-61.
Myers, A.
1977   Rivals to the Dead Sea Scrolls. *Michigan Christian Advocate*, 6 January 1977.
Ogilvy, A.
1976   Interview: Paolo Matthiae and Gabriela Matthiae Scandone. *BA* 39: 90-93.
Pettinato, G.
1975   Testi cuneiformi del 3. millennio in paleo-cananeo rinvenuti nella campagna 1974 a Tell Mardikh = Ebla. *Or* 44: 361-74.
1976a   Ibla (Ebla) A. Philologisch. *RLA* 5: 9-13.
1976b   Il calendario di Ebla al tempo del re Ibbi-Sipiš sulla base di TM 75. G. 427. *AfO* 25: 1-36.
1976c   The Royal Archives of Tell-Mardikh-Ebla. *BA* 39: 44-52.
1976d   Carchemish = Kār-Kamiš, le prime attestazioni del III millennio. *OrAnt* 15: 11-15.
1976e   ED LU E ad Ibla, la riconstruzione delle prime 68 righe sulla base di TM. 75. G. 1488. *OrAnt* 15: 169-78.
1976f   I testi cuneiformi della biblioteca reale di Tell Mardikh-Ebla. Notizia preliminare sulla scuole di Ebla. *Rendiconti della Pontificia Accademia Romana di Archeologia* 48: 47-57.
1976g   Aspetti amministrativi e topografici di Ebla nel III millennio av. C. A. Documentazione Epigrafica. *RSO* 50:1-15.
1977a   Relations entre les royaumes d'Ebla et de Mari du troisième millenaire d'après les archives royales de Tell Mardikh-Ebla. *Akkadica* 2: 20-28.
1977b   Il calendario semitico del 3. millennio ricostruito sulla base dei testi di Ebla. *OrAnt* 16: 257-85.
1977c   Gli archivi reala di Tell Mardikh-Ebla: reflessioni e prospettive. *Rivista biblica italiana* 25: 225-43.
1978a   Liste presargoniche di uccelli nella documentazione di Fara ad Ebla. *OrAnt* 17: 165-78.
1978b   L'Atlante geografico del Vicino Oriente antico attestato ad Ebla e ad Abū Ṣalābīkh I. *Or* 47: 50-73.
1979a   *Catalogo dei testi cuneiformi di Tell Mardikh-Ebla.* (Materiali epigrafici di Ebla 1.) Naples: Istituto Universitario Orientale di Napoli.
1979b   *Ebla: Un impero inciso nell'argilla.* Milan: Mondadori.
1979c   Il commercio internazionale di Ebla. Economia Statale e privata. *State and Temple Economy in the Ancient Near East*, ed. E. Lipiński. Louvain: Gembloux.
Pettinato, G., with Mander, P.
1979   *Culto ufficiale ad Ebla durante il regno di Ibbi-Sipiš.* Orientis Antiqui Collectio 16. Rome: Istituto per l'Oriente = *OrAnt* 18: 85-132.
Pugh, J.
1978   Excitement Grows over Translations of Ebla Tablets. *St. Petersburg Times*, 11 February 1978.
Rainey, A. F.
1977   Queries? and Comments! *Biblical Archaeology Review* 3, No. 1: 38.
Sarna, N. M.
1977   Abraham in History. *Biblical Archaeology Review* 3, No. 4: 5-9.
Shanks, H.
1976a   Ancient Royal Library Found. *Biblical Archaeology Review* 2, No. 2: 25.
1976b   The Ebla Tablets. *Biblical Archaeology Review* 2, No. 3: 36.
1976c   The Promise of Ebla. *Biblical Archaeology Review* 2, No. 4: 32.
1979a   Syria Tries to Influence Ebla Scholarship. *Biblical Archaeology Review* 5, No. 2: 36-50.

1979b   Syrian Ambassador to U.S. Asks BAR to Print Ebla Letter Rejected by New York Times. *Biblical Archaeology Review* 5, No. 4: 15-17.

1979c   Ebla Evidence Evaporates. *Biblical Archaeology Review* 5, No. 6: 52-53.

Ska, J.-L., S.J.

1978   Les découvertes de Tell-Mardikh-Ebla et la Bible. *Nouvelle Revue Théologique* 100: 389-98.

Ullendorff, E.

1978   On Gelb 1977. *JSS* 23: 151-54.

Vacchi, L.

1975   Before the Bible. *Panorama*, 11 December 1975 (Italian).

Veenhof, K. R.

1978   Tell-Mardikh-Ebla. Het oudste Syrie en het Oude Testament. *Nederlands Theologisch Tijdschrift* 32: 1-11.

Vitkus, S. N.

1976   Sargon Unseated. *BA* 39: 114-17.

Weldon, A.

1978   Ebla's Cuneiform Tablets. *St. Petersburg Independent*, 11 February 1978.

Medicine in the Land and Times of the Old Testament

J. V. KINNIER WILSON

University of Cambridge, England

In deliberating upon the style and content of this address, I have allowed myself both a geographical choice and a choice of method. For on the one hand, as one thinks about method, there is the problem of deciding how much, out of a vast array of material, can be included in a statement of this kind. On the other hand, as one thinks about geography, there is the problem that "Medicine in the Land and Times of the Old Testament" is, by this very definition, a subject far-reaching in both time and space.

The conclusion I have come to is that I might usefully attempt to provide a comparative survey of what the ancient Near East contributes to the history of medicine, concentrating particularly on recent advances in knowledge and yet relating this throughout to the major findings of the past. Necessarily one must be quite selective in presenting a survey of such a kind.

But, as to the geographical choice I have not compromised. The phrase "the land and times of the Old Testament" may suitably be interpreted in terms of Egypt, Mesopotamia, and Syria-Palestine itself, and the statement is therefore divided into three parts so that something may be said medically about each of the three areas. I shall not, of course, pretend that I am equally qualified to speak on the medicine and diseases of all of these countries; but to some degree I have researched in them all, and in bringing them together here I believe we may discover something of importance from the comparison itself—we may discover that medically, as in other respects, Egypt, Mesopotamia, and Palestine were three quite different worlds. Each developed along independent lines of thought and was of its own kind.

I EGYPT

Almost every study on Egyptian medicine gives some place to the vizier Imhotep, who lived in the times of the IIIrd Dynasty. His name became a legend in Egyptian medicine, and museums in many countries have examples of the bronze statuettes which were made of him in the later periods.[1]

---

[1]The most scholarly study is undoubtedly by D. Wildung, *Imhotep und Amenhotep:*

In general, however, medicine in Egypt was in the hands of two kinds of doctors. There was the *heri-ha'ab* (written *ḥry-ḥꜣb*), and the *seynu* (written *synw*). The first of these means "carrier of the ritual book," by which is meant the book of magic or incantation, by means of which diseases might be countered magically. As such, and as recently pointed out by Elmar Edel,[2] the *heri-ha'ab* was the equivalent of the Akkadian *āšipu*, the "exorcist" or "incantation-priest."[3] The *seynu*, on the other hand, was the practical physician or surgeon, and still today the Coptic *seyn* is the normal word for "doctor." He corresponds very largely to the Akkadian *asû*, usually translated "physician." As to their books, two in particular are well known and will require no introduction in this account.

There is firstly the Papyrus Ebers, the most important and impressive of all the medical papyri, published in a superb edition in 1875.[4] It is over 20 meters long and consists of 110 columns of writing which have been divided into 877 sections. From a short calendar written on the reverse of the papyrus, it can be dated to about 1550 B.C., but is based on much earlier originals.

The text is almost entirely a collection of prescriptions for bodily ailments. Treatments[5] involving pills, powders, liquid medicines, ointments, and suppositories were all prescribed. The drugs, as one might expect, were commonly of vegetable origin, but animals, reptiles, birds, and even fish were used, as well as certain mineral substances such as verdigris and sulphur. Commonly a number of prescriptions were offered for the treatment of a single illness. This may be seen, for instance, in the column of text reproduced on Plate 1. In that text the word which stands alone in lines 3, 10, and 18 means "another (remedy)," and thus the three prescriptions which follow are part of a series begun on an earlier column. In each case the drugs are listed in black ink on the right of the column, and the measures, or fractions, are placed opposite them in red ink on the left. There then follows a short instruction on the preparation and application of the remedy.

One principle of treatment is known, namely, that many diseases were thought to be caused by superfluous food remaining in the body. As a

---

Gottwerdung im alten Ägypten (Münchner ägyptologische Studien 36, 1977). Cf. also the same writer's article, "Imhotep," *LÄ* 3 (1977) 145-48.

[2] *Ägyptische Ärzte und ägyptische Medizin am hethitischen Königshof* (Göttingen, 1976) 55-56 and 61.

[3] Cf. further below in Section 2.

[4] The full title is *Papyrus Ebers: das hermetische Buch über die Arzeneimittel der alten Ägypter in hieratischer Schrift*, herausgegeben ... von Georg Ebers. It was published in Leipzig in two volumes.

[5] A standard source is still W. R. Dawson, *Magician and Leech: a Study in the Beginnings of Medicine, with Special Reference to Ancient Egypt* (London, 1929), Ch. 7: "Drugs and Doses." Of more recent date is P. Ghalioungui, *Magic and Medical Science in Ancient Egypt* (London, 1963), Ch. 9: "*Materia Medica* and Dispensing."

Pl. 1.

A column of text from the Ebers Papyrus reproduced from the edition by Dr. Georg Ebers, published in Leipzig in 1875.

result, "quite excessive reliance was placed upon emetics, purges and enemas."[6] Among the diseases which are mentioned, the Eg. $ḥf^3.t$ and pnd may be identified as round worm and tapeworm infection,[7] and trachoma ($nḥ^3.t$) has been recognized among the serious eye diseases.[8] Prominent also is a known urinary condition which is written with the letters ^cayin, ^aleph and ^cayin ($^c\exists^c$) and which has understandably, if not altogether scientifically, been called the "Aaa-disease." It has long been accepted as referring to Bilharzia.[9]

The second of the important texts is the Edwin Smith Surgical Papyrus, published by James Henry Breasted in 1930.[10] This was a most accomplished edition, with full text, translation, and commentary, and in Volume I of his *History of Medicine*, Henry Sigerist took almost half a page to record the immediate medical and scholarly reaction to the appearance of this unique manuscript.[11]

As to its content, the papyrus is almost exclusively concerned with what has been called "wound surgery." The procedures are described for treating wounds and injuries of many kinds, including fractures. If a wound could be treated, then the immediate action often involved stitching. This was so, for example, in Case No. 26, which is one of these shown on Plate 2, which reproduces Column IX of the papyrus. It advocates stitching in the case of a bad wound in the upper lip of an injured person.

The manuscript is not complete. After describing the procedures to be adopted in some 48 cases which begin at the head and continue systematically downwards towards the lower part of the back, the text suddenly breaks off, actually in the middle of a sentence.

---

[6]J. R. Harris, ed., *The Legacy of Egypt* (2nd ed.; Oxford, 1971) 128. The basis for this conclusion are statements made by Herodotus and Diodorus.

[7]So according to E. Ebbell, *Altägyptische Bezeichnungen für Krankheiten und Symptome* (Oslo, 1938) 34; cf. von Deines and Westendorf, *Wörterbuch der medizinischen Texte* 2 (Berlin, 1961-62) 594f. and ibid. 1, 267, respectively.

[8]Ebbell, *Bezeichnungen*, 26-27, accepted by von Deines and Westendorf, *Wörterbuch*, 472. The argument is that the term in question, a known eye disease, means literally "Rauheit" or "Unebenheit" and will refer to the follicles or granulations which occur characteristically in trachoma (this word itself being a derivative from the Gk. τραχύς, "rough").

[9]In a "Note on the presence of 'Bilharzia haematobia' in Egyptian mummies of the Twentieth Dynasty," *British Medical Journal* (1910/1) 16, M. A. Ruffer reported on the discovery of calcified eggs of *Bilharzia haematobia* in a microscopic section of the kidneys of two XXth Dynasty mummies, some of whose organs he had been able to examine. The existence of Bilharzia in ancient Egypt has never since been in doubt. For the latest statement with all intervening references, cf. A. T. Sandison, *LÄ* 1 (1975) 813.

[10]The work appeared in the University of Chicago OIP series, Vols. 3 and 4.

[11]H. Sigerist, *History of Medicine* 1 (Oxford, 1951) 360, n. 17. Sigerist's own description will be found on pp. 303-11.

Pl. 2.

Column IX of the Edwin Smith Surgical Papyrus, reproduced from the edition of James Henry Breasted (Chicago, 1930). (Courtesy, The Oriental Institute, Chicago).

The Egyptian Medical Papyri

Name	Dynasty	Subject-matter
1 The Ebers Papyrus	XVIII	General
2 The Edwin Smith Papyrus	XVIII	Injuries and wounds
3 The Ramesseum Papyri III, IV, and V	XII/XIII	III Miscellaneous IV Pregnacy and birth V Muscular complaints
4 The Kahun Papyrus	XII	Gynecology
5 The Hearst Papyrus	XVIII	Similar to the Ebers Papyrus
6 The Chester-Beatty Papyri	XX	Medico-magical recipes
7 The Berlin Medical Papyrus	XIX	Similar to the Ebers and Hearst Papyri
8 The London Medical Papyrus	XVIII	Medico-magical recipes
9 The Carlsberg Papyrus	XVIII	A fragment. Eyes; birth prognoses
10 Collections of Magical Papyri	Various	Magical prescriptions
11 The Brooklyn Papyrus	Late	(Not yet published)
12 Coptic and Greek Papyri	Late	Various

Fig. 1

At this point attention may be drawn to the table of Egyptian Medical Papyri, which is set out at Fig. 1.[12] To the nonspecialist the table may give some impression of how extensive the medical textual material really is. It lists the Ramesseum Papyri, which are so-called because they were found beneath the foundations of the great mortuary temple of Ramesses II. These are among the oldest known medical papyri.[13] The Kahun Papyrus was discovered in 1889; the importance of the document lies in the attempt that it made to systematize diseases of women and matters relating to pregnancy.[14] To select one further category, it will be noticed that items 6, 8, and 10 contain a strong magical element. This also had its place in the treatment of disease.[15]

---

[12]The table owes much to W. R. Dawson, "The Egyptian Medical Papyri," first published in *Science, Medicine and History: Essays on the Evolution of Scientific Thought and Medical Practice, Written in Honour of Charles Singer* 1 (Oxford, 1953) 47-60. The study has been republished in D. Brothwell and A. T. Sandison, eds., *Diseases in Antiquity* (Springfield, Ill., 1967), Ch. 7.

[13]For more detailed discussion, cf. J. W. B. Barns, *Five Ramesseum Papyri* (Oxford, 1956) nos. III to V.

[14]For further discussion cf., *int. al.*, P. Ghalioungui, *Magic and Medical Science*, 118-20 (section on Gynaecology).

[15]In general on this subject, reference may be made to the article "Krankheitsabwehr" by I. E. S. Edwards, *LÄ* 3 (1979) 759-62. There is an extensive bibliography.

It will be realized that it is the list *as a whole* which is important for the purpose of this survey, and its witness to the richness of the Egyptian medical sources. To emphasize their contribution, it should be said that numerous aspects of these sources have been examined, amongst others, by Hermann Grapow, Hildegard von Deines, and Wolfhart Westendorf, in a basic series "Grundriss der Medizin der alten Ägypter" (Berlin, 1954-1973). It will long remain an indispensable source of knowledge on the meaning and interpretation of the texts.

From texts we pass to mummies, and also to "palaeopathology," that is, the study of disease in ancient human remains. The term palaeopathology was in fact introduced by Sir Marc Ruffer, one of the great names in Egyptian medicine. His collected papers under the title *Studies in the Palaeopathology of Egypt* (Chicago, 1921) were published shortly after his death in 1917.

Mummies have actually been studied medically since 1820,[16] but the name that is most associated with early work is that of Sir Grafton Elliot Smith, sometime Professor of Anatomy at Cairo. He is said to have examined over 25,000 skeletons, skulls, and mummies brought to light by archaeologists in Egypt and Nubia, and his study on *The Royal Mummies*, published in 1912, is still a standard work of reference.

In more recent years a valuable aid to palaeopathology has been found in radiology. The first mummy was X-rayed in Cairo in 1904.[17] Since then mummies in the collections of the Field Museum at Chicago and of the British Museum in London have been radiographed. In 1966 a team of specialists from the University of Michigan began re-studying the mummies in the Cairo Museum, and *X-Raying the Pharaohs* (London, 1973) by James Harris and Kent Weeks gives an account of their work. Mummies belonging to Manchester University have also been recently investigated by a research team under Dr. Rosalie David.[18]

A few examples may now serve to show the importance of this work in historical medical studies. Thus, the probable existence of smallpox in ancient Egypt was communicated by Ruffer and Ferguson in a study entitled "An Eruption Resembling That of Variola in the Skin of a Mummy of the Twentieth Dynasty."[19] Both the form of the eruption and the general distribution of the spots made the case for the diagnosis, and when the Michigan Expedition re-examined the mummy towards the end of the

---

[16]W. R. Dawson, in his Foreward to *Diseases in Antiquity*, viii.

[17]Dawson, ibid., ix. The mummy was in fact that of the Pharaoh Tuthmose IV (XVIIIth Dynasty).

[18]Cf. further below.

[19]*Journal of Pathology and Bacteriology* 15 (1911) 1ff., reprinted in *Diseases in Antiquity*, Ch. 25.

1960s no alternative diagnosis could be suggested.[20] By the time of the latter examination the mummy in question had been determined as that of the Pharaoh Ramesses V.

More commonly, the evidence for ancient disease derives from bones. In this category we may first include the congenital club-foot, or *talipes equinus*, of the Pharaoh Merneptah-Siptah of the XIXth Dynasty, as illustrated in Elliot Smith's catalogue of the royal mummies at Cairo, published in 1912.[21]

The necropolis at Gizeh has also produced an extraordinary early example of a large tumor of the thigh bone. The bone is reproduced in Plate 3 from an original photograph in *Egyptian Mummies* by Elliot Smith and Warren Dawson, published in 1924.[22]

And something in particular must be said about tuberculosis, especially tuberculosis of the spine, or "Pott's disease." Tuberculosis of both the spine and the lungs was known to Hippocrates and was described in his *Epidemics*, Book I.[23] As "the wasting disease" it is likely to have been the *šaḥepet* (שחפת) of Lev 26:16 and Deut 28:22.

What happens, so far as the spinal condition is concerned, is that the disease destroys the calcium in the vertebrae; the spine accordingly becomes weak, and in serious cases it can no longer support the weight of the body. A characteristic "angular deformity" then develops, causing the back to become very rounded and the neck also to be bent forwards. It is this angular deformity in specimens of vertebrae which makes the case for the identification, and numerous examples of it have now been found, notably from graves in Nubia.[24]

Moreover, the matter is even capable of proof, and in this connection attention may be drawn to Plate 4, which reproduces two views of the mummy of a priest of Amen of the XXIst Dynasty. The original illustration may be found in the already cited Smith and Dawson volume on

---

[20] See J. E. Harris and K. R. Weeks, *X-Raying the Pharaohs* (London, 1973) 166.

[21] The reference is to pl. LXII of G. E. Smith, *The Royal Mummies*, Catalogue du Musée du Caire. The condition has been thought by some authorities to be that of poliomyelitis, on which cf. further below.

[22] The reference is to fig. 64 of *Egyptian Mummies*, and there is a brief description of the bone, thought to be of Vth Dynasty date, on p. 157.

[23] Two standard sources are R. H. Major, *Classical Descriptions of Disease* (Springfield, Ill., 1945) 52-53, and J. Chadwick and W. N. Mann, *The Medical Works of Hippocrates* (Oxford, 1950) 30-31. According to Morse (cf. n. 24) many other Classical writers refer also to the disease.

[24] Cf. D. Morse, "Tuberculosis," Brothwell and Sandison, *Diseases in Antiquity*, Ch. 19 with fig. 6. In addition, the chapter ably summarises and evaluates the secondary evidence for spinal tuberculosis deriving from statuettes and certain other representations of the human figure found in Egypt.

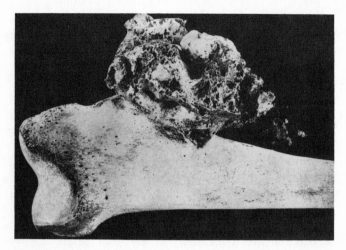

Pl. 3.

A large tumor of the thigh-bone from the Necropolis at Gizeh, Vth Dynasty. Reproduced from Elliot Smith and Warren Dawson, *Egyptian Mummies*, fig. 64.

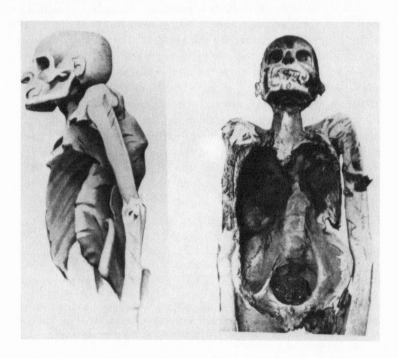

Pl. 4.

Mummy (right) and sketch of a priest of Amen of the XXIst Dynasty showing evidence of spinal tuberculosis or Pott's disease. Reproduced from Elliot Smith and Warren Dawson, *Egyptian Mummies*, fig. 62.

Egyptian Mummies[25] and it is well known. To describe it, one notices on the right, in the center of the mummy, that the spinal column has been partly destroyed. A large abscess is also located in the upper pelvic region, on the left-hand side as the body is viewed from the front, and an abscess of this kind occurs typically with tuberculosis. The illustration on the left is a drawing, but shows again that angular deformity of the spine which, as we have seen, is altogether typical of Pott's disease.

As to the X-ray side of palaeopathology, there is much that is of interest in Dr. David's *Mysteries of the Mummies* (London, 1978), and this study is of additional importance in that it provides much information on the equipment and technology now available to the modern radiologist. However, it was unexpected that radiographs of the principal mummy of the investigation, thought to have been that of a young girl aged 13 or 14, should reveal that the two legs had been respectively broken through the thigh bone and the shin bone, and that the bone below the breaks was altogether missing.[26] The book discusses the various theories which might account for this finding,[27] which clearly belongs to the history of injury.[28]

In general it may be emphasized that medicine is not the only interest in the radiological examination of mummies, but it has provided much information on teeth and dentistry,[29] and at least one parasite, a calcified guinea-worm, was first detected by this means.[30] There may, however, be a case for caution in connection with some aspects of X-ray diagnosis.

I refer to the plate on page 34 of the Harris and Weeks study on *X-Raying the Pharaohs*. The plate in question shows a chest X-ray of Meryet-Amon, the wife and sister of Amenhotep I, and the authors state that it "reveals arthritis and scoliosis (abnormal curvature of the spine)— ailments also known to modern man." However, I have discussed the matter with a radiologist of my acquaintance at Addenbrooke's Hospital in Cambridge, and his opinion was that the apparent curvature of the spine may simply have been a matter of posture, and due only to the way that the body happened to be lying when it was X-rayed.

---

[25]Fig. 62.

[26]For the full account cf. pp. 91-92 with the illustrations presented on pp. 125-26.

[27]Pp. 97 and 99.

[28]Principally it was thought that the girl might either have suffered a fatal accident from falling masonry or the like, or else—since there appeared to be some evidence that the body, before mummification, may have lain for a time in water (and conceivably the River Nile)— that crocodiles might have removed the missing limbs.

[29]Cf. particularly Harris and Weeks, *X-Raying the Pharaohs*, 62-66 and *passim* elsewhere, the whole project having been undertaken under the direction of the University of Michigan's School of Dentistry. Information on the ages at which various pharaohs died has also been obtained from this work.

[30]Cf. David, *Mysteries*, 91 and 124.

Moreover, the presumed arthritis is also questionable. The evidence for it shows up on X-rays as a whitening of the discs between the vertebrae. But, this whitening—which in fact indicates calcification—has now been reported in the X-rays of mummies on a scale which enormously exceeds the present day frequency for arthritis. There is an important chapter by Dr. P. H. K. Gray in Brothwell and Sandison's *Diseases in Antiquity* on precisely this point.[31] It would, therefore, be wise if we were to wait until the problem is better understood. It still seems uncertain whether anything in the embalming process is implicated and might explain the phenomenon.[32]

This brief statement on medicine and disease in ancient Egypt requires a short appendix. The funerary stele of the priest Ruma of the XVIIIth Dynasty, now in the Carlsberg Glyptothek at Copenhagen, has been often reproduced in medical studies.[33] The priest is shown with a long staff held under the left arm—evidently to assist forward movement or to support the body when at rest—and, as in the case of the Pharaoh Siptah, there is a marked condition of *talipes equinus* with associated muscular wasting in the right leg. The condition *may* have been that of poliomyelitis, as some authorities declare. However, my understanding is that the paralysis may equally have been of congenital origin, in which case one must leave the matter open.[34]

II MESOPOTAMIA

We may now turn to Mesopotamia, that is, to Sumer and the later Babylonia and Assyria. Mesopotamia has left no visual record of her doctors, but the impression of a Sumerian cylinder seal (cf. Plate 5 [a]) from the collection of the Louvre in Paris, may in some part serve instead. The text informs us that the seal belonged to a certain Ur-lugal-edinna, who was a physician (*azu*). He is represented on the seal by his forceps, together with other symbols which, however, are of gods and not medical. In fact, the scene is probably an "introduction," with the two maces representing a seated deity[35] and the third symbol of the series representing the "introducer" (also a deity). The standing figure will have been an

---

[31]The study is entitled "Calcinosis intervertebralis, with special reference to similar changes found in mummies of Ancient Egyptians," and it is published on pp. 20-30 of the volume cited.

[32]Gray, "Calcinosis intervertebralis," 25-28.

[33]For a basic source cf. M. Mogensen, *La Glyptothèque Ny Carlsberg: la collection égyptienne* (Copenhagen, 1930), pl. CVII, with discussion, p. 99, under 'A 724.'

[34]Cf. amongst others H. Sigerist, *History of Medicine*, 64, and S. A. Kinnier Wilson, *Neurology* (2nd ed.; London, 1954) 246.

[35]Probably or possibly of a Nergal type, if the arguments which I put forward in *The Rebel Lands* (Cambridge, 1979) 50, may be considered relevant.

Pl. 5.

(a) Seal of the Sumerian physician Ur-lugal-edinna, who is evidently represented on the seal by his forceps in what is probably an "introduction" scene. (Courtesy, Musée du Louvre).

(b) A *lamashtu* amulet from Nippur, illustrating the "folk-medicine" of the times. Originally published in Brothwell and Sandison, eds., *Diseases in Antiquity* (1967) 195.

attendant deity who is probably portrayed in the act of blessing the physician.

The seal is Sumerian, and in Sumerian times—as it would seem—the *azu* was the only doctor who was prominent in society. It is only at a later period, in Babylonia, that one meets the *āšipu*, a specialist in incantations and a kind of medical "diviner," capable of reading the "signs" of suffering or of divine punishment. In using the term "punishment," we may recognize a link with the Old Testament, but the matter became more involved in Babylonia because of its many gods. Many names of diseases in fact incorporated the name of a god, as *qāt Ištar*, "the disease of Ishtar," or *qāt Šamaš*, "the disease of Shamash,"[36] Some diseases were also named after demons, and there was a *qāt eṭimmi*, or "the disease of the ghosts."[37]

In general, there was probably much superstition and much ignorance, and, as one might expect under such conditions, "folk-medicine" also flourished among the people. The amulet shown on Plate 5 (b) may tell something of the folk-medicine of the day. It was first published in my chapter on "Organic diseases of ancient Mesopotamia" in the Brothwell-Sandison volume on *Diseases in Antiquity*, and is now in the Royal Ontario Museum in Toronto.[38] It depicts the demoness Lamashtu surrounded by several animals of the lower orders, including (lower right) the *ascaris*(?), one of the intestinal worms of Iraq and of many tropical countries.

Additionally, the amulet seems also to have proteced from scorpion sting and snake-bite. The snake is the "triangle and tail" which is shown to the right center of the field, and it almost certainly denotes the viper[39] which has a flat triangular head. The small animal beneath it, half turning, as it would seem, towards the snake, I am tempted to think may be a representation of the mongoose—the Akkadian *šikkû*, after Landsberger's identification.[40] Their bones have been found in several Babylonian houses, where they were evidently kept as pets.

It could be mentioned that some limestone jewelry molds have been found which suggest that small Lamashtu amulets of probably beaten copper might sometimes be worn around the neck.[41] The stone amulet

---

[36]In fact Akk. *qātu*, lit. "hand," may be thought to express the idea of both "disease" and "punishment" in such contexts. Particularly relevant is *Ludlul bēl nēmeqi* III 1, where the Righteous Suffer declares: *kab-ta-at qāt-su ul a-le-'-i na-šá-šá*, "So heavy was (Marduk's) 'hand' upon me that I could not bear it."

[37]Previously translated "hand of a ghost," but since all other names of the type are particular and not general, we prefer to give the grammmatically singular *eṭimmu* a plural meaning (like *ilu* as "the gods").

[38]The amulet was bought locally from a dealer by late Prof. Th. J. Meek of the University of Toronto, and is thought therefore to have come from Nippur in southern Babylonia. It is probably datable to the first millennium B.C.

[39]*Cerastes cornutus*, sometimes known as the "horned viper."

[40]B. Landsberger, *Die Fauna des alten Mesopotamien* (Leipzig, 1934) 110-11.

[41]Details of the British Museum collection may be found in *A Guide to the Babylonian and Assyrian Antiquities* (3rd ed.; London, 1922) 188-89.

discussed above would probably have been hung up at the entrance of a house.

But, it is time to turn to the scribes. The medical texts were of many kinds, but in the first place there necessarily belongs that large compendium of tablets, concerned with physical diseases of all kinds, whose ancient name is still unknown and which is referred to simply as "The Assyrian Medical Texts." A small section of this material was assembled and published by Friedrich Küchler in 1904,[42] but in the 1920s the matter was taken up anew by R. Campbell Thompson of Merton College, Oxford, and several important books[43] and some fourteen basic medical studies[44] resulted from his work. At the present time the extensive Assur material, in some part begun by E. Ebeling in his *KAR* volumes,[45] is being systematically copied and published by Franz Köcher.[46]

Most probably the compendium was a combined *asû* and *āšipu* series.[47] It was put together from a number of different sources in the late Old Babylonian period,[48] and included both prescriptions and incantations. As with the Papyrus Ebers, numerous plant and animal products, and some minerals, were used in the prescriptions. These were to be dried and pounded or the like, and then usually mixed with a liquid such as beer, honey, oil or milk, before application. In most cases we are largely ignorant of the principles which were at work in the formulation of the different treatments, but occasionally, when only one plant or drug is prescribed, a medical principle may indeed be involved. Long ago Campbell Thompson noted the sensible use of sulphur for certain skin diseases;[49] I have also noted the interesting use of Solanum berries, which have antispasmodic properties, in cases of difficult childbirth.[50]

It could be mentioned that the earliest medical text so far known is written in Sumerian, and has been published by Miguel Civil in *RA* 54

---

[42] *Beiträge zur Kenntnis der assyrisch-babylonischen Medizin* (Leipzig).

[43] *Assyrian Medical Texts* (1923), *The Assyrian Herbal* (1924), and *On the Chemistry of the Ancient Assyrians* (1925) appeared first; the latter two developed eventually into *A Dictionary of Assyrian Botany* (London, 1949), and *A Dictionary of Assyrian Chemistry and Geology* (Oxford, 1936).

[44] These appeared in *The Proceedings of the Royal Society of Medicine, JRAS, RA, AJSL, AfO* (one), and *Babyloniaca* (one), between the years 1924 and 1937.

[45] That is, *Keilschrifttexte aus Assur religiösen Inhalts* (Leipzig, 1919-23).

[46] *Die babylonisch-assyrische Medizin in Texten und Untersuchungen* (Berlin, 1963-). Four volumes have so far been published in this series.

[47] Cf. especially E. K. Ritter, "Magical-expert (= *āšipu*) and Physician (= *asû*): Notes on Two Complementary Professions in Babylonian Medicine," *Studies in Honor of B. Landsberger* (AS 16, 1965) 299-322. The two kinds of doctor and their work has been further studied by R. D. Biggs "Babylonien," *Krankheit, Heilkunst, Heilung* (eds. H. Schipperges, E. Seidler, and P. U. Unschuld; Freiburg/München, 1978) 101-109.

[48] On this point cf. A. L. Oppenheim, "Mesopotamian Medicine," *Bulletin of the History of Medicine* 36/2 (1962) 101 and *Ancient Mesopotamia* (Chicago, 1964) 290-91 and 295.

[49] In *CAH* 3 (1925) 240.

[50] In *Diseases in Antiquity*, 203.

(1960) 57-72. It consists of a number of prescriptions for mainly external use, classified according to type but without obvious indication of the condition to be treated.

By comparison, the series "Sa-gig," or, in Akkadian, *sakikkū*, which is known also by its first line *enūma ana bīt marṣi āšipu illaku*, "When an *āšipu* is going to the house of a sick man," has virtually no therapeutic content. It treats exclusively of diagnosis, prognosis, and the symptoms of disease, and the term sa-gig, or *sakikkū*, no doubt properly means "The Symptoms." When complete the series was 40 tablets long, and a first edition was published in 1951 by the French Assyriologist, René Labat.[51]

By way of illustration, Plate 6 shows a new text of Tablet XXV of the series,[52] here published with the kind permission of the Trustees of the British Museum. Its main concern is with epilepsy, called in Akkadian *miqtu*, and the symptoms are altogether clear. There is reference to the fall, the deviation of the eyes, the muscular spasm, the turning of the body, and foaming at the mouth. Certain kinds of "aura" which precede the attack are also mentioned; they include the feeling of numbness, described as "coldness," in the tips of the fingers and toes.[53] Also interesting is line 18 of the text shown on Plate 6, which begins; *šumma u₈-a-a-i iš/ltanassi* (KA.KA-si), "If he (the patient) cries out 'uā'i'." With little doubt, here is the first reference in history to the "epileptic cry."

It seems likely that at least one text derives from an earlier form of the series,[54] and it should be mentioned that a Catalogue of the series is known which includes also a list of the Tablets of "Physiognomical omens."[55] These are concerned with features or characteristics of the body of a permanent nature, and although much is not strictly medical, the omens, as in Sa-gig, are still concerned with the meaning of "signs." An example of the series is shown on Plate 7 and deals with certain grain-like marks on the skin (Akk. *še'u*).[56] The numerous parts of the body where the mark might be found are given, one after the other, on the left-hand side of the tablet, and the supposed meaning of this, in each case, is stated confidently on the right.

---

[51] *Traité akkadien de diagnostics et pronostics medicaux* 1-2 (Paris, 1951). An Appendix to this work is entitled "Pronostics akkadiens et pronostics grècs," and lists numerous points of comparison between the Akkadian series and certain works of Hippocrates.

[52] The Tablet (BM 47753) is represented otherwise by O. R. Gurney, *The Sultantepe Tablets* 1 (London, 1957) no. 91 plus ibid. 2, no. 287, but has not yet been edited.

[53] Rev. 5 and 8.

[54] *The Sultantepe Tablets* 1, no. 89.

[55] Cf. J. V. Kinnier Wilson, "The Nimrud Catalogue of Medical and Physiognomical Omina," *Iraq* 24 (1962) 52-62. The total number of Tablets in the series was there suggested as 22, but it may rather have been 24 (revised estimate).

[56] I am indebted to the Trustees of the British Museum for permission to reproduce the photograph (BM 64513, reverse). Some duplicate texts have been published by F. R. Kraus, *Texte zur babylonischen Physiognomatik* (Berlin, 1939) nos. 44-48.

Pl. 6.

The reverse of an unpublished tablet belonging to the series "Sa-gig" (Tablet XXV). It is largely concerned with the symptoms of epilepsy (BM 47753).

Pl. 7.

An unpublished tablet of *šumma liptu*, one of the sub-series of the physiogonomical omina. The text is concerned with cysts or the like (Akk. *še'u*) situated in different parts of the body (BM 64513).

For the vast collection of texts on psychological medicine, still in many cases quite difficult to interpret, I hope it will be sufficient to refer to my own two studies in this direction,[57] especially as the subject is hardly capable of easy summary. A major problem rests in the difficulty of separating medical aspects of witchcraft from those which are the legitimate interest of social anthropology,[58] and possibly no one at the present time has found the right balance to this problem.

But, we ought now to turn to physical disease, and perhaps the first thing to say is that, unlike the situation in Egypt, there is no real "palaeopathology" of ancient Mesopotamia. It could begin, one may suppose, almost at any time, but in general conditions are unfavorable: the climate is wetter, the soil is more acid, the skeletons are fewer, and mummies do not exist. Nevertheless, Assyriology has other means of finding out at least something about the ancient disease picture, and there are three diseases out of many which may be discussed here.

The first of these is leprosy. There will be something more to say of this when we turn to the Old Testament, but I believe that the argument properly begins in Mesopotamia.

The essential problem regarding leprosy is that there is everywhere a shortage of symptoms. The text presented on Plate 8 may, however, supply some secure information. It is taken from an Old Babylonian omen tablet published some years ago by Franz Köcher and A. Leo Oppenheim.[59] The copy is that of Köcher; the transliteration and translation are Oppenheim's.

As to the meaning of the text, a first investigation appeared in my "Leprosy in Ancient Mesopotamia" published in *RA* 60 (1966) 47-58, although some refinements to the argument are incorporated here. The implied reference to excommunication (lines 44 and 45) is initially of importance, but the main argument concerns the point that leprosy may develop in one of two ways—or in two ways at different times—depending upon the resistance of the body to the disease. Thus, where there is strong resistance "nerve" leprosy may develop, resulting in the formation on the skin of one or more whitish or depigmented areas, and these I would identify with the *pūṣu* or "white spot(s)" (the word is actually singular in the text). On the other hand, where there is poor resistance "nodular" or "lepromatous" leprosy may develop, and such nodules, I suggest, could well be the *nuqdū*. The two types often co-exist, resulting in mixed cases.

---

[57]"An Introduction to Babylonian Psychiatry," *Studies in Honor of B. Landsberger* (AS 16, 1965) 289-98, and "Mental Diseases of Ancient Mesopotamia," *Diseases in Antiquity*, Ch. 56.

[58]For the latter, cf. especially E. Reiner, *La magie babylonienne: le monde du sorcier* (Paris, 1966); T. Abusch, "Mesopotamian Anti-Witchcraft Literature: Texts and Studies, Part I," *JNES* 33 (1974) 251-62; and R. D. Biggs in the work cited in n. 47.

[59]F. Köcher and A. L. Oppenheim, "The Old-Babylonian Omen Text VAT 7525," *AfO* 18 (1957/58) 62-77.

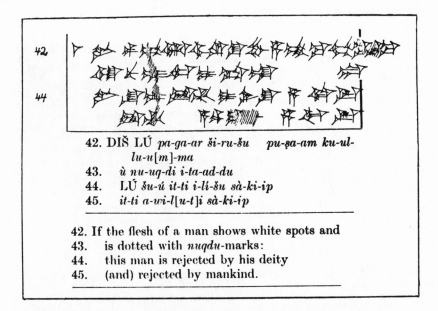

42. DIŠ LÚ *pa-ga-ar ši-ru-šu*   *pu-ṣa-am ku-ul-*
    lu-u[m]-ma
43. *ù nu-uq-di i-ta-ad-du*
44. LÚ *šu-ú it-ti i-li-šu sà-ki-ip*
45. *it-ti a-wi-l[u-t]i sà-ki-ip*

42. If the flesh of a man shows white spots and
43. is dotted with *nuqdu*-marks:
44. this man is rejected by his deity
45. (and) rejected by mankind.

Pl. 8.

Evidence for leprosy in the Old Babylonian period. The relevant lines of an OB omen text
published by Franz Köcher and A. L. Oppenheim, *AfO* 18 (1958) 62ff.

Plate 9 provides a modern example of even such a mixed case. The
large depigmented area on the left of the patient belongs to nerve leprosy,
and the nodules on the right, most clearly seen on the lower part of the
back, belong to the nodular leprosy. We suggest that the one was a *pūṣu*
and that the other were *nuqdū*. There would perhaps remain the difficulty
of deciding why *only* dimorphous leprosy should be mentioned, if this is
the correct interpretation of the text. Otherwise the correspondence would
seem good and without obvious alternative.[60]

The second disease which we discuss here is in a sense related to
leprosy since it has been confused with it. It is *saḥaršuppû*, which has long
been known from the penalty clauses on boundary stones to have been an
incurable skin condition requiring excommunication.[61] However, an argument against its meaning "leprosy" is that the word itself will not suit, for
saḥaršuppû derives from the Sumerian saḥar-šub-ba, which means (as it

---

[60]It may be added that there is evidence from a NB historical text—discussed in my study
on "Leprosy in Ancient Mesopotamia," *RA* 60 (1966) 50—that *pūṣu* as a term might be used
of a large white spot on the skin of a bull, so that something of its possible size is indicated
accordingly.

[61]References on this point have been gathered by J. Nougayrol, "*Sirrimu* (non **purîmu*)
'âne sauvage'," *JCS* 2 (1948) 207-208. Cf. also *RA* 60 (1966) 49, n. 3.

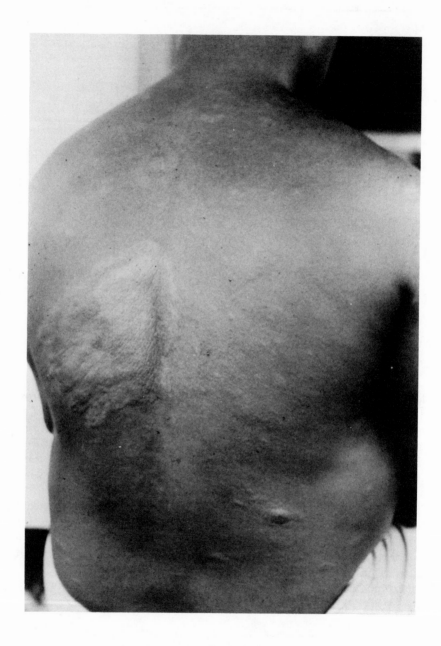

Pl. 9.

A case of dimorphous or "mixed type" leprosy showing, on the left, a large depigmented area which may be identified with the *pūṣu* of the Köcher-Oppenheim text, and nodules which will have been the *nuqdū*. (Courtesy, Dr. T. F. Davey, CBE).

would seem) either "dust-fall" or "fallen dust."[62] This would be a poor name for leprosy.[63]

In fact, such a name would far more accurately suit the initial skin condition of scurvy. In this disease, caused by lack of Vitamin C, "petechial haemorrhages" may be found in almost any part of the body, and an old account describes how the legs "shrivelled up and became covered with black spots and spots of the colour of earth, like an old boot."[64] Further support then comes from the lexical entry

saḫar-šub-ba = ga-ra-bu

as compared also with the entries

gig-ḫab = ga-ra-bu
gig-ḫab = bu-šá-a-nu,[65]

for scurvy is above all an "evil-smelling disease" (this with reference to the breath), which is the meaning of both the Sumerian gig-ḫab and the Akkadian būšānu. That both saḫaršuppû and garābu may possibly have had an association also with pellagra[66] is an idea that may be considered in the light of the Old Testament evidence discussed below.

As an introduction to the third disease which we discuss here, reference may first be made to an article by Dr. Hanna Zakaria of the College of Medicine in Baghdad entitled "Historical Study of *Schistosoma Haematobium* and Its Immediate Host, *Bulinus Truncatus*, in Central Iraq." It was published in 1959 in the *Journal of the Faculty of Medicine, Baghdad*, NS I, pp. 2-10.

In this study Dr. Zakaria investigates the possible early occurrence of Bilharzia, or Schistosomiasis, in ancient Iraq (it may be recalled that Bilharzia—to use the original name—was mentioned earlier in this study in connection with the Egyptian "Aaa-disease"). As is now widely known, Bilharzia, possibly the greatest medical problem of the modern Middle East, is caused by a parasite called *schistosoma*, which lives in canals and drains in close association with a certain kind of snail, the *bulinus truncatus*. What Dr. Zakaria did was to discover shells of this snail in the mud-brick walls of Babylon, in the side of excavation cuts at Tell ᶜAqeir, and in the bricks of the ziggurat at ᶜAqar Quf (some 30 km west of

---

[62] The latter translation is that of R. D. Biggs, "Medicine in Ancient Mesopotamia," *History of Science* 8 (1969) 102.

[63] On this point, cf. my note in *RA* 61 (1967) 190, and R. D. Biggs, *History of Science* 8 (1969) 102.

[64] The observation is taken from the translation of a manuscript by Jean, Sire de Joinville (1224-1319), as cited by R. H. Major, *Classical Descriptions of Disease* (Springfield, Ill., 1945) 586.

[65] For the sources, see *RA* 60 (1966) 51.

[66] A deficiency disease which may often complicate scurvy in famine conditions.

Baghdad). This information establishes the antiquity of the snail, and, as I have myself argued in two subsequent studies,[67] an Akkadian word *mūṣu*, which occurs in the urinary texts and is associated with both haematuria and "stones" (*calculi*), goes a long way towards establishing the antiquity of the disease.

Reference to the map reinforces the identification. The disease—or actually two slightly different forms of it—is securely recorded for both Egypt and Iraq, so that the geography is correct accordingly. As to Israel, which is also today involved in the disease, I believe that the Hebrew זוֹב (*zôb*) of Lev 15:2 may well have referred to infectious urinary Bilharzia. *Zôb* was a "discharge" of some kind, but it cannot have denoted a venereal disease—which is the usual interpretation—since there is no evidence that this existed anywhere in the ancient Near East. זוב = to flow, gush

In any event, this would be an appropriate place to shift the focus of attention to ancient Israel which forms the third part of this account.

III ISRAEL AND THE OLD TESTAMENT

We may begin this Old Testament section with a quotation which actually stands outside the period under review. It will be already familiar.

> Honor the doctor for his services,
>   for the Lord hath appointed him;
> His skill comes from the Most High,
>   and even kings reward him (for healing them).

The Book is *Ecclesiasticus*, dated to about 190 B.C., and the cited verses (38:1-2) are important because they are pleading for a new attitude towards medicine. The doctor, says Ben Sira, should be honored; he is an agent of God; he and his medicines should not be despised. The passage contrasts vividly with Old Testament attitudes where disease was largely regarded as a punishment for sin, and where God himself was the great healer and deliverer.

For this and other aspects of disease and its "treatment" in ancient Israel, reference may be made to the writings of such scholars as J. Preuss,[68] C. J. Brim,[69] P. Humbert,[70] J. O. Leibowitz,[71] M. Sussman,[72] F. Rosner,[73] and others, which in many ways must be called upon to supplement the somewhat restricted coverage of this account. However, from the viewpoint

---

[67]"Gleanings from the Iraq Medical Journals," *JNES* 27 (1968) 246 and *Diseases in Antiquity*, 195-96.

[68]*Biblisch-Talmudische Medizin* (Berlin, 1911).

[69]*Medicine in the Bible* (New York, 1936).

[70]"Maladie et médecine dans l'Ancien Testament," *RHPR* 44 (1964) 1-29.

[71]"רפואה," *EncBib* 7 (1976) 407-25 (Hebrew).

[72]"Diseases in the Bible and the Talmud," *Diseases in Antiquity*, Ch. 16.

[73]*Medicine in the Bible and Talmud* (New York, 1977), a somewhat traditional approach.

of the documentation which, as for the two previous sections, we discuss first, there is one matter in particular which has not, as it seems to me, been much stressed or even understood. We take up the matter here.

It is concerned with the idea that some of the Hebrew psalms are to be regarded as "medical" documents in that their whole purpose was to help or sustain a person in his suffering. Already in his *Das Gebet des Kranken im Alten Testament: Untersuchungen zur Bestimmung und Zuordnung der Krankheits- und Heilungspsalmen* (Stuttgart, 1973), K. Seybold has begun to look at certain psalms in this way, especially as they may be thought to concern physical disorders, and since 1965[74] I have myself argued that several were composed to help persons suffering from psychological disorders. An example not previously discussed is Psalm 56. It begins (*NEB* translation):

Be gracious to me, O God, for the enemy persecute me,
My assailants harass me all day long.

In this verse "all day long" is already curious, and in any normal situation it might be thought unrealistic. However, the psalm continues:

All the day long my watchful foes persecute me;
Countless are those who assail me.

Here again the verse might seem to lack realism, until, that is, it is seen that the situation *is* unreal and relates to a person suffering from ideas or delusions of persecution. Typically in this condition the patient thinks that he is surrounded by countless enemies and conspirators,[75] but they exist only in the mind and not in fact.

It is of much interest that the psalm seeks to help the patient by calling upon him to put his whole hope and confidence in God, saying (vv. 4 and 11): "In God I trust and shall not be afraid." However, this instruction is both totally expected and in keeping with the general attitude since trust in God lies absolutely at the heart of Old Testament medicine.

In saying this one has not quite said everything, for it is likely that strict hygiene and sensible food laws played an essential part also in the maintenance of health standards. But, unlike the case in both Egypt and Mesopotamia, there were no prescriptions, so that we may usefully now turn our attention to some individual problems and diseases. The statement which follows relates principally to identifiable diseases and has been tabulated under headings for the sake of brevity and convenience. It necessarily reflects the chance nature of the source material.

---

[74]Firstly in "An Introduction to Babylonian Psychiatry," (AS 16) 298, and secondly, in *Diseases in Antiquity*, 731.

[75]They appear to be summarized as ᶜ*ammîm* in v. 7 (Hebrew v. 8), so that "the nations" (*NEB*) will not suit here. The sense is rather: "O God, in thy anger bring ruin upon the(se) outcasts."

(1) Scurvy

The following lines are from the Book of Lamentations (4:5 and 8). They describe Jerusalem in the early sixth century B.C., during the long and cruel siege of the city by Nebuchadnezzar II of Babylon.

> Those who had fed on luxuries went scavenging[76] in the streets,
> Those brought up in purple embraced the refuge-dumps. . . .
> They went unrecognized in the streets, their faces blacker than charcoal,
> Their skin shrivelled upon their bones and dry as (tinder-)wood.

It must have been a pitiable scene. These were indeed famine conditions, with much protein deficiency (v. 8b) and scurvy (v. 8a). The latter proposal I first advanced in *Diseases in Antiquity*, 194, and it is based entirely on the reference to the blackness of the skin. Scurvy, as we have seen, is a deficiency disease, and the symptoms include sore gums, an evil-smelling breath, and spots on the skin. However, in severe cases, at a terminal stage, there occur also large-scale haemorrhages under the skin. It is these which impart the black color, as we read in the account.

(2) Scurvy and Pellagra

The following quotations are from the Book of Job:

19:17 "My breath is abhorred of my wife,
And I am become loathsome to the sons of my mother."

19:20 *Pelli meae, consumptis carnibus, adhaesit os meum,
et derelicta sunt tantummodo labia circa dentes meos.*
"My bone adheres to my skin, the flesh having wasted,
And in like manner are rotton the 'lips' (gums) around my teeth."

16:15 "I have sewn sackcloth upon my skin."

30:18 "(The disease) bindeth me about as the collar of my coat."

We suggest that the first two symptoms are those of scurvy. Job had an evil-smelling breath, and, at least according to the Vulgate, a degenerating gum condition around the teeth. By contrast, it would seem likely that the second pair of symptoms are those of pellagra. Pellagra is similarly a deficiency disease, caused by a deficiency of "B" vitamins. It commonly co-exists with scurvy. The word itself is derived from two Italian words meaning "rough skin," and this would be appropriate to the "sackcloth" of 16:15 as well as to the extensive dermatitis mentioned in Chapter 2. The final phrase, "It bindeth me about like the collar of my coat," brings to mind a particular skin feature of the disease known as "Casal's collar"

---

[76]For this meaning of the Heb. שׁסם, interpreted through the Akk. *ḫamāmu*, "to gather up," *ḫummumu*, "to pick up (litter, scraps)," cf. the writer's comment in *JSS* 7 (1962) 178.

(being so named after the Spanish court physician, Gaspar Casal, who first described it).

It may be mentioned that since the action of the Book of Job takes place *outside* the city, pellagra like leprosy may have been an "excommunication" disease—and it possibly drove even Nabonidus into exile.[77] It is perhaps also important that, when the dead skin has peeled off, the facial scars in pellagra appear remarkably white, for the regulation of Lev 13:13 is that "If (the diseased skin) has all turned white, then he is clean."

(3) Blindness following Vitamin A Deficiency.

Under this heading there are two texts which we may consider. They translate as follows:

(i) The Lord will smite you with madness and blindness and with confusion of mind, and you will become one who gropes about at noonday, as the blind man gropes about in darkness.

Deut 28:28-29

(ii) The wild asses stand still upon the bare heights,
Sniffing the wind for scent, like wolves (when they hunt for prey);
Their sight has failed, for there is no grass.

Jer 14:6

The first of these passages is part of a curse which might fall upon any member of the community who violated the Covenant,[78] and although it is necessarily theoretical in such a context, it is likely to reflect observed experience. In this case the basic condition may possibly be that of day-blindness—"you will become one who gropes about a noonday"—which is caused by a serious lack of Vitamin A. To this state both the "madness" (שגעון) and the "mental confusion" (תמהון לבב) are likely to be related— the combination would be a strange one otherwise—and, as two medical colleagues have suggested to me, could be explainable on the basis of an associated deficiency of Vitamin B.

The second text comes from Jeremiah and is part of the description of a serious drought which fell sometime upon Jerusalem and, indeed, the whole of Judah. Everything dried up, there was no water, there was not

---

[77]This proposal, which could be regarded as something of a "missing link" in the strange story of the Babylonian king, follows from the Aramaic "Prayer of Nabonidus" found at Qumran and published by J. T. Milik, "'Prière de Nabonide,' et autres écrits d'un cycle de Daniel: Fragments araméens de Qumrân 4," *RB* 63 (1956) 407-15. It is there stated that Nabonidus, much as Job, became afflicted with באישא שחנא. Cf. further M. Weinfeld, *Deuteronomy and the Deuteronomic School* (Oxford, 1972) 121, n. 2.

[78]Cf. amongst others M. Weinfeld, *Deuteronomy and the Deuteronomic School*, Part 1, Ch. 2, and the same writer's "The Loyalty Oath in the Ancient Near East," *UF* 8 (1976) 397-401.

even any grass. An additional observation is that the wild asses went blind—"their sight has failed, for there is no grass."

In modern terms this observation may be entirely understood. As it has been explained to me by F. R. Spratling of the Cambridge Veterinary School (whose idea it is), grass contains a substance called "carotene," which is broken down in the process of digestion into Vitamin A, and Vitamin A is necessary for healthy vision. As for the detail that the asses were seen to be "sniffing the wind for scent, like wolves," it has been observed that certainly cattle[79] under such circumstances must sniff around for food with their heads low towards the ground, for in their blindness they have necessarily to rely on their faculty of smell and not of sight.

(4) Oriental Sore.

The Hebrew *šĕḥîn miṣrayim* (שחין מצרים), which occurs in Deut 28:27, is translated "the botch of Egypt" by the Authorised Version, and mainly "the boil of Egypt" elsewhere.

For this condition one disease qualifies as does none other, namely, the so-called Oriental (or Tropical) Sore, known medically as cutaneous Leishmaniasis. The identification is altogether suitable, since the Sore is well-known in Egypt, being in fact recorded for North Africa, Egypt, Ethiopia, as well as many countries of western and central Asia. Moreover, since "boil" is at least one of the acceptable translations of the Hebrew *šĕḥîn*, it is relevant that "Aleppo Boil," "Baghdad Boil," and "Delhi Boil" are three of the local names which the disease has in these particular areas.

There can be little doubt that, in its origin, the phrase goes back to the tradition of the Plague of Boils described in Exod 9:9-10, but something quite specific and recognizable would seem to be necessary to explain the allusion in Deuteronomy. It was already S. R. Driver's opinion in the ICC *Commentary on Deuteronomy*, p. 310, that "some kind of endemic boil or malignant pustule ... may be intended."[80]

(5) Bubonic Plague

This most serious disease is initially transmitted to man by means of rat fleas, or occasionally by the fleas of other small animals, but if it should then involve the lungs and become "pneumonic," it may spread rapidly by droplet infection from the mouth and kill thousands or even tens of thousands before running its course. Opinion is not unanimous, but it nevertheless seems probable that 1 Samuel 5 and 6, with its account of a

---

[79]On this point I have been referred to T. Moore, *Vitamin A* (Amsterdam/London, etc., 1957) Ch. 34, "Vitamin A in farm and domestic animals," and pl. 40.

[80]I have noticed that S. Muntner, "Medicine," *EncJud* 11 (1972) 1179 gives the Hebrew *ᶜopālîm* as the equivalent term to the modern Leishmaniasis. This cannot, however, be correct, as may be sufficiently clear from the following section.

pestilence which struck the cities of Philistia about the year 1040 B.C., was describing even such a "pandemic" of bubonic plague.

The case is essentially threefold. First, there is mention (1 Sam 5:6) of either rats or mice as "ravaging the land" (LXX only), although their part in the outbreak was clearly not understood. Second, all five cities of the Philistines were involved in the plague (cf. 1 Sam 6:4 and 17) so that its scale may be gauged accordingly. Thirdly, the much-featured ᶜopālîm will not have been "haemorrhoids," as suggested by the early commentators (and unfortunately retained by the *NEB* in 6:11 and 17), but those buboes which give the disease its distinctive name. The bubo, from the Gk. βουβών "groin," is a swollen lymphatic gland, and, according to the textbooks, it is found in the groin or armpit, or, rarely, in the neck, or some 75 per cent of cases in a serious outbreak. It does not of itself endanger life, so that the observation of 1 Sam 5:12, "Even those who did not die were plagued with the buboes," would be correct accordingly.[81]

(6) Leprosy.

There will be space to make a short statement in the continuing debate.

There is early evidence for leprosy in India,[82] but if we should confine the inquiry to the ancient Near East it may be said that, whatever its origins, leprosy appears to have been present in Babylonia in the Old Babylonian period.[83] It may also have been present in Judah in the eighth century B.C., that is, if one should consider that King Uzziah of Judah was a genuine early case. According to the account in 2 Chronicles 26, there was an occasion in the temple in Jerusalem when Uzziah became angry with his priests, whereupon "leprosy broke out on his forehead" (v. 19).

---

[81]On a related matter it may be said that I do not personally subscribe to the view that an outbreak of plague forced Sennacherib and his army to leave the outskirts of Jerusalem in the year 701(?) B.C. It is far more likely that they left in a panic after some alarmist rumor had spread through the camp. A clue to what happened is surely to be seen in 2 Kgs 19:7, "Behold, I shall put a spirit in him, so that he shall hear a rumor and return to his own land"; in this case the *original* meaning of 2 Kgs 19:35 (= Isa 37:36) may have been: "And that night the Angel of the Lord went forth and smote the hundred and eighty-five thousand of the camp of the Assyrians (into thinking [add: ויאמרו?] that) even if they should depart early in the morning they would be all dead men." Indeed, I have sometimes wondered whether the well-known incident of the field mice that gnawed the bow-strings and shield straps (Herodotus ii:141) was not itself the *sign* which made the omen-conscious Assyrians strike camp in haste and without even waiting for another sun to rise.

[82]The standard source is J. Lowe, "Comments on the History of Leprosy," *Indian Medical Gazette* 77 (1942) 180, reprinted in *Leprosy Review* 18 (1947) 54. The evidence derives from a Sanskrit work entitled *Suśruta-saṃhitā* ("The Collection of Suśruta"), which "under different heads, describes most of the signs and symptoms of leprosy even in its milder forms with which we are familiar today." The date is uncertain.

[83]Cf. above in the Mesopotamian section. It is notable that no *name* accompanies the presumed description of leprosy in the OB text, so that it may possibly have been quite rare at the time.

Presumably the meaning is that leprosy *was discovered* to have broken out on his forehead; it is not difficult to think that the king may have covered or veiled his face in some way so as to hide his disfigurement from the gaze of men. In any event, reference to any textbook will indicate how completely the forehead can be involved in the disease. From this point of view the identification suits very well.

Having said this, I would certainly agree with those writers who believe that true leprosy is not visible in the regulations of Leviticus 13 and 14.[84] There are in particular no words which easily qualify to express the nodules and lepromata which characterize at least this form of the disease. All one can say is that, if Leviticus at all reflects the situation of the Exodus period, we should not really *expect* to find leprosy discussed in the book. On the best evidence available, leprosy arrived very late in Egypt[85] and came probably into Israel and Judah by way of the Fertile Crescent and not from Egypt.

It may be added that the above list does not overlook the importance of certain terminal illnesses, namely, those of Nabal (1 Sam 25:36-38), Asa (1 Kgs 15:23 and 2 Chr 16:12), and Jehoram (2 Chr 21:19, cf. also v. 15), but the shortage of essential details makes it difficult to reach firm conclusions. So far as the first of these is concerned, it is the opinion of Leibowitz[86] that Nabal died of a heart attack, but the old idea that he had a stroke (due to brain haemorrhage) would account more easily for the way that "he lay there like a stone" (1 Sam 25:37), so that this explanation would still seem to be preferable.[87] Both Asa and Jehoram have been discussed by G. R. Driver,[88] although it may be said firstly that if Asa's foot ailment was indeed senile gangrene *at the end*, the basic trouble must have been vascular since it is not true of gangrene that "lingering cases are known."[89] The main problem in the case of Jehoram is that, while we learn that "his bowels prolapsed because of the disease" (2 Chr 21:19), it cannot be known what that disease was. It may have been dysentery.[90]

---

[84]Cf. in particular all three editions of S. R. Browne, *Leprosy in the Bible* (3d ed.; London, 1979), and—as I owe to Dr. H. Williamson—E. V. Hulse, "The Nature of Biblical Leprosy," *PEQ* 107 (1975) 87-105.

[85]The earliest known skeletal evidence for leprosy derives from a Coptic mummy from Nubia of the 6th century A.D., first described by G. Elliot Smith and D. E. Derry, *Anatomical Report, Bulletin No. 6, Archaeological Survey of Nubia* (Cairo, 1910). Cf. also Elliot Smith and W. R. Dawson, *Egyptian Mummies*, 152, fig. 66, and V. Møller-Christensen, "Evidence for Leprosy in Earlier Peoples," *Diseases in Antiquity*, 300.

[86]In *The History of Coronary Heart Disease* (London/Berkeley, 1970) 39-40, and *EncBib* 7 (1976) 415 (Hebrew).

[87]Cf. already in the first edition of J. Hastings, ed., *Dictionary of the Bible* (Edinburgh, 1909) 599.

[88]"Ancient Lore and Modern Knowledge," *Hommages à A. Dupont-Sommer* (Paris, 1971) 283-84.

[89]Owed personally to Dr. Anthony Walker (Cambridge).

[90]Suggested also in "Medicine," *Dictionary of the Bible* (ed. J. Hastings; 2nd ed.; Edinburgh, 1963) 638.

It may be admitted in conclusion that, in later times, Greek philosophy was to bring new insights and maturer judgments into man's understanding of the nature of health and disease. The Greeks had a different approach, and pathology became something new in their medical schools and in daily life. But the ancient Near East—Egypt, Mesopotamia and Israel—has its own story to tell, and indeed it is three stories, for surely each makes a unique contribution to the history of medicine. They have here for the first time been studied together.

Indexes

INDEXES

I. TEXTS

A. BIBLICAL AND JEWISH TEXTS

1. The Hebrew Bible (MT)

Genesis

1 . . . . . 58, 61, 69
1:7 119
1:14-19 119
1:26 125
2 . . . . 58, 73
2-3 60
2-11* 62
2:1 110
2:4bff. 69
2:5 71
2:5-3:23 61
2:7 . . . . . . 59, 70
2:8-9 72
2:9 64
2:15 . . . . . 71, 72
2:16-17 59
2:17 . . . 59, 64, 71
2:18 . . . . . 59, 61
2:18ff. 72
2:19 70
2:19-20 71
2:23 59
2:23-24 61
3 . . . . 60, 61
3:5 64
3:7 64
3:14 61
3:14ff. 59, 61
3:15 73
3:16b 61
3:17 61
3:17ff. 60
3:19 . . . . . 70, 71
3:21 . . . . . 60, 72
3:22 . . . . 71, 125
3:24 . . . . 73, 113
4 . . . . 60, 61
4:6-7 . . . . . 60, 61

Genesis (cont.)

4:7 71
4:11 . . . . . 60, 61
4:13ff. 60, 71
4:15 72
5:29 61
6-8 58
6:3 71
6:5 71
6:5-6 61
6:7 72
6:8 71
6:9 71
7:1 71
7:4 71
7:11 71
8:20 61
8:21 71
8:21-22 61
8:22 . . . . . 61, 71
8:28 71
9:22ff. 66
9:25 61
9:25ff. 262
9:25-26 . . . 66, 72
9:26 66
10 330
10:8ff. 68
10:24-25 328
10:26-30 202
11 . . . . . . 61, 330
11:4 72
11:5 58
11:7 . . 58, 61, 125
11:14-16 328
11:16-26 329
11:28 58
12 63
12:1 . . . 58, 62, 64

Genesis (cont.)

12:1-3 . . . . . 61, 62
12:2 . . . . . . 62, 63
12:2-3 . . . . . 68, 72
12:3 . . . 57, 61, 62
72, 73
12:3a 62
12:6 66
12:7 64
12:10ff. 58, 71
12:11 64
12:17 . . . . . 58, 72
13:1 63
13:13 71
14 . . . . 72, 328-330
14 and 18-19 . . 328
14:2 328
14:3 329
14:4 252
14:13ff. 69
14:15 329
14:18 328
14:19-22 134
16:7 59
16:7a 72
16:11ff. 72
17 56
18-19 . . . . 71, 328
18:1 59
18:3 71
18:14 72
18:18 . . . . . 62, 63
18:20 71
18:21 58
18:22ff. 62
19 65
19:19 71
19:24 . . . . . 71, 72
20:1ff. 58

Genesis (cont.)

20:5 71
20:12 71
21:11-12 71
21:22-24 78
21:23 78
21:25 78
21:25-26 78
21:27 78
21:28 62
21:28-31 78
21:32 78
22:15ff. 64
22:15-18 62
22:18 62
23:14 62
25:21 58
25:23 66
26 68
26:1ff. 58
26:3 72
26:4 62
26:10 66
26:20 78
26:22 72
26:26-31 78
26:28 72
26:29 . . . . . . 77, 78
27 180
27:4 72
27:7 72
27:20 72
27:29 62
27:29a 66
27:30 71
27:37 66
27:40b 66
28:11ff. 57
28:12 57
28:13 . . . . . 57, 63
28:14 . . . . . 57, 62
28:15 72
28:16 . . . . . 57, 64
28:17 . . . . . 57, 130
28:18 57
28:20 57
29ff. 68
29:31 72

Genesis (cont.)

29:31ff. 57, 58
29:32-33 72
30:2 58
30:17ff. 58
30:22 58
30:23 58
30:24 58
30:27 72
30:30 72
31:3 . . . . . 58, 72
31:13 58
31:31 57
31:44ff. 68
31:*44-32:3 78
32:10 63
32:11 73
34 65
34:7 65
35:3 57
35:7 57
37-50 15
38:7 72
38:10 72
38:26 71
39:2-3 72
39:21 72
39:23 72
41:42-43 224
41:46 125
46:3 . . . . . . 62, 63
49:15 262
50:20 63

Exodus

1:7 63
1:9 63
1:11 . 67, 227, 263
1:11-12 63
1:20 63
2:11ff. 71
2:22 67
2:23-25 56
3 . . . . 56, 57,
                63, 127
3ff. 56

Exodus (cont.)

3:1 . . . . . 59, 100
3:2a 59
3:2b 59
3:3 59
3:4 57
3:4a 57
3:4b 57
3:7 63
3:7-8 56
3:8 . . . . . 58, 63,
             70, 72
3:9-10 56
3:15 127
3:16 63
3:16-17 70
3:17 63
5-14 63-64
5:2 . . . . . . 64, 73
6 . . . . 56, 57
6:2ff. 56
7:17 . . . . . 64, 72
8:4 64
8:4-5 58
8:6 64
8:18 64
8:24 . . . . . 58, 64
9:9-10 362
9:14 64
9:27 . . . . . 64, 71
9:28 64
10:2 64
10:16 64
10:16-17 71
10:17 64
10:28 59
12:32 . . . 62, 64, 73
14 58
14:13-14 72
15 96
15:3 95
15:3-4 224
15:6-7a 95
15:7b 95
15:9 95
15:10-13 95
15:15ab 95
15:16a 95

Exodus (cont.)

15:17 . . . . 100, 106
15:17-18 95
15:18 . . . . . 94, 95
15:25a 71
16:4 71
16:10 137
18:5 100
19 64
19:3b-8 90
19:11 58
19:18 58
19:18-19 100
19:20 58
20:22 100
22:20 67
22:21 . . . . . 84, 85
22:22 85
23:6 84
23:9 85
23:20-33 90
24:1 75
24:4b 75
24:5-6 75
24:8 75
24:9-11 75
24:13 100
25:20 116
25:22 . . . . 116, 137
28:11 213
29:43 137
32 256
32-34 89
32:8 256
34 64
34:5 58
37:9 116

Leviticus

10:1 255
13 364
13:13 361
14 364
15:2 358
16:2 116
18 65
19:9-10 84

Leviticus (cont.)

19:33-34 85
23:22 84
25:35 84
26:16 344

Numbers

7:89 . . . . 116, 137
10:29-30 64
10:30 58
10:33 100
10:35 106
10:35-36 81
11:18 71
11:23 72
13:16 127
14:10 137
16:19 137
16:28 64
16:30 64
17:7 137
20:6 137
21:13 211
21:15 211
21:28 211
22-24 64
22:6 63
22:28 72
22:31 72
22:34 71
22:36 211
23:8 97
23:10 6
23:21 . . . . 95, 129
24:6ff. 66
24:7 66
24:9 62
24:16 . . 64, 97, 134
24:17 66
24:18 66
27:40a 66
32:1 212

Deuteronomy

1:38 125
2:36 . . . . 210, 211

Deuteronomy (cont.)

3:16 211
4:19 124
4:29-31 89
10:1-5 137
11:24 212
15:7-8 84
17:3 124
17:16 231
20:11 . . . . 263, 266
24:14 85
24:19-22 84
28:22 344
28:27 362
28:28-29 361
30 89
32:8 . . . . . 97, 134
33:2 100
33:4-5 96
33:5 95
33:26 . . . . 106, 122

Joshua

1:4 212
5:13-15 124
7:7 2
8 78
12:2 211
13 211
13:9 . . . . 210, 211
13:16 . . . . 210, 211
13:25 212
15:21 177
15:21-63 265
15:51 177
16:10 262
17:13 262
18:1 130
19 . . . . . 211, 212
19:28-29 212
19:29 212
19:37 . . . . 208, 210,
                    212
19:46 235
19:51 130
22:22 252

Joshua (cont.)

22:29 252
24:2-24,(28) . . . 90

Judges

1 195
1:21-33 208
1:28 262
1:30 262
1:33 262
1:35 262
4-5 217
5 . . . . 2, 84, 107
5:4 100
5:4-5 106
8:14 . . . . . 25, 86
8:22 241
8:33 128
9 69
9:4 128
9:27 129
9:37 130
11:8 240
11:11 243
11:24 97
19:23-24 65
20:6 65
20:10 241
21:19-23 129

1 Samuel

1:1 131
1:3 . . 111, 128, 136
1:9 129
1:11 . . . . 111, 128,
                130
1:24 129
2:3 134
2:10 134
2:22 130
3 131
3:3 129
3:15 129
4:1-7:1 47
4:4 . . 111-113, 127,
            128, 136
4:5-6 129

1 Samuel (cont.)

4:18 129
4:21-22 129
4:22 129
5 362
5:6 363
5:12 363
6 362
6:4 363
6:11 363
6:17 363
6:20 129
8 83
8:5 . . . . . 80, 182
8:11 . . . . 90, 224
8:11-17 . . . 83, 260
                265
8:11-12:14 79
8:16 260
8:20 . . . . 80, 182
9:16 80
10 86
10:1 80
10:6 81
10:7 72
10:10 81
10:24 129
10:25 . . . . . 83, 90
11:6 81
11:12a 78
12 88-91
12:1-5 88
12:2-5 88
12:6-15 88
12:7abA 88, 89
12:8a 88
12:8b 89
12:8bC 88
12:9b-11a 88
12:11b 89
12:12 . . . . . 88, 182
12:13 . . . . . 88, 89
12:14 89
12:14-15 89
12:14b 89
12:*16-20 89
12:16-25 88
12:21-25 89
12:22b 89

1 Samuel (cont.)

13:5 195
13:19-20 195
14:*4-14 80
14:47 192
15 84
15:2 136
15:10-35 187
16ff. 69
16:1-13 80
16:13 81
16:18 72
16:21-22 125
17-20 79
17:37 72
17:45 . . . . 127, 136
18:1 79
18:1-5 80
18:3 79
18:12 72
18:14 72
18:28 72
20:5 80
20:8 79
20:12-17 80
20:41 80
20:42 79
21:2-10 135
22:1-2 178
22:6-23 135
22:7 . . . . . 79, 83
22:8 252
22:9 129
22:13 252
22:20 129
22:34 192
23:24 247
24:4 82
25:36-38 364
25:37 364
28:9 82
29:9 82

2 Samuel

2 Sam + Kgs 1-2 . .
                239
1:6 195

2 Samuel (cont.)

1:14 82
1:16 82
1:18ff. 2
1:19-27 4
1:21 3
1:26 3-5
2 44
2-3 187
2-4 . . . . . 29, 47,
52, 53
2-7 . . . . . 29, 181
2:1-5:3 29
2:4 80
2:4b-7 79
2:5-6 79
2:6 77
2:8 44
2:8-9 185
2:8-32 45
2:8-4:12
(or 5:3) 28
2:9 44
2:10b 44
2:12 . . . . . 44, 79
2:13-16 44
2:17-28 44
2:29-32 44
3 45
3-4 . . . . . . 44, 45
3:1-6a 45
3:1a 45
3:2a 45
3:3 192
3:5b 45
3:6-4:12 28
3:6a 45
3:6b 45
3:6bff. 45
3:6b-11 45
3:6b-39 45
3:9 . . . . . . 52, 84
3:9b 79
3:10 45
3:11 45
3:12a-21f 45
3:12e 45
3:13c 45
3:13d-19 45

2 Samuel (cont.)

3:17-19 79
3:18 84
3:18b 79
3:20 79
3:21 79
3:21e 45
3:21g 45
3:21g-h 45
3:21h 45
3:22a 46
3:22a-c 45
3:22b 46
3:22c 46
3:22d 46
3:22d-e 46
3:22e 46
3:23-25 46
3:23d 46
3:23e 46
3:23f 46
3:24d 46
3:24e 46
3:24f 46
3:25b 46
3:25c 46
3:25d 46
3:26-39 46
3:27 . . . . . 79, 183
3:33-34 4
4 . . . . 45, 46
4:1 46
4:2a-d 46
4:2d-4 46
4:4 49
4:5a 46
4:5a-8a 46
4:5b 46
4:5c 46
4:6b 46
4:6c 47
4:7b 47
4:7c 47
4:7g 47
4:8a 47
4:8b-11c 47
4:8c 47
4:8d 47
4:9 . . . . . . 47, 52

2 Samuel (cont.)

4:9c 47
4:11b 47
4:12a-d 47
4:12e-f 47
5 84
5:1-3 . . . . 47, 183,
240, 253
5:2b 79
5:2b-3 84
5:3 . . . 28, 79, 80,
90, 243, 248
5:4-5 47
5:6-9(10) 47
5:9b 212
5:10 . . . . 72, 136
5:11 . . . 206, 209,
212, 213
5:13-16 47
5:17 194
5:17ff. 68
5:17-6:1 47
6 . . . . 27, 47, 81
6:2 . . . . 113, 128,
135, 136
6:13-19 47
6:13-23 47
6:13a 47
6:13b 47
6:14a 48
6:14b 48
6:15 129
6:15a 48
6:16 . . . . . 27, 47
6:16a 48
6:16b 48
6:16c 48
6:16d 48
6:17a 48
6:17c 48
6:18 . . . . 113, 128
136
6:18a 48
6:18b 48
6:19a 48
6:19b 48
6:20 196
6:20-23 . . . . 27, 47
6:20a 48

2 Samuel (cont.)

6:20b	48
6:20c	48
6:20d	48
6:21a	48
6:21b	48
6:21e	48
6:22a	48
6:22b	48
6:22c	48
6:23	48
7	27, 47, 86
	105, 187
7:1-4a	86
7:1-17	86
7:1a	86
7:2	212
7:2-5	86
7:2-7	86
7:3	72, 86
7:7	86
7:8	86, 113, 136
7:8-9	72
7:8a	86
7:9	72, 86
7:10	86
7:11b	27, 86
7:12	86, 91
7;12-14a	86
7:13a	187
7:14	86
7:14b-15	86
7:15	86
7:16	27, 86
7:*16	86
7:17	86
7:18-22a	86
7:26	113, 136
7:27	113, 136
7:27-29	86
7:28	87
8:1	208
8:1-14	47
8:2	66, 79, 195
	208
8:2-12	208
8:3-4	195
8:4	217

2 Samuel (cont.)

8:6	79
8:9-10	237
8:13-14	66, 208
8:14	195
8:15	182, 185
8:15-18	47
8:16-18	266
8:18	178
8:18b	82
9	44, 45, 47, 48,
	52, 53, 79
9-10	28
9-20 + 1 Kgs 1-2	
	15, 27, 29,
	52, 69, 175
9-24	29, 181
9:1	48
9:1c	48
9:2-5	48
9:3c	48
9:6-8	49
9:7c	49
9:7e	49
9:9-11c	49
9:10d	49
9:11d	49
9:11d-13	49
9:12c	49
9:13a	49
9:13b	49
9:13c	49
10	44, 53
10-13	38
10-14	38
10:1	80
10:1-5	44, 46
10:1-14	45
10:1-14	
(15-19d)	38
10:1-11:1	208
10:2	192
10:2b	44
10:2c	44
10:2d	44
10:3	44
10:4	44
10:4b	44

2 Samuel (cont.)

10:4d	44
10:5f	44
10:6-7	44
10:6-14	44
10:6c-7b	44
10:8-11	44
10:8b	44
10:9d	44
10:10b	44
10:11-12	44
10:13-14	44
10:13-14c	44
10:13b	44
10:14c	44
10:14d	44
10:14f	44
10:15-19a	44
10:19	79
10:19b	44, 45
10:19e	38
11-12	28, 38,
	42-44, 53
11-14	45
11:1	43
11:1-12:31	38
11:2-5	43, 52
11:2-27	29, 182
11:3	177, 247
11:6-13	43, 44
11:6-17	43
11:8	43
11:9	43
11:10	43
11:11	184
11:13	43
11:14-21	182
11:14-24	43, 44
11:16-27	208
11:17	43
11:18-25	43
11:21	43
11:24	43
11:25-27	43, 44
11:25c	43
11:26-27a	43
11:27	31, 54, 187
11:27b-12:15a	43

2 Samuel (cont.)

11:27f	43
12	87
12:1-7a	87
12:1-13	85
12:1-15a	43
12:1-25	187
12:7-15	182
12:10-11	187
12:13-15a	87
12:15b-20	43, 44
12:15b-23	43
12:15b-25	29
12:18	43
12:19	43
12:21-23	43, 44
12:24	31, 54
12:24-25	43, 44, 187
12:26-31	43, 44, 208
12:28	184
12:30	195
12:31	266
13-14	29, 38, 44, 53
13-20	28, 38
13:1b	39
13:1c	39
13:1d	39
13:1-4	39
13:1-22	38, 39
13:2a	39
13:3a	39
13:3b	39
13:3c	39
13:4e	39
13:5-11a	39
13:5a	39
13:5b	39
13:5c	39
13:5d	39
13:5e	39
13:5f	39
13:5g	39
13:5h	39
13:6	39
13:6-7	182

2 Samuel (cont.)

13:6a	39
13:6b	39
13:6c	39
13:6d	39
13:6e	39
13:6f	39
13:6g	39
13:7-11a	40
13:7c	40
13:7d	40
13:8e	40
13:9c	40
13:10b	40
13:10c	40
13:10e	40
13:11a	40
13:11b	40
13:11b-14	40
13:11c	40
13:11d	40
13:11e	40
13:12	65
13:12-13	40
13:14a	39-41
13:14b	40
13:14c	40
13:14d	40
13:15a	40, 41
13:15a-b	40
13:15b	40, 41
13:15c-17	40
13:15d	40
13:15e	40
13:16a	39
13:16a-b	40
13:16c	40, 41
13:17c	40
13:17d	40
13:18-19	41
13:20-22	41
13:23-37(38)	38
13:23-38	46
13:23a	41
13:23a-29b	41
13:23a-38b	41
13:25e	41
13:26-27	182

2 Samuel (cont.)

13:27a	41
13:27b	41
13:28a	41
13:29b	41
13:29c	41
13:30-31	41
13:32c-d	41
13:32-33	41
13:33a	41
13:33c	41
13:34a	41
13:34a-d	41
13:34b	41
13:34c	41
13:34d	41
13:35a-36b	41
13:35b	41
13:36	182
13:36b	41
13:36c-e	42
13:37-38b	42
13:37a	42
13:37b	42
13:38a	42
13:38b	42
13:38c-14:20	42
13:38c-14:33	42
14	25
14:17	82
14:20	82
14:21-23b	42
14:23c	42
14:23c-28	42
14:24b	42
14:24c	42
14:24d	42
14:24e	42
14:25	52
14:25-27	42
14:25a	42
14:27c	42
14:28a	42
14:28b	42
14:29-32	42
14:33	42, 183
15	243
15ff.	38, 267

2 Samuel (cont.)

15-20 . . . 29, 31, 34
38, 54
15:1 . . . . . 52, 224
15:1-6 . . . 208, 248
15:1-12 31
15:1-17 . . . . 34, 45
15:1-17:29 31
15:2-4 183
15:6 183
15:7 128
15:7-9 182
15:10 . . . . 183, 243
15:12 . . . . . 52, 252
15:13 241
15:13-16:14 31
15:18 . . . . . 33, 34,
178, 195
15:18-19:41 . . . 33,
34, 45
15:19 31
15:19-22 31
15:19-37a . . . 31-33
15:19-37b 34
15:19ff. 32
15:20 . . . . . 31, 208
15:21 31
15:22 31
15:23 31
15:25 31
15:29 31
15:30 . . . . . . 5, 31
15:31 252
15:31ff. 32
15:31-36 31
15:37a 31
15:37b 31, 32
15:37bff. 32
15:37b-16:15 . . . 31
15:37b-
17:23 . . . . 33, 34
15:37b-17:23(29) . . .
32
16:1-4 32
16:3 186
16:5-8 186
16:5-14 32
16:5d 32

2 Samuel (cont.)

16:5e 32
16:7a 32
16:7b-c 32
16:7c 32
16:8a 32
16:8b 32
16:8d 32
16:10c 32
16:10d 32
16:11e 32
16:11f 32
16:12a 32
16:12b 32
16:15 . . . . . 31, 32
246
16:15-17:23 31
16:16ff. 32
16:16-19 33
16:16-17:23 . . 32, 33
16:20-23 33
16:20b 33
16:23a 33
16:23b 33
17 25
17:1 245
17:1-4 33
17:3 246
17:5-10 33
17:7b 33
17:8b 33
17:8c 33
17:10b 33
17:10c 33
17:11-14b 33
17:14 . . . 31, 54, 70
17:14c-d 33
17:15-21(23) . . . 33
17:24-29 34
17:24a 33
17:24b 33
17:24-19:9 31
17:25 . . . . . 33, 183
17:26a 33
17:27a 33
18:1 . . . . 178, 184
18:1-2d 34
18:1-4 36

2 Samuel (cont.)

18:1-4c 34
18:1-19:9 . . 33, 34,
36, 42
18:2f 34
18:2-3 34
18:3b 34
18:4 184
18:4c 34
18:4d 35
18:4d-
17(18) 34-36
18:5 184
18:5a 35
18:5a-b 35
18:5b 35
18:5c 35
18:6 246
18:6a 35
18:6b 35
18:6-8 183
18:7 242
18:8a 35
18:8b 35
18:9-11 35
18:9-15 183
18:12 178
18:12d 35
18:12d-e 35
18:12e 35
18:12f 35
18:14-17(18) . . . 35
18:19 36
18:19-23 36
18:19-32 36
18:19b 36
18:19c 36
18:19d 36
18:20 36
18:20b 36
18:20d 36
18:20e 36
18:21 37
18:22 37
18:22c 37
18:22d 37
18:22e 37
18:22f 37

2 Samuel (cont.)

18:23a	37
18:23b	37
18:24	38
18:24-27	36, 38
18:24e	38
18:25	52
18:25a	38
18:25d	38
18:25e	38
18:26	38, 52
18:26b	38
18:26d	38
18:26f	38
18:27	52
18:28-30	36, 37
18:28-32	36, 37
18:28f	37
18:28g	37
18:29	37
18:29b	36, 37
18:29d	37
18:29f	37
18:30	37
18:31-32	36, 37
18:31c	37
18:31d	37
18:32	37
18:32b	36, 37
18:32d	37
19:1	5, 181
19:1-5	35, 36
19:1e	35
19:1f	35
19:1h	35
19:3-4	35
19:5c	35
19:5d	35
19:6-8	181
19:6-9	34, 36
19:7	34
19:9-41	31
19:9-20:22	31
19:10	249
19:10-11	183, 243
19:10-16b	34
19:13	248
19:14	183, 248

2 Samuel (cont.)

19:15	248
19:16a-24	33
19:16c-24	34
19:22	82
19:23	183
19:25ff.	32
19:25-31	79
19:25-39	33, 34
19:28	82
19:40-41	33, 34
19:42-44	34, 183
19:42-	
- 20:22	31, 45
20	34, 267
20:1	183, 249, 252
20:1-2	183, 186
20:2	249
20:3	212
20:4-5	183
20:4-22	250
20:6	34
20:6-7	178
20:7	178
20:10b	178
20:10-11a	79
20:21	252
20:23a	185
20:23b	178
20:23ff.	248
20:23-26	185
20:24	259, 264, 266
20:41	249
20:42-43	249
20:44	249
21	82
21:1-10	208
21:1-14	28, 78
22:11	122
23:1b-3	88
23:1b-3a	88
23:1b-7	87
23:3b	88
23:4	88
23:5	88, 90, 91
23:5-7	88

2 Samuel (cont.)

23:5a=bD	88
23:5a-bAB	88
23:5b	88
23:5bA-B	88
23:5bAB-C	88
23:6	88
23:6a-b	88
23:7a	88
23:7a-b	88
23:7aA-B	88
23:8-39	177
23:19	178
23:20	177
23:23	178
23:34	177
24:1	211
24:1-9	211
24:2	211, 212
24:4	211
24:5	210, 211
24:5-6	212
24:5-7	206, 209, 211-213
24:6	210-212
24:7	195, 210-212
24:8	211
24:14-25	136
24:25	82

1 Kings

1	49, 187
1-2	28, 45, 49 53, 176, 179
1-13	19
1:1-4	49, 51, 52, 178, 185
1:1-2:12	49, 52
1:2	125
1:5	52, 179, 223
1:5-10	49
1:5-27	51
1:5a	53
1:5c	49
1:6	52

1 Kings (cont.)

1:7-8 . . . . . 49, 176
1:8 176
1:9 . . . . . 52, 178
1:9a 49
1:9b 49
1:10 . . . . 49, 176
1:11 178
1:11-21 50
1:11d 50
1:11e 50
1:13 . . . 178, 179
1:13d 50
1:13e 50
1:13f 50
1:13g 50
1:13h 50
1:16 179
1:17 179
1:17b 50
1:17c 50
1:17d 50
1:18 178
1:18a 50
1:18b 50
1:19 176
1:19a 50
1:19b 50
1:19c 50
1:20 . . . . . 28, 179
1:20d 50
1:22-27 50
1:24 179
1:24-25 178
1:24d 50
1:25-26 176
1:25b 50
1:25c 50
1:26 50
1:27 179
1:27c 50
1:28-31 . . . . 50, 52
1:29 52
1:29c 50
1:30 . . . . . 52, 179
1:30a 50
1:30b 50
1:30c 50

1 Kings (cont.)

1:30d 50
1:30e 50
1:32 176
1:32-37 50
1:32-53 52
1:33b 50
1:33c 50
1:33d 50
1:34a 51
1:34b 51
1:34c 51
1:34d 51
1:35 179
1:35a 51
1:35c 51
1:35d 51
1:36 51
1:36-37 179
1:37 181
1:38 176
1:38-40 51
1:38a 51
1:38b 51
1:38c 51
1:39a 51
1:39b 51
1:39c 51
1:39d 51
1:39e 51
1:40a 51
1:40b-c 51
1:41-53 51
1:41c-e 51
1:42 52
1:43d 51
1:44 176
1:44a 51
1:44b 51
1:45a 51
1:45b 51
1:46 51
1:47 . 72, 179, 181
1:47-48 51
1:48 179
1:49 51
1:50-53 51
2:1-2a 49, 51

1 Kings (cont.)

2:1-12 52
2:4 179
2:10 . . . . . 49, 51
2:12 . . . . 49, 51,
            179, 187
2:12a 51
2:13-46 186
2:15 178-180
2:22 . . . . 176, 179
2:24 179
2:28 176
2:28b 183
2:31-33 186
2:33 179
2:35 177
2:45 179
2:46b 187
3 . . . . . . 66, 180
3-11 . . . . . 18, 19
3:1 227
3:13 219
4 265
4:1 185
4:4 250
4:6 . . . . . 259, 264
4:7-19 . . . 208, 209
            218, 292
4:12 292
4:20 219
4:26 218
5 . . . . . . 66, 265
5:1 . . 196, 199, 223
5:3 . . . . 219, 220
5:4 . . 196, 199, 234
5:5 219
5:7-8 218
5:8 . . . . . 209, 236
5:8ff. 297
5:9-14 19
5:14 223
5:15 212
5:15-26 . . 116, 207,
        208, 212, 213
5:15-7:51 81
5:16-18 219
5:17 . . . . 212, 297
5:19 213

1 Kings (cont.)

5:20 213
5:20-23 235
5:22 213
5:24 . . . 207, 213
5:27 67
5:27ff 209
5:27-28 . . 259, 264,
266
5:28-29 67
5:29 260
5:30 260
5:32 . 207, 212, 213
6-8 295
6:1 203
6:15-18 297
6:18 297
6:23-28 . . 116, 298,
303
6:27 116
6:29 297
6:37-38 203
6:38b 207
7:1 . . . . 203, 207
7:2ff 219
7:9-10 303
7:9-12 297
7:11-12 303
7:12 136
7:13-14 116
7:15-22 297
7:40 302
7:45 302
7:45-46 194
8:7 116
8:11 116
8:12 69
8:12-13 106
8:13 . . . 104, 117
8:64 82
9 . . . . . . 67, 292
9:10 203
9:10ff. 204
9:10-11a 207
9:10-14 207
9:11 213
9:11b 207, 235
9:11-13 235

1 Kings (cont.)

9:12-13 207
9:13 207
9:14 207
9:15 . . . 67, 259,
275
9:15ff. 67, 209
9:15-17 . . 289, 290
9:15-18 . . 203, 209
9:15a 264
9:15b 264
9:16 . . . . . 199, 227
9:17-19 264
9:18 237
9:19 . . . . 67, 209
9:20 195
9:20ff 67
9:20-21 . . 265, 266
9:20-22 . . 259, 264
9:21 . . . 264, 266
9:22 209
9:23 260
9:24 203
9:26-28 . . 207, 234
9:26-29 201
9:27 260
9:28 190
10:1-10 . . 19, 223
10:1-13 191
10:4ff. 204
10:4-5 306
10:11 . . . 190, 207,
234
10:11-12 . . 190, 201,
220
10:14-21 219
10:22 . . . 190, 201,
207, 219, 234
10:23 219
10:25 223
10:26 . . . 209, 218,
223
10:27 223
10:28 . . . 215, 216,
229, 231
10:28-29 . . 190, 201,
215
10:29 . . . 215, 216,

1 Kings (cont.)

223, 225, 226,
229, 231, 234
11:14ff. 66
11:14-22 . . 201, 209
11:23-25 209
11:26 . . . 209, 250
11:26-28 . . 203, 251
11:28 . . . . 67, 260
11:40 203
11:42 207
12 . . . 69, 83, 90,
244 252,
253, 267
12:1 252
12:2-3a 255
12:4 254
12:4ff. 67
12:6 125
12:7 254
12:8 264
12:12 255
12:18 259
12:19 252
12:20 255
12:26-33 81
12:28 256
13 19
14:6-16 187
14:25 203
15:20 210
15:22 267
15:23 364
15:27 244
16:16 . . . 244, 252
17:1 125
18-19 87
18:5 218
18:15 125
19:4 6
19:15 259
19:20-22 259
20:7 240
21:8-13 241
22:19 . . . 124, 125,
127
22:19-23 124
22:48 234

1 Kings (cont.)

22:49 201
23-24 19

2 Kings

1:2 128
1:3 128
1:6 128
1:16 128
3:5 252
3:14 125
5:9 223
5:16 125
5:20 213
8:20ff. 66
8:22 252
9:1-13 244
9:14 252
10:9 252
11 90
11:4 78
11:7 253
11:14 252
11:17 90
12:4-15 81
12:12 213
12:13-16 82
12:20 90
12:21 252
13:14 110
14:19-21 90
15:29 210
16:10-16 82
17:16 124
18:7 252
19:7 363
19:15 113
19:35 363
21:3 124
21:5 124
21:23-24 90
23:2 240
23:3 90
23:3-7 81
23:4-5 124
24:20 252

Isaiah

1-39 109
1:2 252
1:7 70
1:9 70
1:25 . . . . 102, 107
2:2 100
2:12 137
2:16 103
3:26 119
6 . . . 117, 118, 125
6:1 . . . . 107, 125
6:2 125
6:3 . . . . 112, 118,
          125, 129
6:5 . . 112, 118, 125
6:8 125
8:18 . . . . 107, 112
9:5 118
10:16-17 107
10:23 127
11:2 118
11:6ff. 73
11:8 73
12:6 107
13:4 . . . 124, 127,
          137
13:13 . . . . 127, 137
14:13-14 . . 100, 121
14:14 134
14:24 118
14:24-25 107
14:24-27 . . 118, 127
14:27 118
17:12-14 . . 102, 107
17:13 103
18:7 137
19:1 122
19:11-12 20
19:12 118
19:16 127
19:17 118
19:24-25 73
20:1-6 20
22:5 . . . . 127, 137
22:8 219
22:12 137

Isaiah (cont.)

22:14 137
22:18 224
23:9 118
24:21-23 127
24:23 . . . . 112, 118,
            137
25:6 . . . . 112, 118
27:13 100
28:23-29 86
28:29 118
29:1-4 107
29:1-8 107
29:6 . . . 102, 103
          127
29:7-8 127
30:1-7 20
30:27-30 102
31:1 . . . . 20, 231
31:2 20
31:4 . . . 127, 137
31:4-5 103
31:8 263
31:8-9 107
31:9 102
33 . . . 101, 107, 108
33:1-24 107
33:3 103
33:3-5 108
33:4 104
33:5 103
33:13-16 104
33:14 102
33:17-24 104
33:20-22 117
33:21 103
33:21-23a 101
33:23 104
34:2 110
36:4 118
36:5 252
36:13 118
37:16 . . . . 113, 118
37:36 363
40:26 124
44:13 213
45:12 124

Isaiah (cont.)

47:1 119
51:15 137
52:7-10 117
54:5 137
55:3 91
65:25 73
66:20 . . . . 100, 223

Jeremiah

2:13 101
3:16-17 117
7:10-14 128
8:2 124
8:19 117
10:16 137
11:20 118
14:6 361
14:21 117
15:19 125
17:12 117
17:12-13 101
17:25 223
18:3-4 70
19:13 124
20:12 118
22:4 223
23:18 125
23:22 125
25:30 122
27:2 86
27:9 86
31:35 137
32:17 137
32:18 . . . . 127, 137
33:8 252
41:4-5 81
46:10 137
46:18 118
48:15 118
50:25 . . . . 127, 137
50:34 137
51:19 137
51:56 134
51:57 118
52:12 125

Ezekiel

1 122
1:1 122
1:4 122
1:11 116
1:22 122
1:22-28 122
1:23 116
1:28 138
3:13 116
8:4 137
9:3 138
10:4 138
10:15 122
10:18 138
10:19 138
10:20 122
11:22 137
11:23 137
14:14 71
14:20 71
27:14 232
28 60
28:11ff. 60
28:14-16 101
39:9-10 104
40:2 100
41:17-19 113
43:4-5 137
43:7 117
43:13-17 302
44:4 137
47:1-12 101

Hosea

1:9 127
5:13 197
8:1 252
10:6 197
12 70
12:6 127
12:14 70

Joel

4:16 . . . . 103, 122
4:18 101

Amos

1:2 . . . . . 103, 122
3:2 61
4:13 137
6:13 73
9:5 137

Micah

1:13 218
3:10 104
4:7 117

Nahum

2:14 127
3:5 127

Habakkuk

3:3 100

Zephaniah

1:5 124
3:14-15 117

Haggai

1:2-11 104

Zechariah

1-8 . . . . 125, 126
1:7-15 126
1:12 126
1:14 126
1:17 126
2:12 126
2:13 126
2:15 126
3:1-10 126
3:4 125
3:6-7 126
4:9 126
4:14 125
6:1-8 126

Zechariah (cont.)

6:5	125
6:15	126
7:3	126
8:2	126
8:3	112, 126
8:9	126
8:13	73
8:21-22	126
12	107
14	107
14:8	101
14:8-9	117
14:10	100
14:14	104
14:16-17	112, 118, 137
14:16-19	104
14:21	137

Malachi

1:14	118

Psalms

2	107
2:1-3	98
2:4-5	103
2:6	100
2:7b-8	82
7:10	118
9:3	134
9:5	119
15	85
16	9, 10
16:2	9
16:5-6	9
16:6	9
16:7	9
16:9	9, 10
18	10, 85, 86, 103
18:7	103
18:10	122
18:11	122
18:14	103, 134
18:17	103

Psalms (cont.)

18:21-27	85
19A	69
19:2	129
20:3	122
20:7	122
24	85
24:2	69
24:3-4	104
24:7	129
24:8	127
24:10	113, 118, 127, 138
26:2	118
29	96
29:1-2	125
29:1-3	129
29:9	129
29:10	119, 122
33:6	61, 124
33:9	61
46	101, 104
46:2-4	102
46:3	101
46:5	94, 99
46:6	99
46:7	102, 103
46:8	102, 112, 127, 136, 138
46:10	104
46:12	112, 127, 136, 138
47	94, 98, 107
47:2	129
47:3	94, 97, 134
47:6	129
48	94, 104, 107, 108
48:2	122
48:2-3	99, 121
48:3	94, 100, 118, 122, 197
48:4	99, 102
48:5-7	102
48:6	103
48:8	103
48:8-9	99
48:9	99, 108,

Psalms (cont.)

	112, 118, 138
48:12-14	104
50:2	103, 122
51:20	99
56	359
56:5	359
56:8	359
56:12	359
57:3	134
59:6	127, 138
63	10
68	105-107
68:2	106
68:5	122
68:7	107
68:8-10	106
68:9	106
68:15	107
68:16-17	107
68:17	100
68:18-19	107
68:19c	107
68:21b-24	106
68:22-24	107
68:25-28	106, 107
68:29	106
68:29-33	107
68:30	105, 107
68:34	122
68:34-35	106
69:7	138
72	82, 85, 91, 182
72:1	197
72:4	84
72:8	197
72:10-11	197
72:12-14	84
72:17	72
73:11	134
74	117
76	103, 107
76:3	99
76:4	104, 107
76:5-6	104
76:6-8	102
76:7	103

Psalms (cont.)

76:9 . . . . 103, 104
76:10-13 107
76:11 104
76:11-13 104
78:17-18 134
78:35 134
78:54 100
78:59-72 128
78:68 . . . . . 99, 105
78:68-69 100
78:69 . . . . 99, 103, 104
80:2 113
80:5 . . . . 113, 138
80:8 . . . . 113, 138
80:15 . . . . 113, 138
80:20 . . . . 113, 138
81:6 127
82 . . . . 82, 98, 107
82:6 134
84:2 . . . . 112, 138
84:4 . . . . 112, 118, 138
84:9 . . . . 112, 138
84:13 . . . . 112, 138
87:1 . . . . . 99, 100
87:2 99
87:5 99
89 136
89:6-8 . . . 118, 125
89:6-9 . . . 125, 136
89:6-19 . . 125, 136
89:7 125
89:9 . . . . 118, 125, 138
89:10-11 136
89:15 118
89:15-16 125
89:16 129
89:19 125
89:20-28 136
89:26 136
89:28 . . . . 82, 125, 136
94:1 134
97:6 129
97:9 . . . 4, 94, 134

Psalms (cont.)

98:6 129
99:1 113
99:9 100
101 . . . . . . 84, 85
101:8 104
102:17 99
103:19 124
103:19-22 124
104:3 122
104:29 70
107:11 134
132:7 116
132:10-18 105
132:13 99
132:13-18 104
133:3 104
135:10-11 197
136:17-19 197
146 117
147:2 99
147:13 104
148:1-5 124
148:5 61
149 117

Proverbs

1-9 15
1:1 . . . . . . 19, 67
5:18-19 7
8 . . . . 10, 17
8:17 11
8:30 11
8:34 11
9 17
10-29 . . . . . 15-23, 25, 26
10:1 19
10:13 21
12:24 263
14:31 69
16:2 71
17:10 21
20:9 71
21:2 71
22:17-23:11 18
25:1 . . . 19, 26, 67

Job

2 360
6:16 122
16:15 360
19:17 360
19:20 360
30:18 360
37:10 122

The Song of Songs
(Canticles)

1:1 7
1:2-2:6 6
1:9 224
2:3 . . . . 8, 9
2:10-13 8
4:4 212
4:6 . . . . 8, 9
4:8 9
8:4-14 6
8:6b 8

Lamentations

1:1 263
4:5 360
4:8 360
4:8a 360
4:8b 360

Ecclesiastes

2:4-6 220

Esther

8:10 218
10:1 263

Daniel

1:5 125
8 124
8:10-13 124
8:11-13 124

Ezra

2:55-58 260
5:11 197

Nehemiah

3:16 212
3:19 212
3:25 212
7:57-60 260
9:6 124
11:3 260
11:25 177

1 Chronicles

11:10-47 177
11:22 177
12:1 178
12:8 178
12:16 178
12:20 178
13:6 113
14:1 213
18:10 237
18:14 185

1 Chronicles (cont.)

21 211
21:16 136
22:15 213
23-28 81
28:2 116

2 Chronicles

1:16-17 . . 201, 215
2:1 260
2:7 220
2:15 235
2:16-17 . . 259, 264
2:17 260
3:12 116
3:13 116
8:3 238
8:3-4 237
8:4 67
8:6 67
8:8 264

2 Chronicles (cont.)

8:8-10 . . . 259, 264
8:11 196
8:17-18 201
8:18 260
9:10 260
9:10-11 201
9:21 . . . . 190, 201
9:26 199
9:28 201
10:1-3 255
10:18 259
12:2 203
16:12 364
17:12 67
18:10 264
18:18-22 124
19:8-11 83
20:36-38 234
21:15 364
21:19 364
26 363

2. The Greek Bible (LXX)

1 Samuel

5:6 363

2 Samuel

13:21 182
24:5 (LXX^L) . . 210
24:6 210
24:6 (LXX^L) . . 210

24:7 210

1 Kings

10:22a-c
(LXX^B) 259,
264, 266
11:25 209
12:2-3 255
12:12 255

12:20 255
12:24^{a-z} 251

2 Kings

5:20 213

Daniel

3:55 113

3. The Vulgate

2 Samuel

6 210

4. The Apocrypha

Ecclesiasticus

38:1-2 358

Wisdom of Solomon

18:24 122

5. The New Testament

Matthew

6:29 205

Luke

1:19 125

Romans

5:12 71
6:23 71

Revelation

15:2 122
21:1 122

6. The Mishnah

Yoma

5:2 122

B. NON-BIBLICAL TEXTS

1. Akkadian Texts

ABL

241 223
241 rev. 16'-
    19' 223
414 237
1201:4-5 218

ADD

698 232

AfO 8

196:19 222

AfO 14

44-45 228

AfO 18

62-77 . . . . 354, 355

AKA

367:III 68 222

ANET

83-84 222
259a 222
259b 229
292b 216
295a 223, 224
559 221

AnSt 6

154:81, 83 . . . 222

AOAT 8

24-27 . . . . 261, 262

ARAB

1 § 603 232
1 § 611 236
2 § 510 223
2 § 556 216
2 § 744 222
2 § 778 229
2 § 905 222
2 § 981 232

ARI 2

§ 46 219

ARI 2 (cont.)

§ 47 221
§ 48 219
§ 80 233
§ 82 232
§ 95 232
§ 97 233
§ 227 220
§ 247 219
§ 426 220
§ 429 222
§ 435 219
§ 436 220
§ 583 220
§ 584 222
§ 585 236
§ 586 220
§ 598 220
§ 678 221

ARM 2

no. 75:1-21 . . . 243
no. 95 243

ARM 5

37, no. 20 . . . 236
20:18ff. . . 226, 229

BBSt

39:1 230
39:15 . . . . 225, 226
39:16 . . . . 226, 230

*Beiträge zur Assyri-
ologie 2*

639, obv. ii 27 . . 99

BM

47753 . . . 351, 352
64513 . . . 351, 353

BO 28

11, 17, iii 21'-
22' 99

Borger, *Asarhaddon*

47:63-64 223
112:12 216
112:15 . . . 215, 216

Code of Hammu-
rabi

i 1-52 99
v 14-24 99

CT IV

29d 226, 230

EA

7:58 221
14 col. 2:15-
16 224
16:9-11 221
17:36-40 221
19:84 221
22:1-4 221
22:3 225
32:21-22 228
205:6 135
266:26-33 221

GCCI 1

269 229-230
269:1-2 226

Goetze, *The Laws
of Eshnunna*

64-65 229
111-112 229

Iraq 13

23 228

Iraq 14

32:40ff. 221

Iraq 17

71 237
80 237
136 237
139-140 237

Iraq 18

125 228

Iraq 25

79 237
79-80 237

JCS 12

78:10-11 228

JEN

515:3 226

K

286 232
1044 223
2401 ii 10'-32' . . . 99

KBo I

10, rev.
62-65 228

Kohler-Ungnad,
Rechtsurkunden

62 no. 91 230

Kraus, *Physiogno-
matik*

nos. 44-48 . . . 351

Lie, *Sargon*

80:17 229

MVAG 41/3

8-9, line 29 . . . 99

ND

421 222
2437 237
2437:31-33 . . . 237
2437:rev. 37 . . 237
2495:10-14 . . . 237
2495:15-16 . . . 237
2647 237
2765 229
2766 236
2766:rev. 13' . . 237

Rost, *Tigl. III*

14:69 222
24 236
85 236

Seidmann, *Adadni-
râri II*

24:71 222

Streck, *Assurbani-
pal 2*

14:II 8-14 222
16:II 40 229

Tadmor, *Tigl. III*

Ann. 17:12′ ..	222
Ann. 19	236
Summ. 5 II	
16-24	236

Tadmor, *Tigl. III* (cont.)

Summ. 8:7′ ...	228
Summ. 9:8′ ...	228

Weidner, *Mannu-ki-Aššur*

16	223

2. Hittite Texts

ANET

192	231
195-196	231
196	231

HL

§ 58	231
§ 178	231
§ 180 .. 226, 230,	231
§ 181 ... 226, 230	

JCS 15

78	230

KUB

III 27 Rs. 17 ..	228

3. West Semitic Texts

ANET

135	102
653	219
655	87

CTA

2 iii 4	101
3B ii 3-39	102
3C iii 10-15 ...	104
3D iii 43-iv 47	102
3D iv 51-54 ...	104
3D iv 71-75 ...	104
3E v 14-15 ...	101
4 iv 21-22	101
4 vii 30-37 ...	102
5 vi 2*-1*	101
6 i 33-34	101
17 vi 47-48 ...	101

CUL

3(ᶜnt).2.22	135
7.1(131).5	135
14(KRT).2 lines 86, 88 ...	135
14(KRT).4 lines 176-178 .	135
15(128).5.19 ...	135
16.1(125).36 ...	135

CUL (cont.)

19(1 AQHT). 4.209	135
35(3).47	135
35(3).53	135
79(83) lines 1, 7, 10	135
143.3-4	135
535	134
2004.15	134
APP.II(173) 51	135

Fitzmyer, *Sefîre*

12:5	216

KAI

15, 1	121

KTU

1.3.II.22	135
1.7.5	135
1.15.V.19	135
1.16.I.36-37 ...	135
1.19.IV.47	135
1.41.47	135
1.41.53	135
1.78.3-4	135

KTU (cont.)

1.87.51	135
1.91.15	134
4.40 lines 1, 7, 10	135

Moabite Stone

12	127
17-18	127

PRU 3

16:180	226
41	232
41:5-7	229

PRU 6

7B:12	226
7B:10-12	230

Ugaritica 5

no. 7 (RS 24.244) 3	101

UT

1012:22-25	236
1127:6 ... 226, 230	
Glossary no. 2138	135

4. Egyptian Texts

ANET

19 77
25ff. 234
26 87
29 77
237 217
246b 217
247b 217
478a 217

MIO 1

15 224

Papyrus Anastasi III

1,2-3 227
6,7-8 . . . . 225, 226

Papyrus Anastasi IV

16,7-10 225
17,8-9 227

Papyrus Bologna 1094

15:4,3-5 227

5. Greek and Latin Texts

Eusebius, Praep. evangelica

I 10.9 121

Herodotus, Historiae

1.74 77
2.141 363
3.8 77
3.90 232
4.70 77

Josephus, Ant.

8.2.9=§58 265
8.5.3 208

Josephus, Ant. (cont.)

8.6.3=§160 . . . 266

Josephus, Bell. Jud.

2.18.9 208
3.3.1 208
5.5.4 122
5.5.5 122

Josephus, Con. Ap.

1.17 208

Josephus, Vita

43-44 208

Philo Byblius

10.18 135
10.20 135

Tacitus, Germania

13-14 77

Xenophon, Anabasis

2.2 77
2.9 77

II. WORDS AND TERMS

A. SUMERIAN

azu 347, 349
gig-ḫab 357

sa-gig 351

saḫar-šub-ba 355

B. AKKADIAN

asû 338, 350
āšipu 338, 349-351
bīt ḫilāni 292, 293, 295, 302
būšānu 357
garābu 357
massu 260, 263
miqtu 351

mīšarum 254
mūṣu 358
nuqdū 354-356
pūṣu 354-356
qāt eṭimmi, Ištar, Šamaš 349
saḫaršuppû 355, 357
sakikkū 351

šarru rabû 94, 190, 197
šibšu 218
šikkû 349
tibnu 218
zabālu 260

C. EBLAITE

nabiᵓutum 326

maḫḫu 326

D. UGARITIC AND OTHER WEST SEMITICS

mlk rb 197
sablum 260
ᶜrb špš 135

ṣ-b-ᵓ 111, 123, 134
ṣbu 135
ṣbu špš 134, 135

rkb ᶜrpt 134
ršp ṣbi 134, 135

E. HEBREW

ᵓalmug, ᵓalmuggîm 202, 220
ᵓeleph 245
ᵓašer ᶜal habbayit 224
zôb 358
zbl 260
ḥokmah 16, 239

ṭôbâ 77
melek gadol 197
melek yareb 197
melek rab 197
maṣṣēbāh 304
merkābāh 223, 224
māšāl 8
ᶜibri, ᶜibrîm 328

ᶜopālîm 362, 363
ᶜarê hamiskᵉnôt 238
rekeb 223
rekeš 218
šēḥîn miṣrayim 362
šaḥepet 344
tukkiyîm 219

F. EGYPTIAN

ibr 217
wrr.t 217
mrkbt 217

ḥry-ḥ3b 338
synw 338
śśm.t 217

kp rdwy 117

G. WORDS IN HEBREW LETTERS

אהל מועד 130
איש ישראל 241, 242, 244
אל גמלות 134
אל דעות 134
אל נקמות 134
אלמג/אלגם 191, 202
אלפים 130
אשר על המס 248
בני אלים 123, 125
בעל ברית 128

בעל זבוב 128
ברית 78, 79, 84, 88, 90, 91
ברית עולם 88
גוי 63
היכל 117, 129, 131
הרים 252
וירם יד ב— 250
זוב 358
חסד 79
טבור הארץ 130

טוב 77
טובה 77, 79, 87
ישב הכרבים 112, 113, 134
כבוד 129, 131, 137, 138
כל ישראל 241
כפרת 116, 117
כרת ברית 78, 79
מבול 119
מחיר 229

מלך גדול 94, 197	עדה 241	קרח 122
מלך רב 94, 118, 197	עדת אל 123	קשר 252
מם 67, 248, 259-267	עליון 94, 134, 136	רקיע 122
מם עובד 259-267	עם 63, 241	שגעון 361
מרד 252	עם הארץ 90	שוט 211
משפט המלך/המלכה 83, 90	עצה 118	שופט 182
נדון 243	עם ישראל 241	שחין מצרים 362
נער 25	פשע 252	שחפת 344
נשבע 78, 84	צבאות, צבא 109-111, 123-127	שלח יד ב— 252 2
סבל 67, 251, 260	צבא השמים 124, 135	שם 137, 138
סוד קדשים 123, 125	צפון 100, 122	שתיה 122
	קהל 241	תכי 191
	קהל קדשים 125	תמהון לבב 361
		תרועה 129

III. AUTHORS

Aberbach, A. 255
Abusch, T. 354
Ackroyd, P. 79
Adams, J. E. 331
Aharoni, Y. 204, 207, 209, 210, 218, 235, 253, 270, 272, 277, 281, 283, 284, 286, 289, 296, 302, 304-306
Ahituv, S. 217, 227
Ahlström, G. W. 121, 129, 130, 176
Albright, W. F. 3, 10, 17, 24, 94, 106, 140, 157, 171, 172, 191, 216, 218-220, 225, 234, 253, 255, 265, 270, 275, 277, 281, 287, 303
Alonso-Schökel, L. 30
Alt, A. 18, 117, 130, 179, 194, 206, 208, 209, 218, 247, 253, 265, 277
Althann, R. 331
Amiran, R. 270, 277, 281
Amoz, J. 331
Anati, E. 235, 276
Andersen, F. I. 331
Archi, A. 331
Arnold, W. R. 110, 127
Astour, M. C. 236
Avigad, N. 156, 235, 266, 278

Bächli, O. 24
Baldacci, M. 331

Ball, E. 197
Barag, D. 161
Barnett, R. D. 220, 302
Barns, J. W. B. 341
Barr, J. 75, 126
Barrelet, M. Th. 164
Barrois, G. A. 302
Barstad, H. M. 331
Bartlett, J. R. 201, 209
Barucq, A. 20
Bass, G. F. 234
Baumgärtel, F. 109, 112, 125, 137
Baumgartner, W. 16
Beck, P. 279
Begrich, J. 119
Ben-Arie, S. 161
Ben-Barak, Z. 89
Ben-Dor, I. 164
Bermant, Ch. 331
Bertholet, A. 128
Beyerlin, W. 256
Biggs, R. D. 332, 350, 354, 357
Bing, J. 233
Biram, A. 262
Biran, A. 272, 275
Birch, B. C. 80
Bisi, A. M. 131, 172
Blenkinsopp, J. 28-30, 78, 175
Boardman, J. 165
Bogoslouskya, I. V. 164
Bogoslousky, E. S. 164
Boling, R. 78, 97

Borchert, O. 123
Borger, R. 99, 215, 220, 223
Bothmer, B. V. 145
Bowra, C. M. 77
Breasted, J. H. 216, 217, 340
Brekelmans, C. 90
Bright, J. 179, 189, 216-218, 256
Brim, C. J. 358
Brinkman, J. A. 220, 225
Brooke, A. G. 251
Broshi, M. 235
Brovarski, E. 121
Browne, S. R. 364
Brueggemann, W. 27, 29, 66
Brunner, H. 121
Buber, M. 256
Buccellati, G. 194
Budde, K. 4, 210
Budge, E. 222
Buhl, M.-L. 129
Bunnens, G. 190
Busink, Th. A. 305
Butzer, K. W. 227

Callaway, J. A. 286
Caminos, R. 225, 227
Campbell, A. F. 128
Caneiro, R. L. 196
Caquot, A. 251
Carlson, R. A. 29, 76, 175, 181
Carratelli, G. P. 230
Cassin, E. 228
Cazelles, H. 16, 17, 24, 78
Černý, J. 121
Chadwick, H. M. 79, 88
Chadwick, K. J. 344
Chadwick, N. K. 79, 88
Chéhab, M. 234, 165
Childs, B. 75
Chipiez, C. 170
Cintas, P. 131
Civil, M. 350
Clamer, Ch. 161
Clark, W. M. 60
Clements, R. E. 83, 121, 135
Clifford, R. J. 121, 130
Coats, G. E. 55
Cody, A. 176
Cogan, M. 229, 235

Cohen, R. 251, 284, 286, 289
Cole, S. D. 332
Conrad, D. 135
Conroy, C. 27, 30, 31, 38, 39, 52, 76
Cooley, R. E. 286
Corswant, W. 298
Couturier, G. 16
Crawford, J. 194
Crenshaw, J. L. 16, 137
Cross, D. 230
Cross, F. M. 86, 94-96, 106, 110,
    130, 131 134, 219, 224, 227,
    231, 256, 284
Crowfoot, J. W. 302
Crown, A. D. 215, 234
Crüsemann, F. 66, 72, 130, 240-
    242, 245, 247, 250, 252, 254,
    255, 265, 267
Culican, W. 131, 170
Curtis, E. L. 231

Dahood, M. 9, 106, 332
Davey, T. F. 356
David, R. 343, 346
Dawson, W. R. 338, 342-345, 364
Debus, D. 251
von Deines, H. 216, 217, 224, 225,
    340, 343
Delekat, L. 28, 53, 127, 175, 180,
    186
Derry, D. E. 364
Dever, W. G. 198, 277-280, 288-
    290, 292, 295, 297, 299, 303,
    304
Diakonoff, I. M. 242
Dietrich, W. 60
Diringer, D. 302
Doi, K. 7
Donner, H. 190, 209
Dossin, G. 229, 232, 236
Dothan, M. 164, 172, 204, 275,
    284, 286, 290
Dothan, T. 145, 235, 280, 305
Dougherty, R. P. 229
Driver, G. R. 128, 364
Driver, S. R. 101, 217, 231, 267,
    362
Dubberstien, W. H. 230
Dumermuth, F. 137

Dunayevsky, I. 275, 280, 305

Eaton, J. 84
Ebbell, E. 340
Ebeling, E. 350
Eben-Shoshan, A. 261
Ebers, G. 338, 339
Edel, E. 228
Edelstein, G. 161, 275
Edgerton, W. F. 201
Edwards, I. E. S. 164, 342
Eisenstadt, S. N. 196
Eissfeldt, O. 91, 97, 110, 112, 113, 117, 127, 128, 135, 136, 255, 261
Elat, M. 191, 215, 216, 234
Elgavish, Y. 276
Eliot, G. 76
Elliger, K. 210
Eph^cal, I. 257
Erman, A. 18, 121, 217, 225
Evans, S. 242
Exum, J. C. 6, 7

Fabry, H. J. 123
Fales, F. M. 232
Fallon, F. T. 138
Fensham, F. C. 206
Ferguson, 343
Finkelstein, J. J. 234, 254
Fischer, R. 82
Fisher, C. S. 275
Fitzgerald, A. 96
Fitzmyer, J. A. 216
Flanagan, J. W. 28, 30, 175
Fohrer, G. 7, 16, 90, 175, 253
Forrer, E. 238
Franken, H. J. 9-11
Frankfort, H. 182
Freedman, D. N. 86, 88, 94, 95, 100, 189, 217, 224, 332
Freedman, N. 332
Friedrich, J. 230
Fritz, V. 64, 71, 73, 80, 284, 288
Fronzaroli, P. 332
Fulco, W. J. 135
Fuss, W. 211

Galling, K. 135, 190, 216
Gamberoni, J. 117

Garber, P. 303
Garbini, G. 332
Gardiner, A. 201, 225
Garelli, P. 215
Garsiel, M. 247
Gasche, H. 164
Gaster, L. M. 332
Gaubert, H. 234
Geckeler, H. 111
Gehman, H. S. 215, 216, 218, 219, 229, 235, 251, 255
Gelb, I. J. 332
Gerleman, G. 7, 117
Gerstenberger, E. 17, 22, 23
Gevirtz, S. 2, 3
Ghalioungui, P. 338, 342
Ghirshman, R. 164
Gichon, M. 209
Gilbert, G. 332
Ginsberg, H. L. 102
Gitton, M. 227
von Glahn, G. 195
Glock, A. E. 275, 304
Glueck, N. 194, 284
Goetze, A. 229, 231, 233
Gooding, D. W. 252, 255, 266
Goodwin, D. W. 95
Gordis, R. 241
Gordon, C. H. 332
Gordon, R. P. 252
Görg, M. 113, 117, 137, 200
Gottwald, N. K. 95, 261, 262
Gradwohl, G. R. 255
Grant, E. 278
Grapow, H. 121, 217, 225, 343
Grätz, H. 210
Gray, J. 24, 81, 87, 117, 134, 135, 175, 176, 179, 185, 191, 215, 218, 219, 229, 234, 255
Gray, P. H. K. 347
Grayson, A. K. 220, 223, 225
Green, A. R. 198, 200, 203
Greenfield, J. C. 191, 197, 220
Grintz, E. S. J. 242
Gros Louis, K. R. R. 181
Guerard, A. 1
Gunkel, H. 22, 62, 65, 68, 111
Gunn, D. M. 5, 13, 27-30, 44, 47, 53, 76, 79, 175, 176, 239

Gunneweg, A. H. J. 266
Gurney, O. R. 222, 230, 351
Güterbock, H. G. 230, 231, 233
Guy, P. L. O. 275

Habel, N. 80
Hachlili, R. 122
Hachmann, R. 164
Hagan, H. 180
Halbe, J. 75, 78, 85
Hallo, W. W. 234
Halpern, B. 78, 134, 203, 256
Hamilton, R. W. 276
Hanslik, R. 202
Hanson, P. D. 3
Haran, M. 113, 116, 129, 253
Har-El, M. 194
Harris, J. E. 343, 346
Hartum, E. S. 225
Hatano, K. 30
Hauer, C. 195
Hawkins, J. D. 219, 231-234
Hayes, A. D. H. 89
Heaton, E. W. 200
Helck, W. 95, 217, 221, 224, 225, 227
Held, M. 117, 248, 260
Heltzer, M. 230
Hempel, J. 16, 66
Henry, M. L. 73
Hermisson, H.-J. 22, 25, 53
Hermann, A. 7
Herrmann, S. 86, 189, 210, 215, 265
Hertzberg, H. W. 34
Herzog, R. 202
Herzog, Z. 281, 291, 295
Hoenig, S. B. 190
Hofer, J. 121
Hoffner, H. J. 230
Holladay, J. S. 295
Holladay, W. 2, 3, 5
Holm-Nielsen, S. 129
Hölscher, W. 145, 201
Holzinger, H. 58
Houtman, C. 130
Huffmon, H. B. 23, 86, 99
Hulse, E. V. 364
Hulst, A. R. 63

Humbert, P. 129, 358
Hurvitz, A. 241

Ikeda, Y. 190, 195, 217, 220, 231-237
Irwin, W. H. 101
Ishida, T. 81, 130, 136, 177, 179, 181, 184, 186, 197, 239-241, 244, 245, 247, 256, 266

Jackson, J. J. 29
Jacob, E. 5
Jacobsen, T. 182, 242
Jahnow, H. 4
Jakobson, R. 1, 4, 9
James, F. 217, 224
Jaritz, K. 219
Jaroš, K. 130
Jean, C. 243
Jellinek, G. 194
Jeremias, Chr. 126
Jeremias, J. 113
Jobling, D. 80, 89
Jolles, A. 7
Jones, H. L. 236
Jüngling, H.-W. 98

Kahana, A. 263
Kaiser, O. 20, 65
Kallai, Z. 210, 217, 245
Kalluveetil, P. 78, 90
Kammenhuber, A. 216, 230
Kantor, H. J. 302
Katzenstein, H. J. 206, 215, 234
Kaufman, S. A. 216
Kayatz, C. 10, 15
Kayser, W. 5
Keel, O. 113, 116, 122, 131
Kees, H. 227
Kegler, J. 191, 207
Kempinski, A. 216, 284, 288
Kenik, H. 84-86
Kenyon, K. M. 277, 278
Kessler, W. 110, 137
King, L. W. 119, 222, 225, 230
Kinnier Wilson, J. V. 222, 237, 351, 354, 355, 357, 358, 360
Kinnier Wilson, S. A. 347
Kitchen, K. A. 200-204, 215, 222, 227
Kittel, R. 9, 205

Klein, R. W. 255
Klostermann, A. 210
Kochavi, M. 86, 279, 284, 286
Köcher, F. 350, 354, 355
Kohler, J. 230
Kraus, F. R. 351
Kraus, H.-J. 9, 253-255
Krinetzki, L. 7
Küchler, F. 350
Kühne, H. 161
Künstlinger, D. 263
Kupper, J.-R. 232
Kutsch, E. 75, 81

Labat, R. 233, 351
Laessøe, J. 243
LaFay, H. 332
Laffey, A. 86
de Lagarde, P. 210
Lambdin, T. O. 224
Lamon, R. S. 275
Lance, H. D. 199, 227, 278, 279
Landsberger, B. 228, 229, 254, 349
Lang, B. 15
de Langhe, R. 260
Langlamet, F. 13, 28, 55, 175, 180, 186, 246
Lapp, N. W. 278, 284, 289
Lapp, P. W. 172, 275, 277-279, 304
Laroche, E. 231
Larsen, M. T. 196, 242
Leach, E. R. 27
Leibovitch, J. 157
Leibowitz, J. O. 358, 364
Levenson, J. 76, 92
Levy, S. 275
Liddell-Hart, B. H. 192
Lie, A. G. 229
Lipiński, E. 129, 130, 216
Liver, J. 229, 239, 245
Liverani, M. 134, 233
von Loewenclau, I. 60, 61
Löhr, M. 127
Lord, A. B. 20
Loretz, O. 3, 16, 17
Loud, G. 113, 116, 275, 302, 304
Lowe, J. 363
Luckenbill, D. D. 228
Luther, B. 241
Lyons, J. 111, 123

Maag, V. 111, 124, 127, 130
Macalister, R. A. S. 278, 290, 293
McCarthy, D. J. 75, 77-79, 86, 89, 90, 332
McCown, C. C. 287
McIntire, C. 332
McLean, N. 251
McKane, W. 55, 240, 246
Magri, E. 332
Maier, J. 109, 113, 116, 122, 128
de Maigret, A. 332
Maisler, B. (see also Mazar) 177
Major, R. H. 344, 357
Malamat, A. 83, 94, 189, 191, 193-196, 198, 203, 206, 217, 220, 224, 227, 232-234, 237, 249, 253, 262
Mallowan, M. E. L. 233
Maloney, P. C. 332
Mander, P. 332, 334
Mann, W. N. 344
Margalit, O. 333
Martin, W. J. 223
Matthiae, P. 309, 312, 315, 333
Matthiae Scandone, G. 312
May, H. G. 171, 172
Mayes, A. D. H. 24
Mayrhofer, M. 191, 220
Mazar, A. 195, 279, 280, 305
Mazar, B. (see also Maisler) 178, 189, 192, 197, 204, 218, 235, 237, 238, 240, 253, 272, 275, 276, 278-280
Mazzoni, S. 333
Meek, Th. J. 349
Meissner, B. 221, 228, 230
Mendelsohn, I. 209, 248, 259-263, 265
Mendenhall, G. E. 24, 206, 245
de Merzenfeld, C. 302
Meshel, Z. 285
Mettinger, T. N. D. 28, 80-82, 88, 100, 116, 136, 138, 175, 180, 185, 200, 209, 218, 224, 239, 240, 244, 248, 249, 253, 259, 260, 263-266
Metzger, M. 119, 121, 122
Meyer, E. 251
Meyers, C. 286
Mikaya, A. 334

Milgrom, J. 241
Milik, J. T. 361
Millard, A. R. 197, 334
Miller, J. M. 286, 288
Miller, P. D. 96, 110, 123-125, 134, 135
Mogensen, M. 347
Møller-Christensen, V. 364
Montet, P. 113
Montgomery, J. A. 215, 216, 218, 219, 229, 235, 251, 255
del Monte, G. F. 232
Moore, T. 362
Moran, W. L. 86, 260
Morentz, S. 24
Morpurgo-Davies, A. 231
Morse, D. 344
Moscati, S. 165, 206
Mowinckel, S. 88, 216, 217
Muilenburg, J. 90
Müller, Ch. 225
Müller, H. P. 65, 129
Müller, K. 99
Müller, V. 140
Müller, W. W. 202
Munn-Rankin, J. M. 228
Muntner, S. 362
Myers, A. 334
Myers, J. M. 216, 229, 234, 238

Naʾaman, N. 215, 216, 221, 228, 229, 234, 236
Nagel, W. 216
Naville, E. 202
Negbi, O. 161, 171
Nielsen, E. 253
von Nordheim, E. 82
Norin, S. 95, 127
Noth, M. 19, 24, 58, 65, 67, 82, 129, 176, 186, 191, 207, 208, 210-212, 215, 216, 218, 219, 223, 229, 234, 235, 238, 239, 247, 255, 261, 265
Nougayrol, J. 229, 230, 232, 355
Nyberg, H. S. 134

Obbink, K. M. 255
O'Ceallaigh, C. G. 267
Oded, B. 210, 237
Ogilvy, A. 334

Ohata, K. 157
Oppenheim, A. L. 216, 221, 222, 224, 228-230, 350, 354, 355
Oppenheim, L. 194, 195
Oren, E. 217, 281
Otten, H. 231, 232
Otto, E. 55, 128, 135, 217, 225
Ottosson, M. 117, 123, 210

Parrot, A. 165
Peckham, B. 215, 234
Perlitt, L. 75
Perrot, G. 170
Petrie, W. M. 145
Pettinato, G. 310, 315-318, 333, 334
Pilz, E. 140
du Plat, T. J. 235
Plein, I. 83
Pope, M. H. 130
Porteous, N. W. 82
Posener, G. 67
Postgate, J. N. 218, 221-223, 229, 237
Potratz, H. A. 228
Poulssen, N. 136
Preuss, H. D. 136
Preuss, J. 358
Pritchard, J. B. 140, 170, 223, 277, 295
Pugh, J. 334
du Purry, A. 65

Rabin, Ch. 220
Rachmani, L. Y. 157
von Rad, G. 11, 14-20, 27, 28, 31, 54, 90, 111
Rainey, A. F. 209, 248, 261, 262, 334
Ramlot, L. 87
Ranke, H. 216
Ratié, S. 202
Redford, D. B. 200, 218
Reiner, E. 354
Rendtorff, R. 28, 55, 58-63, 65, 71
Reviv, H. 240, 242
Richardson, H. N. 88
Richter, W. 23, 30, 80, 112
Ridderbos, N. H. 3, 4
Ridout, G. P. 27, 28, 30, 32, 38, 39, 42, 43

Riesner, I.   259, 261
Riis, P. J.   164, 235, 236
Ringgren, H.   121
Ritter, K.   350
Robert, A.   11
Roberts, J. J. M.   93, 97, 98, 100, 102, 136, 138
Robertson, D. A.   94, 95
Rokland, E.   93
Rose, M.   127
Rosenthal, F.   219
Rosner, F.   358
Ross, J. P.   110-112, 117, 123
Rost, L.   15, 18, 27, 28, 31, 44, 47, 53, 66, 86, 87, 175
Rost, P.   222, 236
Roth, W. M. W.   246
Roux, G.   233
Rowe, A.   156, 161, 172
Rowton, M. B.   228
Rudolph, W.   7, 211, 229, 231, 265
Ruffer, M. A.   340, 343
Rupprecht, K.   212
Ruprecht, E.   62, 63
Ryckmans, G.   202

Sacon, K. K.   30
Sadgrove, M.   8
Saggs, H. W. F.   237
Salonen, A.   217, 222
Saltz, D. L.   235
Šanda, A.   215
Sandison, A. T.   340
Sarna, N. M.   334
Sasson, J. M.   227
de Saussure, F.   30
Säve-Söderbergh, T.   202
Sawyer, J. F. A.   111, 126
Sayed, A. M. A. H.   202
Schaeffer, C. F. A.   131
Schicklberger, F.   80
Schmid, H. H.   55, 57, 62, 63, 65, 69
Schmidt, H.   113
Schmidt, L.   62-64, 72, 73, 80
Schmidt, W. H.   13, 57, 59, 63, 75, 130
Schmitt, H. C.   56, 62, 64, 65, 67, 68, 73

Schmitt, R.   109
Schoff, W. H.   202
Schottroff, W.   60, 66
Schreiden, K.   260
Schulman, A. R.   198
Schulte, H.   28, 29, 53, 54, 64, 76, 175, 182, 186
Schwartz, E.   54
Scott, R. B. Y.   19, 239
Seebass, H.   55, 73, 81, 251
Segal, M. H.   7, 28
Seger, J. D.   277
Seidemann, J.   222
Sekine, M.   6, 11
Sellin, E.   304
van Seters, J.   55, 62, 65, 78
Seux, M.-J.   94, 197
Seybold, K.   61, 66, 359
Seyrig, H.   116, 131
Shanks, H.   334
Shiloh, Y.   276-278, 280, 281, 287, 288, 295, 298, 302, 304
Shipton, G. M.   275
Siegerist, H.   340, 347
Simpson, W. K.   145, 149
Sinclair, L. A.   277, 278
Ska, J. L.   335
Skehan, P. W.   210
Skinner, J.   251
Smend, R.   113
Smith, G. E.   343-345, 364
Smolar, L.   255
von Soden, W.   66, 98, 225
Soggin, J. A.   28, 134, 175, 189, 207, 215, 244, 247, 248, 261, 262, 265, 266, 269
Sommer, F.   228
Spalinger, A.   217
Speiser, E. A.   224, 328
Spiegelberg, W.   121
Spratling, F. R.   362
Staiger, E.   1, 4, 5, 9
Stamm, J. J.   129
Starkey, J.   280
Steck, O. H.   60, 62, 66, 68, 123
Steele, F. R.   230
Stefanini, R.   233
Steuernagel, C.   128
Stève, M. G.   164

Stieglitz, R. R. 230
Stoebe, H. J. 80, 83
Stolz, F. 128
Streck, M. 222, 229
Strong, S. A. 99
Sussman, M. 358

Tadmor, H. 215, 216, 220, 222, 224, 228, 229, 231-233, 235-237, 241, 242, 244, 247, 254, 256
Tadmor, M. 173
Tallqvist, K. L. 237
Talmon, S. 122, 130, 256
Terrien, S. 130
Thackeray, H, St. J. 251
Théodoridès, A. 202
Thompson, J. A. 79, 123
Thompson, R. C. 350
Thomsen, P. 216
Thureau-Dangin, F. 302
Tidwell, N. L. 192
Tischler, J. 232
Tsevat, M. 110, 127, 128
Tsukimoto, A. 176
Tufnell, O. 157
Tur-Sinai, N. H. 220
Tzori, N. 156

Ullendorff, E. 335
Ullmann, S. 126
Ungnad, A. 230
Ussishkin, D. 161, 231, 233, 235, 281, 282, 292-295, 298, 303, 304

Vacchi, L. 335
Van-Buren, E. D. 156
Vanel, A. 131
Vannoy, J. R. 89
de Vaux, R. 24, 56, 81, 95, 113, 172, 184, 217-219, 255, 261, 277, 287
Veenhof, K. R. 335
Veijola, T. 13, 76, 86, 89, 175, 239, 266
Verga, G. 86
Vetter, D. 6
Vitkus, S. N. 335
Vogt, H. C. M. 257
Vorländer, H. 65-67, 69
de Vrie, S. 76

Wagner, N. E. 55
Walker, A. 364
Wambacq, B. N. 110
Watsuji, T. 10
Weeks, K. R. 343, 346
Weidner, E. 219, 222, 223, 228, 229, 232
Weimar, P. 60
Weinberg, S. S. 170
Weinfeld, M. 75, 77, 83, 124, 137, 231, 254, 361
Weippert, M. 237, 255, 286
Weisman, Z. 80, 244
Weitzman, M. 331
Weldon, A. 335
Wellhausen, J. 27
Welten, P. 113, 238, 305
Westendorf, W. 340, 343
Westermann, C. 20, 56, 60, 203
Westphal, G. 124
White, J. B. 6-8
Whybray, R. N. 15, 23, 27, 28, 53, 55, 86, 175, 239
Widengren, G. 121
Wiklander, B. 109
Wildberger, H. 20
Wildung, D. 337, 338
Willi, Th. 211
Williams, R. J. 16, 227
Wilson, J. A. 201, 217
Winckler, H. 215
Winnet, F. V. 65
Winter, I. J. 302
Wiseman, D. J. 221, 228
Wolff, H. W. 17, 62, 73, 112, 127
Wooley, C. L. 235
Worrell, J. E. 281
Wright, G. E. 209, 218, 253, 275, 277-279, 281, 302, 303
Wright, G. R. H. 130
Würthwein, E. 7, 13, 28, 43, 67, 116, 175, 180, 186, 191, 239, 266
Wüst, M. 211, 212

Yadin, Y. 130, 172, 195, 203, 204, 216, 217, 224, 272, 274-276, 283, 290, 292-295, 297, 302, 304, 305

Yeivin, S. 200, 224, 234
Yoyotte, J. 217, 227-229
Yiinuma, J. 10

Zakaria, H. 357

Zeuger, E. 55, 61
Zibelius, K. 201, 202
Zimmerli, W. 64
Zobel, H.-J. 81

IV. PROPER NAMES

A. PERSONAL NAMES

Aaron 255
Abd el-Malik, Caliph 295
Abiathar 31, 82, 135, 176-178, 186,
  247
Abihu, the Levite 255
Abijah, son of Jeroboam 255
Abimelech, king of the Philstines
  78
Abimelech, son of Gideon 78, 80
Abishag, the Shunamite 185, 186
Abishai 32, 34, 178, 184
Abner 45-47, 52, 53, 79, 80, 185-
  187, 193
Abraham 58, 61-64, 69-72, 78, 327-
  330
Abram (in Ebla tablets) 327
Absalom 6, 32, 33, 35-38, 41, 42,
  182-184, 192, 224, 242-245, 247,
  252
Adad-nirari II 219, 220, 222
Adad-nirari III 223
Adiyabu, prince of Guzana 223
Adonijah 49, 51, 53, 176-180, 185,
  186
Adoniram (= Adoram) 248, 254
Ahab 189, 218, 240, 252, 274, 295
Ahaz 82
Ahijah, the Shilonite 187, 251
Ahimaaz 36, 37
Ahithophel 25, 31-34, 245-247
Akhenaton (= Amenhotep IV) 221,
  331
Amasa 33, 34, 79, 183-186, 247
  248, 250
Amenhotep I 346
Amenhotep II 217
Amenhotep III 221
Amenhotep IV (=
Akhenaton) 221,
  224
Amnon 182, 187

Amos 73
Ar-en-num, king of Ebla 311, 323,
  324
Asa 267, 364
Asahel 79
Ashurbanipal 222, 224, 229, 232
Ashur-bel-kala 219
Ashurnasirpal II 220-222, 236
Ashur-rabi II 233
Ashuruballit 221
Athaliah 90, 253
Azitawada, king of Adana 219

Baalam 6, 72
Baᶜana, son of Ahilud 292
Baanah, son of Rimmon 47
Baᵓlu, ruler of Tyre 216
Baasha 244
Bar-Rakkib, king of Samᶜal 292,
  294, 303
Barzillai 33, 34
Bathsheba 43, 44, 50-53, 177-179,
  182, 184, 187, 247
Bedan 90
Benaiah, ben Jehoiada 51, 176-
  179, 181, 185, 186, 248, 250
Ben-Hadad, king of Aram 246
Burnaburiash, king of Babylon 224

Canaan 66, 72

Danel 130
David (in Ebla tablets) 327
Diodorus 340
Dubuḫu-Ada, prince of Ebla 323
Dudiya (= Tudiya), king of Assyria
  324, 325

Eber 328, 329
Ebrium, king of Ebla 322-324,
  328, 329
Eliam, son of Ahithophel 177, 247

Elijah 6, 125
Elisha 110, 125, 244
Eni-il, king of Hamath 237
Enna-Dagan, king of Mari 311, 322, 324
Esarhaddon 99
Esau 76, 180
Esau (in Ebla tablets) 327
Eshbaᶜal (= Ishbaal, Ishbosheth) 45-47, 53, 79, 185, 187, 193, 247

Gideon 25, 86, 241
Giluhepa, princess of Mitanni 221

Hadad, the Edomite 201
Hadadezer 196, 237
Hadoram (= Joram) 237
Haggith 177
Hammurabi, king of Babylon 84, 105, 242, 243, 324, 331
Hanun 44
Hatshepsut, queen of Egypt 202, 225
Hattusili III 228
Herodotus 76, 198, 340
Hezekiah 19, 20, 26, 90, 107, 118, 224
Hippocrates 344, 351
Hiram, king of Tyre 190, 201, 206-209, 212, 213, 234, 260
Hosea 11
Hushai, the Archite 25, 31-34, 246

Ibbi-Sipiš, king of Ebla 323
Ibbit-lim, king of Ebla 315
Igriš-Ḥalam, king of Ebla 323
Iblul-il, king of Mari 311, 322, 324
Imhotep, Pharaoh 337
Ini-Teshub, king of Carchemish 232
Irhuleni, king of Hamath 236
Irkab-Damu, king of Ebla 323
Isaac 63, 66, 72, 78, 180, 327
Ishbaal (= Ishbosheth, Eshbaal) 45-47, 53, 79, 185, 187, 193, 247
Ishmael (in Ebla tablets) 327
Ishme-Dagan 226
Israel (in Ebla tablets) 326, 327
Ittai, the Gittite 31, 34, 178

Jacob 57, 62, 63, 66, 71, 72, 76, 130, 180, 327

Jehoash, king of Judah 253
Jehoram, king of Judah 364
Jehoshaphat 83, 189, 234
Jehu 90, 244
Jephthah 97, 240, 243, 245
Jeroboam I 187, 203, 244, 254-256, 272
Jeroboam II 274
Jezebel 87
Joab 29, 34-37, 42-47, 79, 176-179, 181-187, 209, 211, 248, 250
Joash, king of Israel 110
Job 360, 361
Jonadab 39, 41
Jonathan, son of Saul 3, 79, 80
Jonathan, son of Abiathar 51, 53
Joram (= Hadoram) 237
Josiah, king of Judah 68, 91, 137, 240, 265
Joshua 2

Kadashman-Enlil II 228
Keret 130
Kilamua, king of Samᶜal 292, 294, 303

Laban 76
Leah 58
Lot 328
Lubarna, king of Pattin 236

Maacah, daughter of Talmai 192
Marduk-nadin-ahhe, king of Babylon 225, 226
Melchizedek 69
Meribbaal (= Mephiboshet) 32-34, 48, 49, 79, 186
Merneptah-Siptah, Pharaoh 344
Meryet-Amon, wife and sister of Amenhotep I 346
Mesha 252
Michael (in Ebla tablets) 326, 327
Micah, the prophet 104, 108
Micaiah, ben Imlah 124
Micaiah (in Ebla tablets) 326, 327
Michal 47, 48
Moses 56-58, 63, 64, 70-72, 95
Mugallu, king of Tabal 232

Naᵓid-Marduk 223
Nabal 364
Nabonidus 226, 229, 361

Naboth, the Jezreelite 241
Nabuapaliddina, king of Babylon 119, 120
Nadab, the Levite 255
Nadab, king of Israel 244, 255
Nahash 78, 80
Nahor 329
Naram-Sin 315
Nathan 43, 50, 51, 53, 81, 176-179, 182, 187
Nebuchadnezzar II 360
Necho, Pharaoh 222
Noah 71
Nur-Adad, prince of Hanigalbat 222

Obadiah, official of Ahab 218
Og, king of Bashan 197
Omri 244

Peleg 329

Rachel 58
Ramesses II 67, 227, 228, 342
Ramesses III 201, 202
Ramesses V 344
Rebecca 180
Rechab, son of Rimmon 47
Rehoboam 81, 83, 203, 244, 246, 252-254, 267, 323
Reu, ancestor of Abraham 329
Ruma, priest of Egypt 347

Sahure, Pharaoh 202
Samuel 80, 83, 88, 131, 182, 187, 265
Sangara, king of Carchemish 222
Sarah 58
Sargon, king of Akkad 98, 311, 315, 331
Sargon II, king of Assyria 223, 228, 229
Saul 66, 79-81, 83, 187, 206, 247, 250, 269, 271, 277-279
Saul (in Ebla tablets) 327
Seleucus I Nicator 226, 230, 236
Sennacherib 98, 108, 363

Serug, ancestor of Abraham 329
Shalmaneser III 236
Shamshi-Adad I, king of Assyria 243
Sheba, son of Bichri 183, 185, 250, 252
Shebnah 224
Shemaᶜiah, prophet 251
Shihon, king of Amorites 197
Shilkani, Pharaoh 228
Shimei 32, 34, 186, 187
Shishak, Pharaoh 199-201, 203, 204, 251, 271, 277
Siamun, Pharaoh 198-201, 227
Simon Maccabeus 290
Sinuhe 77, 80
Siptah, Pharaoh 347
Šura-Damu, prince of Ebla 322, 324
Tagu, prince of Gath-Carmel 221
Talmai, king of Geshur 192
Tamar, daughter of David 39, 40, 182, 187
Terah 329
Thuthmose III 216
Thuthmose IV 343
Tiglath-pileser I 219, 220, 232, 233
Tiglath-pileser III 222, 228, 237
Tirhakah 216
Tōᶜi, king of Hamath 209, 237
Tudiya (= Dudiya), king of Assyria 324
Tutankh-amun 314
Tushratta, king of Mitanni 221, 225

Uriah, the Hittite 43, 44, 177, 182, 184, 187
Uzziah, king of Judah 363

Wenamon 77

Zadok 31, 34, 82, 176, 177, 247
Ziba 32, 34, 48, 49, 186
Zimri-Lim 243
Zizi, king of Hamazi in Elam 323

B. DEITIES

Adad (= Hadad) 325
Amen 344, 345

Anat, ᶜAnath, Anath, goddess 102, 104, 164, 217

Ashur 98, 99
Astarte, ᶜAstarte, goddess 149, 161, 164, 217, 275, 304
Ašera, goddess 325
Aštar, goddess 325
Aštarta, goddess 325
Baal 96, 97, 100, 102, 104, 131, 134, 325
Baal-Berith 78
Bara, goddess 325
Chemosh 97, 325
Dagan 323, 325
Damu 326
El 96-98, 100, 101, 129-131, 133-135, 325
El-Berith 78
El Elyon 69, 134
Elohim (= Yahweh) 56-58
Elyon 97
Enlil 222, 325
Hadad (= Adad) 325
Inanna, goddess 325
Ishtar, goddess 98, 119, 221

Jupiter 325
Kamiš 325
Lamashtu, demoness 348, 349
Malik 325, 326
Marduk 98, 99, 349
Mot 106
Nergal 325, 347
Qudshu, goddess 164
Rašap 323, 325, 326
Reshep 135
Shaddai 326
Shamash 119, 120
Sin 119
Sipiš 324, 325
Utu 325
Yahweh (YHWH, Lord) 5, 32, 33, 36, 43, 44, 52, 56-61, 63, 68, 70-73, 79, 84, 86-89, 91, 94-108, 177, 180, 187, 207, 211, 243, 255, 256, 304, 324
YHWH Sabaoth 109-138
Yamm 102, 106

C. Cities, Lands and Nations

Abel of Beth-maacah 250
Abu-Salabikh 316
Acco (= Ptolemais) 208, 322, 328
Acco (Bay of) 275, 276
ᶜAd (in Koran and Ebla tablets) 330
Adab 322
Adana 219, 233
Adullam (cave of) 178
Admah 328
Aegean 271, 288
Africa 201
    North Africa 362
ᶜAi 286
ᶜAin Farᶜah 277
Ajalon Valley 278
Akhshak 322
Akkad 322
Alalakh, Alalaḫ 77, 260, 267
Alashia (= Cyprus) 228, 231, 311
Aleppo 94, 312, 322, 328
Al-Mina 235
Amanus 235

Ammon, Ammonites 38-41, 44, 78, 86, 97, 192, 195, 198, 208, 229, 240, 273
Amorites 2, 24, 242, 264
Amuq 235
Anathoth 186
Anatolia 189, 190, 195, 215, 226, 230, 232, 289, 292, 293, 302, 322
Anti-Lebanon 238
Apamea 236
Aphek 139, 271, 273, 279, 286
Aqaba 284
ᶜAqar Quf 357
Arabia, Arabs 77, 191, 202
    South Arabia 203, 204
Arabia Felix 311
Arad 271, 273, 283, 284, 289, 304-306
Aram, Aramaeans (= Syrians) 24, 68, 106, 107, 192, 195, 196, 209, 217, 231, 233, 271
Aram-Damascus 208

Aram-Zobah, Aram-Ṣōbā 193, 196, 208, 209
Aribua 236
Aroer 210, 211
Arslan-Tash 297
Ashdod 172, 203, 204, 271, 281, 290, 291, 322, 328
Ashur 220, 311, 322, 324, 325
Assyria, Assyrians 68, 77, 80, 87, 99, 118, 191, 197, 219-222, 228, 229, 233, 236-238, 243, 271, 298, 324, 325, 347, 363
Athens 10, 242
Baalath 203
Bab-edh-Dhra 330
Babylon 98, 99, 105, 223, 242, 357, 360
Babylonia, Babylonians 77, 224-227, 230, 271, 295, 347, 349, 363
Southern Babylonia 349
Bagdad 10
Bashan 273
Mt. Bashan 106
Beᶜer Hafir 285
Beᶜerotayim 285
Beersheba 210-212, 271-273, 281, 283-287, 289, 302
Bela 328
Bethel 68, 130, 134
Beth-horon 203
Beth-Shean 156, 172, 275
Beth-Shemesh 271, 273, 278, 287, 289
Biqaᶜ 237
Bit-Adini 220, 231
Byblos 86, 87, 113, 114, 213, 322, 328
Cabul 204, 207, 208
Cairo 10, 343
Calah 220, 229
Canaan, Canaanites 6, 24, 66, 72, 121, 130, 135, 139-173, 194, 195, 199, 208, 210, 212, 216-218, 225, 261-263, 265, 266, 277, 286, 327
Cape Guardafui 202
Carchemish 222, 226, 231-234 322
Carmel 322, 328
Mt. Carmel 208, 275

Carthage 165
Cilicia (= Que) 215, 227, 232
Coastal Plain (of Palestine) 278-280
Crete 271
Cush (sons of) 202
Cyprus (= Alashia) 228, 231, 271, 311
Damascus 209, 312, 322, 328-330
Dan 210, 211, 271-273, 289
Dead Sea 273, 329, 330
Debir 281
Deir el-Bahri 202
Deir el-Balaḥ 141, 145, 149, 156, 157, 170, 172
Dimona 285
Djibouti 202
Dor 328
Ebla 77, 297, 309-335
Edom, Edomites 66, 86, 104, 107, 195, 198, 201, 208, 209, 252
Eglon 281
Egypt, Egyptians 7, 10, 20, 63, 64, 67, 77, 80, 88, 95, 118, 121, 139, 144, 145, 161, 170, 189-204, 215-217, 219, 221-227, 229, 231, 232, 263, 271, 279, 311, 337-347, 354, 358, 359, 362, 364, 365
ᶜEin Qadeis 285
Elah (Vale of) 278
Elam 99, 311, 322, 323
el-ᶜAmarna 260, 267
Elat 10, 284
ᶜEn-gev 271-273
En Rogel 178, 179
Ephraim (forest of) 183
Ephraim (mountains of) 177
Erma (= Iram, in Ebla tablets) 330
Ezion-Geber 201, 204, 234, 284
Ethiopia 362
Fara 316
Gad 210, 212
Galilee 207, 272-276, 286
Lower Galilee 208
Upper Galilee 207, 250, 271, 272, 286
Western Galilee 204, 235
Galilee (Sea of) 272, 273
Gath-Carmel 221

Gaulan 192
Gaza 141, 196, 199, 229, 322, 328
Geshur 42, 192
Gezer 198-200, 203, 227, 271, 273, 278-281, 288-292
Gibbethon 244
Gibeah 271, 273, 277, 279
Gibeon, Gibeonites 80, 82, 271, 273, 277
Gib^cot Mesora 285
Gilboa 3
Gilead 210, 212, 240, 243, 246, 273
Gilgal 249
Gittites 195
Gizeh 344, 345
Gomorrah 328, 330
Gozan, Guzana (= Tell Halaf) 223, 292, 302
Greece, Greeks 77, 81, 139, 165, 365
Gurgum 231, 232
Hadrumetum-Sousse 131, 132
Hama 236, 312, 322, 328
Hamath 86, 87, 104, 209, 235-238
Hamath-Rabbah 236
Hamath-Zoba 237
Hamazi (in Elam) 311, 323
Hanigalbat 222
Haran 316, 322, 327
Har Boger 285
Haro^ɔa 285
Har Raviv 285
Harsamna 232
H. Halvqim 285
H. Rogem 285
H. Uza 285
Hatira 285
Hatti, the land of Hatti 77, 221
Hattusha 311
Havilah 202
Hazor 129, 139, 172, 203, 271-274, 281, 288-292, 297, 322
Hebrews 67, 328
Hebron 45-47, 177, 192, 193, 240, 243, 247-249, 253
Heliopolis 121
Hiesa 237
Hill Country (of Palestine) 286
Hittites 80, 191, 228, 264
Hivites 210, 212, 264

Homs 322, 328
Horeb 6, 100
Hormah (= Tell Masos?) 284
Horn of Africa 203, 234
Huleh basin 272
Ibiza 165
Iram (= Erma) 330
Iran 164, 170
^cIyyōn 210
Izbet Sarteh 286
Jabesh-gilead, Jabeshites 78-80
Jabla 235, 236
Jaffa, Joppa 217, 234, 235, 273
Jebusites 177, 264
Jekabzeel 177
Jericho 10, 288
Jerusalem 5, 10, 31, 32, 42, 43 66, 68, 69, 81, 94, 99-108, 112, 122, 126, 128, 129, 135, 136, 177, 181, 186, 190, 192, 197, 199, 207, 209, 223, 235, 240, 241, 246, 248, 249, 254, 255, 273, 277, 278, 280, 286, 289, 295, 302-304, 306, 322, 328, 360, 361, 363
Jezreel valley 195, 275
Joktan (sons of) 202
Jordan 2, 210, 241, 249, 273
Jordan basin 329
Judah, Judea 229, 280, 281, 361
Judah (mountains of) 177
Kabzeel 177
Kadesh-barnea (Qadesh Barnea) 284, 285
Kadesh in Naphtali (= Qadas) 210, 212
Kadesh on the Orontes (= Tell Nabī Mind) 210
Kanish 311
Karatepe 292, 302
Karnaim 73
Karnak 121, 203
Kh. el-Asheq (= ^cEn-Gev) 272
Kh. el-Meshâsh (= Tell Masos, Hormah) 284
Kh. Raddana 286
Kiryath-Sefer 281
Kish 310, 311, 318, 322
Kishon River 276
Kulania 235

Kurdistan 243
Kusû (land of) 229
La°ana 285
Laba°u (= Lebo-Hamath) 237
Lachish 157, 161, 271, 273, 280-
    282, 287, 290, 291, 295, 304,
    305
Lebanon 165, 220, 234, 235, 264,
    266, 272, 297
Lebo-Hamath (= Laba°u) 237
Libyans 201, 203
Luhute 236
Makmish 156, 172
Malhata 271, 273
Mamre 59, 68
Mari 77, 232, 311, 314, 316, 322,
    324
Marseille 10
Mediterranean 103, 191, 234, 236,
    311
    eastern Mediterranean 9, 165,
        170
    northern Mediterranean 10
    western Mediterranean 190
Mediterranean shores 156
Mediterranean sphere, world 77,
    235, 288
Megiddo 113, 115, 172, 195, 203,
    216, 217, 271-273, 275, 276, 278,
    281, 287, 289-295, 297, 302, 304,
    322
Meluḫḫa 216
Meshwesh 201
Mesopotamia 10, 94, 105, 121, 139,
    164, 170, 189, 230, 232, 236,
    242, 271, 292, 310, 316, 322,
    337, 347-359, 365
    southern Mesopotamia 323
    Upper Mesopotamia 311, 322
Midianites 241
Mitanni 191, 221, 225
Mizpah 243, 287
Mizpe Ramon 285
Moab, Moabites 66, 86, 97, 192,
    195, 198, 208, 229, 273, 288,
    325
Muṣri 215, 216
Mutkinu 232
Mycenae 139
ǫ Hammadi 314

Nahal Loz 285
Nahariyah 164
Nairi 232
Nazareth 10
Negev 177, 271, 273, 281-286, 289
    northern Negev 273, 286
    southern Negev 204
Neirab 165
Neo-Hittites 198, 231, 232, 271
Nimrud 297
Nineveh 223, 322
Nippur 222, 348, 349
Nob 129
Nubia 201, 203, 343, 344, 364
Nuzi 226, 314
Ophir 190, 191, 201, 202, 207, 219,
    234
Orontes river 210
Palestine 199, 203, 208, 211, 212,
    271, 297
    North Palestine 225
Pattin 220, 236
Perezzites 264
Per-Ramesses (= Raamses) 227
Persians 77
Persian Gulf 311
Philistia, Philistines 68, 78, 80, 83,
    86, 87, 107, 194-196, 199-201,
    208, 235, 243, 244, 278, 279,
    286, 288, 290, 363
Phoenicia, Phoenicians 77, 86, 121,
    170, 234, 235, 293
Phoenician coast 195, 198, 205-214,
    220
Pithom 67, 227
Pitru 232
Pizzo Cannita 165
Ptolemais (= Acco) 208
Punt 201, 202
Qa (city of) 242, 243
Qatna 226, 236
Qidisi 236
Que (= Cilicia) 190, 195, 201, 215,
    216, 233, 234, 238
Qumran 314, 361
Quseima 285
Raamses (= Per-Ramesses) 67
Rabbah, Rabbath Ammon 43, 44,
    184
Rabla (= Ribla) 236

Ramot Gilead 244
Râs el-ᶜAin (= Aphek) 279
Ras Shamrah (= Ugarit) 235, 316
Red Sea 190, 191, 196, 201, 202, 204, 220, 234, 284
Refed 285
Retenu (= Syria-Palestine) 217
Revivim 285
Ribla (=Rabla) 237
Ritma 285
Rome 10, 77, 81
Saᶜad 285
Sabastiyeh (= Samaria) 277
Sais 222
Sakçegözü 292, 302
Salem 328
Samᶜal (= Zinjirli) 292, 302
Samaria 218, 271, 273, 277, 278, 297, 300, 301
Sardinia 131
Sareira (= Zeredah, MT) 251
Scythians 77
Sea-Peoples 195, 200, 235, 288
Seba 197
Sede-Boqer 285
Shamutu (in Ebla tablets) 330
Sharon plain 195
Sheba 190, 191, 197, 202
Shechem 78, 130, 244 250-254, 271, 273, 277, 288, 289, 297, 299
Shemshara (= Shushara) 77, 243
Shephelah 199, 223, 278-280, 286
Shiloh 111, 112, 116, 117, 128-131, 134
Shiqmona 271, 273, 275, 276, 289
Shushara (= Shemshara) 243
Sianu 236
Sisily 165
Sidon 121, 165, 206, 210-213, 328
Sinai 322, 328
    eastern Sinai 284
Sinai (Mount) 58, 100, 107
Sippar 119, 120
Sodom 71, 328, 330
Somalia 202
Spain 165, 190
Ṣubate (= Zobah) 237
Succoth 25, 86, 194
Sukas 235, 236

Sukki 203
Sumer, Sumerians 347, 348
Syria 77, 157, 161, 164, 165, 171, 190, 196, 226, 231, 235, 271, 289, 292, 297, 316, 322, 328, 330
    Middle Syria 209
    North Syria 231, 292, 293, 302, 309
    Northwest Syria 311
Syrians (= Aramaeans) 209
Syria-Palestine 77, 191, 196, 217, 261, 263, 267, 310, 322, 327, 329, 337
Taanach, Taᶜanach 172, 271, 273, 275, 289, 304
Tabal 232
Tadmor 237, 238
Taḥtīm Ḥådšī 210
Tall Nabī mind (= Kadesh on the Orontes) 210
Tamar 203
Tanis 198
Tarshish 197, 207, 234
Taurus 232
Tell Abu Hawam 235, 271, 273, 276, 295, 296
Tel ᶜAmal 271, 273, 275
Tell ᶜAqeir 357
Tell ᶜArad (= Arad) 283, 285
Tell Balâṭah (= Shechem) 277
Tell Beit Mirsim (= Kiryath-Sefer) 140, 157, 171, 271, 273, 281, 287-289
Tell Daruk (= Usnu?) 236
Tell ed-Duweir (= Lachish) 280
Tell el-Farᶜah N. (= Tirzah) 172, 271, 273, 277, 288
Tell el-Fûl (= Gibeah) 277
Tell el-Ḥesi (= Eglon?) 271, 281, 287, 288, 295, 296
Tell el-Jîb (= Gibeon) 277
Tell el-Kheleifeh (= Ezion-Geber) 171, 284, 289
Tell el-Milḥ (= Tel Malḥata) 284
Tell el-Mutesellim (= Megiddo) 275
Tell el-Qadaḥ 272
Tell el-Qadi (= Dan) 272
Tell el-Qudeirat (= Kadesh-barnea) 284

Tell el-Naṣbeh (= Mizpah) 287
Tell el-Rumeileh (= Beth-shemesh) 278
Tell el-Samak (= Shiqmona) 275
Tell el-Seba^c (= Beersheba) 281
Tell esh-Shariᵓa (Tel Seraᵓ) 281
Tell Halaf (= Guzan) 223, 292, 302
Tell Jemmeh 271
Tell Kudadi 235
Tel Malḥata (= Tell el-Milḥ) 284
Tell Mardikh (= Ebla) 297, 309-335
Tel Masad 156
Tel Masoa (= Kh. el-Meshâsh, Hormah?) 271, 284, 286, 288
Tel Mikhal 156
Tell Qasile 195, 235, 271, 273, 279, 287, 289, 295, 296, 305
Tel Seraᵓ (= Tell esh-Shariᵓa) 281
Tel Ṣippor 271
Tell Ta^{c}anach (= Ta^{c}anach) 275
Tell Taᵓyinat, Tell Tayinat 235, 292, 297, 302
Tel Zeror 156, 157, 171
Thamudu 330
Thebes 198, 201
Til-Barsip 231
Tiphsah 196, 199
Tirzah 277, 287

Togarma 232
Transjordania, Transjordan (= east side of Jordan) 86, 177, 194, 266, 288
Tyre 60, 86, 87, 101, 190-192, 195, 200, 201, 204, 206-213, 215, 216, 234, 235, 273
Ugarit 77, 133, 226, 230, 235, 236, 260, 267, 314, 322, 328
Unqi/Pattin 235
Ur 310
Urartu 222
Uruk 310
Usnu (= Tell Daruk?) 236
Van 233
Wadi Gawasis 202
Yarkon River 235, 279
Ya^{c}zēr 210, 212
Yeroham 285
Zeboiim 328
Ziklag 178
Zinjirli (= Sam^{c}al) 292, 294, 302, 303
Zion 91, 93-108, 112, 117, 118, 121, 122, 126, 136
Zoar 328
Zobah (Ṣubate) 237, 238

V. SUBJECTS

Aaa-disease 340, 357
Aaronid 82
Absalom's rebellion 5, 34, 52, 82, 83, 178, 183, 241, 246-250, 256
African proverbs 20, 21
Ahiram's sarcophagus 113, 114
Akkad (First Dynasty of) 311, 315, 316, 322
Akkadian 94, 190, 197, 218, 316, 317
Albright school 3
Amarna letters 81, 139, 198
Amenope (Instruction of) 18
Ammonite war 184
Amorite 316, 318
amphictyony 24
anointing 80, 81
    priestly anointing 76
apodictic laws 22

Arabic 135
Aramaic 94, 197, 316, 361
Ark 31, 47, 81, 100, 105, 108, 112, 116, 117, 122, 128, 129, 131, 135-137
assonance 2, 3, 21, 22
Assyrian King Lists 324
Assyrian Medical Texts 350
Assyrian Text (Marduk's trial before Ashur) 98
Assyro-Babylonian literature 6
Astarte figurines 140, 149, 170
Baal epic, myth 101-103, 106
Babylon (First Dynasty of) 324
Babylonian exile 68, 257
Balaam oracles 88, 97
Banquet Stele (of Ashurnasirpal II) 221
blessings 75, 84, 88, 89, 94

Book of the Covenant 67
Broken Obelisk 219
Cain narrative 60
Canaanite cities, city-states 16, 17, 24, 66
Canaanite culture, tradition, etc. 9, 17, 25, 65, 95, 103, 104, 129, 131, 134, 288, 289
Canaanite dialects 316
paleo-Canaanite 316, 317
Canaanite literature, myth, mythology 17, 102, 105
Canaanite monarchies 81
Canaanite-Phoenician sources 17
Canaanite religion, deities, pantheon, polytheism 95, 96, 100, 111, 326
Canaanite-style temple 76, 297
Cherethites and Pelethites 176, 178, 195, 250
Cherubim, cherubim throne 109-138, 255, 298, 301, 303
chiasmus, chiastic 3, 31, 38, 41
Chronicler 67, 83, 265
climatology 10
concentric structure 31, 33, 36, 38, 41, 42, 46, 49, 54
Coptic 338
Coptos ships 201
Court History (of David) 239, 246
Covenant 75-92, 96, 99, 193, 240, 252-254, 256, 361
creation story (biblical) 59, 69, 70, 326
curse 75, 82, 88, 89
David (house of, dynasty of) 81, 90, 180, 185-187, 250, 253-256, 265, 323
Davidides 86, 180, 253
David's heroes 176-178
David's lament (over the death of Abner) 2, 4, 5
David's lament (over the death of Saul and Jonathan) 2, 4, 5
David's Last Words 87
David's Rise (story of) 18, 72, 136, 181
Deutero-Isaiah 69
deuteronomic, deuteronomistic 45, 58, 63, 64, 69, 70, 75, 76,

78, 83, 86-89, 92, 100, 123, 127, 136, 137, 207, 212, 213, 252
post-deuteronomic 19, 68, 89, 213, 265
pre-deuteronomic 19, 78, 89-92, 106, 198
proto-deuteronomic 127
Deuteronomist(s), Dtr. 88, 124, 137, 208, 256, 265, 266
Dtr^G 86
Dtr^N 76
Dtr^P 76
Deuteronomistic Historical Work 67, 92, 137, 269
Deuteronomy 85, 137, 263, 362
Urdeuteronomy 91, 92
divine (heavenly) assembly, council, court 123-127, 131, 134, 136, 324
Eblaite 316-321, 325, 327
Egyptian 117, 357
Egyptian art, figurines, etc. 156, 157, 164, 170, 171, 302
Egyptian culture, influence, models, etc. 14, 16, 19, 25, 81, 86
Egyptian literature, love lyric 6-8
Egyptian wisdom, wisdom literature 15, 20, 24
elders 83, 193, 194, 240-248, 253, 257
Elohist 57, 62-64, 68, 70, 71, 78
Gilgamesh (Epic of) 221
God of Abraham 56
God of the Fathers 63
Golden Calf (story of) 255
great king (= šarru rabû) 94, 98, 118, 197
Greco-Phoenician art 172
Greek drama 7
Greek states 76
Hannah's prayer 130
Hathor wig 149, 161, 164
Hebrew 3, 316-319, 324
Homeric poems 20
horses
Anatolian 227-229, 232-234, 238
Assyrian 236
Egyptian 228, 229
Mesaean 229
Nubian 229

Hurrian 243
inclusio 2, 6, 8, 31-33, 37, 39, 42, 44, 45, 88
Isaiah Apocalypse 112
Jebusite-Canaanite religion 176, 177
Jeroboam's revolt, rebellion 246, 247, 250-252
Jerusalem cult, cultic tradition, liturgy 91, 117-119, 121, 123, 125, 126
Joseph Narrative, Story 15, 18, 72, 224
King's Highway 196
Kingship 75-92, 96, 99
Kojiki 1
Königsnovelle 86
Koran 327, 330
Levites 68
Luwian (hieroglyphic) 219, 231, 233
Manner of the king 223
Manyōshū 1, 2
Mediterranean-Canaanite influence 10
Mesopotamian art, figurines 156, 157, 302
Mesopotamian culture, influence, models 16, 17, 25
Mesopotamian hymns 107
Mesopotamian texts 224
Mesopotamian wisdom literature 24
messianic king 118
Nathan's dynastic promise 86, 91
Neo-Assyrian empire 209, 213
Nimrud ivory 197
nō-play 7
Norito 2
oath 77, 78, 82-84, 99, 252
Omrides 277
palaeopathology 343, 346, 354
Papyrus, Papyri
    Berlin Medical Papyrus 342
    Carlsberg Papyrus 342
    Chester-Beatty Papyri 342
    Ebers Papyrus 338, 339, 342, 350
    Edwin Smith Surgical Papyrus 340-342
    Hearst Papyrus 342
    Kahun Papyrus 342
    London Medical Papyrus 342
    Ramesseum Papyri 342
Paradise story (biblical) 59, 70
parallelism 21, 22, 88
Persian empire 263
Philistine temples 280, 305
Phoenician 219, 316
Phoenician art, style, etc. 172, 297, 298
Phoenician temple 302
Poor Man of Nippur 222
Prayer of Nabonidus (from Qumran) 361
Priestly Code 137
Priestly literature, writer 57, 58, 63, 64, 68-70, 88, 106, 116, 122, 129
primitive democracy 242
Punic inscriptions 131, 132, 165, 170
qina-meter 4
Rahab (mythological dragon) 136
Ras Shamra texts (= Ugaritic texts) 139
rhetorical analysis, criticism 27, 30, 39
Roman law 76, 261
royal psalms 85
Sa-gig (series) 351, 352
Saul (house of, kingdom of) 2, 47, 48, 186
scribal schools 86, 318, 326
scribes 25, 66, 318, 320, 321, 350
Sefire inscriptions 197
Semitic 316-321, 326, 327
    East Semitic 316, 317
    West Semitic 100, 260, 316, 317, 327
Semitic deities 325
Sheba (Queen of) 191, 204, 223, 306
Sheba's rebellion, revolt 34, 178, 184, 186, 245-249, 253
Sinai pericope, traditions 58, 64, 75
Solomonic administrative districts 218, 253
Solomonic enlightenment 14, 15,

17, 18, 20, 23
Song of Deborah 2, 127, 217
Song of the Sea 95, 224
Succession Narrative 5, 13-15, 18, 25, 27-54, 175-187
Suhi dynasty (in Carchemish) 233
Sumerian 316, 317, 319-321, 326, 349, 350
Sumerian cities, city-states 77, 310
Sumerian culture 315, 318
Sumerian deities 325
Sumerian King Lists 322
Suśruta-saṃhitā (Sanskrit) 363
Taanach correspondence 139
Table of Nations 202
Tarshish (ships of) 103, 190, 201, 219, 234
Tekoa (woman of) 25, 182, 183
Temple (Jerusalem Temple) 69, 81, 88, 89, 91, 99, 103, 105-108, 112, 116-119, 121, 123, 125, 126, 128, 129, 131, 136-138, 187, 197, 207, 208, 212, 213, 220, 235, 265, 278, 295, 297, 298, 302, 304, 305, 363
Ugaritic 3, 94, 100, 104, 117, 131, 134, 197, 316-319, 324
Ugaritic texts (= Ras Shamra texts) 129, 135
Ura-Tarhunda dynasty (in Carchemish) 233
Wenamon story 87, 234
Wisdom 10, 11, 13-26, 66, 69, 85, 86, 88
Solomon's wisdom 19, 20
wordplay 2, 3, 21, 22, 127
Yahwism 85, 176
Yahwist 13, 18, 55-73, 75, 78, 85
Zaphon 100, 102, 121, 122